# Programming iOS 4

# Programming iOS 4

*Matt Neuburg*

O'REILLY®

Beijing • Cambridge • Farnham • Köln • Sebastopol • Tokyo

**Programming iOS 4**
by Matt Neuburg

Published by O'Reilly Media, Inc., 1005 Gravenstein Highway North, Sebastopol, CA 95472.

O'Reilly books may be purchased for educational, business, or sales promotional use. Online editions are also available for most titles (*http://my.safaribooksonline.com*). For more information, contact our corporate/institutional sales department: (800) 998-9938 or *corporate@oreilly.com*.

| | | | |
|---|---|---|---|
| **Editor:** | Brian Jepson | **Cover Designer:** | Karen Montgomery |
| **Production Editor:** | Teresa Elsey | **Interior Designer:** | David Futato |
| **Proofreader:** | Nancy Kotary | **Illustrator:** | Robert Romano |

**Printing History:**

    May 2011:        First Edition.

ISBN: 978-1-449-38843-0

[LSI]

1305160664

# Table of Contents

## Part III.  Cocoa

# Part IV.    Views

## Part V.   Interface

# Part VII.   Final Topics

# Preface

With the advent of version 2 of the iPhone system, Apple proved they could do a remarkable thing — adapt their existing Cocoa computer application programming framework to make applications for a touch-based device with limited memory and speed and a dauntingly tiny display. The resulting Cocoa Touch framework, in fact, turned out to be in many ways better than the original Cocoa.

A programming framework has a kind of personality, an overall flavor that provides an insight into the goals and mindset of those who created it. When I first encountered Cocoa Touch, my assessment of its personality was: "Wow, the people who wrote this are really clever!" On the one hand, the number of built-in interface widgets was severely and deliberately limited; on the other hand, the power and flexibility of some of those widgets, especially such things as UITableView, was greatly enhanced over their Mac OS X counterparts. Even more important, Apple created a particularly brilliant way (UIViewController) to help the programmer make entire blocks of interface come and go and supplant one another in a controlled, hierarchical manner, thus allowing that tiny iPhone display to unfold virtually into multiple interface worlds within a single app without the user becoming lost or confused.

Even more impressive, Apple took the opportunity to recreate and rationalize Cocoa from the ground up as Cocoa Touch. Cocoa itself is very old, having begun life as NeXTStep before Mac OS X even existed. It has grown by accretion and with a certain conservatism in order to maintain something like backward compatibility. With Cocoa Touch, on the other hand, Apple had the opportunity to throw out the baby with the bath water, and they seized this opportunity with both hands.

So, although Cocoa Touch is conceptually based on Mac OS X Cocoa, it is very clearly *not* Mac OS X Cocoa, nor is it limited or defined by Mac OS X Cocoa. It's an independent creature, a leaner, meaner, smarter Cocoa. I could praise Cocoa Touch's deliberate use of systematization (and its healthy respect for Occam's Razor) through numerous examples. Where Mac OS X's animation layers are glommed onto views as a kind of afterthought, a Cocoa Touch view always has an animation layer counterpart.

Memory management policies, such as how top-level objects are managed when a nib loads, are simplified and clarified. And so on.

At the same time, Cocoa Touch is still a form of Cocoa. It still requires a knowledge of Objective-C. It is not a scripting language; it is certainly not aimed at nonprogrammers, like HyperCard's HyperTalk or Apple's AppleScript. It is still huge and complicated. In fact, it's rather difficult.

Meanwhile, Cocoa Touch itself evolves and changes. The iPhone System 2 matured into the iPhone System 3. Then there was a sudden sally in a new direction when the iPad introduced a larger screen and iPhone System 3.2. The iPhone 4 and its double-resolution Retina display also ran on a major system increment, now dubbed iOS 4. Every one of these changes has brought new complexities for the programmer to deal with. To give just one simple example, users rightly complained that switching between apps on the iPhone meant quitting one app and launching another. So Apple gave the iPhone 4 the power of multitasking; the user can switch away from an app and then return to it later to find it still running and in the state it was left previously. All well and good, but now programmers must scurry to make their apps compatible with multitasking, which is not at all trivial.

The popularity of the iPhone, with its largely free or very inexpensive apps, and the subsequent popularity of the iPad, have brought and will continue to bring into the fold many new programmers who see programming for these devices as worthwhile and doable, even though they may not have felt the same way about Mac OS X. Apple's own annual WWDC developer conventions have reflected this trend, with their emphasis shifted from Mac OS X to iOS instruction.

The widespread eagerness to program iOS, however, though delightful on the one hand, has also fostered a certain tendency to try to run without first learning to walk. iOS gives the programmer mighty powers that can seem as limitless as imagination itself, but it also has fundamentals. I often see questions online from programmers who are evidently deep into the creation of some interesting app, but who are stymied in a way that reveals quite clearly that they are unfamiliar with the basics of the very world in which they are so happily cavorting.

It is this state of affairs that has motivated me to write this book, which is intended to ground the reader in the fundamentals of iOS. I love Cocoa and have long wished to write about it, but it is iOS and its popularity that has given me a proximate excuse to do so. Indeed, my working title was "Fundamentals of Cocoa Touch Programming." Here I have attempted to marshal and expound, in what I hope is a pedagogically helpful and instructive yet ruthlessly Euclidean and logical order, the principles on which sound iOS programming rests, including a good basic knowledge of Objective-C (starting with C itself) and the nature of object-oriented programming, advice on the use of the tools, the full story on how Cocoa objects are instantiated, referred to, put in communication with one another, and managed over their lifetimes, and a survey of the primary interface widgets and other common tasks. My hope, as with my previous books, is that you will both read this book cover to cover (learning something new often enough to keep you turning the pages) and keep it by you as a handy reference.

This book is not intended to disparage Apple's own documentation and example projects. They are wonderful resources and have become more wonderful as time goes on. I have depended heavily on them in the preparation of this book. But I also find that they don't fulfill the same function as a reasoned, ordered presentation of the facts. The online documentation must make assumptions as to how much you already know; it can't guarantee that you'll approach it in a given order. And online documentation is more suitable to reference than to instruction. A fully written example, no matter how well commented, is difficult to follow; it demonstrates, but it does not teach.

A book, on the other hand, has numbered chapters and sequential pages; I can assume you know C before you know Objective-C for the simple reason that Chapter 1 precedes Chapter 2. And along with facts, I also bring to the table a degree of experience, which I try to communicate to you. Throughout this book you'll see me referring to "common beginner mistakes"; in most cases, these are mistakes that I have made myself, in addition to seeing others make them. I try to tell you what the pitfalls are because I assume that, in the course of things, you will otherwise fall into them just as naturally as I did as I was learning. You'll also see me construct many examples piece by piece or extract and explain just one tiny portion of a larger app. It is not a massive finished program that teaches programming, but an exposition of the thought process that developed that program. It is this thought process, more than anything else, that I hope you will gain from reading this book.

iOS is huge, massive, immense. It's far too big to be encompassed in a book even of this size. And in any case, that would be inappropriate and unnecessary. There are entire areas of Cocoa Touch that I have ruthlessly avoided discussing. Some of them would require an entire book of their own. Others you can pick up well enough, when the time comes, from the documentation. This book is only a beginning — the fundamentals. But I hope that it will be the firm foundation that will make it easier for you to tackle whatever lies beyond, in your own fun and rewarding iOS programming future.

In closing, some version numbers, so that you know what assumptions I am making. At the time I started writing this book, system versions 3.1.3 (on the iPhone) and 3.2 (on the iPad) were most recent. As I was working on the book, iOS 4 and the iPhone 4 came into being, but it didn't yet run on the iPad. Subsequently iOS 4.2 emerged: the first system able to run on both the iPhone and the iPad. At the same time, Xcode was improved up to 3.2.5.

Then, just in time for my final revisions, Xcode 3.2.6 and iOS 4.3 were released, along with the first public version of the long-awaited Xcode 4. Xcode 4 is a thorough overhaul of the IDE: menus, windows, and preferences are quite different from Xcode 3.2.x. At the same time, both Xcode 4 and Xcode 3.2.x can coexist on the same machine and can be used to work on the same project; moreover, Xcode 3.2.x has some specialized capabilities that Xcode 4 lacks, so some long-standing developers may well continue to use it. This situation presents a dilemma for an author describing the development process. However, for iOS programming, I recommend adoption of Xcode 4, and this book assumes that you have adopted it.

## Conventions Used in This Book

The following typographical conventions are used in this book:

*Italic*

> Indicates new terms, URLs, email addresses, filenames, and file extensions.

`Constant width`

> Used for program listings, as well as within paragraphs to refer to program elements such as variable or function names, databases, data types, environment variables, statements, and keywords.

**`Constant width bold`**

> Shows commands or other text that should be typed literally by the user.

`Constant width italic`

> Shows text that should be replaced with user-supplied values or by values determined by context.

 This icon signifies a tip, suggestion, or general note.

 This icon indicates a warning or caution.

## Using Code Examples

This book is here to help you get your job done. In general, you may use the code in this book in your programs and documentation. You do not need to contact us for permission unless you're reproducing a significant portion of the code. For example, writing a program that uses several chunks of code from this book does not require permission. Selling or distributing a CD-ROM of examples from O'Reilly books does require permission. Answering a question by citing this book and quoting example code does not require permission. Incorporating a significant amount of example code from this book into your product's documentation does require permission.

We appreciate, but do not require, attribution. An attribution usually includes the title, author, publisher, and ISBN. For example: "*Programming iOS 4* by Matt Neuburg (O'Reilly). Copyright 2011 Matt Neuburg, 978-1-449-38843-0."

If you feel your use of code examples falls outside fair use or the permission given above, feel free to contact us at *permissions@oreilly.com*.

## Safari® Books Online

Safari Books Online is an on-demand digital library that lets you easily search over 7,500 technology and creative reference books and videos to find the answers you need quickly.

With a subscription, you can read any page and watch any video from our library online. Read books on your cell phone and mobile devices. Access new titles before they are available for print, and get exclusive access to manuscripts in development and post feedback for the authors. Copy and paste code samples, organize your favorites, download chapters, bookmark key sections, create notes, print out pages, and benefit from tons of other time-saving features.

O'Reilly Media has uploaded this book to the Safari Books Online service. To have full digital access to this book and others on similar topics from O'Reilly and other publishers, sign up for free at *http://my.safaribooksonline.com*.

## How to Contact Us

Please address comments and questions concerning this book to the publisher:

O'Reilly Media, Inc.
1005 Gravenstein Highway North
Sebastopol, CA 95472
800-998-9938 (in the United States or Canada)
707-829-0515 (international or local)
707-829-0104 (fax)

We have a web page for this book, where we list errata, examples, and any additional information. You can access this page at:

*http://oreilly.com/catalog/0636920010258/*

To comment or ask technical questions about this book, send email to:

*bookquestions@oreilly.com*

For more information about our books, courses, conferences, and news, see our website at *http://www.oreilly.com*.

Find us on Facebook: *http://facebook.com/oreilly*

Follow us on Twitter: *http://twitter.com/oreillymedia*

Watch us on YouTube: *http://www.youtube.com/oreillymedia*

## Acknowledgments

It's a poor craftsman who blames his tools. No blame attaches to the really great tools by which I have been assisted in the writing of this book. I am particularly grateful to the Unicomp Model M keyboard (*http://pckeyboard.com*), without which I could not have produced so large a book so painlessly. I was also aided by wonderful software, including TextMate (*http://macromates.com*) and AsciiDoc (*http://www.methods.co.nz/asciidoc*). BBEdit (*http://www.barebones.com*) helped with its `diff` display. Screenshots were created with Snapz Pro X (*http://www.ambrosiasw.com*) and GraphicConverter (*http://www.lemkesoft.com*); diagrams were drawn with OmniGraffle (*http://www.om nigroup.com*).

The splendid O'Reilly production process converted my AsciiDoc text files into PDF while I worked, allowing me to proofread in simulated book format. Were it not for this, and the Early Release program that permitted me to provide my readers with periodic updates of the book as it grew, I would never have agreed to undertake this project in the first place. I would like particularly to thank Tools maven Abby Fox for her constant assistance.

I have taken advice from two tech reviewers, Dave Smith and David Rowland, and have been assisted materially and spiritually by many readers who submitted errata and encouragement. I was particularly fortunate in having Brian Jepson as editor; he provided enthusiasm for the O'Reilly tools and the electronic book formats, a watchful eye, and a trusting attitude; he also endured the role of communications pipeline when I needed to prod various parts of the O'Reilly machine. I have never written an O'Reilly book without the help of Nancy Kotary, and I didn't intend to start now; her sharp eye has smoothed the bristles of my punctuation-laden style. For errors that remain, I take responsibility, of course.

# PART I

# Language

Apple has provided a vast toolbox for programming iOS to make an app come to life and behave the way you want it to. That toolbox is the *API* (application programming interface). To use the API, you must speak the API's language. That language, for the most part, is Objective-C, which itself is built on top of C; some pieces of the API use C itself. This part of the book instructs you in the basics of these languages:

- Chapter 1 explains C. In general, you will probably not need to know all the ins and outs of C, so this chapter restricts itself to those aspects of C that you need to know in order to use both Objective-C and the C-based areas of the API.

- Objective-C adds object-based programming features to C. Chapter 2 discusses object-based programming in general architectural terms. It also explains some extremely important terms that will be used throughout the book, along with the concepts that lie behind them.

- Chapter 3 introduces the basic syntax of Objective-C.

- Chapter 4 continues the explanation of Objective-C, discussing the nature of Objective-C classes, with emphasis on how to create a class in code.

- Chapter 5 completes the introduction to Objective-C, discussing how instances are created and initialized, along with an explanation of such related topics as polymorphism, instance variables, accessors, `self` and `super`, key–value coding, and properties.

Even at this point, our discussion of Objective-C is not yet complete; we'll return in Part III to a description of further aspects of the language: those that are particularly bound up with the Cocoa frameworks.

# Just Enough C

*Do you believe in C? Do you believe in anything that has*
*to do with me?*

—Leonard Bernstein and Stephen Schwartz, *Mass*

To program for iOS, you need some knowledge of the C programming language, for two reasons:

- Most of your iOS programming will be in the Objective-C language, and Objective-C is a superset of C. This means that Objective-C presupposes C; everything that is true of C trickles up to Objective-C. A common mistake is to forget that "Objective-C is C" and to neglect a basic understanding of C.

- Some of the iOS API involves C rather than Objective-C. Even in Objective-C code, you often need to use C data structures and C function calls. For example, a rectangle is represented as a CGRect, which is a C *struct*, and to create a CGRect from four numbers you call CGRectMake, which is a C *function*. The iOS API documentation will very often show you C expressions and expect you to understand them.

The best way to learn C is to read *The C Programming Language* (PTR Prentice Hall, 1988) by Brian W. Kernighan and Dennis M. Ritchie, commonly called K&R (Ritchie was the creator of C). It is one of the best computer books ever written: brief, dense, and stunningly precise and clear. K&R is so important for effective iOS (and Mac OS X) programming that I keep a physical copy beside me at all times while coding, and I recommend that you do the same. Another useful manual is *The C Book*, by Mike Banahan, Declan Brady and Mark Doran, available online at *http://publications.gbdirect .co.uk/c_book/*.

You don't have to know *all* about C in order to use Objective-C effectively, though; and that's a good thing. C is not a large or difficult language, but it has some tricky corners and can be extremely subtle, powerful, and low-level. Also, it would be impossible, and unnecessary, for me to describe all of C in a single chapter. C is described far more fully and correctly in K&R, *The C Book*, and elsewhere than I could possibly do it. Sooner or later, you're probably going to have technical questions about C that this chapter doesn't (and shouldn't) make any attempt to answer. So I emphasize that you really, really ought to have K&R or something similar at hand and resort to it as needed.

What I can do, and what this chapter will attempt to do, is tell you what aspects of C are important to understand at the outset, before you even start using Objective-C for iOS programming. That's why this chapter is "Just Enough C": it's just enough to get you going, comfortably and safely.

If you know no C at all, I suggest that, as an accompaniment to this chapter, you also read parts of K&R (think of this as "C: The Good Parts Version"). Here's my proposed K&R syllabus:

- Quickly skim K&R Chapter 1, the tutorial.
- Carefully read K&R Chapters 2 through 4.
- Read the first three sections of K&R Chapter 5 on pointers and arrays. You don't need to read the rest of Chapter 5 because you won't typically be doing any pointer arithmetic, but you do need to understand clearly what a pointer is, as Objective-C is all about objects and every reference to an object is a pointer; you'll be seeing and using that * character constantly.
- Read also the first section of K&R Chapter 6, on structures (structs); as a beginner, you probably won't define any structs, but you will use them quite a lot, so you'll need to know the notation (for example, as I've already said, a CGRect is a struct).
- Glance over K&R Appendix B, which covers the standard library, because you may find yourself making certain standard library calls, such as the mathematical functions; forgetting that the library exists is a typical beginner mistake.

Just to make things a little more confusing, the C defined in K&R is not precisely the C that forms the basis of Objective-C. Developments subsequent to K&R have resulted in further C standards (ANSI C, C89, C99), and the Xcode compiler extends the C language in its own ways. By default, Xcode projects are treated as C99 (though you could specify another C standard if you really wanted to). Fortunately, the most important differences between K&R's C and Xcode's C are small, convenient improvements that are easily remembered, so K&R remains the best and most reliable C reference.

## Compilation, Statements, and Comments

C is a compiled language. You write your program as text; to run the program, things proceed in two stages. First your text is compiled into machine instructions; then those machine instructions are executed. Thus, as with any compiled language, you can make two kinds of mistake:

- Any purely syntactic errors (meaning that you spoke the C language incorrectly) will be caught by the compiler, and the program won't even begin to run.
- If your program gets past the compiler, then it will run, but there is no guarantee that you haven't made some other sort of mistake, which can be detected only by noticing that the program doesn't behave as intended.

The C compiler is fussy, but you should accept its interference with good grace. The compiler is your friend: learn to love it. It may emit what looks like an irrelevant or incomprehensible error message, but when it does, the fact is that you've done something wrong and the compiler has helpfully caught it for you. Also, the compiler can warn you if something seems like a possible mistake, even though it isn't strictly illegal; these warnings, which differ from outright errors, are also helpful and should not be ignored.

I have said that running a program requires a preceding stage: compilation. But in fact there is a third stage that precedes compilation: preprocessing. (It doesn't really matter whether you think of preprocessing as a stage preceding compilation or as the first stage of compilation.) Preprocessing modifies your text, so when your text is handed to the compiler, it is not identical to the text you wrote. Preprocessing might sound tricky and intrusive, but in fact it proceeds only according to your instructions and is helpful for making your code clearer and more compact.

C is a statement-based language; every statement ends in a semicolon. (Forgetting the semicolon is a common beginner's mistake and is liable to get you a completely irrelevant and incomprehensible error message from the compiler.) For readability, programs are mostly written with one statement per line, but this is by no means a hard and fast rule: long statements (which, unfortunately, arise very commonly because of Objective-C's verbosity) are commonly split over multiple lines, and extremely short statements are sometimes written two or three to a line. You cannot split a line just anywhere, however; for example, a literal string can't contain a return character. Indentation is linguistically meaningless and is purely a matter of convention (and C programmers argue over those conventions with near-religious fervor); Xcode helps "intelligently" by indenting automatically, and you can use its automatic indentation both to keep your code readable and to confirm that you're not making any basic syntactic mistakes.

Comments are delimited in K&R C by /* ... */; the material between the delimiters can consist of multiple lines (K&R 1.2). In modern versions of C, a comment also can be denoted by two slashes (//); the rule is that if two slashes appear, they and everything after them on the same line are ignored:

```
int lower = 0; // lower limit of temperature table
```

These are sometimes called C++-style comments and are much more convenient for brief comments than the K&R comment syntax.

Throughout the C language (and therefore, throughout Objective-C as well), capitalization matters. All names are case-sensitive. There is no such data type as Int; it's lowercase "int." If you declare an int called `lower` and then try to speak of the same variable as `Lower`, the compiler will complain. By convention, variable names tend to start with a lowercase letter.

# Variable Declaration, Initialization, and Data Types

C is a strongly typed language. Every variable must be declared, indicating its data type, before it can be used. Declaration can also involve explicit initialization; a variable that is declared but not explicitly initialized is of uncertain value (and should be regarded as dangerous until it *is* initialized). In K&R C, declarations must precede all other statements, but in modern versions of C, this rule is relaxed so that you don't have to declare a variable until just before you start using it. The usual convention is thus to declare a variable and assign it a value as it makes its first appearance on the scene:

```
int height = 2;
int width = height * 2;
height = height + 1;
int area = height * width;
```

The basic built-in C data types are all numeric: char (one byte), int (four bytes), float and double (floating-point numbers), and varieties such as short (short integer), long (long integer), unsigned short, and so on. iOS makes use of some further numeric types derived from the C numeric types (by way of the `typedef` statement, K&R 6.7); the most important of these are NSInteger (along with NSUInteger) and CGFloat. You don't need to use these explicitly unless an API tells you to, and even when you do, just think of NSInteger as int and CGFloat as float, and you'll be fine.

To *cast* (or *typecast*) a variable's value explicitly to another type, precede the variable's name with the other type's name in parentheses:

```
int height = 2;
float fheight = (float)height;
```

In that particular example, the explicit cast is unnecessary because the integer value will be cast to a float implicitly as it is assigned to a float variable, but it illustrates the notation. You'll find yourself typecasting quite a bit in Objective-C, mostly in order to subdue the worries of the compiler (examples appear in Chapter 3).

Another form of numeric initialization is the enum (K&R 2.3). It's a way of assigning names to a sequence of numeric values and is useful when a value represents one of several possible options. The Cocoa API uses this device a lot. For example, the three possible types of status bar animation are defined like this:

```
typedef enum {
    UIStatusBarAnimationNone,
    UIStatusBarAnimationFade,
    UIStatusBarAnimationSlide,
} UIStatusBarAnimation;
```

That definition assigns the value 0 to the name UIStatusBarAnimationNone, the value 1 to the name UIStatusBarAnimationFade, and the value 2 to the name UIStatusBarAnimationSlide. The upshot is, however, that you can use the suggestively meaningful names without caring about, or even knowing, the arbitrary numeric values they represent. It's a useful idiom, and you may well have reason to define enums in your own code.

There appears to be a native text type (a string) in C, but this is something of an illusion; behind the scenes, it is actually a null-terminated array of char. For example, in C you can write a string literal like this:

```
"string"
```

But in fact this is stored as 7 bytes, the numeric (ASCII) equivalents of each letter followed by a byte consisting of 0 to signal the end of the string. This data structure, called a C string, is rather tricky, and if you're lucky you'll rarely or never encounter one while programming iOS. In general, when working with strings, you'll use an Objective-C object type called NSString. An NSString is totally different from a C string; it happens, however, that Objective-C lets you write a literal NSString in a way that looks very like a C string:

```
@"string"
```

Notice the at-sign! This expression is actually a directive to the Objective-C compiler to form an NSString object. A common mistake is forgetting the at-sign, thus causing your expression to be interpreted as a C string, which is a completely different animal.

Because the notation for literal NSStrings is modeled on the notation for C strings, it is worth knowing something about C strings, even though you won't generally encounter them. For example, K&R lists a number of escaped characters (K&R 2.3), which you can also use in a literal NSString, including the following:

\n

A Unix newline character

\t

A tab character

\"

A quotation mark (escaped to show that this is not the end of the string literal)

\\

A backslash

 NSStrings are natively Unicode-based, but because Objective-C is C, including non-ASCII characters in a literal NSString was, until quite recently, remarkably tricky, and you needed to know about such things as the \x and \u escape sequences. Now, however, it is perfectly legal to type a bullet or any other non-ASCII character directly into an NSString literal, and you should ignore old Internet postings (and even an occasional sentence in Apple's own documentation) warning that it is not.

K&R also mention a notation for concatenating string literals, in which multiple string literals separated only by white space are automatically concatenated and treated as a single string literal. This notation is useful for splitting a long string into multiple lines for legibility, and Objective-C copies this convention for literal NSStrings as well, except that you have to remember the at-sign:

```
@"This is a big long literal string "
@"which I have broken over two lines of code.";
```

# Structs

C offers few simple native data types, so how are more complex data types made? There are three ways: structures, pointers, and arrays. Both structures and pointers are going to be crucial when you're programming iOS. You're less likely to need a C array, because Objective-C has its own NSArray object type, but it will arise in a couple of examples later in this book.

A C structure, usually called a struct (K&R 6.1), is a compound data type: it combines multiple data types into a single type, which can be passed around as a single entity. Moreover, the elements constituting the compound entity have names and can be accessed by those names through the compound entity, using dot-notation. For example, the iOS documentation tells you that a CGPoint is defined as follows:

```
struct CGPoint {
    CGFloat x;
    CGFloat y;
};
typedef struct CGPoint CGPoint;
```

Recall that a CGFloat is basically a float, so this is a compound data type made up of two simple native data types; in effect, a CGPoint has two CGFloat parts, and their names are x and y. (The rather odd-looking last line merely asserts that one can use the term CGPoint instead of the more verbose struct CGPoint.) So we can write:

```
CGPoint myPoint;
myPoint.x = 4.3;
myPoint.y = 7.1;
```

Just as we can assign to myPoint.x in order to *set* this part of the struct, we can say myPoint.x to *get* this part of the struct. It's as if myPoint.x were the name of a variable. Moreover, an element of a struct can itself be a struct, and the dot-notation can be chained. To illustrate, first note the existence of another iOS struct, CGSize:

```
struct CGSize {
    CGFloat width;
    CGFloat height;
};
typedef struct CGSize CGSize;
```

Put a CGPoint and a CGSize together and you've got a CGRect:

```
struct CGRect {
    CGPoint origin;
    CGSize size;
};
typedef struct CGRect CGRect;
```

So suppose we've got a CGRect variable called myRect, already initialized. Then myRect.origin is a CGPoint, and myRect.origin.x is a CGFloat. Similarly, myRect.size is a CGSize, and myRect.size.width is a CGFloat. You could change just the width part of our CGRect directly, like this:

```
myRect.size.width = 8.6;
```

Instead of initializing a struct by assigning to each of its elements, you can initialize it at declaration time by assigning values for all its elements at once, in curly braces, separated by commas, like this:

```
CGPoint myPoint = { 4.3, 7.1 };
```

The iOS API has many commonly used structs, typically accompanied by convenience functions for working with them.

# Pointers

The other big way that C extends its range of data types is by means of pointers (K&R 5.1). A pointer is an integer (of some size or other) with a meaning: it designates the location in memory where the real data is to be found. Knowing the structure of that data and how to work with it, as well as allocating a block of memory of the required size beforehand and disposing of that block of memory when it's no longer needed, is a very complicated business. Luckily, this is exactly the sort of complicated business that Objective-C is going to take care of for us. So all you really have to know in order to use pointers is what they are and what notation is used to refer to them.

Let's start with a simple declaration. If we wanted to declare an integer in C, we could say:

```
int i;
```

That line says, "i is an integer." Now let's instead declare a *pointer* to an integer:

```
int* intPtr;
```

That line says, "intPtr is a pointer to an integer." Never mind how we know there really is going to be an integer at the address designated by this point; here, I'm concerned only with the notation. It is permitted to place the asterisk in the declaration before the name rather than after the type:

```
int *intPtr;
```

I don't generally use that second form when declaring a pointer, but it does come in handy when declaring several variables of the same type in a single statement. Here's what I mean. It is legal, though I did not mention this earlier, to declare multiple variables of a single type in one statement, like this:

```
int i, j, k;
```

By the same token, it is possible to declare multiple pointers to the same type in one statement by attaching the asterisk to the variable name (repeatedly):

```
int *intPtr1, *intPtr2, *intPtr3;
```

However, the name of the type is still int*. If you are asked what type is intPtr is, the answer is int* (a pointer to an int); the asterisk is part of the name of the type of this variable. If you needed to cast a variable p to this type, you'd cast like this: (int*)p.

Pointers are very important in Objective-C, because Objective-C is all about objects (Chapter 2), and every variable referring to an object is itself a pointer. For example, I've already mentioned that the Objective-C string type is called NSString. So the way to declare an NSString variable is as a pointer to an NSString:

```
NSString* s;
```

An NSString literal is an NSString value, so we can even declare and initialize this NSString object, thus writing a seriously useful line of Objective-C code:

---

```
NSString* s = @"Hello, world!";
```

In pure C, having declared a pointer-to-integer called `intPtr`, you are liable to speak later in your code of `*intPtr`. This notation, outside of a declaration, means "the thing pointed to by the pointer `intPtr`." You speak of `*intPtr` because you wish to access the integer at the far end of the pointer.

But in Objective-C, this is generally *not* the case. In your code, you'll be treating the pointer to an object as the object. So, for example, having declared `s` as a pointer to an NSString, you will *not* then proceed to speak of `*s`; rather, you will speak simply of `s`, as if it *were* the string. All the Objective-C stuff you'll want to do with an object will expect the pointer, not the object at the far end of the pointer; behind the scenes, Objective-C itself will take care of the messy business of following the pointer to its block of memory and doing whatever needs to be done in that block of memory. This fact is extremely convenient for you as a programmer, but it does cause Objective-C users to speak a little loosely; we tend to say that "`s` is an NSString," when of course it is actually a pointer to an NSString.

You must never let this convenience lull you into forgetting the crucial fact that a pointer is a pointer. The logic of how pointers work is different from the logic of how simple data types work. The difference is particularly evident with assignment. Assignment to a simple data type changes the data value. Assignment to a pointer repoints the pointer. Suppose `ptr1` and `ptr2` are both pointers, and you say:

```
ptr1 = ptr2;
```

Now `ptr1` and `ptr2` are pointing at the same thing. Any change to the thing pointed to by `ptr1` will also change the thing pointed to by `ptr2`, because they are the same thing. Meanwhile, whatever `ptr1` was pointing to before the assignment is now not being pointed to by `ptr1`; it might, indeed, be pointed to by nothing (which could be bad). A firm understanding of these facts is crucial when working in Objective-C (Figure 1-1).

The most general type of pointer is *pointer-to-void* (`void*`), the *generic pointer*. It is legal to use a generic pointer wherever a specific type of pointer is expected. In effect, pointer-to-void casts away type checking as to what's at the far end of the pointer. Thus, the following is legal:

```
int* p1; // and pretend p1 has a value
void* p2;
p2 = p1;
p1 = p2;
```

# Arrays

A C array (K&R 5.3) consists of multiple elements of the same data type. An array declaration states the data type of the elements, followed by the name of the array, along with square brackets containing the number of elements:

```
int arr[3]; // means: arr is an array consisting of 3 ints
```

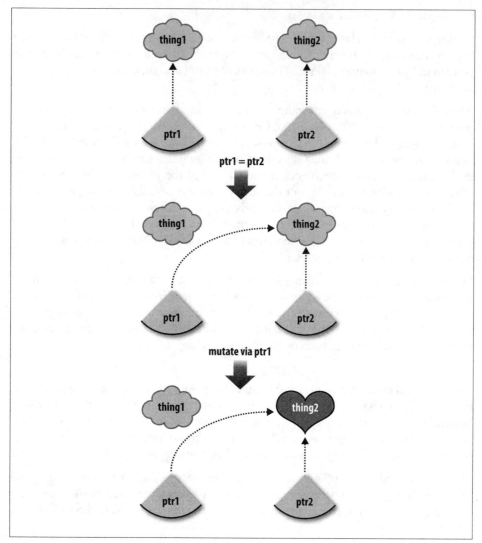

*Figure 1-1. Pointers and assignment*

To refer to an element of an array, use the array's name followed by the element number in square brackets. The first element of an array is numbered 0. So we can initialize an array by assigning values to each element in turn:

```
int arr[3];
arr[0] = 123;
arr[1] = 456;
arr[2] = 789;
```

Alternatively, you can initialize an array at declaration time by assigning a list of values in curly braces, just as with a struct. In this case, the size of the array can be omitted from the declaration, because it is implicit in the initialization (K&R 4.9):

```
int arr[] = {123, 456, 789};
```

Curiously, the name of an array is the name of a pointer (to the first element of the array). Thus, for example, having declared `arr` as in the preceding examples, you can use `arr` wherever a value of type `int*` (a pointer to an int) is expected. This fact is the basis of some highly sophisticated C idioms that you almost certainly won't need to know about (which is why I don't recommend that you read any of K&R Chapter 5 beyond section 3).

C arrays rarely arise in practice when programming iOS, because you'll work mostly with the NSArray object type instead. But here's a case where they do. The function `CGContextStrokeLineSegments` is declared like this:

```
void CGContextStrokeLineSegments (
    CGContextRef c,
    const CGPoint points[],
    size_t count
);
```

The second parameter is an array (meaning a C array) of CGPoints. That's what the square brackets tell you. So to call this function, you'd need to know at least how to make an array of CGPoints. You might do it like this:

```
CGPoint arr[] = {{4,5}, {6,7}, {8,9}, {10,11}};
```

Having done that, you can pass `arr` as the second argument in a call to `CGContextStrokeLineSegments`.

Also, a C string, as I've already mentioned, is actually an array. For example, the NSString method `stringWithUTF8String:` takes (according to the documentation) "a NULL-terminated C array of bytes in UTF8 encoding;" but the parameter is declared not as an array, but as a `char*`. Those are the same thing, and are both ways of saying that this method takes a C string.

## Operators

Arithmetic operators are straightforward (K&R 2.5), but watch out for the rule that "integer division truncates any fractional part." This rule is the cause of much novice error in C. If you have two integers and you want to divide them in such a way as to get a fractional result, you must represent at least one of them as a float:

```
int i = 3;
float f = i/2; // beware! not 1.5
```

To get 1.5, you should have written `i/2.0` or `(float)i/2`.

The integer increment and decrement operators (K&R 2.8), ++ and --, work differently depending on whether they precede or follow their variable. The expression ++i replaces the value of i by 1 more than its current value and then uses the resulting value; the expression i++ uses the current value of i and then replaces it with 1 more than its current value. This is one of C's coolest features.

C also provides bitwise operators (K&R 2.9), such as bitwise-and (&) and bitwise-or (|); they operate on the individual binary bits that constitute integers. Of these, the one you are most likely to need is bitwise-or, because the Cocoa API often uses bits as switches when multiple options are to be specified simultaneously. For example, there are various ways in which a UIView can be resized automatically as its superview is resized, and you're supposed to provide one or more of these when setting a UIView's autoresizingMask property. The autoresizing options are listed in the documentation as follows:

```
enum {
    UIViewAutoresizingNone              = 0,
    UIViewAutoresizingFlexibleLeftMargin    = 1 << 0,
    UIViewAutoresizingFlexibleWidth         = 1 << 1,
    UIViewAutoresizingFlexibleRightMargin   = 1 << 2,
    UIViewAutoresizingFlexibleTopMargin     = 1 << 3,
    UIViewAutoresizingFlexibleHeight        = 1 << 4,
    UIViewAutoresizingFlexibleBottomMargin  = 1 << 5
};
typedef NSUInteger UIViewAutoresizing;
```

The << symbol is the left shift operator; the right operand says how many bits to shift the left operand. So pretend that an NSUInteger is 8 bits (it isn't, but let's keep things simple and short). Then this enum means that the following name–value pairs are defined (using binary notation for the values):

UIViewAutoresizingNone
    00000000

UIViewAutoresizingFlexibleLeftMargin
    00000001

UIViewAutoresizingFlexibleWidth
    00000010

UIViewAutoresizingFlexibleRightMargin
    00000100

UIViewAutoresizingFlexibleTopMargin
    00001000

and so on. The reason for this bit-based representation is that these values can be combined into a single value (a *bitmask*) that you pass to set the autoresizingMask. All Cocoa has to do in order to understand your intentions is to look to see which bits in the value that you pass are set to 1. So, for example, 00001010 would mean that UIView-

`AutoresizingFlexibleTopMargin` and `UIViewAutoresizingFlexibleWidth` are true (and that the others, by implication, are all false).

The question is how to form the value 00001010 in order to pass it. You could just do the math, figure out that binary 00001010 is decimal 10, and set the `autoresizingMask` property to 10, but that's not what you're supposed to do, and it's not a very good idea, because it's error-prone and makes your code incomprehensible. Instead, use the bitwise-or operator to combine the desired options:

```
myView.autoresizingMask =
    UIViewAutoresizingFlexibleTopMargin | UIViewAutoresizingFlexibleWidth;
```

This notation works because the bitwise-or operator combines its operands by setting in the result any bits that are set in either of the operands, so 00001000 | 00000010 is 00001010, which is just the value we're trying to convey.

Simple assignment (K&R 2.10) is by the equal sign. But there are also compound assignment operators that combine assignment with some other operation. For example:

```
height *= 2; // same as saying: height = height * 2;
```

The ternary operator (?:) is a way of specifying one of two values depending on a condition (K&R 2.11). The scheme is as follows:

```
(condition) ? exp1 : exp2
```

If the condition is true (see the next section for what that means), the expression *exp1* is evaluated and the result is used; otherwise, the expression *exp2* is evaluated and the result is used. For example, you might use the ternary operator while performing an assignment, using this schema:

```
myVariable = (condition) ? exp1 : exp2;
```

What gets assigned to `myVariable` depends on the truth value of the condition. There's nothing happening here that couldn't be accomplished more verbosely with flow control (see the next section), but the ternary operator can greatly improve clarity, and I use it a lot.

# Flow Control and Conditions

Basic flow control is fairly simple and usually involves a condition in parentheses and a block of conditionally executed code in curly braces. These curly braces constitute a new scope, into which new variables can be introduced. So, for example:

```
if (x == 7) {
    int i = 0;
    i += 1;
}
```

After the closing curly brace in the fourth line, the `i` introduced in the second line has ceased to exist, because its scope is the inside of the curly braces. If the contents of the curly braces consist of a single statement, the curly braces can be omitted, but I would advise beginners against this shorthand, as you can confuse yourself. A common beginner mistake (which will be caught by the compiler) is forgetting the parentheses around the condition. The full set of flow control statements is given in K&R Chapter 3, and I'll just summarize them schematically here (Example 1-1).

*Example 1-1. The C flow control constructs*

```
if (condition) {
    statements;
}

if (condition) {
    statements;
} else {
    statements;
}

if (condition) {
    statements;
else if (condition) {
    statements;
} else {
    statements;
}

while (condition) {
    statements;
}

do {
    statements;
} while (condition);

for (before-all; condition; after-each) {
    statements;
}
```

The if...else if...else structure can have as many else if blocks as needed, and the else block is optional. Instead of an extended if...else if...else if...else structure, when the conditions would consist of comparing various values against a single value, you can use the switch statement; however, I never use it, and I don't recommend that you do either, as it is rather confusing and can easily go wrong. See K&R 3.4 if you're interested.

The C for loop needs some elaboration for beginners (Example 1-1). The *before-all* statement is executed once as the for loop is first encountered and is usually used for initialization of the counter. The condition is then tested, and if true, the block is executed; the condition is usually used to test whether the counter has reached its limit. The *after-each* statement is then executed, and is usually used to increment or decrement the counter; the condition is then immediately tested again. Thus, to execute a block using integer values 1, 2, 3, 4, and 5 for i, the notation is:

```
int i;
for (i = 1; i < 6; i++) {
    // ... statements ...
}
```

The need for a counter intended to exist solely within the for loop is so common that C99 permits the declaration of the counter as part of the *before-all* statement; the declared variable's scope is then inside the curly braces:

```
for (int i = 1; i < 6; i++) {
    // ... statements ...
}
```

The for loop is one of the few areas in which Objective-C extends C's flow-control syntax. Certain Objective-C objects represent enumerable collections of other objects; "enumerable" basically means that you can cycle through the collection, and cycling through a collection is called *enumerating* the collection. To make enumerating easy, Objective-C provides a for...in operator, which works like a for loop:

```
SomeType* oneItem;
for (oneItem in myCollection) {
    // ... statements ....
}
```

On each pass through the loop, the variable oneItem (or whatever you call it) takes on the next value from within the collection. As with the C99 for loop, oneItem can be declared in the for statement, limiting its scope to the curly braces:

```
for (SomeType* oneItem in myCollection) {
    // ... statements ....
}
```

To abort a loop from inside the curly braces, use the break statement. To abort the current iteration from within the curly braces and proceed to the next iteration, use the continue statement. In the case of while and do, continue means to perform immediately the conditional test; in the case of a for loop, continue means to perform immediately the *after-each* statement and then the conditional test.

C also has a goto statement that allows you to jump to a named (labeled) line in your code (K&R 3.8); even though goto is notoriously "considered harmful," there are situations in which it is pretty much necessary, especially because C's flow control is otherwise so primitive.

 It is permissible for a C statement to be compounded of multiple statements, separated by commas, to be executed sequentially. The last of the multiple statements is the value of the compound statement as a whole. This construct, for instance, lets you perform some secondary action before each test of a condition or perform more than one *after-each* action (an example appears in Chapter 17).

We can now turn to the question of what a condition consists of. C has no separate boolean type; a condition either evaluates to 0, in which case it is considered false, or it doesn't, in which case it is true. Comparisons are performed using the equality and relational operators (K&R 2.6); for example, == compares for equality, and < compares for whether the first operand is less than the second. Logical expressions can be combined using the logical-and operator (&&) and the logical-or operator (||); using these along with parentheses and the not operator (!) you can form complex conditions. Evaluation of logical-and and logical-or expressions is short-circuited, meaning that if the left condition settles the question, the right condition is never even evaluated.

 Don't confuse the logical-and operator (&&) and the logical-or operator (||) with the bitwise-and operator (&) and the bitwise-or operator (|) discussed earlier. Writing & when you mean && (or *vice versa*) can result in surprising behavior.

The operator for testing basic equality, ==, is not a simple equal sign; forgetting the difference is a common novice mistake. The problem is that such code is legal: simple assignment, which is what the equal sign means, has a value, and any value is legal in a condition. So consider this piece of (nonsense) code:

```
int i = 0;
while (i = 1) {
    i = 0;
}
```

You might think that the while condition tests whether i is 1. You might then think: i is 0, so the while body will never be performed. Right? Wrong. The while condition does not test whether i is 1; it assigns 1 to i. The value of that assignment is also 1, so the condition evaluates to 1, which means true. So the while body *is* performed. Moreover, even though the while body assigns 0 to i, the condition is then evaluated again and assigns 1 to i a second time, which means true yet again. And so on, forever; we've written an endless loop, and the program will hang. (And, depending on what compiler and settings you're using, you might not even get a warning of trouble ahead.)

C programmers actually revel in the fact that testing for zero and testing for false are the same thing and use it to create compact conditional expressions, which are considered elegant and idiomatic. I don't recommend that you make use of such idioms, as they can be confusing, but I must admit that even I do occasionally resort to this sort of thing:

```
NSString* s = nil;
// ...
if (s) {
    // ...
}
```

The idea of that code is to test whether the NSString object s, between the time it was declared and the start of the if-block, has been set to an actual string. Because nil is a form of 0, the condition is asking whether s is non-nil. Some Objective-C programmers would take me to task for this style of writing code; if I want to test whether s is nil, they would say, I should test it explicitly:

```
if (s == nil)
```

In fact, some would say, it is even better to write the terms of the comparison in the opposite order:

```
if (nil == s)
```

Why? Because if I were to omit accidentally the second equal sign, thus turning the equality comparison into an assignment, the first expression would compile (and misbehave, because I am now assigning nil to s), but the second expression would certainly be caught by the compiler as an error, because assigning a value to nil is illegal.

Objective-C introduces a BOOL type, which you should use if you need to capture or maintain a condition's value as a variable, along with constants YES and NO (actually representing 1 and 0), which you should use when setting a boolean value. Don't compare anything against a BOOL, not even YES or NO, because a value like 2 is true in a condition but is not equal to YES or NO. Just use the BOOL directly as a condition, or as part of a complex condition, and all will be well. For example:

```
BOOL snil = (nil == s);
// ...
if (snil) // ... not: if (snil == YES)
```

# Functions

C is a function-based language (K&R 4.1). A *function* is a block of code defining what should happen; when other code *calls* (invokes) that function, the function's code does happen. A function returns a value, which is substituted for the call to that function.

Here's a definition of a function that accepts an integer and returns its square:

```
int square(int i) {
    return i * i;
}
```

Now I'll call that function:

```
int i = square(3);
```

Because of the way square is defined, that is exactly like saying:

```
int i = 9;
```

That example is extremely simple, but it illustrates many key aspects of functions.

Let's analyze how a function is defined:

```
int❶ square❷(❸int i) {❹
    return i * i;
}
```

❶ We start with the type of value that the function returns; here, it returns an int.

❷ Then we have the name of the function, which is `square`.

❸ Then we have parentheses, and here we place the data type and name of any values that this function expects to receive. Here, `square` expects to receive one value, an int, which we are calling `i`. The name `i` (along with its expected data type) is a *parameter*; when the function is called, its value will be supplied as an *argument*. If a function expects to receive more than one value, multiple parameters in its definition are separated by a comma (and when the function is called, the arguments supplied are likewise separated by a comma).

❹ Finally, we have curly braces containing the statements that are to be executed when the function is called.

Those curly braces constitute a scope; variables declared within them are local to the function. The names used for the parameters in the function definition are also local to the function; in other words, the `i` in the first line of the function definition is the same as the `i` in the second line of the function definition, but it has nothing to do with any `i` used outside the function definition (as when the result of the function call is assigned to a variable called `i`). The value of the `i` parameter in the function definition is assigned from the corresponding argument when the function is actually called; in the previous example, it is 3, which is why the function result is 9. Supplying a function call with arguments is thus a form of assignment. Suppose a function is defined like this:

```
int myfunction(int i, int j) { // ...
```

And suppose we call that function:

```
int result = myfunction(3, 4);
```

That function call effectively assigns 3 to the function's `i` parameter and 4 to the function's `j` parameter.

When a `return` statement is encountered, the value accompanying it is handed back as the result of the function call, and the function terminates. It is legal for a function to return no value; in such a case, the `return` statement has no accompanying value, and the definition states the type of value returned by the function as `void`. It is also legal to call a function and ignore its return value even if it has one. For example, we could say:

```
square(3);
```

That would be a somewhat silly thing to say, because we have gone to all the trouble of calling the function and having it generate the square of 3 — namely 9 — but we have done nothing to *capture* that 9. It is exactly as if we had said:

```
9;
```

You're allowed to say that, but it doesn't seem to serve much purpose. On the other hand, the point of a function might be not so much the value it returns as other things it does as it is executing, so then it might make perfect sense to ignore its result.

The parentheses in a function's syntax are crucial. Parentheses are how C knows there's a function. Parentheses after the function name in the function *definition* are how C knows this is a function definition, and they are needed even if this function takes no parameters. Parentheses after the function name in the function *call* are how C knows this is a function call, and they are needed even if this function call supplies no arguments. Using the bare name of a function is possible, because the name is effectively a kind of variable (and I'll talk later about why you might want to do that), but it doesn't call the function.

Let's return to the simple C function definition and call that I used as my example earlier. Suppose we combine that function definition and the call to that function into a single program:

```
int square(int i) {
    return i * i;
}
int i = square(3);
```

That is a legal program, but only because the definition of the square function precedes the call to that function. If we wanted to place the definition of the square function elsewhere, such as after the call to it, we would need at least to precede the call with a declaration of the square function (Example 1-2). The declaration looks just like the first line of the definition, but it is a statement, ending with a semicolon, rather than a left curly brace.

*Example 1-2. Declaring, calling, and defining a function*

```
int square(int i);
int i = square(3);
int square(int i) {
    return i * i;
}
```

The parameter names in the declaration do not have to match the parameter names in the definition, but all the types (and, of course, the name of the function) must match. The types constitute the *signature* of this function. In other words, it does not matter if the first line, the declaration, is rewritten thus:

```
int square(int j);
```

What does matter is that, both in the declaration and in the definition, square is a function taking one int parameter and returning an int.

In Objective-C, when you're sending a message to an object (Chapter 2), you won't use a function call; you'll use a method call (Chapter 3). But you will most definitely use plenty of C function calls as well. For example, earlier we initialized a CGPoint by setting its x element and its y element and by assigning its elements values in curly braces. But what you'll usually do to make a new CGPoint is to call `CGPointMake`, which is declared like this:

```
CGPoint CGPointMake (
    CGFloat x,
    CGFloat y
);
```

Despite its multiple lines and its indentations, this is indeed a C function declaration, just like the declaration for our simple `square` function. It says that `CGPointMake` is a C function that takes two CGFloat parameters and returns a CGPoint. So now you know (I hope) that it would be legal (and typical) to write this sort of thing:

```
CGPoint myPoint = CGPointMake(4.3, 7.1);
```

# Pointer Parameters and the Address Operator

I've mentioned several times that your variables referring to Objective-C objects are going to be pointers:

```
NSString* s = @"Hello, world!";
```

Although it is common to speak loosely of `s` as an NSString (or just as a string), it is actually an `NSString*` — a pointer to an NSString. Therefore, when a C function or an Objective-C method expects an `NSString*` parameter, there's no problem, because that's exactly what you've got. For example, one way to concatenate two NSStrings is to call the NSString method `stringByAppendingString:` (that's not a misprint; the colon is part of the name), which the documentation tells you is declared as follows:

```
- (NSString *)stringByAppendingString:(NSString *)aString
```

The space between the class name and the asterisk is optional, so this declaration is telling you (after you allow for the Objective-C syntax) that this method expects one `NSString*` parameter and returns an `NSString*`. That's splendid because those kinds of pointers are just what you've got and just what you want. So this code would be legal:

```
NSString* s1 = @"Hello, ";
NSString* s2 = @"World!"
NSString* s3 = [s1 stringByAppendingString: s2];
```

The idea, then, is that although Objective-C is chock-a-block with pointers and asterisks, they don't make things more complicated, as long as you remember that they *are* pointers.

Sometimes, however, a function expects as a parameter a pointer to something, but what you've got is not a pointer but the thing itself. Thus, you need a way to create a pointer to that thing. The solution is the address operator (K&R 5.1), which is an ampersand before the name of the thing.

For example, there's an NSString method for reading from a file into an NSString, which is declared like this:

```
+ (id)stringWithContentsOfFile:(NSString *)path
                    encoding:(NSStringEncoding)enc
                       error:(NSError **)error
```

Now, never mind what an `id` is, and don't worry about the Objective-C method declaration syntax. Just consider the types of the parameters. The first one is an `NSString*`; that's no problem, as every reference to an NSString is actually a pointer to an NSString. An NSStringEncoding turns out to be merely an alias to a primitive data type, an NSUInteger, so that's no problem either. But what on earth is an `NSError**`?

By all logic, it looks like an `NSError**` should be a pointer to a pointer to an NSError. And that's exactly what it is. This method is asking to be passed a pointer to a pointer to an NSError. Well, it's easy to declare a pointer to an NSError:

```
NSError* myError;
```

But how can we obtain a pointer to that? With the address operator! So our code might look, schematically, like this:

```
NSString* myPath = // something or other;
NSStringEncoding myEnc = // something or other;
NSError* myError = nil;
NSString* result = [NSString stringWithContentsOfFile: myPath
                                             encoding: myEnc
                                                error: &myError];
```

The important thing to notice is the ampersand. Because `myError` is a pointer to an NSError, `&myError` is a pointer to a pointer to an NSError, which is just what we're expected to provide. Thus, everything goes swimmingly.

This device lets Cocoa effectively return *two* results from this method call. It returns a real result, which we have captured by assigning it to the NSString pointer we're calling `result`. But if there's an error, it also wants to set the value of another object, an NSError object; the idea is that you can then study that NSError object to find out what went wrong. (Perhaps the file wasn't where you said it was, or it wasn't stored in the encoding you claimed it was.) By passing a pointer to a pointer to an NSError, you give the method free rein to do that. Before the call to `stringWithContentsOfFile:`, `myError` was uninitialized; during the call to `stringWithContentsOfFile:`, Cocoa can, if it likes, repoint the pointer, thus giving `myError` an actual value.

So the idea is that you first check `result` to see whether it's nil. If it isn't, fine; it's the string you asked for. If it is, you then study the NSError that `myError` is now pointing to, to learn what went wrong. This pattern is frequently used in Cocoa.

You can use the address operator to create a pointer to any named variable. A C function is technically a kind of named variable, so you can even create a pointer to a function! This is an example of when you'd use the name of the function without the parentheses: you aren't calling the function, you're talking about it. For example, `&square` is a pointer to the `square` function. In Chapter 9, I describe a situation in which this is a useful thing to do.

Another operator used in connection with pointers, or when memory must be allocated dynamically, is `sizeof`. It may be followed by a type name in parentheses or by a variable name; a variable name needn't be in parentheses, but it *can* be, so most programmers ignore the distinction and use parentheses routinely, as if `sizeof` were a function.

For example, the documentation shows the declaration for `AudioSessionSetProperty` like this:

```
OSStatus AudioSessionSetProperty (
    AudioSessionPropertyID    inID,
    UInt32                    inDataSize,
    const void                *inData
);
```

Never mind what an AudioSessionPropertyID is; it's merely a value that you obtain and pass on. UInt32 is one of those derived numeric types I mentioned earlier. The discussion has already dealt with pointer-to-void and how to derive a pointer using the address operator. But look at the *name* of the second parameter; the function is asking for the size of the thing pointed to by the third parameter. Here's an actual call to this function (from Chapter 27):

```
UInt32 ambi = kAudioSessionCategory_AmbientSound;
AudioSessionSetProperty(kAudioSessionProperty_AudioCategory, sizeof(ambi), &ambi);
```

# Files

The little dance of declaring a function before calling it (Example 1-2) may seem rather absurd, but it is of tremendous importance in the C language, because it is what allows a C program to be arbitrarily large and complex.

As your program grows, you can divide and organize it into multiple files. This kind of organization can make a large program much more maintainable — easier to read, easier to understand, easier to change without accidentally breaking things. A large C program therefore usually consists of two kinds of file: code files, whose filename extension is *.c*, and header files, whose filename extension is *.h*. The build system will automatically "see" all the files and will know that together they constitute a single program, but there is also a rule in C that code inside one file cannot "see" another file unless it is explicitly told to do so. Thus, a file itself constitutes a scope; this is a deliberate and valuable feature of C, because it helps you keep things nicely pigeonholed.

The way you tell a C file to "see" another file is with the `#include` directive. The hash sign in the term `#include` is a signal that this line is an instruction to the preprocessor. In this case, the word `#include` is followed by the name of another file, and the directive means that the preprocessor should simply replace the directive by the entire contents of the file that's named.

So the strategy for constructing a large C program is something like this:

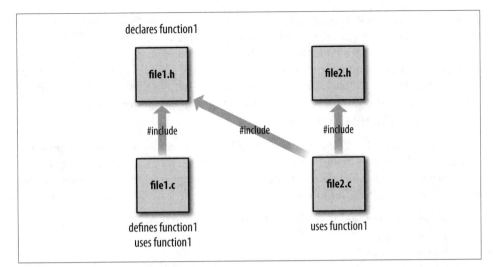

declares function1

file1.h

file2.h

#include    #include    #include

file1.c

file2.c

defines function1
uses function1

uses function1

*Figure 1-2. How a large C program is divided into files*

- In each .*c* file, put the code that only this file needs to know about; typically, each file's code consists of related functionality.

- In each .*h* file, put the function declarations that multiple .*c* files might need to know about.

- Have each .*c* file include those .*h* files containing the declarations it needs to know about.

So, for example, if function1 is defined in *file1.c*, but *file2.c* might need to call function1, the declaration for function1 can go in *file1.h*. Now *file1.c* can include *file1.h*, so all of its functions, regardless of order, can call function1, and *file2.c* can also include *file1.h*, so all of *its* functions can call function1 (Figure 1-2). In short, header files are a way of letting code files share knowledge about one another without actually sharing code (because, if they did share code, that would violate the entire point of keeping the code in separate files).

But how does the compiler know where, among all these multiple .*c* files, to begin execution? Every real C program contains, somewhere, exactly one function called main, and this is always the entry point for the program as a whole: the compiler sets things up so that when the program executes, main is called.

The organization for large C programs that I've just described will also be, in effect, the organization for your iOS programs. (The chief difference will be that instead of .*c* files, you'll use .*m* files, because .*m* is the conventional filename extension for telling Xcode that your files are written in Objective-C, not pure C.) Moreover, if you look at any iOS Xcode project, you'll discover that it contains a file called *main.m*; and if you look at that file, you'll find that it contains a function called main. That's the entry point to your application's code when it runs.

Furthermore, your iOS programs consist not only of *your* code files and their corresponding *.h* files, but also of Apple's code files and *their* corresponding *.h* files. The difference is that Apple's code files (which are what constitutes Cocoa) have already been compiled. But your code must still `#include` Apple's *.h* files so as to be able to see Apple's declarations. If you look at an iOS Xcode project, you'll find that any *.h* files it contains by default, as well as its *main.m* file, contain a line of this form:

```
#import <UIKit/UIKit.h>
```

That line is essentially a single massive `#include` that copies into your program the declarations for the entire basic iOS API. Moreover, each of your *.m* files `#import`s its corresponding *.h* file, including whatever the *.h* file `#import`s. Thus, all your code files include the basic iOS declarations.

For example, earlier I said that CGPoint was defined like this:

```
struct CGPoint {
  CGFloat x;
  CGFloat y;
};
typedef struct CGPoint CGPoint;
```

After the preprocessor operates on all your files, your *.m* files actually *contain* that definition of CGPoint. (In Xcode 3.2.x, you can even choose Build → Preprocess to confirm that this is true.) And that is why your code is able to use a CGPoint!

The `#import` preprocessor directive is not mentioned in K&R. It's an Objective-C addition to the language. It's based on `#include`, but it is used instead of `#include` because it (`#import`) contains some logic for making sure that the same material is not included more than once. Such repeated inclusion is a danger whenever there are many cross-dependent header files; use of `#import` solves the problem neatly.

The `#import` directive, like the `#include` directive (K&R 4.11), can specify a file in angle brackets or in quotation marks:

```
#import <UIKit/UIKit.h>
#import "MyHeader.h"
```

The quotation marks form means "look for the named file in the same folder as this file" (the *.m* file in which the `#import` line occurs). The angle brackets form means to look among the various header search paths supplied in the build settings; these search paths are set for you automatically, and you normally won't need to modify them. In general, the distinction means that you'll use angle brackets to refer to a header file owned by the Cocoa API and quotation marks to refer to a header file that you wrote. If you're curious as to what an `#import` directive imports, select it (in Xcode) and choose File → Open Quickly to display the contents of the designated header file.

# The Standard Library

You also have at your disposal a large collection of built-in C library files. A library file is a centrally located collection of C functions, along with a *.h* file that you can include in order to make those functions available to your code.

For example, suppose you want to round a float up to the next highest integer. The way to do this is to call some variety of the `ceil` function. You can read the `ceil` man page in Xcode, or by typing `man ceil` in the Terminal. The documentation tells you what `#include` to use to incorporate the correct header and also shows you the function declarations and tells you what those functions do. A small pure C program might thus look like this:

```
#include <math.h>
float f = 4.5;
int i = ceilf(f); // now i is 5
```

In your iOS programs, *math.h* is included for you as part of the massive UIKit `#import`, so there's no need to include it again. But some library functions might require an explicit `#import`.

The standard library is discussed in K&R Appendix B. But the modern standard library has evolved since K&R; it is a superset of K&R's library. The `ceil` function, for example, is listed in K&R appendix B, but the `ceilf` function is not. Similarly, if you wanted to generate a random number (which is likely if you're writing a game program that needs to incorporate some unpredictable behavior), you probably wouldn't use the `rand` function listed in K&R; you'd use the `random` function, which supersedes it.

Forgetting that Objective-C is C and that the C library functions are available to your code is a common beginner mistake.

# More Preprocessor Directives

Of the many other available preprocessor directives, the one you'll use most often is `#define`. It is followed by a name and a value; at preprocess time, the value is substituted for the name down through this code file. As K&R very well explain (K&R 1.4), this is a good way to prevent "magic numbers" from being hidden and hard-coded into your program in a way that makes the program difficult to understand and maintain.

For example, in an iOS app that lays out some text fields vertically, I might want them all to have the same space between them. Let's say this space is 3.0. I shouldn't write 3.0 repeatedly throughout my code as I calculate the layout; instead, I write:

```
#define MIDSPACE 3.0
```

Now instead of the "magic number" 3.0, my code uses a meaningful name, `MIDSPACE`; at preprocessor time, the text `MIDSPACE` is replaced with the text `3.0`. So it amounts to the same thing, but if I decide to change this value and try a different one, all I have to do change is the #define line, not every occurrence of the number 3.0.

A #define simply performs text substitution, so any expression can be used as the value. Sometimes you'll want that expression to be an NSString literal. In Cocoa, NSString literals can be used as a key to a dictionary or the name of a notification. (Never mind for now what a dictionary or a notification is.) This situation is an invitation to error. If you have a dictionary containing a key @"mykey" and you mistype this elsewhere in your code as @"myKey" or @"mikey", the compiler won't complain, but your program will misbehave. The solution is to define a name for this literal string:

```
#define MYKEY @"mykey"
```

Now use MYKEY throughout your code instead of @"mykey", and if you mistype MYKEY the preprocess substitution won't be performed and the compiler *will* complain, catching the mistake for you.

The #define directive can also be used to create a macro (K&R 4.11.2), a more elaborate form of text substitution. You'll encounter a few Cocoa macros in the course of this book, but they will appear indistinguishable from functions; their secret identity as macros won't concern you.

There is also a #pragma mark directive that's useful with Xcode; I talk about it when discussing the Xcode programming environment (Chapter 9).

## Data Type Qualifiers

A variable's data type can be declared with a qualifier before the name of the type, modifying something about how that variable is to be used. For example, the declaration can be preceded by the term const, which means (K&R 2.4) that it is illegal to change the variable's value; the variable must be initialized in the same line as the declaration, and that's the only value it can ever have.

You can use a const variable as an alternative way (instead of #define) to prevent "magic numbers" and similar expressions. For example:

```
const NSString* MYKEY = @"Howdy";
```

The Cocoa API itself makes heavy use of this device. For example, in some circumstances Cocoa will pass a dictionary of information to your code. The documentation tells you what keys this dictionary contains. But instead of telling you a key as a string, the documentation tells you the key as a const NSString variable name:

```
UIKIT_EXTERN NSString *const UIApplicationStatusBarOrientationUserInfoKey;
```

(Never mind what UIKIT_EXTERN means.) This declaration tells you that UIApplicationStatusBarOrientationUserInfoKey is the name of an NSString, and you are to trust that its value is set for you. You are to go ahead and use this name whenever you want to speak of this particular key, secure in the knowledge that the actual key name string will be substituted. You do not have to know what that actual key name string is. In this way, if you make a mistake in typing the variable name, the compiler will catch the mistake because you'll be using the name of an undefined variable.

Another commonly used qualifier is `static`. This term is unfortunately used in two rather different ways in C; the way I commonly use it is inside a function. Inside a function, `static` indicates that the memory set aside for a variable should not be released after the function returns; rather, the variable remains and maintains its value for the next time the function is called. A static variable is useful, for example, when you want to call a function many times without the overhead of calculating the result each time (after the first time). First test to see whether the static value has already been calculated: if it hasn't, this must be the first time the function is being called, so you calculate it; if it has, you just return it. Here's a schematic version:

```
int myfunction() {
    static int result = 0; // 0 means we haven't done the calculation yet
    if (result == 0) {
        // calculate result and set it
    }
    return result;
}
```

A very common use of a static variable in Objective-C is to implement a singleton instance returned by a class factory method. If that sounds complicated, don't worry; it isn't. Here's an example from my own code, which you can grasp even though we haven't discussed Objective-C yet:

```
+ (CardPainter*) sharedPainter {
    static CardPainter* sp = nil;
    if (nil == sp)
        sp = [[CardPainter alloc] init];
    return sp;
}
```

That code says: If the CardPainter instance `sp` has never been created, create it, and in any case, now return it. Thus, no matter how many times this method is called, the instance will be created just once and that same instance will be returned every time.

# CHAPTER 2

# Object-Based Programming

*My object all sublime.*

—W. S. Gilbert, *The Mikado*

Objective-C, the native language for programming the Cocoa API, is an object-oriented language; in order to use it, the programmer must have an appreciation of the nature of objects and object-based programming. There's little point in learning the syntax of Objective-C message sending or instantiation without a clear understanding of what a message or an instance is. That is what this chapter is about.

## Objects

An object, in programming, is based on the concept of an object in the real world. It's an independent, self-contained thing. These objects, unlike purely inert objects in the real world, have abilities. So an object in programming is more like a clock than a rock; it doesn't just sit there, but actually does something. Perhaps one could compare an object in programming more to the animate objects of the real world, as opposed to the inanimate objects, except that — unlike real-world animate things — a programming object is supposed to be predictable: in particular, it does what you tell it. In the real world, you tell a dog to sit and anything can happen; in the programming world, you tell a dog to sit and it sits. (This is why so many of us prefer programming to dealing with the real world.)

In object-based programming, a program is organized into many discrete objects. This organization can make life much easier for the programmer. Each object has abilities that are specialized for that object. You can think of this as being a little like how an automobile assembly line works. Each worker or station along the line does one thing (screw on the bumpers, or paint the door, or whatever) and does it well. You can see immediately how this organization helps the programmer. If the car is coming off the assembly line with the door badly painted, it is very likely that the blame lies with the door-painting object, so we know where to look for the bug in our code. Or, if we decide to change the color that the door is to be painted, we have but to make a small change in the door-painting object. Meanwhile, other objects just go on doing what they do. They neither know nor care what the door-painting object does or how it works.

Objects, then, are an organizational tool, a set of boxes for encapsulating the code that accomplishes a particular task. They are also a conceptual tool. The programmer, being forced to think in terms of discrete objects, must divide the goals and behaviors of the program into discrete tasks, each task being assigned to an appropriate object. Of course, objects can cooperate with one another, and the ways in which this cooperation can be arranged are innumerable. The assembly-line analogy illustrates one such arrangement — first, object 1 operates upon the end-product; then it hands it off to object 2, and object 2 operates upon the end-product, and so on — but that arrangement won't be appropriate to most tasks. Coming up with an appropriate arrangement — an *architecture* — for the cooperative and orderly relationship between objects is one of the most challenging aspects of object-based programming.

## Messages and Methods

Nothing in a computer program happens unless it is instructed to happen. In a C program, all code belongs to a function and doesn't run unless that function is called. In an object-based program, all code belongs to an object, and doesn't run unless that object is told to run that code. All the action in an object-based program happens because an object was told to act. What does it mean to tell an object something?

An object, in object-based programming, has a well-defined set of abilities — things it knows how to do. For example, imagine an object that is to represent a dog. We can design a highly simplified, schematic dog that knows how to do an extremely limited range of things: eat, come for a walk, bark, sit, lie down, sleep. The purpose of these abilities is so that the object can be told, as appropriate, to exercise them. So, again, we can imagine our schematic dog, rather like some child's toy robot, responding to simple commands: Eat! Come for a walk! Bark!

In object-based programming, a command directed to an object is called a *message*. To make the dog object eat, we send the eat message to the dog object. This mechanism of message sending is the basis of all activity in the program. The program consists entirely of objects, so its activity consists entirely of objects sending messages to one another.

For objects to send messages to one another, objects must know about one another in some appropriate way at some appropriate time. Ensuring such mutual knowledge is part of the architectural design process I spoke of earlier. Returning for a moment to the assembly-line architecture, it's no use saying that object 1 operates on the end-product and then object 2 operates on the end-product; that isn't going to happen all by itself. It has to be arranged somehow. We can imagine various architectures for arranging it. Perhaps we will set things up so that object 1 knows about object 2, and as the last step in its own operation, sends a message to object 2, handing it the end-product and telling it to commence its own operation. Or perhaps we will have a conveyor-belt object, which will hand the end-product to object 1 and tell it to commence its operation, wait until object 1 finishes with it, and then hand the end-product to object 2 and tell *it* to commence its operation. Each of these is a perfectly reasonable architectural pattern, and many others are possible; it is the programmer's job to implement an architecture that not only makes the program work appropriately, but also makes the program itself clear and easy for the programmer to work on. But the problem of making sure that within that architecture, each object knows about — technically, has a *reference* to — any other object to which it might need to send a message can be quite tricky (so much so, indeed, that an entire chapter of this book, Chapter 13, is devoted to it).

A moment ago, I said that in a C program, all code belongs to a function. The object-based analogue to a function is called a *method*. So, for example, a dog object might have an **eat** method. When the dog object is sent the **eat** message, it responds by calling the **eat** method.

It may sound as if I'm not drawing any clear distinction between a message and a method. But there is a difference. A message is what one object says to another. A method is a bundle of code that gets called. The connection between the two is not perfectly direct. You might send a message to an object that corresponds to no method of object. For example, you might tell the dog to recite the soliloquy from Hamlet. I'm not sure what will happen if you do that; the details are implementation-dependent. (The dog might just sit there silently. Or it might get annoyed and bite you. Or, I suppose, it might nip off, read Hamlet, memorize the soliloquy, and recite it.) But that implementation-dependence is exactly the point of the distinction between message and method.

Nevertheless, in general the distinction between sending a message and calling a method won't usually be important in real life. Most of the time, when you're using Objective-C, your reason for sending a message to an object will be that that object implements the corresponding method and you are expecting to call that method. So sending a message to an object and calling a method of an object will appear to be the same act.

# Classes and Instances

We come now to an extremely characteristic and profound feature of object-based programming. Just like in the real world, every object in the object-based programming world is of some type. This type, called a *class*, is the object-based analogy to the data type in C. Just as a simple variable in C might be an int or a float, an object in the object-based programming world might be a Dog (or an NSString). In the object-based programming world, the idea of this arrangement is to ensure that more than one individual object can be relied upon to act the same way.

There can, for example, be more than one dog. You might have a dog called Fido and I might have a dog called Rover. But both dogs know how to eat, come for a walk, and bark. In object-based programming, they know that because they both belong to the Dog class. The knowledge of how to eat, come for a walk, and bark is part of the Dog class. Your dog Fido and my dog Rover possess this knowledge solely by virtue of being Dog objects.

From the programmer's point of view, what this means is simple: all the code you write is put into a class. All the methods you write will be part of some class or other. You don't program an individual dog object: you program the Dog class.

But I just got through saying that an object-based program works through the sending of messages to individual objects. So even though the programmer does not write the code for an individual dog object, there still needs to *be* an individual dog object in order for there to be something to send a message to. It is the Dog class that knows how to bark, but it is an individual dog object that is told to bark, and that actually does bark. So the question is: if all Dog code lives in a Dog class, where do individual dogs come from?

The answer is that they have to be created in the course of the program as it runs. When the program starts out, it contains code for a Dog class, but no individual dog objects. If any barking by any dogs is to be done, the program must first create an individual dog object. This object will belong to the Dog class, so it can be sent the bark message. An individual object belonging to the Dog class (or any class) is an *instance* of that class. To manufacture, from a class, an actual individual object that is an instance of that class, is to *instantiate* that class.

So every individual object, such as I talked about in the preceding sections — every individual object, that is, to which a message can be sent — is an instance of some class. Classes exist from the get-go, as part of the fact that the program exists in the first place; they are where the code is. Instances are manufactured, deliberately and individually, as the program runs. Each instance is manufactured *from* a class, it is an instance *of* that class, and it has methods by virtue of the fact that the class has those methods. The instance can then be sent a message; what it will do in response depends on what code the class contains in its methods. The instance is the individual thing that can be sent messages; the class, with its methods, is the locus of the thing's ability to respond to messages (Figure 2-1).

This relationship between instance and class begins to sound rather ethereal or metaphysical. Instances and classes seem to be programming-language analogies to what a philosopher would call particulars and universals. Indeed, the whole setup reminds one of nothing so much as Plato's theory of Forms. For Plato, this world of ours is the world of individual things, but those things derive their natures by virtue of archetypal Forms that live off in another world. I'm not the only person ever to make this comparison to Platonic Forms — it is, indeed, implicit in the design of object-based languages and has been evoked explicitly in discussions of such languages ever since

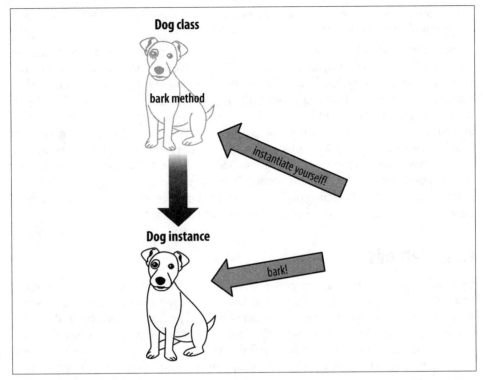

*Figure 2-1. Class and instance*

Smalltalk. But the comparison is still an apt one. As I said many years ago in my book REALbasic: The Definitive Guide:

> Indeed, object-oriented programming seems to fulfill Plato's philosophical program announced in the *Euthyphro* (6e, my translation):
>
> SOCRATES. Now, you recall that I asked you to explain to me, not this or that particular pious thing, but that Form Itself through which all pious things are pious? You did say, I believe, that it was through one Form that impious things are impious and pious things are pious; don't you remember?
>
> EUTHYPHRO. Yes, I do.
>
> SOCRATES. All right, then; so, explain to me what is this Form Itself, so that by keeping my eyes upon it and using it as a model, I may declare that whatever you or anyone else does that is of this sort, is pious, and that whatever is not, is not.
>
> The problems with Plato's characterization are well known: the Form seems to be a "thing" separate from the particular things of the world around us, the notion "through" is crucial but slippery, and Plato seems to equivocate rather glibly between the Form's being responsible for a thing's being such and such and our ability to know that a thing is such and such; thus, his program is almost certainly doomed to failure as an explanation of how the world works. But he is perfectly accurate about how an object-oriented

program works! If an instance is of the Pious type, there really is a separate Pious class that really is responsible for the instance being such as it is.

Because every individual object is an instance of a class, to know what messages you can officially send to that object, you need to know at least what methods its class has endowed it with. The public knowledge of this information is that class's API. (A class may also have methods that you're not really supposed to call from outside that object; these would not be public and other objects couldn't officially send those messages to an instance of that class.) That's why Apple's own Cocoa documentation consists largely of pages listing and describing the methods supplied by some class. For example, to know what messages you can send to an NSString object (instance), you'd start by studying the NSString class documentation. That page is really just a big list of methods, so it tells you what an NSString object can do. That isn't everything in the world there is to know about an NSString, but it's a big percentage of it.

# Class Methods

Up to now I've been keeping something back, and if you've been paying close attention, you may have caught me at it, because it looks as though I've contradicted myself. I said that nothing happens in a program unless a message is sent to an object. But I also said that there are no instances until they are created as the program runs. The contradiction is that if messages can be sent only to instances, it appears that no instances can ever be created (because, when the program starts up, there are no instances to which you can send the message asking for an instance to be created).

The truth that I've been keeping back, which complicates things only a little, is that classes are themselves objects and can be sent messages. This revelation solves the contradiction completely. No instances exist as the program starts up, but the classes do. The classes may live off in a world of Platonic Forms, but they can still be sent messages. And one of the most important things you can ask a class to do by sending it a message is to instantiate itself.

You cannot, however, ask an instance to instantiate itself. It thus begins to look as if there must be two kinds of message: messages that you are allowed to send to a class (such as telling the Dog class to instantiate itself) and messages that you are allowed to send to an instance (such as telling an individual dog to bark). That is exactly true. More precisely, all code lives as a method in a class, but methods are of two kinds: class methods and instance methods. If a method is a class method, you can send that message to the class. If a method is an instance method, you can send that message to an instance of the class.

In Objective-C syntax, class methods and instance methods are distinguished by the use of a plus sign or a minus sign. For example, Apple's NSString class documentation page listing the methods of the NSString class starts out like this:

```
+ string
- init
```

The `string` method is a class method. The `init` method is an instance method.

In general, though not exclusively, class methods tend to be factory methods — that is, methods for generating an instance. This makes sense, because making an instance of itself is one of the main things you're likely to want to ask a class to do. You might think that a class really needs only *one* class method for generating an instance of itself, and that is rigorously true, but classes tend to provide multiple factory methods purely as a convenience to the programmer. For example, here are three NSString class methods:

```
+ string
+ stringWithFormat:
+ stringWithContentsOfFile:encoding:error:
```

They all make instances. The first class method, `string`, generates an empty NSString instance (a string with no text). The second class method, `stringWithFormat:`, generates an NSString instance based on text that you provide, which can include transforming other values into text; for example, you might use it to start with an integer 9 and generate an NSString instance @"9". The third class method reads the contents of a file and generates an NSString instance from those contents. When you come to write your own classes, you too might well create multiple class methods that act as instance factories for your own future programming convenience.

## Instance Variables

Now that I've revealed that classes are objects and can be sent messages, you might be wondering why there need to be instances at all. Why doesn't the mere existence of classes as objects suffice for object-based programming? Why would you ever bother to instantiate any of the classes? Why wouldn't you write all your code as class methods, have the program send messages from one class object to another, and be done with it?

The answer is that instances have a feature that classes do not: instance variables. An instance variable is just what the name suggests: it's a variable belonging to an instance. Like instance methods, instance variables are defined as part of the class. But the *value* of an instance variable is set as the program runs and belongs to one instance alone. In other words, different instances can have different values for the same instance variable.

For example, suppose we have a Dog class and we decide that it might be a good idea for every dog to have a name. Just as you can learn a real-world dog's name by reading the tag on its collar, we want to be able to assign every dog instance a name and, subsequently, to learn what that name is. So, in designing the Dog class, we declare that this class has an instance variable called name, whose value is a string (probably an NSString, as we're using Objective-C). Now when our program runs we can instantiate Dog and assign the resulting dog instance a name (that is, we can assign its name instance variable a value). We can also instantiate Dog again and assign *that* resulting dog in-

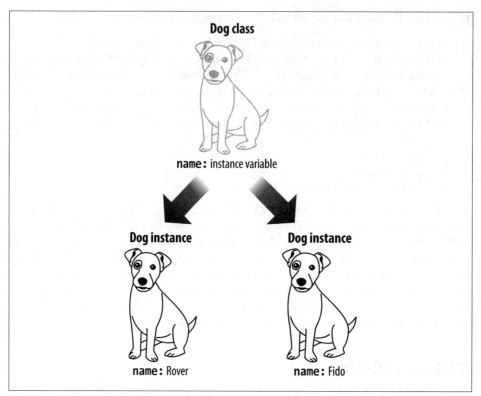

*Figure 2-2. Instance variables*

stance a name. Let's say these are two different names: one is `@"Rover"` and one is `@"Fido"`. Then we've got two instances of Dog, and they are significantly different; they differ in the value of their `name` instance variables (Figure 2-2).

So an instance is a reflection of the instance methods of its class, but that isn't *all* it is; it's also a collection of instance variables. The class is responsible for what instance variables the instance has, but not for the values of those variables. The values can change as the program runs and apply only to a particular instance. An instance is a cluster of particular instance variable values.

In short, an instance is both code and data. The code it gets from its class and in a sense is shared with all other instances of that class, but the data belong to it alone. The data can persist as long as the instance persists. The instance has, at every moment, a state — the complete collection of its own personal instance variable values. An instance is a device for maintaining state. It's a box for storage of data.

# The Object-Based Philosophy

In my REALbasic book, I summarized the nature of objects in two phrases: encapsulation of functionality, and maintenance of state:

*Encapsulation of functionality*

Each object does its own job, and presents to the rest of the world — to other objects, and indeed in a sense to the programmer — an opaque wall whose only entrances are the methods to which it promises to respond and the actions it promises to perform when the corresponding messages are sent to it. The details of how, behind the scenes, it actually implements those actions are secreted within itself; no other object needs to know them.

*Maintenance of state*

Each individual instance is a bundle of data that it maintains. Typically that data is private, which means that it's encapsulated as well; no other object knows what that data is or in what form it is kept. The only way to discover from outside what data an object is maintaining is if there's a method that reveals it.

As an example, imagine an object whose job is to implement a stack — it might be an instance of a Stack class. A *stack* is a data structure that maintains a set of data in LIFO order (last in, first out). It responds to just two messages: push and pop. Push means to add a given piece of data to the set. Pop means to remove from the set the piece of data that was most recently pushed and hand it out. It's like a stack of plates: plates are placed onto the top of the stack or removed from the top of the stack one by one, so the first plate to go onto the stack can't be retrieved until all other subsequently added plates have been removed (Figure 2-3).

The stack object illustrates encapsulation of functionality because the outside world knows nothing of how the stack is actually implemented. It might be an array, it might be a linked list, it might be any of a number of other implementations. But a client object — an object that actually sends a push or pop message to the stack object — knows nothing of this and cares less, provided the stack object adheres to its contract of behaving like a stack. This is also good for the programmer, who can, as the program develops, safely substitute one implementation for another without harming the vast machinery of the program as a whole. And just the other way round, the stack object knows nothing and cares less about who is telling it to push or to pop, and why. It just hums along and does its job in its reliable little way.

The stack object illustrates maintenance of state because it isn't just the gateway to the stack data — it *is* the stack data. Every object that has a reference to the stack object has the same access to its data, the same ability to push or to pop. (And that's all it can do. The stack data is effectively inside the stack object; no one else can see it. All that another object can do is push or pop.) If a certain object is at the top of our stack object's stack right now, then whatever object sends the pop message to this stack object will

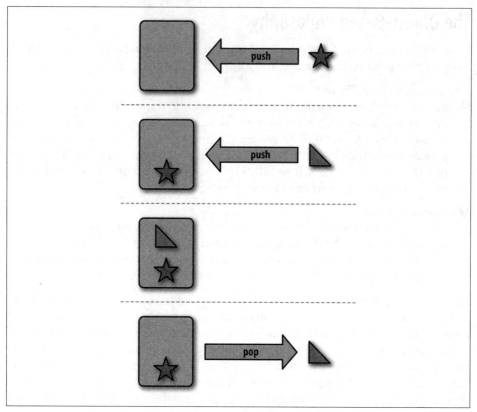

*Figure 2-3. A stack*

receive that object in return. If no object sends the pop message to this stack object, then the object at the top of the stack will just sit there, waiting.

As a second example of the philosophy and nature of object-based programming at work, I'll revert to another imaginary scenario I used in my REALbasic book. Pretend we're writing an arcade game where the user is to "shoot" at moving "targets," and the score increases every time a target is hit. We immediately have a sense of how we might organize our code using object-based programming and can see how object-based programming will fulfill its nature and purpose:

- There will be a Target class. Every target object will be an instance of this class. This decision makes sense because we want every target to behave the same way. A target will need to know how to draw itself; that knowledge will be part of the Target class, which makes sense because all targets will draw themselves in the same way. Thus we have the relationship between class and instance.

- Targets may draw themselves the same way, but they may also differ in appearance. Perhaps some targets are blue, others are red, and so on. This difference between individual targets can be expressed as an instance variable. Call it color. Every time we instantiate a target, we'll assign it a color. The Target class's code for drawing an individual target will look at that target's `color` instance variable and use it when filling in the target's shape. Clearly, we could extend this individualization as much as we like: targets could have different sizes, different shapes, and so on, and all of these parametric distinctions could be made on an individual basis through the use of instance variables. Thus we have both encapsulation of functionality and maintenance of state. A target has a state, the parameters that describe how it should look, and also has the ability to draw itself, expressing that state visually.

- When a target is hit by the user, it will explode. So perhaps the Target class will have an `explode` instance method; thus, every target knows how to explode. One thing that should happen whenever a target explodes is that the user's score should increase. So let's imagine a score object — an instance of the Score class. Give every target object a reference to this score object so that it can send a message to it. When a target explodes, one of things its `explode` instance method will do is send an `increase` message to the score object. Thus we have both encapsulation of functionality and maintenance of state. The score object responds indifferently to any object that sends it the `increase` message; it doesn't need to know why it's being sent that message. Nor does the score object even need to know that targets exist, or indeed that it's part of a game. It just sits there maintaining the score, and when it receives the `increase` message, it increases it.

This chapter has described only the rudiments of object-based philosophy — enough to communicate the correct mind-set. Using object-based programming effectively to make a program clear and maintainable is something of an art; your abilities will improve with experience. Eventually, you may want to do some further reading on how to construct an object-based program most effectively. I recommend in particular two classic, favorite books. *Refactoring*, by Martin Fowler (Addison-Wesley, 1999), describes how you can get a sense that you might need to rearrange what methods belong to what classes (and how to conquer your fear of doing so). *Design Patterns*, by Erich Gamma, Richard Helm, Ralph Johnson, and John Vlissides (also known as "the Gang of Four"), is the bible on architecting object-based programs, listing all the ways you can arrange objects with the right powers and the right knowledge of one another (Addison-Wesley, 1994).

# CHAPTER 3

# Objective-C Objects and Messages

One of the first object-based programming languages to achieve maturity and wide-spread dissemination was Smalltalk. It was developed during the 1970s at Xerox PARC under the leadership of Alan Kay and started becoming widely known in 1980. The purpose of Objective-C, created by Brad Cox and Tom Love in 1986, was to build Smalltalk-like syntax and behavior on top of C. Objective-C was licensed by NeXT in 1988 and was the basis for its application framework API, NeXTStep. Eventually, NeXT and Apple merged, and the NeXT application framework evolved into Cocoa, the framework for Mac OS X applications, still revolving around Objective-C. That history explains why Objective-C is the base language for iOS programming. (It also explains why Cocoa class names often begin with "NS" — it stands for "NeXTStep.")

Having learned the basics of C (Chapter 1) and the nature of object-based programming (Chapter 2), you are ready to meet Objective-C. This chapter describes Objective-C structural fundamentals; the next two chapters provide more detail about how Objective-C classes and instances work. (A few additional features of the language are discussed in Chapter 10.) As with the C language, my intention is not to describe the Objective-C language completely, but to provide a practical linguistic grounding, founded on my own experience of those aspects of the language that need to be firmly understood as a basis for iOS programming.

## An Instance Reference Is a Pointer

In C, every variable must be declared to be of some type. In an object-based language such as Objective-C, an instance's type is its class. The C language includes very few basic data types. To facilitate the multiplicity of class types required by its object-based nature, Objective-C takes advantage of C pointers. So, in Objective-C, if a variable is an instance of the class MyClass, that variable is of type `MyClass*` — a pointer to a MyClass. In general, in Objective-C, a reference to an instance is a pointer and the name of the data type of what's at the far end of that pointer is the name of the instance's class.

Note the convention for capitalization. Variable names tend to start with a lowercase letter; class names tend to start with an uppercase letter.

As I mentioned in Chapter 1, the fact that a reference to an instance is a pointer in Objective-C will generally not cause you any difficulties, because pointers are used consistently throughout the language. For example, a message to an instance is directed at the pointer, so there is no need to dereference the pointer. Indeed, having established that a variable representing an instance is a pointer, you're likely to forget that this variable even *is* a pointer and just work directly with that variable:

```
NSString* s = @"Hello, world!";
NSString* s2 = [s uppercaseString];
```

Having established that s is an NSString*, you would never dereference s (that is, you would never speak of *s) to access the "real" NSString. So it feels as if the pointer *is* the real NSString. Thus, in the previous example, once the variable s is declared as a pointer to an NSString, the uppercaseString message is sent directly to the variable s. (The uppercaseString message asks an NSString to generate and return an uppercase version of itself; so, after that code, s2 is @"HELLO, WORLD!")

The tie between a pointer, an instance, and the class of that instance is so close that it is natural to speak of an expression like MyClass* as meaning "a MyClass instance," and of a MyClass* value as "a MyClass." A Objective-C programmer will say simply that, in the previous example, s *is* an NSString, that uppercaseString returns "an NSString," and so forth. It is fine to speak like that, and I do it myself (and will do it in this book) — provided you remember that this is a shorthand. Such an expression means "an NSString instance," and because an instance is represented as a C pointer, it means an NSString*, a pointer to an NSString.

Although the fact that instance references in Objective-C are pointers does not cause any special difficulty, you must still be conscious of what pointers are and how they work. As I emphasized in Chapter 1, when you're working with pointers, you must keep in mind the special meaning of your actions. So here are some basic facts about pointers that you should keep in mind when working with instance references in Objective-C.

## Instance References, Initialization, and nil

Merely declaring an instance reference's type doesn't bring any instance into existence. For example:

```
NSString* s; // only a declaration; no instance is pointed to
```

After that declaration, s is *typed* as a pointer to an NSString, but it is not *in fact* pointing to an NSString. You have created a pointer, but you haven't supplied an NSString for it to point to. It's just sitting there, waiting for you to point it at an NSString, typically by assignment (as we did with @"Hello, world!" earlier). Such assignment *initializes* the variable, giving it an actual meaningful value of the proper type.

You can declare an instance variable in one line of code and initialize it later, like this:

```
NSString* s;
// ... time passes ...
s = @"Hello, world!";
```

But this is not common, nor is it wise. It is much more common to declare and initialize a variable all in one line of code:

```
NSString* s = @"Hello, world!";
```

Declaration without initialization, on the other hand, creates a dangerous situation:

```
NSString* s;
```

What *is* s after a mere declaration like that? It could be anything. But it is *claiming* to be a pointer to an NSString, and so your code might proceed to *treat* it as a pointer to an NSString. But it is pointing at garbage. A pointer pointing at garbage is liable to cause serious trouble down the road when you accidentally try to use it as an instance. Sending a message to a garbage pointer, or otherwise treating it as a meaningful instance, can crash your program. Even worse, it might *not* crash your program: it might cause your program to behave very, very oddly instead — and figuring out why can be difficult.

For this reason, if you *aren't* going to initialize an instance reference pointer at the moment you declare it by assigning it a real value, it's a good idea to assign it nil:

```
NSString* s = nil;
```

What is nil? It's simply a form of zero — the form of zero appropriate to an instance reference. The nil value simply means: "This instance reference isn't pointing to any instance." Indeed, you can test an instance reference against nil as a way of finding out whether it is in fact pointing to a real instance. This is an extremely common thing to do:

```
if (nil == s) // ...
```

As I mentioned in Chapter 1, the explicit comparison with nil isn't strictly necessary; because nil is a form of zero, and because zero means false in a condition, you can perform the same test like this:

```
if (!s) // ...
```

I do in fact write nil tests in that second form all the time, but some programmers would take me to task for bad style. The first form has the advantage that its real meaning is made explicit, rather than relying on a cute implicit feature of C. The first form places nil first in the comparison so that if the programmer accidentally omits an equal sign, performing an assignment instead of a comparison, the compiler will catch the error (because assignment to nil is illegal).

Many Cocoa methods use a return value of nil, instead of an expected instance, to signify that something went wrong. You are supposed to capture this return value and test it for nil in order to discover whether something *did* go wrong. For example, the documentation for the NSString class method `stringWithContentsOfFile:encoding:error:` says that it returns "a string created by reading data from the file named by path using the encoding, enc. If the file can't be opened or there is an encoding error, returns nil." So, as I described in Chapter 1, your next move after calling this method and capturing the result should be to test that result against nil, just to make sure you've really got an instance now:

```
NSString* path = // ... whatever;
NSStringEncoding enc = // ... whatever;
NSError* err = nil;
NSString* s = [NSString stringWithContentsOfFile:path encoding:enc error:&err];
if (nil == s) // oops! something went wrong...
```

You should now be wondering about the implications of a nil-value pointer for sending a message to a noninstance. For example, you can send a message to an NSString instance like this:

```
NSString* s2 = [s uppercaseString];
```

That code sends the `uppercaseString` message to s. So s is supposedly an NSString instance. But what if s is nil? With some object-based programming languages, sending a message to nil constitutes a runtime error and will cause your program to terminate prematurely (REALbasic and Ruby are examples). But Objective-C doesn't work like that. In Objective-C, sending a message to nil is legal and does not interrupt execution. Moreover, if you capture the result of the method call, it will be a form of zero — which means that if you assign that result to an instance reference pointer, it too will be nil:

```
NSString* s = nil; // now s is nil
NSString* s2 = [s uppercaseString]; // now s2 is nil
```

Whether this behavior of Objective-C is a good thing is a quasi-religious issue and a subject of vociferous debate among programmers. It is useful, but it also extremely easy to be tricked by it. The usual scenario is that you accidentally send a message to a nil reference without realizing it, and then later your program doesn't behave as expected. Because the point where the unexpected behavior occurs is later than the moment when the nil pointer arose in the first place, the genesis of the nil pointer can be difficult to track down (indeed, it often fails to occur to the programmer that a nil pointer is the cause of the trouble in the first place).

Short of peppering your code with tests to ascertain that your instance reference pointers are not accidentally nil, which is not generally a good idea, there isn't much you can do about this. This behavior is strongly built into the language and is not going to change. It's just something you need to be aware of.

To sum up the lessons of this section:

- Don't let any time elapse between the moment you declare an instance pointer variable and the moment you assign it an actual object value. In the modern C language, you can wait until just before you need a variable and declare it at that moment. So always declare a variable and initialize it in the same line (or in the very next line) if at all possible. If you can't initialize it to a meaningful object value, initialize it to nil.

- If a method call can return nil, be conscious of that fact. Don't assume that everything will go well and that it won't return nil. On the contrary, if something can go wrong, it probably will. For example, to omit the nil test after calling `stringWith-ContentsOfFile:encoding:error:` is just stupid. I don't care if you know perfectly well that the file exists and the encoding is what you say it is — test the result for nil!

## Instance References and Assignment

As I said in Chapter 1, assigning to a pointer does not mutate the value at the far end of the pointer; rather, it repoints the pointer. Moreover, assigning one pointer to another repoints the pointer in such a way that both pointers are now pointing to the very same thing. Failure to keep these simple facts firmly in mind can have results that range from surprising to disastrous.

For example, instances in general are usually mutable: they typically have instance variables that can change. If two references are pointing at one and the same instance, then when the instance is mutated by way of one reference, that mutation also affects the instance as seen by the other reference. To illustrate, pretend that we've implemented the Stack class described in the previous chapter:

```
Stack* myStack1 = // ... create Stack instance and initialize myStack1 ... ;
Stack* myStack2 = myStack1;
[myStack1 push: @"Hello"];
[myStack1 push: @"World"];
NSString* s = [myStack2 pop];
```

After we pop myStack2, s is @"World" even though nothing was ever pushed onto myStack2 (and the stack myStack1 contains only @"Hello" even though nothing was ever popped off of myStack1). That's because we did push two strings onto myStack1 and then pop one string off myStack2, and myStack1 *is* myStack2 — in the sense that they are both pointers to the very same stack instance. That's perfectly fine, as long as you understand and intend this behavior.

In real life, you're likely to pass an instance off to some other object, or to receive it from some other object:

```
Stack* myStack = // ... create Stack instance and initialize myStack ... ;
// ... more code might go here ...
[myObject doSomethingWithThis: myStack]; // pass myStack to myObject
```

After that code, myObject has a pointer to the very same instance we're already pointing to as myStack. So we must be careful and thoughtful. The object myObject might mutate

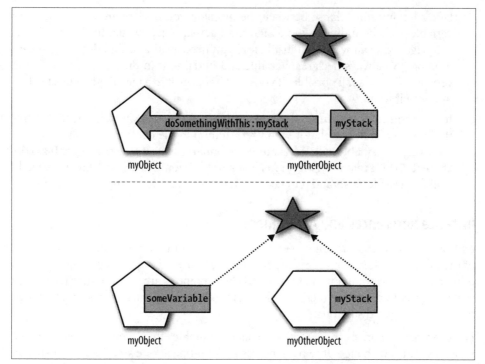

*Figure 3-1. Two instances end up with pointers to the same third instance*

myStack right under our very noses. Even more, the object myObject might *keep* its reference to the stack instance and mutate it *later* — possibly much later, in a way that could surprise us. This is possible because instances can have instance variables that point to other objects, and those pointers can persist as long as the instances themselves do. This kind of shared referent situation can be intentional, but it is also something to watch out for and be conscious of (Figure 3-1).

Another possible misunderstanding is to imagine that the assignment myStack2 = myStack1 somehow makes a new, separate instance that duplicates myStack1. That's not at all the case. It doesn't make a new instance; it just points myStack2 at the very same instance that myStack1 is pointing at. It may be possible to make a new instance that duplicates a given instance, but the ability to do so is not a given and it is not going to happen through mere assignment. (For how a separate duplicate instance might be generated, see the NSCopying protocol and the copy method mentioned in Chapter 10.)

## Instance References and Memory Management

The pointer nature of instance references in Objective-C also has implications for management of memory. The scope, and in particular the lifetime, of variables in pure C is typically quite straightforward: if you bring a piece of variable storage into existence by declaring that variable within a certain scope, then when that scope ceases to exist, the variable storage ceases to exist. That sort of variable is called *automatic* (K&R 1.10). So, for example:

```
void myFunction() {
    int i; // storage for an int is set aside
    i = 7; // 7 is placed in that storage
} // the scope ends, so the int storage and its contents vanish
```

But in the case of a pointer, there are two pieces of memory to worry about: the pointer itself, which is an integer signifying an address in memory, and whatever is at the far end of that pointer. Nothing about the C language causes the destruction of what a pointer points to when the pointer itself is automatically destroyed as it goes out of scope:

```
void myFunction() {
    NSString* s = @"Hello, world!"; // storage for a pointer is set aside
    NSString* s2 = [s uppercaseString]; // storage for another pointer is set aside
} // the two pointers go out of existence...
// ... but what about the two NSStrings they point to?
```

Some object-based programming languages in which a reference to an instance is a pointer do manage automatically the memory pointed to by instance references (REALbasic and Ruby are examples). But Objective-C, at least the way it's implemented when you're programming for iOS, is not one of those languages. Because the C language has nothing to say about the automatic destruction of what is pointed to by a reference to an instance, Objective-C implements an explicit mechanism for the management of memory. I'll talk in a later chapter (Chapter 12) about what that mechanism is and what responsibilities for the programmer it entails.

# Messages and Methods

An Objective-C method is defined as part of a class. It has three aspects:

*Whether it's a class method or an instance method*
    If it's a class method, you call it by sending a message to the class itself. If it's an instance method, you call it by sending a message to an instance of the class.

*Its parameters and return value*
    As with a C function, an Objective-C method takes some number of parameters; each parameter is of some specified type. And, as with a C function, it may return a value, which is also of some specified type; if the method returns nothing, its return type is declared as void.

*Its name*
    An Objective-C method's name must contain as many colons as it takes parameters. The name is split after each colon in a method call or declaration, so it is usual for the part of the name preceding each colon to describe the corresponding parameter.

## Sending a Message

As you've doubtless gathered, the syntax for sending a message to an object involves square brackets. The first thing in the square brackets is the object to which the message is to be sent; this object is the message's *receiver*. Then follows the message:

```
NSString* s2 = [s uppercaseString]; // send "uppercaseString" message to s ...
// ... (and assign result to s2)
```

If the message is a method that takes parameters, each corresponding argument value comes after a colon:

```
[myStack1 push: @"Hello"]; // send "push:" message to myStack1 ...
// ...with one argument, the NSString @"Hello"
```

To send a message to a class (calling a class method), you can represent the class by the literal name of the class:

```
NSString* s = [NSString string]; // send "string" message to NSString class
```

To send a message to an instance (calling an instance method), you'll need a reference to an instance, which (as you know) is a pointer:

```
NSString* s = @"Hello, world!"; // and now s is initialized as an NSString instance
NSString* s2 = [s uppercaseString]; // send "uppercaseString" message to s
```

You can send a class method to a class, and an instance method to an instance, no matter how you got hold of and represent the class or the instance. For example, @"Hello, world!" is itself an NSString instance, so it's legal to say:

```
NSString* s2 = [@"Hello, world!" uppercaseString];
```

If a method takes no parameters, then its name contains no colons, like the NSString instance method uppercaseString. If a method takes one parameter, then its name contains one colon, which is the final character of the method name, like the hypothetical Stack instance method push:. If a method takes two or more parameters, its name contains that number of colons. In the minimal case, its name ends with that number of colons. For example, a method taking three parameters might be called hereAreThreeStrings:::. To call it, we split the name after each colon and follow each colon with an argument, which looks like this:

```
[someObject hereAreThreeStrings: @"string1" : @"string2" : @"string3"];
```

That's a legal way to name a method, but it isn't very common, mostly because it isn't very informative. Usually the name will have more text; in particular, the part before each colon will describe the parameter that follows that colon.

For example, there's a UIColor class method for generating an instance of a UIColor from four CGFloat numbers representing its red, green, blue, and alpha (transparency) components, and it's called colorWithRed:green:blue:alpha:. Notice the clever construction of this name. The colorWith part tells something about the method's purpose: it generates a *color*, starting *with* some set of information. All the rest of the name, Red:green:blue:alpha:, describes the meaning of each parameter. And you call it like this:

```
UIColor* c = [UIColor colorWithRed: 0.0 green: 0.5 blue: 0.25 alpha: 1.0];
```

The space after each colon in the method call is optional. (Space before a colon is also legal, though in practice one rarely sees this.)

The rules for naming an Objective-C method, along with the conventions governing such names (like trying to make the name informative about the method's purpose and the meanings of its parameters), lead to some rather long and unwieldy method names, such as `getBytes:maxLength:usedLength:encoding:options:range:remainingRange:`. Such verbosity of nomenclature is characteristic of Objective-C. Method calls, and even method declarations, are often split across multiple lines to prevent a single line of code from becoming so long that it wraps within the editor, as well as for clarity.

## Declaring a Method

The declaration for a method has three parts:

- Either + or -, meaning that the method is a class method or an instance method, respectively.
- The data type of the return value, in parentheses.
- The name of the method, split after each colon. Following each colon is the corresponding parameter, expressed as the data type of the parameter, in parentheses, followed by a placeholder name for the parameter.

So, for example, Apple's documentation tells us that the declaration for the UIColor class method `colorWithRed:green:blue:alpha:` is:

```
+ (UIColor*) colorWithRed: (CGFloat) red green: (CGFloat) green
              blue: (CGFloat) blue alpha: (CGFloat) alpha
```

(Note that I've split the declaration into two lines, for legibility and to fit onto this page. The documentation puts it all on a single line.)

Make very sure you can read this declaration! You should be able to look at it and say to yourself instantly, "The name of this method is `colorWithRed:green:blue:alpha:`. It's a class method that returns a UIColor and takes four CGFloat parameters."

It is not uncommon, outside of code, to write a method's name along with the plus sign or the minus sign, to make it clear whether this is a class method or an instance method. So you might speak informally of "-uppercaseString," just as a way of reminding yourself or a reader that this is an instance method. Again outside of code, it is not uncommon, especially when communicating with other Objective-C programmers, to speak of a method's name along with the class in which this method is defined. So you might say "NSString's -uppercaseString," or even something like "-[NSString uppercaseString]." Notice that that isn't code, or even pseudo-code, because you are not actually speaking of a method call, and in any case you could never send the `uppercaseString` message to the NSString class; it's just a compact way of saying, "I'm talking about the `uppercaseString` that's an instance method of NSString."

## Nesting Method Calls

Wherever in a method call an object of a certain type is supposed to appear, you can put another method call that returns that type. Thus you can nest method calls. A method call can appear as the message's receiver:

```
NSString* s = [[NSString string] uppercaseString]; // silly but legal
```

That's legal because NSString's class method **string** returns an NSString instance (formally, an **NSString\*** value, remember), so we can send an NSString instance method to that result. Similarly, a method call can appear as an argument in a method call:

```
[myStack push: [NSString string]]; // ok if push: expects an NSString* parameter
```

However, I must caution you against overdoing that sort of thing. Code with a lot of nested square brackets is very difficult to read (and to write). Furthermore, if one of the nested method calls happens to return nil unexpectedly, you have no way to detect this fact. It is often better, then, to be even more verbose and declare a temporary variable for each piece of the method call. Just to take an example from my own code, instead of writing this:

```
NSArray* arr = [[MPMediaQuery albumsQuery] collections];
```

I might write this:

```
MPMediaQuery* query = [MPMediaQuery albumsQuery];
NSArray* arr = [query collections];
```

Even though the first version is quite short and legible, and even though the variable **query** will never be used again — it exists solely in order to be the receiver of the **collections** message in the second line — it is worth creating it as a separate variable. For one thing, it makes this code far easier to step through in the debugger later on, when I want to pause after the **albumsQuery** call and see whether the expected sort of result is being returned.

## No Overloading

The data type returned by a method, together with the data types of each of its parameters in order, constitute that method's *signature*. It is illegal for two methods of the same type (class method or instance method) to exist in the same class with the same name but different signatures.

So, for example, you could not have two MyClass instance methods called **myMethod**, one of which returns void and one of which returns an NSString. Similarly, you could not have two MyClass instance methods called **myMethod:**, both returning void, one taking a CGFloat parameter and one taking an NSString parameter. An attempt to violate this rule will be stopped dead in its tracks by the compiler, which will announce a "conflicting types" or "duplicate declaration" error. The reason for this rule is that if two such conflicting methods were allowed to exist, there would be no way to determine from a method call to one of them *which* method was being called.

You might think that the issue could be decided by looking at the types involved in the call. If one `myMethod:` takes a CGFloat parameter and the other `myMethod:` takes an NSString parameter, you might think that when `myMethod:` is called, Objective-C could look at the actual argument and realize that the former method is meant if the argument is a CGFloat and the latter if the argument is an NSString. But Objective-C doesn't work that way. There are languages that permit this feature, called *overloading*, but Objective-C is not one of them.

## Parameter Lists

It isn't uncommon for an Objective-C method to require an unknown number of parameters. A good example is the NSArray class method `arrayWithObjects:`, which looks from the name as if it takes one parameter but in fact takes any number of parameters, separated by comma. The parameters are the objects of which the NSArray is to consist. The trick here, however, which you must discover by reading the documentation, is that the list must end with nil. The nil is not one of the objects to go into the NSArray (nil isn't an object, so an NSArray can't contain nil); it's to show where the list ends.

So, here's a correct way to call the `arrayWithObjects:` method:

```
NSArray* pep = [NSArray arrayWithObjects:@"Manny", @"Moe", @"Jack", nil];
```

The declaration for `arrayWithObjects:` uses three dots to show that a comma-separated list is legal:

```
+ (id)arrayWithObjects:(id)firstObj, ... ;
```

Without the nil terminator, the program will not know where the list ends, and bad things will happen when the program runs, as it goes hunting off into the weeds of memory, incorporating all sorts of garbage into the NSArray that you never meant to have incorporated. Forgetting the nil terminator is a common beginner error, but not as common as it used to be: by a bit of deep-C voodoo, the Objective-C compiler now notices if you've forgotten the nil, and warns you ("missing sentinel in function call").

The C language has explicit provision for argument lists of unspecified length, which Objective-C methods such as `arrayWithObjects:` are using behind the scenes. I'm not going to explain the C mechanism, because I don't expect you'll ever write a method or function that requires it; see K&R 7.3 if you need the gory details.

## Unrecognized Selectors

Objective-C messaging is dynamic, meaning that the compiler takes no formal responsibility for whether a particular object is a legal recipient of a given message. That's because whether an object can deal with a message sent to it isn't decided until the program actually runs and the message actually arrives. Objective-C has various devices for dealing at runtime with a message that doesn't correspond directly to a method, and for all the compiler knows, one of them might come into play in this case. For example, at the time the program runs, the recipient of the message might be nil — and it's harmless to send *any* message to nil.

Thus, it is legal to direct a message at an object with no corresponding method. The only guardian against this possibility is the compiler, but it isn't a very strong guardian. For example:

```
NSString* s = @"Hello, world!";
[s rockTheCasbah]; // compiler warns
```

An NSString has no method `rockTheCasbah`. But the compiler will not stop you from running a program containing this code; it's legal. The compiler will *warn* you, but it won't stop you. The warning, if you're using the GCC parser, reads: "Warning: 'NSString' may not respond to '-rockTheCasbah' (messages without a matching method signature will be assumed to return 'id' and accept '...' as arguments.)" The LLVM parser says that same thing more tersely: "Warning: method '-rockTheCasbah' not found (return type defaults to 'id')." Without going into the details, what the compiler means is: "I know of no instance method `rockTheCasbah`, so I can't check its signature against the return type and arguments you're actually using, so I'll just make some loose assumptions and let it pass."

This is a good example of what I meant in Chapter 2 when I said that sending a message and calling a method were not the same thing. The compiler is saying that NSString has no `rockTheCasbah` instance method, but that it isn't going to stop you from sending an NSString a `rockTheCasbah` message. At runtime, the object that receives the `rockThe-Casbah` message might be able to deal with it, for all the compiler knows.

However, if you *do* send a message to an object that really *can't* deal with it, your program will crash at that moment. So, for example, our attempt to send an NSString the `rockTheCasbah` message will crash our program, with a message (in the console log) of this form: "-[NSCFString rockTheCasbah]: unrecognized selector sent to instance 0x3048."

The important thing here is the phrase *unrecognized selector*. The term "selector" is roughly equivalent to "message," so this is a way of saying a certain instance was sent a message it couldn't deal with. The console message also tries to tell us *what* instance this was. 0x3048 is the value of the instance pointer; it is the address in memory to which our `NSString*` variable `s` was actually pointing. (Never mind why the NSString is described as an NSCFString; this has to do with NSString's implementation behind the scenes.)

(Strictly speaking, I should not say that a situation like this will "crash our program." What it will actually do is to generate an *exception*, an internal message as the program runs signifying that something bad has happened. It is possible for Objective-C code to "catch" an exception, in which case the program will not crash. The reason the program crashes, technically, is not that a message was sent to an object that couldn't handle it, but that the exception generated in response wasn't caught. That's why the crash log also says, "Terminating app due to uncaught exception.")

For this reason, you should generally not ignore a compiler warning that a certain class "may not respond to" a certain message. You should fix your program so that the compiler does not warn.

# Typecasting and the id Type

One way to silence the compiler when it warns in the way I've just described is by typecasting. A typecast, however, is not a viable way of fixing the problem unless it also tells the truth. It is perfectly possible to lie to the compiler by typecasting; this is not nice, and is not likely to yield nice consequences.

For example, suppose we've defined a class MyClass that does contain an instance method rockTheCasbah. As a result, it is fine with the compiler if you send the rockThe-Casbah message to a MyClass, although it is not fine to send the rockTheCasbah message to an NSString. So you can silence the compiler by claiming that an NSString instance *is* a MyClass instance:

```
NSString* s = @"Hello, world!";
[(MyClass*)s rockTheCasbah];
```

The typecast silences the compiler; there is no warning. Notice that the typecast is not a value conversion; it's merely a claim about what the type will turn out to be at runtime. You're saying that when the program runs, s will magically turn out to be a MyClass instance. Because MyClass has a rockTheCasbah instance method, that silences the compiler. Of course, you've lied to the compiler, so when the program runs it will crash anyway, in exactly the same way as before! You're still sending an NSString a message it can't deal with, so the very same exception about sending an unrecognized selector to an NSCFString instance will result. So don't do that!

Sometimes, however, typecasting to silence the compiler is exactly what you do want to do. This situation quite often arises in connection with class inheritance. We haven't discussed class inheritance yet, but I'll give an example anyway. Let's take the built-in Cocoa class UINavigationController. Its topViewController method is declared to return a UIViewController instance. In real life, though, it is likely to return an instance of some class you've created. So in order to call a method of the class you've created on the instance returned by topViewController without upsetting the compiler, you have to reassure the compiler that this instance really will be an instance of the class you've created. That's what I'm doing in this line from one of my own apps:

```
[((RootViewController*)[navigationController topViewController]) setAlbums: arr];
```

The expression (RootViewController*) is a typecast in which I'm assuring the compiler that at this moment in the program, the value returned by the topViewController method call will in fact be an instance of RootViewController, which is my own defined class. The typecast silences the compiler when I send this instance the setAlbums: message, because my RootViewController class has a setAlbums: instance method and the compiler knows this. And the program doesn't crash, because I'm not lying: this top-ViewController method call really *will* return a RootViewController instance.

Objective-C also provides a special type designed to silence the compiler's worries about object data types altogether. This is the id type. An id is a pointer, so you don't say id*. It is defined to mean "an object pointer," plain and simple, with no further specification. Thus, every instance reference is also an id.

Use of the id type causes the compiler to stop worrying about the relationship between object types and messages. The compiler can't know anything about what the object will really be, so it throws up its hands and doesn't warn about anything. Moreover, any object value can be assigned or typecast to an id, and *vice versa*. The notion of assignment includes parameter passing. So you can pass a value typed as an id as an argument where a parameter of some particular object type is expected, and you can pass any object as an argument where a parameter of type id is expected. (I like to think of an id as analogous to both type AB blood and type O blood: it is both a universal recipient and a universal donor.) So, for example:

```
NSString* s = @"Hello, world!";
id unk = s;
[unk rockTheCasbah];
```

The second line is legal, because any object value can be assigned to an id. The third line doesn't generate any compiler warning, because any message can be sent to an id. (Of course the program will *still* crash when it actually runs and unk turns out to be an NSString and incapable of receiving of the rockTheCasbah message.)

If an id's ability to receive any message reminds you of nil, it should. I have already said that nil is a form of zero; I can now specify what form of zero it is. It's zero cast as an id. Of course, it still makes a difference at runtime whether an id is nil or something else; sending a message to nil won't crash the program, but sending an unknown message to an actual object will.

Thus, id is a device for turning off the compiler's type checking altogether. Concerns about what type an object is are postponed until the program is actually running. Note that they would have been postponed anyway! As I've already said, Objective-C's message sending mechanism is dynamic. The compiler is merely a gatekeeper in this regard; that's why it can only issue warnings. All the compiler can do is intelligently analyze your code to see if you *might* be making a mistake that could matter at runtime. Using id turns off this part of the compiler's intelligence and leaves you to your own devices.

I do not recommend that you make extensive use of id to live in a world of pure dynamism. The compiler is your friend; you should let it use what intelligence it has to catch mistakes in your code. Thus, I almost never declare a variable or parameter as an id. I want my object types to be specific, so that the compiler can help check my code.

On the other hand, the Cocoa API does make frequent use of id, because it has to. For example, consider the NSArray class, which is the object-based version of an array. In pure C, you have to declare what type of thing lives in an array; for example, you could have "an array of int." In Objective-C, using an NSArray, you can't do that. Every NSArray is an array of id, meaning that every element of the array can be of any object type. You can put a specific type of object into an NSArray because any specific type of object can be assigned to an id (id is the universal recipient). You can get any specific type of object back out of an NSArray because an id can be assigned to any specific type of object (id is the universal donor).

So, for example, NSArray's lastObject method is defined as returning an id. So, given an NSArray arr, I can fetch its last element like this:

```
id unk = [arr lastObject];
```

However, after that code, unk can now be sent any message at all, and we are dispensing with the compiler's type checking. Therefore, if I happen to *know* what type of object an array element is, I always assign or cast it to that type. For example, let's say I happen to know that arr contains nothing but NSString instances (because I put them there in the first place). Then I will say:

```
NSString* s = [arr lastObject];
```

The compiler doesn't complain, because an id can be assigned to any specific type of object (id is the universal donor). Moreover, from here on in, the compiler regards s as an NSString, and uses its type checking abilities to make sure I don't send s any non-NSString messages, which is just what I wanted. And I didn't lie to the compiler; at runtime, s really *is* an NSString, so everything is fine.

The compiler's type checking is called *static typing*, as opposed to the dynamic behavior that takes place when the program actually runs. What I'm saying here, then, is that I prefer to take advantage of static typing as much as possible.

The Cocoa API will sometimes return an id from a method call where you might not expect it. It's good to be conscious of this, because otherwise the compiler can mislead you into thinking you're doing something safe when you're not. For example, consider this code:

```
UIColor* c = [NSString string];
```

This is clearly a mistake — you're assigning an NSString to a UIColor variable, which is likely to lead to a crash later on — but the compiler is silent. Why doesn't the compiler warn here? It's because the NSString string class method is declared like this:

```
+ (id)string
```

The string method returns an NSString, but its return value is typed as an id. An id can be assigned where any object type is expected, so the compiler doesn't complain when it's assigned to a UIColor variable. (As for *why* the string method returns an id instead of an NSString, that's a different matter; it has to do with NSString's underlying implementation as something called a class cluster, which we don't need to go into here; Chapter 10 has a bit more to say about class clusters.)

Earlier, I said that it is illegal for the same class to define methods of the same type (class method or instance method) with the same name but different signatures. But I did not say what happens when two *different* classes declare conflicting signatures for the same method name. This is another case in which it matters whether you're using static or dynamic typing. If you're using static typing — that is, the type of the object receiving the message is specified — there's no problem, because there's no doubt which method is being called (it's the one in that object's class). But if you're using dynamic typing, where the object receiving the message is an id, you might get a warning from the compiler. In general, having two different classes that declare conflicting signatures for the same method name is not necessarily problematic, and Cocoa does it quite a bit internally. But it's just as well to avoid it, and the need to avoid it is another reason why method names are so verbose: it's in order to make each method name unique.

 Accidentally defining your own method with the same name as an existing Cocoa method can cause mysterious problems. For example, in a recent online query, a programmer was confused because the compiler complained that his call to initWithObjects: lacked a nil terminator, even though his initWithObjects: didn't need a nil terminator. No, *his* initWithObjects: didn't, but *Cocoa's* did, and the compiler couldn't distinguish them because this message was being sent to an id. He should have picked a different name.

## Messages as Data Type

Objective-C is so dynamic that it doesn't have to know until runtime what message to send to an object or what object to send it to. Certain important methods actually accept both pieces of information as parameters. For example, consider this method declaration from Cocoa's NSNotificationCenter class:

```
- (void)addObserver:(id)notificationObserver selector:(SEL)notificationSelector
         name:(NSString *)notificationName object:(id)notificationSender
```

We'll discuss later what this method does (when we talk about notifications in Chapter 11), but the important thing to understand here is that it constitutes an instruction to send a certain message to a certain object at some later, appropriate time. For example, our purpose in calling this method might be to arrange to have the message tickleMeElmo: sent at some later, appropriate time to the object myObject.

So let's consider how we might actually make this method call. The object to which the message will be sent is here called notificationObserver, and is typed as an id (making it possible to specify any type of object to send the message to). So, for the notificationObserver parameter, we're going to pass myObject. The message itself is the notificationSelector parameter, which has a special data type, SEL (for "selector," the technical term for a message name). The question now is how to express the message name tickleMeElmo:.

You can't just put `tickleMeElmo:` as a bare term; that doesn't work syntactically. You might think you could express it as an NSString, `@"tickleMeElmo:"`, but surprisingly, that doesn't work either. It turns out that the correct way to do it is like this:

```
@selector(tickleMeElmo:)
```

The term `@selector()` is a directive to the compiler, telling it that what's in parentheses is a message name. Notice that what's in parentheses is not an NSString; it's the bare message name. And because it is the name, it must have no spaces and must include any colons that are part of the message name.

So the rule is extremely easy: when a SEL is expected, you'll usually pass a `@selector()` expression. Failure to get this syntax right, however, is a common beginner error. Notice also that this syntax is an invitation to make a typing mistake, especially because there is no checking by the compiler. If `myObject` implements a `tickleMe-Elmo:` method and I accidentally type `@selector(tickleMeElmo)`, forgetting the colon or making any other mistake in specifying the message name, there is no compiler error; the problem won't be discovered until the program runs and something bad happens. (In this case, if the `tickleMeElmo` message without the colon is ever sent to `myObject`, the app will probably crash with an unrecognized selector exception.)

# C Functions and Struct Pointers

Although your code will certainly call many Objective-C methods, it will also probably call quite a few C functions. For example, I mentioned in Chapter 1 that the usual way of initializing a CGPoint based on its x and y values is to call CGPointMake, which is declared like this:

```
CGPoint CGPointMake (
    CGFloat x,
    CGFloat y
);
```

Make certain that you can see at a glance that this *is* a C function, not an Objective-C method, and be sure you understand the difference in the calling syntax. To call an Objective-C method, you send a message to an object, in square brackets, with each argument following a colon in the method's name; to call a C function, you use the function's name followed by parentheses containing the arguments.

Moreover, many Objective-C objects and methods have lower-level C counterparts. For example, besides the Objective-C NSString, there is also something called a CFString; the "CF" stands for "Core Foundation," which is a lower-level C-based API. A CFString is an opaque C struct ("opaque" means that the elements constituting this struct are kept secret, and that you should operate on a CFString only by means of appropriate functions). As with an NSString or any other object, in your code you'll typically refer to a CFString by way of a C pointer; the pointer to a CFString has a type name, CFStringRef (a "reference to a CFString," evidently). You work with a CFString in pure C, by calling functions.

You might, on occasion, actually have to work with a Core Foundation type even when a corresponding object type exists. For example, you might find that NSString, for all its power, fails to implement a needed piece of functionality, which is in fact available for a CFString. Luckily, an NSString (a value typed as `NSString*`) and a CFString (a value typed as `CFStringRef`) are interchangeable: you can use one where the other is expected, though you will have to typecast in order to quiet the worries of the compiler. The documentation describes this interchangeability by saying that NSString and CFString are "toll-free bridged" to one another.

To illustrate, I'll use a CFString to convert an NSString representing an integer to that integer. (This use of CFString is unnecessary, and is just by way of demonstrating the syntax; NSString has an `intValue` method.)

```
NSString* answer = @"42";
int ans = CFStringGetIntValue((CFStringRef)answer);
```

The typecast prevents the compiler from complaining, and works because NSString is toll-free bridged to CFString — in effect, behind the scenes, an NSString *is* a CFString.

 Cocoa defines a number of underlying pointer-to-struct C data types, whose name typically ends in "Ref" (CGColorSpaceRef, CGPathRef, and so on). It is sometimes necessary to assign one of these to an `id` variable or parameter. For example, a CALayer's `setContents:` method expects an `id` parameter, but the actual value must be a CGImageRef. This is legal, because a pointer is just a pointer, but the compiler will complain unless you also typecast to an `id` or a pointer-to-void (`void*`).

You might even have reason to write your own C functions as part of a class, instead of writing a method. A C function has lower overhead than a full-fledged method; so even though it lacks the object-oriented abilities of a method, it is sometimes useful to write one, as when some utility calculation must be called rapidly and frequently. Also, once in a while you might encounter a Cocoa method or function that requires you to supply a C function as a "callback."

An example is the NSArray method `sortedArrayUsingFunction:context:`. The first parameter is typed like this:

```
NSInteger (*)(id, id, void *)
```

That expression denotes, in the rather tricky C syntax used for these things, a pointer to a function that takes three parameters and returns an NSInteger. The three parameters of the function are an `id`, an `id`, and a pointer-to-void (which means any C pointer). The address operator (see Chapter 1) can be used to obtain a pointer to a C function. So to call `sortedArrayUsingFunction:context:` you'd need to write a C function that meets this description, and use its name, preceded by an ampersand, as the first argument.

To illustrate, I'll write a "callback" function to sort an NSArray of NSStrings on the last character of each string. (This would be an odd thing to do, but it's only an example!) The NSInteger returned by the function has a special meaning: it indicates whether the first parameter is to be considered less than, equal to, or larger than the second. I'll obtain it by calling the NSString compare: method, which returns an NSInteger with that same meaning. Here's the function:

```
NSInteger sortByLastCharacter(id string1, id string2, void* context) {
    NSString* s1 = (NSString*) string1;
    NSString* s2 = (NSString*) string2;
    NSString* string1end = [s1 substringFromIndex:[s1 length] - 1];
    NSString* string2end = [s2 substringFromIndex:[s2 length] - 1];
    return [string1end compare:string2end];
}
```

And here's how we'd call sortedArrayUsingFunction:context: with that function as our callback (assume that arr is an NSArray of strings):

```
NSArray* arr2 = [arr sortedArrayUsingFunction:&sortByLastCharacter context:NULL];
```

# Blocks

A *block* is an extension to the C language, introduced in Mac OS X 10.6 and available if you're compiling for iOS 4.0 or later. It's a way of bundling up some code and handing off that entire bundle as an argument to a C function or Objective-C method. This is similar to what we did at the end of the preceding section, handing off a pointer to a function as an argument, but instead we're handing off the code *itself*. The latter has some major advantages over the former, which I'll discuss in a moment.

As an example, I'll rewrite the preceding example to use a block instead of a function pointer. Instead of calling sortedArrayUsingFunction:context:, I'll call sortedArray-UsingComparator:, which takes a block as its parameter. The block is typed like this:

```
NSComparisonResult (^)(id obj1, id obj2)
```

That's similar to the syntax for specifying the type of a pointer to a function, but a caret character is used instead of an asterisk character. So this means a block that takes two id parameters and returns an NSComparisonResult (which is merely an NSInteger, with just the same meaning as in the previous example). We can define the block and hand it off as the argument to sortedArrayUsingComparator: all in a single move, like this:

```
NSArray* arr2 = [arr sortedArrayUsingComparator: ^(id obj1, id obj2) {
    NSString* s1 = (NSString*) obj1;
    NSString* s2 = (NSString*) obj2;
    NSString* string1end = [s1 substringFromIndex:[s1 length] - 1];
    NSString* string2end = [s2 substringFromIndex:[s2 length] - 1];
    return [string1end compare:string2end];
}];
```

The syntax of the inline block definition is:

```
^❶(id obj1, id obj2)❷ {❸
```

❶ First, the caret character.

❷ Then, parentheses containing the parameters.

❸ Finally, curly braces containing the block's content.

Thanks to the block, as you can see, we've combined the definition of the callback function with its use. Of course, you might object that this means the callback isn't reusable; if we had *two* calls to sortedArrayUsingComparator: using the same callback, we'd have to write out the callback in full twice. To avoid such repetition, a block can be assigned to a variable:

```
NSComparisonResult (^sortByLastCharacter)(id, id) = ^(id obj1, id obj2) {
    NSString* s1 = (NSString*) obj1;
    NSString* s2 = (NSString*) obj2;
    NSString* string1end = [s1 substringFromIndex:[s1 length] - 1];
    NSString* string2end = [s2 substringFromIndex:[s2 length] - 1];
    return [string1end compare:string2end];
};
NSArray* arr2 = [arr sortedArrayUsingComparator: sortByLastCharacter];
NSArray* arr4 = [arr3 sortedArrayUsingComparator: sortByLastCharacter];
```

 The return type in an inline block definition is usually omitted. If included, it *follows* the caret character, *not* in parentheses. If omitted, you may have to use typecasting in the return line to make the returned type match the expected type. For a complete technical syntax specification for blocks, see *http://clang.llvm.org/docs/BlockLanguageSpec.txt*.

The power of blocks really starts to emerge when they are used instead of a selector name. In an example earlier in this chapter, we talked about how you could pass @selector(tickleMeElmo:) as the second argument to addObserver:selector:name: object: as a way of saying, "When the time comes, please call my tickleMeElmo: method." We also talked about how error-prone this syntax was: make a typing error, and your tickleMeElmo: method mysteriously won't be called. Moreover, such code is hard to maintain; there's the tickleMeElmo: method sitting there, completely separate from the code that calls addObserver:selector:name:object:, yet existing only to specify what should happen at the later time when our message arrives. (I'll talk about this problem again in Chapter 11.) It might well be clearer and more compact to call add-

`ObserverForName:object:queue:usingBlock:` and specify there and then as a block what should happen at message time, with no separate method callback.

Variables in scope at the point where a block is defined keep their meaning within the block at that moment, even though the block may be executed at some later moment. (Technically, we say that a block is a *closure*.) It is this aspect of blocks that makes them useful for specifying functionality to be executed at some later time, or even in some other thread.

Variables in scope whose meaning is captured by the closure are protected from direct assignment from within the block, unless you deliberately turn off this protection. Thus, if code inside a block tries to assign directly to a variable whose meaning comes from outside the block, the compiler will prevent it. To turn off this protection, declare the variable using the __block qualifier. But of course if such a variable is an object reference, messages can be sent to it and the object may be mutated (because message sending is not assignment) even without the __block qualifier.

Examples in this book may or may not use blocks, depending on the system version for which the example is written. If I quote code from one of my apps that runs on a pre-4.0 version of the system, that code can't involve blocks. If I write an example targeted purely at iOS 4.0 or later, I'll feel free to use blocks.

# CHAPTER 4

# Objective-C Classes

This chapter describes some linguistic and structural features of Objective-C having to do with classes; in the next chapter, we'll do the same for instances.

## Class and Superclass

In Objective-C, as in many other object-oriented languages, a mechanism is provided for specifying a relationship between two classes: they can be *subclass* and *superclass* of one another. For example, we might have a class Quadruped and a class Dog and make Quadruped the superclass of Dog. A class may have many subclasses, but a class can have only one immediate superclass. (I say "immediate" because that superclass might itself have a superclass, and so on in a rising chain, until we get to the ultimate superclass, called the *base class*, or *root class*.)

Because a class can have many subclasses but only one superclass, we can imagine all classes in a program as being arranged in a tree that splits into branches, such that each branch splits into smaller branches, each smaller branch splits into even smaller branches, and so on. Or we can imagine all the classes arranged in a hierarchy, such as might be displayed in an outline, with a single ultimate superclass, then all of its immediate subclasses in the next level below that, then each of *their* immediate subclasses in the next level below that, and so on. Indeed, before you write a line of your own code, Cocoa already consists of exactly such a vast repertoire of classes arranged in exactly such a hierarchical relationship. Xcode will actually display this relationship for you: choose View → Navigators → Symbol and click Hierarchical, with only the second icon in the filter bar darkened (Figure 4-1). (In Xcode 3.2.x, choose Project → Class Browser and switch to "Hierarchy, all classes.")

The reason for the class–subclass relationship is to allow related classes to share functionality. Suppose, for example, we have a Dog class and a Cat class, and we are considering defining a `walk` method for both of them. We might reason that both a dog and a cat walk in pretty much the same way, by virtue of both being quadrupeds. So it might make sense to define `walk` as a method of the Quadruped class, and make both

*Figure 4-1. Browsing the built-in class hierarchy in Xcode 4*

Dog and Cat subclasses of Quadruped. The result is that both Dog and Cat can be sent the `walk` message, even if neither of them has a `walk` method, because each of them has a superclass that *does* have a walk method. We say that a subclass *inherits* the methods of its superclass.

The purpose of subclassing is not merely so that a class can inherit another class's methods; it's so that it can define methods of its own. Typically, a subclass consists of the methods inherited from its superclass *and then some*. If Dog has no methods of its own, it is hard to see why it should exist separately from Quadruped. But if a Dog knows how to do something that not every Quadruped knows how to do — let's say, bark — then it makes sense as a separate class. If we define `bark` in the Dog class, and `walk` in the Quadruped class, and make Dog a subclass of Quadruped, then Dog inherits the ability to walk from the Quadruped class and also knows how to bark.

It is also permitted for a subclass to redefine a method inherited from its superclass. For example, perhaps some dogs bark differently from other dogs. We might have a class NoisyDog, for instance, that is a subclass of Dog. Dog defines `bark`, but NoisyDog also defines `bark`, and defines it differently from how Dog defines it. This is called *overriding*. The very natural rule is that if a subclass overrides a method inherited from its superclass, then when the corresponding message is sent to an instance of that subclass, it is the subclass's version of that method that is called.

## Interface and Implementation

As you already know from Chapter 2, all your code is going to go into some class or other. So the first thing we must do is specify what is meant by putting code "into a class" in Objective-C. How does Objective-C say, linguistically and structurally, "This is the code for such-and-such a class"?

To write the code for class, you must actually provide two chunks or sections of code, called the *interface* and the *implementation*. Here's the complete minimum code required to define a class called MyClass. This class is so minimal that it doesn't even have any methods of its own:

```
@interface MyClass
@end
@implementation MyClass
@end
```

The `@interface` and `@implementation` compiler directives show the compiler where the interface and implementation sections begin for the class that's being defined, MyClass; the corresponding `@end` lines show where each of those sections end.

In real life, the implementation section is where any methods for MyClass would be defined. So here's a class that's actually defined to do something:

```
@interface MyClass
@end
@implementation MyClass
- (NSString*) sayGoodnightGracie {
    return @"Good night, Gracie!";
}
@end
```

Observe how a method is defined. The first line is just like the method declaration, stating the type of method (class or instance), the type of value returned, and the name of the method along with the types of any parameters and local names for those parameters (see Chapter 3). Then come curly braces containing the code to be executed when the method is called, just as with a C function (see Chapter 1).

However, this class is still pretty much useless, because it can't be instantiated. In Cocoa, knowledge of how to be instantiated, plus how to do a number of other things that any class should know how to do, resides in the base class, which is the NSObject class. Therefore, all Cocoa classes must be based ultimately on the NSObject class, by declaring as the superclass for your class either NSObject or some other class that inherits from NSObject (as just about any other Cocoa class does). The syntax for this declaration is a colon followed by the superclass name in the `@interface` line, like this:

```
@interface MyClass : NSObject
@end
@implementation MyClass
- (NSString*) sayGoodnightGracie {
    return @"Good night, Gracie!";
}
@end
```

 NSObject is not the only Cocoa base class. It used to be, but there is now another, NSProxy. NSProxy is used only in very special circumstances and is not discussed in this book. If you have no reason for your class to inherit from any other class, make it inherit from NSObject.

In its fullest form, the interface section might contain some more material. In particular, there are two main types of stuff that the interface section might contain:

*Instance variables*

> If our class is to have any instance variables (other than those inherited from its superclass), they must be declared in the interface section.

*Method declarations*

> If we want to declare our methods, those method declarations go into the interface section. Method declarations are not required, but without a method declaration, a method cannot be "seen" by other methods defined before it in the same class.

So here is MyClass defined in what we might term canonical form:

```
@interface MyClass : NSObject {
    // instance variable declarations go here
}
- (NSString*) sayGoodnightGracie;
@end
@implementation MyClass
- (NSString*) sayGoodnightGracie {
    return @"Good night, Gracie!";
}
@end
```

There are no instance variable declarations in our class, so I've used a comment to show where they go; notice the curly braces surrounding the place. I'll go into detail about instance variables in the next chapter. The method declaration matches the name and signature for the method definition and ends with a semicolon (required).

# Header File and Implementation File

It's perfectly possible for the interface and implementation of a class to appear in the same file, or for multiple classes to be defined in a single file, but this is not the usual convention. The usual convention is one class, two files: one file containing the interface section, the other file containing the implementation section. For example, let's suppose you are defining a class MyClass. Then you have two files, *MyClass.h* and *My-Class.m*. (The file naming is not magical or necessary; it's just part of the convention. The file extensions are pretty much necessary, though, because the build process and Xcode itself rely on them.) The interface section goes into *MyClass.h*, which is called the *header file*. The implementation section goes into *MyClass.m*, which is called the *implementation file*. This separation into two files is not inconvenient, because Xcode, expecting you to follow this convention, makes it easy to jump from editing a *.h* file to the corresponding *.m* file and *vice versa* (Navigate → Jump to Next Counterpart; in Xcode 3.2.x, View → Switch to Header/Source File). Finally, the implementation file imports the header file (see Chapter 1 on the `#import` directive); this effectively unites the full class definition, making the definition legal even though it is split between two files, and allowing the implementation section to "see" any method declarations in the interface section.

With this arrangement in place, further imports become easy to configure. The header file imports the basic header file for the entire Cocoa framework; in the case of an iOS program, that's *UIKit.h* (again, see Chapter 1). There is no need for the implementation file to import *UIKit.h*, because the header file imports it, and the implementation file imports the header file. If a class needs to know about another class that isn't already imported in this way, its implementation file imports that class's header file. Example 4-1 summarizes this conventional schema.

*Example 4-1. Conventional schema for defining a class*

```
// [MyClass.h]

#import <UIKit/UIKit.h>

@interface MyClass : NSObject {
    // instance variable declarations go here
}
- (NSString*) sayGoodnightGracie;
@end

// [MyClass.m]

#import "MyClass.h"
#import "OtherClass.h"

@implementation MyClass
- (NSString*) sayGoodnightGracie {
    return @"Good night, Gracie!";
}
@end
```

The result of this arrangement is that everything has the right visibility. No file ever imports an implementation file; that way, what's inside a class's implementation file is private to that class. If something about a class needs to be public, such as a method that you want other classes to be able to call, it is declared in the header file, and other classes import that header file in their implementation files (as I do with *Other-Class.h* in Example 4-1); this keeps the chain of imports clear and simple.

A header file is also an appropriate place to define constants. In Chapter 1, for example, I talked about the problem of mistyping the name of a notification or dictionary key, which is a literal NSString, and how you could solve this problem by defining a name for such a string:

```
#define MYKEY @"mykey"
```

The question then arises of where to put that definition. If only one class needs to know about it, the definition can go near the start of its implementation file (it doesn't need to be inside the implementation section). But if multiple classes need to know about this name, then a header file is an appropriate location; every implementation file that imports this header file will acquire the definition, and you can use the name MYKEY in that implementation file.

A slight problem arises when a header file needs to mention one of your other classes. Suppose, for example, that MyClass has a public method that takes or returns an instance of MyOtherClass, or that MyClass has an instance variable whose type is MyOtherClass. So *MyClass.h* needs to speak of `MyOtherClass*`. But *MyClass.h* does not import *MyOtherClass.h*, so *MyClass.h* doesn't know about MyOtherClass, and the compiler will complain. To silence the compiler without violating the arrangement of imports (by importing *MyOtherClass.h* in the header file *MyClass.h*), use the `@class` directive. The word `@class` is followed by a comma-separated list of class names, ending with a semicolon. So *MyClass.h* might start out like this:

```
#import <UIKit/UIKit.h>
@class MyOtherClass;
```

Then the interface section would follow, as before. The `@class` directive simply tells the compiler, "Don't worry, MyOtherClass really is the name of a class." That's all the compiler needs to know in order to permit the mention of the type `MyOtherClass*` in the header file.

If, on the other hand, MyClass is to be a subclass of some other class, then MyClass's header file must import that superclass's header file (or some other header file that imports that superclass's header file). Thus, for example, in Example 4-1, *MyClass.h* imports *UIKit.h*; thus it knows about NSObject, so that MyClass can declare NSObject as its superclass.

A question that may occur to you at this point is how to declare a method without making it public. For example, let's say that many methods in MyClass need to call `myCoolMethod`, which is also a MyClass method. To make `myCoolMethod` visible to all MyClass methods, regardless of the order in which they are defined in the implementation section, you can declare `myCoolMethod` in the interface section. But this effectively "publishes" `myCoolMethod`, because any other class that imports *MyClass.h* will now know about it. If that isn't something you want to do, there's a trick for creating a second interface section that only MyClass's implementation section can see (Chapter 10).

**The Global Namespace**

When defining classes, choose your class names wisely to prevent name collisions. Objective-C has no namespaces; there's a single vast namespace containing all names. You don't want your own class name (or, for that matter, any other top-level constant name) to match a name defined in Cocoa. Instead of namespaces, there's a convention: each Cocoa framework prefixes its names with a particular pair of capital letters (NSString and NSArray, CGFloat and CGRect, and so on). Apple suggests that you use a prefix of your own as well. Don't use any of Apple's prefixes. Nothing limits your prefix to two letters, or requires that both letters be uppercase. In fact, because all of Apple's own prefixes *are* two uppercase letters, "My" as a prefix is safe.

# Class Methods

Class methods are useful in general for two main purposes:

*Factory methods*
> A factory method is a method that dispenses an instance of that class. For example, the UIFont class has a class method `fontWithName:Size:`. You supply a name and a size, and the UIFont class hands you back a UIFont instance corresponding to a font with that name and size.

*Global utility methods*
> Classes are global (visible from all code), so a class is a good place to put a utility method that anyone might need to call and that doesn't require the overhead of an instance. For example, the UIFont class has a class method `familyNames`. It returns an array of strings (that is, an NSArray of NSString instances) consisting of the names of the font families installed on this device. Because this method has to do with fonts, the UIFont class is as good a place as any to put it.

Most methods that you write will be instance methods, but now and then you might write a class method. When you do, your purpose will probably be similar to those examples.

# The Secret Life of Classes

A class method may be called by sending a message directly to the name of a class. For example, the `familyNames` class method of UIFont that I mentioned a moment ago might be called like this:

```
NSArray* fams = [UIFont familyNames];
```

Clearly, this is possible because a class is an object (Chapter 2), and the name of the class here represents that object.

You don't have to do anything to create a class object. One class object for every class your program defines is created for you automatically as the program starts up. (This includes the classes your program imports, so there's a MyClass class object because you defined MyClass, and there's an NSString class object because you imported *UIKit.h* and the whole Cocoa framework.) It is to this class object that you're referring when you send a message to the name of the class.

Your ability to send a message directly to the bare name of a class is due to a kind of syntactic shorthand. You can use the bare class name only in two ways (and we already know about both of them):

*To send a message to*
In the expression [UIFont familyNames], the bare name UIFont is sent the family-Names message.

*To specify an instance type*
In the expression NSString*, the bare name NSString is followed by an asterisk to signify a pointer to an instance of this class.

Otherwise, to speak of a class object, you need to obtain that object formally. One way to do this is to send the class message to a class or instance. For example, [MyClass class] returns the actual class object. Some built-in Cocoa methods expect a class object parameter (whose type is described as Class). To supply this as an argument, you'd need to obtain a class object formally. Take, for example, introspection on an object to inquire what its class is. The isKindOfClass: instance method is declared like this:

```
- (BOOL)isKindOfClass:(Class)aClass
```

So that means you could call it like this:

```
if ([someObject isKindOfClass: [MyClass class]]) // ...
```

A class object is not an instance, but it is definitely a full-fledged object. Therefore, a class object can be used wherever an object can be used. For example, it can be assigned to a variable of type id:

```
id classObject = [MyClass class];
```

You could then call a class method by sending a message to that object, because it is the class object:

```
id classObject = [MyClass class];
[classObject someClassMethod];
```

All class objects are also members of the Class class, so you could say this:

```
Class classObject = [MyClass class];
[classObject someClassMethod];
```

# CHAPTER 5

# Objective-C Instances

Instances are the heart of the action in an Objective-C program. Most of the methods you'll define when creating your own classes will be instance methods; most of the messages you'll send in your code will call instance methods. This chapter describes how instances come into existence and how they work.

## How Instances Are Created

Your class objects are created for you automatically as your program starts up, but instances must be created deliberately as the program runs. The entire question of where instances come from is thus crucial. Ultimately, every instance comes into existence in just one way: someone turns to a class and ask that class to instantiate itself. But there are three different ways in which this can occur: ready-made instances, instantiation from scratch, and nib-based instantiation.

### Ready-Made Instances

One way to create an instance is indirectly, by calling code that does the instantiation for you. You can think of an instance obtained in this indirect manner as a "ready-made instance." (That's my made-up phrase, not an official technical term.) For example, consider this simple code:

```
NSString* s2 = [s uppercaseString];
```

The documentation for the NSString instance method uppercaseString says that it returns an NSString* that is "an uppercased representation of the receiver." In other words, you send the uppercaseString message to an NSString, and you get back a *different*, newly created NSString. After that line of code, s2 points to an NSString instance that didn't exist beforehand.

The NSString produced by the uppercaseString method is a ready-made NSString instance. Your code didn't say anything about instantiation; it just sent the uppercase-String message. But clearly *someone* said something about instantiation, because instantiation took place; this is a newly minted NSString instance. That someone is presumably some code inside the NSString class. But we don't have to worry about the details. We are guaranteed of receiving a complete ready-made ready-to-roll NSString, and that's all we care about.

Similarly, any class factory method instantiates the class and dispenses the resulting instance as a ready-made instance. So, for example, the NSString class method `string-WithContentsOfFile:encoding:error:` reads a file and produces an NSString representing its contents. All the work of instantiation has been done for you. You just accept the resulting string and away you go.

Not every method that returns an instance returns a new instance, of course. For example, this is how you ask an array (an NSArray) for its last element:

```
id last = [myArray lastObject];
```

The NSArray `myArray` didn't *create* the object that it hands you. That object already existed; `myArray` was merely containing it, as it were — it was holding the object, pointing to it. Now it's sharing that object with you, that's all.

Similarly, many classes dispense one particular object. For example, your app has exactly one instance of the UIApplication class (we call this the *singleton* UIApplication instance); to access it, you send the `sharedApplication` class method to the UIApplication class:

```
UIApplication* theApp = [UIApplication sharedApplication];
```

This singleton instance existed before you asked for it; indeed, it existed before any code of yours could possibly run. You don't care how it was brought into being (though in fact the details are quite interesting, as you'll see in Chapter 7); all you care is that you can get hold of it when you want it. I'll talk more about globally available singleton objects of this kind in Chapter 13.

## Instantiation from Scratch

The alternative to requesting a ready-made instance is to tell a class, yourself, directly, to instantiate itself. There is basically one way to do this: you send a class the `alloc` message. The `alloc` class method is implemented by the NSObject class, the root class from which all other classes inherit. It causes memory to be set aside for the instance so that an instance pointer can point to it. (Management of that memory is a separate issue, discussed in Chapter 12.)

You must never, never, *never* call `alloc` by itself. You must *immediately* call another method, an instance method that *initializes* the newly created instance, placing it into a known valid state so that it can be sent other messages. Such a method is called an *initializer*. Moreover, an initializer returns an instance — usually the same instance, initialized. Therefore you can, and always should, call `alloc` and the initializer in the same line of code. The minimal initializer is `init`. So the basic pattern, known informally as "alloc-init," looks like Example 5-1.

*Example 5-1. The basic pattern for instantiation from scratch*

```
SomeClass* aVariable = [[SomeClass alloc] init];
```

You cannot instantiate from scratch if you do not also know how to initialize, so we turn immediately to a discussion of initialization.

## Initialization

Every class defines (or inherits) at least one initializer. This is an instance method; the instance has just been created (by calling `alloc` on the class), and it is to this newly minted instance that the initializer message must be sent. An initialization message must be sent to an instance immediately after that instance is created by means of the `alloc` message, and it must not be sent to an instance at any other time.

The basic initialization pattern, as shown in Example 5-1, is to nest the `alloc` call in the initialization call, assigning the result of the *initialization* (not the `alloc`!) to a variable. One reason for this is that if something goes wrong and the instance can't be created or initialized, the initializer will return nil; therefore it's important to capture the result of the initializer and treat that, not the result of `alloc`, as the pointer to the instance.

To help you identify initializers, all initializers are named in a conventional manner. The convention is that all initializers, and only initializers, begin with the word `init`. The ultimate bare-bones initializer is called simply `init`, and takes no parameters. Other initializers do take parameters, and usually begin with the phrase `initWith` followed by descriptions of their parameters. For example, the NSArray class documentation lists these methods:

```
- initWithArray:
- initWithArray:copyItems:
- initWithContentsOfFile:
- initWithContentsOfURL:
- initWithObjects:
- initWithObjects:count:
```

Let's try a real example. A particularly easy and generally useful initializer for NSArray is `initWithObjects:`. It takes a list of objects; the list must be terminated by nil. In Chapter 3, we illustrated this by creating an NSArray from three strings, by means of a class factory method that returned a ready-made instance:

```
NSArray* pep = [NSArray arrayWithObjects:@"Manny", @"Moe", @"Jack", nil];
```

Now we'll do what amounts to exactly the same thing, except that we'll create the instance ourselves, from scratch:

```
NSArray* pep = [[NSArray alloc] initWithObjects:@"Manny", @"Moe", @"Jack", nil];
```

In that particular case, there exist both a factory method and an initializer that work from the same set of data. Ultimately, it makes no difference which you use; given the same arguments, both approaches result in NSArray* instances that are indistinguishable from one another. It will turn out in the discussion of memory management (Chapter 12) that there might be a reason to choose instantiation from scratch over ready-made instances.

In looking for an initializer, don't forget to look upward through the class hierarchy. For example, the class documentation for UIWebView lists no initializers, but UIWebView inherits from UIView, and in UIView's class documentation you'll discover init-WithFrame:. Moreover, the init method is defined as an instance method of the NSObject class, so every class inherits it and every newly minted instance can be sent the init message. Thus it is a given that if a class defines no initializers of its own, you can initialize an instance of it with init. For example, the UIResponder class documentation lists no initializers at all (and no factory methods). So to create a UIResponder instance from scratch, you'd call alloc and init.

### The designated initializer

If a class does define initializers, one of them may be described in the documentation as the *designated initializer*. (There's nothing about a method's name that tells you it's the designated initializer; you must peruse the documentation to find out.) For example, in the UIView class documentation, the initWithFrame: method is described as the designated initializer. A class that does not define a designated initializer inherits its designated initializer; the ultimate designated initializer, inherited by all classes without any other designated initializer anywhere in their superclass chain, is init.

The designated initializer is the initializer on which any other initializers depend, in this class or any subclasses: ultimately, they *must* call it. The designated initializer might have the most parameters, allowing the most instance variables to be set explicitly, with the other initializers supplying default values for some instance variables, for convenience. Or it might just be the most basic form of initialization. But in any case, it is a bottleneck through which all other initializers pass. Here are some examples:

- The NSDate class documentation says that initWithTimeIntervalSinceReference-Date: is the designated initializer, and that initWithTimeIntervalSinceNow: calls it.

- The UIView class documentation says that initWithFrame: is the designated initializer. UIView contains no other initializers, but some of its subclasses do. UIWebView, a UIView subclass, has no initializer, so initWithFrame: is its inherited designated initializer. UIImageView, a UIView subclass, has initializers such as initWithImage:, but none of them is a designated initializer; so initWithFrame: is its inherited designated initializer as well, and initWithImage: must call initWith-Frame:.

Moreover, a class that implements a designated initializer will override the designated initializer inherited from its superclass. The idea is typically that even the inherited

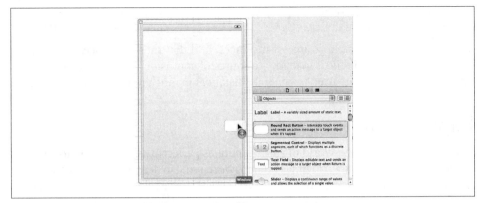

*Figure 5-1. Dragging a button into a window*

designated initializer, if called, will call this class's designated initializer. For example, UIView overrides the inherited `init` to call its own designated initializer, `initWith-Frame:`, with a value of `CGRectMake(0,0,0,0)`.

## Nib-Based Instantiation

The third means of instantiation is through a nib file. A nib file (whose extension may be *.nib* or *.xib*) is where Xcode lets you "draw" parts of the user interface. Most Xcode projects will include at least one nib file, which will be built into the app bundle, and will then be loaded as the app runs. A nib file consists, in a sense, of the names of classes along with instructions for instantiating and initializing them. When the app runs and a nib file is loaded, those instructions are carried out — those classes *are* instantiated and initialized.

For example, suppose you'd like the user to be presented with a window containing a button whose title is "Howdy." Xcode lets you arrange this graphically by editing a nib file: you drag a button from the Object library into the window, place it at a certain position in the window, and then set its title to "Howdy" (Figure 5-1). In effect, you create a drawing of what you want the window and its contents to look like.

When the app runs, the nib file loads, and that drawing is turned into reality. To do this, the drawing is treated as a set of instructions for instantiating objects. The button that you dragged into the window is treated as a representative of the UIButton class. The UIButton class is told to instantiate itself, and that instance is then initialized, giving it the same position you gave it in the drawing (the instance's `frame`), the same title you gave it in the drawing (the instance's `title`), and putting it into the window. In effect, the loading of your nib file is equivalent to this code (assuming that `window` is a reference to the window object):

```
UIButton* b =
    [UIButton buttonWithType:UIButtonTypeRoundedRect]; // factory method, instantiate
[b setTitle:@"Howdy!" forState:UIControlStateNormal]; // set up title
```

```
[b setFrame: CGRectMake(100,100,100,35)];          // set up frame
[window addSubview:b];                             // place button in window
```

The fact that nib files are a source of instances, and that those instances are brought into existence as the nib file is loaded, is a source of confusion to beginners. I'll discuss nib files and how they are used to generate instances in much more detail in Chapter 7.

# Polymorphism

The compiler, even in the world of static typing, is perfectly happy for you to supply a subclass instance where a superclass type is declared. To see this, let's start with the first line of the previous example:

```
UIButton* b = [UIButton buttonWithType:UIButtonTypeRoundedRect];
```

UIButton is a subclass of UIControl, which is a subclass of UIView. So it would be perfectly legal and acceptable to say this:

```
UIButton* b = [UIButton buttonWithType:UIButtonTypeRoundedRect];
UIView* v = b;
```

The variable b is a UIButton instance, but I'm assigning it to a variable declared as a UIView. That's legal and acceptable because UIView is an ancestor (up the superclass chain) of UIButton. Putting it another way, I'm behaving as if a UIButton were a UI-View, and the compiler accepts this because a UIButton *is* a UIView.

What's important when the app runs, however, is not the declared class of a variable, but the actual class of the object to which that variable points. Even if I assign the UIButton instance b to a UIView variable v, the object to which the variable v points is still a UIButton. So I can send it messages appropriate to a UIButton. For example:

```
UIButton* b = [UIButton buttonWithType:UIButtonTypeRoundedRect];
UIView* v = b;
[v setTitle:@"Howdy!" forState:UIControlStateNormal];
```

That code will cause the compiler to complain, because UIView doesn't implement set-Title:forState:. So I'll calm the compiler's fears by typecasting:

```
UIButton* b = [UIButton buttonWithType:UIButtonTypeRoundedRect];
UIView* v = b;
[(UIButton*)v setTitle:@"Howdy!" forState:UIControlStateNormal];
```

The typecast calms the compiler's fears, but the important thing is what happens when the program runs. What happens is that this code works just fine! It works fine not because I typecast v to a UIButton (typecasting doesn't convert magically convert anything to anything else; it's just a hint to the compiler), but because v really *is* a UIButton. So when the message setTitle:forState: arrives at the object pointed to by v, everything is fine. (If v had been a UIView but not a UIButton, on the other hand, the program would have crashed at that moment.)

An object, then, responds to a message sent to it on the basis of what it really is, not on the basis of anything said about what it is — and what it really is cannot be known until the program actually runs and the message is actually sent to that object.

Now let's turn the tables. We called a UIButton a UIView and sent it a UIButton message. Now we're going to call a UIButton a UIButton and send it a UIView message.

What an object really is depends not just upon its class but also upon that class's inheritance. A message is acceptable even if an object's own class doesn't implement a corresponding method, provided that the method is implemented somewhere up the superclass chain. For example, returning again to the same code:

```
UIButton* b = [UIButton buttonWithType:UIButtonTypeRoundedRect];
[b setFrame: CGRectMake(100,100,100,35)];
```

This code works fine, too. But you won't find `setFrame:` in the documentation for the UIButton class. That's because you're looking in the wrong place. A UIButton is a UIControl, and a UIControl is a UIView. To find out about `setFrame:`, look in the UIView class's documentation. (Okay, it's more complicated than that; you won't find `setFrame:` there either. But you will find a term `frame` which is called a "property," and this amounts to the same thing, as I'll explain later in this chapter.) So the `setFrame:` message is sent to a UIButton, but it corresponds to a method defined on a UIView. Yet it works fine, because a UIButton *is* a UIView.

A common beginner mistake is to consult the documentation without following the superclass chain. If you want to know what you can say to a UIButton, don't just look in the UIButton class documentation: also look in the UIControl class documentation, the UIView class documentation, and so on.

To sum up: we treated a UIButton object as a UIView, yet we were still able to send it a UIButton message. We treated a UIButton as a UIButton, yet we were still able to send it a UIView message. What matters when a message is sent to an object is not how the variable pointing to that object is declared but what class the object really is. What an object really is depends upon its class, along with that class's inheritance from the superclass chain; these facts are innate to the object and are independent of how the variable pointing to the object presents itself to the world. This independent maintenance of object type integrity is the basis of what is called *polymorphism*.

But it is not quite the whole of polymorphism. To understand the whole of polymorphism, we must go further into the dynamics of message sending.

# The Keyword self

A common situation is that code in an instance method defined in a class must call another instance method defined within the same class. We have not yet discussed how to do this. A method is called by sending a message to an object; in this situation, what object would that be? The answer is supplied by a special keyword, self. Here's a simple example:

```
@implementation MyClass

- (NSString*) greeting {
    return @"Goodnight, Gracie!";
}

- (NSString*) sayGoodnightGracie {
    return [self greeting];
}

@end
```

When the sayGoodnightGracie message is sent to a MyClass instance, the sayGoodnight-Gracie method runs. It sends the greeting message to self. As a result, the greeting instance method is called; it returns the string @"Goodnight, Gracie!", and this same string is then returned from the sayGoodnightGracie method.

The example seems straightforward enough, and it is. In real life, your code when you define a class will sometimes consist of a few public instance methods along with lots of other instance methods on which they rely. The instance methods within this class will be calling each other constantly. They do this by sending messages to self.

Behind this simple example, though, is a subtle and important mechanism having to do with the real meaning of the keyword self. The keyword self does not actually mean "in the same class." It's an instance, after all, not a class. What instance? It's this same instance. The same as what? The same instance to which the message was sent that resulted in the keyword self being encountered in the first place.

So let's consider in more detail what happens when we instantiate MyClass and send the sayGoodnightGracie message to that instance:

```
MyClass* thing = [[MyClass alloc] init];
NSString* s = [thing sayGoodnightGracie];
```

We instantiate MyClass and assign the instance to a variable thing. We then send the sayGoodnightGracie message to thing, the instance we just created. The message arrives, and it turns out this instance is a MyClass. Sure enough, MyClass implements a say-GoodnightGracie method, and this method is called. As it runs, the keyword self is encountered. It means "the instance to which the original message was sent in the first place." That, as it happens, is the instance pointed to by the variable thing. So now the greeting message is sent to that instance (Figure 5-2).

This mechanism may seem rather elaborate, considering that the outcome is just what you'd intuitively expect. But the mechanism *needs* to be elaborate in order to get the right outcome. This is particularly evident when superclasses are involved and a class overrides a method of its superclass. To illustrate, suppose we have a class Dog with an instance method bark. And suppose Dog also has an instance method speak, which

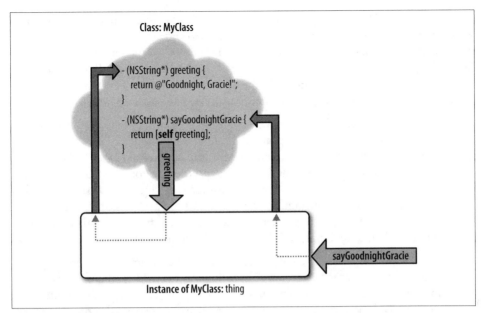

*Figure 5-2. The meaning of self*

simply calls **bark**. Now suppose we subclass Dog with a class Basenji, which overrides **bark** (because Basenjis can't bark). What happens when we send the **speak** message to a Basenji instance, as in Example 5-2?

*Example 5-2. Polymorphism in action*

```
@implementation Dog

- (NSString*) bark {
    return @"Woof!";
}

- (NSString*) speak {
    return [self bark];
}

@end

@implementation Basenji : Dog

- (NSString*) bark {
    return @""; // empty string, Basenjis can't bark
}

@end

// [so, in some other class...]

Basenji* b = [[Basenji alloc] init];
NSString* s = [b speak];
```

If the keyword self meant "the same class where this keyword appears," then when we send the speak message to a Basenji instance, we would arrive at the implementation of speak in the Dog class, and the Dog class's bark method would be called. This would be terrible, because it would make nonsense of the notion of overriding; we'd return @"Woof!", which is wrong for a Basenji. But that is *not* what the keyword self means. It has to do with the instance, not the class.

So here's what happens. The speak message is sent to our Basenji instance, b. The Basenji class doesn't implement a speak method, so we look upward in the class hierarchy and discover that speak is implemented in the superclass, Dog. We call Dog's instance method speak, the speak method runs, and the keyword self is encountered. It means "the instance to which the original message was sent in the first place." That instance is still our Basenji instance b. So we send the bark message to the Basenji instance b. The Basenji class implements a bark instance method, so this method is found and called, and the empty string is returned (Figure 5-3).

Of course, if the Basenji class had *not* overridden bark, then when the bark message was sent to the Basenji instance, we would have looked upward in the class hierarchy *again* and found the bark method implemented in the Dog class and called that. Thus, thanks to the way the keyword self works, inheritance works correctly both when there is overriding and when there is not.

If you understand that example, you understand polymorphism. The mechanism I've just described is crucial to polymorphism and is the basis of object-oriented programming. (Observe that I now speak of object-oriented programming, not just object-based programming as in Chapter 2. That's because, in my view, the addition of polymorphism is what turns object-based programming into object-oriented programming.)

## The Keyword super

Sometimes (quite often, in Cocoa programming) you want to override an inherited method but still access the overridden functionality. To do so, you'll use the keyword super. Like self, the keyword super is something you send a message to. But its meaning has nothing to do with "this instance" or any other instance. The keyword super is class-based, and it means: "Start the search for messages I receive in the superclass of this class" (where "this class" is the class where the keyword super appears).

You can do anything you like with super, but its primary purpose, as I've already said, is to access overridden functionality — typically from within the very functionality that does the overriding, so as to get both the overridden functionality and some additional functionality.

For example, suppose we define a class NoisyDog, a subclass of Dog. When told to bark, it barks twice:

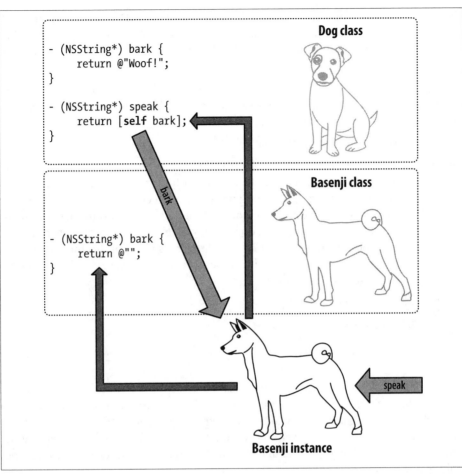

```objc
- (NSString*) bark {
    return @"Woof!";
}

- (NSString*) speak {
    return [self bark];
}
```

**Dog class**

**Basenji class**

```objc
- (NSString*) bark {
    return @"";
}
```

bark

speak

**Basenji instance**

*Figure 5-3. Class inheritance, overriding, self, and polymorphism*

```objc
@implementation NoisyDog : Dog

- (NSString*) bark {
    return [NSString stringWithFormat: @"%@ %@", [super bark], [super bark]];
}

@end
```

That code calls super's implementation of bark, twice; it assembles the two resulting strings into a single string with a space between, and returns that (using the stringWith-Format: method). Because Dog's bark method returns @"Woof!", NoisyDog's bark method returns @"Woof! Woof!". Notice that there is no circularity or recursion here: NoisyDog's bark method will never call itself.

A nice feature of this architecture is that by sending a message to the keyword super, rather than hard-coding @"Woof!" into NoisyDog's bark method, we ensure maintainability: if Dog's **bark** method is changed, the result of NoisyDog's **bark** method will change to match. For example, if we later go back and change Dog's **bark** method to return @"Arf!", NoisyDog's **bark** method will return @"Arf! Arf!" with no further change on our part.

In real Cocoa programming, it will very often be Cocoa's own methods that you're overriding. For example, the UIViewController class, which is built into Cocoa, implements a method **viewDidAppear:**, defined as follows:

```
- (void)viewDidAppear:(BOOL)animated
```

The documentation says that UIViewController is a class for which you are very likely to define a subclass (so as to get all of UIViewController's mighty powers — we'll find out what they are in Chapter 19 — along with your own custom behavior). The documentation proceeds to suggest that in your subclass of UIViewController you might want to override this method, but cautions that if you do, "you must call **super** at some point in your implementation." The phrase "call **super**" is a kind of shorthand, meaning "pass on to **super** the very same call and arguments that were sent to you." So your own implementation might look like this:

```
@implementation MyViewController : UIViewController
// ...
- (void) viewDidAppear: (BOOL) animated {
    [super viewDidAppear: animated];
    // ... do more stuff here ...
}
```

The result is that when **viewDidAppear:** is called in a MyViewController instance, we do both the standard stuff that its superclass UIViewController does in response to **viewDidAppear:** and the custom stuff pertaining our own class MyViewController. In this particular case, we don't even know exactly what the UIViewController stuff is, and we don't care. When the documentation tells you to call **super** when overriding, call **super** when overriding!

# Instance Variables and Accessors

In Chapter 3, I explained that one of the main reasons there are instances and not just classes is that instances can have instance variables. Instance variables, you remember, are declared when you define the class, and in Chapter 4 I said that these declarations go into the curly-braces part of the class's interface section. But the value of an instance variable differs for each instance.

The term "instance variable" arises so often that it is often abbreviated to *ivar*. I'll use both terms indiscriminately from now on.

Let's write a class that uses an instance variable. Suppose we have a Dog class and we want every Dog instance to have a number, which should be an int. (For example, this number might correspond to the dog's license number, or something like that.) So the interface section for the Dog class might look like this:

```
@interface Dog : NSObject {
    int number;
}
// public method declarations go here
@end
```

(You might ask why, for this example, I don't use instead the concept of giving the dog a name. The reason is that a name would be an NSString instance, which is an object; instance variables that are pointers to objects raise issues of memory management I don't want to get into now. But instance variables that are simple C data types raise no such issues. We'll return to this matter in Chapter 12.)

By default, instance variables are *protected*, meaning that other classes (except for subclasses) can't see them. So if, somewhere else, I instantiate a Dog, I won't be able to access that Dog instance's `number` instance variable. This is a deliberate feature of Objective-C; you can work around it if you like, but in general you should not. Instead, if you want to provide public access to an instance variable, write an accessor method and make the method declaration public.

Within a class, on the other hand, that class's own instance variables are global. Any Dog method can just use the variable name `number` and access this instance variable, just like any other variable. But global variables can be confusing when you're reading code; suddenly there's a variable called `number` and you don't understand what it is, because there's no declaration for it (the declaration is stashed away in the interface section, which is in a different file). So I often use a different notation, like this: `self->ivarName`. The "arrow" operator, formed by a minus sign and a greater-than sign, is called the *structure pointer* operator, because of its original use in C (K&R 6.2).

So let's write, in Dog's implementation section, a method that allows setting a value for the `number` ivar:

```
- (void) setNumber: (int) n {
    self->number = n;
}
```

Of course, we must also declare `setNumber:` in Dog's interface section:

```
@interface Dog : NSObject {
    int number;
}
- (void) setNumber: (int) n;
@end
```

We can now instantiate a Dog and assign that instance a number:

```
Dog* fido = [[Dog alloc] init];
[fido setNumber: 42];
```

We can now set a Dog's number, but we can't get it (from outside that Dog instance). To correct this problem, we'll write a second accessor method, one that allows for getting the value of the number ivar:

```
- (int) number {
    return self->number;
}
```

Again, we declare the number method in Dog's interface section. (You're not going to be confused, are you, by the fact that Dog has both a number method and a number instance variable? This doesn't confuse the compiler, because they are used in completely different ways in code, so it shouldn't confuse you either.) Now we can both set and get a Dog instance's number:

```
Dog* fido = [[Dog alloc] init];
[fido setNumber: 42];
int n = [fido number];
// sure enough, n is now 42!
```

This architecture is very typical. Your class can have as many ivars as you like, but if you want them to be publicly accessible, you must provide accessor methods. Luckily, Objective-C 2.0 — which is what you're using to program for iOS — provides a mechanism for generating accessor methods automatically (discussed in Chapter 12), so you won't have to go through the tedium of writing them by hand every time you want to make an ivar publicly accessible. (Though, to be honest, I don't see why you shouldn't have to go through that tedium; before Objective-C 2.0, we all had to, so why shouldn't you? We also had to clean the roads with our tongues on the way to school. And we liked it! You kids today, you don't know what real programming is.)

## Key–Value Coding

Objective-C provides a means for translating from a string to an instance variable accessor, called *key–value coding*. Such translation is useful, for example, when the name of the desired instance variable will not be known until runtime. So, for example, instead of calling [fido number], we might have a string @"number" that tells us what accessor to call. This string is the "key." To use key–value coding to get the value of the number instance variable from the fido instance, we would say:

```
int n = [fido valueForKey: @"number"];
```

Similarly, to use key–value coding to set the value of the number instance variable in the fido instance, we would say:

```
[fido setValue: 42 forKey: @"number"];
```

In this case there is no advantage to using key–value coding over just calling the accessors. But suppose we had received the value @"number" in a variable (as the result of a method call, perhaps). Suppose that variable is called something. Then we could say:

```
int n = [fido valueForKey: something];
```

Thus we could access a different instance variable under different circumstances. This powerful flexibility is possible because Objective-C is such a dynamic language that a message to be sent to an object does not have be formed until the program is already running.

When you call `valueForKey:` or `setValue:forKey:`, the correct accessor method is called if there is one. Thus, when we use `@"number"` as the key, a `number` method and a `set-Number:` method are called if they exist. (This is one reason why your accessors should be properly named.) On the other hand, if there isn't an accessor method, the instance variable is accessed directly. Such direct access violates the privacy of instance variables, so there's a way to turn off this feature for a particular class if you don't like it. (I'll explain what it is, with more about key–value coding, in Chapter 12.)

# Properties

A *property* is a syntactical feature of Objective-C 2.0 designed to provide an alternative to the standard syntax for calling an instance variable accessor. In other words, a property is merely syntactic sugar for calling an instance variable's accessors. I'll use the Dog class as an example. If the Dog class has an instance variable `number` and a getter method called `number` and a setter method called `setNumber:`, then the Dog class might also declare a `number` property. If it does, then instead of saying things like this:

```
[fido setNumber: 42];
int n = [fido number];
```

You can talk like this:

```
fido.number = 42;
int n = fido.number;
```

As you can see, this is a very pleasant syntax. You use dot-notation to chain the property name to the instance, and you can use the resulting expression either on the left side of an equal sign (to set the instance variable's value) or elsewhere (to fetch the instance variable's value). Remember, though, that you can do this only if the class you're talking to has declared a property corresponding to the instance variable in question. Remember also that your use of property syntax is not compulsory. If Dog has a `number` property, it has getter and setter methods `number` and `setNumber:`, and you are free to call them directly if you like. When you use a property in code, it is translated behind the scenes into a call to the corresponding getter or setter method, so it's all the same if you call the corresponding getter or setter method explicitly.

To use a property within the class that declares that property, you must use `self` explicitly. So, for example:

```
self.number = 42;
```

Do not confuse a property with an instance variable. An expression like `self->number = n`, or even simply `number = n`, sets the instance variable directly (and is possible only within the class, because instance variables are protected by default). An expression like `fido.number` or `self.number` involves a property and is equivalent to calling a getter or setter method. That getter or setter method may access an instance variable, and that instance variable may have the same name as the property, but that doesn't make them the same thing.

I have not yet told you *how* to declare a property corresponding to an instance variable. Plus, there are many options when declaring a property that affect how it can be used and what it means. All of that will be taken up in Chapter 12. But I'm telling you about properties now because they are so widely used in Cocoa and because you'll see them so frequently in the documentation. For example, in Chapter 1, I talked about setting a UIView's `autoresizingMask` property:

```
myView.autoresizingMask =
    UIViewAutoresizingFlexibleTopMargin | UIViewAutoresizingFlexibleWidth;
```

How did I know I could talk that way? Because the UIView documentation says that UIView declares an `autoresizingMask` property. Near the top of the documentation page, we see this line:

autoresizingMask *property*

And further down, we get the details:

**autoresizingMask**

An integer bit mask that determines how the receiver resizes itself when its bounds change.

```
@property(nonatomic) UIViewAutoresizing autoresizingMask
```

That last line *is* the property declaration. Never mind for now what `nonatomic` means; the point is that `autoresizingMask` is a property. That's how I knew I could use property syntax as a way of calling a setter method; alternatively, I could have called the `setAutoresizingMask:` method explicitly.

Similarly, earlier in this chapter I called UIView's `setFrame:` method, even though no such method is mentioned in the UIView documentation. What the UIView documentation does say is this:

**frame**

The receiver's frame rectangle.

```
@property(nonatomic) CGRect frame
```

The documentation is telling me that I can call a UIView setter method either by assigning to a `frame` property using dot-notation or by calling `setFrame:` explicitly.

Objective-C uses dot-notation for properties, and C uses dot-notation for structs; these can be chained. So, for example, UIView's `frame` is a property whose value is a struct (a CGRect); thus, you can say `myView.frame.size.height`, where `frame` is a property that returns a struct, `size` is a component of that struct, and `height` is a component of *that* struct. But a struct is not a pointer, so you cannot (for example) *set* a frame's height directly through a chain starting with the UIView, like this:

```
myView.frame.size.height = 36.0; // compile error
```

Instead, if you want to change a component of a struct property, you must fetch the property value into a struct variable, change the struct variable's value, and set the entire property value from the struct variable:

```
CGRect f = myView.frame;
f.size.height = 0;
myView.frame = f;
```

# How to Write an Initializer

Now that you know about `self` and `super` and instance variables, we can return to a topic that I blithely skipped over earlier. I described how to initialize a newly minted instance by calling an initializer, and emphasized that you must always do so, but I said nothing about how to write an initializer in your own classes. You will wish to do so only when you want your class to provide a convenient initializer that goes beyond the functionality of the inherited initializers. Often your purpose will be to accept some parameters and use them to set the initial values of some instance variables.

For example, in our example of a Dog with a number, let's say we don't want any Dog instances to come into existence without a number; every Dog *must* have one. So having a value for its `number` ivar is a *sine qua non* of a Dog being instantiated in the first place. An initializer publicizes this rule and helps to enforce it — especially if it is the class's designated initializer. So let's decide that this initializer will be Dog's designated initializer.

Moreover, let's say that a Dog's number should not be changed. Once the Dog has come into existence, along with a number, that number should remain attached to that Dog instance for as long as that Dog instance persists.

So delete the `setNumber:` method and its declaration, thus destroying any ability of other classes to set a Dog instance's `number` after it has been initialized. Instead, we're going to set a Dog's `number` as it is initialized, using a method we'll declare like this:

```
- (id) initWithNumber: (int) n
```

Our return value is typed as `id`, not as a pointer to a Dog, even though in fact we will return a Dog object. This is a convention that we should obey. The name is conventional as well; as you know, the `init` beginning tells the world this is an initializer.

Now I'm just going to show you the actual code for the initializer (Example 5-3). Much of this code is conventional — a dance you are required to do. You should not question this dance: just do it. I'll describe the meaning of the code, but I'm not going to try to justify all the parts of the convention.

*Example 5-3. Conventional schema for an initializer*

```
- (id) initWithNumber: (int) n {
    self = [super init]; ❶ ❷
    if (self) {
        self->number = n; ❸
    }
    return self; ❹
}
```

The parts of the convention are:

❶ We send some sort of initialization message, calling a designated initializer. If this is our class's designated initializer, this message is sent to super and calls the super-class's designated initializer. Otherwise, it is sent to self and calls either this class's designated initializer or another initializer that calls this class's designated initializer. In this case, this is our class's designated initializer, and the superclass's designated initializer is init.

❷ We capture the result of the initialization message to super, and assign that result to self. It comes as a surprise to many beginners (and not-so-beginners) that one can assign to self at all or that it would make sense to do so. But one can assign to self (because of how Objective-C messaging works behind the scenes), and it makes sense to do so because in certain cases the instance returned from the call to super might not be same as the self we started with.

❸ If self is not nil, we initialize any instance variables we care to. This part of the code is typically the only part you'll customize; the rest will be according to the pattern. Observe that I don't use any setter methods; in initializing an instance variable not inherited from the superclass, you should assign directly to the instance variable (and if it's an object, you'll also have to do some memory management, to be explained in Chapter 12).

❹ We return self.

All instance variables are set to a form of zero by alloc. Therefore, any instance variables not initialized explicitly in an initializer remain 0. This means, among other things, that by default a BOOL instance variable is NO and an object reference instance variable is nil. It is common practice to take advantage of these defaults in your program; if the default values are satisfactory initial values, you won't bother to set them in your designated initializer.

But we are not finished. Recall from earlier in this chapter that a class that defines a designated initializer should also override the inherited designated initializer (in this case, `init`). And you can see why: if we don't, someone could say `[[Dog alloc] init]` and create a dog without a number — the very thing our initializer is trying to prevent. Just for the sake of the example, I'll make the overridden `init` assign a negative number as a signal that there's a problem. Notice that we're still obeying the rules: this initializer is not the designated initializer, so it calls this class's designated initializer.

```
- (id) init {
    return [self initWithNumber: -9999];
}
```

Just to complete the story, here's some code showing how we now would instantiate a Dog:

```
Dog* fido = [[Dog alloc] initWithNumber:42];
int n = [fido number];
// n is now 42; our initialization worked!
```

# PART II

# IDE

By now, you're doubtless anxious to jump in and start writing an app. To do that, you need a solid grounding in the tools you'll be using. The heart and soul of those tools can be summed up in one word: Xcode. In this part of the book we explore Xcode, the *IDE* (integrated development environment) in which you'll be programming iOS. Xcode is a big program, and writing an app involves coordinating a lot of pieces; this part of the book will help you become comfortable with Xcode. Along the way, we'll generate a simple working app through some hands-on tutorials.

- Chapter 6 tours Xcode and explains the architecture of the *project*, the collection of files from which an app is generated.

- Chapter 7 is about nibs. A *nib* is a file containing a drawing of your interface. Understanding nibs — knowing how they work and how they relate to your code — is crucial to your use of Xcode and to proper development of just about any app.

- Chapter 8 pauses to discuss the Xcode documentation and other sources of information on the API.

- Chapter 9 explains editing your code, testing and debugging your code, and the various steps you'll take on the way to submitting your app to the App Store.

# CHAPTER 6

# Anatomy of an Xcode Project

*Xcode* is the application used to develop an iOS app. An Xcode *project* is the entire collection of files and settings needed in order to construct an app. The source for an app is an Xcode project. To develop and maintain an app, you must know how to manipulate an Xcode project. That means you must know your way around a project, as displayed by Xcode. By the same token, you must know your way around Xcode sufficiently to manipulate a project.

 The term "Xcode" is actually used in two ways. It's the name for the entire suite of developer tools — the Xcode tools — and it's the name of one application within that suite, the application in which you edit and build your app. This ambiguity should generally present little difficulty.

Xcode is a powerful, complex, and extremely large program. My approach when introducing Xcode to new users is to suggest that they adopt a kind of deliberate tunnel vision: if you don't understand something, don't worry about it, and don't even look at it (and don't touch it, because you might change something important). That's the approach I'll take here. This and subsequent chapters will undertake a simplified survey of Xcode, charting a somewhat restricted path, focusing on aspects of Xcode that you most need to understand immediately and resolutely ignoring those that you don't.

For full information, study Apple's own documentation (choose Help → Xcode Help); it may seem overwhelming at first, but what you need to know is probably in there somewhere. There are also entire books devoted to describing and explaining Xcode.

 This chapter describes Xcode 4. Earlier versions, designated generically as Xcode 3.2.x, are very different.

# New Project

Even before you've written any code, an Xcode project is quite elaborate. To see this, let's make a new, essentially "empty" project; you'll see instantly that it isn't empty at all.

1. Start up Xcode and choose File → New → New Project.

2. The "Choose a template" dialog appears. The template is your project's initial set of files and settings. When you pick a template, you're really picking an existing folder full of files; it will be one of the folders at some depth inside */Developer/ Platforms/iPhoneOS.platform/Developer/Library/Xcode/Project Templates* (I use the folder name */Developer* on the assumption that when you installed the Xcode tools you accepted the default and installed into a top-level */Developer* folder). This folder will essentially be copied, and a few values will be filled in, in order to create your project.

   So, in this case, on the left, under iOS (not Mac OS X!), choose Application. On the right, select Window-based Application. Click Next.

3. You are now asked to provide a name for your project (Product Name). Let's call our new project *Empty Window*.

   In a real project, you should give some thought to the project's name, as you're going to be living in close quarters with it. As Xcode copies the template folder, it's going to use the project's name to "fill in the blank" in several places, including some filenames and some settings, such as the name of the app. Thus, whatever you type at this moment is something you'll be seeing in a lot of places throughout your project, for as long as you work with this project. So use a name that is either your app's final name or at least approximates it.

   It's fine to use spaces in a project name. Wherever it is used as part of the name of various files and the value of certain settings, the name you type as the Product Name will have its spaces converted to underscores (where the template uses the term `___PROJECTNAMEASIDENTIFIER___`). But your spaces will remain in the folder name, the project name, and the app name (where the template uses the term `___PROJECTNAME___`).

4. Just below the Product Name field is the Company Identifier field. The first time you create a project, this field will be blank, and you should fill it in. The goal here is to create a unique string; your app's bundle identifier, which is shown in gray below the company identifier, will consist of the company identifier plus a version of the project's name, and because every project should have a unique name, the bundle identifier will also be unique and will thus uniquely identify this project along with the app that it produces and everything else connected with it. The convention is to start the company identifier with `com.` and to follow it with a string (possibly with multiple dot-components) that no one else is likely to use. For example, I use `com.neuburg.matt`.

---

5. Make sure the Device Family pop-up menu is set to iPhone and that both checkboxes are unchecked. Click Next.

6. You've now told Xcode how to construct your project. Basically, it's going to copy the folder at *Application/Window-based Application/Window-based iPhone Application* from within the *Project Templates* folder I mentioned earlier. But you need to tell it where to copy this folder to. That's why Xcode is now presenting a Save As dialog. You are to specify the location of a folder that is about to be created — a folder that will be the *project folder* for this project.

   The project folder can go just about anywhere, and you can move it after creating it. So the location doesn't matter much; I usually create new projects on the Desktop.

7. Xcode 4 also offers to create a git repository for your project. In real life, this can be a great convenience, but for now, uncheck that checkbox. Click Create.

8. The *Empty Window* project folder is created on disk (on the Desktop, if that's the location you just specified), and the project window for the Empty Window project opens in Xcode.

The project we've just created is a working project; it really does build an iOS app called Empty Window. To see this, make sure that in the Scheme pop-up menu in the project window's toolbar there's a checkmark next to iPhone 4.3 Simulator (though the exact system version number might be different), and choose Product → Run. After a while, the iOS Simulator application opens and displays your app running — an empty white screen.

 To *build* a project is to compile its code and assemble the compiled code, together with various resources, into the actual app. Typically, if you want to know whether your code compiles and your project is consistently and correctly constructed, you'll build the project (Product → Build). To *run* a project is to launch the built app, in the Simulator or on a connected device; if you want to know whether your code works as expected, you'll run the project (Product → Run), which automatically builds first if necessary.

# The Project Window

An Xcode project must embody a lot of information about what files constitute the project and how they are to be used when building the app, such as:

- The source files (your code) that are to be compiled
- Any resources, such as icons, images, or sound files, as well as nib files, that are to be part of the app
- Any frameworks to which the code must be linked as the app is built

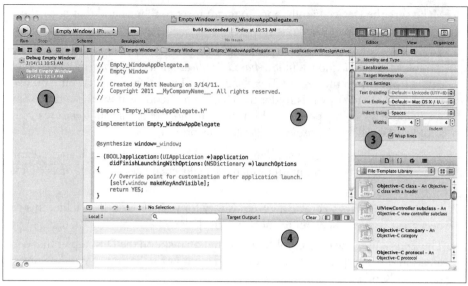

*Figure 6-1. The project window, on steroids*

- All settings (instructions to the compiler, to the linker, and so on) that are to be obeyed as the app is built

Xcode presents this information in graphical form, and this is one reason why a project window is so elaborate, and why learning to navigate and understand it takes time. Also, this single window must let you access, edit, and navigate your code, as well as reporting the progress and results of such procedures as building or debugging an app. In short, the single project window displays a lot of information and embodies a lot of functionality. You won't lose your way, however, if you just take a moment to explore this window and see how it is constructed.

Figure 6-1 shows the project window, configured in rather an extreme manner, in order to display as many parts of the window as possible. In real life, you'd probably never show all these parts of the window at the same time, except very briefly, unless you had a really big monitor.

1. On the left is the Navigator pane. Show and hide it with View → Navigators → Show/Hide Navigator (Command-0) or with the first button in the View segmented control in the toolbar.

2. In the middle is the Editor pane (or simply "editor"). A project window always contains at least one Editor pane. I could have displayed this window with multiple Editor panes, but I was afraid that might make you run screaming from the room.

3. On the right is the Utilities pane. Show and hide it with View → Utilities → Show/Hide Utilities (Command-Option-0) or with the third button in the View segmented control in the toolbar.

4. At the bottom is the Debugger pane. Show and hide it with View → Show/Hide Debug Area (Shift-Command-Y) or with the second button in the View segmented control in the toolbar.

 All Xcode keyboard shortcuts can be customized; see the Key Bindings pane of the Preferences window. Keyboard shortcuts that I cite are the defaults.

## The Navigator Pane

All navigation of the project window begins ultimately with the Navigator pane, the column of information at the left of the window. It is possible to toggle the visibility of the Navigator pane (View → Navigators → Hide/Show Navigator, or Command-0); for example, once you've used the Navigator pane to reach the item you want to see or work on, you might hide the Navigator pane temporarily to maximize your screen real estate (especially on a smaller monitor). You can change the Navigator pane's width by dragging the vertical line at its right edge.

The Navigator pane itself can display seven different sets of information; thus, there are actually seven navigators. These are represented by the seven icons across its top; to switch among them, use these icons or their keyboard shortcuts (Command-1, Command-2, and so on). You will quickly become adept at switching to the navigator you want; their keyboard shortcuts will become second nature. If the Navigator pane is hidden, pressing a navigator's keyboard shortcut both shows the Navigator pane and switches to that navigator.

Depending on your settings in the Behaviors pane of Xcode's preferences, a navigator might show itself automatically when you perform a certain action. For example, by default, when you build your project, if warning messages or error messages are generated, the Issue navigator will appear. This automatic behavior will not prove troublesome, because it is generally precisely the behavior you want, and if it isn't, you can change it; plus you can easily switch to a different navigator at any time.

The most important general use pattern for the Navigator pane is: you select something in the Navigator pane, and that thing is displayed in the main area of the project window. Let's begin experimenting immediately with the various navigators:

*Project navigator (Command-1)*
Click here for basic navigation through the files that constitute your project. For example, in the Empty Window folder (these folder-like things in the Project navigator are actually called *groups*) click *Empty_WindowAppDelegate.m* to view its code (Figure 6-2).

At the top level of the Project navigator, with a blue Xcode icon, is the Empty Window project itself; click it to view the settings associated with your project and

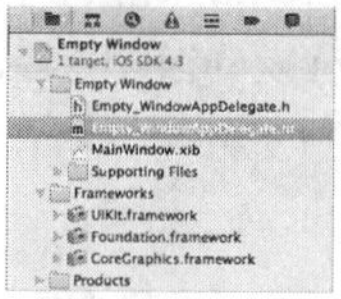

*Figure 6-2. The Project navigator*

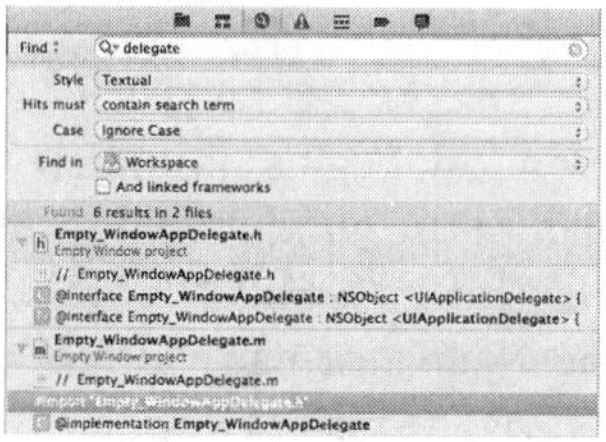

*Figure 6-3. The Search navigator*

its targets. Don't change anything here without knowing what you're doing! I'll talk later in this chapter about what these settings are for.

*Symbol navigator (Command-2)*

A *symbol* is a name, typically the name of a class or method. Depending on which of the three icons in the filter bar at the bottom of the Symbol navigator you highlight, you can view Cocoa's built-in symbols or the symbols defined in your project. The former can be a useful form of documentation; the latter can be helpful for navigating your code. For example, highlight the first two icons in the in the filter bar (the first two are light-colored, the third is dark), and see how quickly you can reach the definition of the `applicationDidBecomeActive:` method.

Feel free to highlight the filter bar icons in various ways to see how the contents of the Symbol navigator change. Note too that you can type in the search field in the filter bar to limit what appears in the Symbol navigator; for example, try typing "active" in the search field, and see what happens.

*Search navigator (Command-3)*

This is a powerful search facility for finding text globally in your project, and even in the headers of Cocoa frameworks. You can also summon the Search navigator with Edit → Find → Find in Workspace (Shift-Command-F). To access the full set of options, click the magnifying glass and choose Show Find Options. For example, try searching for "delegate" (Figure 6-3). Click a search result to jump to it in your code.

*Issue navigator (Command-4)*

You'll need this navigator primarily when your code has issues. This doesn't refer to emotional instability; it's Xcode's term for warning and error messages emitted when you build your project.

To see the Issue navigator in action, you'll need to give your code an issue. For example, navigate (as you already know how to do, in at least three different ways) to the file *Empty_WindowAppDelegate.m*, and in the blank line after the last comment at the top of the file, above the `#import` line, type howdy. Save (Command-S) and build (Command-B). The Issue navigator will display five error messages, showing that the compiler is totally unable to cope with this illegal word appearing in an illegal place. Click an issue to see it within its file. (Now that you've made Xcode miserable, select "howdy" and delete it; build again, and your issues will be gone. If only real life were this easy!)

*Debug navigator (Command-5)*

By default, this navigator will appear when your code is paused while you're debugging it. There is not a strong distinction in Xcode between running and debugging; the milieu is the same. (The difference is mostly a matter of whether breakpoints are obeyed; more about that, and about debugging in general, in Chapter 9.) However, if your code runs and doesn't pause, the Debug navigator by default won't come into play.

To see the Debug navigator in action, you'll need to give your code a breakpoint. Navigate once more to the file *Empty_WindowAppDelegate.m*, select in the line that says `return YES`, and choose Product → Debug → Add Breakpoint at Current Line to make a blue breakpoint arrow appear on that line. Run the project. (If the project is already running, the Stop dialog will appear; click Stop to terminate the current run and begin a new one.) By default, as the breakpoint is encountered, the Navigator pane switches to the Debug navigator, and the Debug pane appears at the bottom of the window.

This overall layout (Figure 6-4) will rapidly become familiar as you debug your projects. The Navigator pane displays the call stack, with the names of the nested methods in which the pause occurs; as you would expect, you can click on a method name to navigate to it. You can shorten or lengthen the list with the slider at the bottom of the pane. The Debug pane, which can be shown or hidden at will (View → Hide/Show Debug Area, or Shift-Command-Y) consists of two subpanes, either of which can be hidden using the segmented control at the top right of the pane.

- On the left, the variables list is populated with the variables in scope for the selected method in the call stack (and you can optionally display processor registers as well).

- On the right is the console, where the debugger displays text messages; that's how you learn of exceptions thrown by your running app. Exceptions are ex-

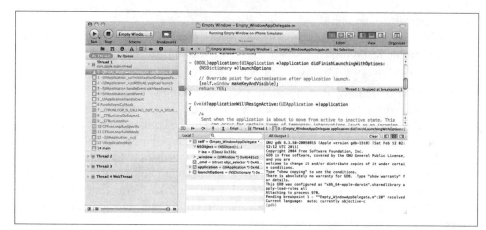

*Figure 6-4. The Debug layout*

tremely important to know about, and this is your only way to know about them, so keep an eye on the console as your app runs.

You can also use the console to communicate via text with the debugger. This can often be a better way to explore variable values during a pause than the variables list.

*Breakpoint navigator (Command-6)*
This navigator lists all your breakpoints. At the moment you've only one, but when you're actively debugging a large project, you'll be glad of this navigator. Also, this is where you create special breakpoints (such as symbolic breakpoints), and in general it's your center for managing existing breakpoints. We'll return to this topic in Chapter 9.

*Log navigator (Command-7)*
This navigator lists your recent major actions, such as building or running (debugging) your project. Click on a listing to see the log file generated when you performed that action. The log file might contain information that isn't displayed in any other way, and also it lets you dredge up messages from the recent past ("What was that exception I got while debugging a moment ago?").

For example, by clicking on the listing for a successful build, and by choosing to display All and All Messages using the filter switches at the top of the log, we can see the steps by which a build takes place (Figure 6-5). To reveal the full text of a step, click on that step and then click the Expand Transcript button that appears at the far right (and see also the menu items in the Editor menu).

When navigating by clicking in the Navigator pane, modifications to your click can determine where navigation takes place. For the settings that govern these click modifications, see the General pane of Xcode's preferences. For example, if you haven't

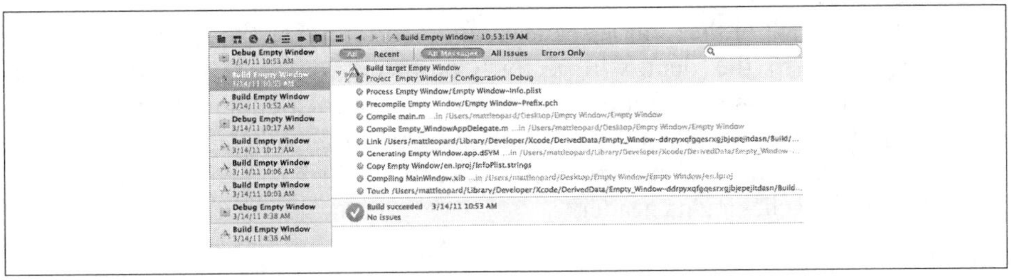

*Figure 6-5. Viewing a log*

changed the original settings, Option-click navigates in an assistant pane (discussed later in this chapter), and double-click navigates by opening a new window.

## The Utilities Pane

The Utilities pane, the column at the right of the project window, consists partly of inspectors that provide information about, and in some cases let you change the specifications of, the current selection, and partly of libraries that function as a source of objects you may need while editing your project. Its importance emerges mostly when you're working in the nib editor (Chapter 7), and you'll probably keep it hidden the rest of the time. But if you have sufficient screen real estate, you might like to keep it open while editing code, because Quick Help, a form of documentation (Chapter 8), is displayed here as well; plus, the Utilities pane is the source of code snippets (Chapter 9). To toggle the visibility of the Utilities pane, choose View → Utilities → Hide/Show Utilities (Command-Option-0). You can change the Utilities pane's width by dragging the vertical line at its left edge.

Many individual inspectors and libraries are discussed in subsequent chapters. Here, I'll just describe the overall physical characteristics of the Utilities pane.

The Utilities pane consists of a set of palettes. Actually, there are so many of these palettes that they are clumped into multiple sets, divided into two major groups: the top half of the pane and the bottom half of the pane. You can change the relative heights of these two halves by dragging the horizontal line that separates them.

*The top half*
What appears in the top half of the Utilities pane depends on what's selected in the current editor. There are two main cases:

*A code file is being edited*
The top half of the Utilities pane shows either the File inspector or Quick Help. Toggle between them with the icons at the top of this half of the Utilities pane, or with their keyboard shortcuts (Command-Option-1, Command-Option-2). The File inspector is rarely needed, but Quick Help can be useful as documentation. The File inspector consists of multiple sections, each of which can be expanded or collapsed by clicking its header.

*A nib file is being edited*

The top half of the Utilities pane shows, in addition to the File inspector and Quick Help, the Identity inspector (Command-Option-3), the Attributes inspector (Command-Option-4), the Size inspector (Command-Option-5), and the Connections inspector (Command-Option-6). Like the File inspector, these can consist of multiple sections, each of which can be expanded or collapsed by clicking its header.

*The bottom half*

The bottom half of the Utilities pane shows one of four libraries. Toggle between them with the icons at the top of this half of the Utilities pane, or with their keyboard shortcuts. They are the File Template library (Command-Option-Control-1), the Code Snippet library (Command-Option-Control-2), the Object library (Command-Option-Control-3), and the Media library (Command-Option-Control-4). The Object library is the most important; you'll use it heavily when editing a nib.

To see a help pop-up describing the currently selected item in a library, press Spacebar.

## The Editor

In the middle of the project window is the *editor*. This is where you get actual work done, reading and writing your code (Chapter 9), or designing your interface in a nib file (Chapter 7). The editor is the core of the project window. You can eliminate the Navigator pane, the Utilities pane, and the Debug pane, but there is no such thing as a project window without an editor (though you can cover the editor completely with the Debug pane).

The editor provides its own form of navigation, the *jump bar* across the top. I'll talk more later about the jump bar, but for now, observe that not only does it show you hierarchically what file is currently being edited, but also it allows you to switch to a different file. In particular, each path component in the jump bar is also a pop-up menu. These pop-up menus can be summoned by clicking on a path component, or by using keyboard shortcuts (shown in the second section of the View → Editor submenu). For example, Control-4 summons a hierarchical pop-up menu, which can be navigated entirely with the keyboard, allowing you to choose a different file in your project to edit. Thus you can navigate your project even if the Project navigator isn't showing.

It is extremely likely, as you develop a project, that you'll want to edit more than one file simultaneously, or obtain multiple views of a single file so that you can edit two areas of it simultaneously. This can be achieved in three ways: assistants, tabs, and secondary windows.

*Assistants*

You can split the editor into multiple editors by summoning an *assistant* pane. To do so, click the second button in the Editor segmented control in the toolbar, or choose View → Editor → Assistant (Command-Option-Return). Also, by default, adding the Option key to navigation opens an assistant pane; for example, Option-click in the Navigator pane, or Option-choose in the jump bar, to navigate by opening an assistant pane (or to navigate in an existing assistant pane if there is one). To remove the assistant pane, click the first button in the Editor segmented control in the toolbar, or choose View → Editor → Standard (Command-Return).

Your first task will be to decide how you want multiple editor panes arranged with respect to one another. To do so, choose from the View → Assistant Layout submenu. I usually prefer All Editors Stacked Vertically, but it's purely a matter of personal taste and convenience.

Once you've summoned an assistant pane, you can split it further into additional assistant panes. To do so, click the "+" button at the top right of an assistant pane. To dismiss a secondary assistant pane, click the "x" button at its top right. Note, however, that clicking the "x" button at the top right does *not* work to dismiss the *last* remaining assistant pane; you have to switch to Standard view (View → Editor → Standard or Command-Return).

An assistant pane is not merely split-pane editing; an assistant pane can bear a special relationship to the primary editor pane. The primary editor pane is the one whose contents, by default, are determined by what you click on in the Navigator pane; an assistant pane, meanwhile, can respond to what file is being edited in the primary editor pane by changing intelligently what file it (the assistant pane) is editing. This is called *tracking*.

To see tracking in action, open a single assistant pane and set the first component in its jump bar to Counterparts (Figure 6-6). Now use the Project navigator to select *Empty_WindowAppDelegate.m*; the primary editor pane displays this file, and the assistant automatically displays *Empty_WindowAppDelegate.h*. Next, use the Project navigator to select *Empty_WindowAppDelegate.h*; the primary editor pane displays this file, and the assistant automatically displays *Empty_WindowAppDelegate.m*. There's a lot of convenience and power lurking here, which you'll explore as you need it.

*Tabs*

You can embody the entire project window interface as a tab. To do so, choose File → New → New Tab (Command -T), revealing the tab bar (just below the toolbar) if it wasn't showing already. Use of a tabbed interface will likely be familiar from applications such as Safari. You can switch between tabs by clicking on a tab, or with Command-Shift-}. At first, your new tab will look identical to the original window from which it was spawned. But now you can make changes in a tab —

*Figure 6-6. Telling an assistant pane to display counterparts*

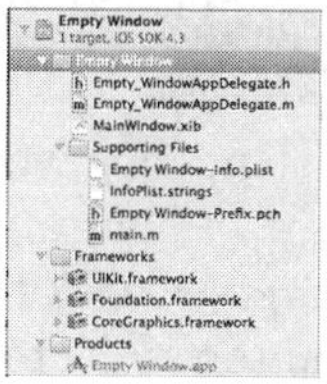

*Figure 6-7. The Project navigator again*

change what panes are showing or what file is being edited, for example — without affecting any other tabs. Thus you can get multiple views of your project.

*Secondary windows*

A secondary project window is similar to a tab, but it appears as a separate window instead of a tab in the same window. To create one, choose File → New → New Window (Command-Shift-T). Alternatively, you can promote a tab to be a window by dragging it right out of its current window. Yet another way to make a secondary project window is to choose Navigate → Open In and navigate left in the resulting dialog until the dialog offers to make a new window.

There isn't a strong difference between a tab and a secondary window; which you use, and for what, will be a matter of taste and convenience. I find that the advantage of a secondary window is that you can see it at the same time as the main window, and that it can be small. Thus, when I have a file I frequently want to refer to, I often spawn into a secondary window an editor displaying that file, making it fairly small and without any additional panes.

# The Project File and Its Dependents

The first item in the Project navigator (Command-1) represents the project file on disk (in our new project, this is called Empty Window). Hierarchically dependent upon it are items that contribute to the building of the project (Figure 6-7).

---

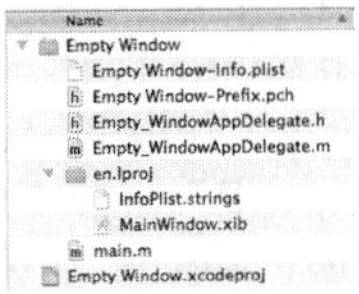

Name
▼ 📁 Empty Window
    📄 Empty Window-Info.plist
    📄 Empty Window-Prefix.pch
    📄 Empty_WindowAppDelegate.h
    📄 Empty_WindowAppDelegate.m
▼ 📁 en.lproj
    📄 InfoPlist.strings
    📄 MainWindow.xib
    📄 main.m
📄 Empty Window.xcodeproj

*Figure 6-8. The project folder*

Many of these items, including the project file itself, correspond to items on disk in the project folder. To survey this correspondence, let's examine the project folder in the Finder simultaneously with the Xcode project window. Select the project file listing in the Project navigator and choose File → Show in Finder.

The Finder displays the contents of your project folder (Figure 6-8). The most important of these is *Empty Window.xcodeproj*. This is the project file. All Xcode's knowledge about your project — what files it consists of and how to build the project — is stored in this file.

To open a project from the Finder, double-click the project file. This will launch Xcode if it isn't already running.

Never, never, *never* touch anything in a project folder by way of the Finder, except for double-clicking the project file to open the project. Don't put anything directly into a project folder. Don't remove anything from a project folder. Don't rename anything in a project folder. Don't touch anything in a project folder! Do all your interaction with the project through the project window in Xcode.

The reason for the foregoing warning is that in order to work properly, the project expects things in the project folder to be a certain way. If you make any alterations to the project folder directly in the Finder, behind the project's back, you can upset those expectations and break the project. When you work in the project window, it is Xcode itself that makes any necessary changes in the project folder, and all will be well. (When you're an Xcode power user, you'll know when you can disobey this rule. Until then, just obey it blindly and rigorously.)

Consider now the groups and files shown in the Project navigator as hierarchically dependent upon the project file, and how they correspond to reality on disk as portrayed in the Finder. (Recall that *group* is the technical term for the folder-like objects shown in the Project navigator.)

The first thing you'll notice is that groups in the Project navigator don't necessarily correspond to folders on disk in the Finder, and folders on disk in the Finder don't necessarily correspond to groups in the Project navigator.

- The Empty Window group is, to some extent, real; it corresponds directly to the *Empty Window* folder on disk. If you were to create additional files (which, in real life, you would almost certainly do in the course of developing your project), you would likely put them in the Empty Window group in the Project navigator so that they'd be in the *Empty Window* folder on disk. (Doing so, however, is not a requirement; your files can live anywhere and your project will still work fine.)

- The Supporting Files group, on the other hand, corresponds to nothing on disk; it's just a way of clumping some items together in the Project navigator, so that they can be located easily and can be shown or hidden together. The things *inside* this group are real, however; you can see that the four files *Empty_Window-Info.plist*, *InfoPlist.strings*, *Empty_Window_Prefix.pch*, and *main.m* do exist on disk — they're just not inside anything called *Supporting Files*. Rather, they're at the top level of the *Empty Window* folder — except that two of them are inside a folder called *en.lproj*, which doesn't appear in the Project navigator! (The folder *en.lproj* has to do with *localization*, which I'll discuss in Chapter 9.)

You may be tempted to find all this confusing. Don't! Remember what I said about not involving yourself with the project folder on disk in the Finder. Keep your attention on the Project navigator, make your modifications to the project there, and all will be well.

By convention, as you add other files to your project that are not code but need to be copied into the app as it is built, such as sound and image files, you would usually put them into yet another group — probably, though not necessarily, a group inside the Empty Window group. You might call this group Resources. (I usually do.) And as your project grows further, you should feel free to create even more groups to help organize your files. To make a new group, choose File → New → New Group. To rename a group, select it in the Project navigator and press Return to make the name editable.

When I say "feel free," I mean it. You want navigating your project to be easy and intuitive. That's what groups are for. They are just ways of making the Project navigator work well for you. As we've seen, they don't necessarily affect how the actual files are stored on disk. Even more important, they don't affect how the app is built. It is not the placement of files in groups or in the Finder that causes them to be built into the app; it's their inclusion in the appropriate target build phase, as I'll explain later in this chapter.

The things in the Frameworks group and the Products group don't correspond to anything in the project folder, but they do correspond to real things that the project needs to know about in order to build and run:

*Frameworks*

This group, by convention, lists frameworks (Cocoa code) that your code calls. Frameworks exist on disk, but they are not built into your app when it is constructed; they don't have to be, because they are present on the target device (an iPhone, iPod touch, or iPad). Instead, the frameworks are *linked* to the app, meaning that the app knows about them and expects to find them on the device when it runs. Thus, all the framework code is omitted from the app itself, saving considerable space.

*Products*
> This group, by convention, holds an automatically generated reference to the built app.

# The Target

A *target* is a collection of parts along with rules and settings for how to build a product from them. It is a major determinant of how an app is built. Whenever you build, what you're really building is a target.

Select the Empty Window project in the Project navigator, and you'll see two things on the left side of the editor: the project itself, and a list of your targets. In this case, there is only one target, called Empty Window (just like the project itself). But there *could* be more than one target, under certain circumstances. For example, you might want to write an app that can be built as an iPhone app or as an iPad app — two different apps that share a lot of the same code. So you might want one project containing two targets.

If you select the project in the left side of the editor, you *edit the project*. If you select the target in the left side of the editor, you *edit the target*. I'll use those expressions a lot in later instructions.

## Build Phases

Edit the target and click Build Phases at the top of the editor (Figure 6-9). These are the stages by which your app is built. By default, there are three of them with content — Compile Sources, Link Binary With Libraries, and Copy Bundle Resources — and those are the only stages you'll usually need, though you can add others. The build phases are both a report to you on how the target will be built and a set of instructions to Xcode on how to build the target; if you change the build phases, you change the build process.

The meanings of the three build phases are pretty straightforward:

*Compile Sources*
> Certain files (your code) are compiled, and the resulting compiled code (a single file called the *binary*) is copied into the app.

*Link Binary With Libraries*
> Certain libraries, usually frameworks, are linked to the compiled code, so that it will expect them to be present on the device when the app runs.

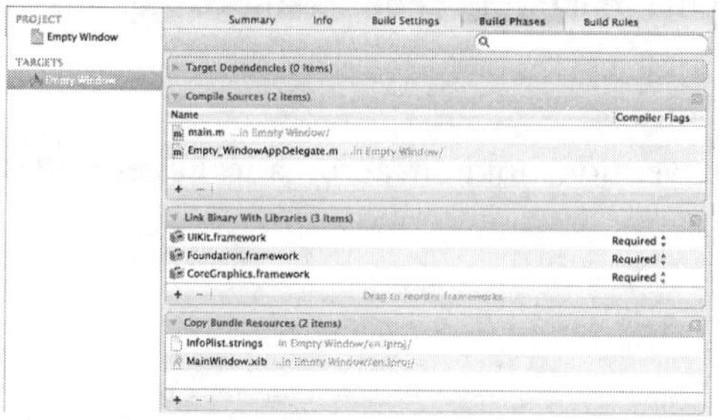

*Figure 6-9. Build phases*

Copy Bundle Resources

> Certain files are copied into the app, so that your code or the system can find them there when the app runs. For example, if your app had an icon, it would need to be copied into the app so the device could find and display it.

By opening the build phases in the editor, you can see the files to which each phase applies. The first phase, Compile Sources, presently compiles two files (*main.m* and *Empty_WindowAppDelegate.m*). The second phase, Link Binary With Libraries, presently links three libraries (frameworks). The third phase, Copy Bundle Resources, presently copies two files (*InfoPlist.strings*, along with *MainWindow.xib*, the nib file).

You can alter these lists. If something in your project was not in Copy Bundle Resources and you wanted it copied into the app during the build process, you could drag it from the Project navigator into the Copy Bundle Resources list, or (easier) click the "+" button beneath the Copy Bundle Resources list to get a helpful dialog listing everything in your project. If something in your project was in Copy Bundle Resources and you didn't want it copied in the app, you would delete it from the list; this would not delete it from your project, from the Project navigator, or from the Finder.

## Build Settings

Build phases are only one aspect of how a target knows how to build the app. The other aspect is build settings. To see them, select this project's single target in the editor, and click Build Settings at the top of the editor (Figure 6-10). Here you'll find a long list of settings, most of which you'll never touch. But Xcode examines this list in order to know what to do at various stages of the build process. Build settings are the reason your project compiles and builds the way it does.

You can determine what build settings are displayed by clicking Basic or All. The settings are combined into categories, and you can close or open each category heading to save room. If you know something about a setting you want to see, such as its name, you can use the search field at the top right to filter what settings are shown.

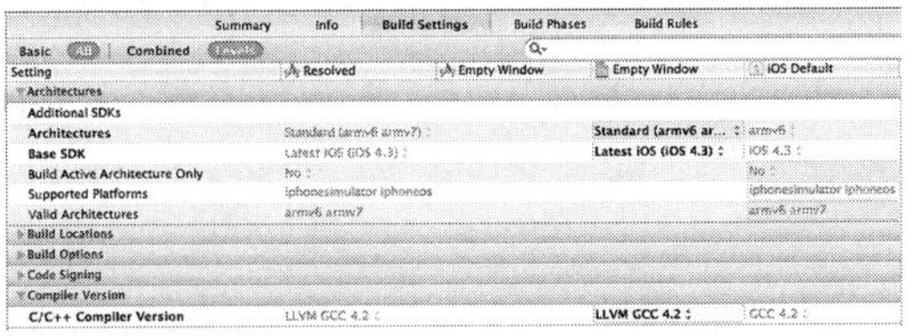

*Figure 6-10. Target build settings*

You can determine how build settings are displayed by clicking Combined or Levels; in Figure 6-10, I've clicked Levels, in order to discuss what levels are. It turns out that not only does a target contain values for the build settings, but the project also contains values for the same build settings; furthermore, Xcode has certain built-in default build setting values. The Levels display shows all of these levels at once, so you can understand the derivation of the actual values used for every build setting.

To understand the chart, read from right to left. For example, the C/C++ Compiler Version build setting, which determines what compiler is used (see "Choosing a Compiler" on page 6), is set to be GCC 4.2 by the built-in Xcode default (the rightmost column). Then, however, the project comes along with a different value for this build setting, namely LLVM GCC 4.2 (second column from the right). The target does not override this value (third column from the right). Therefore the actual value used will be LLVM GCC 4.2 (fourth column from the right, "Resolved").

If you wanted to change this value, you could, here and now. You could change the value at the project level or at the target level. I'm not suggesting that you should do so; indeed, you will rarely have occasion to manipulate build settings directly, as the defaults are usually acceptable. Nevertheless, you *can* change build setting values, and this is where you would do so. For details on what the various build settings are, consult Apple's documentation, especially the *Xcode Build Setting Reference*. Also, you can select a build setting and show Quick Help in the Utilities pane to learn more about it.

## Configurations

There are actually multiple lists of build setting values — though only one such list applies when a build is performed. Each such list is called a *configuration*. Multiple configurations are needed because you build in different ways at different times for different purposes, and thus you'll want certain build settings to take on different values under different circumstances.

By default, there are two configurations:

*Debug*
   This configuration is used throughout the development process, as you write and run your app.

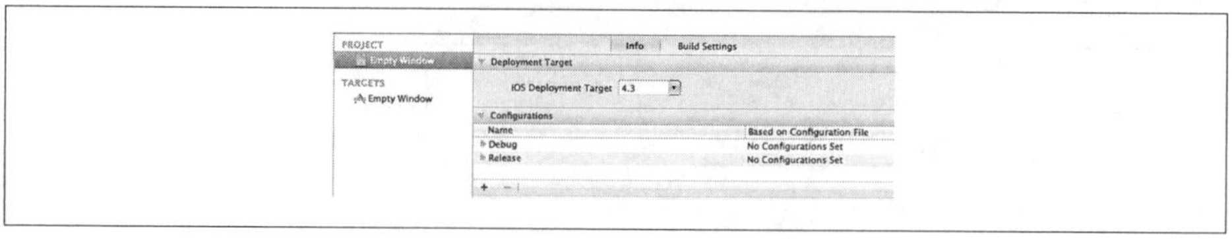

*Figure 6-11. Configurations*

*Release*

This configuration is used for late-stage testing, when you want to check performance on a device.

Configurations exist at all because the project says so. To see where the project says so, select the project in the editor and click Info at the top of the editor (Figure 6-11). Note that these configurations are just names. You can make additional configurations, and when you do, you're just adding to a list of names. The importance of configurations emerges only when those names are coupled with build setting values. Configurations can affect build setting values both at the project level and at the target level.

For example, return to the target build settings (Figure 6-10) and type "Strip" into the search field to filter the list of settings. You'll immediately spot the Strip Debug Symbols During Copy build setting. It has *two* values: one for the Debug configuration, one for the Release configuration. When you make a debug build, you use the Debug configuration, and the value for this setting is No; that way, debugging is possible because the needed names are included in the built app. When you make a release build, you use the Release configuration, and the value for this setting is Yes; that way, the app is smaller, but debugging isn't possible because the needed names aren't present.

Here's another example. Type "Optim" into the search field. Now you can look at the Optimization Level build setting. The Debug configuration value for Optimization Level is None: while you're developing your app, your code is just compiled line by line in a straightforward way. The Release configuration value for Optimization Level is Fastest, Smallest; the resulting binary is faster and smaller, which is great when the app runs on a device, but would be no good while you're developing the app because breakpoints and stepping in the debugger wouldn't work properly. (A not uncommon beginner error is building with the Release configuration and then wondering why the debugger isn't pausing at breakpoints any more.)

## Schemes and Destinations

So far, I have said that there are configurations, and I have explained that you may need to switch between configurations in order to get the build setting values appropriate for your current purpose. But I have not said how the configuration is determined as you actually build. It's determined by a scheme.

A *scheme* unites a target (or multiple targets) to be built with a build configuration, with respect to the purpose for which you're building. A new project, such as Empty

*Figure 6-12. The scheme editor*

Window, comes by default with a single scheme, named after the project's single target. Thus this project's single scheme is called, by default, Empty Window. To see it, choose Product → Edit Scheme. The scheme editor dialog opens. Make sure that Info at the top of the dialog is selected.

On the left side of the scheme editor are listed various actions you might perform from the Product menu. Click an action to see its corresponding settings in this scheme. Of these actions, Build and Run are the most common, and the only ones I've discussed up to now, so we'll concentrate on them. The Build action is different from the other actions, because it is common to all of them (the other actions all implicitly involve building); thus the Build action merely determines what target(s) will be built when each of the other actions is performed, and for our simple project this is trivial, because we've only one target and we always need it built. So, now consider the Run action.

When you click the Run action at the left, the editor displays the settings that will be used when you build and run (Figure 6-12). As you can see, the Build Configuration pop-up menu is set to Debug. That explains where the current build configuration comes from. At the moment, whenever you build and run, you're using the Debug build configuration and the build setting values that correspond to it, because you're using this scheme, and that's what this scheme says to do when you build and run.

Now dismiss the scheme editor, and consider this question: suppose you wanted to build and run using the Release build configuration. (The Debug build configuration settings may affect the behavior of the built app, so you want to test the app as an actual user would experience it.) How would you do this? One way would be to return to the scheme editor and change the build configuration for this scheme. Xcode makes this convenient: hold the Option key as you choose Product → Run (or as you click the Run button in the toolbar). The scheme editor appears, containing a Run button. So now you can make any changes you like, such as setting the Build Configuration pop-up menu to Release for the Run action, and proceed directly to build and run the app by clicking Run.

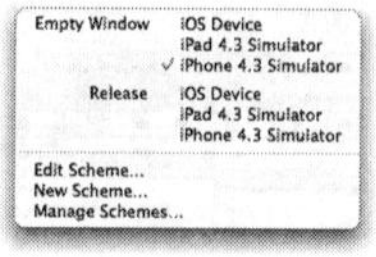

*Figure 6-13. The Scheme pop-up menu*

(If you're following along and you did make this change, open the scheme editor again and set the Build Configuration pop-up for the Run action in our Empty Window scheme back to Debug.)

On the other hand, if you were to find yourself often wanting to switch between building and running with the Debug configuration and building and running with the Release configuration, you might make a distinct scheme that uses the Release debug configuration for the Run action. This is easy to do: in the scheme editor, click Duplicate Scheme. The name of the new scheme is editable; let's call it Release. Change the Build Configuration pop-up for the Run action in our new scheme to Release, and dismiss the scheme editor.

Now you have two schemes, Empty Window (whose build configuration for running is Debug) and Release (whose build configuration for running is Release). To switch between them easily, you can use the Scheme pop-up menu in the project window toolbar (Figure 6-13) before you build and run.

The Scheme pop-up menu lists each scheme, along with each *destination* on which you might run your built app. A destination is effectively a machine that can run your app. For example, you might want to run the app in the Simulator or on a physical device. There is no configuration of destinations; you are automatically assigned destinations, depending on what system your project is set to run on and what devices are connected to your computer. Destinations and schemes have nothing to do with one another; your app is built the same way regardless of your chosen destination. The presence of destinations in the Scheme pop-up menu is intended as a convenience, allowing you to use the pop-up menu to choose either a scheme or a destination, or both, in a single move.

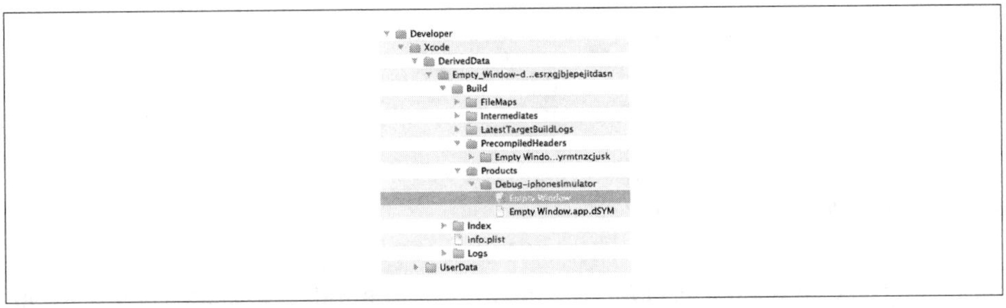

*Figure 6-14. The built app, in the Finder*

The listing of destinations together with schemes in a single pop-up menu may be *intended* as a convenience, but the repetition of all destinations for every scheme can make the Scheme pop-up menu long and unwieldy. Moreover, it's confusing, because destinations and schemes have nothing to do with one another (they are orthogonal, independent settings), and yet here they are together in a single menu. It would have been better to have two pop-up menus, one for choosing a scheme, and another for choosing a destination. In fact, in the scheme editor, that's exactly what you see! For this reason, you may find it more useful to switch among schemes or among destinations by using the scheme editor. Pressing Command-Option-R to pass through the scheme editor on your way to building and running your app will quickly become second nature.

# From Project to App

An app file is really a special kind of folder called a *package* (and a special kind of package called a *bundle*). The Finder normally disguises a package as a file and does not dive into it to reveal its contents to the user, but you can bypass this protection and investigate an app bundle with the Show Package Contents command. By doing so, you can study the structure of your built app bundle.

We'll use the Empty Window app that we built earlier as a sample minimal app to investigate. You'll have to locate it in the Finder; by default, it should be somewhere in your user *Library/Developer/Xcode/DerivedData* folder, as shown in Figure 6-14. (In theory, you should be able to select the app under Products in the Navigation pane and choose File → Show in Finder, but there seems to be a bug preventing this.)

In the Finder, Control-click the Empty Window app and choose Show Package Contents from the contextual menu.

Looking inside our minimal app bundle (Figure 6-15), we see that it contains just five files:

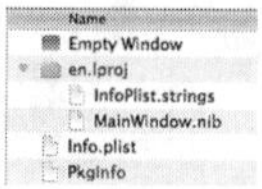

*Figure 6-15. Contents of the app package*

*PkgInfo*

> A tiny text file reading `APPL????`, signifying the type and creator codes for this app. The *PkgInfo* file something of a dinosaur; it isn't really necessary for the functioning of an iOS app and is generated automatically. You'll never need to touch it.

*InfoPlist.strings*

> A text file intended for text appearing in our app that might need to be translated into different languages. It is copied directly from *InfoPlist.strings* in the project. We haven't edited this file, and our app currently appears only in English, so this file is of no interest at the moment.

*MainWindow.nib*

> Currently, our app's only nib file. It contains instructions for generating an instance of our app's main window (currently just a white rectangle — an empty window). It is created ("compiled") from the *MainWindow.xib* file in the project; a *.xib* file and a *.nib* file are different forms of the same thing. This particular nib file is the *main nib file*, which means that when the app is launched, this nib file is loaded automatically so that the window it describes is instantiated and can be displayed.

*Empty Window*

> Our app's compiled code (the binary). When the app is launched, the binary is linked to the various frameworks, and the code begins to run (starting with the entry point in the `main` function).

*Info.plist*

> A configuration file in a strict text format (a *property list* file). It is derived from the project file *Empty_WindowInfo.plist*. It contains instructions to the system about how to treat and launch the app. For example, if our app had an icon, *Info.plist* would tell the system its name, so that the system could dive into the app bundle, find it, and display it. It also tells the system things like the name of the binary and the name of the main nib file, so that the system can find them and launch the app correctly.

In real life, an app bundle will contain more files, but the difference will mostly be one of degree, not kind. For example, our project might have additional nib files, icon image files, and image or sound files. All of these would make their way into the app bundle.

You are now in a position to appreciate, in a general sense, how the components of our project are treated and assembled into an app, and what responsibilities accrue to you, the programmer, in order to ensure that the app is built correctly. The rest of this chapter outlines what goes into the building of an app from a project.

## Build Settings

We have already talked about how build settings are determined. Xcode itself, the project, and the target all contribute to the resolved build setting values, some of which may differ depending on the build configuration. Before building, you, the programmer, will have already specified a scheme; the scheme determines the build configuration, the specific set of build setting values that will apply as the build proceeds.

## Property List Settings

Your project contains a property list file that will be used to generate the built app's *Info.plist* file. The target knows what file it is because it is named in the Info.plist File build setting. For example, in our project, the value of the Info.plist File build setting has been set automatically to *Empty Window/Empty_Window-Info.plist*. (Take a look at the build settings and see!)

 Because the name of the file in your project from which the built app's *Info.plist* file is generated will vary, depending on the name of the project, I'll refer to it generically as the project's *Info.plist*.

The property list file is a collection of key–value pairs. You can edit it, and will probably need to do so. There are two main ways to edit your project's *Info.plist*:

- Select the file in the Project navigator and edit in the editor. By default, the key names (and some of the values) are displayed descriptively, in terms of their functionality; for example, it says "Bundle name" instead of the actual key, which is CFBundleName. But you can view the actual keys by choosing Editor → Show Raw Keys & Values (you might have to click in the editor to enable this menu item).

- Edit the target, and click Info at the top of the editor. This pane shows effectively the same information as editing the *Info.plist* in the editor.

I'm not going to enumerate all the key–value pairs you might want to edit in your project's property list file, but I'll just call attention to a few that you will almost certainly want to edit (and I'll talk about others in Chapter 9 and elsewhere):

*Bundle display name* (CFBundleDisplayName)
    The name that appears under your app's icon on the device screen; this name needs to be short in order to avoid truncation.

*Bundle identifier (*`CFBundleIdentifier`*)*

> Your app's unique identifier, used throughout the development process and when submitting to the App Store. I talked earlier in this chapter about how this is derived from your company name when you create a project.

*Bundle version (*`CFBundleVersion`*)*

> A version string, which will appear at the App Store. You should increment the version when you develop and submit an update to an existing app.

For a complete list of the possible keys and their meanings, see Apple's document *Information Property List Key Reference.*

## Nib Files

You edit a nib file (technically, this will probably be a *.xib* file) to describe graphically some objects that you want instantiated when the nib file loads (Chapter 5). Your app is likely to have at least one nib file. By breaking your interface into multiple nib files, you simplify the relationship between each nib file and your code; also, if nibs that aren't needed when your app launches aren't loaded until they *are* needed, you speed up your app's launch time, and you streamline your app's memory usage (because nib objects are not instantiated until the nib is loaded, and can then be destroyed when they are no longer needed).

The target knows about your nib files because they appear in its Copy Bundle Resources build phase. In the case of a nib file in *.xib* format, the file is not merely copied into the app bundle; Xcode also translates (compiles) it into a *.nib* file (using the `ibtool` tool).

Nib files located inside your app bundle are loaded when they are needed as the app runs, usually because code tells them to load. However, one nib file is special: the main nib file. It must load before any code has a chance to tell it to do so. The main nib file is designated by the *Info.plist* key "Main nib file base name" (`NSMainNibFile`); the system sees this and loads the main nib file automatically as the app launches.

A universal app — that is, an app that runs both on the iPad and on the iPhone — typically has *two* main nib files; the main nib file to be loaded when the app runs on an iPad is specified by the *Info.plist* key "Main nib file base name (iPad)" (`NSMainNibFile~ipad`). Thus the app can have different basic interfaces on the two different types of device.

See Chapter 7 for more details about nib files.

## Other Resources

Our app doesn't currently have any additional resources — not even an icon file. But if it did, the target would know about them because they appear in its Copy Bundle

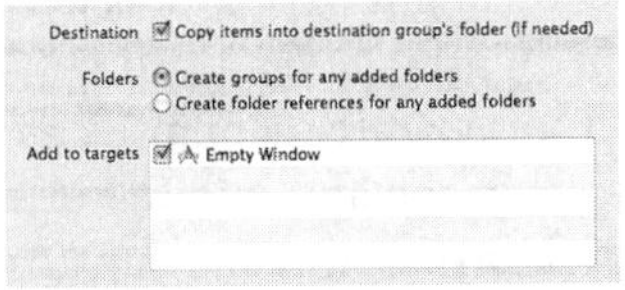

*Figure 6-16. Options when adding a resource to a project*

Resources build phase. In general, such resources would be copied unchanged into the app bundle.

With the exception of the app's icon and some images with standardized names, all of which are found and used by the system, additional resources are present because you want your running app to be able to fetch them out of its bundle. For example, if your app needs to display a certain image, you'd add the image to your project and make sure it appears in the Copy Bundle Resources build phase. When the app runs, your code (or possibly the code implied by a loaded nib file) reaches into the app bundle, locates the image, and displays it (Chapter 15).

To add a resource to your project, start in the Project navigator and choose File → Add Files to Empty Window (or whatever the name of the project is). Alternatively, drag the resource from the Finder into the Project navigator. Either way, a dialog appears (Figure 6-16) containing a pane in which you make the following settings:

*Copy items into destination group's folder (if needed)*
> You should almost certainly check this checkbox. Doing so causes the resource to be copied into the project folder. If you leave this checkbox unchecked, your project will be relying on a file that's outside the project folder and that you might delete or change unintentionally. Keeping everything your project needs inside the project folder is far safer.

*Folders*
> This choice matters only if what you're adding to the project is a folder. In both cases, whether the folder is copied into the project folder depends on whether you checked the checkbox discussed in the previous paragraph; the difference is in how the project references the folder contents:

*Create groups for any added folders*
> The folder is expressed as a group within the Project navigator, but its contents all appear individually in the Copy Bundle Resources build phase, so they will all be copied individually into the app bundle.

*Create folder references for any added folders*
> The folder itself is shown in blue in the Project navigator and appears as a folder in the Copy Bundle Resources build phase; thus, the build process will copy the entire folder and its contents into the app bundle. This means that the resources inside the folder won't be at the top level of the bundle, but in a

subfolder of it; your code might have to specify the folder name when loading such a resource. Such an arrangement can be valuable if you have many resources and you want to separate them into categories (rather than clumping them all at the top level of the app bundle) or if the folder hierarchy among resources is meaningful to your app.

*Add to Targets*

Checking this checkbox causes the resource to be added to the target's Copy Bundle Resources build phase. Thus you will almost certainly want to check it; why else would you be adding this resource to the project? But if this checkbox is unchecked and you realize later that a resource listed in the Project navigator needs to be added to the Copy Bundle Resources build phase, you can add it manually, as I described earlier.

An alternative way to copy resources from your project into the app bundle is through a custom Copy Files build phase that you add to your target. To do so, edit the target, switch to Build Phases, and click Add Build Phase (at the lower right) and choose Add Copy Files. A Copy Files build phase appears; open its triangle, and you'll find you can specify a custom path within the app bundle. For example, if you leave the Destination pop-up menu set to Resources and type "Pix" in the Subpath field, then any resources you add to this build phase will be copied into a folder called *Pix* in the app bundle.

A custom Copy Files build phase of this sort can be a good way of keeping resources organized by folder inside your app bundle; I frequently use it for this purpose. Bear in mind, however, that it is entirely up to you to make sure that the desired resources are placed inside the appropriate Copy Files build phase (and that they are not placed in the normal Copy Bundle Resources build phase, because if they are, you'll end up with two copies of the resource in your app bundle). Also, your code may have to specify the path in order to fetch the resource from inside the app bundle.

## Code

Code declaring a single class, Empty_WindowAppDelegate, was created for you when the project was created; the implementation file for this class (*Empty_WindowAppDelegate.m*) appears in the target's Compile Sources build phase. If you create any further class files, you'll specify that they should be added to the target, and they too will then have their implementation files listed in the Compile Sources build phase. This (the contents of the Compile Sources build phase) is how your target knows what files to compile to create the app's binary.

The binary that results from compilation of these files is your project's *executable*, and is placed into the app bundle, with its name being by default the same as the name of the target. The app bundle's *Info.plist* file has an "Executable file" (CFBundle-Executable) key whose value is the name of the binary; this is how the system knows how to locate the executable and launch the app.

Besides the class code files you create (or that Xcode creates for you), your project contains a *main.m* file. This too is in the Compile Sources build phase; it had better be, because this file contains the all-important `main` function, the entry point to your app's code! Here are its contents:

```
int main(int argc, char *argv[])
{
    NSAutoreleasePool *pool = [[NSAutoreleasePool alloc] init];
    int retVal = UIApplicationMain(argc, argv, nil, nil);
    [pool release];
    return retVal;
}
```

The `main` function is very simple, but it's crucial. It calls `UIApplicationMain`, which sets everything else in motion, creating your first object (the shared UIApplication instance), loading the main nib file, calling any appropriate delegate code (which is responsible for presenting the initial interface, as I'll explain in Chapter 7), and then just sitting there, watching for the user to do something (the *event loop*). The call to `UIApplication-Main` is wrapped in some memory management functionality (the `pool` stuff) that I'll explain in Chapter 12.

Finally, notice the file *Empty_Window_Prefix.pch* in the Project navigator. This is your project's *precompiled header* file. It isn't listed in the Compile Sources build phase because it is actually compiled *before* that build phase; the target knows about it because it is pointed to by the Prefix Header build setting.

The precompiled header is a device for making compilation go faster. It's a header file; it is compiled once (or at least, very infrequently) and the results are cached (off in */var/folders/*) and are implicitly imported by all your code files. So the precompiled header should consist primarily of `#import` directives for headers that never change (such as the built-in Cocoa headers); it is also a reasonable place to put `#defines` that will never change and that are to be shared by all your code.

The default precompiled header file imports `<Foundation/Foundation.h>` (the Core Foundation framework header) and `<UIKit/UIKit.h>` (the Cocoa framework).

## Frameworks and SDKs

A *framework* is a library of compiled code used by your code. Most of the frameworks you are likely to use will be Apple's built-in frameworks; they are built-in in the sense that they are part of the system on the device where your app will run — they live in */System/Library/Frameworks*, though you can't tell that on an iPhone or iPad because there's no way to view the filesystem directly.

However, your code needs to use these frameworks not only when running on a device but also when building and when running in the Simulator. To make this possible, part of the device's system — in particular, the part containing its frameworks — is duplicated on your computer, in the */Developer* folder. This duplicated subset of the device's system is called an *SDK* (for "software development kit") and is something you can see directly in the Finder. For example, look at */Developer/Platforms/iPhoneOS.platform/ Developer/SDKs/iPhoneOS4.3.sdk/System/Library/Frameworks*; behold, there are the frameworks included on a device running iOS 4.3.

To use a framework in your code, you must do two things:

*Import the framework's header*

A framework has a header file, which provides (usually by importing other header files within the framework) the interface information about classes in that framework. Your code needs this information in order to *compile* successfully. You import the header with an appropriate #import directive.

*Link to the framework*

A framework is a package; you must instruct the build system to associate this package with your app's executable binary, so that your binary's calls to code within that framework can be routed into the framework's compiled code. This is necessary in order for your app to *run* successfully. Such an association is called *linking* the binary with the framework, and you instruct the build system to do this by including the framework in the target's Link Binary With Libraries build phase.

You might think that linkage is impossible because the framework to which we ultimately want to link is off on a target device somewhere. But linkage is path-based, and the path is determined relative to the current SDK. Thus, the linkage to the UIKit framework uses the path *System/Library/Frameworks/UIKit.frame-work*. This path is relative to the current SDK, so if you're using the iOS 4.3 SDK, the path during development will be */Developer/Platforms/iPhoneOS.platform/De-veloper/SDKs/iPhoneOS4.3.sdk/System/Library/Frameworks/UIKit.framework*. But when the app runs on the device, there is no SDK, and the path becomes absolute, starting at the top level of the device. Thus, when the app runs in the Simulator, the framework is found successfully on your computer, and when the app runs on a device, the framework is found successfully on the device.

By default, three frameworks are linked into your target:

*Foundation*

Many basic Cocoa classes, such as NSString and NSArray and others whose names begin with "NS," are part of the Foundation framework. The Foundation framework is imported in the precompiled header file (and, by default, in the headers of new classes that you create). In turn, it imports the Core Foundation headers and loads the Core Foundation framework as a subframework; thus, there is no need for you to import or link explicitly to the Core Foundation framework (which is full of functions and pointer types whose names begin with "CF," such as CFString-Ref).

*UIKit*
>    Cocoa classes that are specialized for iOS, whose names begin with "UI," are part of the UIKit framework. The UIKit framework is imported in the precompiled header file (and by templated class code files such as *Empty_WindowAppDelegate.h*).

*Core Graphics*
>    The Core Graphics framework defines many structs and functions connected with drawing, whose names begin with "CG." It is imported by many UIKit headers, so you won't need to import it explicitly.

You might find that the three default frameworks are sufficient to your needs, or you might find that you need other frameworks to provide additional functionality. How will you know that a class or function you want to use resides outside the three default frameworks? You might get a clue from its name, which won't begin with "NS," "UI," or "CG", but more often, if you're like me, you'll be alerted by banging up against the compiler.

For example, let's say you've just found out about animation (Chapter 17) and you're raring to try it in your app. So, in your code, you create a CABasicAnimation:

```
CABasicAnimation* anim = [CABasicAnimation animation];
```

The next time you try to build your app, the compiler complains that CABasicAnimation is undeclared (and that it therefore can't make sense of `anim` either). That's when you realize you need to import a framework header. Near the start of the CABasicAnimation class documentation is a line announcing that it's in *QuartzCore.framework*. You might guess (correctly) that the way to import the main Quartz Core framework header is to put this line near the start of your implementation file:

```
#import <QuartzCore/QuartzCore.h>
```

This works to quiet the compiler. Remember, though, that I said that using a framework requires two things; we've done only one of them. So your code *still* doesn't build. This time, you get a build error during the link phase of the build process complaining about `_OBJC_CLASS_$_CABasicAnimation` and saying, "Symbol(s) not found." That mysterious-sounding error merely means that you've forgotten to link your target to the Quartz Core framework.

To link your target to a framework, edit the target, click Build Phases at the top of the editor, open the Link Binary with Libraries build phase, and click the "+" button at the bottom of the build phase. A dialog appears nicely listing the existing frameworks that are part of the active SDK. Select *QuartzCore.framework* and click Add. The Quartz Core framework is added to the target's Link Binary With Libraries build phase. (It also appears in the Project navigator; you might like to drag it manually into the Frameworks group, for the sake of neatness.) Now you can build (and run) your app.

You might wonder why the project isn't linked by default to *all* the frameworks, so that you don't have to go through this process every time you stray beyond the default three frameworks. It's just a matter of time and resources. Importing headers increases the size of your code; linking to frameworks slows down your app's launch time. You should link to only the frameworks needed for your code to run.

Where you import a framework header depends on how you intend to use it. It's simply a matter of scope. If a framework's classes are to be mentioned only within a single implementation file, then you can import it at the start of that implementation file. If you want to subclass one of the framework's classes, you'll need to import it at the start of the interface file that declares the subclass; in that case, every implementation file that imports this interface file imports the framework header, and there's no need to import the framework header separately in the implementation file. Of course, for maximum scope, you can simply import the framework header in the precompiled header file, making that framework available throughout your code.

# CHAPTER 7

# Nib Management

A *nib file*, or simply *nib*, is a file containing a drawing of a piece of your interface. The term *nib* is not really an English word (it has nothing to do with fountain pens, for example); it is based on the file extension *.nib* that is used to signify this type of file, an extension that originated as an acronym (for "NeXTStep Interface Builder"). Nowadays, you will usually develop your interface using a file format whose extension is *.xib*; when your app is built, your target's *.xib* files are translated ("compiled") into *.nib* format (Chapter 6). But a *.xib* file is still referred to as a nib file. I will speak of the same nib file as having either a *.xib* extension (if you're editing it) or a *.nib* extension (if it's in the built app).

You construct your program in two ways — writing code, and drawing the interface. But these are really two ways of accomplishing the same ends; drawing the interface *is* a way of writing code. When the app runs and your drawing of the interface in a nib file is loaded, it is translated into instructions for instantiating and initializing the objects in the nib file. You could equally have instantiated and initialized those same objects in code. (This point is crucial; see "Nib-Based Instantiation" on page 77.) Indeed, deciding whether to create an interface object in code or through a nib file is not always easy; each approach has its advantages. The important thing is to understand how interface objects drawn in a nib file are instantiated and connected to your code when the app runs.

 This chapter describes Xcode 4. Earlier versions, designated generically as Xcode 3.2.x, are very different. Up through Xcode 3.2.x, nib editing was performed in a separate application, Interface Builder. Starting in Xcode 4, the functionality of Interface Builder is rolled into Xcode itself.

## A Tour of the Nib-Editing Interface

Let's use an actual nib file to explore the Xcode nib-editing interface. In Chapter 6, we created a simple Xcode project, Empty Window; it contains a nib file, so we'll use that.

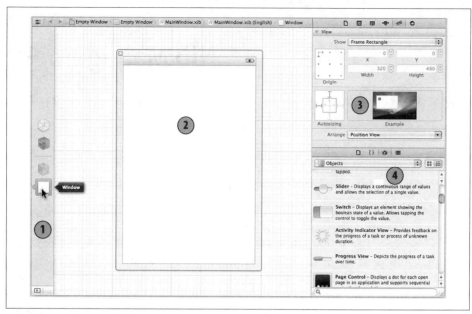

*Figure 7-1. Editing a nib file*

In Xcode, open the Empty Window project, locate the *MainWindow.xib* listing in the Project navigator, and click it to edit it.

Figure 7-1 shows the project window after selecting *MainWindow.xib* and making some additional adjustments. The Navigator pane is hidden; the Utilities pane is showing. Within the Utilities pane, the Size inspector and the Object library are showing. The interface may be considered in four pieces:

1. At the left of the editor is the *dock*, showing the nib's top-level objects. The dock can be expanded by dragging its right edge or by clicking the tiny arrow button at the lower left; then it shows *all* of the nib's objects hierarchically.

2. The remainder of the editor is devoted to the *canvas*, where you physically design your app's interface. The canvas portrays views in your app's interface and things that can contain views. (A *view* is an interface object, which draws itself into a rectangular area. The phrase "things that can contain views" is my way of including view controllers, which are represented in the canvas even though they are not drawn in your app's interface.)

3. The inspectors in the Utilities pane are where you view and edit details of the currently selected object.

4. The libraries in the Utilities pane, especially the Object library, are your source for interface objects to be added to the nib.

# The Dock

The dock, as I've already said, shows the nib's *top-level objects*. To see what this means, you need first to envision the nib as containing objects. Some of these objects — those that represent views — are arranged in a hierarchy of containment. Objects that are contained by no other object are top-level objects.

A view can contain other views (its *subviews*) and can be contained by another view (its *superview*); for example, a button might be a subview of a window, and that window would be that button's superview. One view can contain many subviews, which might themselves contain subviews. But each view can have only one immediate superview. Thus there is a hierarchical tree of subviews contained by their superviews with a single object at the top. The highest superview of any such hierarchy in the nib is a top-level object and appears in the dock. That's why the window object (labeled Window in Figure 7-1) appears in this nib's dock: it is a view contained by no other view.

A nib file can actually contain two types of top-level object:

*Placeholders (proxy objects)*
> A placeholder, or *proxy object*, represents an object that already exists in your app's code at the time the nib is loaded. Proxy objects appear in a nib file chiefly so that you can provide communication between objects in your app's code and objects instantiated from the nib. You can't create or delete a proxy object; the dock is populated automatically with them. Proxy objects are shown above the dividing line in the dock.

*Nib objects*
> A nib object is an object that is instantiated by the nib — that is, the instance it represents will be created when your code runs and the nib loads. You can create new nib objects. Top-level nib objects are shown below the dividing line in the dock.

The dock can be expanded (by clicking the tiny triangle button at its bottom left); it then portrays objects by name (label), and shows as an outline the full hierarchy of objects in this nib (Figure 7-2). At present, expanding the dock may seem silly, because there is no hierarchy; all objects in this nib are top-level objects. But when a nib contains many levels of hierarchically arranged objects, you're going to be very glad of the ability to survey them all in a nice outline, and to select the one you're after, thanks to the expanded dock. You can also rearrange the hierarchy here; for example, if you've made an object a subview of the wrong view, you can drag it onto the view it should be a subview of within this outline.

You can also select objects using the jump bar at the top of the editor. First, click on the canvas background so that no object is selected; the entire hierarchy of the objects in your nib is then shown as a set of hierarchical menus off the rightmost jump bar path component (Control-6). Again, this may seem like small potatoes now, when your nib

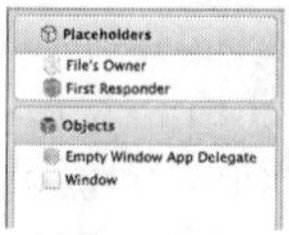

*Figure 7-2. The dock, expanded*

contains just four top-level objects and nothing more, but it will be valuable when you've many nib objects in a hierarchy.

The names (labels) by which nib objects are designated are meaningful only while editing a nib file; they have no relationship to your code. When the dock is expanded, each object is portrayed by its label, as shown in Figure 7-2. When the dock is collapsed, you can see a top-level object's label by hovering the mouse over it, as shown in Figure 7-1. If you find an object's label unhelpful, you can change it in the expanded dock; select the object and press Return to make its label editable. Alternatively, select the object and edit the Label field of the Identity section of the Identity inspector (Command-Option-3).

## Canvas

The canvas presents a graphical representation of a top-level nib object along with its subviews, similar to what you're probably accustomed to in any drawing program. If a top-level nib object has a graphical representation (not every top-level nib object has one), you can click on it in the dock to display that representation in the canvas. A little dot to the left of a top-level object in the collapsed dock indicates that it is currently being displayed graphically in the canvas.

To remove the canvas representation of a top-level nib object, click the "x" at its upper left; this merely clears the representation from the canvas — it does not remove the top-level nib object from the dock (or from the nib), and of course you can always bring back the graphical representation by clicking that nib object in the dock again. On the other hand, the canvas is scrollable and automatically accommodates all graphical representations within it, so you can keep as many graphical representations open in the canvas as you like, side by side, and scroll to see each one, regardless of the size of your monitor; thus you might never need to remove the canvas representation of a top-level nib object at all.

Our simple Empty Window project's *MainWindow.xib* contains just one top-level nib object that has a graphical representation — the app's window, called Window. Because this is our app's window, any changes you make here will be reflected in the app's user interface when you run it. To see this, we're going to add a subview to it:

1. Ensure that the Window in the dock is being displayed in the canvas.
2. Look at the Object library (Control-Option-Command-3). Click the second button in the segmented control to put the Object library into list view, if it isn't in list

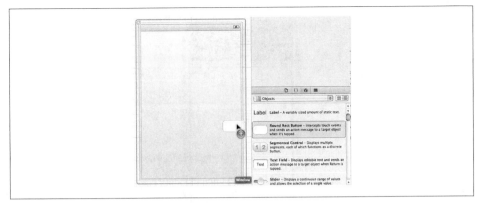

*Figure 7-3. Dragging a button into a window*

view already. Locate the Round Rect Button (you can type "button" into the filter bar at the bottom of the library as a shortcut).

3. Drag the Round Rect Button from the Object library into the Window in the canvas (Figure 7-3). Don't accidentally drop the button onto the canvas background, outside of the window! This would cause the button to become a top-level object, which is not what you want. If that happens, select the button in the dock and press Delete, and try again.

A button now appears in the window in the canvas. The move we've just performed — dragging from the Object library into the canvas — is extremely characteristic; you'll do it often as you design your interface. Here are two alternative ways to do the same thing:

- Double-click an object in the Object library; if a view (such as our window) is already selected in the canvas, a copy of that object becomes a subview of it.

- Type some part of an object's name in the filter bar; you can then use arrow keys to select the correct object, if needed, and finally press Return to copy the object into the canvas. You can switch to the Object library with Control-Option-Command-3, and this also puts focus in the filter bar, so the whole operation can be performed with the keyboard.

Next, play around with the button in the window. Much as in a drawing program, the nib editor provides features to aid you in designing your interface. Here are some things to try:

- Select it: resizing handles appear.
- Resize it to make it wider: dimension information appears.
- Drag it near the edge of the window: a guideline appears, showing a standard margin space between the edge of the button and the edge of the window.
- With the button selected, hold down the Option key and hover the mouse outside the button: arrows and numbers appear showing the pixel distance between the

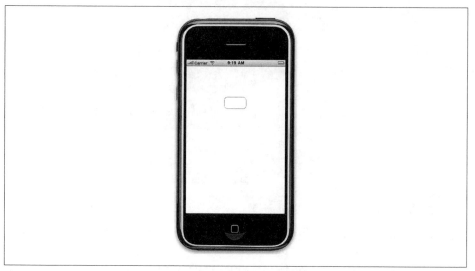

*Figure 7-4. The Empty Window app's window is empty no longer*

button and the edges of the window. (If you accidentally clicked and dragged while you were holding Option, you'll now have two buttons. That's because Option-dragging an object duplicates it. Select the unwanted button and press Delete to remove it.)

- Shift-Control-click on the button: a menu appears, letting you select the button or whatever's behind it (in this case, the window).

Let's prove that we really are designing our app's interface. We'll run the app to see that its interface has changed.

1. Make sure that the Breakpoints button in the window toolbar is *not* selected, as we don't want to pause at any breakpoints you may have created while reading the previous chapter.
2. Make sure the destination in the Scheme pop-up menu is the iPhone Simulator.
3. Choose Product → Run (or click the Run button in the toolbar).

After a heart-stopping pause, the iOS Simulator opens, and presto, our empty window is empty no longer (Figure 7-4); it contains a round rect button! You can tap this button with the mouse, emulating what the user would do with a finger; the button highlights as you tap it.

## Inspectors and Libraries

There are four inspectors that appear only when you're editing a nib and apply to whatever object is selected in the dock or canvas:

*Identity inspector (Command-Option-3)*

Far and away the most important section of this inspector is the first one, the Custom Class. The selected object's Class setting tells you the object's class, and you can use it to change the object's class. Some situations in which you'll need to change the class of an object in the nib appear later in this chapter.

*Attributes inspector (Command-Option-4)*

Settings here correspond to properties and methods that you might use to configure the object in code. For example, the Type pop-up menu in the Attributes inspector for the button in our window says this UIButton's Type is Rounded Rect; this corresponds to calling `buttonWithType:` with an argument value of `UIButtonType-RoundedRect`. Similarly, typing a value in the Title field is like calling the button's `setTitle:forState:` method. The UIButton Attributes inspector has three sections, corresponding to UIButton's class inheritance — a UIButton is also a UIControl ("Control" in the inspector) and a UIView ("View" in the inspector).

> The correspondence between Attributes inspector settings and Objective-C methods is mostly a matter of guesswork. The Attributes inspector doesn't always tell you, and there's no way to see the code generated when the nib actually loads.

*Size inspector (Command-Option-5)*

The X, Y, Width, and Height fields determine the object's frame (its position and size within its superview), corresponding to its `frame` property in code; you can equally do this in the design window by dragging and resizing, but numeric precision can be desirable. The Autosizing box corresponds to the `autoresizingMask` property, determining how the object will be repositioned and resized when its superview is resized; a delightful animation demonstrates visually the implications of your settings. The Arrange pop-up menu contains useful commands for positioning the selected object.

*Connections inspector (Command-Option-6)*

I'll discuss this later in this chapter.

There are two libraries that are of particular importance when you're editing a nib:

*Object library (Control-Option-Command-3)*

This library, as we've already seen, is your source for types of object that you want to copy into the nib.

*Media library (Control-Option-Command-4)*

This library lists media in your project, such as images that you might want to drag into a UIImageView or directly into your interface (in which case a UIImageView is created for you).

# Nib Loading and File's Owner

A nib file is useless until your app runs and the nib file is *loaded*. One nib, designated by the *Info.plist* key "Main nib file base name" (`NSMainNibFile`, see Chapter 6), is loaded automatically as the app launches. Other nibs are loaded explicitly as needed while the app runs.

For example, imagine our app has two complete sets of interface, and the user might never ask to see the second one. It makes obvious sense not to load a nib containing the second set of interface until the user *does* ask to see it. By this strategy, a nib is loaded when its instances are needed, and those instances are destroyed when they are no longer needed. Thus memory usage is kept to a minimum, which is important because memory is at a premium in a mobile device. Also, loading a nib takes time, so loading fewer nibs at launch time makes launching faster.

*When a nib loads, some already existing instance is designated its owner.* A nib cannot load without an owner, and the owner must exist before the nib can load.

In the case of the automatically loaded main nib file, the owner is the single UIApplication instance created automatically as the app launches (the *shared application* object). In other cases, the nib's owner must be specified in order to load the nib. It will often be a UIViewController instance, because a UIViewController already knows how to load a nib and manage a view that it contains (Chapter 19), but it can be an instance of any class.

The File's Owner top-level object in a nib file is a proxy for the instance that will be the nib's owner when the nib loads, and its class should be set to that instance's class. In the case of our Empty Window project's *MainWindow.xib*, the File's Owner's class has been correctly set in advance: its class is UIApplication (do you see how to confirm this?), corresponding to the fact that a UIApplication instance will be the nib's owner when it loads. For nibs that you create, the File's Owner's class might not be set correctly, and you'll have to set it yourself using the Identity inspector.

*When a nib loads, its nib objects are instantiated*, meaning its top-level nib objects and all deeper-level nib objects hierarchically dependent on them. (Proxy objects, by definition, exist before the nib loads; nib loading does not instantiate them.) For example, in our nib, the window is instantiated when the nib loads, bringing with it the button inside it. (Again, see "Nib-Based Instantiation" on page 77; make very sure you understand this point!) This is what nibs are for — to instantiate objects when they load. To put it another way, that is what nib loading is — it is the instantiation of the nib objects described in the nib. At that point, having loaded, the nib's work is done; the nib does not, for example, have to be "unloaded."

The same nib can be loaded multiple times, generating an entirely new set of instances each time. A common beginner question is, "I have a view in a nib; how do I make multiple copies of this view?" The simple solution is to load that nib multiple times. This is common practice. For example, consider table view cells. Every "row" of a table view is a table view cell. Let's say there's a certain look and behavior you want each "row" to have. You design the cell in a nib of its own as a UITable-ViewCell. If the table has to display ten rows, you load that nib ten times (Chapter 21).

# Default Instances in the Main Nib File

Instances are where the action is in an Objective-C program. An app's main nib file (*MainWindow.xib*, in our case) is crucially responsible for how the app comes to have any instances at all. To see this, we'll analyze what happens as the app launches and the main nib file loads.

As the app launches, UIApplicationMain is called in *main.m*, which causes the UIApplication class to be instantiated to create our app's one "shared application" instance. Now our app has its first instance, so we have something that can serve as the main nib file's owner. So now the main nib file is loaded with the shared application instance as its owner. This causes the nib objects in the main nib file to be instantiated. By default, there are two of them:

*The window*
> An instance of the UIWindow class. This is the container of the entire interface to be displayed to the user. In an iOS app, there is exactly one main window instance, and this is it. It is the object whose contents appear on the device's screen (after it is sent the makeKeyAndVisible message). All other visible interface is visible purely by virtue of being a subview of this window.

*The app delegate*
> In our app, an instance of the Empty_WindowAppDelegate class (and labeled, by default, Empty Window App Delegate). This class was defined for us as part of the project template (in the code files *Empty_WindowAppDelegate.h* and *Empty_WindowAppDelegate.m*). This class is our app's earliest opportunity to run custom code: its application:didFinishLaunchingWithOptions: method is called automatically (by a mechanism that I'll explain in Chapter 11) as soon as the application is ready to display its interface and receive input from the user. By default, this method calls makeKeyAndVisible on the UIWindow instance that was just generated by the loading of the main nib, thus causing the interface to be displayed.

The Xcode app template thus implements for us a bootstrapping strategy that gets our app rolling:

1. The main function is called, as with any C program.

2. The `main` function calls `UIApplicationMain`.

3. `UIApplicationMain` creates the shared application instance, which by default is an instance of UIApplication.

4. `UIApplicationMain` consults *Info.plist* to learn the name of the main nib file, and loads it with the shared application instance as owner.

5. The app's single UIWindow object is instantiated from the nib.

6. The app's single Empty_WindowAppDelegate object is instantiated from the nib.

7. The app finishes its internal setup, and `application:didFinishLaunchingWith-Options:` is sent to the Empty_WindowAppDelegate instance.

8. Empty_WindowAppDelegate sends `makeKeyAndVisible` to the UIWindow instance, causing the interface to appear. The app is now ready to receive user input.

All further initialization as an app starts up is an elaboration on this built-in bootstrapping strategy.

 The Empty_WindowAppDelegate instance generated by the loading of the main nib is intended to be the *only* instance of this class. Do not instantiate Empty_WindowAppDelegate again later in the program. And don't delete the Empty_WindowAppDelegate instance from the main nib, or otherwise interfere with the bootstrapping operation I've just described; if you do, your app won't launch properly.

# Making and Loading a Nib

Nib files other than the main nib file must be loaded explicitly as the app runs. This can happen semiautomatically through the instantiation of an object that incorporates nib-loading behavior, such as a UIViewController (Chapter 19); or it can happen completely manually, through explicit nib-loading code that you write.

Let's illustrate nib-loading code. To do so, we'll need a second nib file in our project. We'll also need an instance to act as the nib's owner. To illustrate the procedure fully, we'll start by creating a class whose sole purpose is to be instantiated so that this instance can act as the owner of the nib file as it loads:

1. In the Empty Window project in Xcode, choose File → New → New File. The "Choose a template" dialog for files appears.

2. At the left of the dialog, under iOS (not Mac OS X!) select Cocoa Touch, and select Objective-C Class in the main part of the dialog. Click Next.

3. The dialog now offers you a chance to specify what superclass the new class should be a subclass of. Make sure this is NSObject. Click Next.

4. Name the file *MyClass*; make sure you're saving into the Empty Window project folder, that the group is Empty Window, and that the target is Empty Window (and checked). Click Save.

We've now created files *MyClass.h* and *MyClass.m* declaring a class called MyClass. Next, we'll make the nib:

1. Choose File → New → New File.
2. At the left of the dialog, under iOS, choose User Interface, and select View in the main part of the dialog. Click Next.
3. For the Device Family, specify iPhone. Click Next.
4. Name the file *MyNib*; make sure you're saving into the Empty Window project folder, that the group is Empty Window, and that the target is Empty Window (and checked). Click Save.

We've now created a nib file, *MyNib.xib*, containing a single top-level nib object, a UIView. Look at *MyNib.xib* in the editor to see that this is true.

Next, we'll write code that will load our new nib when the app runs. Our little app has only one place where code is guaranteed to run: the Empty_WindowAppDelegate instance method `application:didFinishLaunchingWithOptions:` (in the file *Empty_WindowAppDelegate.m*). So let's put our code there. Just before or after the call to `makeKeyAndVisible`, insert this code to instantiate MyClass and load *MyNib.nib* with that instance as its owner:

```
MyClass* mc = [[MyClass alloc] init];
[[NSBundle mainBundle] loadNibNamed:@"MyNib" owner:mc options:nil];
```

Xcode will complain about this, because you can't speak of MyClass without importing its declaration, so after the existing `#import` at the start of this file, add this line:

```
#import "MyClass.h"
```

Now build and run the project. Our new *MyNib.nib* file loads, and its UIView top-level nib object is instantiated. Unfortunately, you can't *see* that this is true! The next section explains how to obtain visible proof that our nib is loading and that its top-level nib objects are being instantiated.

# Outlet Connections

You know how to load a nib file, thus instantiating its top-level nib objects. But those instances are useless to you if you don't know how to get a reference to any of them in your code. To refer in code to instances generated from nib objects when the nib loads, you need an outlet connection from a proxy object in the same nib.

A *connection* is a named unidirectional linkage from one object in a nib file (the connection's source) to another object in the same nib file (the connection's target). An *outlet* is a connection whose name corresponds to an instance variable in the source object. When the nib loads, and the target object is instantiated, the value of the instance variable is set to the target object. Thus the source object winds up with a reference to the target object as the value of one of its instance variables.

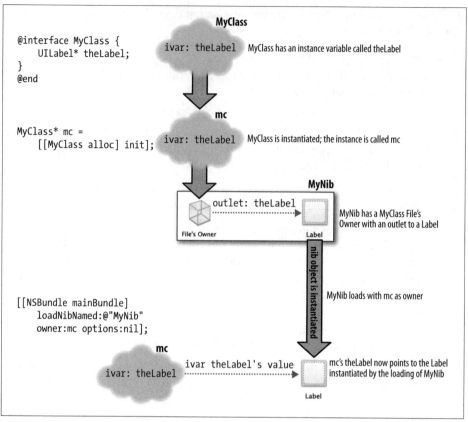

*Figure 7-5. How an outlet provides a reference to a nib-instantiated object*

Connections can link any two objects in a nib file, but a proxy object as the source of a connection is special because it represents an object that exists before the nib loads. Thus an outlet from a proxy object causes an object that exists *before* the nib loads to end up with an instance variable whose value is an object that doesn't exist until *after* the nib loads — an object that is in fact instantiated by the loading of the nib.

In the most typical configuration, the proxy object will be the File's Owner. The instance that owns the nib has an instance variable, and the File's Owner in the nib has a corresponding outlet to a nib object; the nib loads, and the owner instance ends up with an instance variable that refers to the instance generated from the nib object (Figure 7-5).

To demonstrate, we'll implement exactly the schema illustrated in Figure 7-5, by making an outlet from the File's Owner to a nib object in *MyNib.xib*. First, we need a nib object in *MyNib.xib* to make an outlet to. For visual impact, we'll replace the existing top-level view with a top-level label, which will draw some text:

1. In Xcode, click *MyNib.xib* to edit it.

2. In the dock, select the View object and delete it.

3. Drag a Label object (UILabel) from the Object library into the dock to become a new top-level object. Its graphical representation appears in the canvas.

4. Double-click the word "Label" in the label's graphical representation and type "Hello, world!" Hit Return to stop editing and to make the label the size of its text.

The object that will own the nib file when it loads is a MyClass instance. But the nib doesn't know this; we need to tell it:

1. Select the File's Owner proxy object and look at the Identity inspector.

2. The Class, under Custom Class, is NSObject. Change this to MyClass. (If you type "My," the word "MyClass" should just appear, as it's the only class Xcode knows about whose name starts with "My." Accept this by pressing Return.)

Now comes the really crucial part. We need two things, in two different places:

*The instance variable*
    In its code, MyClass needs an instance variable whose value will be the label.

*The outlet*
    In the nib, the File's Owner proxy, representing a MyClass instance, needs an outlet pointing at the label — an outlet with the same name as the instance variable.

When the app runs and *MyNib.nib* is loaded with a MyClass instance as its owner, as we arranged in the preceding section, those two pairs of things will be effectively equated:

- The MyClass instance will be equated with the File's Owner proxy in the nib, because it *will* be the nib's owner as it loads.

- MyClass's instance variable will be equated with the File's Owner outlet pointing at the label, because *they have the same name.*

 I'm oversimplifying. It isn't really the identity of the instance variable's name with that of the outlet that makes the match. It's more complicated than that; the match is made using key–value coding. The rigorous details appear in Chapter 12.

You thus need to work in two places at once: the nib, and MyClass's code. Before Xcode 4, this required working separately in two *different* places, Xcode (where the code was edited) and Interface Builder (where the nib was edited). But in Xcode 4, the same program edits both the code and the nib, and furthermore you can see the code and the nib *at the same time*, all of which will make creating this pair of things, the instance variable and the outlet, much easier than it once was.

I want you now to arrange to see two things at once: *MyClass.h* (the MyClass header file, where we'll declare the instance variable) and *MyNib.xib* (where we'll create the

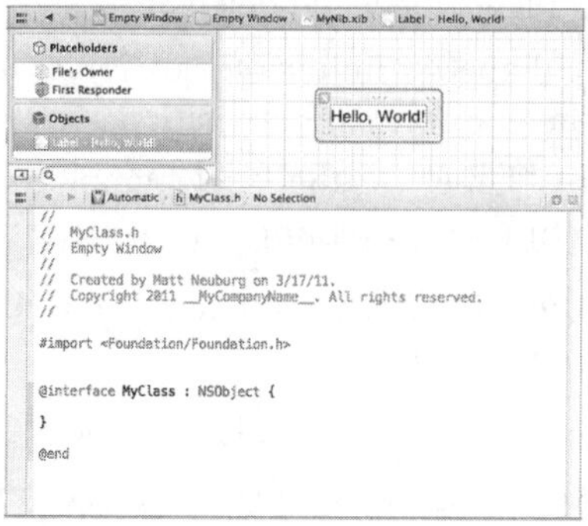

*Figure 7-6. Editing a nib, with code in the assistant pane*

outlet). You could use two project windows if you wanted, but for simplicity, let's use an assistant: while editing *MyNib.xib*, switch to Assistant view (View → Editor → Assistant) as in Figure 7-6.

> If your experience is like mine, when you chose View → Editor → Assistant, the assistant appeared with MyClass's header file showing. Xcode has guessed (correctly) what code you want to see when a UILabel is selected in the nib. If that isn't the case, use the jump bar in the assistant pane to make the assistant pane show *MyClass.h*.

In *MyClass.h* (in the assistant pane), in the interface section, between the curly braces, declare a UILabel instance variable:

```
IBOutlet UILabel* theLabel;
```

The term `IBOutlet` is linguistically meaningless; it is `#defined` as an empty string, so it is deleted before the compiler ever sees it. It's purely a hint to Xcode to make it easy for you to create the outlet. We have typed the instance variable as a `UILabel*`, because we happen to know that this is the type of object that this instance variable will be pointing to; we could also use `id`, or any superclass of UILabel. If we do not use one of these alternatives (`id`, UILabel, or a superclass of UILabel), we will not be able to form the connection to a UILabel in the nib.

We have accomplished half our task: we've made the instance variable. Now we're ready for the other half, namely, to make the outlet connection. There are several ways to do this, so I'll just pick one for now and demonstrate the others later:

1. Select File's Owner in the nib and switch to the Connections inspector. Lo and behold, the name of our instance variable, `theLabel`, is listed here! This is the work of the `IBOutlet` hint we typed earlier.

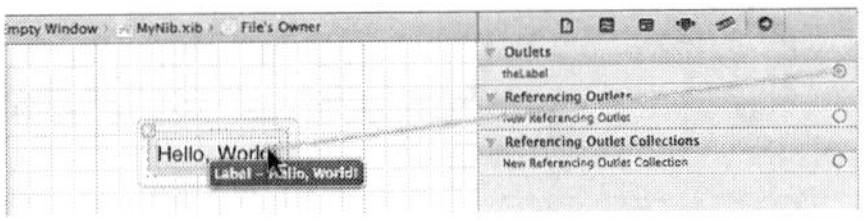

*Figure 7-7. Connecting an outlet from the Connections inspector*

2. Click in the empty circle to the right of `theLabel`, drag to the Label object in the canvas (Figure 7-7), and release the mouse. (A kind of elastic line follows the mouse as you drag from the circle to show that you're creating a connection.)

With the File's Owner object selected, look again at the Connections inspector; it shows that `theLabel` is connected to the Label nib object! We have made an outlet connection from the File's Owner to the Label object, and this outlet connection has the same name as the instance variable `theLabel` in MyClass. So when the nib loads and a MyClass instance is the nib's owner, its `theLabel` instance variable will be set to the UILabel object that will be instantiated through the loading of the nib.

To prove that this is the case, we'll do something with that instance variable in our code. In particular, we'll stick the UILabel into our main window interface, thus making it visible. Its visibility will prove that the nib is loading and that the instance variable is being set by the outlet.

Return to *Empty_WindowAppDelegate.m* and modify the nib-loading code like this (you added the first two lines earlier):

```
MyClass* mc = [[MyClass alloc] init];
[[NSBundle mainBundle] loadNibNamed:@"MyNib" owner:mc options:nil];
UILabel* lab = [mc valueForKey: @"theLabel"];
[self.window addSubview: lab];
lab.center = CGPointMake(100,100);
```

(We haven't written an accessor method in MyClass for `theLabel`, so to save time I used key–value coding.) Build and run the app. The words "Hello, world!" appear in the window! This proves that our outlet worked. We loaded a nib and, using an outlet, we obtained a reference to a nib object.

> Making an instance variable and giving it an `IBOutlet` hint, but forgetting to connect the outlet to anything in the nib, is an unbelievably common beginner (and not-so-beginner) mistake. Had we made this mistake, our code would have run without error, but "Hello, world!" would not appear in the window because `lab` would be nil.

## More Ways to Create Outlets

I said a moment ago that there were other ways to create the outlet. Let's try some of them. Return to our assistant-paned nib editor, select the File's Owner, switch to the Connections inspector, and delete the outlet by clicking the little "x" to its left. We're going to make this outlet again, a different way:

*Figure 7-8. Connecting an outlet by Control-dragging from the source object*

*Figure 7-9. Connecting an outlet by dragging from the Connections HUD*

1. Select the File's Owner in the dock.
2. Hold down the Control key and drag from the File's Owner to the label. An elastic line follows the mouse.
3. A little window (called a HUD, for "heads-up display") appears, titled Outlets, listing `theLabel` as a possibility (Figure 7-8). Click `theLabel`.

Once again, look at the Connections inspector with the File's Owner selected to confirm that this worked. You can even build and run the project again, to prove it to yourself if you're in any doubt. Now delete the outlet *again*; we're going to make this outlet in yet a *different* way:

1. Select the File's Owner in the dock.
2. Control-click the File's Owner in the dock. A HUD appears, looking a lot like the Connections inspector.
3. Drag from the circle to the right of `theLabel` to the label (Figure 7-9).

Now delete the outlet *again*; we're going to make this outlet in *another* way. This time, we're going to operate from the point of view of the label. The Connections inspector shows all connections emanating *from* the selected object; it also shows all connections linking *to* the selected object. So, select the label and look at the Connections inspector. It lists "New Referencing Outlet." This means an outlet *from* something else *to* the thing we're inspecting, the label. So:

1. From the circle at the right of "New Referencing Outlet," drag to the File's Owner. An elastic line follows the mouse.
2. A HUD saying `theLabel` appears. Click it.

Confirm that, once again, we've made an outlet from the File's Owner to the label. (And we could also have done the same thing by Control-clicking the label to start with, to show its Connections HUD.) Now delete the outlet *again*; we're going to make this outlet in *another* way. This time, we're going to start with the label, but we're going to connect directly to the *code* which is sitting in the assistant pane:

1. Select the label.

2. Make sure that *MyClass.h* is showing in the assistant pane and that you can see the `IBOutlet` line declaring the instance variable `theLabel`.

3. Hold down the Control key and drag from the label to that line of code. An elastic line follows the mouse.

4. When you've got the mouse positioned correctly, the words Connect Outlet will appear. Release the mouse.

Yet again, confirm that we've successfully made the desired outlet. Now delete the outlet one last time, and (get this) *delete the line of code* declaring the instance variable. We're going to create the outlet and the instance variable declaration, all in a single amazing move:

1. Select the label.

2. Make sure *MyClass.h* is showing in the assistant pane.

3. Hold down the Control key and drag from the label to the area between the curly braces. An elastic line follows the mouse.

4. A little HUD appears, asking for the name of the instance variable that's about to be created. Call it `theLabel` (and make sure the type is UILabel), and press Return. The `IBOutlet` line declaring the instance variable is created, and the outlet is formed to match it.

That last way of making an outlet was extremely cool and convenient, but a word of warning: coolness and convenience do not relieve you of the necessity of understanding what an outlet is and how it works. No matter what physical gesture you make in Xcode, the conditions must ultimately be the same: there must be an instance variable in a class, and an outlet in the nib, *with the same name*, and *to an instance of that class*. Otherwise, the instance variable won't be properly set when the nib loads.

## More About Outlets

At the risk of seeming to repeat myself, let me emphasize an important thing to remember about outlets (and nib connections generally) that often confuses beginners: they apply to specific instances. Outlets appear in a nib, but a nib is just a template for specific instances. At the moment a nib loads, then and only then, the one specific instance which is the nib's owner (represented by the File's Owner in the nib) and the specific instances generated from the nib objects are all in existence together and are hooked together by their outlets.

All our examples so far have involved a proxy object, but an outlet connection can connect any two objects in the nib. The only requirement is that the source object be of a class that has an instance variable whose type matches the class of the target object.

Nothing in the documentation for a built-in Cocoa class tells you which of its instance variables are available as outlets. In general, the only way to learn what outlets a built-in class provides is to examine a representative of that class in a nib.

The outlet mechanism explains some missing steps in our Empty Window app's bootstrapping sequence described earlier in this chapter, with regard to the main nib (*MainWindow.xib*, in the case of our Empty Window app):

- After the main nib loads, the app's single UIApplication instance sends `application:didFinishLaunchingWithOptions:` to the Empty_WindowAppDelegate object that was instantiated from the nib. But how does it get a reference to that instance? It's an outlet.

  In the main nib, the File's Owner, which is a proxy for the UIApplication instance, has an outlet (called `delegate`) to the Empty Window App Delegate nib object, whose class is Empty_WindowAppDelegate. So after the nib loads, the UIApplication instance's `delegate` instance variable is pointing to that Empty_Window-AppDelegate instance.

- In its implementation of the `application:didFinishLaunchingWithOptions:` method, Empty_WindowAppDelegate calls `makeKeyAndVisible` on the UIWindow instance loaded from the nib. But how does it get a reference to that instance? It's an outlet.

  In the main nib, the Empty Window App Delegate nib object has an outlet (called `window`) to the Window nib object, whose class is UIWindow. So when the nib loads and they are both instantiated, the Empty_WindowAppDelegate instance's `window` instance variable (technically named `_window`, by a means that I'll explain in Chapter 12) is pointing to that UIWindow instance.

It is also possible to create an *outlet collection*. This is an NSArray instance variable matched by multiple connections to objects of the same type. For example, suppose a class contains this instance variable declaration:

```
IBOutletCollection(UILabel) NSArray* labels;
```

Then it is possible to form multiple `labels` outlets from an instance of that class in a nib, each one to a different UILabel in that nib. When the nib loads, those UILabel instances become the elements of the NSArray `labels`. The order in which the outlets are formed is the order of the elements in the array. This is a new feature and I haven't written any code that uses it.

## Action Connections

An *action* is a message emitted automatically by a Cocoa UIControl interface object (a *control*) when the user does something to it, such as tapping the control. The various

## Connections Between Nibs

You cannot draw a connection from an object in one nib to an object in another nib. If you expect to be able to do this, you haven't understood what a nib is! An object in a nib is only a potential object, becoming a real object when the nib is loaded and the object is instantiated. This potentiality can be realized never, once, or many times. Two objects in the same nib will be instantiated together, so it's clear what a connection means. But a connection from an object in one nib to an object in another nib would be meaningless, because there's no way to say what actual future instances the connection is supposed to connect. The problem of communicating between an instance instantiated from one nib and an instance instantiated from another nib is just a special case of the more general problem of how to communicate between instances in a program and is discussed in Chapter 13.

user behaviors that will cause a control to emit an action message are called *events*. To see a list of possible events, look at the UIControl class documentation, under "Control Events." For example, in the case of a UIButton, the user tapping the button corresponds to the UIControlEventTouchUpInside event. In the case of a UITextField, the user typing or deleting or cutting or pasting corresponds to the UIControlEventEditing-Changed event. A complete list of UIControls and what events they respond to is provided in Chapter 11.

An action message, then, is a way for your code to respond when the user does something to a control in the interface, such as tapping a button. But your code will not receive an action message from a control unless you explicitly make prior arrangements with that control. You must tell the control what event should trigger an action message, what instance to send the action message to, and what the action message's name should be. There are two ways to make this arrangement: in code, or in a nib.

Either way, we're going to need a method for the action message to call. There are three standard signatures for a method that is to be called through an action message; the most commonly used one takes a single parameter, which will be a reference to the object that emitted the action message. (For full details, see Chapter 11.) So, for example, you could have a method like this (let's agree to put it in the app delegate, *Empty_WindowAppDelegate.m*):

```
- (void) buttonPressed: (id) sender {
    UIAlertView* av = [[UIAlertView alloc] initWithTitle:@"Howdy!"
                                    message:@"You tapped me."
                                    delegate:nil
                         cancelButtonTitle:@"Cool"
                         otherButtonTitles:nil];
    [av show];
}
```

Here's how you might arrange *in code* for `buttonPressed:` to be called when the user taps a button. The following example (perhaps part of the app delegate's `application:didFinishLaunchingWithOptions:`) creates a button in code, puts it into the app's window, and arranges that when the user taps the button, the button should send this instance the `buttonPressed:` message:

```
UIButton* b = [UIButton buttonWithType:UIButtonTypeRoundedRect];
[b setTitle:@"Howdy!" forState:UIControlStateNormal];
[b setFrame: CGRectMake(100,100,100,35)];
[self.window addSubview:b];
[b addTarget:self action:@selector(buttonPressed:)
        forControlEvents:UIControlEventTouchUpInside];
```

That last line means: "Hey there, button! When the user taps on you (`UIControlEventTouchUpInside`), send me (`self`) a `buttonPressed:` message." (See Chapter 3 if you've forgotten about the `@selector` directive.) Of course, such an instruction assumes that this object (`self`) really does implement a `buttonPressed:` method. (If it doesn't, then when the user taps the button, the app will crash.)

Feel free to run the app and confirm that this works. But when you've done that, delete the code just above (but leave the `buttonPressed:` implementation in place, as we're still going to need it). Instead of creating a button in code and arranging in code for its action message to be `buttonPressed:`, we're going to use the *existing* button in *MainWindow.xib* and arrange *in the nib* for *its* action message to be `buttonPressed:`. We're going to form an *action connection* in the nib.

As with outlets, there are several ways to do this; I'll just show you the main ones and leave you to discover the rest. (They are all directly comparable to the many ways of creating an outlet connection.)

1. We need a hint, in our code, that a method with the expected signature exists. This hint involves substituting `IBAction` for the method's **void** return type. (The substitution is legal because `IBAction` is `#defined` as **void**; Xcode can see the hint in your code, but the preprocessor will turn `IBAction` back to **void** before the compiler ever sees it.) So, in *Empty_WindowAppDelegate.m*, change the first line of our `buttonPressed:` method implementation to look like this, and then save (File → Save):

   ```
   - (IBAction) buttonPressed: (id) sender {
   ```

2. Now edit *MainWindow.xib*, select the button in the window, and look at the Connections inspector. The event for which we'd like to send the action message is Touch Up Inside. Drag from its circle to the Empty Window App Delegate nib object in the dock, which is to receive the message (Figure 7-10).

3. A little window listing possible Empty_WindowAppDelegate action methods appears; in this case, it lists only `buttonPressed:`. Click on `buttonPressed:` to form the connection.

To see that the action connection has been formed, look at the Connections inspector. If you select the button, the Connections inspector reports that the button's Touch Up

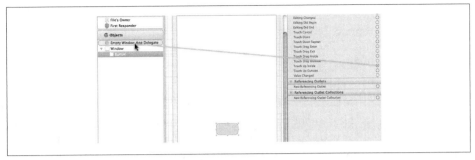

*Figure 7-10. Connecting an action from the Connections inspector*

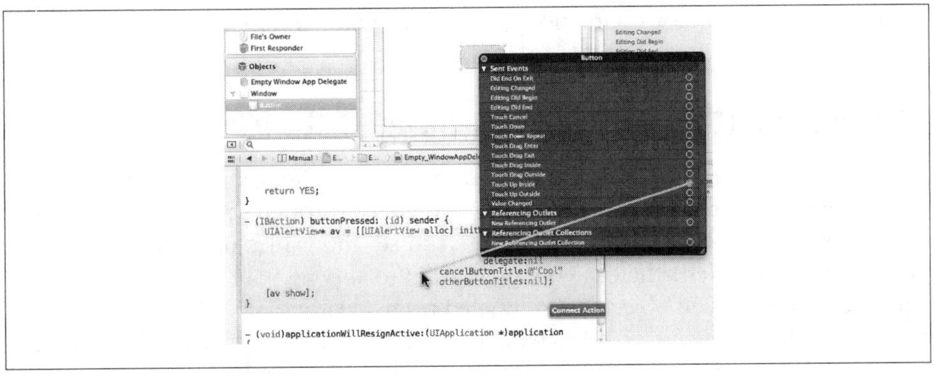

*Figure 7-11. Connecting an action to a method implementation*

Inside event is connected to the Empty Window App Delegate's `buttonPressed:` method. If you select the Empty Window App Delegate object, the Connections inspector reports a Received Action where `buttonPressed:` is called by the Rounded Rect Button's Touch Up Inside event.

At this point, you can also build and run the project to confirm that the action connection is working. In the running app, the button inside the window now actually does something when the user taps it: it summons an alert.

As with outlets, we could have formed the action connection by Control-dragging from the button directly to the Empty Window App Delegate object, instead of involving the Connections inspector. And, as with outlets, there are two ways to do this. If you *just* Control-drag, Interface Builder assumes a default event for you (in this case, it would assume Touch Up Inside). If that isn't what you want, start by Control-clicking on the button to summon a temporary version of the Connections inspector, and drag from the desired event's circle just as you would do from the real Connections inspector.

As with outlets, you can also form the action connection directly to code. In Figure 7-11, we've Control-clicked the button to summon its Connections HUD, and dragged from the Touch Up Inside circle to the `buttonPressed:` implementation.

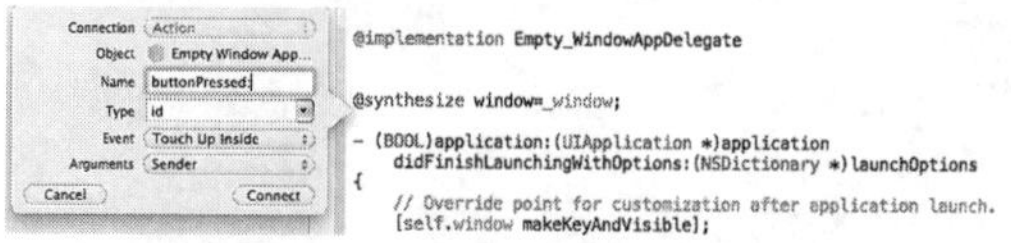

*Figure 7-12. Connecting an action and creating a method implemention*

But wait, there's more! Instead of writing the action method ahead of time, you can ask Xcode to stub it out for you. To do so, drag to an empty spot in the implementation; a dialog appears, letting you specify the name of the action method, the number of arguments it should take, and the control event to be used as a trigger (Figure 7-12). Xcode inserts the method implementation, but doesn't put any code between the curly braces; it's smart, but not smart enough to guess what you want the method to do!

# Additional Initialization of Nib-Based Instances

By the time a nib finishes loading, its instances are fully fledged; they have been initialized and configured with all the attributes dictated through the Attributes and Size inspectors, and their outlets have been used to set the values of the corresponding instance variables. Nevertheless, you might want to append your own code to the initialization process as an object is instantiated from a loading nib. Most commonly, to do this, you'll implement `awakeFromNib`. The `awakeFromNib` message is sent to all nib-instantiated objects just after they are instantiated by the loading of the nib: at the point where this happens, the object has been initialized and configured and its connections are operational.

For example, our Empty Window app is loading *MyNib.xib*, extracting a UILabel from it, and inserting that label into our interface; the result is that the words "Hello, world!" appear in our window. Let's modify the behavior of this UILabel so that it does some additional self-initialization in code. To do that, we will need a class of our own to which our UILabel will belong. Clearly, this needs to be a UILabel subclass. So:

1. In Xcode, choose File → New → New File and specify that you want a Cocoa Touch Objective-C class. Click Next.

2. Make the new class a subclass of UILabel. Click Next.

3. Call it MyLabel. Make sure you're saving into the project folder; set the Empty Window group and the Empty Window target. Click Save.

4. In *MyLabel.m*, somewhere in the implementation section, implement `awakeFromNib`:

```
- (void) awakeFromNib {
    [super awakeFromNib];
    self.text = @"I initialized myself!";
}
```

5. That code won't apply to the label in *MyNib.xib* unless that label *is* a MyLabel, so edit *MyNib.xib* and change the label's class to MyLabel (in the Identity inspector).

Now build and run the project. Instead of "Hello, world!" we now see "I initialized myself!" in the window.

**Mac OS X Programmer Alert**

If you're an experienced Mac OS X programmer, you may be accustomed to rarely or never calling super from awakeFromNib; doing so used to raise an exception, in fact. In iOS, you must always call super in awakeFromNib. Another major difference is that in Mac OS X, a nib owner's awakeFromNib is called when the nib loads, so it's possible for an object to be sent awakeFromNib multiple times; in iOS, awakeFromNib is sent to an object only when that object is itself instantiated from a nib, so it can be sent to an object a maximum of once.

Much more rarely, you might need to interfere with a nib object's initialization at an even earlier stage. If this object is a UIView or UIViewController (or a subclass of either), you can implement initWithCoder:. In your implementation, be sure to call super and return self as you would do in any initializer. Your purpose here would typically be to initialize additional instance variables that your subclass has declared, as with any initializer.

Suppose, for example, that MyLabel declares an instance variable that is an int called num. Then:

```
- (id) initWithCoder:(NSCoder *)aDecoder {
    self = [super initWithCoder:aDecoder];
    if (self) {
        self->num = 42;
    }
    return self;
}

- (void) awakeFromNib {
    [super awakeFromNib];
    self.text = [NSString stringWithFormat: @"The answer is %i", self->num];
}
```

That's trivial and unnecessary, but it illustrates the principle.

# CHAPTER 8

# Documentation

*Knowledge is of two kinds. We know a subject ourselves,*
*or we know where we can find information upon it.*

—Samuel Johnson, *Boswell's Life of Johnson*

*You don't remember Cocoa; you look it up!*

—Anonymous programmer, cited by
Beam and Davidson, *Cocoa in a Nutshell*

No aspect of Cocoa programming is more important than a fluid and nimble relationship with the documentation. There is a huge number of built-in classes, with many methods and properties and other details. Apple's documentation, whatever its flaws, is the definitive official word on how you can expect Cocoa to behave and on the contractual rules incumbent upon you in working with this massive framework whose inner workings you cannot see directly.

The Xcode documentation installed on your machine comes in large chunks called *documentation sets* (or *doc sets*, also called *libraries*). You do not merely install a documentation set; you subscribe to it, so that when Apple releases a documentation update (because a new version of iOS has been released, or because there has been an incremental revision of the documentation), you can obtain the updated version.

When you first install the Xcode tools, assuming that you checked Documentation in the installer, you should start up Xcode to let it download and install your initial documentation sets. The process can be monitored, to some extent, in the Documentation pane of the Preferences window; you can also specify here whether you want updates installed automatically or whether you want to press Check and Install Now manually from time to time. This is also where you specify which doc sets you want; I believe that in Xcode 4 the iOS 4.3 Library and the Xcode 4.0 Developer Library are all you need for iOS development (you may have to click Get to obtain them), and that any doc sets you don't download can still be accessed via the Internet. You may have to provide your machine's admin password when a doc set is first installed.

This chapter describes Xcode 4. Earlier versions, designated generically as Xcode 3.2.x, are very different.

# The Documentation Window

Your primary access to the documentation is in Xcode, through the Documentation tab of the Organizer window (Help → Documentation and API Reference). I'll refer to this as the *documentation window*, even though it's really an aspect of the Organizer window.

The documentation window behaves basically as a glorified web browser, because the documentation consists essentially of web pages. Indeed, most of the same pages can be accessed at Apple's developer site, *http://developer.apple.com*. And any page open in the documentation window can be opened instead in your web browser: Control-click for the contextual menu and choose Open Page in Browser. Notice too the contextual menu for links within a documentation window. When you're trying to figure something out, the ability to spawn off a page as a secondary window in a browser while you go on searching in the Xcode documentation window can be very useful.

Each doc set has a home page, which you access from the Browse navigator (Editor → Explore Documentation) or from the first component of the jump bar (Control-4). A typical home page presents a full list of documents, which can be sorted by column and filtered by keyword. Some home pages, such as the iOS Library home page, also have a broad categorical list down the left side, which can similarly be used to filter the document list. In practice I rarely use these home pages, though they can come in handy when you're looking for broad topic introductions (click Guides on the left). The Browse navigator (and the jump bar) can also be used to explore a doc set by category.

When you encounter a documentation page to which you're likely to want to return, make it a bookmark (Editor → Add Bookmark). Bookmarks are accessed through the Bookmarks navigator (Editor → Documentation Bookmarks). Documentation bookmark management is simple but effective: you can rearrange bookmarks or delete a bookmark, and that's all.

My chief way into the documentation — and, I suspect, most users' chief way — is by searching (Editor → Search Documentation). Type a term into the search field (Shift-Option-Command-?). Click the magnifying glass to choose Show Find Options. It's important to set these options correctly:

*Match Type*
Your choices are Contains, Prefix, and Exact. These determine how your search terms are understood (as middles of words, starts of words, or whole words, respectively), and you'll probably want to switch among them fairly often, depending on what you're searching for. For example, if you are typing the start of the name

of a class you want to search for, do a Prefix search, not a Contains search. Fortunately, as you type into the search bar, a pop-up menu lets you change match type on the fly using the keyboard.

*Doc Sets*

Check only those doc sets that interest you; if you're doing iOS development, for example, uncheck any Mac OS X libraries to eliminate inapplicable and duplicate results.

*Languages*

Check only those languages you're likely to be interested in (probably Objective-C and C).

Once you've entered settings that you like, you can hide the find options to save space; the one option you're likely to change most often, Match Type, can be changed on the fly, as I've already said.

In Xcode 4, the search doesn't take place until you press Return. Search results are displayed in categories, in relevance order, in the navigation pane; click a result to see that page.

Alternatively, if you're editing code, select a term in the editor and choose Help → Search Documentation for Selected Text (Control-Option-Command-/). This command switches to the documentation window, enters the selected term into the search field, and performs the search using the current find options, in a single move.

 Results are presented hierarchically with the hierarchy triangles closed. You have to click triangles to expand the results, in order to see and navigate to the actual pages that contain your search term.

Don't confuse searching the documentation with finding within the current page. To find within the current documentation page, make sure the focus is within the page itself, and then use the Edit → Find menu commands. Command-F summons a find bar, as in Safari.

A major difference between the display of a documentation page in Xcode and its display in Safari is that the latter often shows a Table of Contents column at the left side. In Xcode, this Table of Contents column is suppressed, which saves space, but makes it harder to get a sense for where you are in a document or a set of related documents. The intention is presumably that you should use the jump bar both to get your bearings and to navigate. The last component in the jump bar may show headings within the current document; the next-to-last component may show related documents in the same collection.

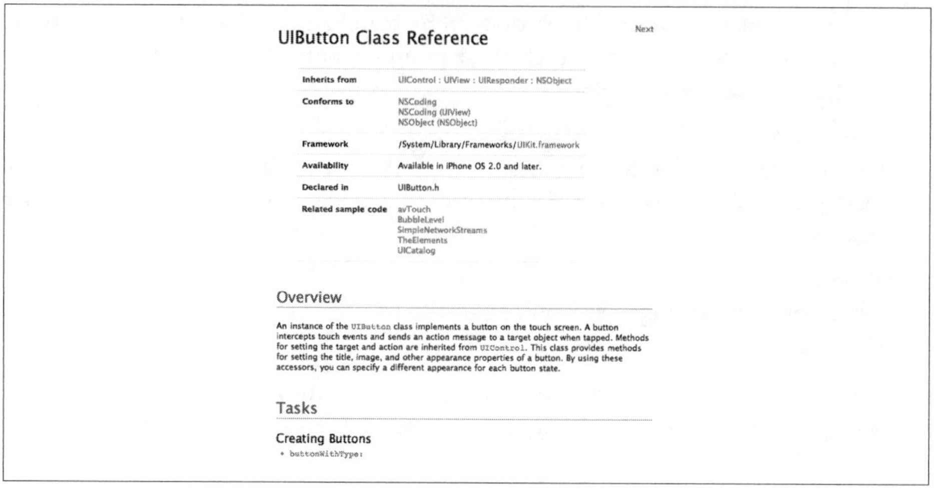

Figure 8-1. The start of a typical class documentation page

# Class Documentation Pages

In the vast majority of cases, your target documentation page will be the documentation for a class. I have frequently spoken already of the importance of class documentation pages. A common move on your part will be to search on a class name in the documentation window. If you search on, say, NSString, the search result whose title is *NSString Class Reference* is the class documentation for NSString.

Let's pause to notice the key features of a class documentation page. I'll use UIButton as an example (Figure 8-1):

*Inherits from*
> Lists, and links to, the chain of superclasses. One of the biggest beginner mistakes is failing to read the documentation up the superclass chain. A class inherits from its superclasses, so the functionality or information you're looking for may be in a superclass. You won't find out about `addTarget:action:forControlEvents:` from the UIButton class page; that information is in the UIControl class page. You won't find out that a UIButton has a `frame` property from the UIButton class page; that information is in the UIView class page.

*Conforms to*
> Lists, and links to, the protocols implemented by this class. Protocols are discussed in Chapter 10. Fortunately, a class that conforms to a formal protocol usually lists that protocol's required methods as links (though the methods themselves are documented on the protocol's documentation page).

Methods injected into a class by a category (Chapter 10) are often *not* listed on that class's documentation page and can be very difficult to discover. This is a major weakness in Apple's organization and display of the documentation. A third-party documentation display application such as AppKiDo can be helpful here (*http://homepage.mac.com/aglee/downloads/appkido.html*).

*Framework*

Tells what framework this class is part of. Your code must link to this framework in order to use this class (see Chapter 6).

*Availability*

States the earliest version of the operating system where this class is implemented. For example, EKEventViewController, along with the whole EventKit framework (consisting of classes for querying the user's calendar; see Chapter 32) wasn't invented until iOS 4.0. So if you want to use this feature in your app, you must make sure either that your app targets only iOS 4.0 or later or that you take precautions not to call into this framework on earlier versions of the operating system. The availability information also confirms that you're looking at the right documentation page; if you're doing iOS programming and this class is available only on Mac OS X, reading this page is pointless. Note that individual methods also have availability information.

*Companion guide*

If a class documentation page lists a companion guide, you might want to click that link and read that guide. Guides are broad surveys of a topic; they provide important information (including, often, useful code examples), and they can serve to orient your thinking and make you aware of your options. (See the UIView class page for an example.)

*Related sample code*

If a class documentation page links to sample code, you might want to examine that code. (But see my remarks on sample code in the next section of this chapter.)

*Overview*

Some class pages provide extremely important introductory information in the Overview section, including links to related guides and further information. (See the UIView class page for an example.)

*Tasks*

This section lists in categorical order, and links to, the properties and methods that appear later on the page. (Recall from Chapter 5 that a property is a syntactic shortcut for calling an accessor method; the documentation lists the property rather than the accessor.) Often, just looking over this list can give you the hint you're looking for.

*Properties, Class Methods, Instance Methods*

These sections provide the full documentation for this class's methods. In recent years, this part of the documentation has become quite splendid, with good hyperlinks. Note the following subsections:

*The property or method name*

This name is suitable for copying and pasting into your code (if, for example, you need to enter the name of a selector).

*The property or method's purpose*

A short summary of what it does.

*The formal declaration for the property or method*

Read this to learn things like the method's parameters and return type. (Chapter 12 explains how to read a property declaration.) Suitable for copying and pasting into your code in order to enter a call to this method, though you are more likely to use Xcode's code completion feature where possible (see Chapter 9).

*Parameters and return value*

Precise information on the meaning and purpose of these.

*Discussion*

Often contains extremely important further details about how this method behaves. Always pay attention to this section!

*Availability*

An old class can acquire new methods as the operating system advances; if a newer method is crucial to your app, you might want to exclude your app from running on older operating systems that don't implement the method.

*See also*

Lists and links to related methods. Very helpful for giving you a larger perspective on how this method fits into the overall behavior of this class.

*Related sample code*

It can sometimes be worth consulting the sample code to see an example of how this particular method is used.

*Declared in*

The relevant header file. It can sometimes be worth looking at the header file, which may contain helpful comments or other details. Unfortunately, the listing of a header file in the documentation window is not a clickable link. You can open the header file from your project window, as explained later in this chapter.

*Constants*

Many classes define constants that accompany particular methods. For example, to create a UIButton instance in code, you call the `buttonWithType:` class method;

the argument value will be a constant, listed under UIButtonType in the Constants section. (To help you get there, there's a link from the `buttonWithType:` method to the UIButtonType section in Constants.) There's a formal definition of the constant; you won't usually care about this (but do see Chapter 1 if you don't know how to read it). Then each value is explained, and the value name is suitable for copying and pasting into your code.

## Sample Code

Apple provides plenty of sample code projects. You can view the code directly in the documentation window; sometimes this will be sufficient, but you can see only one class implementation or header file at a time, so it's difficult to get an overview. The alternative is to open the sample code project in Xcode.

When you look at a sample code page from your browser, there's a button that reads Download Sample Code. In fact, the sample code may already be on your computer. When you look at the same sample code page in the documentation window, the same button will read Open Project. The sample code on your hard disk is zipped, so even if the code is already on your computer, you are first asked to specify a "download folder" in which to save the unzipped project folder. This policy of keeping the sample code projects zipped on your hard disk is a good one, as it prevents you from accidentally altering the original, and you are free to experiment with the unzipped copy.

 If a sample code project was linked against the frameworks of an older SDK that isn't installed on your computer, you won't be able to build and run the project, and features that depend on indexing won't work. This situation is easy to detect and easy to fix. The chief sign is that the project will be described in the Project navigator with the words "missing base SDK," and the Issue navigator will show a Target Integrity warning. To solve the problem, click that issue in the Issue navigator to edit the build settings, and change the outdated Base SDK setting to Latest iOS.

As a form of documentation, sample code is both good and bad. It can be a superb source of working code that you can often copy and paste and use with very little alteration in your own projects. It is usually heavily commented, because the Apple folks are aware, as they write the code, that it is intended for instructional purposes. Sample code also illustrates concepts that users have difficulty extracting from the documentation. (Users who have not grasped UITouch handling, for instance, often find that the lightbulb goes on when they discover the MoveMe example.) But the logic of a project is often spread over multiple files, and nothing is more difficult to understand than someone else's code (except, perhaps, your own code). Moreover, what learners most need is not the fait accompli of a fully written project but the reasoning process that constructed the project, which no amount of commentary can provide.

My own assessment is that Apple's sample code is generally very thoughtful and instructive and definitely a major component of the documentation, and that it deserves more appreciation and usage than it seems to get. But it is most useful, I think, after you've reached a certain level of competence and comfort.

# Other Resources

Here is a survey of other useful resources that supplement the documentation.

## Quick Help

Quick Help is a condensed rendering of the documentation on some single topic, usually a symbol name (a class or method). It appears with regard to the current selection or insertion point automatically in the Quick Help inspector (Option-Command-2) if the inspector is showing. Thus, for example, if you're editing code and the insertion point or selection is within the term `CGPointMake`, documentation for `CGPointMake` appears in the Quick Help inspector if it is visible.

A slightly reduced version of the same Quick Help documentation can displayed as a small floating window, without the Quick Help inspector, by Option-clicking on a term in code. Alternatively, select a term and choose Help → Quick Help for Selected Item (Shift-Control-Command-?). In the Quick Help window, click the "book" icon to open the full documentation in the documentation window; click the "H" icon to open the appropriate header file.

Both the Quick Help inspector and the Quick Help window may also contain links. Some of these may be to various other documentation aids, such as sample code. The most important link will probably be the first one, the name of the symbol being documented; this links to the appropriate spot in the full documentation in the documentation window.

Xcode 4 provides no *direct* path from a symbol in code to its documentation in the documentation window. You must pass through Quick Help to get there. You can select a term and choose Help → Search Documentation for Selected Text (Control-Option-Command-/), but this is hardly the same thing, as it doesn't jump to the actual API linked from Quick Help.

If you hold down Option and hover the mouse over code, the term that Quick Help would document if you were to click at that point appears with a dotted underline.

Quick Help is also available during code completion (Chapter 9), concerning the term currently being proposed as a completion; the question-mark icon at the right side of the code completion pop-up menu summons the Quick Help window. Plus, Quick

Help is available in the Quick Help inspector for interface objects selected while editing a nib, for build settings while editing a project or target, and so forth.

## Symbols

A *symbol* is a nonlocally defined term, such as the name of a class, method, or instance variable. If you can see the name of a symbol in your code in an editor in Xcode, Command-click it to jump to the definition for that symbol. Alternatively, select text and choose Navigate → Jump to Definition (Control-Command-D). If there are multiple definitions for a term, when you Command-click you'll get a little pop-up window where you can pick which one to jump to. If you hold down Command and hover the mouse over code, the symbol whose definition would be shown if you were to click at that point appears with a solid underline.

If the symbol is defined in a Cocoa framework, you jump to the header file. If the symbol is defined in your code, you jump to the class or method definition. This can be very helpful not only for understanding your code but also for navigating it. For example, suppose you realize that for memory management reasons you need to modify the `dealloc` method in one of your classes. If you can see the word `dealloc` anywhere in the current editor, you can Command-click it to jump to any other `dealloc` method in your project.

The precise meaning of the notion "jump" depends upon the modifier keys you use in addition to the Command key, and on your settings in the General pane of Xcode's preferences. For example, if you haven't changed these settings from the default, Command-click jumps in the same editor, Command-Option-click jumps in an assistant pane, and Command-double-click jumps in a new window. Similarly, Control-Option-Command-D jumps in an assistant pane to the definition of the selected term.

Another way to see a list of your project's symbols, and navigate to a symbol definition, is with the Symbol navigator (Chapter 6).

## Header Files

Sometimes a header file can be a useful form of documentation. It compactly summarizes a class's instance variables and methods and may contain comments and other helpful information. A single header file can contain declarations for multiple class interfaces and protocols. So it can be an excellent quick reference.

There are various ways to see a header file from an Xcode editor:

- If the class is your own and you're in the implementation file, choose Navigation → Jump to Next Counterpart (Control-Command-Up).
- Click the Related Files button at the left of the jump bar (Control-1). The menu lets you jump to any header files imported in the current file (as well as any files

that import the current file) and to the header files of the current class file's super-classes and subclasses and so forth. Hold Option to jump in an assistant pane.

- Select text and choose File → Open Quickly (Shift-Command-O). This command brings up a dialog listing all source and header files containing a given symbol.

- Command-click a symbol, choose Navigate → Jump to Definition, or pass through Quick Help, as described in the previous sections.

- Use the Symbol navigator (Chapter 6).

## Internet Resources

Programming has become a lot easier since the Internet came along and Google started indexing it. It's amazing what you can find out with a Google search. Your problem is very likely a problem someone else has faced, solved, and written about on the Internet. Often you'll find sample code that you can paste into your project and adapt.

Apple's documentation resources are available at *http://developer.apple.com*. These resources are updated before the changes are rolled into your doc sets for download. There are also some materials here that aren't part of the Xcode documentation on your computer. As a registered iOS developer, you have access to iTunes videos, including the videos for all WWDC 2010 sessions, and to Apple's developer forums (*https://devforums.apple.com*).

Apple maintains some public mailing lists (*http://lists.apple.com/mailman/listinfo*). I have long subscribed to the Xcode-users group (for questions about use of the Xcode tools) and the Cocoa-dev group (for questions about programming Cocoa). Cocoa-dev does now permit iOS questions, but it is not heavily used for these. The lists are searchable, but Apple's own search doesn't work very well; you're better off using Google with a site:lists.apple.com term, or *http://www.cocoabuilder.com*, which archives the lists. Apple has not added a mailing list devoted to iOS programming; that's what the developer forums are supposed to be for, though the interface for these is extraordinarily clunky in my view, and this — plus the lack of openness (to Google and to the world in general) — has limited their usefulness.

Other online resources, such as forums, have sprung up spontaneously as iOS programming has become more popular, and lots of iOS and Cocoa programmers blog about their experiences. I am particularly fond of Stack Overflow (*http://www.stackoverflow.com*); of course it isn't devoted exclusively to iOS programming, but lots of iOS programmers hang out there, questions are answered succinctly and correctly, and the interface lets you focus on the right answer quickly and easily.

# CHAPTER 9

# Life Cycle of a Project

This chapter surveys some of the main stages in the life cycle of a project, from inception to submission at the App Store. This survey will provide an opportunity to discuss some additional features of the Xcode development environment. You already know how to create a project, define a class, and link to a framework (Chapter 6), as well as how to create and edit a nib (Chapter 7) and how to use the documentation (Chapter 8).

 This chapter describes Xcode 4. Earlier versions, designated generically as Xcode 3.2.x, are very different.

## Choosing a Device Architecture

As you create a project, after you pick a project template, in the part of the dialog where you name your project, the Device Family pop-up menu may offer a choice of iPhone or iPad. Some templates offer no choice, as they are by nature applicable to only one type of device. The Window-based Application template offers a third choice — Universal (meaning both iPhone and iPad).

You are not tied forever to your initial decision, but your life will be easier if you decide correctly from the outset. The iPhone and iPad differ in their physical environments as well as their programming interfaces. The iPad has a larger window size, along with some built-in interface features that don't exist on the iPhone, such as split views and popovers (Chapter 22); thus an iPad project's nib files and some other resources will differ from those of an iPhone project.

Different types of device may also be running different versions of the operating system. iOS 4.2 and later runs on both iPhone and iPad, but prior to that the two devices ran different systems: iOS 3.1.3 and before, plus iOS 4.0 and 4.1, were iPhone only, while iOS 3.2.x was iPad only.

Your choice in the Device Family pop-up menu, then, affects what template your new project will be based on. It also affects your target's Targeted Device Family build setting:

*iPad*
> The app will run only on an iPad.

*iPhone*
> The app will run on an iPhone or iPod touch; it can also run on an iPad, but not as a native iPad app (it runs in a reduced enlargeable window, which I call the *iPhone Emulator*; Apple sometimes refers to this as "compatibility mode").

*iPhone/iPad*
> The app will run natively on both kinds of device, and should be structured as a universal app. A *universal app* is a single app built from a single target, but it contains some resources that are loaded only on one type of device or the other.

Two additional build settings work together and in conjunction with the Targeted Device Family to determine what systems your device will run on:

*Base SDK*
> The *latest* system your app can run on: in Xcode 4, you have just one choice, iOS 4.3. Actually, there is an alternative, Latest iOS; the advantage of this is that if you update Xcode to develop for a subsequent system, your existing projects will build in that updated Xcode without your also having to update their Base SDK setting. Latest iOS is the default when you create a new project.

*iOS Deployment Target*
> The *earliest* system your app can run on: this can be any iOS system number from the current 4.3 all the way back to 3.0. (iOS 3.0 is also the earliest system on which a universal app will run.) You can change the iOS Deployment Target setting easily by editing your project; see the iOS Deployment Target pop-up menu in the Info tab.

Writing an app whose Deployment Target differs from its Base SDK is something of a challenge. The problem is that Xcode will happily allow you to use any features of the Base SDK, but an actual device will not. If you use any features that are not supported on a particular device under a particular system, the app will crash on that device.

To see this, create (in Xcode 4) a new iPhone project using the View-based Application template and set the iOS Deployment Target to 3.2. You can build an app from this project and load it into an iPad running iOS 3.2, but the app will crash on launch, because the template contains this line, which is encountered as the app starts up:

```
self.window.rootViewController = self.viewController;
```

The problem is that the window `rootViewController` property wasn't invented until iOS 4.0.

However, you might not own an iPad running iOS 3.2 to test on, and the prospect that a bug like this might not be discovered until the app has been let loose upon a world of users is highly unsettling — indeed, you might decide that attempting backward-compatibility simply isn't worth the gamble. Fortunately, in this case there is a way to discover the problem from within Xcode, because the Simulator lets you specify what device and system version to simulate, as far back as iOS 3.2 (choose iPad 3.2 Simulator as your destination in the Scheme pop-up menu before you build and run). So you could test in the Simulator, telling the Simulator to behave as an iPad running iOS 3.2, and discover the crash.

Writing a universal app compounds the challenge, thanks to the environmental differences between iPhone and iPad. As you develop, you must juggle two versions of many files, such as nibs and the app delegate classes. You'll want to share some code between the iPhone and the iPad version of the app, but other pieces of code you'll probably want to keep separate, because they must behave differently; for example, you can't summon a popover on an iPhone.

There are various programming devices to govern dynamically what code is encountered, based on what system or device type the app is running on; thus you can avoid executing code that will cause a crash in a particular environment (see also Example 29-1):

- The UIDevice class lets you query the current device as [UIDevice currentDevice] to learn its system version (systemVersion) and type (userInterfaceIdiom, either UIUserInterfaceIdiomPhone or UIUserInterfaceIdiomPad; available in iOS 3.2 and later). This query is also packaged as a convenience function (actually a macro), UI_USER_INTERFACE_IDIOM.

- You can test for the existence of a method using respondsToSelector: and related NSObject calls.

- You can test for the existence of a class using the NSClassFromString function, which yields nil if the class doesn't exist.

- You can test for the existence of a constant name, including the name of a C function, by taking the name's address and testing against zero. For example:

```
if (&UIApplicationWillEnterForegroundNotification) // ...
```

If that condition is true, it's okay to refer to UIApplicationWillEnterForegroundNotification.

If you write an app for just iPhone and decide later to make it universal or to create a separate iPad app based initially on the same code, you can edit the target and (in the Summary tab) change the Devices pop-up menu. A dialog ("Transition to Universal Target") offers to copy and adjust your interface for you, and you should probably accept; in general I find that this feature is quite clever about such things as giving you good initial alternative nib files, so that you can build and start developing for iPad immediately, whereas you'd be very unlikely to perform this migration successfully on your own.

# Localization

A device can be set by the user to prefer a certain language as its primary language. You might like the text in your app's interface to respond to this situation by appearing in that language. This is achieved by *localizing* the app for that language.

Localization works through localization folders in your project and in the built app bundle. Every resource in one of these localization folders has a counterpart in the other localization folders. Then, when your app goes to load such a resource, it automatically loads the one appropriate to the user's preferred language. For example, if there's a copy of *MainWindow.nib* in the English localization folder and a copy of *Main-Window.nib* in the French localization folder, the latter will be loaded as the app launches on a device on which French is the preferred language. So the two copies of *MainWindow.nib* should be identical except that all the text the user will see in the interface should be in French in the French version.

This approach solves the problem for resources that are physically loaded, such as nib files and images and sound files, but it doesn't deal with strings generated from within your code, such as the text of an alert message. Surely you don't want your code to consist of a bunch of massive `if` clauses every time there's text to display. The problem is solved through the use of a strings file. A *strings file* is a specially formatted text file whose file extension is *.strings*; by default the name of the file is *Localizable.strings* (that is, this file will be sought by default, if no filename is specified), but you can use another name if you like. As with other localized resources, the strings file exists in multiple copies, one for each language. The strings file consists of key–value pairs; the keys are the same in all copies, but the values differ, depending on the target language. So instead of entering a string directly in your code, you tell your code to fetch the correct value from the appropriate strings file, based on the key:

```
NSString* myAlertText = NSLocalizedString(@"alertTextKey", nil);
```

Another specially named *.strings* file, *InfoPlist.strings*, stores localized versions of *Info.plist* key values. So, for example, the value of the `CFBundleDisplayName` key, as set in your project's *Info.plist* file, appears under your app's icon on the user's device (Chapter 6); to change this name depending on the user's primary language setting, you'd include appropriate key–value pairs in *InfoPlist.strings* files.

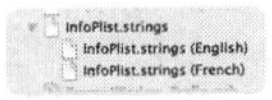

*Figure 9-1. How a localized strings file is represented in Xcode*

Localization explains the *en.lproj* folder seen in the Finder in our Empty Window project folder (Figure 6-8). That's an English localization folder; its contents, *Main-Window.xib* and *InfoPlist.strings*, are localized for English. In Xcode, however, nothing seems to indicate this; you wouldn't know, from looking at the Project navigator, that there's anything special about these two files. That's because there's only one localization. As soon as a file has more than one localization, it's shown in the Project navigator as a kind of folder, inverted from how it's shown in the Finder: the file name contains hierarchically the names of the localizations (Figure 9-1). This makes it easy to find and edit the correct copy of the file.

To get started with localization in your project, select in the Project navigator a file that you want to localize and examine it in the Localization section of the File inspector (Command-Option-1). It is obvious how to add and remove localization languages here.

For full discussion, see Apple's *Internationalization Programming Topics*.

# Editing Your Code

Many aspects of Xcode's editing environment can be modified to suit your tastes. Your first step should be to pick a font face and size you like in the Fonts & Colors preference pane. Nothing is so important as being able to read and write code comfortably! I like a largish size (14 or even 16) and a pleasant monospaced font such as Monaco, Menlo, or Consolas (or the freeware Inconsolata).

Xcode has some formatting, autotyping, and text selection features adapted for Objective-C. Exactly how these behave depends upon your settings in the Editing and Indentation tabs of Xcode's Text Editing preference pane. I'm not going to describe these settings in detail, but I urge you to take advantage of them. Under Editing, I like to check just about everything, including Line Numbers; visible line numbers are useful when debugging. Under Indentation, I like to have just about everything checked too; I find the way Xcode lays out Objective-C code to be excellent with these settings.

If you like Xcode's smart syntax-aware indenting, but you find that once in a while a line of code isn't indenting itself correctly, try choosing Editor → Structure → Re-indent (Control-I), which autoindents the current line. (Autoindent problems can also be caused by incorrect syntax earlier in the file, so hunt for that too.)

Under Editing, notice "Balance brackets in Objective-C method calls." If this option is checked, then when you type a closing square bracket after some text, Xcode intelli-

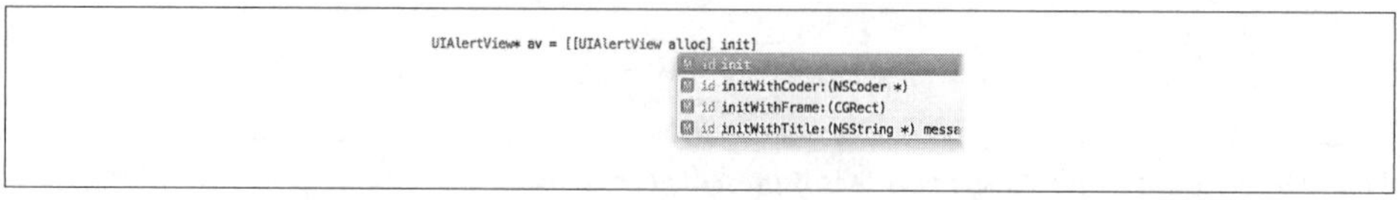

```
UIAlertView* av = [[UIAlertView alloc] init]
    id init
    id initWithCoder:(NSCoder *)
    id initWithFrame:(CGRect)
    id initWithTitle:(NSString *) messa
```

*Figure 9-2. The autocompletion menu*

gently inserts the opening square bracket before the text. I like this feature, as it allows me to type nested square brackets without planning ahead. For example, I type this:

```
UIAlertView* av = [UIAlertView alloc
```

I now type the right square bracket *twice*. The first right square bracket closes the open left square bracket (which highlights to indicate this). The second right square bracket also inserts a space before itself, plus the missing left square bracket:

```
UIAlertView* av = [[UIAlertView alloc] ]
//            insertion point is here: ^
```

The insertion point is positioned before the second right square bracket, ready for me to type `init`.

## Autocompletion

As you write code, you'll take advantage of Xcode's autocompletion feature. Objective-C is a verbose language, and whatever reduces your time and effort typing will be a relief. However, I personally do *not* check "Suggest completions while typing" under Editing; when I want autocompletion to happen, I ask for it manually, by pressing Esc.

For example, suppose my code is as displayed in the previous example, with the insertion point before the second right square bracket. I now type `init` and then press Esc, and a little menu pops up, listing the four `init` methods appropriate to a UIAlertView (Figure 9-2). You can navigate this menu, dismiss it, or accept the selection, using only the keyboard. So I would navigate to `initWithTitle:...` (no need, actually, as it is selected by default) and press Return to accept the selected choice.

Alternatively, I might press Control-Period instead of Esc. Pressing Control-Period repeatedly cycles through the alternatives. Again, press Return to accept the selected choice.

The template for the correct method call is now entered in my code (I've broken it manually into multiple lines to show it here):

```
[[UIAlertView alloc] initWithTitle:<#(NSString *)#>
                    message:<#(NSString *)#>
                    delegate:<#(id)#>
            cancelButtonTitle:<#(NSString *)#>
            otherButtonTitles:<#(NSString *), ...#>, nil]
```

The expressions in `<#...#>` are *placeholders*, showing the type of each parameter; you can select the next placeholder with Tab (if the insertion point is in the neighborhood of a placeholder) or by choosing Navigate → Jump to Next Placeholder (Control-Slash).

Thus I can select a placeholder and type in its place the actual value I wish to pass, select the next placeholder and type its value, and so forth.

 Placeholders are delimited by `<#...#>` behind the scenes, but they appear as "text tokens" to prevent them from being edited accidentally. To convert a placeholder to a normal string without the delimiters, select it and press Return, or double-click it.

Autocompletion also works for method declarations. You don't have to know or enter a method's return type beforehand. Just type the initial - or + (to indicate an instance method or a class method) followed by the first few letters of the method's name. For example, in my app delegate I might type:

```
- appli
```

If I then press Esc, I see a list of methods such as `application:didChangeStatusBar-Frame:`; these are methods that might be sent to my app delegate (by virtue of its being the app delegate, as discussed in Chapter 11). When I choose one, the declaration is filled in for me, including the return type and the parameter names:

```
- (void)application:(UIApplication *)application
    didChangeStatusBarFrame:(CGRect)oldStatusBarFrame
```

At this point I'm ready to type the left curly brace, followed by a Return character; this causes the matching right curly brace to appear, with the insertion point positioned between them, ready for me to start typing the body of this method.

## Snippets

Code autocompletion is supplemented by code snippets, which are text constructs with an abbreviation. Code snippets are kept in the Code Snippet library (Control-Option-Command-2). You type the abbreviation and the macro is included among the possible completions. For example, to enter an `if` block, I would type `if` and press Esc and then Return; the construct appears in my code, and the condition area (between the parentheses) and statements area (between the curly braces) are placeholders.

To learn a snippet's abbreviation, you must open its editing window (select the snippet in the Code Snippet library and press Spacebar) and click Edit. You can add your own snippets, which will be categorized as User snippets; the easiest way is to drag text into the Code Snippet library. Edit to suit your taste, providing a name, a description, and an abbreviation; use the `<#...#>` construct to form any desired placeholders.

If learning a snippet's abbreviation is too much trouble, simply drag it from the Code Snippet library into your text.

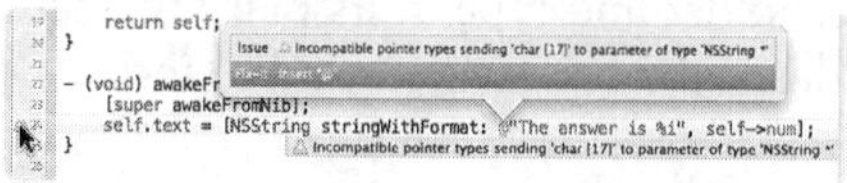

*Figure 9-3. A warning with a Fix-it suggestion*

## Live Syntax Checking

Xcode 4 introduces live syntax checking as you type. This feature can save you from mistakes; in addition, the extremely cool "Fix-it" feature can actually make *and implement* positive suggestions on how to avert a problem.

For instance, in Figure 9-3 I've accidentally omitted the @ before an Objective-C NSString literal, and the compiler is warning (because what I've typed is a C string literal, a very different thing). By clicking on the warning symbol in the gutter, I've summoned a little dialog that not only describes the mistake but tells me how to fix it. Not only that: it has tentatively inserted the missing @ into my code. (Note that @ is a faded gray color. It's not part of what I typed; Xcode has added it.) Not only *that*: if I press Return, or double-click the "Fix-it" button in the dialog, Xcode *really* inserts the missing @ into my code — and the warning vanishes, because the problem is solved. If I'm confident that Xcode will do the right thing, I can choose Editor → Fix All in Scope (Control-Command-F), and Xcode will implement *all* nearby Fix-it suggestions without my even having to show the dialog.

Live syntax checking can be toggled on or off using the Enable Live Issues In Editors checkbox in the General preference pane. I'm of two minds about this feature. On the one hand I'm tempted to turn it off, as I find it intrusive. My code is almost never valid while I'm typing, because the terms and parentheses are always half-finished; that's what it means to be typing. For example, merely typing a left parenthesis will instantly cause the syntax checker to complain of a parse error (until I type the corresponding right parenthesis). On the other hand, turning off live syntax checking turns off Fix-it, and it's a pity to lose something so convenient.

## Navigating Your Code

Developing an Xcode project involves editing code in many files at once. Xcode provides numerous ways to navigate your code. Many of these have been mentioned in previous chapters.

*The Project navigator*
    If you know something about the name of a file, you can find it quickly in the Project navigator (Command-1) by typing into the search field in the filter bar at the bottom of the navigator (Edit → Filter → Filter in Navigator, Command-Option-J). For example, type xib to see just your nib files. Moreover, after using the filter

bar, you can press Tab and then the Up or Down arrow key to navigate the Project navigator. Thus you can reach the desired nib file with the keyboard alone.

*The Symbol navigator*

As with the Project navigator, the filter bar can quickly get you where you want to go. For example, to see all `dealloc` implementations in your code, highlight the first two icons (the first two are light, the third is dark) and type `deall` in the search field.

*The jump bar*

Every path component of the jump bar is a menu:

*The bottom level*

At the bottom level (farthest right) in the jump bar is a list of your file's method and function declarations and definitions, in the order in which they appear (hold Command while choosing the menu to see them in alphabetical order); choose one to navigate to it.

You can add your own entries to this bottom-level menu using the `#pragma mark` directive. For example:

```
#pragma mark Memory Management
- (void)dealloc {
    [window release];
    [super dealloc];
}
```

The result is that the "dealloc" item in the bottom-level menu falls within a "Memory Management" section. To make a section divider line in the menu, type a `#pragma mark` directive whose value is a hyphen.

*Higher levels*

Higher-level path components are hierarchical menus; thus you can use any of them to work your way down the file hierarchy.

*History*

Each editor pane remembers the names of files you've edited in it. The Back and Forward triangles are both buttons and pop-up menus (or choose Navigate → Go Back and Navigate → Go Forward, Control-Command-Left and Control-Command-Right).

*Related items*

The leftmost button in the jump bar summons a hierarchical menu of files related to the current file, such as counterparts, superclasses, and included files.

*The Assistant pane*

The Assistant allows you to be in two places at once. Hold Option while navigating to open something in an Assistant pane instead of the main or current editor pane.

The first path component in an Assistant pane's jump bar sets its automatic relationship to the main pane (*tracking*). If that relationship involves multiple files, triangle buttons appear at the right end of the jump bar, letting you navigate between them; or choose from the second path component's pop-up menu (Control-5). (For example, show *Empty_WindowAppDelegate.m* in the main pane and switch the assistant pane's related items pop-up menu to Includes.)

You can also be in two places at once by opening a tab or a separate window.

*Jump to definition*

Navigate → Jump to Definition (Control-Command-D) lets you jump to the definition or implementation of the symbol already selected in your code.

*Open quickly*

File → Open Quickly (Shift-Command-O) searches in a dialog for a symbol in your code and the Cocoa headers. You can type the symbol in the search field, or, if a symbol is selected when you summon the dialog, it will be entered in the search field for you (and you can then navigate the dialog entirely with the keyboard).

*Breakpoints*

The Breakpoint navigator lists all breakpoints in your code. Xcode 4 lacks code bookmarks, but you can misuse a disabled breakpoint as a bookmark.

*Finding*

Finding is a form of navigation. Xcode has both a global find (Edit → Find → Find in Workspace, Shift-Command-F, which is the same as using the Search navigator) and an editor-level find (Edit → Find → Find, Command-F); don't confuse them.

Find options are all-important. Both sorts of find have options settings that you can summon by clicking the magnifying glass. The global find options (Figure 6-3) allow you to specify the scope of a search (which files will be searched) in sophisticated ways: choose Custom in the "Find in" pop-up menu to create a scope. The global find search bar also pops down a menu automatically as you type, letting you switch among the most important options. You can also find using regular expressions. There's a lot of power lurking here.

To replace text, click on the word Find next to the search bar to summon the pop-up menu, and choose Replace. (It may be necessary to perform a global find first, before a global replace on the same search term will work.) You can replace all occurrences, or select particular find results in the Search navigator and replace only those (click Replace instead of Replace All). Even better, click Preview; it summons a dialog that shows you the effect of each possible replacement, and lets you check or uncheck particular replacements in advance of performing the replacement.

A sophisticated form of editor-level find is Editor → Edit All In Scope, which finds simultaneously all occurrences of the currently selected term (usually a variable name) within the current set of curly braces; you can use this to change the variable's name throughout its scope, or just to survey how the name is used. To change a symbol's name throughout your code, use Xcode's Refactoring feature (see "Making Global Changes to Your Code" in the *Xcode 4 User Guide*).

# Debugging

Debugging is the art of figuring out what's wrong with the behavior of your app as it runs. I divide this art into two main techniques: caveman debugging and pausing your running app.

## Caveman Debugging

*Caveman debugging* consists of altering your code, usually temporarily, typically by adding code to dump informative messages into the console.

 To see the console as a full window, open a second project window or tab, show the Debug pane (View → Show Debug Area), and slide the top of the Debug pane all the way up to cover the editor. Eliminate the Navigator and Organizer panes, and the variables list. Now this window or tab contains nothing but the console. Switch to this window or tab when you want to read the console, but don't run or stop while viewing it, as doing so may cause the Debug pane to close or change size.

The standard command for sending a message to the console is NSLog. It's a C function, and it takes an NSString which operates as a format string, followed by the format arguments.

A *format string* is a string (here, an NSString) containing symbols called *format specifiers*, for which values (the format arguments) will be substituted at runtime. All format specifiers begin with a percent sign (%), so the only way to enter a literal percent sign in a format string is as a double percent sign (%%). The character(s) following the percent sign specify the type of value that will be supplied at runtime. The most common format specifiers are %@ (an object reference), %i (an integer), %f (a float), and %p (a pointer, usually an object reference, shown as the address in memory pointed to, useful for making certain that two references refer to the same instance). For example:

```
NSLog(@"the window: %@", self.window);
```

In that example, `self.window` is the first (and only) format argument, so its value will be substituted for the first (and only) format specifier, %@, when the format string is printed in the console. Thus the console output looks something like this:

```
the window: <UIWindow: 0x391e740; frame = (0 0; 320 480); opaque = NO;
autoresize = RM+BM; layer = <CALayer: 0x391f4c0>>
```

This nice display of information is due to UIWindow's implementation of the `description` method: an object's `description` method is called when that object is used with the %@ format specifier. For this reason, you will probably want to implement `description` in your own classes, so that you can investigate an instance with a simple NSLog call.

For the complete repertory of format specifiers available in a format string, read Apple's document *String Format Specifiers*. The format specifiers are largely based on those of the C `printf` standard library function; see K&R B1.2, the `sprintf` man page, and the IEEE `printf` specification linked from the documentation.

> If an object reference has been set to nil, NSLog will report it as (`null`). But if an object reference is uninitialized, an NSLog call referring to it will probably fail silently, or even crash the debugger. This is very frustrating; indeed, the fact that this object reference is uninitialized is probably just what you were trying to debug. This is another good reason to initialize your variables explicitly as you declare them.

The main ways to go wrong with NSLog (or any format string) are to supply a different number of format arguments from the number of format specifiers in the string, or to supply an argument value different from the type declared by the corresponding format specifier. These mistakes can send your app off into the weeds, or at least give misleading results. I often see beginners claim that logging shows a certain value to be nonsense, when in fact it is their NSLog call that is nonsense; for example, a format specifier was %i but the value of the corresponding argument was a float.

C structs are not objects, so to see a struct's value with NSLog you must somehow disassemble or translate the struct. Common Cocoa structs usually supply convenience functions for this purpose. For example:

```
NSLog(@"%@", NSStringFromCGRect(self.window.frame)); // {{0, 0}, {320, 480}}
```

Purists may scoff at caveman debugging, but I use it heavily: it's easy, informative, and lightweight. And sometimes it's the only way. Unlike the debugger, NSLog works with any build configuration (Debug or Release) and wherever your app runs (in the Simulator or on a device). It even works on someone else's device, such as a tester to whom you've distributed your app. It's a little tricky for a tester to get a look at the console so as to be able to report back to you, but it can be done: the tester can connect the device to a computer and view its log in Xcode's Organizer window or with Apple's iPhone Configuration Utility; there's also a free utility app called Console that displays the log right on the device.

Remember to remove or comment out NSLog calls before shipping your app, as you probably don't want your finished app to dump lots of messages into the console. A useful trick (shamelessly stolen from Jens Alfke) is to call MyLog instead of NSLog, and define MyLog like this in your precompiled header:

```
#define MyLog if(0); else NSLog
```

When it's time to stop logging, change the 0 to 1.

A useful fact when logging is that the variable name _cmd holds the selector for the current method. Thus a single form of statement can signal where you are:

```
NSLog(@"Starting %@ in %@", NSStringFromSelector(_cmd), self);
```

Another sort of call with which you can pepper your code is *asserts*. Asserts are conditions that you claim (assert) are true at that moment — and you feel so strongly about this that you want your app to crash if you're wrong. Asserts are a very good way to confirm that the situation matches your expectations, not just now as you write your code, but in the future as the app develops. Some developers even think that asserts should be allowed to remain in your code when your app is finished.

The simplest form of assert is the C function (actually it's a macro) assert(), to which you pass one argument, a condition — something that can be evaluated as false (0) or true (some other value). If it's false, your app will crash when this line is encountered, along with a nice explanation in the log. For example, suppose we assert NO, which is false and will certainly cause a crash. Then when this line is encountered we crash with this log message:

```
Assertion failed: (NO),
function -[testAssertAppDelegate application:didFinishLaunchingWithOptions:],
file /Users/mattleopard/Desktop/testAssert/testAssert/testAssertAppDelegate.m,
line 26.
```

That's plenty for us to track down the assertion failure: we know the assertion condition, the method in which the assertion occurred, the file containing that method, and the line number.

For higher-level asserts, look at NSAssert (used in Objective-C methods) and NSCAssert (used in C functions) and their relatives; they allow you to form your own log message, and the relatives allow the log message to be a format string. For example, NSAssert3 takes a condition along with a format string containing three format specifiers, followed by the values to be substituted for each format specifier.

## The Xcode Debugger

When you're building and running in Xcode, you can pause in the debugger and use Xcode's debugging facilities. There isn't a strong difference between running and debugging in Xcode 4; the main distinction is whether breakpoints are activated (activated breakpoints are obeyed, whereas deactivated breakpoints are ignored).

The important thing, if you want to use the debugger, is that the app should be built with the Debug build configuration. The debugger is not very helpful against an app built with the Release build configuration, not least because compiler optimizations can destroy the correspondence between steps in the compiled code and lines in your code. Trying to debug a Release build is a common beginner error (though it's less likely

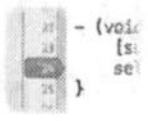

*Figure 9-4. A breakpoint*

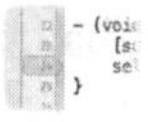

*Figure 9-5. A disabled breakpoint*

to occur accidentally in Xcode 4, in which by default a scheme's Run action uses the Debug build configuration).

To create a breakpoint (Figure 9-4), select in the editor the line where you want to pause, and choose Product → Debug → Add Breakpoint at Current Line (Command-Backslash). This keyboard shortcut toggles between adding and removing a breakpoint for the current line. The breakpoint is symbolized by an arrow in the gutter. Alternatively, a simple click in the gutter adds a breakpoint; to remove a breakpoint gesturally, drag it out of the gutter.

A breakpoint can be disabled. This means that even if breakpoints are activated, we won't pause at this one. That way, you can leave in place a breakpoint that you might need later without pausing at it every time it's encountered. To disable a breakpoint at the current line, click on the breakpoint in the gutter to toggle its enabled status. Alternatively, Control-click on the breakpoint and choose Disable Breakpoint in the contextual menu. A dark breakpoint is enabled; a light breakpoint is disabled (Figure 9-5).

Once you have some breakpoints in your code, you'll want to survey and manage them. That's what the Breakpoint navigator is for. Here you can navigate to a breakpoint, enable or disable a breakpoint by clicking on its arrow in the navigator, and delete a breakpoint.

You can also edit a breakpoint's behavior. Control-click on the breakpoint, in the gutter or in the Breakpoint navigator, and choose Edit Breakpoint. This is a very powerful facility: you can have a breakpoint pause only under a certain condition or after it has been encountered a certain number of times, and you can have a breakpoint perform a certain action when it is encountered, such as logging or running a script.

A breakpoint can be configured to continue automatically after performing its action when it is encountered. This can be an excellent alternative to caveman debugging: Instead of inserting an NSLog call, which must be compiled into your code and later removed when the app is released, you can set a breakpoint that logs and continues, which operates only when you're debugging.

In the Breakpoint navigator, you can create two kinds of breakpoint that you can't create in a code editor: exception breakpoints and symbolic breakpoints. Click the "+" button at the bottom of the navigator and choose from its pop-up menu.

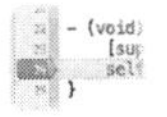

*Figure 9-6. Paused at a breakpoint*

*Exception breakpoint*

An exception breakpoint causes your app to pause at the time an exception is thrown or caught, without regard to whether the exception would crash your app later. I recommend that you create an exception breakpoint to catch all exceptions when they are thrown, because this gives the best view of the call stack and variable values at the moment of the exception (rather than later when the crash actually occurs); you can see where you are in your code, and you can examine variable values, which may help you understand the cause of the problem. If you do create such an exception breakpoint, I also suggest that you use the contextual menu to say Move Breakpoint To → User, which makes this breakpoint permanent and global to all your projects.

*Symbolic breakpoint*

A symbolic breakpoint causes your app to pause when a certain method is called, regardless of what object called it or to what object the message is sent. The method name is entered in a special way — the instance method or class method symbol (- or +) followed by square brackets containing the class name and the method name. For example, to learn where in my app the `beginReceivingRemoteControl-Events` message was being sent to my shared application instance, I configured a symbolic breakpoint like this:

```
-[UIApplication beginReceivingRemoteControlEvents]
```

Breakpoints as a whole can be active or inactive: click the Breakpoints button in the project window toolbar or choose Product → Debug → Activate/Deactivate Breakpoints (Command-Y). The active status of breakpoints as a whole doesn't affect the enabled or disabled status of any breakpoints; if breakpoints are inactive, they are simply ignored en masse, and no pausing at breakpoints takes place. Breakpoint arrows are blue if breakpoints are active, gray if they are inactive.

When the app runs with breakpoints active and an enabled breakpoint is encountered (and assuming its conditions are met, and so on), the app pauses. In the active project window, the editor shows the file containing the point of execution, which will usually be the file containing the breakpoint. The point of execution is shown as a green arrow; this is the line that is *about* to be executed (Figure 9-6). Depending on the settings for "Run pauses" in the Behaviors preference pane, the Debug navigator and the Debug pane will also appear.

Here are some things you might like to do while paused at a breakpoint:

*See where you are*

One common reason for setting a breakpoint is to make sure that the path of ex-ecution is passing through a certain line. You can see where you are in any of your methods by clicking on the method name in the call stack, shown in the Debug navigator.

Methods listed in the call stack with a User icon, with the text in black, are yours; click one to see where you are paused in that method. Other methods, with the text in gray, are methods for which you have no source code, so there would be little point clicking one unless you know something about assembly language. The slider at the bottom of the navigator hides chunks of the call chain, to save space, starting with the methods for which you have no source. Highlight (lighten) the "Σ" icon at the bottom left of the navigator to hide all threads for which you have no source.

 You can also navigate the call stack using the jump bar at the top of the Debug pane.

*Study variable values*

This is a very common reason for pausing. In the Debug pane, variable values for the current scope (corresponding to what's selected in the call stack) are visible in the variables list. You can see additional object features, such as collection ele-ments, instance variables, and even some private information, by opening triangles. Switch the pop-up menu above the variables list to Auto to see only those variables that Xcode thinks will interest you (because their value has been recently changed, for instance); if you're after completeness, Local will probably be the best setting. You can use the search field to filter variables by name or value.

In some cases, unchecking Enable Data Formatters in the contextual menu can cause display of variables to be more reliable. However, in that case some object variable values may not be displayed in useful form. But you can always send `description` to an object variable and view the output in the console by selecting Print Description from the contextual menu.

*Set a watchpoint*

A watchpoint is like a breakpoint, but instead of depending on a certain line of code it depends on a variable's value: the debugger pauses whenever the variable's value changes. You can set a watchpoint only while paused in the debugger. Control-click on the variable in the variables list and choose Watch Address of [Variable]. Watchpoints, once created, are listed and managed in the Breakpoint navigator.

*Manage expressions*

An expression is code to be added to the variables list and evaluated every time we pause. Choose Add Expression from the contextual menu in the variables list.

*Talk to the debugger*

You can communicate verbally with the debugger in the console. The most common command is `po` (for "print object") followed by an object variable's name or a method call that returns an object; it calls the object's `description` method, just like NSLog.

> Xcode's debugger is a front end to an open source third-party command-line debugger tool. Thus, by talking directly to that command-line tool you can do everything that you can do through the Xcode debugger interface, and more. Throughout the history of Xcode up through through Xcode 3.2.x, the debugger tool has been GDB; see *Debugging with GDB*. Starting in Xcode 4.0, the debugger LLDB is available as an alternative (*http://lldb.llvm.org*), but at the time of this writing it is not yet enabled for iOS projects, so this book assumes you're using GDB.

*Fiddle with breakpoints*

You are free to create, destroy, enable and disable, and otherwise manage breakpoints dynamically even though your app is running, which is useful because where you'd like to pause next might depend on what you learn while you're paused here.

*Step or continue*

To proceed with your app, you can either resume running (Product → Debug → Continue) until the next breakpoint is encountered or take one step and pause again. Also, if you hover the mouse over the gutter, a green Continue to Here button lets you resume and then pause at the line you specified, treating the line temporarily as it if had a breakpoint without actually setting a breakpoint there.

The stepping commands (under Product → Debug) are:

*Step Over*

Pause at the next line.

*Step Into*

Pause in your method that the current line calls, if there is one; otherwise, pause at the next line.

*Step Out*

Pause when we return from the current method.

You can access these commands through convenient buttons at the top of the Debug pane. Even if the Debug pane is collapsed, the part containing the buttons appears while running. You can also float the project window over everything else on your computer by choosing Product → Window Behavior → Xcode In Front;

after you then switch to the Simulator, you can interact with the Xcode window without giving it focus. If you do want to give it focus, to type in a filter bar for instance, click Focus in the toolbar. This mode of working could be useful while you're interacting with the Simulator, so as not to have keep switching between the Simulator and Xcode. To end it, choose Normal from the Debugging pop-up menu in the window toolbar.

 Step Over and Step Into have advanced forms where you hold Control to step by machine-level instruction, and Control-Shift to step while blocking all other threads.

*Start over, or abort*

To kill the running app, click Stop in the toolbar (Product → Stop, Command-Period). To kill the running app and relaunch it without rebuilding it, Control-click Run in the toolbar (Product → Perform Action → Run Without Building, Control-Command-R). You can make changes to your code while the app is running or paused, but they are not magically communicated to the running app; you must run in the normal way (which includes building) to see your changes in action.

 Clicking the Home button in the Simulator or on the device does *not* stop the running app in the iOS 4 multitasking world.

# Static Analyzer

From time to time, you should use the static analyzer to look for possible sources of error in your code; choose Product → Analyze (Shift-Command-B). This command causes your code to be compiled, and the static analyzer studies it and reports its findings in the Issue navigator and in your code.

The static analyzer is static — it's analyzing your code, not debugging in real time — but it is remarkably intelligent and may well alert you to potential problems that could otherwise escape your notice. For example, there are two memory leaks in the Empty Window project as we've developed it in previous chapters; this is deliberate, because we haven't yet discussed memory management (we'll discuss it, and fix these leaks, in Chapter 12). The static analyzer correctly reports them.

The static analyzer isn't perfect, and can result in false warnings, but think of it as notifying you of things to think about rather than as listing definite issues. For more about the static analyzer, see *http://clang-analyzer.llvm.org*.

# Clean

From time to time, during repeated testing and debugging, and before making a different sort of build (switching from Debug to Release, or running on a device instead of the Simulator), it is a good idea to *clean* your target. This means that existing builds will be removed and caches will be cleared, so that all code will be considered to be in need of compilation and the next build will build your app from scratch.

The first build of your app after you clean will take longer than usual. But it's worth it, because cleaning removes the cruft, quite literally. For example, suppose you have been including a certain resource in your app, and you decide it is no longer needed. You can remove it from the Copy Bundle Resources build phase, but that doesn't remove it from your built app. Only cleaning will do that, because it removes the built app completely.

To clean, choose Product → Clean. For more complete cleaning, hold Option to get Product → Clean Build Folder.

You should also from time to time remove all versions of your built app from the Simulator cache. Choose iOS Simulator → Reset Content and Settings. Alternatively, you can clean the cache by hand. To do so, first quit the Simulator if it's running. Then find the cache in *~/Library/Application Support/iPhone Simulator*, followed by the system version of the SDK (for example, there might be a folder called *4.3*); within this, find the *Applications* folder, and move the contents of that folder to the trash.

In addition, Xcode 4 stores builds and project indexes in *~/Library/Developer/Xcode/ DerivedData*. From time to time, with Xcode not running, I like to move the contents of that folder to the trash. A project will take longer to open for the first time afterward, because its index must be rebuilt, and it will take longer to build, because its build information has been removed. But the space savings on your hard disk can be significant.

# Running in the Simulator

When you build and run with Simulator as the destination, you run in the iOS Simulator application. There's little to say about running in the Simulator, because it's so intuitive. The Simulator window represents a device, and you can interact with it in some of the same basic ways as you would a device. Using the mouse, you can press the Home button and tap on the device's screen; hold Option to make the mouse represent two fingers and Option-Shift to move those fingers in parallel. Menu items let you perform hardware gestures such as rotating the device, shaking it, and locking its screen; you can also test your app by simulating certain rare events, such as a low-memory situation.

What hardware and system the Simulator simulates depends upon your choices in Hardware → Device and Hardware → Version. If your app runs on either iPhone or iPad, you can choose which device is simulated as you choose your destination. The iPhone

4 device, Hardware → Device → iPhone (Retina), is displayed at double size, so that each pixel of the Retina display corresponds to a pixel of your computer's monitor. The iPad device can be displayed at half or full size (choose from Window → Scale).

# Running on a Device

Sooner or later, you're going to want to switch from running and testing and debugging in the Simulator to running and testing and debugging on a real device. The Simulator is nice, but it's only a simulation; there are many differences between the Simulator and a real device. The Simulator is really your computer, which is fast and has lots of memory, so problems with memory management and speed won't be exposed until you run on a device. User interaction with the Simulator is limited to what can be done with a mouse: you can click, you can drag, you can hold Option to simulate use of two fingers, but more elaborate gestures can be performed only on an actual device. And many iOS facilities, such as the accelerometer and access to the music library, are not present on the Simulator at all, so that testing an app that uses them is possible *only* on a device.

Don't even think of developing an app without testing it on a device. You have no idea how your app *really* looks and behaves until you run it on a device. Submitting to the App Store an app that you have not run on a device is asking for trouble.

Before you can run your app on a device, even just to test, you must join the iOS Developer Program by paying the annual fee. (Yes, this is infuriating. Now get over it.) Only in this way can you obtain and provide to Xcode the credentials for running on a device. Once you have joined the iOS Developer Program, obtaining these credentials involves use of the iOS Provisioning Portal, which is accessed online, through your web browser (or, for certain actions, through Xcode itself).

To reach the iOS Provisioning Portal in your browser (once you're an iOS Developer Program member), go to *http://developer.apple.com/dev center/ios*. Click Log In to log in, and then click iOS Provisioning Portal at the upper right.

You will need to perform the following steps just once:

1. Join the iOS Developer Program (*http://developer.apple.com/programs/ios*). This requires filling out a form and paying the annual fee. Unless you have multiple developers, all of whom might need to build and run on their own devices, the Individual program is sufficient. The Company program costs no more, but adds the ability to privilege additional developers in various roles. (You do *not* need the

Company program just in order to distribute your built app to other users for testing.)

2. Obtain a *development certificate* that identifies and authorizes your computer. This is the computer to which you'll be attaching the device so you can run on it. Basically, this certificate matches the person who uses your computer to the person interacting with the iOS Provisioning Portal. The certificate will be stored in your computer's keychain, where Xcode will be able to see it automatically.

The certificate depends upon a private–public key pair. The private key will live in your keychain; the public key will be handed over to the iOS Provisioning Portal, to be built into the certificate. The way you give the Portal your public key is through a *request* for the certificate. So, you generate the private–public key pair; your keychain keeps the private key; the public key goes into the certificate request; you submit the request, containing the public key, to the Portal; and the Portal sends back the certificate, also containing the public key, which also goes into your keychain, where it is matched with the private key, thus ensuring that you are you.

Detailed instructions for generating the private–public key pair and the certificate request are available once you've joined the iOS Developer Program and have logged in at Apple's developer site. (A video review of the steps involved is available to anyone at *http://developer.apple.com/ios/videos/popupcerts.action*.) Basically, you start up Keychain Access and choose Keychain Access → Certificate Assistant → Request a Certificate from a Certificate Authority. Using your name and email address as identifiers, you generate and save to disk a 2048-bit RSA certificate request file. Your private key is stored in your keychain then and there; the certificate request contains your public key.

You then go to the iOS Provisioning Portal in your browser. At the Portal, upload the certificate request file using the Development (not Distribution!) tab of the Certificates section. You may have to approve your own request.

 If this is your very, very first time obtaining any certificate from the Portal, you will need *another* certificate: the WWDR Intermediate Certificate. This is the certificate that certifies that certificates issued by WWDR (the Apple Worldwide Developer Relations Certification Authority) are to be trusted. (You can't make this stuff up.) You'll see a link for this intermediate certificate; click it to download the intermediate certificate. Double-click the intermediate certificate file; it is imported by your keychain. You can then throw the file away.

When the development certificate itself is ready, you download it and double-click it; Keychain Access automatically imports the certificate and stores it in your keychain. You do not need to keep the certificate request file or the development certificate file; your keychain contains all the needed credentials. If this has worked, you can see the certificate in your keychain, read its details, and observe that it is valid and linked to

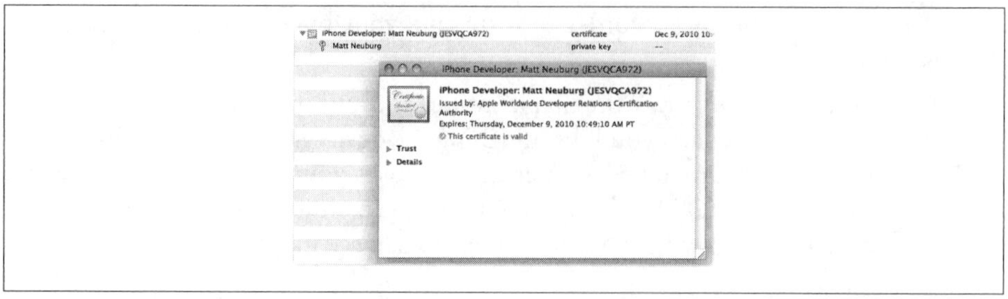

*Figure 9-7. A valid development certificate, as shown in Keychain Access*

your private key (Figure 9-7). After you've done this once, your development certificate is good for all your app development from now on. (However, your development certificate expires when your year of iOS Developer Program membership expires; if you renew your membership, you'll have to revoke your current development certificate at the Portal, delete it from your keychain, and repeat the process of obtaining a new one.)

With your development certificate in place, you need to register a device for development use, meaning that you'll be able to build and run from Xcode onto that device rather than the Simulator. This can be done entirely from within Xcode. Open the Organizer window (Window → Organizer) and switch to the Devices tab. Select Provisioning Profiles at the left, and make sure Automatic Device Provisioning is checked at the bottom of the window. Attach your device to the computer; the device name appears at the left under Devices. Select it, and click Use For Development. You'll be asked for your Portal username and password. Xcode connects to the Portal via the Internet and does two things:

- It registers your device at the Portal by its name and unique identifier number. You could have done this yourself in your browser (at the Portal, under Devices), but this way it is done for you.

- It creates and downloads from the Portal a universal development provisioning profile (referred to as a Team Provisioning Profile) for development on this device. This is something you can't do at the Portal yourself. A development provisioning profile created manually at the Portal applies to a single app; in the past, when the Portal was the only way to obtain a development provisioning profile, you had to generate a new development provisioning profile for each app you wanted to test on a device, which was very inconvenient. But the development provisioning profile generated by Xcode applies to all apps, now and in the future (until it expires, at which time it can be easily regenerated). The universal development provisioning profile appears in the Organizer, under Provisioning Profiles; you can identify it because it is called Team Provisioning Profile and has an app identifier consisting of just a key and an asterisk, like this: B398E68A3D.*.

If you develop an app that uses certain specialized features, such as push notifications (Chapter 37) or in-app purchases, you must generate a development provisioning profile the old way, manually at the Portal. To do so, first enter your app by name and bundle id in the App IDs section of the Portal. Now go to Provisioning and the Development section and generate a new provisioning profile, specifying that app and your device(s). You can then download the provisioning profile in the Organizer window, under Provisioning Profiles, by clicking the Refresh button.

You can install the provisioning profile onto your device manually in the Organizer window by dragging its listing (under Provisioning Profiles) onto the device's name (under Devices). Alternatively, you can just start building and running on the device. Start with a project window. With the device attached to the computer, pick the destination in the Scheme pop-up menu corresponding to your device; then build and run. If Xcode complains that your device doesn't contain a copy of the provisioning profile, and offers to install it for you, accept that offer.

The app is built, loaded onto your device, and runs. As long as you launch the app from Xcode, everything is just as it was before: you can run, or you can debug, and the running app is in communication with Xcode, so that you can stop at breakpoints, read messages in the console, and so on. The outward difference is that to interact physically with the app, you use the device, not the Simulator.

## Device Management

Your central location for management of identities (certificates), provisioning profiles, and devices is the Devices tab of the Organizer window (Window → Organizer). Under Library, select Developer Profile to see your identities and provisioning profiles. Select Provisioning Profiles for another list of profiles.

When your device is attached to the computer, it is listed with a green dot under Devices. Click its name to access information on the device. You can see the device's unique identifier. You can see provisioning profiles that have been installed on the device. You can view the device's console log in real time, just as if you were running the Console application to view your computer's logs. You can see log reports for crashes that took place on the device. And you can take screenshots that image your device's screen; you'll need to do this for your app when you submit it to the App Store. Crash reports and screenshots are also available under Library.

## Version Control

Various systems of *version control* exist for taking periodic snapshots (technically called *commits*) of your project. The value of such a system to you will depend on what system you use and how you use it; for example, you might use version control because it lets you store your commits in a repository offsite, so that your code isn't lost in case of a local computer glitch or some equivalent "hit by a bus" scenario, or because it allows multiple developers to access the same code.

To me, personally, the chief value of version control is *freedom from fear*. Having version control actually changes the way I program. A project is a complicated thing, consisting of numerous files. Often, changes must be made in many files before a new feature can be tested. Thus it is all too easy to start down some virtual road involving creating or editing multiple files, only to find yourself at the end of a blind alley and needing to retrace your steps. Version control means that I can easily retrace my steps; I have but to say, in the language of some version control system I've been using, "Forget everything I just did and return the whole project to where it was at such-and-such a commit." I rarely, if ever, *in fact* retrace my steps, but the knowledge that I *could* do so gives me the courage to try some programming strategy whose outcome may not be apparent until after many days of effort. Also, I can ask a version control system, "What the heck are all the changes I've made since the last commit?" In short, without version control I'd be lost, confused, hesitant, rooted to the spot, paralyzed with uncertainty; with it, I forge boldly ahead and get things done. For this reason, my current personal favorite version control system is git (*http://git-scm.com*), whose agile facilities for managing branches give me tremendous license to experiment.

Xcode provides various version control facilities. Starting with Xcode 4, those facilities concentrate on git and Subversion (*http://subversion.apache.org*). This doesn't mean you can't use any other version control system with your projects! It means only that you can't use any other version control system in an integrated fashion from inside Xcode. Personally, I don't find that to be any kind of restriction. For years I've used Subversion, and more recently git, on my Xcode projects from the command line in Terminal, or using other third-party GUI front ends (such as svnX for Subversion, *http://www.lachoseinteractive.net/en/products*). I'm comfortable and nimble at the command line, and access to version control from within Xcode itself is not a priority for me.

At the same time, version control integration in Xcode 4 is greatly improved and far more extensive than previously:

*Automatic git repository creation*
> When you create a new project in Xcode 4, the Save dialog includes a checkbox that offers to place a git repository into your project folder from the outset.

*Automatic repository detection*
> When you open an existing project in Xcode 4, if that project is already managed with Subversion or git, Xcode detects this and is ready instantly to display version control information in its interface.

*Version comparison*
> The Version editor (View → Editor → Version) includes a view similar to that of the File Merge utility, graphically displaying the differences between versions of a file.

*Figure 9-8. Version comparison*

For example, in Figure 9-8, I can see that in the more recent version of this file (on the left) I've shifted a line upward. The Version editor also includes various ways to survey and navigate versions and commit logs.

Without minimizing these features, I've no plans to rely on them exclusively or even primarily (although I'll certainly take advantage of them where convenient). I find version control management through the command line far easier and clearer for many purposes, and Xcode doesn't come close to the command line's power, especially for managing branches (and Xcode has nothing like the visual branch representation of git's own gitk tool).

Version control in general is a large and complicated topic. Use and configuration of any version control system can be tricky and scary at first and always requires some care. So I'm deliberately not going to say anything specific about it; I'm mentioning it at all only because version control of some sort is in fact likely, sooner or later, to play a role in the life cycle of your projects. When it does, you'll want to read up on the use of your chosen version control system, along with "Managing Versions of Your Project" in the *Xcode 4 User Guide*. You'll find Xcode 4's integrated version control facilities in three chief locations:

*The File menu*
The relevant menu items are all under File → Source Control.

*The Version editor*
Choose View → Editor → Version, or click the third button in the Editor segmented control in the project window toolbar.

*The Organizer*
The Repositories tab of the Organizer window lists known repositories and branches for each project, along with their commit logs. Also, use the "+" button at the bottom of the navigator to enter data about a remote repository, so that you can obtain a copy of its contents.

Xcode also contains its own way of taking and storing a snapshot of your project as a whole; this is done using File → Create Snapshot (and, according to your settings, some mass operations such as find-and-replace or refactoring may offer to take a snapshot first). Snapshots themselves are managed in the Projects tab of the Organizer window. Although these snapshots are basically just simple copies of your project, and should not be regarded as any kind of serious version control, they can certainly serve the purpose of giving confidence in advance of performing some change that might subsequently engender regret.

# Instruments

As your app approaches completion, you may wish to fine-tune it for memory usage, speed, and other real-time behavior. Xcode provides a sophisticated and powerful utility application, Instruments, that lets you collect profiling data on your app as it runs. The graphical display and detailed data provided by Instruments may give you the clues you need to optimize your app.

You can use Instruments on the Simulator or the device. The device is where you'll do your ultimate testing, and certain instruments (such as Core Animation) are available only for the device; on the other hand, certain other instruments (such as Zombies) are available only in the Simulator.

To get started with Instruments, set the desired destination in the Scheme pop-up menu in the project window toolbar, and choose Product → Profile. Your app builds using the Profile action for your scheme; by default, this uses the Release build configuration, which is probably what you want. Instruments launches; if your scheme's Instrument pop-up menu for the Profile action is set to Ask on Launch, Instruments presents a dialog where you choose a trace template. With Instruments running, you should interact with your app like a user; Instruments will record its statistics. Once Instruments is running, it can be further customized to profile the kind of data that particularly interests you, and you can save the structure of the Instruments window as a custom template.

Use of Instruments is an advanced topic and beyond the scope of this book. Indeed, an entire book could (and really should) be written about Instruments alone. (But don't be put off by that fact, because Instruments is really useful; it is the best way to discover, for example, that you're leaking memory, or why your app is taking so long to launch.) Instruments 4 (which accompanies Xcode 4) is easier to use than earlier versions, and many interface features will feel similar to Xcode 4 itself. Read Apple's document, *Instruments User Guide*. Also, many WWDC 2010 videos are about Instruments; look for sessions with "Instruments" or "Performance" in their names.

# Distribution

By *distribution* is meant providing your app to others who are not developers on your team. There are two kinds of distribution:

*Ad Hoc distribution*
> You are providing a copy of your app to a limited set of known users so that they can try it on their devices and report bugs, make suggestions, and so forth.

*App Store distribution*
> You are providing the app to the App Store so that anyone can download it (possibly for a fee) and run it.

The Portal imposes a registration limit of 100 devices per year *per developer* (not per app), which limits your number of Ad Hoc testers. Your own devices used for development are counted against this limit.

In order to perform any kind of distribution, you will need a *distribution certificate*, which is different from the development certificate discussed earlier in this chapter. Like the development certificate, you need only one distribution certificate; it identifies you as you. Obtaining a distribution certificate is exactly like obtaining a development certificate, except that, at the iOS Provisioning Portal, under Certificates, you use the Distribution tab instead of the Development tab. (And, like the development certificate, it expires when your year of iOS Developer Program membership expires; if you renew, you'll have to revoke your distribution certificate at the Portal, delete it from your keychain, and obtain a new distribution certificate.)

You will also need a *distribution profile* specifically for this app, which is different from the development profile you obtained earlier. You can't obtain a distribution profile from within Xcode; you must get it at the Portal in your browser. You might need *two* distribution profiles, because the profile for an Ad Hoc distribution is different from the profile for an App Store distribution. Remember, you will need a separate set of distribution profiles for each app you plan to distribute.

When you build for distribution, you'll use the Product → Archive command. Indeed, you can think of *archive* as meaning "build for distribution." (Product → Archive isn't enabled unless your destination in the Scheme pop-up menu is a device.) If you look at the Archive action in your default scheme, you'll discover that it is set to use the Release distribution configuration. But if you examine the Code Signing Identity build setting for your project, you'll see that by default it uses the team development profile. This won't do. When you archive, you want to use a distribution profile. The solution is to create a Distribution build configuration; you can then set the Archive action in your scheme to use the Distribution build configuration, and set the Code Signing Identity build setting to use the distribution profile when the Distribution build configuration is in force.

First, here are the steps for obtaining a distribution profile:

1. To obtain an Ad Hoc distribution profile, collect the unique identifiers of all the devices where this build is to run, and add each of the device identifiers at the Portal under Devices. (For an App Store profile, omit this step.)

2. In the Portal, in the Distribution (not Development!) tab of the Provisioning section, ask for a New Profile. In the New Profile form, ask for an Ad Hoc profile or an App Store profile, depending on which you're after.

3. Describe the profile, giving it a name, and specifying your distribution certificate and this app. For an Ad Hoc profile, also specify all the devices you want the app to run on. Be careful about the profile's name; I suggest that this name should

contain both the name of the app and the term "adhoc" or "appstore," so that you can identify it later easily from within Xcode.

4. Click Submit to generate the profile; you might then have to refresh the browser window to see the Download button next to your new profile. Download the profile and drag it onto Xcode's icon in the Dock. You can now throw the profile away in the Finder; Xcode has kept a copy (which should appear in the Organizer window).

Now here are the steps to create a separate build configuration for your project:

1. Edit the project. In the Info tab, duplicate the Release configuration. Name the new configuration Distribution.

2. Edit the project (still). In the Build Settings tab, locate the Code Signing Identity entry. The Distribution build setting is now listed here. For the subentry Any iOS Device, set the value of this to a distribution profile for this app. (I believe it won't matter which distribution profile you choose; the important thing here is that you're specifying a profile that is tied to your distribution certificate.)

3. Edit the scheme, and switch to the Archive action. Change the build configuration to Distribution, and click OK.

## Ad Hoc Distribution

To create and distribute an Ad Hoc distribution build, first switch to the iOS Device destination in the Scheme pop-up menu in the project window toolbar. Until you do this, the Product → Archive menu item will be disabled. You do *not* have to have a device connected; you are not building to run on a particular device, but to save an archive.

Apple's docs say that an Ad Hoc distribution build should include an icon that will appear in iTunes, but my experience is that this step is optional. If you want to include this icon, it should be a PNG or JPEG file, 512×512 pixels in size, and its name should be *iTunesArtwork*, with *no file extension*. Make sure the icon is included in the build, being present in the Copy Bundle Resources build phase.

Now choose Product → Archive. The build is created and copied into a date folder within *~/Library/Developer/Xcode/Archives*; it also appears in the Organizer window in the Archives tab. Locate the archive in the Organizer window. You can add a comment here; you can also change the archive's name (this won't affect the name of the app).

Select the archive and press the Share button at the upper right of the window. A dialog appears. Here, you are to specify a Contents type; choose iOS App Store Package (the default). You must also choose an Identity; specify the identity associated with the Ad

Hoc distribution profile for this app. (This is the step in which it matters which of the app's distribution profiles you specify.) Click Next.

After a while, a Save dialog appears. Give the file a useful name (again, this won't affect the name of the app). Save the file to disk. It will have the suffix *.ipa* ("iPhone app").

Locate in the Finder the file you just saved. Provide this file to your users with instructions. A user should launch iTunes and drag the *.ipa* file onto the iTunes icon in the Dock. Then the user should connect the device to the computer, make certain the app is present *and checked* in the list of apps for this device, and sync the device to cause the app to be copied to it.

If you listed your own device as one of the devices for which this Ad Hoc distribution profile was to be enabled, you can obey these instructions yourself to make sure the Ad Hoc distribution is working as expected. First, remove from your device any previous copies of this app (such as development copies). Then copy the app onto your device by syncing with iTunes as just described. The app should run on your device, and you should see the Ad Hoc distribution profile on your device (in the Settings app, under General → Profiles). Because you are not privileged over your other Ad Hoc testers, what works for you should work for them.

# Final App Preparations

As the day approaches when you're thinking of submitting your app to the App Store, don't let the prospect of huge fame or big profits hasten you past the all-important final stages of app preparation. Apple has a lot of requirements for your app, such as icons and launch images, and failure to meet them can cause your app to be rejected. Take your time. Make a checklist and go through it carefully. See the *iOS Application Programming Guide* for full details.

Xcode 4 makes it easier than in the past for you to fulfill these requirements, by providing interface for doing so. Edit the target, and switch to the Summary tab; there are spaces where for an iPhone app you can drag-and-drop normal and double-resolution icons, and normal and double-resolution launch images, and for an iPad app you can drag-and-drop an iPad icon along with portrait and landscape launch images.

At various stages, you can also obtain validation of your app to confirm that you haven't omitted certain requirements. For example, by default, a new project's Release build configuration has the Validate Build Product build setting set to Yes. Thus, when I do a build of the Empty Window app we've developed in previous chapters, if that build uses the Release build configuration (or the Distribution build configuration duplicated from it), Xcode warns that the app has no icon. When you submit your app to the App Store, it will be subjected to even more rigorous validation.

## Icons in the App

An icon file must be a PNG file, without any alpha transparency, with an exact pixel size. It should be a full square, without shading (the "shine" effect that you see in the upper part of icons on your device); the rounding of the corners and shine will be added for you. You can prevent the shine effect from being added to the icon for your App Store build by defining and checking the "Icon already includes gloss and bevel effects" (UIPrerenderedIcon) key in your *Info.plist*. Make sure that the icon is copied into the built app by inclusion in the Copy Bundle Resources build phase. The required size is as follows:

- For an iPhone app that is to run on iOS 3.1.3 or before, the icon file should be 57×57 pixels in size.
- For an iPad app, the icon file should be 72×72 pixels in size.
- For an iPhone app that is to run on iOS 4, there should be two primary app icons, one 57×57 pixels, the other 114×114 pixels (for use on the double-resolution Retina display). A double-resolution variant of an icon should have the same name as the single-resolution variant, except for the addition of @2x to its name.

As I mentioned earlier, in Xcode 4 you can drag-and-drop the required icons into the appropriate spaces in the Summary tab when you're editing the target, and Xcode itself will incorporate them into the project and the target and configure the *Info.plist* for you. For example, if I drop a 57×57 PNG file called *myDumbIcon.png* onto the first icon space, it is copied into the project and added to the target, and the first element in the "Icon files" key in my *Info.plist* becomes myDumbIcon.png.

Alternatively, you can specify the icon file(s) manually using the *Info.plist*. In this case, you will have to add the relevant key–value pairs manually. The keys work as follows:

- If the app is to run on iOS 3.1.3 or before, set the "Icon file" (CFBundleIconFile) key's value in your *Info.plist* to the name of the icon (including the file extension).
- If the app is to run on iOS 3.2 or later, set the "Icon files" key's value (CFBundle-IconFiles, and notice the plural!); this value is an array, so you can list multiple icons.
- If the app is to run both on iOS 3.1.3 or before and on iOS 3.2 or later, use *both* keys.

You may also optionally include smaller versions of your icon to appear when the user does a search on the device (and in the Settings app, if you include a settings bundle, Chapter 36). The smaller icon sizes are 29×29 pixels (for an iPhone app), 50×50 pixels (for an iPad app), and 58×58 pixels (for an iPhone 4 app, on the double-resolution display). List the icons in the "Icon files" key. If the app is to run on iOS 3.1.3 or before, the 29×29 icon must be named *Icon-Small.png*.

The system determines which icon listed under the "Icon files" key to use under what circumstances by examining their sizes. That's one reason why the sizes must be exactly correct.

For more information, see Apple's tech note QA1686, "App Icons on iPad and iPhone."

## Other Icons

When you submit the app to the App Store, you will be asked to supply a 512×512 PNG, JPEG, or TIFF icon to be displayed at the App Store. Have this icon ready before submission. Apple's guidelines say that it should not merely be a scaled-up version of your app's icon, but it must not differ perceptibly from your app's icon, either, or your app will be rejected (I know this from experience).

The App Store icon does *not* need to be built into your app; indeed, it should not be, as it will merely swell the built app's size unnecessarily (remember that space is at a premium on a device, and that your app must be downloaded from the App Store, so users appreciate your keeping your app as small as possible). On the other hand, you will probably want to keep it in your project (and in your project folder) so that you can find and maintain it easily. So create it and import it into your project, but do *not* add it to any target.

 If you created a 512×512 icon file for Ad Hoc distribution, you may wish to delete it from the Copy Bundle Resources build phase now so that it doesn't swell the final app's size unnecessarily.

## Launch Images

There may be a delay between the moment when the user taps your app's icon to launch it and the moment when your app is up and running and displaying its initial window. To cover this delay and give the user the sense that something is happening, you should provide a launch image to be displayed during that interval.

The launch image might be just a blank depiction of the main elements or regions of the app's interface, so that when the actual window appears, those elements or regions will seem to be filled in. The best way to create such a launch image is to start with a screenshot of your app's actual initial interface. That way, all you have to do is blank out the details. You don't need to blank out the status bar area; it will be covered by the real status bar. Taking screenshots is covered in the next section.

For an iPhone app, the launch image should be a PNG image, 320×480 pixels in size. It should be named *Default.png*. Create the launch image, import it into the project, and make sure it is built into the app, being present in the Copy Bundle Resources build phase. For iOS 4 and the double-resolution Retina display, provide a second version of the launch image, 640×960 pixels, called *Default@2x.png*.

For an iPad app, you will probably provide at least *two* launch images. Here's why. On the iPhone, you get to dictate the orientation in which the app should launch (landscape or portrait), so you can be certain that the default image matches this. But on the iPad, you're not supposed to do that; your app should be prepared to launch in whatever orientation the device happens to be. Thus, you need a launch image for landscape orientation and a launch image for portrait orientation. The landscape image should be called *Default-Landscape.png*; it should be 748 pixels high and 1024 pixels wide. The portrait image should be called *Default-Portrait.png*; it should be 1004 pixels high and 768 pixels wide. Observe that these sizes omit the status bar area, unlike the iPhone launch image.

You can use the orientation suffixes in the names of launch images on iOS 4 as well. To distinguish between a launch image to be used on the iPhone and a launch image with the same orientation suffix to be used on the iPad, use additional suffixes ~ipad and ~iphone. Thus you can end up with file names like *Default-Portrait@2x~ipad.png*. To make things even more confusing, you can replace *Default* with some other base name by creating the "Launch image" key in your *Info.plist* file and setting its value appropriately — but only on iOS 3.2 and later.

As I mentioned earlier, in Xcode 4 you can drag-and-drop the required icons into the appropriate spaces in the Summary tab when you're editing the target. For example, if I drop a 320×480 PNG file called *myLaunchImage.png* onto the first launch image space, it is copied into the project and added to the target, and the copy is renamed *Default.png*.

## Screenshots

When you submit the app to the App Store, you will be asked for one or more screenshots of your app in action to be displayed at the App Store. You should take these screenshots beforehand and be prepared to provide them during the app submission process.

The best way to obtain these screenshots is through the Organizer window in Xcode. Connect your device to your computer and run the app. Get it into a state suitable for display at the App Store. In the Organizer window, locate your device under Devices and click Screenshots. Click New Screenshot, at the lower right of the window, to capture an image. Repeat until you have gathered the desired screenshots.

To make screenshots available for upload, select each one in the left side of the window and click Export to save it with a nice filename into the Finder. Apple asks that if the status bar is visible in a screenshot, you remove it. And you may need to rotate a screenshot to get it into the correct orientation.

To make a screenshot a launch image (see the previous section), select it in the list and click Save as Launch Image. A dialog will ask you what name to assign to it and what open project to add it to.

# Property List Settings

A number of settings in *Info.plist* are crucial to the proper behavior of your app. You should peruse Apple's *Information Property List Key Reference* for full information. Most of the required keys are created as part of the template, and are given reasonable default values, but you should check them anyway. In addition to those already mentioned in Chapter 6, the following are particularly worthy of attention:

*Bundle version* (CFBundleVersion)
> A version string, such as "1.0". This version number will appear at the App Store, and you should increment it when you develop and submit an update to an existing app. Failure to increment the version string when submitting an update will cause the update to be rejected.

*Status bar style* (UIStatusBarStyle)
> On the iPhone and iPod touch, the look of the status bar. (On the iPad, the status bar is always black opaque.) Your choices are "Gray style" (UIStatusBarStyle-Default), "Opaque black style" (UIStatusBarStyleBlackOpaque), and "Transparent black style" (UIStatusBarStyleBlackTranslucent). This setting will be used in conjunction with your launch image, even before the app is actually running. If the status bar is to be hidden initially, set "Status bar is initially hidden" (UIStatusBar-Hidden) instead.

*Supported interface orientations* (UISupportedInterfaceOrientations)
> The initial orientation(s) in which the app is permitted to launch. (The app may support additional orientations later as it runs.) In Xcode 4, you can perform this setting graphically in the Summary tab when editing your target.

*Required device capabilities* (UIRequiredDeviceCapabilities)
> You should set this key if the app requires capabilities that are not present on all devices. Be sure to look over the list of possible values. Don't use this key unless it makes no sense for your app to run *at all* on a device lacking the specified capabilities.

Property list settings can adopt different values depending on what device type you're running on. To specify that a property list setting applies only on a particular type of device, you add to its key the suffix ~iphone, ~ipod, or ~ipad. This feature is typically useful in a universal app, in which the distinction will be between iPhone and iPod, on the one hand, and iPad on the other. The general setting is used unless there is an applicable specific case, so in a universal app you might have one setting with no suffix and a second setting with the ~ipad suffix. Thus, for example, you could have a different set of supported initial interface orientations on the iPad by adding settings for "Supported interface orientations (iPad)" (UISupportedInterfaceOrientations~ipad).

# Submission to the App Store

When you're satisfied that your app works well, and you've installed or collected all the necessary resources, you're ready to submit your app to the App Store for distribution. The primary way to submit your app is through a website called iTunes Connect. You can find a link to it on the iOS developer pages when you've logged in at Apple's site. You can go directly to *http://itunesconnect.apple.com*, but you'll still need to log in with your iOS Developer username and password.

The first thing you should do at iTunes Connect is download the *iTunes Connect Developer Guide*. It's a PDF that gives you a good idea what to expect when you submit your app, as well as later when you return for financial and other reports, and when you update your app.

You should also go to the Contracts section at iTunes Connect and complete submission of your contract if you haven't already done so. You can't offer any apps for sale until you do, and even free apps require completion of a contractual form.

When you submit an app to iTunes Connect, you will have to supply a description of fewer than 4,000 characters; Apple recommends fewer than 580 characters, and the first paragraph is the most important, because this may be all that users see when they visit the App Store. It must be pure text, without HTML and without character styling.

You will also be asked for a list of keywords: a comma-separated list shorter than 100 characters. These keywords will be used, in addition to your app's name, to help users discover your app through the Search feature of the App Store.

iTunes Connect will also expect you to provide a website where users can find more information about your app; it's good to have that ready in advance.

Now build the app. The procedure is exactly as for an Ad Hoc build. Set the destination to iOS Device in the Scheme pop-up menu in the project window toolbar, and choose Product → Archive.

The archived build that appears in the Organizer window can be used to generate either an Ad Hoc build or an App Store build. You can't test an App Store build. So if you want to test one last time, use this archived build to generate an Ad Hoc build and test with that. When you generate the App Store build, you use the exact same binary, so you are guaranteed that its behavior will be exactly the same as the build you tested. (That is one of the purposes of archiving.)

Enter your app's information at the iTunes Connect website. I'm not going to recite all the steps you have to go through, as these are described thoroughly in the *iTunes Connect Developer Guide*. But I'll just mention a few possible pitfalls:

*Your app's name*
> This is the name that will appear at the App Store; it need not be identical to the short name that will appear under the app's icon on the device, dictated by the

Bundle Display Name setting in your *Info.plist* file. This name can be up to 70 characters long, though Apple recommends that you limit it to 35 characters. You can get a rude shock when you submit your app's information to iTunes Connect and discover that the name you wanted is already taken. There is no reliable way to learn this in advance, and such a discovery can require a certain amount of scrambling on your part: you might have to Build and Archive your app yet again with a new name and possibly other last-minute changes.

*Copyright*
> Do not include a copyright symbol in this string; it will be added for you at the App Store.

*SKU number*
> This is unimportant, so don't get nervous about it. It's just a unique identifier, unique within the world of your own apps. It's convenient if it has something to do with your app's name. It needn't be a number; it can actually be any string.

*Price*
> You don't get to make up a price. You have to choose from a list of pricing "tiers."

*Availability Date*
> This setting has caused much consternation and confusion among developers. Apple suggests that you set the availability date to the date you submit the app; that way, when it is approved, it will be available immediately. The problem is that developers have complained that this limits the app's discoverability, because when the app is approved it doesn't appear in the App Store's list of new apps (because the availability date is too far in the distant past). The current consensus seems to be that this is not the issue it once was, and that you should just take Apple's advice and make it available now.

When you've submitted the information for your app, you can do a final validation check: return to the Organizer window, select the archived build, and click Validate. (This feature has not worked well for me in the past, however.)

Finally, when you're ready to upload the app for which you've already submitted the information at iTunes Connect, and when the iTunes Connect status for your app is "Waiting for Upload," you can perform the upload using Xcode. Select the archived build in the Organizer and click Submit, specifying the App Store distribution profile.

Alternatively, you can use Application Loader, an application located in */Developer/ Applications/Utilities/*, to upload the app. Application Loader first checks with iTunes Connect to see what apps are awaiting upload; pick the right one. In the Organizer, click Share and specify the App Store distribution profile. Find the exported app in the Finder and compress it; hand the resulting *.zip* file to Application Loader.

You will subsequently receive emails from Apple informing you of your app's status as it passes through various stages: "Waiting For Review," "In Review," and finally, if all has gone well, "Ready For Sale" (even if it's a free app). Your app will then appear at the App Store.

# PART III

# Cocoa

When you program for iOS, you take advantage of a suite of frameworks provided by Apple. These frameworks, taken together, constitute *Cocoa*; the brand of Cocoa that provides the API for programming iOS is *Cocoa Touch*. Cocoa thus plays an important and fundamental role in iOS programming; your code will ultimately be almost entirely about communicating with Cocoa — interacting with the frameworks provided by Apple, in order to make an app that does what you want it to do.

The Cocoa Touch frameworks are a huge boon to you, the programmer, because they provide the underlying functionality that any iOS app needs to have. Your app can put up a window, show the interface containing a button, respond to that button being tapped by the user, and so forth, because Cocoa knows how to do those things. But with the great advantages of working with a framework come great responsibilities. You have to think the way the framework thinks, put your code where the framework expects it, and fulfill many obligations imposed on you by the framework.

- Chapter 10 picks up where Chapter 5 left off, describing some Objective-C linguistic features used by Cocoa, such as categories and protocols; it also surveys some important fundamental classes.

- An *event* is a message sent by Cocoa to your code. Cocoa is event-based; if Cocoa doesn't send your code an event, your code doesn't run. Getting your code to run at the appropriate moment is all about knowing what events you can expect Cocoa to send you and when. Chapter 11 describes Cocoa's event-driven model, along with its major design patterns.

- Chapter 12 describes your responsibilities for making your instances nicely encapsulated and good memory-management citizens in the world of Cocoa objects.

- Chapter 13 surveys some answers to the question of how your objects are going to see and communicate with one another within the Cocoa-based world.

# Cocoa Classes

Using the Cocoa frameworks requires an understanding of how those frameworks organize their classes. Cocoa class organization depends upon certain Objective-C language features that are introduced in this chapter. The chapter also surveys some commonly used Cocoa utility classes, along with a discussion of the Cocoa root class.

## Subclassing

Cocoa effectively hands you a large repertory of objects that already know how to behave in certain desirable ways. A UIButton, for example, knows how to draw itself and how to respond when the user taps it; a UITextField knows how to summon the keyboard when the user taps in it, how to accept keyboard input, and how to respond when the user finishes inputting text.

Often, the default behavior or appearance of an object supplied by Cocoa won't be quite what you're after, and you'll want to customize it. Cocoa classes are heavily endowed with methods and properties for precisely this purpose, and these will be your first resort. Always study the documentation for a Cocoa class to see whether instances can already be made to do what you want. For example, the class documentation for UILabel (Chapter 27) shows that you can set the font, size, color, line-breaking behavior, and horizontal alignment of its text, among other things.

Nevertheless, sometimes setting properties and calling methods won't suffice to customize an instance the way you want to. In such cases, Cocoa may provide methods that are called internally as an instance does its thing, and whose behavior you can customize by subclassing and overriding. You don't have the code to any of Cocoa's built-in classes, but you can still subclass them, creating a new class that acts just like a built-in class except for the modifications you provide.

Oddly enough, however (and you might be particularly surprised by this if you've used another object-oriented application framework), subclassing is probably one of the less important ways in which your code will relate to Cocoa. Knowing or deciding when to subclass can be somewhat tricky, but the general rule is that you probably shouldn't subclass unless you're invited to.

A common case involves custom drawing into a UIView. You don't actually draw *into* a UIView; rather, when a UIView needs drawing, its `drawRect:` method is called so that the view can draw itself. So the way to make a UIView that is drawn in some completely custom manner is to subclass UIView and implement `drawRect:` in the subclass. As the documentation says, "Subclasses override this method if they actually draw their views." That's a pretty strong hint that you *need* to subclass UIView in order to do custom drawing into a UIView.

For example, suppose we want our window to contain a horizontal line. There is no horizontal line interface widget, so we'll just have to roll our own — a UIView that draws itself as a horizontal line. Let's try it. First we'll code the class:

1. In our Empty Window example project, choose File → New → New File and specify a Cocoa Touch Objective-C class, and in particular a subclass of UIView. Call it *MyHorizLine*. Xcode creates *MyHorizLine.m* and *MyHorizLine.h*.

2. In *MyHorizLine.m*, remove the comment delimiters from around the `drawRect:` implementation, and make it look like this (without further explanation; you'll know all about this after you read Chapter 15):

   ```
   - (void)drawRect:(CGRect)rect {
       CGContextRef c = UIGraphicsGetCurrentContext();
       CGContextMoveToPoint(c, 0, 0);
       CGContextAddLineToPoint(c, self.bounds.size.width, 0);
       CGContextStrokePath(c);
   }
   ```

3. Edit *MainWindow.xib*. Show the Window top-level object in the canvas. Find UIView in the Object library, and drag it into the Window object in the canvas.

4. Select the UIView in the window and use the Identity inspector to change its class to MyHorizLine.

Build and run the app in the Simulator. You'll see a horizontal line corresponding to the location of the top of the MyHorizLine instance in the window.

In that example, we started with a bare UIView that had no drawing functionality of its own. (That's why there was no need to call `super`; the default implementation of UIView's `drawRect:` does nothing.) But you might also be able to subclass a built-in UIView subclass to modify the way it already draws itself. Again using UILabel as an example, the documentation shows that two methods are present for exactly this purpose. Both `drawTextInRect:` and `textRectForBounds:limitedToNumberOfLines:` explicitly tell us: "You should not call this method directly. This method should only be overridden by subclasses." The implication is that these are methods that will be called for us, automatically, by Cocoa, as a label draws itself; thus, we can subclass UILabel and implement them in our subclass to modify how a particular type of label draws itself.

Here's an example from one of my own apps, in which I subclass UILabel to make a label that draws its own rectangular border and has its content inset somewhat from that border, by overriding `drawTextInRect:`. As the documentation tells us: "In your overridden method, you can configure the current [graphics] context further and then invoke **super** to do the actual drawing [of the text]." Let's try it:

1. In the Empty Window project, make a new class file, a UILabel subclass this time; call it *MyBoundedLabel*.
2. In *MyBoundedLabel.m*, insert this code into the implementation section:

```
- (void)drawTextInRect:(CGRect)rect {
    CGContextRef context = UIGraphicsGetCurrentContext();
    CGContextStrokeRect(context, CGRectInset(self.bounds, 1.0, 1.0));
    [super drawTextInRect:CGRectInset(rect, 5.0, 5.0)];
}
```

3. In *MyNib.xib*, select the UILabel and change its class to MyBoundedLabel.

Build and run the app, and you'll see how the rectangle is drawn and the label's text is inset within it.

Similarly, in a table view (a UITableView) you might very well be able to avoid subclassing the table view cell (UITableViewCell), because it provides so many properties through which you can customize its appearance. If you want text to appear in the cell using a certain font, the built-in cell styles and the ability to access and modify the cell's labels might be quite sufficient. You can directly replace a cell's background or put a checkmark at the right end of the cell. All of that is simply a matter of setting the cell's built-in properties. But if you want a table view cell that doesn't look or behave like any of the built-in cell styles, then you'll have to subclass UITableViewCell. (We'll go deeply into this in Chapter 21.)

You wouldn't subclass UIApplication (the class of the singleton shared application instance) just in order to respond when the application has finished launching, because the delegate mechanism (Chapter 11) provides a way to do that (`application:didFinish-LaunchingWithOptions:`). On the other hand, if you need to perform certain tricky customizations of your app's fundamental event messaging behavior, you'd have to subclass UIApplication in order to override **sendEvent:**. The documentation does tell you this, and it also tells you, rightly, that needing to do this would be fairly rare (though I have had occasion to do it).

 If you do subclass UIApplication, you'll need to change the third argument in the call to `UIApplicationMain` in *main.m* from nil to the NSString name of your subclass. Otherwise your UIApplication subclass won't be instantiated as the shared application instance.

Another set of classes that's commonly subclassed is UIViewController and its built-in subclasses (Chapter 19). And, naturally, any class you write will need to be a subclass of NSObject, if nothing else. You definitely want your class to inherit all of NSObject's yummy goodness, including `alloc` and `init`, which make it possible to instantiate your class in the first place. For more information, see "The Secret Life of NSObject," later in this chapter.

# Categories

A *category* is an Objective-C language feature that allows you to reach right into an existing class and define additional methods. You can do this even if you don't have the code for the class, as with Cocoa's classes. Your instance methods can refer to `self`, and this will mean the instance to which the message was originally sent, as usual. A category, unlike a subclass, cannot define additional instance variables; it can override methods, but you should probably not take advantage of this ability.

Defining a category is just like defining the class on which the category is being defined: you need an interface section and an implementation section, and you'll typically distribute them into the standard *.h* and *.m* class file pair. At the start of both the interface section and the implementation section, where you give the class's name, you add a category name in parentheses. The *.h* file will probably need to import the header for the original class (or the header of the framework that defines it), and the *.m* file will, as usual, import the corresponding header file.

For example, in one of my apps I found myself performing a bunch of string transformations in order to derive the path to various resource files inside the app bundle based on the resource's name and purpose. I ended up with half a dozen utility methods. Given that these methods all operated on an NSString, it was appropriate to implement them as a category of NSString, thus allowing *any* NSString, anywhere in my code, to respond to them.

The code was structured like this (I'll show just one of the methods):

```
// [StringCategories.h]
#import <Foundation/Foundation.h>

@interface NSString (MyStringCategories)
- (NSString*) basePictureName;
@end

// [StringCategories.m]
#import "StringCategories.h"

@implementation NSString (MyStringCategories)
- (NSString*) basePictureName {
    return [self stringByAppendingString:@"IO"];
}
@end
```

If we had written a utility method within some other class, we'd have to pass an NSString to the method that operates on it. But a category is neater and more compact.

We've extended NSString itself to have `basePictureName` as an instance method, so we can send the `basePictureName` message directly *to* the NSString we want to transform:

```
NSString* aName = [someString basePictureName];
```

A category is particularly appropriate in the case of a class like NSString, because the documentation warns us that subclassing NSString is a bad idea. That's because NSString is part of a complex of classes called a *class cluster*, which means that an NSString object's real class might actually be some other class. A category is a much better way to modify a class within a class cluster than subclassing.

## Splitting a Class

A category can be used to split a class over multiple *.h/.m* file pairs. If a class becomes long and unwieldy, yet it clearly needs to be a single class, you can define the basic part of it (including instance variables) in one file pair, and then add another file pair defining a category on your own class to provide further methods.

Cocoa itself takes does this. A good example is NSString. NSString is defined as part of the Foundation framework, and its basic methods are declared in *NSString.h*. Here we find that NSString itself, with no category, has just two methods, `length` and `characterAtIndex:`, because these are regarded as the minimum that a string needs to do in order to be a string. Additional methods — those that create a string — deal with a string's encoding, split a string, search in a string, and so on, are clumped into a category. A string also may serve as a file pathname, so we also find a category on NSString in *NSPathUtilities.h*, where methods are declared for splitting a pathname string into its constituents and the like. Then, in *NSURL.h*, there's another NSString category, declaring a couple of methods for dealing with percent-escaping in a URL string. Finally, off in a completely different framework (UIKit), *UIStringDrawing.h* adds yet another NSString category, with methods for drawing a string in a graphical context.

This organization won't matter to you as a programmer, because an NSString is an NSString, no matter how it acquires its methods, but it can matter when you consult the documentation. The NSString methods declared in *NSString.h*, *NSPathUtilities.h*, and *NSURL.h* are documented in the NSString class documentation page, but the NSString methods declared in *UIStringDrawing.h* are not, presumably because they originate in a different framework. Instead, they appear in a separate document, *NSString UIKit Additions Reference*. As a result, the string drawing methods can be difficult to discover, especially as the NSString class documentation doesn't link to the other document (although it does mention it). I regard this as a flaw in the structure of the Cocoa documentation. A third-party utility such as AppKiDo can be helpful here.

## Private Method Declarations

A problem (already mentioned in Chapter 4) arises when you'd like to declare a method in such a way that all other methods in the same class can see the declaration (and can thus call the method) without putting that declaration in the class's interface section where every other class that imports the header file will *also* be able to see and call it. The solution is to put an interface section for a category on your own class *in the implementation file*, which no one imports (Example 10-1).

*Example 10-1. Declaring a method privately*

```
// [in MyClass.m]
#import "MyClass.h"

@interface MyClass (Tricky)
- (void) myMethod;
@end

@implementation MyClass
// all methods here can call myMethod
@end
```

This trick cannot completely prevent some other class from calling this class's myMethod — Objective-C is too dynamic for that — but at least a normal call to my-Method from some other class will get its hand slapped by the compiler.

In Example 10-1, the compiler will not warn if the methods declared in the category interface section (such as myMethod) are not defined in the implementation section. If this worries you, there are two solutions. One is to provide a named category implementation section, corresponding to the named category interface section; if you fail to implement the category-declared methods in this category implementation section, the compiler *will* warn:

```
@implementation MyClass (Tricky)
// must implement myMethod here, or compiler will warn
@end
```

The other approach is just the opposite, namely to remove the category name altogether from the category implementation section; if you then fail to implement the category-declared methods in the *normal* implementation section, the compiler will warn:

```
@interface MyClass ()
- (void) myMethod;
@end
```

This nameless type of category is called a *class extension*, and I'll discuss a further use of it in Chapter 12, when we talk about Objective-C properties and the @synthesize directive.

# Protocols

Every reasonably sophisticated object-oriented language must face the fact that the hierarchy of subclasses and superclasses is insufficient to express the desired relationships between classes. For example, a Bee object and a Bird object might need to have certain features in common by virtue of the fact that both a bee and a bird can fly. But Bee might inherit from Insect, and not every insect can fly, so how can Bee acquire the aspects of a Flier in a way that isn't completely independent of how Bird acquires them?

Some object-oriented languages solve this problem through *mixin* classes. For example, in Ruby you could define a Flier module, complete with method definitions, and incorporate it into both Bee and Bird. Objective-C uses a simpler, lighter-weight approach — the *protocol*. Cocoa makes heavy use of protocols.

A protocol is just a named list of method declarations, with no implementation. A class may formally declare that it *conforms* to (or *adopts*) a protocol; such conformance is inherited by subclasses. This declaration satisfies the compiler when you try to send a corresponding message. If a protocol declares an instance method `myCoolMethod`, and if MyClass declares conformance to that protocol, then you can send the `myCool-Method` message to a MyClass instance and the compiler won't complain.

Actually implementing the methods declared in a protocol is up to the class that conforms to it. A protocol method may be required or optional. If a protocol method is required, then if a class conforms to that protocol, the compiler will complain if that class fails to implement that method. Implementing optional methods, on the other hand, is optional. (Of course, that's just the compiler's point of view; at runtime, if a message is sent to an object with no implementation for the corresponding method, a crash can result.)

Here's an example of how Cocoa uses a protocol. Some objects can be copied; some can't. This has nothing to do with an object's class heritage. Yet we would like a uniform method to which any object that *can* be copied will respond. So Cocoa defines a protocol named NSCopying, which declares just one method, `copyWithZone:` (required). A class that explicitly conforms to NSCopying is promising that it implements `copyWith-Zone:`.

Here's how the NSCopying protocol is defined (in *NSObject.h*, where your code can see it):

```
@protocol NSCopying
- (id)copyWithZone:(NSZone *)zone;
@end
```

That's all there is to defining a protocol. The definition uses the `@protocol` compiler directive; it states the name of the protocol; it consists entirely of method declarations; and it is terminated by the `@end` compiler directive. A protocol definition will typically appear in a header file, so that classes that need to know about it (in order to call its methods) can import it. A `@protocol` section of a header file is not inside any other section (such as an `@interface` section).

The NSCopying protocol definition in *NSObject.h* is just a definition; it is not a statement that NSObject conforms to NSCopying. Indeed, NSObject does *not* conform to NSCopying. To see this, try sending the `copyWithZone:` method to your own subclass of NSObject:

```
MyClass* mc = [[MyClass alloc] init];
MyClass* mc2 = [mc copyWithZone: [mc zone]];
```

The compiler warns that a MyClass instance may not respond to `copyWithZone:`. If you ignore this warning and run the app, it crashes with an exception when the `copyWith-Zone:` message is sent to an object that can't deal with it.

To conform formally to a protocol, a class's `@interface` section appends the name of the protocol, in angle brackets, after the name of the superclass (or, if this is a category declaration, after the parentheses naming the category). To state that a class conforms to multiple protocols, put multiple protocol names in the angle brackets, separated by comma.

Let's see what happens if you conform formally to the NSCopying protocol. Modify the first line of the `@interface` section of your class as follows:

```
@interface MyClass : NSObject <NSCopying>
```

Now the compiler issues a different warning, namely that MyClass fails to implement `copyWithZone:` and thus does not fully implement the NSCopying protocol (because `copyWithZone:` is a required method of the NSCopying protocol).

The name of a protocol may also be used when specifying an object type. Most often, the object will be typed as an `id`, but with the accompanying proviso that it conforms to a protocol, whose name appears in angle brackets.

To illustrate, let's look at another typical example of how Cocoa uses protocols, namely in connection with a table (UITableView). A UITableView has a `dataSource` property, declared like this:

```
@property (nonatomic, assign) id<UITableViewDataSource> dataSource
```

This property represents an instance variable whose type is `id <UITableViewData-Source>`. This means "I don't care what class my data source belongs to, but whatever it is, it should conform to the UITableViewDataSource protocol." Such conformance constitutes a promise that the data source will implement at least the required instance methods `tableView:numberOfRowsInSection:` and `tableView:cellForRowAtIndexPath:`, which the table view will call when it needs to know what data to display.

If you attempt to set a table view's `dataSource` property to an object that does *not* conform to UITableViewDataSource, you'll get a warning from the compiler:

```
MyClass* mc = [[MyClass alloc] init];
UITableView* tv = [[UITableView alloc] init];
tv.dataSource = mc; // compiler warns
```

To quiet the compiler, MyClass's declaration should state that it conforms to UITa-bleViewDataSource. Now MyClass *is* an `id <UITableViewDataSource>`, and the third line no longer generates a warning. Of course, you must also supply implementations of `tableView:numberOfRowsInSection:` and `tableView:cellForRowAtIndexPath:` in My-Class to avoid the other warning, namely that you're not fully implementing a protocol you've claimed to conform to.

A prevalent use of protocols in Cocoa is in connection with delegate objects. We'll talk in detail about delegates in Chapter 11, but you can readily see that many classes have a `delegate` property and that the class of this property is often `id <SomeProtocol>`. For example, in our Empty Window project, the Empty_WindowAppDelegate class provided by the project template is declared like this:

```
@interface Empty_WindowAppDelegate : NSObject <UIApplicationDelegate>
```

The reason is that Empty_WindowAppDelegate's purpose on earth is to serve as the shared application's delegate. The shared application object is a UIApplication, and a UIApplication's `delegate` property is typed as an `id <UIApplicationDelegate>`. So Empty_WindowAppDelegate announces its role by explicitly conforming to UIApplicationDelegate.

As a programmer, Cocoa's use of protocols will matter to you in two ways. First, when an object value that you wish to supply is typed as `id <SomeProtocol>`, you will need to make sure that that object's class does indeed conform to SomeProtocol (and implements any methods required by that protocol).

Second, you must understand about protocols in order to use the documentation. A protocol has its own documentation page. When the UIApplication class documentation tells you that a UIApplication's `delegate` property is typed as an `id <UIApplicationDelegate>`, it's implicitly telling you that if you want to know what messages a UIApplication's delegate might receive, you need to look in the UIApplicationDelegate protocol documentation.

Similarly, when a class's documentation mentions that the class conforms to a protocol, don't forget to examine that protocol's documentation, because the latter might contain important information about how the class behaves. To learn what messages can be sent to an object, you need to look upward through the inheritance chain (the superclass); you also need to look at any protocols that this object's class conforms to.

Might you ever have cause to define a protocol yourself? Unless you're writing a framework, this probably wouldn't be necessary, but protocols can make your code neater and cleaner, because they effectively allow one class to declare a method that another class is to implement, which is sometimes appropriate architecturally.

For example, in one of my apps I present a modal view, whose code is in a class called ColorPickerController, where the user can move three sliders to choose a color. When the user taps Done or Cancel, the view should be dismissed. It makes sense that the code that presented the view should also be code that dismisses it, so I need to send a message from the ColorPickerController instance to the instance that presented the view. Here is the declaration for that message:

```
- (void) colorPicker:(ColorPickerController*)picker
      didSetColorNamed:(NSString*)theName
             toColor:(UIColor*)theColor;
```

The question is: where should this declaration go? Now, it happens that in my app I know the class of the instance that will present the ColorPickerController's view: it is a SettingsController. So I could simply declare this method in the interface section of SettingsController's heading file (which ColorPickerController would then have to import, in order to send the message). But this feels wrong, for two reasons. First, it should not be up to SettingsController to declare a method that it is defining only in deference to ColorPickerController. Second, it is merely a contingent fact that the instance being sent this message is a SettingsController; it could be *any* class that presents and dismisses the modal view.

So even though we happen to know that ColorPickerController will be sending this message to a SettingsController instance, we should act as though we didn't know it. We want ColorPickerController to declare our method, and we want it to send the message blindly to some receiver, without regard to the class of that receiver. This is precisely what a protocol is for. The solution, therefore, is for ColorPickerController to define a protocol in its header file, with this method as part of that protocol.

# Optional Methods

The careful reader may have noticed that earlier sections of this chapter have listed two ways in which a method can be publicly declared without necessarily being implemented, and without the compiler complaining if it isn't:

- By defining a named category interface section with no corresponding named category implementation section.
- By defining a protocol in which some methods are explicitly designated as optional.

The question thus arises: How, in practice, is such an optional method feasible? We know that if a message is sent to an object and the object can't handle that message, an exception is raised (and your app will likely crash). But a method declaration is a contract suggesting that the object *can* handle that message. If we subvert that contract by declaring a method that might or might not be implemented, aren't we inviting crashes?

The answer is that Objective-C is not only dynamic but also introspective. You can ask an object whether it can deal with a message without actually sending it that message. This makes optional methods quite safe, provided you know that a method is optional.

The key method here is NSObject's `respondsToSelector:`, which takes a selector parameter and returns a BOOL. With it, you can send a message to an object only if it would be safe to do so:

```
MyClass* mc = [[MyClass alloc] init];
if ([mc respondsToSelector:@selector(woohoo)]) {
    [mc woohoo];
}
```

You wouldn't want to do this before sending just any old message, because it isn't necessary except for optional methods, and it slows things down a little. But Cocoa does in fact call `respondsToSelector:` on your objects as a matter of course. To see that this is true, implement `respondsToSelector:` on Empty_WindowAppDelegate in our Empty Window project in such a way as to instrument it with logging:

```
- (BOOL) respondsToSelector: (SEL) sel {
    NSLog(@"%@", NSStringFromSelector(sel));
    return [super respondsToSelector:(sel)];
}
```

Here's the output on my machine, as the Empty Window app launches:

```
application:handleOpenURL:
application:openURL:sourceApplication:annotation:
applicationDidReceiveMemoryWarning:
applicationWillTerminate:
applicationSignificantTimeChange:
application:willChangeStatusBarOrientation:duration:
application:didChangeStatusBarOrientation:
application:willChangeStatusBarFrame:
application:didChangeStatusBarFrame:
application:deviceAccelerated:
application:deviceChangedOrientation:
applicationDidBecomeActive:
applicationWillResignActive:
applicationDidEnterBackground:
applicationWillEnterForeground:
applicationWillSuspend:
application:didResumeWithOptions:
application:didFinishLaunchingWithOptions:
```

That's Cocoa, checking to see which of the optional UIApplicationDelegate protocol methods (including a couple of undocumented methods) are actually implemented by our Empty_WindowAppDelegate instance — which, because it is the UIApplication object's delegate and formally conforms to the UIApplicationDelegate protocol, has explicitly agreed that it *might* be willing to respond to any of those messages. The entire delegate pattern (Chapter 11) depends upon this technique. Observe the policy followed here by Cocoa: it checks all the optional protocol methods once, when it first meets the object in question, and presumably stores the results; thus, the app is slowed a tiny bit by this bombardment of `respondsToSelector:` calls, but now Cocoa knows all the answers and won't have to perform any of these same checks on the same object later on.

# Some Foundation Classes

The Foundation classes of Cocoa provide basic data types and utilities that will form the basis of much that you do in Cocoa. Obviously I can't list all of them, let alone describe them fully, but I can survey a few that I use frequently and that you'll probably want to look into before writing even the simplest Cocoa program. For more information, start with Apple's list of the Foundation classes in the *Foundation Framework Reference*.

## Useful Structs and Constants

NSRange is a struct of importance in dealing with some of the classes I'm about to discuss. Its components are integers (NSUInteger), `location` and `length`. So a range whose `location` is 1 starts at the second element of something (because element counting is always zero-based), and if its `length` is 2 it designates this element and the next. Cocoa also supplies various convenience methods for dealing with a range; you'll use NSMakeRange frequently. (Note that the name, NSMakeRange, is backward compared to names like CGPointMake and CGRectMake.)

NSNotFound is a constant integer indicating that some requested element was not found. For example, if you ask for the index of a certain object in an NSArray and the object isn't present in the array, the result is NSNotFound. The result could not be 0 to indicate the absence of the object, because 0 would indicate the first element of the array. Nor could it be nil, because nil is 0 (and in any case is not appropriate when an integer is expected). The true numeric value of NSNotFound is of no concern to you; always compare against NSNotFound itself, to learn whether a result is a meaningful index.

If a search returns a range and the thing sought is not present, the `location` component of the resulting NSRange will be NSNotFound.

## NSString and Friends

NSString, which has already been used rather liberally in examples earlier in this book, is the Cocoa object version of a string. You can create an NSString through a number of class methods and initializers, or by using the NSString literal notation @"...", which is really a compiler directive. Particularly important is stringWithFormat:, which lets you convert numbers to strings and combine strings; see Chapter 9, where I discussed format strings in connection with NSLog.

```
int x = 5;
NSString* s = @"widgets";
NSString* s2 = [NSString stringWithFormat:@"You have %i %@.", x, s];
```

NSString has a modern, Unicode-based idea of what a string can consist of. A string's "elements" are its characters, whose count is its length. These are not bytes, because the numeric representation of a Unicode character could be multiple bytes, depending on the encoding. Nor are they glyphs, because a composed character sequence that prints as a single "letter" can consist of multiple characters. Thus the length of an NSRange indicating a single "character" might be greater than 1.

An NSString can be searched using various rangeOf... methods, which return an NSRange. In addition, NSScanner lets you walk through a string looking for pieces that fit certain criteria; for example, with NSScanner (and NSCharacterSet) you can skip past everything in a string that precedes a number and then extract the number. Starting with iOS 3.2, the rangeOfString: family of search methods can specify an option NSRegularExpressionSearch, which lets you search using a regular expression; in iOS 4, regular expressions are fully supported as a separate class, NSRegularExpression (which uses NSTextCheckingResult to describe match results).

In this example from one of my apps, the user has tapped a button whose title is something like "5 by 4" or "4 by 3". I want to know both numbers; one tells me how many rows the layout is to have, the other how many columns. I use an NSScanner to locate the two numbers:

```
NSString* s = [as buttonTitleAtIndex:ix];
NSScanner* sc = [NSScanner scannerWithString:s];
int rows, cols;
[sc scanInt:&rows];
[sc scanUpToCharactersFromSet:[NSCharacterSet decimalDigitCharacterSet]
                intoString:nil];
[sc scanInt:&cols];
```

If I were writing this same code to run only on iOS 4, I might do the same thing using a regular expression:

```
NSString* s = [as buttonTitleAtIndex:ix];
int rowcol[2]; int* prowcol = rowcol;
NSError* err = nil;
NSRegularExpression* r = [NSRegularExpression regularExpressionWithPattern:@"\\d"
                                                    options:0
                                                      error:&err];
// error-checking omitted
for (NSTextCheckingResult* match in [r matchesInString:s
                                        options:0
                                          range:NSMakeRange(0, [s length])])
    *prowcol++ = [[s substringWithRange: [match range]] intValue];
```

The syntax seems oddly tortured, though, because we must convert each match from an NSTextCheckingResult to a range, then to a substring of our original string, and finally to an integer.

An NSString object's string is immutable. You can use a string to generate another string in various ways, such as by appending another string or by extracting a substring, but you can't alter the string *itself*. For that, you need NSString's subclass, NSMutableString.

An NSString carries no font and size information. In iOS programming, interface objects that display strings (such as UILabel) have a font property that is a UIFont, which is used to determine the single font and size in which the string will display. String drawing in a graphical context can be performed simply with methods provided through the UIStringDrawing category on NSString (see the *String UIKit Additions Reference*). Complex string layout in a graphical context, including use of styled text, requires Core Text and is a separate topic (Chapter 23).

NSString has convenience utilities for working with a file path string, and is often used in conjunction with NSURL, which is another Foundation class worth looking into. NSString and some other classes discussed in this section provide methods for writing out as a file or reading in a file; when they do, the file can be specified either as an NSString file path or as an NSURL.

## NSDate and Friends

An NSDate is a date and time, represented internally as a number of seconds (NSTimeInterval) since some reference date. Calling [`NSDate date`] gives you a date object for the current date and time; other date operations may involve NSDateComponents and NSCalendar and can be a bit tricky because calendars are complicated (see the *Date and Time Programming Guide*).

You will also likely be concerned with dates represented as strings. Creation and parsing of date strings involves NSDateFormatter, which uses a format string similar to NSString's `stringWithFormat`. A complication is added by the fact that the exact string representation of a date component or format can depend upon the user's locale, consisting of language, region format, and calendar settings. (Actually, locale considerations can also play a role in NSString format strings.)

In this example from one of my apps, I prepare the content of a UILabel reporting the date and time when our data was last updated. The app is not localized — the word "at" appearing in the string is always going to be in English — so I want complete control of the presentation of the date and time components as well. To get it, I have to insist upon a particular locale:

```
NSDateFormatter *df = [[NSDateFormatter alloc] init];
if ([[NSLocale availableLocaleIdentifiers] indexOfObject:@"en_US"] != NSNotFound) {
    NSLocale* loc =
        [[NSLocale alloc] initWithLocaleIdentifier:@"en_US"];
```

```
    [df setLocale:loc]; // force English month name and time zone name if possible
}
[df setDateFormat:@"d MMMM yyyy 'at' h:mm a z"];
NSString* lastUpdated = [df stringFromDate: [NSDate date]];
```

## NSNumber

An NSNumber is an object that wraps a numeric value (including BOOL). Thus, you can use it to store and pass a number where an object is expected. An NSNumber is formed from an actual number with a method that specifies the numeric type; for example, you can call numberWithInt: to form a number from an int:

```
[[NSUserDefaults standardUserDefaults] registerDefaults:
    [NSDictionary dictionaryWithObjectsAndKeys:
        [NSNumber numberWithInt: 4],
        @"cardMatrixRows",
        [NSNumber numberWithInt: 3],
        @"cardMatrixColumns",
        nil]];
```

An NSNumber is not itself a number, so you can't use it in calculations or where an actual number is expected. Instead, you must extract the number from its NSNumber wrapper using the inverse of the method that wrapped the number to begin with. So, for example, if an NSNumber wraps an int, you can call intValue to extract the int:

```
NSUserDefaults* ud = [NSUserDefaults standardUserDefaults];
int therows = [[ud objectForKey:@"cardMatrixRows"] intValue];
int thecols = [[ud objectForKey:@"cardMatrixColumns"] intValue];
```

Actually, this is such a common transformation when communicating with NSUser-Defaults that it provides convenience methods. So I could have written the same thing this way:

```
NSUserDefaults* ud = [NSUserDefaults standardUserDefaults];
int therows = [ud integerForKey:@"cardMatrixRows"];
int thecols = [ud integerForKey:@"cardMatrixColumns"];
```

## NSValue

NSValue is NSNumber's superclass. Use it for wrapping nonnumeric C values such as structs. Convenience methods provided by through the NSValueUIGeometryExtensions category on NSValue (see the *NSValue UIKit Additions Reference*) allow easy wrapping and unwrapping of CGPoint, CGSize, CGRect, CGAffineTransform, and UIEdgeInsets; additional categories allow easy wrapping and unwrapping of CATransform3D, CMTime, CMTimeMapping, and CMTimeRange.

You are unlikely to need to store any other kind of C value in an NSValue, but you can if you need to.

# NSData

NSData is a general sequence of bytes. It is immutable; the mutable version is its subclass NSMutableData.

In practice, NSData tends to arise in two main ways:

- When downloading data from the Internet. For example, the NSURLConnection class supplies whatever it retrieves from the Internet as NSData. Transforming it from there into (let's say) a string, specifying the correct encoding, would then be up to you.

- When storing an object as a file or in user preferences. For example, you can't store a UIColor value directly into user preferences. So if the user has made a color choice and you need to save it, you transform the UIColor into an NSData (using NSKeyedArchiver) and save that:

```
[[NSUserDefaults standardUserDefaults] registerDefaults:
    [NSDictionary dictionaryWithObjectsAndKeys:
        [NSKeyedArchiver archivedDataWithRootObject:[UIColor blueColor]],
        @"myColor",
        nil]];
```

The use of NSKeyedArchiver, and its reversal with NSKeyedUnarchiver, is a separate topic (Chapter 36).

## Equality and Comparison

The foregoing types will quickly come to seem to you like basic data types, but of course they are actually object types. Therefore you cannot compare them with the C operators for testing equality as you would with actual numbers. That's because, in the case of object types, the C operators compare the pointers, not the object content of the instances. For example:

```
NSString* s1 = [NSString stringWithFormat:@"%@, %@", @"Hello", @"world"];
NSString* s2 = [NSString stringWithFormat:@"%@, %@", @"Hello", @"world"];
if (s1 == s2) // false
    // ...
```

The two strings are equivalent (@"Hello, world") but are not the same object. (The example is deliberately elaborate because Cocoa's efficient management of string literals sees to it that two strings initialized directly as @"Hello, world" *are* the same object, which wouldn't illustrate the point I'm making.) It is up to individual classes to implement a test for equality. The general test, isEqual:, is inherited from NSObject and overridden, but some classes also define more specific and efficient tests. Thus, the correct way to perform the above test is like this:

```
if ([s1 isEqualToString: s2])
```

Similarly, it is up to individual classes to supply ordered comparison methods. The standard method is called compare:, and returns one of three constants:

NSOrderedAscending (the receiver is less than the parameter), NSOrderedSame (the receiver is equal to the parameter), or NSOrderedDescending (the receiver is greater than the parameter).

## NSIndexSet

NSIndexSet expresses a collection of ordered integers (so, despite the name, it isn't really a set, because a set is unordered). For example, you might want to speak of elements 1, 2, 3, 4, 8, 9, and 10 of an NSArray. NSIndexSet expresses this notion in some compact implementation that can be readily queried. The actual implementation is opaque, but you can imagine that in this case the set might consist of two NSRange structs, (1,4) and (8,3). NSIndexSet is thus very commonly used with NSArray. For example, to retrieve multiple objects simultaneously from an array, you specify the desired indexes as an NSIndexSet. It is also used with other things that are array-like; for example, you pass an NSIndexSet to a UITableView to indicate what sections to insert or delete.

An NSIndexSet is immutable; its mutable subclass is NSMutableIndexSet. You can form a simple NSIndexSet consisting of just one contiguous range directly, by passing an NSRange to `indexSetWithIndexesInRange:`; but to form a more complex index set you'll need to use NSMutableIndexSet so that you can append additional ranges.

Walking through (enumerating) the index values specified by an NSIndexSet is easy in iOS 4.0, which provides `enumerateIndexesUsingBlock:`. But if your code is to run on earlier systems, you can't use blocks, and no enumerator is provided, so you must resort to a rather clumsy construct (Example 10-2).

*Example 10-2. Enumerating an NSIndexSet*

```
NSIndexSet* ixen = //...;
NSUInteger ix = [ixen firstIndex];
do {
    // ... do something with ix ...
} while ((ix = [ixen indexGreaterThanIndex:ix]) != NSNotFound);
```

## NSArray and NSMutableArray

An NSArray is an ordered collection of objects. Its length is its count, and a particular object can be obtained by index number using objectAtIndex:. The index of the first object is zero, so the index of the last object is count minus one. You can form an NSArray in various ways, but typically you'll start by supplying a list of the objects it is to contain (see Chapter 3).

An NSArray is immutable. This doesn't mean you can't mutate any of the objects it contains; it means that once the NSArray is formed you can't remove an object from it, insert an object into it, or replace an object at a given index. To do those things, you can derive a new array consisting of the original array plus or minus some objects, or use NSArray's subclass, NSMutableArray.

You can walk through (enumerate) every object in an array with the `for...in` construct described in Chapter 1. (You'll get an exception if you try to mutate an array while enumerating it.)

You can seek an object within an array with `indexOfObject:` or `indexOfObjectIdentical-To:`; the former's idea of equality is to call `isEqual:`, whereas the latter uses pointer equality.

Those familiar with other languages may miss such utility array functions as `map`, which builds a new array of the results of calling a method on each object in the array. (`make-ObjectsPerformSelector:` requires a selector that returns no value, and `enumerate-ObjectsUsingBlock:` requires a block function that returns no value.) The usual work-around is to make an empty mutable array and then enumerate the original array, calling a method and appending each result to the mutable array (Example 10-3). It is also sometimes possible to use key–value coding as a `map` substitute (see Chapter 12).

*Example 10-3. Building an array by enumerating another array*

```
NSMutableArray* marr = [NSMutableArray array];
for (id obj in myArray) {
    id result = [obj doSomething];
    [marr addObject: result];
}
```

You can filter an array to produce a new array consisting of just those objects meeting a test that can be described as an NSPredicate:

```
NSArray* pep = [NSArray arrayWithObjects: @"Manny", @"Moe", @"Jack", nil];
NSPredicate* p = [NSPredicate predicateWithFormat:@"self BEGINSWITH[cd] 'm'"];
NSArray* ems = [pep filteredArrayUsingPredicate:p];
```

To filter an array on a more customized test, you can walk through the array applying the test and adding those that meet it to an NSMutableArray (similar to Example 10-3). Alternatively, in iOS 4.0 there is now the ability to filter an array using a block:

```
NSArray* pep = [NSArray arrayWithObjects: @"Manny", @"Moe", @"Jack", nil];
NSArray* ems =
    [pep objectsAtIndexes: [pep indexesOfObjectsPassingTest:
    ^BOOL(id obj, NSUInteger idx, BOOL *stop) {
        return ([(NSString*)obj rangeOfString:@"m"
            options:NSCaseInsensitiveSearch].location == 0);
    }]];
```

You can derive a sorted version of the array, supplying the sorting rules in various ways, or if it's a mutable array, you can sort it directly.

# NSSet and Friends

An NSSet is an unordered collection of distinct objects. This means that no two objects in a set can return YES when they are compared using `isEqual:`. Learning whether an object is present in a set is much more efficient than seeking it in an array, and you can ask whether one set is a subset of, or intersects, another set. You can walk through (enumerate) a set with the `for...in` construct, though the order is of course undefined. You can filter a set, as you can an array. Indeed, much of what you can do with a set is parallel to what you can do with an array, except that of course you can't do anything with a set that involves the notion of ordering.

An NSSet is immutable. You can derive one NSSet from another by adding or removing elements, or you can use its subclass, NSMutableSet.

NSCountedSet, a subclass of NSMutableSet, is a mutable unordered collection of objects that are *not* necessarily distinct (this concept is usually referred to as a *bag*). It is implemented as a set plus a count of how many times each element has been added.

Personally, I don't find myself storing data in sets very much; but many important Cocoa methods use them (such as those involving touch event handling), so you do have to know about them.

# NSDictionary and NSMutableDictionary

An NSDictionary is an unordered collection of key–value pairs. The key is usually an NSString, though it doesn't have to be. The value can be any object. An NSDictionary is immutable; its mutable subclass is NSMutableDictionary.

The keys of a dictionary are distinct (using `isEqual:` for comparison). If you add a key–value pair to an NSMutableDictionary, then if that key is not already present, the key–value pair is simply added, but if the key is already present, then the corresponding value is replaced.

The fundamental use of an NSDictionary is to request an entry's value by key (using `objectForKey:`); if no such key exists, the result is nil, so this is also the way to find out whether a key is present. A dictionary is thus an easy, flexible data storage device, an object-based analogue to a struct. Cocoa often uses a dictionary to provide you with an extra packet of named values, as in the `userInfo` of an NSNotification, the `options` parameter of `application:didFinishLaunchingWithOptions:`, and so on.

Data structures such as an array of dictionaries, a dictionary of dictionaries, and so forth, are extremely common, and will often lie at the heart of an app's functionality. Here's an example from one of my own apps. The app bundle contains a text file laid out like this:

```
chapterNumber [tab] pictureName [return]
chapterNumber [tab] pictureName [return]
```

As the app launches, I load this text file and parse it into a dictionary, each entry of which has the following structure:

```
key: (chapterNumber, as an NSNumber)
value: [Mutable Array]
    (pictureName)
    (pictureName)
    ...
```

Thus, as we walk the text file, we end up with all pictures for a chapter collected under the number of that chapter. This makes it easy for me later to present all the pictures for a given chapter. For each line of the text file, if the dictionary entry for that chapter number doesn't exist, we create it, with an empty mutable array as its value. Whether that dictionary entry existed or not, it does now, and its value is a mutable array, so we append the picture name to that mutable array. Observe how this single typical example (Example 10-4) brings together many of the Foundation classes discussed in this section.

*Example 10-4. Parsing a file with Foundation classes*

```
NSString* f = [[NSBundle mainBundle] pathForResource:@"index" ofType:@"txt"];
NSError* err = nil;
NSString* s = [NSString stringWithContentsOfFile:f
                                        encoding:NSUTF8StringEncoding
                                           error:&err];
// error-checking omitted
NSMutableDictionary* d = [NSMutableDictionary dictionary];
for (NSString* line in [s componentsSeparatedByString:@"\n"]) {
    NSArray* items = [line componentsSeparatedByString:@"\t"];
    NSInteger chnum = [[items objectAtIndex: 0] integerValue];
    NSNumber* key = [NSNumber numberWithInteger:chnum];
    NSMutableArray* marr = [d objectForKey: key];
    if (!marr) { // no such key, create key-value pair
        marr = [NSMutableArray array];
        [d setObject: marr forKey: key];
    }
    // marr is now a mutable array, empty or otherwise
    NSString* picname = [items objectAtIndex: 1];
    [marr addObject: picname];
}
```

You can get from an NSDictionary a list of keys, a sorted list of keys, or a list of values. You can walk through (enumerate) a dictionary by its keys with the for...in construct, though the order is of course undefined. A dictionary also supplies an object-Enumerator, which you can use with the for...in construct to walk through just the values. Starting in iOS 4.0, you can also walk through the key–value pairs together using a block, and you can even filter an NSDictionary by some test against its values.

# NSNull

NSNull does nothing but supply a pointer to a singleton object, [NSNull null]. Use this singleton object to stand for nil in situations where an actual object is required and nil is not permitted. For example, you can't use nil as the value of an element of a collection (such as NSArray, NSSet, or NSDictionary), so you'd use [NSNull null] instead.

Despite what I said earlier about equality, you can test an object against [NSNull null] using the C equality operator, because this is a singleton instance and therefore pointer comparison works.

## Immutable and Mutable

Beginners sometimes have difficulty with the Foundation's immutable/mutable class pairs, so here are some hints.

The documentation may not make it completely obvious that the mutable classes obey and, if appropriate, override the methods of the immutable classes. Thus, for example, [NSArray array] generates an immutable array, but [NSMutableArray array] generates a mutable array. (You will look in vain for the expected [NSMutableArray mutable-Array].) The same is true of all the initializers and convenience class methods for instantiation: they may all have "array" in their name, but when sent to NSMutableArray, they yield a mutable array.

That fact also answers the question of how to make an immutable array mutable, and *vice versa*. If arrayWithArray:, sent to the NSArray class, yields a new immutable array containing the same objects in the same order as the original array, then the same method, arrayWithArray:, sent to the NSMutableArray class, yields a *mutable* array containing the same objects in the same order as the original. Thus this single method can transform an array between immutable and mutable in either direction. You can also use copy (produces an immutable copy) and mutableCopy (produces a mutable copy).

All of the above applies equally, of course, to the other immutable/mutable class pairs. You will often want to work internally and temporarily with a mutable instance but then store (and possibly vend, as an instance variable) an immutable instance, thus protecting the value from being changed accidentally or behind your own back. What matters is not a variable's declared class but what class the instance really is (polymorphism; see Chapter 5), so it's good that you can easily switch between an immutable and a mutable version of the same data.

To test whether an instance is mutable or immutable, do *not* ask for its class. These immutable/mutable class pairs are all implemented as *class clusters*, which means that Cocoa uses a secret class, different from the documented class you work with. This secret class is subject to change without notice, because it's none of your business and you should never have looked at it in the first place. Thus, code of this form is subject to breakage:

```
if ([NSStringFromClass([n class]) isEqualToString: @"NSCFArray"]) // wrong!
```

Instead, to learn whether an object is mutable, ask it whether it responds to a mutability method:

```
if ([n respondsToSelector:@selector(addObject:)]) // right
```

Bear in mind also that just because a collection class is immutable doesn't mean that the objects it collects are immutable. They are still objects and do not lose any of their normal behavior merely because they are pointed to by an immutable collection.

## Property Lists

A *property list* is a string (XML) representation of data. The Foundation classes NSString, NSData, NSArray, and NSDictionary are the only classes that can be converted into a property list. Moreover, an NSArray or NSDictionary can be converted into a property list only if the only classes it collects are these classes, along with NSDate and NSNumber. (This is why, as mentioned earlier, you must convert a UIColor into an NSData in order to store it in user defaults; the user defaults is a property list.)

The primary use of a property list is to store data as a file. NSArray and NSDictionary provide convenience methods writeToFile:atomically: and writeToURL:atomically: that generate property list files given a pathname or file URL, respectively; they also provide inverse convenience methods that initialize an NSArray object or an NSDictionary object based on the property list contents of a given file. For this very reason, you are likely to start with one of these classes when you want to create a property list. (NSString's writeToFile:atomically:encoding:error: and NSData's writeToURL:atomically: just write the data out as a file directly, not as a property list.)

When you initialize an NSArray or NSDictionary from a property list file in this way, the objects in the collection are all immutable. If you want them to be mutable, or if you want to convert an instance of one of the other property list classes to a property list, you'll use the NSPropertyListSerialization class (see the *Property List Programming Guide*).

# The Secret Life of NSObject

Because every class inherits from NSObject, it's worth taking some time to investigate and understand NSObject. NSObject is constructed in a rather elaborate way:

- It defines some native class methods and instance methods having mostly to do with the basics of instantiation and of method sending and resolution. (See the *NSObject Class Reference*.)

- It adopts the NSObject protocol. This protocol declares instance methods having mostly to do with memory management, the relationship between an instance and its class, and introspection. Because all the NSObject protocol methods are required, the NSObject class implements them all. (See the *NSObject Protocol Reference*.) This architecture is what permits NSProxy to be a root class; it, too, adopts the NSObject protocol.

- It implements convenience methods related to the NSCopying, NSMutableCopying, and NSCoding protocols, without formally adopting those protocols. NSObject intentionally doesn't adopt these protocols because this would cause all other classes to adopt them, which would be wrong. But thanks to this architecture, if a class does adopt one of these protocols, you can call the corresponding convenience method. For example, NSObject implements the `copy` instance method, so you can call `copy` on any instance, but you'll crash unless the instance's class adopts the NSCopying protocol and implements `copyWithZone:`.

- A large number of methods are injected into NSObject by more than two dozen informal protocols, which are actually categories on NSObject. For example, `awake-FromNib` (see Chapter 7) comes from the UINibLoadingAdditions category on NSObject, declared in *UINibLoading.h*.

- A class object, as explained in Chapter 4, is an object. Therefore all classes, which are objects of type Class, inherit from NSObject. Therefore, *any method defined as an instance method by NSObject can be called on a class object as a class method!* For example, `respondsToSelector:` is defined as an instance method by NSObject, but it can be treated as a class method and sent to a class object.

The problem for the programmer is that Apple's documentation is rather rigid about classification. When you're trying to work out what you can say to an object, you don't care where that object's methods come from; you just care what you can say. But Apple differentiates methods by where they come from. Even though NSObject is the root class, the most important class, from which all other classes inherit, no single page of the documentation provides a conspectus of all its methods. Instead, you have to look at both the *NSObject Class Reference* and the *NSObject Protocol Reference* simultaneously, plus the pages documenting the NSCopying, NSMutableCopying, and NSCoding protocols (in order to understand how they interact with methods defined by NSObject), plus you have to supply mentally a class method version of every NSObject instance method!

Of the methods injected into NSObject as informal protocols, many are delegate methods (see Chapter 11) and do not need centralized documentation; for example, `animationDidStart:` is documented under the CAAnimation class, quite rightly. Others are documented on the NSObject class documentation page; for example, `cancel-PreviousPerformRequestsWithTarget:` comes from a category declared in *NSRun-Loop.h*, but it is documented under NSObject, quite rightly. However, every object responds to `awakeFromNib`; it's likely to be crucial to every app you write, yet you must learn about it outside of the NSObject documentation. The same goes, it might be argued, for all the key–value coding methods (Chapter 12) and key–value observing methods (Chapter 13).

Once you've collected all the NSObject methods, you can see that they fall into certain categories, much as outlined in Apple's documentation (see also "The Root Class" in the "Cocoa Objects" section of the *Cocoa Fundamentals Guide*):

*Creation, destruction, and memory management*
Methods for creating an instance, such as `alloc` and `copy`, along with methods that you might override in order to learn when something is happening in the lifetime of an object, such as `initialize` (see Chapter 11) and `dealloc` (see Chapter 12), plus methods that manage memory (see Chapter 12).

*Class relationships*
Methods for learning an object's class and inheritance, such as `class`, `superclass`, `isKindOfClass:`, and `isMemberOfClass:`.

To check the class of an instance (or class), use methods such as `isKindOfClass:`. Direct comparison of two class objects, as in `[someObject class] == [otherObject class]`, is rarely advisable, especially because a Cocoa instance's class might be a private, undocumented subclass of the class you expect. I mentioned this already in connection with class clusters, and it can happen in other cases.

*Object introspection and comparison*
Methods for asking what would happen if an object were sent a certain message, such as `respondsToSelector:`; for representing an object as a string (`description`, used in debugging; see Chapter 9); and for comparing objects (`isEqual:`).

*Message response*
Methods for meddling with what does happen when an object is sent a certain message, such as `doesNotRecognizeSelector:`. If you're curious, see the *Objective-C Runtime Programming Guide*. An example appears in Chapter 25.

*Message sending*
Methods for sending a message indirectly. For example, `performSelector:` takes a selector as parameter, and sending it to an object tells that object to perform that selector. This might seem identical to just sending that message to that object, but what if you don't know what message to send until runtime? Moreover, variants on `performSelector:` allow you send a message on a specified thread, or send a message after a certain amount of time has passed (`performSelector:withObject:afterDelay:` and similar); this is called *delayed performance*.

Delayed performance is a valuable technique. You often need to let Cocoa finish doing something, such as laying out interface, before proceeding to a further step; delayed performance with a very short delay (even as short as zero seconds) is enough to postpone a method call until after Cocoa has finished whatever it's in the middle of doing. Technically, it allows the current run loop to finish, completing and unwinding the entire current method call stack, before sending the specified selector. It can also be used for simple timing, such as when you want to do something different depending whether the user taps twice in quick succession or only once; basically, when the user first taps, you respond using delayed performance, to give the user time to tap again if two taps are intended. Examples of both uses appear in later chapters.

# CHAPTER 11

# Cocoa Events

None of your code runs until Cocoa calls it. The art of Cocoa programming consists largely of knowing when and why Cocoa will call your code. If you know this, you can put your code in the correct place, with the correct method name, so that your code runs at the correct moment, and your app behaves the way you intend.

In Chapter 7, for example, we wrote a method to be called when the user taps a certain button in our interface, and we also arranged things so that that method *would* be called when the user taps that button:

```
- (void) buttonPressed: (id) sender {
    // ... react to the button being pressed
}
```

This architecture typifies the underpinnings of a Cocoa program. Your code itself is like a panel of buttons, waiting for Cocoa to press one. If something happens that Cocoa feels your code needs to know about and respond to, it presses the right button — if the right button is there. You organize your code with Cocoa's behavior in mind. Cocoa makes certain promises about how and when it will dispatch messages to your code. These are Cocoa's *events*. You know what these events are, and you arrange your code to be ready when Cocoa delivers them.

Thus, to program for Cocoa, you must, in a sense, surrender control. Your code never gets to run just whenever it feels like it. It can run *only* in response to some kind of event. Something happens, such as the user making a gesture on the screen, or some specific stage arriving in the lifetime of your app, and Cocoa dispatches an event to your code — if your code is prepared to receive it. So you don't write just any old code you want to and put it in any old place. You use the framework, by letting the framework use you. You submit to Cocoa's rules and promises and expectations, so that your code will be called at the right time and in the right way.

The specific events that you can receive are listed in the documentation. The overall architecture of how and when events are dispatched and the ways in which your code arranges to receive them is the subject of this chapter.

# Reasons for Events

Broadly speaking, the reasons you might receive an event may be divided informally into four categories. These categories are not official; I made them up. Often it isn't completely clear which of these categories an event fits into; an event may well appear to fit two categories. But they are still generally useful for visualizing how and why Cocoa interacts with your code.

*User events*
> The user does something interactive, and an event is triggered directly. Obvious examples are events that you get when the user taps or swipes the screen, or types a key on the keyboard.

*Lifetime events*
> These are events notifying you of the arrival of a stage in the life of the app, such as the fact that the app is starting up or is about to go into the background, or of a component of the app, such as the fact that a UIViewController's view has just loaded or is about to be removed from the screen.

*Functional events*
> Cocoa is about to do something, and turns to you in case you want to supply (additional) functionality. I would put into this category things like UIView's `drawRect:` (your chance to have a view draw itself) and UILabel's `drawTextInRect:` (your chance to modify the look of a label), with which we experimented in Chapter 10.

*Query events*
> Cocoa turns to you to ask a question; its behavior will depend upon your answer. For example, the way data appears in a table (a UITableView) is that whenever Cocoa needs a cell for a row of the table, it turns to you and asks for the cell.

# Subclassing

A built-in Cocoa class may define methods that Cocoa itself will call and that you are invited (or required) to override in a subclass. Sometimes you know when the method will be called; at other times you don't know or care exactly when the method is called, but you know that you must override it so that whenever it *is* called, your behavior, and not (merely) the default behavior, will take place.

An example I gave in Chapter 10 was UIView's `drawRect:`. The built-in UIView implementation does nothing, so overriding `drawRect:` in a subclass is your only chance to dictate the full procedure by which a view draws itself. You don't know exactly when this method will be called, and you don't care; when it is, you draw, and this guarantees that the view will always appear the way you want it to. (You never call `drawRect:` yourself; if some underlying condition has changed and you want the view to be redrawn, you call `setNeedsDisplay` and let Cocoa call `drawRect:` in response.)

In addition to UIView, particular built-in UIView subclasses may have methods you'll want to customize through subclassing. Typically this will be in order to change the way the view is drawn. In Chapter 10 I gave an example involving UILabel and its `draw-TextInRect:`. Another example is UISlider, which lets you customize the position and size of the slider's "thumb" by overriding `thumbRectForBounds:trackRect:value:` (Chapter 25).

UIViewController (Chapter 19) is a good example of a class meant for subclassing. Of the methods listed in the UIViewController class documentation, just about all are methods you might have reason to override. If you create a UIViewController subclass in Xcode, you'll see that the template already includes about half a dozen methods for you to uncomment and override if desired.

For example, you must override `loadView` if your UIViewController creates its view in code, and you must create and assign it to this instance's `view` property at this moment. (I'd probably call that a functional event, because your code has a specific job to do, namely, supply the view.) You may override `viewDidLoad` to perform additional initializations as your view is first loaded, whether it comes from a nib or you created it in `loadView`. Methods like `viewWillAppear:` and `viewDidDisappear:` are called as your UIViewController's view takes over the screen or is replaced on the screen by some other view; thus, `viewWillAppear:` is a moment to make sure that whatever happened while your view was offscreen is reflected in how it looks as it comes back onscreen. (Those are obviously lifetime events.)

A method like `shouldAutorotateToInterfaceOrientation:` is what I call a query event. It is passed an orientation parameter and returns a BOOL telling Cocoa whether your view can appear in that orientation. The default, if you don't implement it, is that your view can appear only in portrait orientation. If you want this UIViewController's view to appear in some other orientation, you'll return YES for that orientation. If you return YES for more than one orientation and the user rotates the device, you might then receive messages like `willRotateToInterfaceOrientation:duration:` and `willAnimate-RotationToInterfaceOrientation:duration:`, where you can customize what happens to the view as the orientation changes.

When looking for events that you can receive through subclassing, be sure to look upward though the inheritance hierarchy. For example, if you're wondering how to be notified when the user has tapped on your custom UIView subclass, you won't find the answer in the UIView class documentation; a UIView receives tap events by virtue of being a UIResponder. In the UIResponder class documentation, you'll learn that you can override `touchesBegan:withEvent:` to be notified of a tap (Chapter 18).

Even further up the inheritance hierarchy, you'll find things like NSObject's `initialize` class method. Every class that is actually sent a class method message (including instantiation) is first sent the `initialize` message, once. Thus, `initialize` can be overridden in order to run code extremely early in a class's lifetime (before it even has an instance). Your project's application delegate class (such as Empty_Window-

AppDelegate in our Empty Window project) is instantiated very early in the app's life-time, as the main nib loads, so its `initialize` can be a good place to perform very early app initializations, such as setting default values for any user preferences. For typical code, look at Apple's Metronome example, in *MetronomeAppDelegate.m*. Observe that we test, as a matter of course, whether `self` really is the class in question; otherwise there is a chance that `initialize` will be called again (and our code will run again) if a subclass of this class is used.

# Notifications

Cocoa provides your app with a single instance of NSNotificationCenter, informally called the *notification center*. This instance is the basis of a mechanism for sending messages called *notifications*. A notification includes an instance of NSNotification (a *notification object*). The idea is that any object can be registered with the notification center to receive certain notifications. Another object can hand the notification center a notification object to send out (this is called *posting* the notification). The notification center will then send that notification object, in a notification, to all objects that are registered to receive it.

The notification mechanism is often described as a dispatching or broadcasting mech-anism, and with good reason. It lets an object send a message without knowing or caring what object or how many objects receive it. This relieves your app's architecture from the formal responsibility of somehow hooking up instances just so a message can pass from one to the other. When objects are conceptually "distant" from one another, notifications can be a fairly lightweight way of permitting one to message the other.

An NSNotification object has three pieces of information associated with it, which can be retrieved by instance methods: its `name`, an NSString which identifies it; an `object` associated with the notification (typically the object that posted it); and its `userInfo`. Not every notification has a `userInfo`; it is an NSDictionary, and can contain additional information associated with the notification. What information this NSDictionary will contain, and under what keys, depends on the particular notification; you have to con-sult the documentation. For example, the documentation tells us that UIApplication's `UIApplicationDidChangeStatusBarFrameNotification` includes a `userInfo` dictionary with a key `UIApplicationStatusBarFrameUserInfoKey` whose value is the status bar's frame. When you post a notification yourself, you can put anything you like into the `userInfo` for the notification's recipient(s) to retrieve.

## Receiving a Built-In Notification

Cocoa itself posts notifications through the notification center, and your code can reg-ister to receive them. You'll find a separate Notifications section in the documentation for a class that provides them.

To register for a notification, you use the `addObserver:...` instance method. The instance to which it is sent will typically be the app's single default notification center, `[NSNotificationCenter defaultCenter]`. The parameters are as follows:

`addObserver:`
> The instance to which the notification is to be sent. This will typically be `self`; it isn't usual for one instance to register a different instance as the receiver of a notification.

`selector:`
> The message to be sent to the observer instance when the notification occurs. The designated method should return `void` and should take one parameter, which will be the NSNotification object (so the parameter should be typed as `NSNotification*` or `id`).

`name:`
> The NSString `name` of the notification you'd like to receive. If this parameter is nil, you're asking to receive *all* notifications sent by the object designated in the `object` parameter. A built-in Cocoa notification's name is usually a constant. As I explained in Chapter 1, this is helpful, because if you flub the name of a constant, the compiler will complain, whereas if you enter the name of the notification directly as an NSString literal and you get it wrong, the compiler won't complain but you will mysteriously fail to get any notifications (because no notification has the name you actually entered) — a very difficult sort of mistake to track down.

`object:`
> The `object` of the notification you're interested in, which will usually be the object that posted it. If this is nil, you're asking to receive *all* notifications with the name designated in the `name` parameter. If both the `name` and `object` parameters are nil, you're asking to receive all notifications.

For example, in one of my apps I need to respond, by changing my interface, if the user starts or stops playing a song from the device's music library. The API for the device's built-in music player is the MPMusicPlayerController class; it provides a notification to tell me when the built-in music player changes its playing state, listed under Notifications in the MPMusicPlayerController's class documentation as `MPMusicPlayer-ControllerPlaybackStateDidChangeNotification`.

It turns out, looking at the documentation, that this notification won't be posted at all unless I call MPMusicPlayerController's `beginGeneratingPlaybackNotifications` instance method. This architecture is not uncommon; Cocoa saves itself some time and effort by not sending out certain notifications unless they are switched on, as it were. So my first job is to get an instance of MPMusicPlayerController and call this method:

```
MPMusicPlayerController* mp = [MPMusicPlayerController iPodMusicPlayer];
[mp beginGeneratingPlaybackNotifications];
```

Now I register myself to receive the desired playback notification:

```
[[NSNotificationCenter defaultCenter] addObserver:self
    selector:@selector(playChanged:)
        name:MPMusicPlayerControllerPlaybackStateDidChangeNotification
     object:nil];
```

So now, whenever an `MPMusicPlayerControllerPlaybackStateDidChangeNotification` is posted, my `playChanged:` method will be called:

```
- (void)playChanged:(id) n {
    // ... do something in response ...
}
```

## Unregistering

It is up to you, for every object that you register as a recipient of notifications, to un-register that object before it goes out of existence. If you fail to do this, and if the object does go out of existence, and if a notification for which that object is registered is posted, the notification center will attempt to send the appropriate message to that object, which is now missing in action. The result will be a crash at best, and chaos at worst.

To unregister an object as a recipient of notifications, send the notification center the `removeObserver:` message, whose parameter is the object that is no longer to receive notifications. (Alternatively, you can unregister an object for just a specific set of noti-fications with `removeObserver:name:object:`.) The trick is finding the right moment to do this. In most cases, the easiest solution is the registered instance's `dealloc` method, this being the last event an instance is sent before it goes out of existence (Chapter 12).

Keep it simple, because complicated logic for registering and unregistering for notifi-cations can be difficult to debug, especially as NSNotificationCenter provides no kind of introspection: you cannot ask an NSNotificationCenter what objects are registered with it as notification recipients. I once had a devil of a time understanding why one of my instances was not receiving a notification for which it was registered. Caveman debugging didn't help. Eventually I realized that some code I'd forgotten about was unregistering my instance.

 I am skipping over some other aspects of notifications that you probably won't need to know about. Read Apple's *Notification Programming Topics for Cocoa* if you want the gory details.

## NSTimer

An timer (NSTimer) is not, strictly speaking, a notification; but it behaves very simi-larly. It is an object that gives off a signal (*fires*) after the lapse of a certain time interval. The signal is a message to one of your instances. Thus you can arrange to be notified when a certain time has elapsed. The timing is not perfectly accurate, but it's pretty good.

Timer management is not exactly tricky, but it is a little unusual. A timer that is actively watching the clock is said to be *scheduled*. A timer may fire once, or it may be a *repeating* timer. To make a timer go out of existence, it must be *invalidated*. A timer that is set to fire once is invalidated automatically after it fires; a repeating timer repeats until *you* invalidate it (by sending it the `invalidate` message). An invalidated timer should be regarded as off-limits: you cannot revive it or use it for anything further, and you should probably not send any messages to it.

The straightforward way to create a timer is with the NSTimer class method `scheduled-TimerWithTimeInterval:target:selector:userInfo:repeats:`. This creates the timer and schedules it, so that it begins watching the clock immediately. The target and selector determine what message will be sent to what object when the timer fires; the method in question should take one parameter, which will be a reference to the timer. The `userInfo` is just like the `userInfo` of a notification. (You can see why I categorize timers as being similar to notifications.)

For example, one of my apps is a game with a score; I want to penalize the user, by diminishing the score, for not making a move within ten seconds of the previous move. So each time the user makes a move, I create a repeating timer whose time interval is ten seconds (and I also invalidate any existing timer); in the method that the timer calls, I diminish the score.

# Delegation

*Delegation* is an object-oriented design pattern, a relationship between two objects, in which the first object's behavior is customized or assisted by the second. The second object is the first object's *delegate*. No subclassing is involved, and indeed the first object is agnostic about the second object's class.

As implemented by Cocoa, here's how delegation works. A built-in Cocoa class has an instance variable, usually called `delegate` (it will certainly have `delegate` in its name). For some instance of that Cocoa class, you set the value of this instance variable to an instance of one of *your* classes. At certain moments in its activity, the Cocoa class promises to turn to its delegate for instructions by sending it a certain message: if the Cocoa instance finds that its delegate is not nil, and that its delegate is prepared to receive that message (see Chapter 10 on `respondsToSelector:`), the Cocoa instance sends the message to the delegate.

In the old days, delegate methods were listed in the Cocoa class's documentation, and their method signatures were made known to the compiler through an informal protocol (a category on NSObject). Now, though, a class's delegate methods are usually listed in a genuine protocol with its own documentation. There are over 70 Cocoa delegate protocols, showing how heavily Cocoa relies on delegation. Most delegate methods are optional, but in a few cases you'll discover some that are required.

To customize a Cocoa instance's behavior through delegation, you start with one of your classes, which, if necessary, declares conformance to the relevant delegate protocol. When the app runs, you set the Cocoa instance's `delegate` ivar (or whatever its name is) to an instance of your class. Usually you'll do this by setting a property. Your class will probably do other things besides serving as this instance's delegate. Indeed, one of the nice things about delegation is that it leaves you free to slot delegate code into your class architecture however you like. For example, if a view has a controller (a UIViewController), it will often make sense for the controller to serve also as the view's delegate.

Here's a simple example, involving UIAlertView. If a UIAlertView has no delegate, then when its Cancel button is tapped, the alert view is dismissed. But if you want to *do* something in response to the alert view being dismissed, you need to give it a delegate so that you can receive an event telling you that the alert view *was* dismissed. It's so common to give a UIAlertView a delegate that its designated initializer allows you to supply one; typically, the delegate will be the instance that summoned the alert view in the first place. Moreover, an alert view with a delegate is *so* common that the delegate is typed as a pure `id`; you don't even have to bother conforming formally to the UIAlertViewDelegate protocol:

```
- (void) gameWon {
    UIAlertView* av =
        [[UIAlertView alloc] initWithTitle:@"Congratulations!"
                                   message:@"You won the game. Another game?"
                                  delegate:self
                         cancelButtonTitle:@"No, thanks."
                         otherButtonTitles:@"Sure!", nil];
    [av show];
}

- (void) alertView:(UIAlertView*) av didDismissWithButtonIndex: (NSInteger) ix {
    if (ix == 1) { // user said "Sure!"
        [self newGame];
    }
}
```

The delegation mechanism is the last piece of the puzzle needed to explain the built-in bootstrapping procedure of a minimal app like our Empty Window project (see "Default Instances in the Main Nib File" on page 133). "The app finishes its internal setup, and `application:didFinishLaunchingWithOptions:` is sent to the Empty_WindowApp-Delegate instance." Why? Because a UIApplication instance sends `application:did-FinishLaunchingWithOptions:` to its delegate when the app has finished launching. And (as we also saw in Chapter 7), thanks to an outlet in *MainWindow.xib*, the Empty_Win-dowAppDelegate instance *is* the UIApplication instance's delegate (the *app delegate* — hence the name, Empty_Window*AppDelegate*).

That's why, in many earlier examples using the Empty Window project, we've put our test code in Empty_WindowAppDelegate's `application:didFinishLaunchingWith-Options:`. This is an event message our project template has already arranged for us to receive; we know the message will be sent, and we know it will be sent early in our app's lifetime, so we know *that* this method will run and *when* it will run.

 The UIApplication delegate methods are also provided as notifications. This lets an instance other than the app delegate hear conveniently about application lifetime events, by registering for them. A few other classes provide duplicate events similarly; for example, UITableView's delegate method `tableView:didSelectRowAtIndexPath:` is matched by a notification `UITableViewSelectionDidChangeNotification`.

By convention, many Cocoa delegate method names contain the modal verbs `should`, `will`, or `did`. A `will` message is sent to the delegate just before something happens; a `did` message is sent to the delegate just after something happens. A `should` method is special: it returns a BOOL, and you are expected to respond with YES to permit something or NO to prevent it. The documentation tells you what the default response is; you don't have to implement a `should` method if the default is acceptable. In many cases, a property will control the overall behavior; the delegate message lets you pick and choose the behavior based on circumstances at runtime.

For example, by default the user can tap the status bar to make a scroll view scroll quickly to the top. Even if the scroll view's `scrollsToTop` property is YES, you can prevent this behavior for a particular tap by returning NO from the delegate's `scrollViewShouldScrollToTop:`.

When you're searching the documentation for how you can be notified of a certain event, be sure to consult the corresponding delegate protocol, if there is one. (And don't forget to consult the class's superclasses to see if one of *them* has a corresponding delegate protocol.) You'd like to know when the user taps in a UITextField to start editing it? You won't find anything relevant in the UITextField documentation; what you're after is `textFieldDidBeginEditing:` in the UITextFieldDelegate protocol. You want to respond when the user rearranges items on your tab bar? Look in UITabBarControllerDelegate. You want to know how to make a UITextView zoomable (through the user making a pinch gesture)? A UITextView is a UIScrollView; a scroll view is not zoomable unless its delegate returns a view from `viewForZoomingInScrollView:`, documented under UIScrollViewDelegate.

You can implement the delegation pattern yourself if you like. That's what I do in the ColorPickerController example mentioned in Chapter 10. My ColorPickerController class's header file has a `delegate` instance variable and a ColorPickerDelegate protocol:

```
@protocol ColorPickerDelegate;
@interface ColorPickerController : UIViewController {
    id <ColorPickerDelegate> delegate;
}
@end

@protocol ColorPickerDelegate
```

```
    // color == nil on cancel
    - (void) colorPicker:(ColorPickerController *)picker
        didSetColorNamed:(NSString *)theName
               toColor:(UIColor*)theColor;
@end
```

Notice the use of the @protocol compiler directive in the first line; like the @class directive, this directive merely quiets the compiler by asserting that ColorPickerDelegate *is* a protocol, defined elsewhere (here, in fact, it is defined later in the same file). In the implementation for ColorPickerController, I send the protocol message to the delegate:

```
    - (void) dismissColorPicker: (id) sender { // user has tapped our Done button
        [self.delegate colorPicker:self
                didSetColorNamed:self.colorName
                        toColor:self.color];
    }
```

In this particular case I don't bother to check whether the delegate is nil, because I happen to know it isn't, and besides, if it is there's no harm done, because sending a message to nil does nothing. And I don't bother to check whether the delegate implements this method, because I happen to know that it does. Still, you could argue that I'm just being lazy and that I should do both those things.

# Data Sources

A *data source* is like a delegate, except that its methods supply the data for another object to display. The only Cocoa classes with data sources are UITableView and UIPickerView. A table view displays data in rows; a picker view displays selectable choices using a rotating drum metaphor. In each case, the data source must formally conform to a protocol with required methods (UITableViewDataSource and UIPickerViewDataSource, respectively).

It comes as a surprise to some beginners that a data source is necessary at all. Why isn't a table's data just part of the table? Or why isn't there at least some fixed data structure that contains the data? The reason is that such policies would violate generality. Use of a data source separates the object that displays the data from the object that manages the data, and leaves the latter free to store and obtain that data however it likes (see on model–view–controller in Chapter 12). The only requirement is that the data source must be able to supply information quickly, because it will be asked for it in real time when the data needs displaying.

Another surprise is that the data source is different from the delegate. But this again is only for generality; it's an option, not a requirement. There is no reason why the data source and the delegate should not be the same object, and most of the time they probably will be.

In this simple example, we implement a UIPickerView that allows the user to select by name a day of the week (the Gregorian week, using English day names). The first two methods are UIPickerView data source methods; the third method is a UIPickerView delegate method:

```
- (NSInteger) numberOfComponentsInPickerView: (UIPickerView*) pickerView {
    return 1;
}

- (NSInteger) pickerView: (UIPickerView*) pickerView
 numberOfRowsInComponent: (NSInteger) component {
    return 7;
}

- (NSString*) pickerView:(UIPickerView*)pickerView
            titleForRow:(NSInteger)row
          forComponent:(NSInteger)component {
    NSArray* arr = [NSArray arrayWithObjects:
                    @"Sunday",
                    @"Monday",
                    @"Tuesday",
                    @"Wednesday",
                    @"Thursday",
                    @"Friday",
                    @"Saturday",
                    nil];
    return [arr objectAtIndex: row];
}
```

# Actions

An *action* is a message emitted by an instance of a UIControl subclass (a *control*) to notify you of a significant user event taking place in that control. The UIControl subclasses are all simple things that the user can interact with directly, like a button (UIButton), a switch (UISwitch), a segmented control (UISegmentedControl), a slider (UISlider), or a text field (UITextField).

The significant user events (*control events*) are listed under UIControlEvents in the Constants section of the UIControl class documentation; they also have informal names that are visible in the Connections inspector when you're editing a nib. I'll mostly use the informal names in what follows. Control events fall roughly into three groups: the user has touched the screen (Touch Down, Touch Drag Inside, Touch Up Inside, etc.), edited text (Editing Did Begin, Editing Changed, etc.), or changed the control's value (Value Changed).

Apple's documentation is rather coy about which controls normally emit actions for which control events, so here's a list obtained through experimentation. Keep in mind that Apple's silence on this matter may mean that the details are subject to change:

*UIButton*
All "Touch" events.

*UIDatePicker*
> Value Changed.

*UIPageControl*
> All "Touch" events, Value Changed.

*UISegmentedControl*
> Value Changed.

*UISlider*
> All "Touch" events, Value Changed.

*UISwitch*
> All "Touch" events, Value Changed.

*UITextField*
> All "Touch" events except the "Up" events, and all "Editing" events. The text field is either in touch mode or in edit mode; as it switches from the former to the latter (and the keyboard appears, and Editing Did Begin is triggered), a Touch Cancel event is triggered. If the user stops editing by tapping Return in the keyboard, Did End on Exit is triggered along with Editing Did End.

The way you hear about a control event is through an action message. A control maintains an internal dispatch table: for each control event, there is some number of target–action pairs, of which the *action* is a selector (the name of a method) and the *target* is the object to which that message is to be sent. When a control event occurs, the control consults its dispatch table, finds all the target–action pairs associated with that control event, and sends each action message to the corresponding target. This architecture is reminiscent of a notification (Figure 11-1).

 The action messaging mechanism is actually more complex than I've stated. The UIControl does not really send the action message directly; rather, it tells the shared application to send it. This means that the entire mechanism can itself be customized. But you'll rarely need to do this, and in any case this is a separate topic (I'll return to this matter in Chapter 25).

There are two ways to manipulate a control's action dispatch table: you can configure an action connection in a nib (as explained in Chapter 7), or you can use code. To use code, you send the control the message addTarget:action:forControlEvents:, where the target is an object, the action is a selector, and the control events are designated by a bitmask (see Chapter 1 if you've forgotten how to construct a bitmask). Unlike a notification center, a control has methods for introspecting the dispatch table. Recall the example from Chapter 7 (where b is a reference to a UIButton):

```
[b addTarget:self action:@selector(buttonPressed:)
        forControlEvents:UIControlEventTouchDown];
```

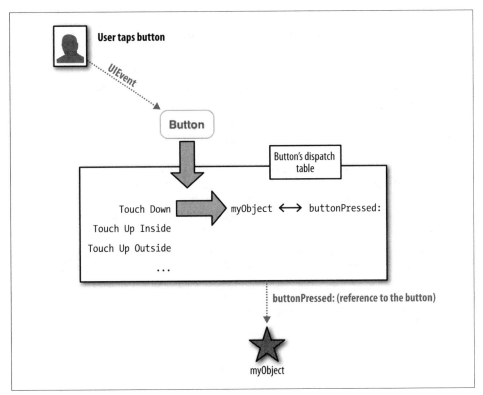

*Figure 11-1. The target–action architecture*

After that, whenever the user taps in the button, our `buttonPressed:` method will be called. It might look like this:

```
- (void) buttonPressed: (id) sender {
    UIAlertView* av = [[UIAlertView alloc] initWithTitle:@"Howdy!"
                                                 message:@"You tapped me."
                                                delegate:nil
                                       cancelButtonTitle:@"Cool"
                                       otherButtonTitles:nil];
    [av show];
}
```

The signature for the action selector can be in any of three forms. The fullest form takes two parameters:

- The control, usually typed as `id`.
- The UIEvent that generated the control event.

A shorter form (the most commonly used form) omits the second parameter; a still shorter form omits both parameters. If you're perfectly certain what control is sending you the message, and you don't need a reference to it, you might not bother with either of the action message's parameters.

**Mac OS X Programmer Alert**

If you're an experienced Mac OS X Cocoa developer, you'll note that there are some major differences between the Mac OS X implementation of actions and the iOS implementation. In Mac OS X, a control has just one action; in iOS, a control may respond to various control events. In Mac OS X, an action has just one target; in iOS, a single event can trigger multiple action messages to multiple targets. In Mac OS X, an action message selector comes in just one form; in iOS, there are three possible forms.

What is the UIEvent, and what is it for? Well, a *touch event* is generated whenever the user does something with a finger (sets it down on the screen, moves it, raises it from the screen). UIEvents are the lowest-level objects charged with communication of touch events to your app. A UIEvent is basically a timestamp (a double) along with a collection (NSSet) of touch events (UITouch). The action mechanism deliberately shields you from the complexities of touch events, but by electing to receive the UIEvent, you can still deal with those complexities if you want to. (See Chapter 18 for full details.)

In this example, I take advantage of the UIEvent's timestamp to do one thing if the user releases a UIButton after holding down a finger for a short time, but a different thing if the user releases the UIButton after holding it down for a longer time. Assume that the UIButton's dispatch table is configured so that its Touch Down control event calls my `buttonDown:event:` method, and its Touch Up Inside control event calls my `buttonUp:event:` method:

```
- (void) buttonDown: (id) sender event: (UIEvent*) e {
    self.downtime = [e timestamp]; // downtime is a property and ivar
}

- (void) buttonUp: (id) sender event: (UIEvent*) e {
    if ([e timestamp] - self.downtime < 0.3) {
        // respond to short tap
    } else {
        // respond to longer hold and release
    }
}
```

# The Responder Chain

A *responder* is an object that knows how to receive UIEvents directly (see the previous section). It knows this because it is an instance of UIResponder or a UIResponder subclass. If you examine the Cocoa class hierarchy, you'll find that just about any class that has anything to do with display on the screen is a responder. A UIView is a responder. A UIWindow is a responder. A UIViewController is a responder. Even a UIApplication is a responder.

If you look in the documentation for the UIResponder class, you'll find that it implements four low-level methods for receiving touch-related UIEvents: `touchesBegan:withEvent:`, `touchesMoved:withEvent:`, `touchesEnded:withEvent:` and `touchesCancelled:withEvent:`. These are called to notify a responder of a touch event. No matter how your code ultimately hears about a user-related touch event — indeed, even if your code *never* hears about a touch event (because Cocoa reacted in some automatic way to the touch, without your code's intervention) — the touch was initially communicated to a responder through one of these methods.

The mechanism for this communication starts by deciding which responder the user touched. The UIView methods `hitTest:withEvent:` and `pointInside:withEvent:` are called until the correct view (the *hit-test view*) is located. Then UIApplication's `sendEvent:` method is called, which calls UIWindow's `sendEvent:`, which calls the correct method of the hit-test view (a responder). I'll cover all this again in full detail in Chapter 18.

The responders in your app participate in a *responder chain*, which essentially links them up through the view hierarchy. A UIView can sit inside another UIView, its *superview*, and so on until we reach the app's UIWindow (a UIView that has no superview). The responder chain, from bottom to top, looks like this:

1. The UIView that we start with (here, the hit-test view).
2. The UIViewController that controls that UIView, if there is one.
3. The UIView's superview, and then *its* UIViewController if there is one. Repeat this step, moving up the superview hierarchy one superview at a time, until we reach...
4. The UIWindow.
5. The UIApplication.

## Deferring Responsibility

The responder chain can be used to let a responder defer responsibility for handling a touch event. If a responder receives a touch event and can't handle it, the event can be passed up the responder chain to look for a responder that *can* handle it. This can happen in two main ways: (1) the responder doesn't implement the relevant method; (2) the responder implements the relevant method to call super.

For example, a plain vanilla UIView has no native implementation of the touch event methods. Thus, by default, even if a UIView is the hit-test view, the touch event effectively falls through the UIView and travels up the responder chain, looking for someone to respond to it. If this UIView is an instance of your own subclass, you might implement the touch event methods in that subclass to catch touch events in the UIView itself; but if the UIView is controlled by a UIViewController, you have already subclassed UIViewController, and that subclass is probably where the interface behavior logic for this UIView is already situated, so you might well prefer to implement the touch event methods there instead. You are thus taking advantage of the responder chain to defer responsibility for handling touch events from the UIView to its UIViewController, in a natural and completely automatic way.

## Nil-Targeted Actions

A *nil-targeted action* is a target–action pair in which the target is nil. There is no designated target object, so the following rule is used: starting with the hit-test view (the view with which the user is interacting), Cocoa looks up the responder chain for an object that can respond to the action message.

Suppose, for example, we have a UIButton inside a UIView. And suppose we run this code early in the button's lifetime, where b is the button:

```
[b addTarget:nil action:@selector(doButton:)
    forControlEvents:UIControlEventTouchUpInside];
```

That's a nil-targeted action. So what happens when the user taps the button? First, Cocoa looks in the UIButton itself to see whether it responds to doButton:. If not, then it looks in the UIView that is its superview. And so on, up the responder chain. If a responder is found that handles doButton:, the action message is sent to that object; otherwise, the message goes unhandled.

Thus, suppose the UIView containing the UIButton is an instance of your own UIView subclass. Let's call it MyView. If MyView implements doButton:, then when the user taps the button, it is MyView's doButton: that will be called.

To create a nil-targeted action in a nib, you form a connection to the First Responder proxy object (in the dock). This is what the First Responder proxy object is for! The First Responder isn't a real object with a known class, so before you can connect an action to it, you have to define the action message within the First Responder proxy object, like this:

1. Select the First Responder proxy, and switch to the Attributes inspector.
2. Click the Plus button and give the new action a signature; it must take a single parameter (so that its name will end with a colon).
3. Now you can Control-drag from a control, such as a UIButton, to the First Responder proxy to specify a nil-targeted action with the signature you specified.

# Application Lifetime Events

As I've already mentioned, events mark certain important stages in the overall lifetime of your application. These events can arrive either as messages to the app delegate (if you implement the appropriate methods) or as notifications to any object (if that object registers for those notifications).

In the old days, before iOS 4, this suite of events was pretty simple:

applicationDidFinishLaunching:
> The app has started up. This, as we have already seen many times, is the earliest opportunity for your code to configure the interface by showing the app's window.

(For reasons that we haven't yet discussed, it is now better for your app delegate to implement `application:didFinishLaunchingWithOptions:` instead.)

`applicationDidBecomeActive:`
> The app has started up; received after `applicationDidFinishLaunching:`. Also received after the end of the situation that caused the app delegate to receive `applicationWillResignActive:`.

`applicationWillResignActive:`
> Something has blocked the app's interface. The most common cause is that the screen has been locked. An alert from outside your app could also cause this event.

`applicationWillTerminate:`
> The app is about to quit. This is your last signal to preserve state (typically, by storing information with NSUserDefaults) and perform other final cleanup tasks.

Starting with iOS 4, however, apps operate in a *multitasking* environment. The Home button doesn't terminate your app; it suspends it. This means that your app is essentially freeze-dried in the background; its process still exists, but it isn't getting any events (though notifications can be stored by the system for later delivery if your app comes to the front once again). You'll probably *never* get `applicationWillTerminate:`, because when your app is terminated by the system, it will already have been suspended.

Thus, you have to worry about what will happen when the app is suspended and when it returns from being suspended (`applicationDidEnterBackground:` and `applicationWillEnterForeground:`, and their corresponding notifications), and the notion of the application becoming inactive or active also takes on increased importance (`applicationWillResignActive:` and `applicationDidBecomeActive:`, and their notifications). Here are some typical scenarios:

*The app launches freshly*
> Your app delegate receives these messages (just as in the premultitasking world):
> - `application:didFinishLaunchingWithOptions:`
> - `applicationDidBecomeActive:`

*The user clicks the Home button*
> If your app is frontmost, it is suspended, and your app delegate receives these messages:
> - `applicationWillResignActive:`
> - `applicationDidEnterBackground:`

*The user summons your suspended app to the front*
> Your app delegate receives these messages:
> - `applicationWillEnterForeground:`
> - `applicationDidBecomeActive:`

*The user double-clicks the Home button*
> The user can now work in the app switcher. If your app is frontmost, your app delegate receives this message:

- `applicationWillResignActive:`

*The user, in the app switcher, taps on your app's window*
> Your app delegate receives this message:

- `applicationDidBecomeActive:`

*The user, in the app switcher, chooses another app*
> If your app is frontmost, your app delegate receives this message:

- `applicationDidEnterBackground:`

*The screen is locked*
> If your app is frontmost, your app delegate receives this message:

- `applicationWillResignActive:`

*The screen is unlocked*
> If your app is frontmost, your app delegate receives this message:

- `applicationDidBecomeActive:`

*The user holds the screen-lock button down*
> The device offers to shut itself down. If your app is frontmost, your app delegate receives this message:

- `applicationWillResignActive:`

*The user, as the device offers to shut itself down, cancels*
> If your app is frontmost, your app delegate receives this message:

- `applicationDidBecomeActive:`

*The user, as the device offers to shut itself down, accepts*
> If your app is frontmost, your app delegate receives these messages:

- `applicationDidEnterBackground:`
- `applicationWillTerminate:` (probably the only way a normal app will receive this message in a multitasking world)

Juggling these events and meeting your responsibilities under all circumstances can be quite tricky. You have, as it were, a lot of bases to cover if you want to make certain that your app is in a known state as it passes through each of its possible lifetime stages. For example, what's a good moment to make certain you've preserved state in case your app is terminated? You're probably not going to be notified by `application-WillTerminate:`, so what should you use instead? Looking over the list of scenarios, you can see that `applicationWillResignActive:` is the broadest signal that *something* might now happen such that your app will subsequently be terminated without further notice, but it is also possible that your app will next become active again. On the other hand, it is very unlikely that your app will be terminated without your receiving `application-`

DidEnterBackground: first, so this is the default signal that you should save state. (You are given a little time to do this before your app is actually suspended; Chapter 38 discusses what to do if you think a little time might not enough.)

Using the existing repertoire of events to work out what's happening isn't always easy. For example, let's say there are things my app wants to do when the user resumes it from a suspended state (`applicationWillEnterForeground:`), and there are things my app wants to do when the user unlocks the screen (`applicationDidBecomeActive:`). Some of these things are the same in both circumstances, but others are not. But the former event is always followed by the latter. So I have to be careful how I respond:

`applicationWillEnterForeground:`
Do things appropriate to resuming from suspension. But do *not* do things that are also appropriate to the user unlocking the screen, because `applicationDidBecomeActive:` is about to be called, so if I do those things here, I'll end up doing them *twice*.

`applicationDidBecomeActive:`
Do things appropriate both when resuming from suspension and when the user unlocks the screen.

Fine, but what about things that are appropriate when the user unlocks the screen but *not* when we resume from suspension? I can't simply put those in `applicationDidBecomeActive:`, which is called when the user unlocks the screen, because it is *also* called when we resume from suspension. Here, Cocoa's notifications are not sufficiently fine-grained. We might have to do a little dance with a flag (a BOOL instance variable) to detect when we become active without having been suspended:

```
- (void)activeButNotForeground {
    // do things for when the screen unlocks
}

- (void)applicationWillEnterForeground:(UIApplication *)application {
    // do things for when we resume from suspension
    self->didForeground = YES;
}

- (void)applicationDidBecomeActive:(UIApplication *)application {
    // do things for when we resume from suspension or the screen unlocks
    if (!self->didForeground)
        [self activeButNotForeground];
    self->didForeground = NO;
}
```

These considerations are of course the same regardless of whether you're the app delegate receiving delegate messages or some other class receiving notifications. Note also that your app will usually be dominated by a UIViewController, whose lifetime events are also of prime importance; some examples appear in the next section, but we won't be discussing UIViewController properly until Chapter 19.

In this section, I've talked as if your app's being backgrounded is identical to its being suspended. However, under highly specialized circumstances (discussed, for instance, in Chapter 27 and Chapter 35), your app can be backgrounded without being suspended. Also, I've talked as if your app has no choice but to participate in the multitasking world, but in fact you can opt out by setting the "Application does not run in background" key (UIApplicationExitsOnSuspend) in your *Info.plist*, thus causing your app to behave in this regard as if it were linked against iOS 3 — when the user clicks the Home button, your app is terminated. For some apps, such as certain games, this might be a reasonable thing to do.

# Swamped by Events

Code that contains multiple entry points — methods that are called through events — can be hard to read, to understand, to maintain, and to debug, even when your classes are relatively small and simple. As you develop a class that's intended to receive more than one or two events, I recommend that you comment your code clearly, so that you know what methods you think Cocoa will be calling and why and when.

To illustrate the problem, I'll list some of the methods in a typical class of mine. This is a small class in a small, simple app. It is a UIViewController subclass; in point of fact, it is a UITableViewController subclass, so it serves not only to load and configure the table view, but also as the table view's delegate and data source. This is an iOS 4 app and therefore participates in multitasking. The app works with the built-in music library and music player, so there are also some notifications from the MPMusicPlayerController class. I omit the class's designated initializer and `dealloc`, as well as various utility methods called by the methods I list.

Here are the methods:

`loadView`

An overridden UIViewController method. Called by Cocoa just after the class is instantiated. Here we create the table view and perform various other view initializations. We also add ourself as observer for four notifications:

```
[[NSNotificationCenter defaultCenter]
    addObserver:self selector:@selector(prepareToForeground:)
        name:UIApplicationWillEnterForegroundNotification
    object:nil];
[[NSNotificationCenter defaultCenter]
    addObserver:self selector:@selector(prepareToSuspend:)
        name:UIApplicationDidEnterBackgroundNotification
    object:nil];
[[NSNotificationCenter defaultCenter]
    addObserver:self selector:@selector(scrollToNow:)
        name:UIApplicationDidBecomeActiveNotification
    object:nil];
[[NSNotificationCenter defaultCenter]
    addObserver:self selector:@selector(reloadData:)
```

```
                  name:MPMusicPlayerControllerNowPlayingItemDidChangeNotification
                  object:nil];
```

scrollToNow:

Called by Cocoa through a notification when the app becomes active (`UIApplicationDidBecomeActiveNotification`), as arranged in `loadView`. This means the app is either starting up, or returning to the foreground after being suspended, or appearing as the user unlocks the screen.

reloadData:

Called by Cocoa through a notification when the currently playing song changes (`MPMusicPlayerControllerNowPlayingItemDidChangeNotification`), as arranged in `loadView`.

prepareToForeground:

Called by Cocoa through a notification when the app returns to the foreground after being suspended (`UIApplicationWillEnterForegroundNotification`), as arranged in `loadView`.

prepareToSuspend:

Called by Cocoa through a notification when the app is suspended (`UIApplication-DidEnterBackgroundNotification`), as arranged in `loadView`.

viewDidLoad

An overridden UIViewController method; called by Cocoa after `loadView`. The view now exists and we can perform further initializations.

viewWillAppear:

An overridden UIViewController method; called by Cocoa when the view is about to appear, presumably because the user has explicitly summoned this view. I use this moment to create a repeating timer (NSTimer), which checks every two seconds to see what fraction of the currently playing song has been played.

checkFraction:

This is the method called every two seconds by the timer created in `viewWill-Appear:`. It updates a UIProgressView to indicate what fraction of the song has played so far. It also changes a button, making it a Play button if the song is paused and a Pause button if the song is playing:

```
UIBarButtonItem* bb =
    [[UIBarButtonItem alloc]
        initWithBarButtonSystemItem:whichButton
                            target:self
                            action:@selector(doPlayPause:)];
```

tableView:heightForRowAtIndexPath:

A table view delegate method; called by Cocoa at unpredictable moments to help configure the table view, because we are the table view's delegate.

---

`numberOfSectionsInTableView:`
> A table view data source method; called by Cocoa at unpredictable moments to help configure the table view, because we are the table view's data source.

`tableView:numberOfRowsInSection:`
> A table view data source method; called by Cocoa at unpredictable moments to help configure the table view, because we are the table view's data source.

`tableView:cellForRowAtIndexPath:`
> A table view data source method; called by Cocoa at unpredictable moments to help configure the table view, because we are the table view's data source.

`tableView:didSelectRowAtIndexPath:`
> A table view delegate method; called by Cocoa when the user taps a table row to select it, because we are the table view's delegate. I respond by starting to play the song represented by this row. I also register to receive a notification if the user stops playing the song:
>
> ```
> [[NSNotificationCenter defaultCenter]
>     addObserver:self selector:@selector(playChanged:)
>         name:MPMusicPlayerControllerPlaybackStateDidChangeNotification
>     object:nil];
> ```

`playChanged:`
> Called by Cocoa through a notification when the currently playing song stops, as arranged in `tableView:didSelectRowAtIndexPath:`.

`tableView:titleForHeaderInSection:`
> A table view data source method; called by Cocoa at unpredictable moments to help configure the table view, because we are the table view's data source.

`doPlayPause:`
> Called by Cocoa when the user taps the Play or Pause button, as arranged in `check-Fraction:`.

One's eyes can easily glaze over at the sight of all these methods called automatically by Cocoa under various circumstances. As a beginner, you might find all of these method names unfamiliar, so my code would be pretty much illegible. Still, experience will teach you about the UIViewController overridden methods, which form a standard sequence of moments in the lifetime of the view controller, and about the table view delegate and data source methods, which — although they are called at unpredictable moments — work together in a reliable and fairly simple way to describe the table and govern its behavior. On the other hand, no amount of experience will tell you that a certain method is called as a button's action or through a notification. You don't know what `prepareToSuspend:` does unless you see the code that arranges for it to be called through a notification, and that code is far away, much earlier in this same class (and could even be in a different class). Thus, comments really help.

Even so, Cocoa is doing the calling and the actual moment when things are called can be unpredictable. Your own code can trigger unintended events. The documentation might not make it clear just when a notification will be sent. There could even be a bug in Cocoa such that events are called in a way that seems to contradict the documentation. Therefore I recommend also that as you develop your app, you instrument your code heavily with caveman debugging (NSLog; see Chapter 9). As you test your code, keep an eye on the console output and check whether the messages make sense.

One problem that can be detected only by logging is that Cocoa might mysteriously call an event too often. This actually happens in my app, where reloadData: is sometimes called twice in quick succession through a notification even though there was just one change in what song is playing. This might be a bug in Cocoa, but the cause isn't important; what matters is how to guard against it. The first question to ask yourself is whether it's worth guarding against. If what I do in reloadData: isn't expensive or sequential in nature, it might not matter if I do it twice in quick succession. But it happens that what I do in reloadData: *is* expensive. So I do a little dance with delayed performance (see Chapter 10, on NSObject) such that if reloadData: is called twice within two-tenths of a second, the first call is effectively thrown away:

```
- (void) reloadData: (NSNotification*) n {
    [UIApplication cancelPreviousPerformRequestsWithTarget:self
                                          selector:
                                              @selector(reallyReloadData)
                                          object:nil];
    [self performSelector:@selector(reallyReloadData)
            withObject:nil
            afterDelay:0.2];
}

- (void) reallyReloadData {
    // do expensive thing here
}
```

Another issue that can arise is that your own code can trigger events unexpectedly. This happened to me in developing a different app, where I suddenly found that in a UIViewController subclass, viewDidLoad was being called twice as the app started up, which should be impossible. Not only that, but — as I discovered after adding some more NSLog messages — it was called while I was still in the middle of executing awakeFromNib, which should *really* be impossible. The reason was that I was making the mistake of mentioning my class's view property during awakeFromNib; this actually causes viewDidLoad to be called. The problem went away when I corrected my mistake. The point is that I wouldn't even have noticed this mistake without NSLog.

The conclusion to which I'm leading is that there's a certain indeterminacy and uncertainty in the nature of events. They bombard your code; they control it. Their relationship can be tricky, and in most cases you shouldn't rely on things happening in a definite order (although you can if the documentation says so, as with applicationWillEnterForeground: being followed by applicationDidBecomeActive:). Your posture will therefore be, to some extent, one of uncertainty and defensiveness. You're like a tennis student being pelted by a ball-serving machine. Without logging, the tennis student is also blindfolded.

# CHAPTER 12

# Accessors and Memory Management

Even when you've understood how to slot in your code so as to get the messages that you want from Cocoa, your obligations to Cocoa and your interactions with the framework are not over. You have additional responsibilities that emerge as you write the code for any class that will be instantiated. There are guidelines for how a well-behaved instance should be structured and how it should act — in fact, I seriously thought of calling this chapter "The Well-Behaved Instance." If you don't follow those guidelines, things can go wrong: outlets aren't set, the wrong methods are called, memory gets used up, your app crashes. This chapter is about those guidelines.

## Accessors

An *accessor* is a method for getting or setting the value of an instance variable. An accessor that gets the instance variable's value is called a *getter*; an accessor that sets the instance variable's value is called a *setter*.

There are naming conventions for accessors, and you should obey them. The conventions are simple:

- A setter's name should start with `set` and be followed by a capitalized version of the instance variable's name. If the instance variable is named `myVar`, the setter should be named `setMyVar:`. The setter should take one parameter: the new value to be assigned to the instance variable.

- A getter should have the same name as the instance variable. If the instance variable is named `myVar`, the getter should be named `myVar`. (This will not cause you or the compiler any confusion, because variable names and method names are used in completely different contexts.)

  You can optionally start the getter's name with `get`, though in fact I never do this. If the instance variable's value is a BOOL, you may optionally start the getter's name with `is` (for example, an ivar `showing` can have a getter `isShowing`), though in fact I never do this.

Accessors are important in part because instance variables are protected, whereas declared methods are public; without accessor methods, a protected instance variable can't be accessed by any other object.

But even apart from this, there is good reason to consider supplying accessors for an instance variable. If an instance variable's value is an object, there are going to be memory management tasks to worry about every time you get and (especially) set that value; the best way to ensure that you're carrying out those tasks reliably and consistently is to pass through an accessor, even in code within the same class (as explained later in this chapter).

Moreover, Cocoa often uses the string name of an instance variable to derive the name of the accessor and call it if it exists. (This conversion is called key–value coding, and is the subject of the next section.) If you don't name your accessors properly, Cocoa can't find them.

A particularly good example is what happens when a nib loads where you've created an outlet in the nib. Suppose you have a class with an instance variable called `myVar` and you've drawn a `myVar` outlet from that class's representative in the nib to a Thing nib object. When the nib loads, the outlet name `myVar` is translated to the method name `setMyVar:`, and your instance's `setMyVar:` method, if it exists, is called with the Thing instance as its parameter, thus setting the value of your instance variable to the Thing (Figure 7-5).

It is important, therefore, to use the accessor names correctly and consistently. You should use accessor names for accessor methods. Just as important, you should *not* use accessor names for methods that aren't accessors! For example, you probably would *not* want to have a method called `setMyVar:` if it is *not* the accessor for the `myVar` instance variable. If you did have such a method, it would be called when the nib loads, the Thing instance would be passed to it, and the Thing instance would *not* be assigned to the `myVar` instance variable! As a result, references in your code to `myVar` would be references to nil.

This example is not at all far-fetched; I very often see beginners complain that they are telling some part of their interface to do something and it isn't doing it. This is frequently because they are accessing the object through an instance variable that is still nil, because it was never set properly through an outlet when the nib loaded, because they misused the name of the setter for some other purpose. (Of course it could also be because they forgot to draw the outlet in the nib in the first place.)

Although I keep saying that the names of the accessor methods use the name of the instance variable, there is no law requiring that they use the name of a *real* instance variable. Quite the contrary: you might deliberately have methods `myVar` and `setMyVar:` when in fact there is no `myVar` instance variable. Perhaps the accessors are masking the real name of the instance variable, which is `slartibartfast`, or perhaps there is no instance variable at all, and these accessors are really doing something quite different behind the scenes. That, indeed, is one of the main reasons for using accessors; they effectively present a façade, as if there were a certain instance variable, shielding the caller from any knowledge of the underlying details.

# Key–Value Coding

The way Cocoa derives the name of an accessor from the name of an instance variable is through a mechanism called *key–value coding*, or simply *KVC*. (See also Chapter 5, where I introduced key–value coding.) A *key* is a string (an NSString) that names the value to be accessed. The basis for key–value coding is the NSKeyValueCoding protocol, an informal protocol (it is actually a category) to which NSObject (and therefore every object) conforms.

The fundamental key–value coding methods are `valueForKey:` and `setValue:forKey:`. When one of these methods is called on an object, the object is introspected. In simplified terms, first the appropriate accessor is sought; if it doesn't exist, the instance variable is accessed directly. So, for example, suppose the call is this:

```
[myObject setValue:@"Hello" forKey:@"greeting"];
```

First, a method `setGreeting:` is sought in `myObject`; if it exists, it is called, passing @"Hello" as its argument. If that fails, but if `myObject` has an instance variable called `greeting`, the value @"Hello" is assigned directly to `myObject`'s `greeting` ivar.

 The key–value coding mechanism can bypass completely the privacy of an instance variable! Cocoa knows that you might not want to allow that, so a class method `accessInstanceVariablesDirectly` is supplied, which you can override to return NO (the default is YES).

Both `valueForKey:` and `setValue:forKey:` require an object as the value. Your accessor's signature (or, if there is no accessor, the instance variable itself) might not use an object as the value, so the key–value coding mechanism converts for you. Numeric types (including BOOL) are expressed as an NSNumber; other types (such as CGRect and CGPoint) are expressed as an NSValue.

As we have seen, Cocoa can access your instances via key–value coding (as it does when a nib containing an outlet is loaded). In addition, you can take advantage of key–value coding in your own code. KVC allows you to decide dynamically, at runtime, what instance variable to access; you obtain the instance variable's name as an NSString and pass that to `valueForKey:` or `setValue:forKey:`.

Also, a number of built-in Cocoa classes permit you to use key–value coding in a special way. If you send `valueForKey:` to an NSArray, it sends `valueForKey:` to each of its elements and returns a new array consisting of the results, an elegant shorthand (and a kind of poor man's `map`). NSSet behaves similarly. NSDictionary implements `valueForKey:` as an alternative to `objectForKey:` (useful particularly if you have an array of dictionaries); so does NSUserDefaults. CALayer (Chapter 16) and CAAnimation (Chapter 17) permit you to use key–value coding to define and retrieve the values for arbitrary keys, as if they were a kind of dictionary; this is useful for attaching identifying and configuration information to one of these instances.

Key–value coding requires caution, because by using an NSString instead of an instance variable or method name, you're throwing away compile-time checking. An attempt to access a nonexistent key through key–value coding will result, by default, in a crash at runtime, with an error message of this form: "This class is not key value coding-compliant for the key myKey." The lack of quotation marks around the word after "the key" has misled many a beginner, so remember: the last word in that error message is the name of the key that gave Cocoa trouble. A common way to encounter this error message is to change the name of an instance variable so that the name of an outlet in a nib no longer matches it; at runtime, when the nib loads, Cocoa will attempt to use key–value coding to set a value in your object based on the name of the outlet, will fail (because there is no longer an instance variable or accessor by that name), and will generate this error.

 A class is *key–value coding compliant* on a given key if it implements the methods, or possesses the instance variable, required for access via that key.

There is also something called a *key path* that allows you to chain keys in a single expression. If an object is key–value coding compliant for a certain key, and if the value of that key is itself an object that is key–value coding compliant for another key, you can chain those keys by calling valueForKeyPath: and setValue:forKeyPath:. A key path string looks like a succession of key names joined with a dot (.). For example, value-ForKeyPath:@"key1.key2" effectively calls valueForKey: on the message receiver, with @"key1" as the key, and then takes the object returned from that call and calls valueFor-Key: on that object, with @"key2" as the key.

To illustrate this shorthand, imagine that our object myObject has an instance variable theData which is an array of dictionaries such that each dictionary has a name key and a description key. I'll show you the actual value of theData as displayed by NSLog:

```
(
    {
        description = "The one with glasses.";
        name = Manny;
    },
    {
        description = "Looks a little like Governor Dewey.";
        name = Moe;
    },
    {
        description = "The one without a mustache.";
        name = Jack;
```

```
      }
   )
```

Then [myObject valueForKeyPath: @"theData.name"] returns an array consisting of the strings @"Manny", @"Moe", and @"Jack". If you don't understand why, review what I said a few paragraphs ago about how NSArray and NSDictionary implement valueForKey:.

Another feature of key–value coding is that it allows an object to implement a key as if its value were an array (or a set), even if it isn't. This is similar to what I said earlier about how accessors function as a façade, putting an instance variable name in front of hidden complexities. To illustrate, I'll add these methods to the class of our object myObject:

```
- (NSUInteger) countOfPepBoys {
    return [self.theData count];
}

- (id) objectInPepBoysAtIndex: (NSUInteger) ix {
    return [self.theData objectAtIndex: ix];
}
```

By implementing countOf... and objectIn...AtIndex:, I'm telling the key–value coding system to act as if the given key (@"pepBoys" in this case) existed and were an array. An attempt to fetch the value of the key @"pepBoys" by way of key–value coding will succeed, and will return an object that can be treated as an array, though in fact it is a proxy object (an NSKeyValueArray). Thus we can now say [myObject valueForKey: @"pepBoys"] to obtain this array proxy, and we can say [myObject valueForKeyPath: @"pepBoys.name"] to get the same array of strings as before. This particular example may seem a little silly because the underlying implementation is already an array instance variable, but you can imagine an implementation whereby the result of objectInPepBoysAtIndex: is obtained through some completely different sort of operation.

The proxy object returned through this sort of façade behaves like an NSArray, not like an NSMutableArray. If you want the caller to be able to manipulate the proxy object provided by a KVC façade as if it were a mutable array, you must implement two more methods, and you must obtain a different proxy object by calling mutableArrayValueForKey:. So, for example:

```
- (void) insertObject: (id) val inPepBoysAtIndex: (NSUInteger) ix {
    [self.theData insertObject:val atIndex:ix];
}

- (void) removeObjectFromPepBoysAtIndex: (NSUInteger) ix {
    [self.theData removeObjectAtIndex: ix];
}
```

Now you can call [myObject mutableArrayValueForKey: @"pepBoys"] to obtain something that acts like a mutable array. (The true usefulness of mutableArrayValueForKey:, however, will be clearer when we talk about key–value observing, later on.)

A complication for the programmer is that none of these method names can be looked up directly in the documentation, because they involve key names that are specific to your object. You can't find out from the documentation what `removeObjectFromPepBoys-AtIndex:` is for; you have to know, in some other way, that it is part of the implementation of key–value coding compliance for a key `@"pepBoys"` that can be obtained as a mutable array. Be sure to comment your code so that you'll be able to understand it later. Another complication, of course, is that getting a method name wrong can cause your object *not* to be key–value coding compliant. Figuring out why things aren't working as expected in a case like that can be tricky.

There is much more to key–value coding; see the *Key-Value Coding Programming Guide* for full information.

# Memory Management

It comes as a surprise to many beginning Cocoa coders that the programmer has an important role to play in the explicit management of memory. What's more, managing memory incorrectly is probably the most frequent cause of crashes — or, inversely, of memory leakage, whereby your app's use of memory increases relentlessly until, in the worst-case scenario, there's no memory left.

The reason why memory must be managed at all is that object references are pointers. As I explained in Chapter 1, the pointers themselves are simple C values (basically they are just integers) and are managed automatically, whereas what an object pointer points to is a hunk of memory that must explicitly be set aside when the object is brought into existence and that must explicitly be freed up when the object goes out of existence. We already know how the memory is set aside — that is what `alloc` does. But how is this memory to be freed up, and when should it happen?

At the very least, an object should certainly go out of existence when no other objects exist that have a pointer to it. An object without a pointer to it is useless; it is occupying memory, but no other object has, or can ever get, a reference to it. This is a *memory leak*. Many computer languages solve this problem through a policy called *garbage collection*. Simply put, the language prevents memory leaks by periodically sweeping through a central list of all objects and destroying those to which no pointer exists. In recent years, Objective-C and Cocoa have developed a form of garbage collection, but this is not available in iOS. Thus, memory must be managed more or less manually.

But manual memory management is no piece of cake, because an object must go out existence neither too late nor too soon. Suppose we endow the language with the ability for one object to command that another object go out of existence now, this instant. But multiple objects can have a pointer (a reference) to the very same object. If both the object Manny and the object Moe have a pointer to the object Jack, and if Manny tells Jack to go out of existence now, poor old Moe is left with a pointer to nothing (or worse, to garbage). A pointer whose object has been destroyed behind the pointer's back is a *dangling pointer*. If Moe subsequently uses that dangling pointer to send a message to the object that it thinks is there, the app will crash.

To prevent both dangling pointers and memory leakage, Objective-C and Cocoa implement a policy of manual memory management based on a number, maintained by every object, called its *retain count*. Other objects can increment or decrement an object's retain count. As long as an object's retain count is positive, the object will persist. No object has the direct power to tell another object to be destroyed; rather, as soon as an object's retain count drops to zero, it is destroyed automatically.

By this policy, every object that needs Jack to persist should increment Jack's retain count, and should decrement it once again when it no longer needs Jack to persist. As long as all objects are well-behaved in accordance with this policy, the problem of memory management is effectively solved:

- There cannot be any dangling pointers, because any object that has a pointer to Jack has incremented Jack's retain count, thus ensuring that Jack persists.
- There cannot be any memory leaks, because any object that no longer needs Jack decrements Jack's retain count, thus ensuring that eventually Jack will go out of existence (when the retain count reaches zero, because no object needs Jack any longer).

Obviously, all of this depends upon all objects cooperating in obedience to this memory management policy. Cocoa's objects (objects that are instances of built-in Cocoa classes) are well-behaved in this regard, but *you* must make sure *your* objects are well-behaved.

## The Golden Rules of Memory Management

Your objects will be well-behaved with respect to memory management as long as you understand the basic concepts of memory management and adhere to certain very simple rules.

Before I tell you the rules, it may help if I remind you (because this is confusing to beginners) that a variable name (including an instance variable) is just a pointer. When you send a message to that pointer, you are really sending a message *through* that pointer, to the object to which it points. The rules for memory management are rules about *objects*, not *names* (references, pointers). You cannot increment or decrement the retain count of a pointer; there is no such thing. The memory occupied by the pointer is managed automatically (and is tiny). What you are concerned with, in managing memory, is the object to which the pointer points.

(That is why I've referred to my example objects by proper names — Manny, Moe, and Jack — and not by variable names. The question of who has retained Jack has nothing to do with what any particular object *calls* Jack.)

## Debugging Memory Management Mistakes

Memory management mistakes are among the most common pitfalls for beginners and even for experienced Cocoa programmers. What experience really teaches is to use every tool at your disposal to ferret them out. Here are some:

- The static analyzer (Product → Analyze) knows a lot about memory management and can help call potential memory management mistakes to your attention.

- Instruments has excellent tools for noticing leaks and tracking memory management of individual objects (Product → Profile).

- Dangling pointers are particularly difficult to track down, but they can often be located by "turning on zombies." This is easy in Instruments with the Zombies template, but unfortunately it doesn't work on a device. For a device, edit the Run action in your scheme, switch to the Arguments tab, and under "Environment Variables" make a new variable whose name is NSZombieEnabled and whose value is YES. The result is that no object ever goes out of existence; instead, it is replaced by a "zombie" that will report to the console if a message is sent to it ("message sent to deallocated instance"). Be sure to turn zombies back off when you've finished tracking down your dangling pointers.

The two things are easily confused, especially because — as I've often pointed out in earlier chapters — the variable name pointing to an object is so often treated as the object that there is a tendency to think that it *is* the object, and to speak as if it were the object. It's clumsy, in fact, to separate talking about the name from talking about the object it points to. But in talking about memory management, I'll try to make that separation, for clarity and correctness, and to prevent confusion.

Here, then, are the golden rules of Cocoa memory management:

- To increment the retain count of any object, send it the **retain** message. This is called *retaining* the object. You should not use **retain** too freely, but you should not hesitate to use it in order to prevent a dangling pointer that would arise if the object should go out of existence while you still need it.

- When you (meaning a certain object) say **alloc** to a class, the resulting instance comes into the world with its retain count already incremented. You do *not* need to retain an object you've just instantiated by saying **alloc** (and you should not). Similarly, when you say **copy** to an instance, the resulting new object (the copy) comes into the world with its retain count already incremented. You do *not* need to retain an object you've just instantiated by saying **copy** (and you should not).

- To decrement the retain count of any object, send it the **release** message. This is called *releasing* the object. If you (meaning a certain object) obtained an object by saying **alloc** or **copy**, or if you said **retain** to an object, you (meaning the same

You must *never* release an object that you have *not* either retained or obtained via `alloc` or `copy`. You must *always* eventually release an object that you *have* either retained or obtained via `alloc` or `copy`.

An easy mnemonic is *ARC*, an acronym for `alloc`, `retain`, and `copy`. These, and only these, are the calls that must be balanced by `release`.

> I have deliberately avoided mentioning `new`, an NSObject class method equivalent to the entire "alloc-init" pattern. It is outmoded and rarely used; I never use it, and I don't think you should either. Nevertheless, you might encounter it in someone else's code (Apple's own sample code occasionally uses it). Because `new` implicitly involves `alloc`, it is covered by the *A* of *ARC*. Or perhaps the mnemonic should be rewritten *NARC*.

object) *must* balance this eventually by saying `release` to that object, *once*. You should assume that thereafter the object may no longer exist.

A general way of understanding memory management policy is to think in terms of *ownership*. If Manny has said `alloc`, `retain`, or `copy` with regard to Jack, Manny has asserted ownership of Jack. More than one object can own Jack at once. It is the responsibility of an owner of Jack eventually to release Jack, and a nonowner of Jack must *never* release Jack.

The moment an object is released, there is a chance it will be destroyed. You should therefore take care not to send any messages subsequently through the pointer that was used to release the object. In effect, you've just turned your *own* pointer into a possible dangling pointer! If there is any danger that you might accidentally attempt to use this dangling pointer, a wise policy is to *nilify* the pointer — that is, to set the pointer itself to nil. A message to nil has no effect, so if you do send a message through that pointer, it won't do any good, but at least it won't do any harm.

## How Cocoa Objects Manage Memory

Built-in Cocoa objects will take ownership of objects you hand them, by retaining them, if it makes sense for them to do so. (Indeed, this is so generally true that if a Cocoa object is *not* going to retain an object you hand it, there will be a note to that effect in the documentation.) Thus, you don't need to worry about managing memory for an object if the only thing you're going to do with it is hand it over to a Cocoa object.

A good example is an NSArray. Consider the following minimal example:

```
NSString* s = [[NSDate date] description];
NSArray* arr = [NSArray arrayWithObject: s];
```

When you hand the string to the array, the array retains the string. As long as the array exists and the string is in the array, the string will exist. When the array goes out of existence, it will also release the string; if no other object is retaining the string, the string will then go out of existence in good order, without leaking, and all will be well. All of this is right and proper; the array could hardly "contain" the string without taking ownership of it.

An NSMutableArray works the same way, with additions. When you add an object to an NSMutableArray, the array retains it. When you remove an object from an NSMutableArray, the array releases it. Again, the array is always doing the right thing.

This is a good example of how you should stay out of, and not worry yourself about, memory management for objects you don't own; the right thing will happen all by itself.

For instance, look back at Example 10-4. Here it is again:

```
NSString* f = [[NSBundle mainBundle] pathForResource:@"index" ofType:@"txt"];
NSError* err = nil;
NSString* s = [NSString stringWithContentsOfFile:f
                                        encoding:NSUTF8StringEncoding
                                           error:&err];
// error-checking omitted
NSMutableDictionary* d = [NSMutableDictionary dictionary];
for (NSString* line in [s componentsSeparatedByString:@"\n"]) {
    NSArray* items = [line componentsSeparatedByString:@"\t"];
    NSInteger chnum = [[items objectAtIndex: 0] integerValue];
    NSNumber* key = [NSNumber numberWithInteger:chnum];
    NSMutableArray* marr = [d objectForKey: key];
    if (!marr) { // no such key, create key-value pair
        marr = [NSMutableArray array];
        [d setObject: marr forKey: key];
    }
    // marr is now a mutable array, empty or otherwise
    NSString* picname = [items objectAtIndex: 1];
    [marr addObject: picname];
}
```

Absolutely no explicit memory management is happening here, because no explicit memory management needs to happen. We're generating a lot of objects, but never do we say alloc (or copy), so we have no ownership, and memory management is therefore not our concern. Moreover, no bad thing is going to happen between one line and the next while this code is running. The mutable dictionary d, for example, generated by calling [NSMutableDictionary dictionary], is not going to vanish mysteriously before we can finish adding objects to it. (I'll say a bit more, later in this chapter, about why I'm so confident of this.)

On the other hand, you still need to think a little, as you interact with them, about how Cocoa objects manage memory. Consider the following:

```
NSString* s = [myMutableArray objectAtIndex: 0];
[myMutableArray removeObjectAtIndex: 0]; // Bad idea!
```

Here we remove a string from an array, keeping a reference to it ourselves as s. But, as I just said, when you remove an object from an NSMutableArray, the array releases it. So the commented line of code in the previous example involves an implicit release of the string in question, and if this reduces the string's retain count to zero, it will be destroyed. In effect, we've just done the thing I warned you about at the end of the previous section: we've turned our own pointer s into a possible dangling pointer, and a crash may be in our future when we try to use it as if it were a string.

The way to ensure against such possible destruction is to retain the object before doing anything that might destroy it:

```
NSString* s = [myMutableArray objectAtIndex: 0];
[s retain];
[myMutableArray removeObjectAtIndex: 0];
```

Of course, now you have made management of this object your business; you have asserted ownership of it, and must make sure that this **retain** is eventually balanced by a subsequent **release**, or the string object may leak.

In general, Cocoa does not retain things like delegates and data sources, action targets, and objects registered to receive a notification. This makes sense from an ownership perspective, but it means that you must take care not to let an object go on thinking that its delegate, data source, action target, or notification recipient exists when it does not, lest it attempt to send a message through a garbage pointer.

Thus, suppose you (a certain object) make yourself some other object's delegate in code, like this:

```
[otherObject setDelegate: self];
```

If you now are about to go out of existence, and if otherObject still exists, you should stop being its delegate. The safe and proper way to do this is to nilify otherObject's delegate pointer:

```
[otherObject setDelegate: nil];
```

Similarly, suppose you (a certain object) have registered yourself to receive a notification, as in Chapter 11:

```
[[NSNotificationCenter defaultCenter] addObserver:self
                        selector:@selector(toggleEnglish:)
                           name:@"toggleEnglish" object:nil];
```

Then if you are now about to go out of existence, and if you are still registered for this notification, you should unregister for it:

```
[[NSNotificationCenter defaultCenter] removeObserver: self];
```

These are tasks that you will handle in your **dealloc** method, if not before; I'll be discussing **dealloc** in the next section.

Be on the lookout for Cocoa objects with unusual memory management behavior. Such behavior will be called out clearly in the documentation. For example, the UIWebView documentation warns: "Before releasing an instance of UIWebView for which you have set a delegate, you must first set its delegate property to nil." And a CAAnimation object retains its delegate; this is exceptional and can cause trouble if you're not conscious of it.

## Memory Management of Instance Variables

As soon as your own instance variables enter the picture, that is a sign to you that you should prick up your memory-management antennae. Return once more, for example, to Example 10-4. As I emphasized in the previous section, there was no need to worry about memory management during this code. We have a mutable dictionary d, which we acquired as a ready-made instance by calling [NSMutableDictionary dictionary], and it isn't going to vanish while we're working with it. Now, however, suppose that in the *next* line we propose to assign d to an instance variable of ours:

```
self->theData = d; // No no no no!
```

That code is a serious potential mistake. If our code now comes to a stop, we're left with a persistent pointer to an object over which we have never asserted ownership; it might vanish, leaving us with a dangling pointer. The solution, obviously, is to retain this object as we assign it to our instance variable. You could do it like this:

```
[d retain];
self->theData = d;
```

Or you could do it like this:

```
self->theData = d;
[self->theData retain];
```

Or, because retain returns self, you could actually do it like this:

```
self->theData = [d retain];
```

(Make sure you understand why those are all equivalent. It's because d and self->theData are just names; they are pointers. What you're retaining is the object pointed to. How you refer to that object, under what name, is neither here nor there.)

So which should you use? Probably none of them. Consider what a lot of trouble it will be if you ever want to assign a *different* value to self->theData. You're going to have to remember to release the object already pointed to (to balance the retain you've used here), and you're going to have to remember to retain the next value as well. It would be much better to encapsulate memory management for this instance variable in an accessor (a setter). That way, as long as you always pass through the accessor, memory will be managed correctly. A standard template for such an accessor might look like Example 12-1.

*Example 12-1. A simple retaining setter*

```
- (void) setTheData: (NSMutableArray*) value {
    if (self->theData != value) {
        [self->theData release];
        self->theData = [value retain];
    }
}
```

In Example 12-1, we release the object currently pointed to by our instance variable (and if that object is nil, no harm done) and retain the incoming value before assigning it to our instance variable. The test for whether the incoming value is the object already pointed to by our instance variable is not just to save a step; it's because if we were to release that object, it could vanish then and there, turning not only self->theData but also value (which points to the same thing) into a dangling pointer.

The setter accessor now manages memory correctly for us; provided we always use it to set our instance variable, all will be well. This is one of the main reasons why accessors are so important! So the assignment to the instance variable in our original code should now look like this:

```
[self setTheData: d];
```

Observe that we can also use this setter subsequently to release the value of the instance variable and nilify the instance variable itself, thus preventing a dangling pointer, all in a single easy step:

```
[self setTheData: nil];
```

So there's yet another benefit of using an accessor to manage memory.

Our memory management for this instance variable is still incomplete, however. We (meaning the object whose instance variable this is) must also remember to release the object pointed to by this instance variable at the last minute before we ourselves go out of existence. Otherwise, if this instance variable points to a retained object, there will be a memory leak. For this very reason, NSObject has an instance method that you will almost always override: dealloc. This method is called as an object goes out of existence. Thus, it is "the last minute."

In dealloc, there is no need to use accessors to refer to an instance variable, and in fact it's not a good idea to do so, because you never know what other side effects an accessor might have. And you must always call super last of all. So here's our implementation of this object's dealloc:

```
- (void) dealloc {
    [self->theData release];
    [super dealloc];
}
```

That completes the memory management for one instance variable. In general, you will need to make sure that *every* object of yours has a dealloc that releases *every* instance variable whose value has been retained.

As mentioned earlier, dealloc is also your last chance to clean up non-retained references to yourself that you have created, such as when you've set yourself to be some other object's delegate, or you've registered with the notification center to receive notifications. Make certain to fulfill these obligations to prevent a message from being sent later to a dangling pointer after you go out of existence.

 Never, never call dealloc in your code, except to call super last of all in your override of dealloc.

Just as it's not a good idea to use your own accessors to refer to your own instance variable in dealloc, so you should not use your own accessors to refer to your own instance variables in an initializer (see Chapter 5). The reason is in part that the object is not yet fully formed, and in part that an accessor can have other side effects. Instead, you must set your instance variables directly, but you must also remember to manage memory.

To illustrate, I'll rewrite the example initializer from Chapter 5 (Example 5-3). This time I'll allow our object (a Dog) to be initialized with a name. The reason I didn't discuss this possibility in Chapter 5 is that a string is an object whose memory must be managed! So, imagine now that we have an instance variable name whose value is an NSString, and we want an initializer that allows the caller to pass in a value for this instance variable. It might look like Example 12-2.

*Example 12-2. A simple initializer that retains an ivar*

```
- (id) initWithName: (NSString*) s {
    self = [super init];
    if (self) {
        self->name = [s retain];
    }
    return self;
}
```

Actually, it is more likely in the case of an NSString that you would copy it rather than merely retain it. The reason is that NSString has a mutable subclass, so some other object might call initWithName: and hand you a mutable string to which it still holds a reference — and then mutate it, thus changing this Dog's name behind your back. So the initializer would look like Example 12-3.

*Example 12-3. A simple initializer that copies an ivar*

```
- (id) initWithName: (NSString*) s {
    self = [super init];
    if (self) {
        self->name = [s copy];
    }
```

```
    return self;
}
```

In Example 12-3, we don't bother to release the existing value of name; it is certainly not pointing to any *previous* value (because there is no previous value), so there's no point.

Thus, memory management for an instance variable may take place in as many as three places: the initializer, the setter, and dealloc. This is a common architecture. It is a lot of work, and a common source of error, having to look in multiple places to check that you are managing memory consistently and correctly, but that's what you must do. Luckily, as I'll point out later in this chapter, Objective-C has the ability to write your accessors for you. But it won't write initializers or dealloc for you, and in any case you should still understand memory management in accessors.

> Earlier, I mentioned that KVC will set an instance variable directly if it can't find a setter corresponding to the key. When it does this, *it retains the incoming value*. This fact is little-known and poorly documented — and scary. The last thing you want is implicit memory management. This is one more reason to provide accessors.

## Instance Variable Memory Management Policies

In the preceding section, we saw that an instance variable might be set by retaining or copying the incoming value. There are in fact three possible memory-management policies for an instance variable:

*retain*
> The incoming value is retained (and the existing value is released).

*copy*
> The incoming value is copied (and the existing value is released). This policy is typical where the class of the instance variable is an immutable class with a mutable subclass (such as NSString, NSArray, or NSDictionary), in case we are handed a mutable instance that might be subsequently mutated by some other object.

*assign*
> The incoming value is directly assigned to the instance variable; it is not retained, nor is the existing value released. This policy is followed when it would be wrong for us to assert ownership of the incoming object. For example, an object would not normally retain its delegate.

The "assign" policy must also be used to prevent a *retain cycle*, a situation in which two objects retain each other. This must never be allowed to happen, because both objects will leak (neither can have its retain count reach zero by normal means). For example, in a system of orders and items, an order needs to know what its items are and an item might need to know what orders it is a part of, but it must not be the case *both* that an order retains its items *and* that an item retains its orders.

Note that you must *not* release, in `dealloc`, an instance variable whose policy is "assign." You would be releasing something you never retained or generated by copying, which is a no-no (and a likely crasher).

## Autorelease

Consider the following situation. Your object has a method that creates and vends an object. It creates the object in a way that calls for release:

```
- (NSArray*) vendArray {
    NSArray* arr = [[NSArray alloc] initWithObjects: @"Hello, world!", nil];
    return arr; // hmmm, not so fast...
}
```

We've got a memory management problem. On the one hand, we generated `arr`'s value by saying `alloc`. This means we must release the object pointed to by `arr`. On the other hand, when are we going to do this? If we do it just *before* returning `arr`, `arr` will be pointing to garbage and we will be vending garbage. We cannot do it just *after* returning `arr`, because our method exits when we say `return`. This is a puzzle. We need a way to vend this object, yet ensure that its retain count *will* be decremented, without decrementing it *now*.

That's what `autorelease` is for:

```
- (NSArray*) vendArray {
    NSArray* arr = [[NSArray alloc] initWithObjects: @"Hello, world!", nil];
    [arr autorelease];
    return arr;
}
```

Or, because `autorelease` returns `self`, we can condense that:

```
- (NSArray*) vendArray {
    NSArray* arr = [[NSArray alloc] initWithObjects: @"Hello, world!", nil];
    return [arr autorelease];
}
```

Here's how `autorelease` works. Your code runs in the presence of something called an *autorelease pool*. (If you look in *main.m*, you can actually see such one such pool being created.) When you send `autorelease` to an object, that object is placed in the autorelease pool, and a number is incremented saying how many times this object has been placed in this autorelease pool. From time to time, when nothing else is going on, the autorelease pool is automatically destroyed and replaced by another. At the moment when an autorelease pool is destroyed, it sends `release` to each of its objects, the same number of times as that object was placed in this autorelease pool. This is called *draining* the pool. If that causes an object's retain count to be zero, fine; the object is destroyed in the usual way. So `autorelease` is just like `release` — effectively, it *is* a form of `release` — but with a proviso, "later, not right this second."

You don't need to know exactly when the current autorelease pool will be drained; indeed, you can't know (unless you force it, as we shall see). The important thing is that in a case like our method vendArray, there will be plenty of time for whoever called vendArray to retain the vended object if desired.

The vended object in a case like our method vendArray is called an *autoreleased object*. The object is not going to vanish right this second, because your code is running. As you vend the object, your code is *still* running. The recipient of the object (whoever called vendArray) needs to bear in mind that this object may be autoreleased. It won't vanish while *that* code is running either, but if the receiving object wants to be sure that the object will persist later on, it should retain it.

In general, the same considerations apply to objects vended by Cocoa. An object you receive by means *other* than those listed in the *ARC* rule isn't under your ownership, so if you want it to persist and you're afraid it might not, you should take ownership of it. But that doesn't mean you need to retain immediately every such object Cocoa hands you, because in general the object will either be owned and retained by some other persistent object, in which case it won't vanish while the other object persists, or it will be independent but autoreleased, in which case it will at least persist while your code continues to run. That's why there's no explicit memory management in Example 10-4 (cited earlier in this chapter): we don't madly retain every object we obtain, because they will all persist long enough for our code to finish.

Sometimes you may wish to drain the autorelease pool immediately. Consider the following:

```
for (NSString* aWord in myArray) {
    NSString* lowerAndShorter = [[aWord lowercaseString] substringFromIndex:1];
    [myMutableArray addObject: lowerAndShorter];
}
```

Every time through that loop, two objects are added to the autorelease pool: the lowercase version of the string we start with, and the shortened version of that. The first object, the lowercase version of the string, is purely an *intermediate object*: as the current iteration of the loop ends, no one except the autorelease pool has a pointer to it. If this loop had very many repetitions, or if these intermediate objects were themselves very large in size, this could add up to a lot of memory. These intermediate objects will all be released when the autorelease pool drains, so they are not leaking; nevertheless, they are accumulating in memory, and in certain cases there could be a danger that we will run out of memory before the autorelease pool drains. The problem can be even more acute than you know, because you might repeatedly call a built-in Cocoa method that itself accumulates a lot of intermediate objects.

The solution is to intervene in the autorelease pool mechanism by supplying your own autorelease pool. This works because the autorelease pool used to store an autoreleased object is the most recently created pool. So you can just create an autorelease pool at the top of the loop and release it at the bottom of the loop, each time through the loop.

When you release an autorelease pool, it is drained, so the objects it contains are sent release then and there:

```
for (NSString* aWord in myArray) {
    NSAutoreleasePool* pool = [[NSAutoreleasePool alloc] init];
    NSString* lowerAndShorter = [[aWord lowercaseString] substringFromIndex:1];
    [myMutableArray addObject: lowerAndShorter];
    [pool release];
}
```

Many classes provide the programmer with two equivalent ways to obtain an object: either an autoreleased object or an object that you create yourself with alloc and some form of init. So, for example, NSArray supplies both the class method arrayWithObjects: and the instance method initWithObjects:. Which should you use? On the whole, Apple would prefer you to lean toward initWithObjects:. In general, where you can generate an object with alloc and some form of init, they'd like you to do so. That way, you are in charge of releasing the object. This policy will prevent your objects from hanging around in the autorelease pool and will keep your use of memory as low as possible.

## Nib Loading and Memory Management

On iOS, when a nib loads, the top-level nib objects that it instantiates are autoreleased. So if someone doesn't retain them, they'll eventually vanish in a puff of smoke. There are two primary strategies for preventing that from happening:

*Outlet graph with retain*
> A memory management graph is formed: every top-level object is retained by another top-level object (without retain cycles, of course), with the File's Owner as the start of the graph. So, the File's Owner proxy has an outlet to a top-level object, and this outlet is backed by an accessor whose setter uses a retain policy. Thus, when the nib loads, the nib owner retains this top-level object (and must, of course, remember to release it before it itself goes out of existence). And so on, for every top-level object (Figure 12-1). This is the strategy you'll typically use when loading a nib.

*Mass retain*
> The call to loadNibNamed:owner:options: (Chapter 7) returns an NSArray of the nib-instantiated objects; retain this NSArray. This is the strategy used by UIApplicationMain when it loads the app's main nib.

Objects in the nib that are *not* top-level objects are already part of a memory management object graph, so there's no need for you to retain them directly. For example, if you have a top-level UIView in the nib, and it contains a UIButton, the UIButton is the UIView's subview — and a view retains its subviews and takes ownership of them. Thus, it is sufficient to manage the UIView's memory and to let the UIView manage the UIButton.

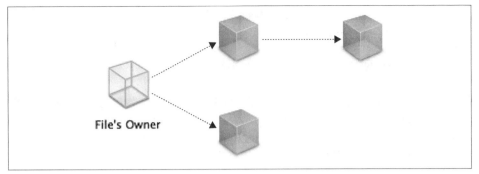

Figure 12-1. *An outlet graph with retain*

However, if you have an outlet to this UIButton, you must be extremely careful! Recall that this outlet will be linked to its source instance at nib-loading time using KVC. This means that if you declare an ivar as an IBOutlet, with no corresponding setter, KVC will add an extra retain to the target instance as it sets the ivar directly, which can cause a memory leak. The best practice, therefore, is always to supply an accessor. An accessor with an assign policy will defend against the entire problem (and this, I'll show later in this chapter, is easy to arrange through a property and a synthesized accessor).

 **Mac OS X Programmer Alert**

Memory management for nib-loaded instances is different on iOS than on Mac OS X. On Mac OS X, nib-loaded instances are not autoreleased, so they don't have to be retained, and memory management is usually automatic in any case because the file's owner is usually an NSWindowController, which takes care of these things for you. On iOS, memory management of top-level nib objects is up to you. On Mac OS X, an outlet to a non-top-level object does not cause an extra retain if there is no accessor for the corresponding ivar; on iOS, it does.

## Memory Management Comments on Earlier Examples

Examples from earlier chapters in this book have omitted memory management, because we hadn't yet discussed it, and are thus incomplete. I don't want you copying incorrect models, so here are some comments on earlier examples.

The singleton vendor from Chapter 1 may appear to leak, because it contains an unbalanced `alloc`:

```
+ (CardPainter*) sharedPainter {
    static CardPainter* sp = nil;
    if (nil == sp)
        sp = [[CardPainter alloc] init];
    return sp;
}
```

In reality, that doesn't count as a leak because it's not an instance method. It's a class method. The instance assigned to sp will persist as long as the class does, which is what we want. It would also persist after the class no longer exists, but there is no such time; if the class no longer exists, it must be because the app has terminated. So there is no leak.

In Example 5-2 and any other example in Chapter 5 where we generated an instance by saying alloc, we should of course be releasing that instance eventually. Similarly, in Chapter 7, we instantiate MyClass only to use it as a nib owner and extract a nib object; when that's done, we should release the instance:

```
MyClass* mc = [[MyClass alloc] init];
[[NSBundle mainBundle] loadNibNamed:@"MyNib" owner:mc options:nil];
UILabel* lab = [mc valueForKey: @"theLabel"];
[self.window addSubview: lab];
lab.center = CGPointMake(100,100);
[mc release];
```

This example from Chapter 7 is more complicated:

```
- (void) buttonPressed: (id) sender {
    UIAlertView* av = [[UIAlertView alloc] initWithTitle:@"Howdy!"
                                         message:@"You tapped me."
                                         delegate:nil
                              cancelButtonTitle:@"Cool"
                              otherButtonTitles:nil];
    [av show];
}
```

How do you manage the memory for a UIAlertView? Can you release it in the same method where it's created? If you do, will the UIAlertView vanish in a puff of smoke while we're still displaying it? Remarkably, it's perfectly safe to say this:

```
- (void) buttonPressed: (id) sender {
    UIAlertView* av = [[UIAlertView alloc] initWithTitle:@"Howdy!"
                                         message:@"You tapped me."
                                         delegate:nil
                              cancelButtonTitle:@"Cool"
                              otherButtonTitles:nil];
    [av show];
    [av release];
}
```

The show method retains the UIAlertView, which is then autoreleased; the autorelease pool is not drained until after the alert is dismissed and its delegate methods have been called. The same applies to the UIAlertView examples in Chapter 11.

In the NSLocale example in Chapter 10, memory management was omitted; here it is again, in its full form:

```
NSDateFormatter *df = [[NSDateFormatter alloc] init];
if ([[NSLocale availableLocaleIdentifiers] indexOfObject:@"en_US"] != NSNotFound) {
    NSLocale* loc =
      [[NSLocale alloc] initWithLocaleIdentifier:@"en_US"];
```

```
    [df setLocale:loc]; // force English month name and time zone name if possible
    [loc release];
}
[df setDateFormat:@"d MMMM yyyy 'at' h:mm a z"];
NSString* lastUpdated = [df stringFromDate: [NSDate date]];
[df release];
```

## Memory Management of Pointer-to-Void Context Info

A number of Cocoa methods take an optional parameter typed as void*, and often called context. You might think that void*, the universal pointer type, would be the same as id, the universal object type, because a reference to an object is a pointer. But an id is a universal *object* type; void* is just a C pointer. This means that Cocoa won't treat this value as an object. So the use of the void* type is a clue to you that Cocoa won't do any memory management on this value. Thus, making sure that it persists long enough to be useful is up to you.

As an example, I'll use beginAnimations:context:. You call this on a UIView before changing one or more of its property values, such as its size, position, or opacity, to make those changes appear animated. Whatever you pass as the context parameter comes back to you later in two delegate messages as the animation proceeds, indicating that the animation is about to start and that the animation has ended; basically, the context is a kind of envelope in which information can be carried from stage to stage during the animation, for any purpose you desire. The context is a void*. So how should you manage its memory?

Let's assume that the void* is in fact an object. A simple solution is to retain it as you hand it to beginAnimations:context: and release it later, when you're done with it. But when exactly is "later," and when are you actually "done with it?" A good answer would appear to be, "When the animation is over," which is when the animationDidStop:finished:context: delegate message arrives. So you could release the context object when you receive it in animationDidStop:finished:context:.

This solution works, but it isn't very maintainable. You're balancing memory-management calls in two very different places, so you can't easily keep an eye on them both. As your code evolves, what if you decide you no longer need to receive animationDidStop:finished:context:, and you delete your implementation of it? If you implement the delegate method for the animation starting, now you have to move the release to that method. If not, you have to eliminate the retain. It's all getting very messy and confusing.

A better approach is to make these context objects persistent, as instance variables or globals, and manage their memory as you would any persistent pointer. A context object will thus persist even after it is no longer needed, but it won't actually leak, provided you release it before you yourself (the managing object) go out of existence. Here's a complete example:

```
static id g_animcontext = nil;

- (void) animate {
    // set up context info pointer with memory management
    [g_animcontext release];
    g_animcontext = [NSDictionary dictionaryWithObject: @"object" forKey: @"key"];
    [g_animcontext retain];
    // prepare animation
    [UIView beginAnimations:@"shrinkImage" context:g_animcontext];
    [UIView setAnimationDelegate:self];
    [UIView setAnimationDidStopSelector:
        @selector(animationDidStop:finished:context:)];
    [imv setAlpha: 0];
    // request animation to start
    [UIView commitAnimations];
}

- (void) animationDidStop:(NSString*)anim
                  finished:(NSNumber *)f context:(void *)c {
    NSDictionary* d = c; // cast back to dictionary, use as desired
    // no memory management for context info here
    // ...
}

- (void)dealloc {
    [g_animcontext release];
    // ... other releases and so forth ...
    [super dealloc];
}
```

Considerations of this sort do not apply to parameters that are typed as objects. For instance, when you call postNotificationName:object:userInfo:, the userInfo is typed as an NSDictionary and is retained for you (and released after the notification is posted); its memory management is not your concern.

## Memory Management of C Struct Pointers

A value obtained through a C function that is a pointer to a struct (its type name will usually end in "Ref") is a kind of object, even though it isn't a full-fledged Cocoa Objective-C object, and it must be managed in much the same way as a Cocoa object. The rule here is that if you obtained such an object through a function whose name contains the word Create or Copy, you are responsible for releasing it. In the case of a Core Foundation object (its type name begins with CF), you'll release it with the CFRelease function; other object creation functions are paired with their own object release functions.

An Objective-C object can be sent messages even if it is nil. But CFRelease cannot take a NULL argument. Be sure that a pointer-to-struct variable is not NULL before releasing it.

The matter is not a complicated one; it's much simpler than memory management of Cocoa objects, and the documentation will usually give you a hint about your memory management responsibilities. As an example, here (without further explanation) is some actual code from one of my apps, strongly modeled on Apple's own example code, in which I set up a base pattern color space (for drawing with a pattern):

```
- (void) addPattern: (CGContextRef) context color: (CGColorRef) incolor {
    CGColorSpaceRef baseSpace;
    CGColorSpaceRef patternSpace;
    baseSpace = CGColorSpaceCreateDeviceRGB ();
    patternSpace = CGColorSpaceCreatePattern (baseSpace);
    CGContextSetFillColorSpace (context, patternSpace);
    CGColorSpaceRelease (patternSpace);
    CGColorSpaceRelease (baseSpace);
    // ...
}
```

Never mind exactly what that code does; the important thing here is that the values for `baseSpace` and `patternSpace` are a "Ref" type (CGColorSpaceRef) obtained through functions with `Create` in their name, so after we're done using them, we release them with the corresponding release function (here, `CGColorSpaceRelease`).

Similarly, you can retain a Core Foundation object, if you are afraid that it might go out of existence while you still need it, with the `CFRetain` function, and you are then, once again, responsible for releasing it with the `CFRelease` function.

When a Core Foundation object type is toll-free bridged with a Cocoa object type, it makes no difference whether you use Core Foundation memory management or Cocoa memory management. For example, if you obtain a CFStringRef and assign it to an NSString variable, sending `release` to it through the NSString variable is just as good as calling `CFRelease` on it.

# Properties

A *property* (see Chapter 5) is syntactic sugar for calling an accessor by using dot-notation. An object does not have a property unless its class (or that class's superclass, of course) declares it. For instance, in a earlier example we had an object with an NSMutableArray instance variable and a setter, which we called like this:

```
[self setTheData: d];
```

If this object's class code declares a property `theData`, we could instead say:

```
self.theData = d;
```

The effect would be exactly the same, because setting a property is just a shorthand for calling the setter. Similarly, suppose we were to say this:

```
NSMutableArray* arr = self.theData;
```

That is exactly the same as calling the getter.

Properties offer certain advantages that accessors, of themselves, do not:

- It is simpler to declare one property than to declare two accessor methods.
- A property declaration includes a statement of the setter's memory management policy. Thus it easy to know, just by glancing at a property declaration, how the incoming value will be treated. You could find this out otherwise only by looking at the setter's code — which, if this is a built-in Cocoa type, you cannot do (and even in the case of your own code, it's a pain having to locate and consult the setter directly).
- With a property declaration, you can ask Cocoa to construct the accessors for you, automatically. Such an automatically constructed accessor is called a *synthesized accessor*. Writing accessors is boring and error-prone; with a property, you write two lines of code (the property declaration, and the request that Cocoa construct its accessors) and that's all: the accessors now exist, without you bothering to write them. The setter produced in this automatic way takes care of managing memory for you, correctly, according to the policy you state in the property declaration.

Thus you will almost certainly want to declare properties for your object-value instance variables. With properties, instance variables become much easier to deal with: you don't have to write accessors for them, you don't have to worry that your accessors might not be handling memory management correctly, and you know at a glance how those accessors do manage memory.

A property is declared in the same part of a class's interface section where you would declare methods. Its syntax schema is as follows:

```
@property (attribute, attribute, ...) type name;
```

Here's a real example, for the NSMutableArray instance variable we were talking about a moment ago:

```
@property (nonatomic, retain) NSMutableArray* theData;
```

The *type* and *name* will usually match the type and name of an instance variable, but what you're really indicating here are the name of the property (as used in dot-notation) and the type of value to be passed to the setter and obtained from the getter.

If this property will be represented by an outlet in a nib, you can say `IBOutlet` before the type. This is a hint to the nib editor and has no formal meaning. The type doesn't have to be an object type; it can be a simple type such as BOOL, CGFloat, or CGSize, but of course in that case no memory management is performed (as none is needed).

The possible attributes are:

`nonatomic`
> If omitted, the synthesized accessors will use locking to ensure correct operation if your app is multithreaded. This will rarely be a concern, and locking slows down the operation of the accessors, so you'll probably specify `nonatomic` most of the time. It's a pity that `nonatomic` isn't the default, but such is life.

retain, copy, *or* assign

These are your choices of memory management policy for the setter (see the discussion of setter memory management policies, earlier in this chapter). If omitted, the default is assign.

readwrite *or* readonly

If omitted, the default is readwrite. If you say readonly, any attempt to use the property as a setter will cause a compiler error (a useful feature), and if the accessors are to be synthesized, no setter is synthesized.

getter=*gname,* setter=*sname*:

By default, the property name is used to derive the names of the getter and setter methods that will be called when the property is used. If the property is named my-Prop, the default getter method name is myProp and the default setter name is set-MyProp:. You can use either or both of these attributes to change that. If you say getter=getALife, you're saying that the getter method corresponding to this property is called getALife (and if the accessors are synthesized, the getter will be given this name).

To request that the accessors be synthesized for you, use the @synthesize directive. It appears anywhere inside the class's implementation section, any number of times, and takes a comma-separated list of property names. The behavior and names of the synthesized accessors will accord with the property declaration attributes I've just talked about. You can state that the synthesized accessors should access an instance variable whose name differs from the property name by using the syntax *propertyName=ivarName* in the property name list.

Thus, using our NSMutableArray instance variable theData as an example, the full code would look like this:

```
// [In the header file]
@interface MyClass : NSObject {
    NSMutableArray* theData;
    // other ivars go here
}
@property (nonatomic, retain) NSMutableArray* theData;
// other properties, method declarations go here
@end

// [In the implementation file]
@implementation MyClass
@synthesize theData
// other code goes here; don't forget to release theData in dealloc
@end
```

If you provide a @property declaration along with a corresponding @synthesize statement, but no corresponding instance variable declaration, the instance variable declaration is implicitly generated for you. This is a *synthesized instance variable.* Thus:

```
@interface MyClass : NSObject {
    // NSMutableArray* theData;
    // omitted, because the implementation says @synthesize theData
}
@property (nonatomic, retain) NSMutableArray* theData;
@end
```

This is a convenient shorthand, and I'll often use it in this book.

 A synthesized instance variable is strictly private, meaning that it is not inherited by subclasses. This fact will rarely prove troublesome, but if it does, simply declare the instance variable explicitly.

You are now in a position to understand the property declaration in the Xcode 4 Window-based Application project template, used by our Empty Window example (the Empty_WindowAppDelegate class). In *Empty_WindowAppDelegate.h*, the interface section declares a property (and an outlet) window, but no instance variable:

```
@property (nonatomic, retain) IBOutlet UIWindow *window;
```

In *Empty_WindowAppDelegate.m*, the implementation synthesizes the accessors, implicitly synthesizing the instance variable declaration, using an alternate name _window for the instance variable:

```
@synthesize window=_window;
```

The result is that we can refer in our code to the property explicitly as self.window, but if we were accidentally to refer to the instance variable directly as window, we'd get a compilation error, because there is no instance variable window (it's called _window). Thus the template adopts a policy designed both to prevent accidental direct access to the instance variable without passing through the accessors and to distinguish clearly in code which names are instance variables — they're the ones starting with an underscore. This can be a useful convention (though this book does not adopt it).

To make a property declaration private, when its accessors are to be synthesized, put it in an anonymous category (a class extension). In this way, this class can access the instance variable through its accessors but other classes cannot (Example 12-4).

*Example 12-4. A private property*

```
// [In the implementation file]
@interface MyClass ()
@property (nonatomic, retain) NSMutableArray* theData;
@end

@implementation MyClass
@synthesize theData
// other code goes here; don't forget to release theData in dealloc
@end
```

Another use of the same structure is to *redeclare* the property. For example, we might want our property to be readonly as far as the rest of the world knows, but readwrite for code within our class. To implement this, declare the property readonly in the interface section in the header file, and then redeclare it as readwrite in the anonymous category interface section in the implementation file. All other attributes must match between both declarations.

If you do not ask explicitly that a declared property's accessors be synthesized, then you must supply them explicitly or the compiler will complain. This is somewhat annoying; one wishes that synthesis of accessors were the default, to save a step when writing and maintaining code. You can turn off this complaint by using @dynamic instead of @synthesize, but this is a promise to generate the accessors in some other way, at runtime, and is rarely used except in connection with Core Animation and Core Data. (An example of @dynamic with Core Animation appears in Chapter 17.)

A useful trick is to take advantage of the @synthesize syntax *propertyName=ivarName* to override the synthesized accessor without losing any of its functionality. What I mean is this. Suppose you want the setter for myIvar to do more than just set myIvar. One possibility is to write your own setter; a synthesized setter does the job correctly, however, while writing a setter from scratch is tedious and error-prone. The solution is to declare a property myIvar along with a corresponding private property (Example 12-4) — let's call it myIvarAlias — and synthesize the private property myIvarAlias to access the myIvar instance variable. You must then write the accessors for myIvar by hand, but all they need to do, at a minimum, is use the myIvarAlias properties to set and get the value of myIvar respectively. The key point is that you can also do *other* stuff in those accessors (Example 12-5); whoever gets or sets the property myIvar will be doing that other stuff.

*Example 12-5. Overriding synthesized accessors*

```
// [In the header file]

@interface MyClass : NSObject {
}
@property (nonatomic, retain) NSNumber* myIvar;
@end

// [In the implementation file]

@interface MyClass ()
@property (nonatomic, retain) NSNumber* myIvarAlias;
@end

@implementation MyClass
@synthesize myIvarAlias=myIvar;

- (void) setMyIvar: (NSNumber*) num {
    // do other stuff here
    self.myIvarAlias = num;
}
```

```
- (NSNumber*) myIvar {
    // do other stuff here
    return self.myIvarAlias;
}
@end
```

A property declaration can also appear in a protocol or category declaration. This makes sense because, with a property declaration, you're really just declaring accessor methods, and these are places where method declarations can go.

Properties make life much easier when dealing with instance variables and their memory management, and you'll doubtless use them all the time. Consider, for example, how trivial it becomes to manage memory for top-level nib objects. Let's say the File's Owner has an outlet to a certain top-level nib object; let's call the outlet myObject. Then the nib owner's interface section contains this line:

```
@property (nonatomic, retain) IBOutlet id myObject;
```

In the implementation section, you say @synthesize myObject, and presto! When the nib loads, the nib's owner retains this nib object.

Do not forget, however, that you must still manage memory when an object goes out of existence. It is up to you to put a release in your dealloc method for any instance variables whose setter uses a retain or copy policy — even if the setter was synthesized and the policy was declared through a property.

 In Xcode 4, when you create an outlet by dragging from a nib object to code in such a way as to generate an instance variable declaration, Xcode creates the instance variable declaration *and* the corresponding release call; when you create an outlet by dragging from a nib object to code in such a way as to generate a property declaration, Xcode creates the property declaration *and* the instance variable declaration *and* the @synthesize directive *and* the corresponding release call. This is cool, but it does make one wonder why Xcode 4 can't do this for *any* property or instance variable you create.

If, at compile time, you get a mysterious error in connection with a property name propertyname, "request for member 'propertyname' in something not a structure or union," this merely means that the object reference to which you have attached this property name by dot-notation has no such property. Probably you mistyped the name of the property. The compiler is talking about "a structure or union" because those are the main things signified by dot-notation. (This error message comes from GCC; if you are using the LLVM parser, you'll get a much more intelligent error message, along with a suggested correction, like this: "Property 'ceter' not found on object of type 'UILabel *'; did you mean 'center'?")

# CHAPTER 13

# Data Communication

As soon as an app grows to more than a few objects, things can become confusing. Beginners are sometimes puzzled about how to communicate data between one piece of code (one object, really) and another. The problem is essentially one of architecture. Constructing your code so that all the pieces fit together and key information can be shared is something of an art. But it isn't difficult. This chapter presents some general considerations that may provide the needed clue.

## Model–View–Controller

In Apple's documentation and online, you will find references to the term *model–view–controller*, or *MVC*. This refers to an architectural goal of maintaining a distinction between three functional aspects of a program that displays information to the user and permits the user to alter that information. The whole notion goes back to the days of Smalltalk, and much has been written about it since then, but informally, here's what the terms mean:

*Model*
> The data and its management (often referred to as the program's "business logic," the hard-core stuff that the program is really all about).

*View*
> What the user sees and interacts with.

*Controller*
> The mediation between the model and the view.

Consider, for example, a game where the current score is displayed to the user:

- A UILabel that shows the user the current score for the game in progress is *view*; it is effectively nothing but a pixel-maker, and its business is to know how to draw itself. The knowledge of *what* it should draw — the score, and the fact that this *is* a score — lies elsewhere. A rookie programmer might try to use the score displayed by the UILabel as the actual score: to increment the score, read the UILabel's

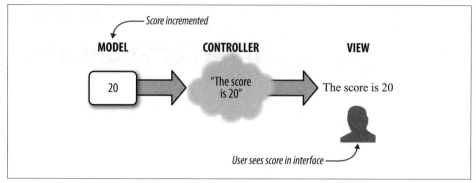

*Figure 13-1. Model–view–controller*

string, turn that string into a number, increment the number, turn the number back into a string, and present that string in place of the previous string. That is a gross violation of the MVC philosophy. The view presented to the user should *reflect* the score; it should not *store* the score.

- The score is data being maintained internally; it is *model*. It could be as simple as an instance variable along with a public `increment` method or as complicated as a Score object with a raft of methods. The score is numeric, whereas a UILabel displays a string; this alone is enough to show that the view and the model are naturally different.

- Telling the score when to change, and seeing that this fact is reflected in the user interface, is the work of the *controller*. This will be particularly clear if we imagine that the model's numeric score needs to be transformed in some way for presentation to the user. For example, suppose the UILabel that presents the score reads: "Your current score is 20". The model is presumably storing and providing the number 20, so what's the source of the phrase "Your current score is..."? Whoever is deciding that this phrase should precede the score in the presentation of the score to the user, and making it so, is a controller.

Even this simplistic example (Figure 13-1) illustrates very well the advantages of MVC. By separating powers in this way, we allow the aspects of the program to evolve with a great degree of independence. Do you want a different font and size in the presentation of the score? Change the view; the model and controller need know nothing about it, but will just go on working exactly as they did before. Do you want to change the phrase that precedes the score? Change the controller; the model and view are unchanged.

Adherence to MVC is particularly appropriate in a Cocoa app, because Cocoa itself adheres to it. The very names of Cocoa classes reveal the MVC philosophy that underlies them. A UIView is a view. A UIViewController is a controller; its purpose is to embody the logic that tells the view how to display itself. In Chapter 11 we saw that a UIPickerView does not hold the data it displays; it gets that data from a data source. So the UIPickerView is a view; the data source is model.

Apple's documentation also points out this telling distinction: true model material and true view material should be quite reusable, in the sense that they can be transferred wholesale into some other app; controller material is generally not reusable, because it is concerned with how *this* app mediates between the model and the view.

In one of my own apps, for example, we download an XML (RSS) news feed and present the article titles to the user as a table. The storage and parsing of the XML are pure model material, and are so reusable that I didn't even write this part of the code (I used some code called FeedParser, by Kevin Ballard). The table is a UITableView, which is obviously reusable, seeing as I obtained it directly from Cocoa. But when the UITable turns to me and asks what I'd like to display in this cell, and I turn to the XML and ask for the title of the article corresponding to this row of the table, that's controller logic.

By keeping the MVC architectural philosophy in mind as you develop your app, you'll implicitly solve one data communication problem. The data will live in the model, the view will be purely presentational in nature, and the communication between them will be handled by your own deliberately written controller code. You'll be communicating between the view and the model because controller code is *about* communicating between the view and model.

## Instance Visibility

The problem of communication often comes down to one object being able to see another: Object Manny needs to be able to find Object Jack repeatedly and reliably over the long term so as to be able to send Jack messages. (This is the same problem I spoke of in Chapter 2 as getting a *reference* to an object.)

An obvious solution is an instance variable of Manny whose value is Jack. This is appropriate particularly when Manny and Jack share certain responsibilities or supplement one another's functionality, and when they will both persist, especially when they will both persist together. A controller whose job is to configure and direct a certain view will need to exist just as long as the view does; they go together. The application object and its delegate, a table view and its data source, a UIViewController and its UIView — these are cases where the former must have an instance variable pointing at the latter.

With instance variables comes the question of memory management policy. Should Manny, which has an instance variable pointing to Jack, also retain Jack? Basically, it depends on how closely allied the objects are. An object does not typically retain its delegate or its data source; it can exist without a delegate or a data source, and the delegate and data source have lives of their own — it is none of this object's business to say whether the delegate or data source should be allowed to go out of existence. This object is therefore always prepared for the possibility that its delegate or data source may be nil. Similarly, an object that implements the target–action pattern, such as a UIControl, does not retain its target. On the other hand, a UIViewController is useless without a UIView to control; its very job is to be coterminous with its view, and to release its view when it itself goes out of existence. Similarly, an object that owns a nib as it loads rules the lifetimes of that nib's top-level objects.

Even when two objects go together closely, it will not necessarily be the case that each holds an instance variable pointing at the other. When each *does* point to the other, you must of course be careful not to let each *retain* the other; that's a retain cycle, and will cause both objects to leak. But if one object is the constant instigator of communication between the two, the first object can simply pass along a reference to itself as a method argument, if it thinks the second object might need this.

This behavior is conventional in a delegate message, for example. The parameter of the delegate message `textFieldShouldBeginEditing:` is a reference to the UITextField that sent the message. The same policy is followed by target–action messages in their fuller forms; the first parameter is a reference to the sender. You can follow a similar policy.

## Visibility by Instantiation

The real question is how one object is to be introduced to the other in the first place. Much of the art of Cocoa programming (and of object-oriented programming generally) lies in getting a reference to a desired object. Every case is different and must be solved separately, but a major clue comes from the fact that every instance comes from somewhere. This means that some object commanded this instance to come into existence in the first place. That object therefore has a reference to the instance at that moment. That is always the starting point.

When Manny instantiates Jack, if it knows that Jack is going to need a reference to itself (Manny) or to some piece of data, it can hand it that reference early in Jack's lifetime. Indeed, you might write Jack with an initializer that will take this reference as a parameter, so that Jack will possess it from the moment it comes into existence. (Compare the approach taken, for example, by UIActionSheet and UIAlertView, where the delegate is one of the initializer's parameters, or by UIBarButtonItem, where the target is one of the initializer's parameters.)

This example, from one of my apps, is from a table view controller. The user has tapped a row of the table. We create a secondary table view controller, handing it the data it will need, and display the secondary table view. I deliberately devised TrackViewController to have a designated initializer `initWithMediaItemCollection:` to make it almost obligatory for a TrackViewController to have access to the data it needs:

```
- (void)showItemsForRow: (NSIndexPath*) indexPath {
    // create subtable of tracks and go there
    TracksViewController *t =
        [[TracksViewController alloc] initWithMediaItemCollection:
            [self.albums objectAtIndex: [indexPath row]]];
    [self.navigationController pushViewController:t animated:YES];
    [t release];
}
```

But what if two objects are conceptually distant from each other? A common case in point is when objects are going to be instantiated from different nibs. How can an instance from one nib get a reference to an instance from another nib? True, you can't draw a connection between an object in nib A and an object in nib B. But someone (Manny) is going to be the file's owner when nib A loads, and someone (Jack) is going to be the file's owner when nib B loads. Those two file's owners might be able to see each other; if so, the problem is solved. Perhaps they are the same object. Perhaps Manny instantiated Jack in the first place. Perhaps they are both instantiated by some third object, which provides a communication path for them.

## Visibility by Relationship

Objects may acquire the ability to see one another automatically by virtue of their position in a built-in structure. Before worrying about how to supply one object with a reference to another, consider whether there may already be a chain of references leading from one to another.

For example, a subview can see its superview. A superview can see all its subviews and can pick out a specific subview through that subview's `tag` property. A subview in a window can see its window. A responder can see the next responder in the responder chain (which also means, because of the structure of the responder chain, that a UIView can see the UIViewController that manages it).

Similarly, if a UIViewController is currently presenting a modal view through a controller, that is its `modalViewController`, and the UIViewController is that controller's `parentViewController`. If it is controlled by a UINavigationController, that is its `navigationController`. A UINavigationController's visible view is controlled by its `visibleViewController`. And from any of these, you can reach the view controller's view, and so forth.

All of these relationships are public. So if you can get a reference to an object within any of these structures or a similar structure, you can effectively navigate the whole structure through a chain of references and lay your hands on any other object within the structure.

## Global Visibility

Some objects are globally visible (that is, visible to all other objects). In general, these are singletons vended by a class method. Some of these objects have properties pointing to other objects, making those other objects likewise globally visible.

For example, any object can see the singleton UIApplication instance by calling `[UIApplication sharedApplication]`. So any object can also see the app's primary window, because that is its `keyWindow` property, and any object can see the app delegate, because that is its `delegate` property. Thus, for example, in our Empty Window project, every object can see the Empty_WindowAppDelegate instance created by the loading of the main nib. This means that any additional object can be made globally visible by designing a globally visible object, such as the app delegate, to hold a reference to it.

Another globally visible object is the shared defaults object obtained by calling [`NSUser-Defaults standardUserDefaults`]. This object is the gateway to storage and retrieval of user defaults, which is similar to a dictionary (a collection of values named by keys). The user defaults are automatically saved when your application quits and are automatically available when your application is launched again later, so they are one of the main ways in which your app maintains state between launches. But, being globally visible, they are also a conduit for communicating values within your app.

For example, in one of my apps there's a setting I call `@"hazyStripy"`. This determines whether a certain visible interface object is drawn with a hazy fill or a stripy fill. This is a setting that the user can change, so there is a preferences interface allowing the user to make this change. When the user displays this preferences interface, I examine the `@"hazyStripy"` setting in the user defaults to configure the interface to reflect it; if the user interacts with the preferences interface to change the `@"hazyStripy"` setting, I respond by changing the actual `@"hazyStripy"` setting in the user defaults.

But the preferences interface is not the only object that uses the `@"hazyStripy"` setting in the user defaults; the drawing code that actually draws the hazy-or-stripy-filled object also uses it, so as to know which way to draw itself. Thus there no need for the object that draws the hazy-or-stripy-filled object and the object that manages the preferences interface to be able to see one another! They can both see this common object, the `@"hazyStripy"` user default (Figure 13-2). Indeed, it is not uncommon to "misuse" the user defaults storage to hold information that is *not* used to maintain state between runs of the app, but is placed there merely because this *is* a location globally visible to all objects.

## Notifications

Notifications (Chapter 11) can be a way to communicate between objects that are conceptually distant from one another without bothering to provide *any* way for one to see the other. Using a notification in this way may seem lazy, an evasion of your responsibility to architect your objects sensibly. But sometimes one object doesn't need to know, and indeed shouldn't know, what object it is sending a message to.

I'll give a specific example. One of my apps consists of a bunch of flashcards. Only one card is showing at any one time, but the cards are actually embedded in a scroll view, so the user can move from one card to the next by swiping the screen. I've supplied classes to manage this interface: each card is managed by a CardController, and the scroll view as a whole is managed by a single ScrollViewController.

The flashcards all have the same layout: a foreign term, along with an English translation. To facilitate learning, the ScrollViewController displays a toolbar with a button

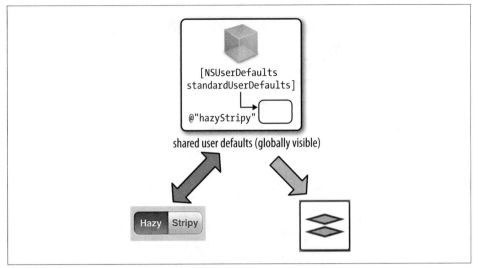

*Figure 13-2. The global visibility of user defaults*

that the user can tap to toggle visibility of the English translation *on all cards*. Thus, the user could hide the English translation and move from card to card, showing the English translation only occasionally to discover a forgotten translation or to confirm a remembered one.

What should happen, exactly, when the user taps the toolbar button? This seems a perfect use of a notification. I could cycle through all the existing CardController instances and tell each one to show or hide the English translation label, but this seems bulky and error-prone. How much simpler to have every CardController, as it comes into existence, register for the @"toggleEnglish" notification. Now the ScrollViewController can post a single notification and all the CardController instances will just hear about it, automatically.

So a CardController has this line of code, early in its lifetime:

```
[[NSNotificationCenter defaultCenter] addObserver:self
                            selector:@selector(toggleEnglish:)
                               name:TOGGLE_ENGLISH object:nil];
```

(TOGGLE_ENGLISH is #defined as @"toggleEnglish" in a header.) When the user taps the button to toggle the visibility of the English translation, the button's action causes the ScrollViewController's toggleEnglish: method to be called. That method contains this line:

```
[[NSNotificationCenter defaultCenter] postNotificationName:TOGGLE_ENGLISH
                                        object:self];
```

So when ScrollViewController's toggleEnglish: method is called, every CardController's toggleEnglish: method is also called — exactly the desired effect.

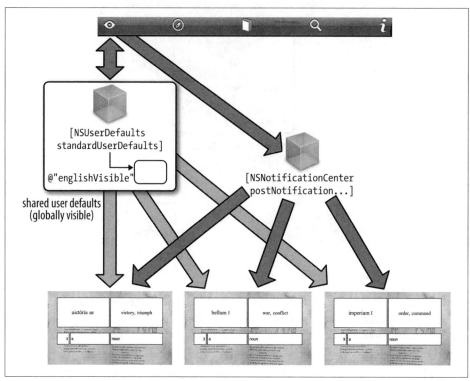

*Figure 13-3. Posting a notification*

This example also involves global storage in user defaults, discussed in the previous section. Just before posting the notification, ScrollViewController stores the desired state of the English translation's visibility in a user preference. Thus, to know what to do in response to the notification, each CardController just consults that preference and obeys it (Figure 13-3). Alternatively, ScrollViewController could have called `post-NotificationName:object:userInfo:` and put this information into the `userInfo`.

# Key–Value Observing

Key–value observing, or *KVO*, is a mechanism somewhat similar to the target–action mechanism, except that it is not limited to controls. (The KVO mechanism is provided through an informal protocol, NSKeyValueObserving, which is actually a set of categories on NSObject and other classes.) The similarity is that objects register with a particular object to be notified when something happens. The "something" is that a certain value in that object is changed.

KVO can be broken down into three stages:

*Registration*

    To hear about a change in a value belonging to object A, object B must be registered with object A.

*Change*

    The change takes place in the value belonging to object A, and it must take place in a special way — a KVO compliant way.

*Notification*

    Object B is notified that the value in object A has changed and can respond as desired.

Here's a simple complete example — a rather silly example, but sufficient to demonstrate the KVO mechanism in action. We have a class MyClass1; this will be the class of object A. We also have a class MyClass2; this will be the class of object B. Finally, we have code that creates a MyClass1 instance called objectA and a MyClass2 instance called objectB; this code registers objectB to hear about changes in an instance variable of objectA called value, and then changes value, and sure enough, objectB is notified of the change:

```
// [In MyClass1.h]

@interface MyClass1 : NSObject {
    NSString* value;
}
@property (nonatomic, copy) NSString* value;
@end


// [In MyClass1.m]

@implementation MyClass1
@synthesize value;
@end


// [In MyClass2.m (in its implementation section)]

- (void) observeValueForKeyPath:(NSString *)keyPath
                       ofObject:(id)object
                         change:(NSDictionary *)change
                        context:(void *)context {
    NSLog(@"I heard about the change!");
}

// [somewhere else entirely]

MyClass1* objectA = [[MyClass1 alloc] init];
MyClass2* objectB = [[MyClass2 alloc] init];
// register for KVO
[objectA addObserver:objectB forKeyPath:@"value" options:0 context:nil]; ❶
// change the value in a KVO compliant way
objectA.value = @"Hello, world!"; ❷
// result: objectB's observeValueForKeyPath:... is called
```

❶ We call `addObserver:forKeyPath:options:context:` to register `objectB` to hear about changes in `objectA`'s `value`. We didn't use any `options` or `context`; I'll talk about the `options` in a moment. (The `context` is for handing in a value that will be provided as part of the notification.)

❷ We change `objectA`'s `value`, and we do it in a KVO compliant way, namely, by passing through the setter (because setting a property is equivalent to passing through the setter). This is another reason why accessors (and properties) are a good thing: they help you guarantee KVO compliance when changing a value.

When we change `objectA`'s `value`, the third stage takes place automatically: a call is made to `objectB`'s `observeValueForKeyPath:...`. We have implemented this method in MyClass2 in order to receive the notification. In this simple example, we expect to receive only one notification, so we just log to indicate that we did indeed receive it. In real life, where a single object might be registered to receive more than one KVO notification, you'd use the incoming parameters to distinguish between different notifications and decide what to do.

At the very least, you'll probably want to know, when `observeValueForKeyPath:...` is called, what the new value is. We can find that out easily, because we are handed a reference to the object that changed, along with the key path for the value within that object. Thus we can use KVC to query the changed object in the most general way:

```
- (void) observeValueForKeyPath:(NSString *)keyPath
                       ofObject:(id)object
                         change:(NSDictionary *)change
                        context:(void *)context {
    id newValue = [object valueForKeyPath:keyPath];
    NSLog(@"The key path %@ changed to %@", keyPath, newValue);
}
```

But it is also possible to request that the new value be included as part of the notification. This depends upon the `options` passed with the original registration. Here, we'll request that both the old and new values be included with the notification:

```
objectA.value = @"Hello";
[objectA addObserver:objectB forKeyPath:@"value"
          options: NSKeyValueObservingOptionNew | NSKeyValueObservingOptionOld
          context:nil];
objectA.value = @"Goodbye"; // notification is triggered
```

When we receive the notification, we fetch the old and new values out of the `change` dictionary:

```
- (void) observeValueForKeyPath:(NSString *)keyPath
                       ofObject:(id)object
                         change:(NSDictionary *)change
                        context:(void *)context {
    id newValue = [change objectForKey: NSKeyValueChangeNewKey];
    id oldValue = [change objectForKey: NSKeyValueChangeOldKey];
    NSLog(@"The key path %@ changed from %@ to %@", keyPath, oldValue, newValue);
}
```

No memory management happens as part of the registration process, so it is incumbent upon you to unregister object B before it is destroyed. Otherwise, object A may later attempt to send a notification to a dangling pointer. This is done by sending object A the `removeObserver:forKeyPath:` message.

Beginners are often confused about how to use KVO to observe changes to a mutable array, to be notified when an object is added to, removed from, or replaced within the array. You can't add an observer to an array itself; you have to observe through an object that has a key path to the array (through accessors, for example). The simple-minded solution is then to access the array using `mutableArrayValueForKey:`, which provides an observable proxy object.

For example, recall how in Chapter 12 we posited an object with an instance variable `theData` which is an array of dictionaries:

```
(
    {
        description = "The one with glasses.";
        name = Manny;
    },
    {
        description = "Looks a little like Governor Dewey.";
        name = Moe;
    },
    {
        description = "The one without a mustache.";
        name = Jack;
    }
)
```

Suppose this is an NSMutableArray. Then we can register with our object to observe the key path `@"theData"`:

```
[objectA addObserver:objectB forKeyPath:@"theData" options:0 context:nil];
```

Now object B will be notified of changes to this mutable array, but only if those changes are performed through the `mutableArrayValueForKey:` proxy object:

```
[[objectA mutableArrayValueForKeyPath:@"theData"] removeObjectAtIndex:0];
// notification is triggered
```

But it seems onerous to require clients to know that they must call `mutableArrayValue-ForKey:`. The simple solution is for our object itself to provide a getter that calls `mutable-ArrayValueForKey:`. Here's a possible implementation:

```
// [In MyClass1, in the header file]

@interface MyClass1 : NSObject {
    NSMutableArray* theData;
}
@property (nonatomic, retain, getter=theDataGetter) NSMutableArray* theData;
@end

// [In MyClass1, in the implementation section]
```

```
@synthesize theData;

- (NSMutableArray*) theDataGetter {
    return [self mutableArrayValueForKey:@"theData"];
}
```

The result is that, as far as any client knows, this object has a key @"theData" and a property theData, and we can register to observe with the key and then access the mutable array through the property:

```
[objectA addObserver:objectB forKeyPath:@"theData"
            options: NSKeyValueObservingOptionNew | NSKeyValueObservingOptionOld
            context:nil];
[objectA.theData removeObjectAtIndex:0]; // notification is triggered
```

If you're going to take this approach, you should really also implement (in MyClass1) the four KVC compliance methods for a mutable array façade (see Chapter 12). Although things will appear to work just fine without them, and although they appear trivial (they are merely delegating to self->theData the equivalent calls), they will be called by the vended proxy object, which increases its efficiency (and, some would argue, its safety). Without these methods, the proxy object resorts to setting the instance variable directly, replacing the entire mutable array, every time a client changes the mutable array:

```
- (NSUInteger) countOfTheData {
    return [self->theData count];
}

- (id) objectInTheDataAtIndex: (NSUInteger) ix {
    return [self->theData objectAtIndex: ix];
}

- (void) insertObject: (id) val inTheDataAtIndex: (NSUInteger) ix {
    [self->theData insertObject:val atIndex:ix];
}

- (void) removeObjectFromTheDataAtIndex: (NSUInteger) ix {
    [self->theData removeObjectAtIndex: ix];
}
```

If what you want to observe are mutations within an individual element of an array, things are more complicated. Suppose our array of dictionaries is an array of mutable dictionaries. To observe changes to the value of the @"description" key of any dictionary in the array, you'd need to register for that key with *each* dictionary in the array, separately. You can do that efficiently with NSArray's instance method addObserver: toObjectsAtIndexes:forKeyPath:options:context:, but if the array *itself* is mutable then you're also going to have to register for that key with any *new* dictionaries that are subsequently added to the array (and unregister when a dictionary is removed from the array). This is doable but daunting, and I'm not going to go into the details here.

The properties of Apple's built-in classes are typically KVO compliant. Indeed, so are many classes that don't use properties per se; for example, NSUserDefaults is KVO compliant. Unfortunately, Apple warns that undocumented KVO compliance can't be counted on.

Key–value observing is a deep mechanism; consult Apple's *Key-Value Observing Guide* for full information. It does have some unfortunate shortcomings — for one thing, it's a pity that all notifications arrive by calling the same method, `observeValue-ForKeyPath:...` — but in general KVO is useful for keeping values coordinated in different objects.

**Mac OS X Programmer Alert**

Mac OS X bindings don't exist on iOS, but you can sometimes use KVO to achieve similar aims.

# PART IV

# Views

This part of the book is about the things that appear in an app's interface. All such things are, ultimately, *views*. A view is a unit of your app that knows how to draw itself. A view also knows how to sense that the user has touched it. Views are what your user sees on the screen, and what your user interacts with by touching the screen. Thus, views are the primary constituent of an app's visible, touchable manifestation. They *are* your app's interface. So it's going to be crucial to know how views work.

- Chapter 14 discusses views in their most general aspect — their hierarchy, position, and visibility.

- A view knows how to draw itself. Chapter 15 is about drawing; it explains how to tell a view what you want it to draw, from simply displaying an already existing image to constructing a drawing line by line.

- The drawing power of a view comes ultimately from its *layer*. To put it another way, a layer is effectively the aspect of a view that knows how to draw — with even more power. Chapter 16 explains about layers.

- A iOS app's interface isn't generally static; it's lively. Much of that liveliness comes from animation. iOS gives you great power to animate your interface with remarkable ease; that power resides ultimately in layers. Now that you know about layers, Chapter 17 tells about animation.

- A view knows how to draw itself; it also knows how to sense that the user is touching it. Chapter 18 is about touches. It explains the iOS view-based mechanisms for sensing and responding to touches, with details on how touches are routed to the appropriate view and how you can customize that routing.

# Views

A *view* (an object whose class is a subclass of UIView) knows how to draw itself into a rectangular area of the interface. Your app has a visible interface thanks to views. Creating and configuring a view can be extremely simple: "Set it and forget it." You've already seen that you can drag an interface widget, such as a UIButton, into your window in the nib; when the app runs, the button appears, and works properly. But you can also manipulate views in powerful ways, in real time. Your code can do some or all of the view's drawing of itself; it can make the view appear and disappear, move, resize itself, and display many other physical changes, possibly with animation.

A view is also a responder (UIView is a subclass of UIResponder). This means that a view is subject to user interactions, such as taps and swipes. Thus, views are the basis not only of the interface that the user sees, but also of the interface that the user touches. Organizing your views so that the correct view reacts to a given touch allows you to allocate your code neatly and efficiently.

The *view hierarchy* is the chief mode of view organization. A view can have subviews; a subview has exactly one immediate superview. Thus there is a tree of views. This hierarchy allows views to come and go together. If a view is removed from the interface, its subviews are removed; if a view is hidden (made invisible), its subviews are hidden; if a view is moved, its subviews move with it; and other changes in a view are likewise shared with its subviews. The view hierarchy is also the basis of, though it is not identical to, the responder chain (Chapter 11).

A view may come from a nib, or you can create it in code. On balance, neither approach is to be preferred over the other; it depends on your needs and inclinations and on the overall architecture of your app.

## The Window

The top of the view hierarchy is the app's window. It is an instance of UIWindow (or your own subclass thereof), which is a UIView subclass. Your app should have exactly one main window. It occupies the entire screen and forms the background to, and the ultimate superview of, all your other visible views. Other views are visible by virtue of being subviews, at some depth, of your app's window. (If your app can display views on an external screen, you'll create an additional UIWindow to contain those views; but in this chapter I'll behave as if there were just one screen, the device's own screen, and just one window.)

The project templates all generate your app's window for you automatically. The window is a top-level nib object in the project's main nib file. This nib file is loaded automatically as the app launches, and the window is instantiated. Another top-level nib object in the main nib file, representing the app delegate, has a `window` outlet pointing to the window. The app delegate instance, which is also generated as the app launches, thus points to the window through its `window` property. (It also retains the window, but it need not do so, as the window is also being retained by the UIApplication instance, the nib's owner.) The app delegate instance is sent the `application:didFinishLaunching-WithOptions:` delegate message by the application instance, and in turn it sends the window instance the `makeKeyAndVisible` message. This causes the window to appear and gives your app a visible manifestation.

In theory, you could modify this process and generate your app's UIWindow in some other way. For example, you could generate the UIWindow instance in code. Apple says to do this by saying:

```
UIWindow* aWindow =
    [[UIWindow alloc] initWithFrame:[[UIScreen mainScreen] bounds]];
```

(The window's designated initializer is `initWithFrame:`; I'll explain in a moment what "frame" and "bounds" are.) You would still need to send the window instance the `make-KeyAndVisible` message in order to make your app's interface appear. In practice, I have never had cause to modify the way the templates generate the window instance.

By virtue of the project templates, the app delegate points to the window as the value of its `window` property; so any code in the app delegate class can refer to the window as `self.window`. Code elsewhere can also get a reference to the app's window; here, I do it by way of the synthesized accessor:

```
UIWindow* theWindow = [[[UIApplication sharedApplication] delegate] window];
```

That code is unusual, though, and may require typecasting to quiet the compiler (because the class of the application's `delegate` property is otherwise unknown). You'd be more likely to use the application's `keyWindow` property:

```
UIWindow* theWindow = [[UIApplication sharedApplication] keyWindow];
```

An even more likely way to get a reference to your app's window would be through a subview of the window, at any depth of the hierarchy. You are very likely to have a reference to at least one such subview, and its `window` property points to the window that contains it, which is the app's window. You can also use a UIView's `window` property as a way of asking whether it is ultimately embedded in a window; if it isn't, its `window` property is nil. A UIView whose `window` property is nil cannot be visible to the user.

Although your app will have exactly one primary window, it may generate other windows of which you are not conscious. For example, if you put up an alert view (UIAlertView), it is displayed in a secondary window that lies on top of your app's window; at that moment, this secondary window is the application's `keyWindow`. You would not be conscious of this fact, however, unless you needed a reference to your app's window while an alert was showing, which is unlikely.

The window's `backgroundColor` property, which it inherits from UIView, affects the appearance of the app if the window is visible behind its subviews. In many cases, though, you are likely to give your window a primary subview that occupies the entire window and blocks it from sight; the window's `backgroundColor` would then make no visible difference. The window would function solely as a container for the app's visible views.

## Subview and Superview

Once upon a time, and not so very long ago, a view owned precisely its rectangular area. No part of any view that was not a subview of this view could appear inside it, because when this view redrew its rectangle, it would erase the overlapping portion of the other view. No part of any subview of this view could appear outside it, because the view took responsibility for its own rectangle and no more.

Those rules, however, were gradually relaxed, and starting in Mac OS X 10.5 Apple introduced an entirely new architecture for view drawing that lifted those restrictions completely. iOS view drawing is based on this revised architecture. So now some or all of a subview can appear outside its superview, and a view can overlap another view and be drawn partially or totally in front of it without being its subview.

So, for example, Figure 14-1 shows three overlapping views. All three views have a background color, so each is completely represented by a colored rectangle. You have no way of knowing, from this visual representation, how the views are related within the view hierarchy. In actual fact, the view in the middle (horizontally) is a sibling view of the view on the left (they are both direct subviews of the window), and the view on the right is a subview of the middle view.

When views are created in the nib, you can examine the view hierarchy in the expanded dock to learn their actual relationship (Figure 14-2). When views are created in code, you know their hierarchical relationship because you created that hierarchy. But the visible interface doesn't tell you, because view overlapping is so flexible.

Nevertheless, a view's position in the view hierarchy does affect how it is drawn. Most important, a view's position in the view hierarchy dictates the *order* in which it is drawn. Sibling subviews of the same superview have a layering order: one is "further back"

*Figure 14-1. Overlapping views*

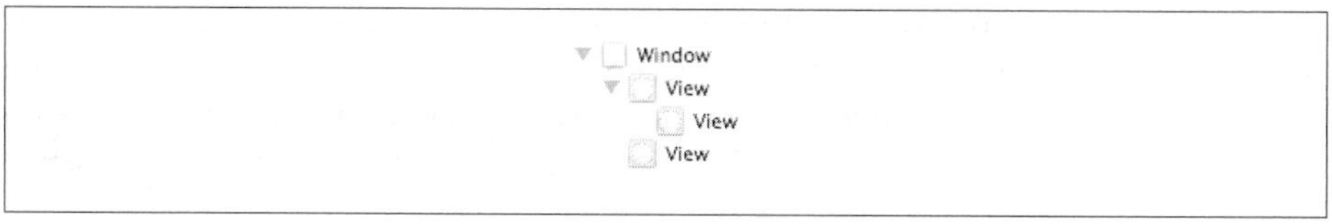

```
▼ ☐ Window
  ▼ ☐ View
        ☐ View
      ☐ View
```

*Figure 14-2. A view hierarchy as displayed in the nib*

than the other. This will make no visible difference if there is no overlap, but the subview that is "further back" is drawn first, so if there *is* overlap, it will appear to be behind its sibling. Similarly, a superview is "further back" than its subviews; the superview is drawn first, so it will appear to be behind its subviews.

You can see this illustrated in Figure 14-1. The view on the right is a subview of the view in the middle and is drawn on top of it. The view on the left is a sibling of the view in the middle, but it is a later sibling, so it is drawn on top of the view in the middle and on top of the view on the right. The view on the left *cannot* appear behind the view on the right but in front of the view in the middle, because those views are subview and superview and are drawn together — both are drawn either before or after the view on the left, depending on the "further back" ordering of the siblings.

This layering order can be governed in the nib either by choosing from the Editor → Arrangement menu (Send to Front, Send to Back, Send Forward, Send Backward) or by arranging the views in the expanded dock. In code, there are methods for arranging the sibling order of views (which we'll come to in a moment).

Here are some other effects of the view hierarchy:

- If a view is removed from or moved within its superview, its subviews go with it.
- If a view's size is changed, its subviews can be resized automatically.
- A view's degree of transparency is inherited by its subviews.
- A view can optionally limit the drawing of its subviews so that any parts of them outside the view are not shown. This is called *clipping* and is set with the view's `clipsToBounds` property.
- A superview *owns* its subviews, in the memory-management sense, much as an NSArray owns its elements; it retains them and is responsible for releasing a sub-

view when that subview ceases to be its subview (it is removed from the collection of this view's subviews) or when it itself goes out of existence.

A UIView has a `superview` property (a UIView) and a `subviews` property (an NSArray of UIViews, in back-to-front order), allowing you to trace the view hierarchy in code. There is also a method `isDescendantOfView:` letting you check whether one view is a subview of another at any depth. If you need a reference to a particular view, you will probably arrange this beforehand as an instance variable, perhaps through an outlet. Alternatively, a view can have a tag (its `tag` property, an integer), and can then be referred to by sending any view further up the view hierarchy the `viewWithTag:` message. Seeing that all tags of interest are unique within their section of the hierarchy is up to you.

Manipulating the view hierarchy in code is easy. This is part of what gives iOS apps their dynamic quality, and it compensates for the fact that there is basically just a single window. It is perfectly reasonable for your code to rip an entire hierarchy of views out of the superview and substitute another. Such behavior can be implemented elegantly by using a UIViewController, a subject to which we'll return later. But you can do it directly, too. The method `addSubview:` makes one view a subview of another; `removeFromSuperview` takes a subview out of its superview's view hierarchy. In both cases, if the superview is part of the visible interface, the subview will appear or disappear; and of course this view may itself have subviews that accompany it. Just remember that removing a subview from its superview releases it; if you intend to reuse that subview later on, you will wish to retain it first. This is often taken care of through a property with a retain policy.

Events inform a view of these dynamic changes. To respond to these events requires subclassing. Then you'll be able to override any of `didAddSubview:` and `willRemoveSubview:`, `didMoveToSuperview` and `willMoveToSuperview:`, `didMoveToWindow` and `willMoveToWindow:`.

When `addSubview:` is called, the view is placed last among its superview's subviews; thus it is drawn last, meaning that it appears frontmost. A view's subviews are indexed, starting at 0, which is rearmost. There are additional methods for inserting a subview at a given index (`insertSubview:atIndex:`), or below (behind) or above (in front of) a specific view (`insertSubview:belowSubview:`, `insertSubview:aboveSubview:`); for swapping two sibling views by index (`exchangeSubviewAtIndex:withSubviewAtIndex:`); and for moving a subview all the way to the front or back among its siblings (`bringSubviewToFront:`, `sendSubviewToBack:`).

Oddly, there is no command for removing all of a view's subviews at once. However, a view's `subviews` array is an immutable copy of the internal list of subviews, so it is legal to cycle through it and remove each subview one at a time:

```
for (UIView* v in view.subviews)
    [v removeFromSuperview];
```

# Frame

A view's `frame` property, a CGRect, is the position of its rectangle within its superview, *in the superview's coordinate system*. By default, the superview's coordinate system will have the origin at the top left, with the x-coordinate growing positively rightward and the y-coordinate growing positively downward.

Setting a view's frame to a different CGRect value repositions the view, or resizes it, or both. If the view is visible, this change will be visibly reflected in the interface. On the other hand, you can also set a view's frame when the view is not visible — for example, when you create the view in code. In that case, the frame describes where the frame *will* be positioned within its superview when it is assigned a superview. UIView's designated initializer is `initWithFrame:`, and you'll often assign a frame this way, especially because the default frame might otherwise be (0,0,0,0), which is rarely what you want.

 Forgetting to assign a view a frame when creating it in code, and then wondering why it isn't appearing when added to a superview, is a common beginner mistake. A view with a zero-size frame is effectively invisible. If a view has a standard size that you want it to adopt, especially in relation to its contents (like a UIButton in relation to its title), an alternative is to send it the `sizeToFit` message.

Knowing this, we can generate programmatically the interface displayed in Figure 14-1. Start with a vanilla iOS app project based on the Window-Based Application template, and make its `application:didFinishLaunchingWithOptions:` method read as follows:

```
UIView* v1 = [[UIView alloc] initWithFrame:CGRectMake(113, 111, 132, 194)];
v1.backgroundColor = [UIColor colorWithRed:1 green:.4 blue:1 alpha:1];
UIView* v2 = [[UIView alloc] initWithFrame:CGRectMake(41, 56, 132, 194)];
v2.backgroundColor = [UIColor colorWithRed:.5 green:1 blue:0 alpha:1];
UIView* v3 = [[UIView alloc] initWithFrame:CGRectMake(43, 197, 160, 230)];
v3.backgroundColor = [UIColor colorWithRed:1 green:0 blue:0 alpha:1];
[self.window addSubview: v1];
[v1 addSubview: v2];
[self.window addSubview: v3];
[v1 release]; [v2 release]; [v3 release];
[self.window makeKeyAndVisible];
```

In that code, we determined the layering order of `v1` and `v3` (the middle and left views, which are sibling subviews of the window) by the order in which we inserted them into the view hierarchy with `addSubview:`.

Part of the app's window may be covered by the status bar, which is actually another window, supplied by the system. This may affect where you want to draw in the window. A view centered within the window will be centered on the screen, but it may not look centered because it isn't centered in the visible part of the window (exclusive of the status bar). Similarly, material drawn in the window at the point (0,0) (in the

---

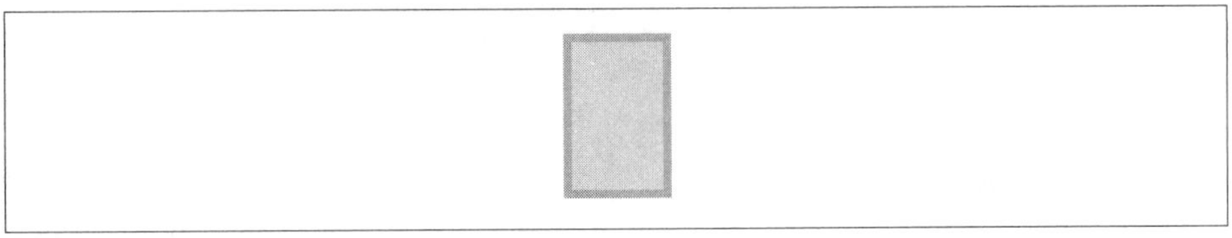

*Figure 14-3. A subview inset from its superview*

window's coordinates) may not be visible, because that point may be covered by the status bar. You can determine the rectangle currently not covered by the status bar as follows:

```
CGRect f = [[UIScreen mainScreen] applicationFrame];
```

Complications are introduced by the possibility of the user rotating the device. This does not change anything about the window's coordinate system, so the window's (0,0) point might be in any corner. This is another reason why you will probably want to cover the window with a single view managed by a UIViewController, which deals seamlessly with rotation. I'll discuss that in Chapter 19; for now, I'll assume that the device is not rotated.

## Bounds and Center

Suppose we wish to give a view a subview inset by 10 pixels, as in Figure 14-3. The utility function CGRectInset makes it easy to derive one rectangle as an inset from another, but *what* rectangle should we use as a basis? Not the superview's frame; the frame represents a view's position within *its* superview, and in that superview's coordinates. What we're after is a CGRect describing our superview's rectangle in its *own* coordinates, because those are the coordinates in which the subview's frame is to be expressed. That CGRect is the view's **bounds** property.

So, the code to generate Figure 14-3 looks like this:

```
UIView* v1 = [[UIView alloc] initWithFrame:CGRectMake(113, 111, 132, 194)];
v1.backgroundColor = [UIColor colorWithRed:1 green:.4 blue:1 alpha:1];
UIView* v2 = [[UIView alloc] initWithFrame:CGRectInset(v1.bounds, 10, 10)];
v2.backgroundColor = [UIColor colorWithRed:.5 green:1 blue:0 alpha:1];
[self.window addSubview: v1];
[v1 addSubview: v2];
[v1 release]; [v2 release];
```

You'll very often use a view's **bounds** in this way. When you need coordinates for drawing inside a view, whether drawing manually or placing a subview, you'll often refer to the view's **bounds**.

*Figure 14-4. A subview exactly covering its superview*

The screen also has bounds, and functions in that sense as the window's superview, even though a UIScreen isn't a view. Moreover, the window's frame is always set to the screen's bounds (see the example earlier in this chapter of creating a window in code). Thus, window coordinates are screen coordinates. For example, when asking the screen for the `applicationFrame`, the answer comes back in screen coordinates, which are also window coordinates, and can thus be used for positioning something within the window.

Interesting things happen when you set a view's bounds. If you change a view's bounds *size*, you change its *frame*. The change in the view's frame takes place around its *center*, which remains unchanged. So, for example:

```
UIView* v1 = [[UIView alloc] initWithFrame:CGRectMake(113, 111, 132, 194)];
v1.backgroundColor = [UIColor colorWithRed:1 green:.4 blue:1 alpha:1];
UIView* v2 = [[UIView alloc] initWithFrame:CGRectInset(v1.bounds, 10, 10)];
v2.backgroundColor = [UIColor colorWithRed:.5 green:1 blue:0 alpha:1];
[self.window addSubview: v1];
[v1 addSubview: v2];
CGRect f = v2.bounds;
f.size.height += 20;
f.size.width += 20;
v2.bounds = f;
[v1 release]; [v2 release];
```

What appears is a single rectangle; the subview completely and exactly covers its superview, its frame being the same as the superview's bounds. The call to `CGRectInset` started with the superview's bounds and shaved 10 points off the left, right, top, and bottom to set the subview's frame (Figure 14-3). But then we added 20 points to the subview's bounds height and width, and thus added 20 points to the subview's frame height and width as well (Figure 14-4). The center didn't move, so we effectively put the 10 points back onto the left, right, top, and bottom of the subview's frame.

When you create a UIView, its bounds coordinate system's (0,0) point is at its top left. If you change a view's bounds *origin*, you move the *origin of its internal coordinate system*. Because a subview is positioned in its superview with respect its superview's coordinate system, such a change will change the apparent position of a subview relative to its superview. To illustrate, we start with our subview inset evenly within its superview, and then change the bounds origin of the superview:

```
UIView* v1 = [[UIView alloc] initWithFrame:CGRectMake(113, 111, 132, 194)];
v1.backgroundColor = [UIColor colorWithRed:1 green:.4 blue:1 alpha:1];
```

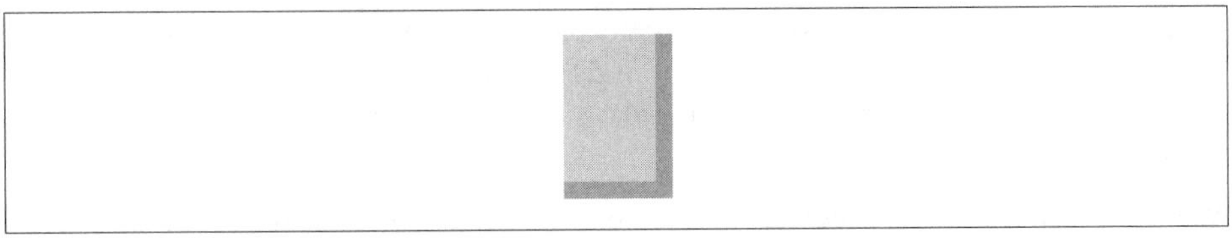

*Figure 14-5. The superview's bounds origin has been shifted*

```
UIView* v2 = [[UIView alloc] initWithFrame:CGRectInset(v1.bounds, 10, 10)];
v2.backgroundColor = [UIColor colorWithRed:.5 green:1 blue:0 alpha:1];
[self.window addSubview: v1];
[v1 addSubview: v2];
CGRect f = v1.bounds;
f.origin.x += 10;
f.origin.y += 10;
v1.bounds = f;
[v1 release]; [v2 release];
```

Nothing happens to the superview's size or position. But the subview has moved up and to the left so that it is flush with its superview's top left corner (Figure 14-5). Basically, what we've done is to say to the superview, "Instead of calling the point at your upper left (0,0), call that point (10,10)." Because the subview's frame origin is itself at (10,10), the subview now touches the superview's top left corner. The effect of changing a view's bounds origin may seem directionally backward — we increased the superview's origin in the positive direction, but the subview moved in the negative direction — but think of it this way: a view's bounds origin point coincides with its frame's top left.

We have seen that changing a view's bounds size affects its frame size. The converse is also true: changing a view's frame size affects its bounds size. What is *not* affected by changing a view's bounds size is the view's center. This property, like the frame property, represents the view's position within its superview, in the superview's coordinates, but it is the position of the bounds center, the point derived from the bounds like this:

```
CGPoint c = CGPointMake(CGRectGetMidX(theView.bounds),
                        CGRectGetMidY(theView.bounds));
```

A view's center is thus a single point establishing the positional relationship between a view's bounds and its superview's bounds. Changing a view's bounds does not change its center (we already saw that when we increased a view's bounds size, its frame expanded around a stationary center); changing a view's center does not change its bounds.

Thus, a view's bounds and center are orthogonal (independent), and describe (among other things) both the view's size and its position within its superview. The view's frame is therefore superfluous! In fact, the frame property is merely a convenient expression of the center and bounds values. In most cases, this won't matter to you; you'll use the frame property anyway. When you first create a view from scratch, the designated initializer is initWithFrame:. You can change the frame, and the bounds size and center will change to match. You can change the bounds size or the center, and the frame will change to match. Nevertheless, the proper and most reliable way to position and size a view within its superview is to use its bounds and center, not its frame; there are some situations in which the frame is meaningless, but the bounds and center will always work.

We have seen that every view has its own coordinate system, expressed by its `bounds`, and that a view's coordinate system has a clear relationship to its superview's coordinate system, expressed by its `center`. This is true of every view in a window, so it is possible to convert between the coordinates of any two views in the same window. Convenience methods are supplied to perform this conversion both for a CGPoint and for a CGRect: `convertPoint:fromView:`, `convertPoint:toView:`, `convertRect:fromView:`, and `convert-Rect:toView:`. If the second parameter is nil, it is taken to be the window.

For example, if `v2` is a subview of `v1`, then to center `v2` within `v1` you could say:

```
v2.center = [v1 convertPoint:v1.center fromView:v1.superview];
```

# Layout

We have seen that a subview moves when its superview's bounds *origin* is changed. But what happens to a subview when its superview's bounds *size* is changed? (And remember, this includes changing the superview's frame size.)

Of its own accord, nothing happens. The subview's bounds and center haven't changed, and the superview's bounds origin hasn't moved, so the subview stays in the same position relative to the top left of its superview. In real life, however, that often won't be what you want. You'll want subviews to be resized and repositioned when their superview's bounds size is changed. This is called *layout*.

The need for layout is obvious in a context such as Mac OS X, where the user can freely resize a window, potentially disturbing your interface. For example, you'd want an OK button near the lower right corner to stay in the lower right corner as the window grows, while a text field at the top of the window should stay at the top of the window, but perhaps should widen as the window widens.

There are no user-resizable windows on an iOS device, but still, a superview might be resized dynamically. For example, you might respond to the user rotating the device 90 degrees by swapping the width and height values of a view; now its subviews should shift to compensate. Or you might want to provide a reusable complex view, such as a table cell containing several subviews, without knowing its precise final dimensions in advance.

Layout is performed in two primary ways, which can be combined:

*Automatic layout*
> Automatic resizing of subviews depends on the superview's `autoresizesSubviews` property. To turn off a view's automatic resizing altogether, set this property to NO. If it is YES, then a subview will respond automatically to its superview's being

resized, in accordance with the rules prescribed by the subview's `autoresizing-Mask` property value.

*Manual layout*

The superview is sent the `layoutSubviews` message whenever it is resized; so, to lay out subviews manually, provide your own subclass and override `layoutSubviews`. If you're going to use both approaches, automatic resizing is performed before `layoutSubviews` is called.

You should never call `layoutSubviews` yourself. Instead, if you wish to trigger layout, send `setNeedsLayout` to the view. This will cause the layout procedures to be followed at the next appropriate moment. Alternatively, if you really need layout to occur right this moment, send the view the `layoutIfNeeded` message; this may cause the layout of the entire view tree, not only below but also above this view, and is probably not a very common thing to do.

Automatic resizing is a matter of conceptually assigning a subview "springs and struts." A spring can stretch; a strut can't. Springs and struts can be assigned internally or externally. Thus you can specify, using internal springs and struts, whether and how the view can be resized, and, using external springs and struts, whether and how the view can be repositioned. For example:

- Imagine a subview that is centered in its superview and is to stay centered, but is to resize itself as the superview is resized. It would have struts externally and springs internally.

- Imagine a subview that is centered in its superview and is to stay centered, and is *not* to resize itself as the superview is resized. It would have springs externally and struts internally.

- Imagine an OK button that is to stay in the lower right of its superview. It would have struts internally, struts externally to its right and bottom, and springs externally to its top and left.

- Imagine a text field that is to stay at the top of its superview. It is to widen as the superview widens. It would have struts externally; internally it would have a vertical strut and a horizontal spring.

When editing a nib file, you can experiment with assigning a view springs and struts in the Size inspector (Autosizing). A solid line externally represents a strut; a solid line internally represents a spring. A helpful animation shows you the effect on your view's position as its superview is resized.

In code, a combination of springs and struts is set through a view's `autoresizingMask` property. It's a bitmask, so you use logical-or to combine options. The options, with names that start with "UIViewAutoresizingFlexible", represent springs; whatever isn't specified is a strut. The default is `UIViewAutoresizingNone`, meaning all struts.

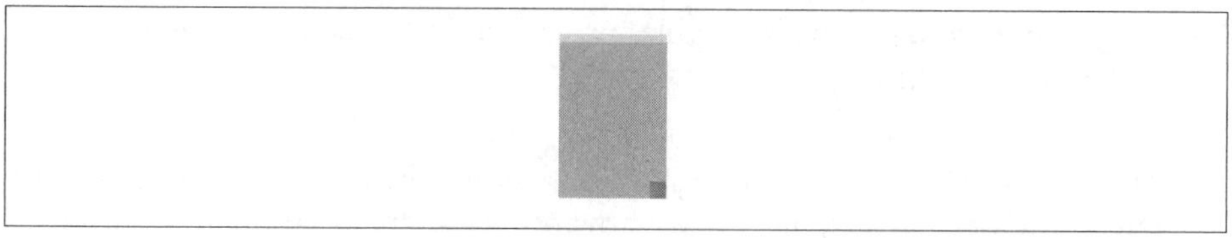

*Figure 14-6. Before autoresizing*

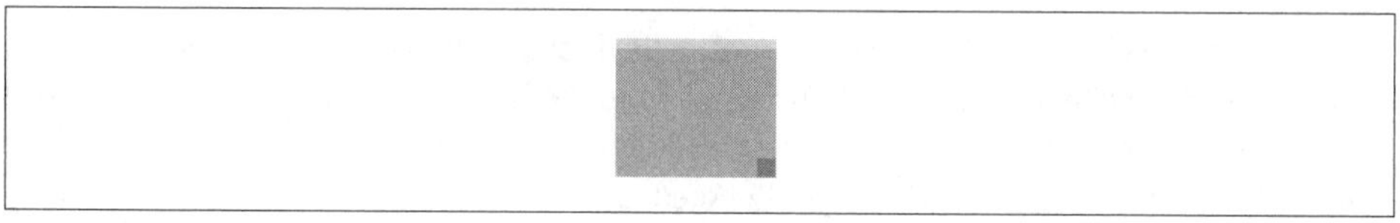

*Figure 14-7. After autoresizing*

To demonstrate autoresizing, I'll start with a view and two subviews, one stretched across the top, the other confined to the lower right (Figure 14-6):

```
UIView* v1 = [[UIView alloc] initWithFrame:CGRectMake(100, 111, 132, 194)];
v1.backgroundColor = [UIColor colorWithRed:1 green:.4 blue:1 alpha:1];
UIView* v2 = [[UIView alloc] initWithFrame:CGRectMake(0, 0, 132, 10)];
v2.backgroundColor = [UIColor colorWithRed:.5 green:1 blue:0 alpha:1];
UIView* v3 =
    [[UIView alloc] initWithFrame:CGRectMake(v1.bounds.size.width-20,
                                             v1.bounds.size.height-20,
                                             20, 20)];
v3.backgroundColor = [UIColor colorWithRed:1 green:0 blue:0 alpha:1];
[self.window addSubview: v1];
[v1 addSubview: v2];
[v1 addSubview: v3];
// ... insert autoresizing settings here ...
[v1 release]; [v2 release]; [v3 release];
```

Into that example, I'll insert code applying strings and struts to the two subviews to make them behave like the text field and the OK button I was hypothesizing earlier:

```
v2.autoresizingMask = UIViewAutoresizingFlexibleWidth;
v3.autoresizingMask =
    UIViewAutoresizingFlexibleTopMargin | UIViewAutoresizingFlexibleLeftMargin;
```

Now I'll resize the superview, thus bringing autoresizing into play; as you can see (Figure 14-7), the subviews remain pinned in their correct relative positions:

```
CGRect f = v1.bounds;
f.size.width += 40;
f.size.height -= 50;
v1.bounds = f;
```

# Transform

A view's `transform` property alters how the view is drawn — it may, for example, change the view's perceived size and orientation — without affecting its bounds and center. A transformed view continues to behave correctly: a rotated button, for example, is still a button, and can be tapped in its apparent location and orientation.

A transform value is a CGAffineTransform, which is a struct representing six of the nine values of a 3×3 transformation matrix (the other three values are constants, so there's no point representing them in the struct). You may have forgotten your high-school linear algebra, so you may not recall what a transformation matrix is. For the details, which are quite simple really, see the "Transforms" chapter of Apple's *Quartz 2D Programming Guide*, especially the section called "The Math Behind the Matrices." But you don't really need to know those details, because convenience functions, whose names start with "CGAffineTransformMake," are provided for creating three of the basic types of transform: rotation, scaling, and translation (i.e., changing the view's apparent position). A fourth basic transform type, skewing or shearing, has no convenience function.

By default, a view's transformation matrix is `CGAffineTransformIdentity`, the identity transform. It has no visible effect, so you're unaware of it. Any transform that you do apply takes place around the view's center, which is held constant.

Here's some code to illustrate use of a transform:

```
UIView* v1 = [[UIView alloc] initWithFrame:CGRectMake(113, 111, 132, 194)];
v1.backgroundColor = [UIColor colorWithRed:1 green:.4 blue:1 alpha:1];
UIView* v2 = [[UIView alloc] initWithFrame:CGRectInset(v1.bounds, 10, 10)];
v2.backgroundColor = [UIColor colorWithRed:.5 green:1 blue:0 alpha:1];
[self.window addSubview: v1];
[v1 addSubview: v2];
v1.transform = CGAffineTransformMakeRotation(45 * M_PI/180.0);
[v1 release]; [v2 release];
```

The `transform` property of the view `v1` is set to a rotation transform. The result (Figure 14-8) is that the view appears to be rocked 45 degrees clockwise. (I think in degrees, but Core Graphics thinks in radians, so my code has to convert.) Observe that the view's `center` property is unaffected, so that the rotation seems to have occurred around the view's center. Moreover, the view's `bounds` property is unaffected; the internal coordinate system is unchanged, so the subview is drawn in the same place relative to its superview. The view's `frame`, however, is now meaningless, as no mere rectangle can describe the region of the superview apparently occupied by the view. The rule is that if a view's `transform` is not the identity transform, you should neither get nor set its `frame`. Also, automatic resizing of a subview requires that the superview's transform be the identity transform.

Suppose, instead of `CGAffineTransformMakeRotation`, we call `CGAffineTransformMake-Scale`, like this:

Figure 14-8. A rotation transform

Figure 14-9. A scale transform

```
v1.transform = CGAffineTransformMakeScale(1.8, 1);
```

The **bounds** property of the view **v1** is still unaffected, so the subview is still drawn in the same place relative to its superview; this means that the two views seem to have stretched horizontally together (Figure 14-9). No bounds or centers were harmed by the application of this transform!

Transformation matrices can be chained. There are convenience functions for applying one transform to another. Their names do *not* contain "Make." These functions are not commutative; that is, order matters. If you start with a transform that translates a view to the right and then apply a rotation of 45 degrees, the rotated view appears to the right of its original position; on the other hand, if you start with a transform that rotates a view 45 degrees and then apply a translation to the right, the meaning of "right" has changed, so the rotated view appears 45 degrees down from its original position. To demonstrate the difference, I'll start with a subview that exactly overlaps its superview:

```
UIView* v1 = [[UIView alloc] initWithFrame:CGRectMake(20, 111, 132, 194)];
v1.backgroundColor = [UIColor colorWithRed:1 green:.4 blue:1 alpha:1];
UIView* v2 = [[UIView alloc] initWithFrame:v1.bounds];
v2.backgroundColor = [UIColor colorWithRed:.5 green:1 blue:0 alpha:1];
```

Then I'll apply two successive transforms to the subview, leaving the superview to show where the subview was originally. In this example, I translate and then rotate (Figure 14-10):

```
v2.transform = CGAffineTransformMakeTranslation(100, 0);
v2.transform = CGAffineTransformRotate(v2.transform, 45 * M_PI/180.0);
```

In this example, I rotate and then translate (Figure 14-11):

```
v2.transform = CGAffineTransformMakeRotation(45 * M_PI/180.0);
v2.transform = CGAffineTransformTranslate(v2.transform, 100, 0);
```

*Figure 14-10. Translation, then rotation*

*Figure 14-11. Rotation, then translation*

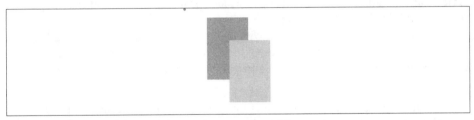

*Figure 14-12. Rotation, then translation, then inversion of the rotation*

The function `CGAffineTransformConcat` concatenates two transform matrices using matrix multiplication. Again, this operation is not commutative. The order is the *opposite* of the order when using convenience functions for applying one transform to another. For example, this gives the same result as Figure 14-11:

```
CGAffineTransform r = CGAffineTransformMakeRotation(45 * M_PI/180.0);
CGAffineTransform t = CGAffineTransformMakeTranslation(100, 0);
v2.transform = CGAffineTransformConcat(t,r); // not r,t
```

To remove a transform from a combination of transforms, apply its inverse. A convenience function lets you obtain the inverse of a given affine transform. Again, order matters. In this example, I rotate the subview and shift it to its "right," and then remove the rotation (Figure 14-12):

```
CGAffineTransform r = CGAffineTransformMakeRotation(45 * M_PI/180.0);
CGAffineTransform t = CGAffineTransformMakeTranslation(100, 0);
v2.transform = CGAffineTransformConcat(t,r);
v2.transform = CGAffineTransformConcat(CGAffineTransformInvert(r), v2.transform);
```

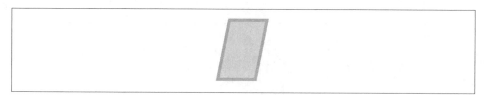

*Figure 14-13. Skew (shear)*

Finally, as there are no convenience methods for creating a skew (shear) transform, I'll illustrate by creating one manually, without further explanation (Figure 14-13):

```
v1.transform = CGAffineTransformMake(1, 0, -0.2, 1, 0, 0);
```

Transforms are useful particularly as temporary visual indicators. For example, you might call attention to a view by applying a transform that scales it up slightly, and then applying the identity transform to restore it to its original size, and animating those changes.

## Visibility and Opacity

A view can be made invisible by setting its `hidden` property to YES, and visible again by setting it to NO. This takes it (and its subviews, of course) out of the visible interface without the overhead of actually removing it from the view hierarchy. A hidden view does not (normally) receive touch events, so to the user it really is as if the view weren't there. But it is there, so it can still participate in layout and can be manipulated in other ways.

A view can be assigned a background color through its `backgroundColor` property, as we've been doing in the examples so far in this chapter — indeed, having a background color is the only thing that made our example views visible and distinguishable. A color is a UIColor; this is not a difficult class to use, and I'm not going to go into details. A view whose background color is nil has a transparent background. It is perfectly reasonable for a view to have a transparent background and to do no additional drawing of its own, just so that it can act as a convenient superview to other views, making them behave together.

A view can be made partially or completely transparent through its `alpha` property: `1.0` means opaque, `0.0` means transparent, and a value may be anywhere between them, inclusive. This affects subviews, as I've already mentioned; if a superview has an `alpha` of `0.5`, none of its subviews can have an *apparent* opacity of more than `0.5`, because whatever `alpha` value they have will be drawn relative to `0.5`. (Just to make matters more complicated, colors have an alpha value as well. So, for example, a view can have an `alpha` of `1.0` but still have a transparent background because its `backgroundColor` has an alpha less than `1.0`.) A view that is completely transparent (or very close to it) is like a view whose `hidden` is YES: it is invisible, along with its subviews, and cannot (normally) be touched.

A view's **opaque** property, on the other hand, is a horse of a different color; changing it has no effect on the view's appearance. Rather, this property is a hint to the drawing system. If a view completely fills its bounds with ultimately opaque material and its **alpha** is **1.0**, so that the view has no effective transparency, then it can be drawn more efficiently (with less drag on performance) if you inform the drawing system of this fact by setting its **opaque** to YES. Otherwise, you should set its **opaque** to NO. The **opaque** value is *not* changed for you when you set a view's **backgroundColor** or **alpha**! Setting it correctly is entirely up to you; the default, perhaps surprisingly, is YES.

# CHAPTER 15

# Drawing

Many UIView subclasses, such as a UIButton or a UITextField, know how to draw themselves; sooner or later, though, you're going to want to do some drawing of your own. A class like UIImageView will display a static image; you can generate that image dynamically by drawing it in code. And a pure UIView does little or no drawing of its own; you can draw its appearance.

Drawing is not difficult, but it is a very large topic. There are some UIKit convenience methods, but the full API is provided by Core Graphics, often referred to as Quartz, or Quartz 2D. Core Graphics is the drawing system that underlies all iOS drawing — UIKit drawing is built on top of it — so it is low-level and consists of C functions, but it isn't entirely alien. This chapter will familiarize you with the fundamentals. For complete information, you'll want to study Apple's *Quartz 2D Programming Guide*.

UIImageView draws an image for you and takes care of all the details. If you want to do any drawing for yourself, however, you must do so in a *graphics context*. A graphics context is basically a place you can draw. In certain situations, a graphics context is provided for you; otherwise, you must obtain or create one for yourself. Either way, this graphics context may also become the *current context*. Core Graphics drawing functions require that you specify a context to draw into; UIKit's Objective-C drawing methods typically draw into the current context. If you have a context that you want to draw into and it isn't the current context, you can make it the current context temporarily by calling `UIGraphicsPushContext` (and be sure to restore things with `UIGraphics-PopContext` later).

## UIImage and UIImageView

If an image does not need to be created dynamically, but has already been created before your app runs, then drawing may be as simple as providing an image file as a resource in your app's bundle. The system knows how to work with many standard image file types, such as TIFF, JPEG, GIF, and PNG.

In the very simplest case, an image in your app's bundle can be obtained through the UIImage class method `imageNamed:`. This method looks for an image file with the supplied name at the top level of your app's bundle and reads it as a UIImage instance. A nice thing about this approach is that memory management is handled for you: the image data may be cached in memory, and if you ask for the same image by calling `imageNamed:` again later, the cached data may be supplied immediately. You can also read an image file from anywhere in your app's bundle using the class method `imageWithContentsOfFile:` or the instance method `initWithContentsOfFile:`. (You can get a reference to your app's bundle with `[NSBundle mainBundle]`, and NSBundle then provides instance methods for getting the pathname of a file within the bundle.) There are various other ways of obtaining a UIImage, but these are the most common.

Once you have a UIImage, displaying it may be as simple as handing it to a UIImageView or some other built-in class that expects a UIImage. If a UIImageView instance begins life in a nib and is to display a UIImage from a file in your app's bundle, you won't even need any code; the UIImageView can be set to that file directly in the nib. (This mechanism works most easily if the file will be at the top level of the app's bundle.)

A UIImageView can actually have *two* images, one assigned to its `image` property and the other assigned to its `highlightedImage` property; which is displayed depends on the value of the UIImageView's `highlighted` property. This notion of highlighting is purely optional, and you can use it however you like; a UIImageView does not automatically highlight itself.

A UIImageView without an image and without a background color is invisible, so you could start with an empty UIImageView in the place where you will later need an image and assign the image in code as needed. An image may have areas that are transparent, and a UIImageView will respect this; thus an image of any shape can appear, without the user being aware that it resides in a rectangular host.

How a UIImageView draws its image depends upon the setting of its `contentMode` property. (The `contentMode` property is inherited from UIView; I'll discuss its more general purpose later in this chapter.) For example, `UIViewContentModeScaleToFill` means the image's width and height are set to the width and height of the view, thus filling the view completely even if this changes the image's aspect ratio; `UIViewContentModeCenter` means the image is drawn centered in the view without altering its size. The best way to get a feel for the meanings of the various `contentMode` settings is to assign a UIImageView a small image in a nib and then, in the Attributes inspector, change the Mode pop-up menu, and see where and how the image draws itself.

When creating a UIImageView in code, you can take advantage of a convenience initializer, `initWithImage:` (or `initWithImage:highlightedImage:`). The default `contentMode` is `UIViewContentModeScaleToFill`, but the image is not initially scaled because the view itself is sized to match to the image. You will still probably need to change the UIImageView's frame, or at least set its center, in order to place it correctly in its superview. In this example, I'll put a picture of the planet Mars in the center of the window:

```
UIImageView* iv =
    [[UIImageView alloc] initWithImage:[UIImage imageNamed:@"Mars.png"]];
[self.window addSubview: iv];
iv.center = self.window.center;
[iv release];
```

On a device with a double-resolution screen (such as the iPhone 4 with Retina display), all these methods of obtaining an image from a file will automatically use, if there is one, a file with the same name extended by @2x, marking it as double-resolution by assigning it a scale property value of 2.0. (So, in this case, we would have a second image file called *Mars@2x.png*.) In this way, your app can contain both a single-resolution and a double-resolution version of an image file; on the double-resolution display device, the double-resolution version of the image is used, and is drawn at the same size as the single-resolution image. Thus your code continues to work without change, but your images look sharper.

The documentation warns that if a UIImageView is to be assigned multiple images (such as an image and a highlightedImage), they must have the same scale property value. This is because the UIImageView gets its own internal scaling information from an image's scale at the time it is assigned to it; it does not change its internal scale merely because you switch the value of its highlighted property.

 Starting in iOS 4, when an image is obtained by name from the bundle, a file with the same name extended by ~ipad will automatically be used if the app is running on an iPad. You can use this in a universal app to supply different images automatically depending on whether the app runs on an iPhone or iPod touch, on the one hand, or on an iPad, on the other. This is true not just for images but for *any* resource obtained by name from the bundle. See Apple's *Resource Programming Guide*.

## UIImage and Graphics Contexts

The function UIGraphicsBeginImageContext creates a graphics context suitable for use as an image and makes it the current context. You then draw into this context to generate the image. When you've done that, you call UIGraphicsGetImageFromCurrentImage-Context to turn the context into a UIImage, and then UIGraphicsEndImageContext to dismiss the context. Now you have a UIImage that you can display in a UIImageView or draw into some other graphics context.

UIImage provides methods for drawing itself into the current context. We now know how to obtain an image context and make it the current context, so we can experiment with these methods. Here, I'll draw two pictures of Mars side by side:

```
UIImage* mars = [UIImage imageNamed:@"Mars.png"];
CGSize sz = [mars size];
```

*Figure 15-1. Two images of Mars combined side by side*

*Figure 15-2. Two images of Mars in different sizes, composited*

```
UIGraphicsBeginImageContext(CGSizeMake(sz.width*2, sz.height));
[mars drawAtPoint:CGPointMake(0,0)];
[mars drawAtPoint:CGPointMake(sz.width,0)];
UIImage* im = UIGraphicsGetImageFromCurrentImageContext();
UIGraphicsEndImageContext();
```

If I now hand this image im over to a visible UIImageView, the image appears onscreen (Figure 15-1). I could do this, for example, by creating the UIImageView in code, as before:

```
UIImageView* iv = [[UIImageView alloc] initWithImage:im];
[self.window addSubview: iv];
iv.center = self.window.center;
[iv release];
```

Additional UIImage methods let you scale an image into a desired rectangle as you draw, and specify the compositing (blend) mode whereby the image should combine with whatever is already present. To illustrate, I'll create an image of Mars centered in another image of Mars that's twice as large, using a blend mode (Figure 15-2):

```
UIImage* mars = [UIImage imageNamed:@"Mars.png"];
CGSize sz = [mars size];
UIGraphicsBeginImageContext(CGSizeMake(sz.width*2, sz.height*2));
[mars drawInRect:CGRectMake(0,0,sz.width*2,sz.height*2)];
[mars drawInRect:CGRectMake(sz.width/2.0, sz.height/2.0, sz.width, sz.height)
        blendMode:kCGBlendModeMultiply alpha:1.0];
UIImage* im = UIGraphicsGetImageFromCurrentImageContext();
UIGraphicsEndImageContext();
```

There is no UIImage method for specifying the source rectangle — that is, for specifying that you want to extract a smaller region of the original image. You can work around this by specifying a smaller graphics context and positioning the image drawing so that the desired region falls into it. For example, to obtain an image of the right half of Mars, you'd make your graphics context half the width of the mars image, and then draw mars shifted left, so that only its right half intersects the graphics context. There is no

*Figure 15-3. Half the original image of Mars*

harm in doing this, and it's a perfectly standard device; the left half of mars simply isn't drawn (Figure 15-3):

```
UIImage* mars = [UIImage imageNamed:@"Mars.png"];
CGSize sz = [mars size];
UIGraphicsBeginImageContext(CGSizeMake(sz.width/2.0, sz.height));
[mars drawAtPoint:CGPointMake(-sz.width/2.0, 0)];
UIImage* im = UIGraphicsGetImageFromCurrentImageContext();
UIGraphicsEndImageContext();
```

On a double-resolution device, the use of UIGraphicsBeginImageContext leads to an undesirable result. The code works, and the image mars will of course be the double-resolution version if there is one but the image ultimately being generated, im, is single-resolution (its scale is 1.0). To generate a double-resolution image as our final output, we must call UIGraphicsBeginImageContextWithOptions instead of UIGraphicsBegin-ImageContext. The third parameter is the scale; if it is 0.0, the correct scale for the current device will be assigned for us. This function was introduced in iOS 4.0, so to run without crashing on an earlier system you'd need to test for its existence:

```
if (&UIGraphicsBeginImageContextWithOptions)
    UIGraphicsBeginImageContextWithOptions(sz, NO, 0.0);
else
    UIGraphicsBeginImageContext(sz);
```

# CGImage

The Core Graphics version of UIImage is CGImage (actually a CGImageRef). They are easily converted to one another: a UIImage has a CGImage property that accesses its Quartz image data, and you can make a UIImage from a CGImage using imageWith-CGImage: or initWithCGImage:.

A CGImage lets you create a new image directly from a rectangular region of the image. (It also lets you apply an image mask, which you can't do with UIImage.) I'll demonstrate by splitting the image of Mars in half and drawing the two halves separately (Figure 15-4):

```
UIImage* mars = [UIImage imageNamed:@"Mars.png"];
// extract each half as a CGImage
CGSize sz = [mars size];
CGImageRef marsLeft = CGImageCreateWithImageInRect([mars CGImage],
                    CGRectMake(0,0,sz.width/2.0,sz.height));
CGImageRef marsRight = CGImageCreateWithImageInRect([mars CGImage],
                    CGRectMake(sz.width/2.0,0,sz.width/2.0,sz.height));
// draw each CGImage into an image context
UIGraphicsBeginImageContext(CGSizeMake(sz.width*1.5, sz.height));
```

*Figure 15-4. Image of Mars split in half*

```
CGContextRef con = UIGraphicsGetCurrentContext();
CGContextDrawImage(con, CGRectMake(0,0,sz.width/2.0,sz.height), marsLeft);
CGContextDrawImage(con, CGRectMake(sz.width,0,sz.width/2.0,sz.height), marsRight);
UIImage* im = UIGraphicsGetImageFromCurrentImageContext();
UIGraphicsEndImageContext();
CGImageRelease(marsLeft); CGImageRelease(marsRight);
```

As already mentioned, Core Graphics functions that operate in a graphics context require us to specify this context; our call to `UIGraphicsBeginImageContext` did not supply us with a reference to the resulting context, but it did make the resulting context the current context, which we can always obtain through `UIGraphicsGetCurrentContext`. Observe also that we must follow the appropriate memory management rules for C functions: wherever we generate something through a function with "Create" in its name, we later call the corresponding "Release" function.

But there's a problem with the previous example: the drawing is upside-down. It isn't rotated; it's mirrored top to bottom, or, to use the technical term, *flipped*. This phenomenon can arise when you create a CGImage and then draw it with CGContext-DrawImage and is due to a mismatch in the native coordinate systems of the source and target contexts.

There are various ways of compensating for this mismatch between the coordinate systems. One is to draw the CGImage into an intermediate UIImage and extract *another* CGImage from that. Example 15-1 presents a utility function for doing this.

*Example 15-1. Utility for flipping an image drawing*

```
CGImageRef flip (CGImageRef im) {
    CGSize sz = CGSizeMake(CGImageGetWidth(im), CGImageGetHeight(im));
    UIGraphicsBeginImageContext(sz);
    CGContextDrawImage(
      UIGraphicsGetCurrentContext(), CGRectMake(0, 0, sz.width, sz.height), im);
    CGImageRef result = [UIGraphicsGetImageFromCurrentImageContext() CGImage];
    UIGraphicsEndImageContext();
    return result;
}
```

Armed with the utility function from Example 15-1, we can now draw the halves of Mars the right way up in the previous example:

```
CGContextDrawImage(
    con, CGRectMake(0,0,sz.width/2.0,sz.height), flip(marsLeft));
CGContextDrawImage(
    con, CGRectMake(sz.width,0,sz.width/2.0,sz.height), flip(marsRight));
```

## Why Flipping Happens

The ultimate source of accidental flipping is that Core Graphics comes from the Mac OS X world, where the coordinate system's origin is located by default at the bottom left and the positive y-direction is upward, whereas on iOS the origin is located by default at the top left and the positive y-direction is downward. In most drawing situations, no problem arises, because the coordinate system of the graphics context is adjusted to compensate. Thus, the default coordinate system for drawing in a Core Graphics context on iOS has the origin at the top left, just as you expect. But creating and drawing a CGImage exposes the issue.

Another solution is to wrap the CGImage in a UIImage and draw using the UIImage drawing methods discussed in the previous section. Those same two lines might then be replaced with this:

```
[[UIImage imageWithCGImage:marsLeft] drawAtPoint:CGPointMake(0,0)];
[[UIImage imageWithCGImage:marsRight] drawAtPoint:CGPointMake(sz.width,0)];
```

Yet another solution is to apply a transform to the graphics context before drawing the CGImage, effectively flipping the context's internal coordinate system. This is elegant, but can be confusing if there are other transforms in play. I'll talk more about graphics context transforms later in this chapter.

A further problem is that our code draws incorrectly on a high-resolution device if there is a high-resolution version of our image file. The reason is that a UIImage has a `scale` property, but a CGImage doesn't. When you call a UIImage's `CGImage` method, therefore, you can't assume that the resulting CGImage is the same size as the original UIImage; a UIImage's `size` property is the same for a single-resolution image and its double-resolution counterpart, but the CGImage of a double-resolution image is twice as large in both dimensions as the CGImage of the corresponding single-resolution image.

So, in extracting a desired piece of the CGImage, we must either multiply all appropriate values by the scale or express ourselves in terms of the CGImage's dimensions. In this case, as we are extracting the left and right halves of the image, the latter is obviously the simpler course. So here's a version of our original code that draws correctly on either a single-resolution or a double-resolution device:

```
UIImage* mars = [UIImage imageNamed:@"Mars.png"];
CGSize sz = [mars size];
// Derive CGImage and use its dimensions to extract its halves
CGImageRef marsCG = [mars CGImage];
CGSize szCG = CGSizeMake(CGImageGetWidth(marsCG), CGImageGetHeight(marsCG));
CGImageRef marsLeft = CGImageCreateWithImageInRect(marsCG,
                    CGRectMake(0,0,szCG.width/2.0,szCG.height));
CGImageRef marsRight = CGImageCreateWithImageInRect(marsCG,
                    CGRectMake(szCG.width/2.0,0,szCG.width/2.0,szCG.height));
// Use double-resolution graphics context if possible
```

```
UIGraphicsBeginImageContextWithOptions(
    CGSizeMake(sz.width*1.5, sz.height), NO, 0.0);
// The rest is as before, calling flip() to compensate for flipping
CGContextRef con = UIGraphicsGetCurrentContext();
CGContextDrawImage(
    con, CGRectMake(0,0,sz.width/2.0,sz.height), flip(marsLeft));
CGContextDrawImage(
    con, CGRectMake(sz.width,0,sz.width/2.0,sz.height), flip(marsRight));
UIImage* im = UIGraphicsGetImageFromCurrentImageContext();
UIGraphicsEndImageContext();
CGImageRelease(marsLeft); CGImageRelease(marsRight);
```

Our flip compensation utility (Example 15-1) works here, but our other solution does not. If you're doing to derive a UIImage from a CGImage where scale matters, you have to provide the scale by calling imageWithCGImage:scale:orientation (only on iOS 4.0 or later) instead of imageWithCGImage:. So our second solution now looks like this:

```
[[UIImage imageWithCGImage:marsLeft
                 scale:[mars scale]
           orientation:UIImageOrientationUp]
  drawAtPoint:CGPointMake(0,0)];
[[UIImage imageWithCGImage:marsRight
                 scale:[mars scale]
           orientation:UIImageOrientationUp]
  drawAtPoint:CGPointMake(sz.width,0)];
```

# Drawing a UIView

The most flexible way to draw a UIView is to draw it yourself. Actually, you don't draw a UIView; you subclass UIView and endow the subclass with the ability to draw itself. When a UIView needs drawing, its drawRect: method is called. Overriding that method is your chance to draw. At the time that drawRect: is called, the current graphics context has already been set to the view. You can use Core Graphics functions or UIKit convenience methods to draw into that context.

You should never call drawRect: yourself. If a view needs updating and you want its drawRect: called, send the view the setNeedsDisplay message. This will cause draw-Rect: to be called at the next proper moment.

 If you subclass a built-in UIView subclass, don't override drawRect: unless you are assured that this is legal. For example, it is not legal to override drawRect: in a subclass of UIImageView; you cannot combine your drawing with that of the UIImageView.

So let's begin again. We'll have a UIView subclass called MyView, in which we'll do all our drawing. How this class gets instantiated, and how the instance gets into our view hierarchy, isn't important. Here, I'll do it in code as the app launches:

```
MyView* mv = [[MyView alloc] initWithFrame:
          CGRectMake(0, 0, self.window.bounds.size.width - 50, 150)];
```

```
mv.center = self.window.center;
[self.window addSubview: mv];
mv.opaque = NO;
[mv release];
```

The only really new thing here is that we set our UIView instance's opaque property to NO. If we don't do this, the view will be drawn with a black background, which isn't what we want. Of course, if the view fills its rectangle with opaque drawing or has an opaque background color, we can leave opaque set to YES and gain some drawing efficiency (see Chapter 14).

The drawing action all takes place in MyView's drawRect: method. At the time draw-Rect: is called, we are guaranteed that the current Core Graphics context is MyView itself, so we can obtain this if we need to with UIGraphicsGetCurrentContext, and then we can do here whatever we did in our earlier examples of drawing in a context. For example, we can draw two halves of Mars, one at each end of the view:

```
- (void)drawRect:(CGRect)rect {
    CGRect b = self.bounds;
    UIImage* mars = [UIImage imageNamed:@"Mars.png"];
    CGSize sz = [mars size];
    CGImageRef marsCG = [mars CGImage];
    CGSize szCG = CGSizeMake(CGImageGetWidth(marsCG), CGImageGetHeight(marsCG));
    CGImageRef marsLeft = CGImageCreateWithImageInRect(marsCG,
                        CGRectMake(0,0,szCG.width/2.0,szCG.height));
    CGImageRef marsRight = CGImageCreateWithImageInRect(marsCG,
                        CGRectMake(szCG.width/2.0,0,szCG.width/2.0,szCG.height));
    CGContextRef con = UIGraphicsGetCurrentContext();
    CGContextDrawImage(con,
        CGRectMake(0,0,sz.width/2.0,sz.height),
        flip(marsLeft));
    CGContextDrawImage(con,
        CGRectMake(b.size.width-sz.width/2.0, 0, sz.width/2.0, sz.height),
        flip(marsRight));
    CGImageRelease(marsLeft); CGImageRelease(marsRight);
}
```

There is no need to call super, because the superclass here is UIView, whose draw-Rect: does nothing.

The need to draw in real time, on demand, surprises some beginners, who worry that drawing may be a time-consuming operation. Equally surprising is the need to draw *repeatedly*; even if the drawing has not changed, you may be called upon to perform the same drawing again. Where drawing is extensive and can be compartmentalized into sections, you may be able to gain some efficiency by paying attention to the rect parameter passed into drawRect:. It designates the region of the view's bounds that needs refreshing. The system knows this either because this is the area that has just been exposed by the removal of some covering view or because you called setNeedsDisplayInRect:, specifying it. Thus, you could call setNeedsDisplayInRect: to tell your drawRect: to redraw a subregion of the view; the rest of the view will be left alone.

## Making a View's Background Transparent

If a view's `backgroundColor` is nil (the default when creating a UIView in code) and its `opaque` is YES (ditto), it will be drawn with a black background; therefore, to make such a view's background transparent, you must set its `opaque` to NO. This problem doesn't arise with a view instantiated from a nib, because you can't assign a view a nil `background-Color` in the nib; it always has *some* background color, even if it is what the nib calls Clear Color ([UIColor clearColor], or transparent black). Thus, assigning [UIColor clearColor] as a code-created view's `backgroundColor` has the same apparent effect, and you may encounter code that does this. But Apple warns that you should *still* set a transparent view's `opaque` to NO, or incorrect drawing may occur.

In general, however, you should not optimize prematurely. What looks like a lengthy drawing operation may be extremely fast. And the iOS drawing system is efficient; it doesn't call `drawRect:` unless it has to (or is told to, through a call to `setNeeds-Display`), and once a view has drawn itself, the result is cached so that the cached drawing can be reused instead of repeating the drawing operation from scratch.

# Graphics Context State

When you draw in a graphics context, the drawing obeys the context's current settings. Thus, the way you draw using Core Graphics functions is to configure the context's settings first, and then draw. For example, to draw a red line followed by a blue line, you would first set the context's line color to red, and then draw the first line; then you'd set the context's line color to blue, and then draw the second line. To the eye, it appears that the redness and blueness are properties of the individual lines, but in fact, at the time you draw each of them, they are properties of the entire graphics context.

A graphics context thus has, at every moment, a *state*, which is the sum total of all its settings; the way a piece of drawing looks is the result of what the graphics context's state was at the moment that piece of drawing was performed. To help you manipulate entire states, the graphics context provides a *stack* for holding states. Every time you call `CGContextSaveGState`, the context pushes the entire current state onto the stack; every time you call `CGContextRestoreGState`, the context retrieves the state from the top of the stack (the state that was most recently pushed) and sets itself to that state.

Many of the settings that constitute a graphics context's state, and that determine the behavior and appearance of drawing performed at that moment, are similar to those of any drawing application. They include (along with some of the commands that determine them):

*Line thickness and dash style*
    `CGContextSetLineWidth, CGContextSetLineDash`

*Line end-cap style and join style*
CGContextSetLineCap, CGContextSetLineJoin, CGContextSetMiterLimit

*Line color or pattern*
CGContextSetRGBStrokeColor, CGContextSetGrayStrokeColor, CGContextSetStroke-ColorWithColor, CGContextSetStrokePattern

*Fill color or pattern*
CGContextSetRGBFillColor, CGContextSetGrayFillColor, CGContextSetFillColor-WithColor, CGContextSetFillPattern

*Shadow*
CGContextSetShadow, CGContextSetShadowWithColor

*Blend mode*
CGContextSetBlendMode (this determines how drawing that you do now will be composited with drawing already present)

*Overall transparency*
CGContextSetAlpha (individual colors also have an alpha component)

*Text features*
CGContextSelectFont, CGContextSetFont, CGContextSetFontSize, CGContextSetText-DrawingMode, CGContextSetCharacterSpacing

*Whether anti-aliasing and font smoothing are in effect*
CGContextSetShouldAntialias, CGContextSetShouldSmoothFonts

Additional settings include:

*Clipping area*
Drawing outside the clipping area is not physically drawn.

*Transform (or "CTM," for "current transform matrix")*
Changes how points that you specify in subsequent drawing commands are mapped onto the physical space of the canvas.

Many (but not all) of these settings will be illustrated by examples later in this chapter.

# Paths

By issuing a series of instructions for moving an imaginary pen, you trace out a *path*. Such a path does *not* constitute drawing! First you provide a path; *then* you draw. Drawing can mean stroking the path or filling the path, or both. Again, this should be a familiar notion from certain drawing applications.

A path is constructed by tracing it out from point to point. Think of the drawing system as holding a pen. Then you must first tell that pen where to position itself, setting the current point; after that, you issue a series of commands telling it how to trace out each subsequent piece of the path. Each additional piece of the path starts at the current point; its end becomes the new current point.

Here are some path-drawing commands you're likely to give:

*Position the current point*
CGContextMoveToPoint

*Trace a line*
CGContextAddLineToPoint, CGContextAddLines

*Trace a rectangle*
CGContextAddRect, CGContextAddRects

*Trace an ellipse or circle*
CGContextAddEllipseInRect

*Trace an arc*
CGContextAddArcToPoint, CGContextAddArc

*Trace a Bezier curve with one or two control points*
CGContextAddQuadCurveToPoint, CGContextAddCurveToPoint

*Close the current path*
CGContextClosePath. This appends a line from the last point of the path to the first point. There's no need to do this if you're about to fill the path, since it's done for you.

*Stroke or fill the current path*
CGContextStrokePath, CGContextFillPath, CGContextEOFillPath, CGContextDraw-Path. Stroking or filling the current path *clears the path*. Use CGContextDrawPath if you want both to fill and to stroke the path in a single command, because if you merely stroke it first with CGContextStrokePath, the path is cleared and you can no longer fill it.

*Erase a rectangle*
CGContextClearRect. This erases all existing drawing in a rectangle. When called on the current context in a view's drawRect:, it erases the view's background color if there is one. If the background color is nil or a color with some transparency, the result will be a transparent rectangle; if the background color is opaque, the result will be a black rectangle.

There are also a lot of convenience functions that create a path and stroke or fill it all in a single move: CGContextStrokeLineSegments, CGContextStrokeRect, CGContextStroke-RectWithWidth, CGContextFillRect, CGContextFillRects, CGContextStrokeEllipseIn-Rect, CGContextFillEllipseInRect.

If you're worried that there might be an existing path, you can call CGContextBegin-Path as you start constructing a new path; many of Apple's examples do this, but in practice I usually do not find it necessary.

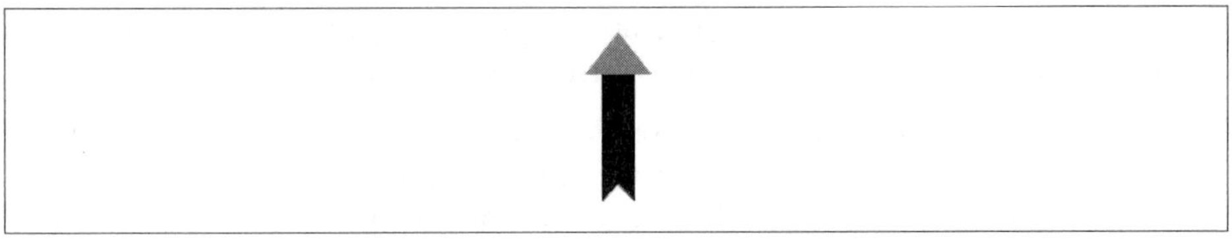

*Figure 15-5. A simple path drawing*

A path can be compound, meaning that it consists of multiple independent pieces. For example, a single path might consist of two separate closed shapes: a rectangle and a circle. When you call `CGContextMoveToPoint` in the middle of constructing a path (that is, after tracing out a path and without clearing it by filling, stroking, or calling `CGContextBeginPath`), you pick up the imaginary pen and move it to a new location without tracing a segment, thus preparing to start an independent piece of the same path.

To illustrate the typical use of path-drawing commands, I'll generate the up-pointing arrow shown in Figure 15-5. This might not be the best way to create the arrow, and I'm deliberately avoiding use of the convenience functions, but it's clear and shows a nice basic variety of typical commands:

```
// obtain the current graphics context
CGContextRef con = UIGraphicsGetCurrentContext();

// draw a black (by default) vertical line, the shaft of the arrow
CGContextMoveToPoint(con, 100, 100);
CGContextAddLineToPoint(con, 100, 19);
CGContextSetLineWidth(con, 20);
CGContextStrokePath(con);

// draw a red triangle, the point of the arrow
CGContextSetFillColorWithColor(con, [[UIColor redColor] CGColor]);
CGContextMoveToPoint(con, 80, 25);
CGContextAddLineToPoint(con, 100, 0);
CGContextAddLineToPoint(con, 120, 25);
CGContextFillPath(con);

// snip a triangle out of the shaft by drawing in Clear blend mode
CGContextMoveToPoint(con, 90, 101);
CGContextAddLineToPoint(con, 100, 90);
CGContextAddLineToPoint(con, 110, 101);
CGContextSetBlendMode(con, kCGBlendModeClear);
CGContextFillPath(con);
```

Properly speaking, we should probably surround our drawing code with calls to `CGContextSaveGState` and `CGContextRestoreGState`, just in case. It probably wouldn't make any difference in this particular example, as the context does not persist between calls to `drawRect:`, but it can't hurt.

If a path needs to be reused, you can save it as a CGPath, which is actually a CGPathRef. You can either copy the graphics context's current path using `CGContextCopyPath`, or you can create a new CGMutablePathRef and construct the path using various CGPath functions that parallel the graphics path-construction functions.

Another nice use of a CGMutablePathRef is to pass it to a method that modifies the path; this can result in an elegant encapsulation of functionality. For example, in one of my apps I draw some cards. Each card consists of one, two, or three repetitions of the same shape. There are three different shapes, and a card draws a shape in a particular color. So I have a class called Shape, and three Shape subclasses. Shape declares a method drawShape:inRect:, like this:

```
- (void) drawShape: (CGMutablePathRef) p inRect: (CGRect) r;
```

Each Shape subclass overrides and implements drawShape: in its own way, depending on what the shape is. For instance, the Ellipse shape implements it like this:

```
- (void) drawShape: (CGMutablePathRef) p inRect: (CGRect) r {
    CGPathAddEllipseInRect(p, NULL, r);
}
```

A card has an instance variable itsShape, which is an instance of one of the three Shape subclasses. So, as part of the process of drawing the card, I simply hand to that card's itsShape a CGMutablePathRef and a CGRect and tell it to draw the shape for me:

```
CGMutablePathRef p = CGPathCreateMutable();
[[theCard itsShape] drawShape: p inRect: theRect];
CGContextAddPath(context, p);
CGPathRelease(p);
// more stuff here...
```

This routine then proceeds to set the graphics context's color and other features, and tells the path to stroke and fill — without knowing anything about what shapes it's drawing! That knowledge resides entirely in the Shape subclasses.

There is also, starting in iOS 3.2, a UIKit class, UIBezierPath, that wraps CGPath. It provides methods for drawing certain path shapes, as well as for stroking, filling, and for accessing certain settings of the current graphics context state. Similarly, UIColor provides methods for setting the current graphics context's stroke and fill colors. Thus we could rewrite our arrow-drawing routine like this:

```
UIBezierPath* p = [UIBezierPath bezierPath];
[p moveToPoint:CGPointMake(100,100)];
[p addLineToPoint:CGPointMake(100, 19)];
[p setLineWidth:20];
[p stroke];

[[UIColor redColor] set];
[p removeAllPoints];
[p moveToPoint:CGPointMake(80,25)];
[p addLineToPoint:CGPointMake(100, 0)];
[p addLineToPoint:CGPointMake(120, 25)];
[p fill];

[p removeAllPoints];
[p moveToPoint:CGPointMake(90,101)];
```

```
[p addLineToPoint:CGPointMake(100, 90)];
[p addLineToPoint:CGPointMake(110, 101)];
[p fillWithBlendMode:kCGBlendModeClear alpha:1.0];
```

There's no savings of code in this particular case, but UIBezierPath still might be useful if you need object features, and it does offer one convenience method, `bezierPathWith-RoundedRect:cornerRadius:`, that is particularly attractive (drawing a rectangle with rounded corners using only Core Graphics function calls is rather tedious).

# Clipping

Another use of a path is to mask out areas, protecting them from future drawing. This is called *clipping*. By default, a graphics context's clipping region is the entire graphics context: you can draw anywhere within the context.

The clipping area is a feature of the context as a whole, and any new clipping area is applied by intersecting it with the existing clipping area; so if you apply your own clipping region, the way to remove it from the graphics context is to wrap things with calls to `CGContextSaveGState` and `CGContextRestoreGState`.

To illustrate, I'll rewrite the code that generated our original arrow (Figure 15-5) to use clipping instead of a blend mode to "punch out" the triangular notch in the tail of the arrow. This is a little tricky, because what we want to clip to is not the region inside the triangle but the region outside it. To express this, we'll use a compound path consisting of more than one closed area — the triangle, and the drawing area as a whole (which we can obtain with `CGContextGetClipBoundingBox`).

Both when filling a compound path and when using it to express a clipping region, the system follows one of two rules:

*Winding rule*
    The fill or clipping area is denoted by an alternation in the direction (clockwise or counterclockwise) of the path demarcating each region.

*Even-odd rule (EO)*
    The fill or clipping area is denoted by a simple count of the paths demarcating each region.

Our situation is extremely simple, so it's easier to use the even-odd rule. So we set up the clipping area using `CGContextEOClip` and then draw the arrow:

```
// obtain the current graphics context
CGContextRef con = UIGraphicsGetCurrentContext();

// punch triangular hole in context clipping region
CGContextMoveToPoint(con, 90, 100);
CGContextAddLineToPoint(con, 100, 90);
CGContextAddLineToPoint(con, 110, 100);
CGContextClosePath(con);
CGContextAddRect(con, CGContextGetClipBoundingBox(con));
```

```
CGContextEOClip(con);

// draw the vertical line
CGContextMoveToPoint(con, 100, 100);
CGContextAddLineToPoint(con, 100, 19);
CGContextSetLineWidth(con, 20);
CGContextStrokePath(con);

// draw the red triangle, the point of the arrow
CGContextSetFillColorWithColor(con, [[UIColor redColor] CGColor]);
CGContextMoveToPoint(con, 80, 25);
CGContextAddLineToPoint(con, 100, 0);
CGContextAddLineToPoint(con, 120, 25);
CGContextFillPath(con);
```

# Gradients

Gradients can range from the simple to the complex. A simple gradient (which is all I'll describe here) is determined by a color at one endpoint along with a color at the other endpoint, plus (optionally) colors at intermediate points; the gradient is then painted either linearly between two points in the context or radially between two circles in the context.

You can't use a gradient as a path's fill color, but you can restrict a gradient to a path's shape by clipping, which amounts to the same thing.

To illustrate, I'll redraw our arrow, using a linear gradient as the "shaft" of the arrow (Figure 15-6):

```
// obtain the current graphics context
CGContextRef con = UIGraphicsGetCurrentContext();
CGContextSaveGState(con);

// punch triangular hole in context clipping region
CGContextMoveToPoint(con, 90, 100);
CGContextAddLineToPoint(con, 100, 90);
CGContextAddLineToPoint(con, 110, 100);
CGContextClosePath(con);
CGContextAddRect(con, CGContextGetClipBoundingBox(con));
```

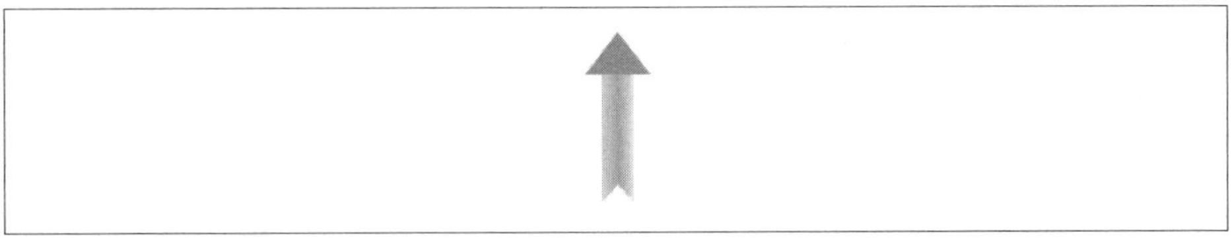

*Figure 15-6. Drawing with a gradient*

```
CGContextEOClip(con);

// draw the vertical line, add its shape to the clipping region
CGContextMoveToPoint(con, 100, 100);
CGContextAddLineToPoint(con, 100, 19);
CGContextSetLineWidth(con, 20);
CGContextReplacePathWithStrokedPath(con);
CGContextClip(con);

// draw the gradient
CGFloat locs[3] = { 0.0, 0.5, 1.0 };
CGFloat colors[12] = {
    0.3,0.3,0.3,0.8, // starting color, transparent gray
    0.0,0.0,0.0,1.0, // intermediate color, black
    0.3,0.3,0.3,0.8 // ending color, transparent gray
};
CGColorSpaceRef sp = CGColorSpaceCreateDeviceGray();
CGGradientRef grad = CGGradientCreateWithColorComponents (sp, colors, locs, 3);
CGContextDrawLinearGradient (con, grad, CGPointMake(89,0), CGPointMake(111,0), 0);
CGColorSpaceRelease(sp);
CGGradientRelease(grad);

CGContextRestoreGState(con); // done clipping

// draw the red triangle, the point of the arrow
CGContextSetFillColorWithColor(con, [[UIColor redColor] CGColor]);
CGContextMoveToPoint(con, 80, 25);
CGContextAddLineToPoint(con, 100, 0);
CGContextAddLineToPoint(con, 120, 25);
CGContextFillPath(con);
```

The call to `CGContextReplacePathWithStrokedPath` pretends to stroke the current path, using the current line width and other line-related context state settings, but then creates a new path representing the outside of that stroked path. Thus, instead of a thick line we have a rectangular region that we can use as the clip region.

We then create the gradient and paint it. The procedure is verbose but simple; everything is boilerplate. We describe the gradient as a set of locations on the continuum between one endpoint (0.0) and the other endpoint (1.0), along with the color to go in each location; in this case, I want the gradient to be lighter at the edges and darker in the middle, so I use three locations, with the dark one at 0.5. We must also supply a color space in order to create the gradient. Finally, we create the gradient, paint it into place, and release the color space and the gradient.

*Figure 15-7. A patterned fill*

# Colors and Patterns

A color is a CGColor (actually a CGColorRef). CGColor is not difficult to work with, and is bridged to UIColor through UIColor's `colorWithCGColor:` and `CGColor` methods.

A pattern, on the other hand, is a CGPattern (actually a CGPatternRef). You can create a pattern and stroke or fill with it. The process is rather elaborate. As an extremely simple example, I'll replace the red triangular arrowhead with a red-and-blue striped triangle (Figure 15-7). To do so, remove this line:

```
CGContextSetFillColorWithColor(con, [[UIColor redColor] CGColor]);
```

In its place, put the following:

```
CGColorSpaceRef sp2 = CGColorSpaceCreatePattern(NULL);
CGContextSetFillColorSpace (con, sp2);
CGColorSpaceRelease (sp2);
CGPatternCallbacks callback = {
    0, &drawStripes, NULL
};
CGAffineTransform tr = CGAffineTransformIdentity;
CGPatternRef patt = CGPatternCreate(NULL,
                    CGRectMake(0,0,4,4),
                    tr,
                    4, 4,
                    kCGPatternTilingConstantSpacingMinimalDistortion,
                    true,
                    &callback);
CGFloat alph = 1.0;
CGContextSetFillPattern(con, patt, &alph);
CGPatternRelease(patt);
```

That code is verbose, but it is almost entirely boilerplate. To understand it, it almost helps to read it backward. What we're leading up to is the call to `CGContextSetFill-Pattern`; instead of setting a fill color, we're setting a fill pattern, to be used the next time we fill a path (in this case, the triangular arrowhead). The third parameter to `CGContextSetFillPattern` is a pointer to a CGFloat, so we have to set up the CGFloat itself beforehand. The second parameter to `CGContextSetFillPattern` is a CGPattern-Ref, so we have to create that CGPatternRef beforehand (and release it afterward).

So now let's talk about the call to `CGPatternCreate`. A pattern is a drawing in a rectangular "cell"; we have to state both the size of the cell (the second argument) and the spacing between origin points of cells (the fourth and fifth arguments). In this case, the cell is 4×4, and every cell exactly touches its neighbors both horizontally and vertically.

We have to supply a transform to be applied to the cell (the third argument); in this case, we're not doing anything with this transform, so we supply the identity transform. We supply a tiling rule (the sixth argument). We have to state whether this is a color pattern or a stencil pattern; it's a color pattern, so the seventh argument is `true`. And we have to supply a pointer to a callback function that actually draws the pattern into its cell (the eighth argument).

Except that that's *not* what we have to supply as the eighth argument. To make matters more complicated, what we actually have to supply here is a pointer to a CGPattern-Callbacks struct. This struct consists of the number 0 and pointers to *two* functions, one called to draw the pattern into its cell, the other called when the pattern is released. We're not specifying the second function, however; it is for memory management, and we don't need it in this simple example.

We have almost worked our way backward to the start of the code. It turns out that before you can call `CGContextSetFillPattern` with a colored pattern, you have to set the context's fill color space to a pattern color space. If you neglect to do this, you'll get an error when you call `CGContextSetFillPattern`. So we create the color space, set it as the context's fill color space, and release it.

But we are *still* not finished, because I haven't shown you the function that actually draws the pattern cell! This is the function whose address is taken as `&drawStripes` in our code. Here it is:

```
void drawStripes (void *info, CGContextRef con) {
    // assume 4 x 4 cell
    CGContextSetFillColorWithColor(con, [[UIColor redColor] CGColor]);
    CGContextFillRect(con, CGRectMake(0,0,4,4));
    CGContextSetFillColorWithColor(con, [[UIColor blueColor] CGColor]);
    CGContextFillRect(con, CGRectMake(0,0,4,2));
}
```

As you can see, the actual pattern-drawing code is very simple. The only tricky issue is that the call to `CGPatternCreate` must be in agreement with the pattern-drawing function as to the size of a cell, or the pattern won't come out the way you expect. We know in this case that the cell is 4×4. So we fill it with red, and then fill its lower half with blue. When these cells are tiled touching each other horizontally and vertically, we get the stripes that you see in Figure 15-7.

Note, finally, that the code as presented has left the graphics context in an undesirable state, with its fill color space set to a pattern color space. This would cause trouble if we were later to try to set the fill color to a normal color. The solution, as usual, is to wrap the code in calls to `CGContextSaveGState` and `CGContextRestoreGState`.

You may have observed in Figure 15-7 that the stripes do not fit neatly inside the triangle of the arrow-head: the bottommost stripe is something like half a blue stripe. This is because a pattern is positioned not with respect to the shape you are filling (or stroking), but with respect to the graphics context as a whole. We could shift the pattern position by calling `CGContextSetPatternPhase` before drawing.

# Graphics Context Transforms

Just as a UIView can have a transform, so can a graphics context. However, applying a transform to a graphics context has no effect on the drawing that's already in it; it affects only the drawing that takes place after it is applied, altering the way the coordinates you provide are mapped onto the graphics context's area. A graphics context's transform is called its CTM, for "current transformation matrix."

It is quite usual to take full advantage of a graphics context's CTM to save yourself from performing even simple calculations. You can multiply the current transform by any CGAffineTransform using `CGContextConcatCTM`; there are also convenience functions for applying a translate, scale, or rotate transform to the current transform.

The base transform for a graphics context is already set for you when you obtain the context; this is how the system is able to map context drawing coordinates onto screen coordinates. Whatever transforms you apply are applied to the current transform, so the base transform remains in effect and drawing continues to work. You can always return to the base transform after applying your own transforms by wrapping your code in calls to `CGContextSaveGState` and `CGContextRestoreGState`.

For example, we have hitherto been drawing our upward-pointing arrow with code that knows how to place that arrow at only one location: the top left of its rectangle is hard-coded at (80,0). This is silly. It makes the code hard to understand, as well as inflexible and difficult to reuse. Surely the sensible thing would be to draw the arrow at (0,0), by subtracting 80 from all the x-values in our existing code. Now it is easy to draw the arrow at *any* position, simply by applying a translation transform beforehand, mapping (0,0) to the desired top left corner of the arrow. So, to draw it at (80,0), we would say:

```
CGContextTranslateCTM(con, 80, 0);
// now draw the arrow at (0,0)
```

A rotate transform is particularly useful, allowing you to draw in a rotated orientation without any nasty trigonometry. However, it's a bit tricky because the point around which the rotation takes place is the origin. This is rarely what you want, so you have apply a translate transform first, to map the origin to the point around which you really want to rotate. But then, after rotating, in order to figure out where to draw you will probably have to reverse your translate transform.

To illustrate, here's code to draw our arrow repeatedly at several angles, pivoting around the end of its tail (Figure 15-8). First, we'll encapsulate the drawing of the arrow as a UIImage. Then we simply draw that UIImage repeatedly:

```
UIGraphicsBeginImageContextWithOptions(CGSizeMake(40,100), NO, 0.0);
CGContextRef con = UIGraphicsGetCurrentContext();

// draw the arrow into the image context
// draw it at (0,0)! adjust all x-values by subtracting 80
// ... actual code omitted ...
```

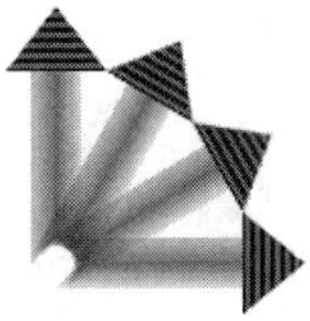

*Figure 15-8. Drawing rotated with a CTM*

```
UIImage* im = UIGraphicsGetImageFromCurrentImageContext();
UIGraphicsEndImageContext();

con = UIGraphicsGetCurrentContext();

[im drawAtPoint:CGPointMake(0,0)];
for (int i=0; i<3; i++) {
    CGContextTranslateCTM(con, 20, 100);
    CGContextRotateCTM(con, 30 * M_PI/180.0);
    CGContextTranslateCTM(con, -20, -100);
    [im drawAtPoint:CGPointMake(0,0)];
}
```

A transform is also one more solution for the "flip" problem we encountered earlier with CGContextDrawImage. Instead of reversing the drawing, we can reverse the context into which we draw it. Essentially, we apply a "flip" transform to the context's coordinate system. You move the context's top downward, and then reverse the direction of the y-coordinate by applying a scale transform whose y-multiplier is -1:

```
CGContextTranslateCTM(con, 0, theHeight);
CGContextScaleCTM(con, 1.0, -1.0);
```

How far down you move the context's top depends on how you intend to draw the image. So, for example, earlier we used a flip utility function to draw the two halves of Mars the right way up:

```
CGContextDrawImage(con,
    CGRectMake(0,0,sz.width/2.0,sz.height),
    flip(marsLeft));
CGContextDrawImage(con,
    CGRectMake(b.size.width-sz.width/2.0, 0, sz.width/2.0, sz.height),
    flip(marsRight));
```

For those two lines, we could substitute this:

```
CGContextTranslateCTM(con, 0, sz.height);
CGContextScaleCTM(con, 1.0, -1.0);
CGContextDrawImage(con,
    CGRectMake(0,0,sz.width/2.0,sz.height),
    marsLeft);
CGContextDrawImage(con,
    CGRectMake(b.size.width-sz.width/2.0, 0, sz.width/2.0, sz.height),
    marsRight);
```

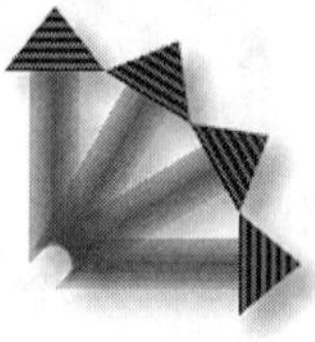

*Figure 15-9. Drawing with a shadow*

## Shadows

To add a shadow to a drawing, give the context a shadow value before drawing. The shadow position is expressed as a CGSize, where the positive direction for both values indicates down and to the right. The blur value is an open-ended positive number; Apple doesn't explain how the scale works, but experimentation shows that 12 is nice and blurry, 99 is so blurry as to be shapeless, and higher values become problematic.

Figure 15-9 shows the result of the same code that generated Figure 15-8, except that before we start drawing the arrow into the real context, we give the real context a shadow with this line:

```
CGContextSetShadow(con, CGSizeMake(7, 7), 12);
```

## Points and Pixels

A point is a dimensionless location described by an x-coordinate and a y-coordinate. When you draw in a graphics context, you specify the points at which to draw, and this works regardless of the device's resolution, because Core Graphics maps your drawing nicely onto the physical output (using the base CTM, along with any anti-aliasing and smoothing). Therefore, throughout this chapter I've concerned myself with graphics context points, disregarding their relationship to screen pixels.

However, pixels do exist. A pixel is a physical, integral, dimensioned unit of display in the real world. Whole-numbered points effectively lie between pixels, and this can matter if you're fussy, especially on a single-resolution device. For example, if a vertical path with whole-number coordinates is stroked with a line width of 1, half the line falls on each side of the path, and the drawn line on the screen of a single-resolution device will seem to be 2 pixels wide (because the device can't illuminate half a pixel).

You will sometimes encounter advice suggesting that if this effect is objectionable, you should try shifting the line's position by 0.5, to center it in its pixels. This advice may appear to work, but it makes some simple-minded assumptions. A more sophisticated approach is to obtain the UIView's `contentScaleFactor` property (on iOS 4.0 and later). This value will be either 1.0 or 2.0, so you can divide by it to convert from pixels to points. Consider also that the most accurate way to draw a vertical or horizontal line is not to stroke a path but to fill a rectangle. So this code will draw a perfect 1-pixel-wide vertical line on any device:

```
CGContextFillRect(con, CGRectMake(100,0,1.0/self.contentScaleFactor,100));
```

# Content Mode

A view that draws something within itself, as opposed to merely having a background color and subviews (as in the previous chapter), has *content*. This means that its `content-Mode` property becomes important whenever the view is resized. As I mentioned earlier, the drawing system will avoid asking a view to redraw itself from scratch if possible; instead, it will use the cached result of the previous drawing operation. So, if the view is resized, the system may simply stretch or shrink or reposition the cached drawing, if your `contentMode` setting instructs it to do so.

It's a little tricky to illustrate this point, because I have to arrange for the view to be resized without also causing it to be redrawn (that is, without triggering a call to `draw-Rect:`). Here's how I'll do that. As the app starts up, I'll create the MyView instance in code and put it in the window, much as before. Then I'll use delayed performance to resize the MyView instance after the window has shown and the interface has been initially displayed:

```
- (BOOL)application:(UIApplication *)application
        didFinishLaunchingWithOptions:(NSDictionary *)launchOptions {
    MyView* mv = [[MyView alloc]
        initWithFrame: CGRectMake(0, 0, self.window.bounds.size.width - 50, 150)];
    mv.center = self.window.center;
    [self.window addSubview: mv];
    mv.opaque = NO;
    mv.tag = 111; // so I can get a reference to this view later
    [mv release];
    [self.window makeKeyAndVisible];
    [self performSelector:@selector(resize:) withObject:nil afterDelay:0.1];
    return YES;
}

- (void) resize: (id) dummy {
    UIView* mv = [self.window viewWithTag:111];
    CGRect f = mv.bounds;
    f.size.height *= 2;
    mv.bounds = f;
}
```

We double the height of the view without causing `drawRect:` to be called. The result is that the view's drawing appears at double its correct height. For example, if our view's `drawRect:` code is the same as the code that generated Figure 15-6, we get Figure 15-10.

This, however, is almost certainly not what we want. Sooner or later `drawRect:` will be called, and the drawing will be refreshed in accordance with our code. Our code doesn't say to draw the arrow at a height that is relative to the height of the view's bounds; it

*Figure 15-10. Automatic stretching of content*

draws the arrow at a fixed height. Thus, not only has the arrow stretched, but at some future time, it will snap back to its original size.

The moral is that our view's `contentMode` property needs to be in agreement with how the view draws itself. For example, our `drawRect:` code dictates the size and position of the arrow relative to the view's bounds origin, its top left. So we could set its `content-Mode` to `UIViewContentModeTopLeft`. Alternatively, and more likely, we could set it to `UIViewContentModeRedraw`; this will cause automatic scaling and repositioning of the cached content to be turned off, and instead the view's `setNeedsDisplay` method will be called, ultimately triggering `drawRect:` to redraw the content.

On the other hand, if a view might be resized only *momentarily* — say, as part of an animation — then stretching behavior might be exactly what you want. Suppose we're going to animate the view by making it get a little larger for a moment and then returning it to its original size, perhaps as a way of attracting the user's attention. Then presumably we do want the view's content to stretch and shrink as the view stretches and shrinks; that's the whole point of the animation. This is precisely what the default `contentMode` value, `UIViewContentModeScaleToFill`, does for us. And remember, it does it efficiently; what's being stretched and shrunk is just a cached image of our view's content.

# CHAPTER 16

# Layers

A UIView has a partner called its *layer*, a CALayer. A UIView does not actually draw itself onto the screen; it draws itself into its layer, and it is the layer that appears on the screen. As already mentioned in the previous two chapters, a view is not redrawn frequently; instead, its drawing is cached, and the cached version of the drawing is used where possible. The cached version is, in fact, the layer.

This might seem like a mere implementation detail, but layers are important and interesting. To understand layers is to understand views more deeply; layers extend the power of views. In particular:

*Layers have properties that affect drawing.*
Layers have drawing-related properties beyond those of a UIView. Because a layer is the recipient and presenter of a view's drawing, you can modify how a view is drawn on the screen by accessing the layer's properties. In other words, by reaching down to the level of its layer, you can make a view do things you can't do through UIView methods alone.

*Layers can be combined within a single view.*
A UIView's partner layer can contain additional layers. Since the purpose of layers is to draw, portraying visible material on the screen, this allows a UIView's drawing to be composited of multiple distinct pieces. This can make drawing easier, with the constituents of a drawing being treated as objects.

*Layers are the basis of animation.*
Animation allows you to add clarity, emphasis, and just plain coolness to your interface. Layers are made to be animated (the "CA" in "CALayer" stands for "Core Animation").

For example, suppose we want to add a compass indicator to our app's interface. Figure 16-1 portrays a simple version of such a compass. It takes advantage of the arrow that we figured out how to draw in Chapter 15; the arrow is drawn into a layer of its own. The other parts of the compass are layers too: the circle is a layer, and each of the cardinal point letters is a layer. The drawing is thus easy to composite in code; even

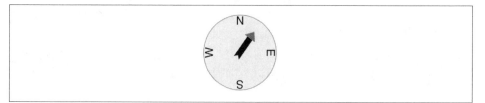

*Figure 16-1. A compass, composed of layers*

more intriguing, the pieces can be repositioned and animated separately, so it's easy to rotate the arrow without moving the circle.

The documentation discusses layers chiefly in connection with animation (in particular, in the *Core Animation Programming Guide*). This categorization gives the impression that layers are of interest only if you intend to animate. That's misleading. Layers are the basis of animation, but they are also the basis of view drawing, and are useful and important even if you don't use them for animation.

CALayer is not part of UIKit. It's part of the Quartz Core framework, which is not linked by default into the project template. Therefore, code that refers to CALayer or related classes must import `<QuartzCore/QuartzCore.h>`, and you must link *Quartz-Core.framework* into the project.

In this chapter, I'll discuss the place of layers in the visual architecture of an iOS app. In the next chapter, I'll talk about animation.

# View and Layer

A UIView instance has an accompanying CALayer instance, accessible as the view's `layer` property. This layer has a special status: it is partnered with this view to embody all of the view's drawing. The layer has no corresponding `view` property, but the view is the layer's `delegate`. The documentation sometimes speaks of this layer as the view's "underlying layer."

By default, when a UIView is instantiated, its layer is an instance of CALayer. But if you subclass UIView and you want your subclass's underlying layer to be an instance of a CALayer subclass (built-in or your own), implement the UIView subclass's `layer-Class` class method.

That, for example, is how the compass in Figure 16-1 is created. We have a UIView subclass, CompassView, and a CALayer subclass, CompassLayer. CompassView contains these lines:

```
+ (Class) layerClass {
    return [CompassLayer class];
}
```

Thus, when CompassView is instantiated, its underlying layer is a CompassLayer. There is no drawing in CompassView; its job is to give CompassLayer a place in the visible interface (because a layer cannot appear without a view). There is no drawing directly into the CompassLayer, either; its job is to assemble, configure, and contain the other layers, which constitute the visible compass interface.

Because every view has an underlying layer, there is a tight integration between the two. The layer is on the screen and portrays all the drawing. The view is the layer's delegate, and if it draws, it does so by contributing to the layer's drawing. And the view's properties are often merely a convenience for accessing the layer's properties. For example, when you set the view's `backgroundColor`, you are really setting the layer's `background-Color`, and if you set the layer's `backgroundColor` directly, the view's `backgroundColor` is set to match. Similarly, the view's `frame` is really the layer's `frame` and *vice versa*.

 A CALayer's `delegate` property is settable, but you must never set the `delegate` property of a view's underlying layer. To do so would be to break this integration between them, thereby causing drawing to stop working correctly.

The view draws into its layer, and the layer caches that drawing; the layer can then be manipulated, changing the view's appearance, without necessarily asking the view to redraw itself. This is a source of great efficiency in the drawing system. It also explains such phenomena as the content stretching that we encountered in the last section of Chapter 15: when the view's bounds size changes, the drawing system simply stretches or repositions the cached layer image, until such time as the view is told to generate a new drawing of itself (`drawRect:`) to replace the layer's contents.

 **Mac OS X Programmer Alert**

On Mac OS X, NSView existed long before CALayer was introduced, so today a view might have no layer, or, if it does have a layer, it might relate to it in various ways. You may be accustomed to terms like *layer-backed view* or *layer-hosting view*. On iOS, layers were incorporated from the outset: every UIView has an underlying layer and relates to it in the same way.

## Layers and Sublayers

A layer can have sublayers, and a layer has at most one superlayer. Thus there is a tree of layers. This is similar and parallel to the tree of views (Chapter 14). In fact, so tight is the integration between a view and its underlying layer, that these hierarchies are effectively the same hierarchy. Given a view and its underlying layer, that layer's superlayer is the view's superview's underlying layer, and that layer has as sublayers all the underlying layers of all the view's subviews. Indeed, because the layers are how the views actually get drawn, one might say that the view hierarchy really *is* a layer hierarchy (Figure 16-2).

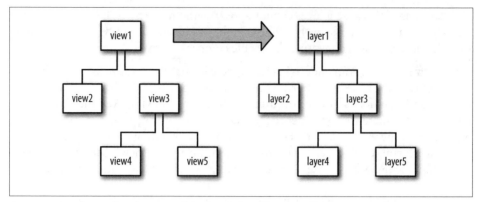

*Figure 16-2. A hierarchy of views and the hierarchy of layers underlying it*

At the same time, the layer hierarchy can go beyond the view hierarchy. A view has exactly one underlying layer, but a layer can have sublayers that are not the underlying layers of any view. So the hierarchy of layers that underlie views exactly matches the hierarchy of views (Figure 16-2), but the total layer tree may be a superset of that hierarchy.

From a visual standpoint, there may be nothing to distinguish a hierarchy of views from a hierarchy of layers. For example, in Chapter 14 we drew three overlapping rectangles using a hierarchy of views (Figure 14-1). This code gives exactly the same visible display by manipulating layers:

```
CALayer* lay1 = [[CALayer alloc] init];
lay1.frame = CGRectMake(113, 111, 132, 194);
lay1.backgroundColor = [[UIColor colorWithRed:1 green:.4 blue:1 alpha:1] CGColor];
[self.window.layer addSublayer:lay1];
CALayer* lay2 = [[CALayer alloc] init];
lay2.backgroundColor = [[UIColor colorWithRed:.5 green:1 blue:0 alpha:1] CGColor];
lay2.frame = CGRectMake(41, 56, 132, 194);
[lay1 addSublayer:lay2];
CALayer* lay3 = [[CALayer alloc] init];
lay3.backgroundColor = [[UIColor colorWithRed:1 green:0 blue:0 alpha:1] CGColor];
lay3.frame = CGRectMake(43, 197, 160, 230);
[self.window.layer addSublayer:lay3];
[lay1 release]; [lay2 release]; [lay3 release];
[self.window makeKeyAndVisible];
```

There are, indeed, situations in which it is not clear whether a piece of interface should be constructed as a view hierarchy or a layer hierarchy. Several of my apps have an interface that is a rectangular grid of objects of the same type; in some cases, I implement these as layers, in some cases I implement them as views, and sometimes it isn't clear to me that my choice is much more than arbitrary. A layer on its own is more lightweight than a view; on the other hand, a view is a UIResponder, so it can respond to touches, and layers lack automatic layout (as implemented through a UIView's `autoresizingMask`).

## Manipulating the Layer Hierarchy

Layers come with a full set of methods for reading and manipulating the layer hierarchy, parallel to the methods for reading and manipulating the view hierarchy. A layer has a `superlayer` property and a `sublayers` property; there are methods `addSublayer:`, `insertSublayer:atIndex:`, `insertSublayer:below:`, `insertSublayer:above:`, `replaceSublayer:with:`, and `removeFromSuperlayer`.

Unlike a view's `subviews` property, a layer's `sublayers` property is writable; thus, you can give a layer multiple sublayers in a single move, by assigning to its `sublayers` property. To remove all of a layer's sublayers, set its `sublayers` property to nil.

Although a layer's sublayers have an order, reflected in the `sublayers` order and regulated with the methods I've just mentioned, this is not necessarily the same as their back-to-front drawing order. By default, it is, but a layer also has a `zPosition` property, a CGFloat, and this also determines drawing order. The rule is that all sublayers with the same `zPosition` are drawn in the order they are listed among their `sublayers` siblings, but lower `zPosition` siblings are drawn before higher `zPosition` siblings. (The default `zPosition` is 0.)

Sometimes, the `zPosition` property is a more convenient way of dictating drawing order than sibling order is. For example, if layers represent playing cards laid out in a solitaire game, it will likely be a lot easier and more flexible to determine how the cards overlap by setting their `zPosition` than by rearranging their sibling order.

Methods are also provided for converting between the coordinate systems of layers within the same layer hierarchy: `convertPoint:fromLayer:`, `convertPoint:toLayer:`, `convertRect:fromLayer:`, and `convertRect:toLayer:`.

## Positioning a Sublayer

Layer coordinate systems and positioning are similar to those of views. A layer's own internal coordinate system is expressed by its `bounds`, just like a view; its size is its bounds size, and its bounds origin is the internal coordinate at its top left.

However, a sublayer's position within its superlayer is not described by its `center`, like a view; a layer does not have a `center`. Instead, a sublayer's position within its superlayer is defined by a combination of two properties, its `position` and its `anchorPoint`. Think of the sublayer as pinned to its superlayer; then you have to say both where the pin passes through the sublayer and where it passes through the superlayer. (I didn't make up that analogy, but it's pretty apt.)

position
   A point expressed in the superlayer's coordinate system.

anchorPoint
   Where the `position` point is with respect to the layer's own bounds. It is a pair of floating-point numbers (a CGPoint) describing a fraction (or multiple) of the layer's

own bounds width and bounds height. Thus, for example, (0,0) is the layer's top left, and (1,1) is its bottom right.

If the anchorPoint is (0.5,0.5) (the default), the position property works like a view's center property. A view's center is thus a special case of a layer's position. This is quite typical of the relationship between view properties and layer properties; the view properties are often a simpler, more convenient, and less powerful version of the layer properties.

A layer's position and anchorPoint are orthogonal (independent); changing one does not change the other. Therefore, changing either of them without changing the other changes where the layer is drawn within its superlayer.

For example, in Figure 16-1, the most important point in the circle is its center; all the other objects need to be positioned with respect to it. Therefore they all have the same position: the center of the circle. But they differ in their anchorPoint. For example, the arrow's anchorPoint is (0.5,0.8), the middle of the shaft, near the end. On the other hand, the anchorPoint of a cardinal point letter is more like (0.5,3.8), well outside the letter's bounds, so as to place the letter near the edge of the circle.

A layer's frame is a purely derived property. When you get the frame, it is calculated from the bounds size along with the position and anchorPoint. When you set the frame, you set the bounds size and position. In general, you should regard the frame as a convenient façade and no more. Nevertheless, it is convenient! For example, to position a sublayer so that it exactly overlaps its superlayer, you can just set the sublayer's frame to the superlayer's bounds.

 A layer created in code (as opposed to a view's underlying layer) has a frame and bounds of (0,0,0,0) and will not be visible on the screen even when you add it to a superlayer that is on the screen. Be sure to give your layer a nonzero width and height if you want to be able to see it.

## CAScrollLayer

If you're going to be moving a layer's bounds origin as a way of repositioning its sublayers *en masse*, you might like to make the layer a CAScrollLayer, a CALayer subclass that provides convenience methods for this sort of thing. (Despite the name, a CAScrollLayer provides no scrolling interface; the user can't scroll it by dragging, for example.) By default, a CAScrollLayer's masksToBounds property is YES; thus, the CAScrollLayer acts like a window through which you see can only what is within its bounds. (You can set its masksToBounds to NO, but this would be an odd thing to do, as it somewhat defeats the purpose.)

To move the CAScrollLayer's bounds, you can talk either to it or to a sublayer (at any depth):

*Talking to the superlayer (the CAScrollLayer)*
> `scrollToPoint:` changes the CAScrollLayer's bounds origin to that point. `scrollTo-Rect:` changes the CAScrollLayer's bounds origin minimally so that the given portion of the bounds rect is visible.

*Talking to a sublayer*
> `scrollPoint:` changes the CAScrollLayer's bounds origin so that the given point *of the sublayer* is at the top left of the CAScrollLayer. `scrollRectToVisible:` changes the CAScrollLayer's bounds origin so that the given rect *of the sublayer's bounds* is within the CAScrollLayer's bounds area. You can also ask the sublayer for its `visibleRect`, the part of this sublayer now within the CAScrollLayer's bounds.

## Layout of Sublayers

The only option for layout of sublayers on iOS is manual layout. When a layer needs layout, either because its bounds have changed or because you called `setNeedsLayout`, its `layoutSublayers` method is called; it's up to you to override this in your CALayer subclass. Alternatively, implement `layoutSublayersOfLayer:` in the layer's delegate; a typical situation is that the layer is a view's underlying layer, and you implement `layoutSublayersOfLayer:` in your UIView subclass.

To do effective manual layout of sublayers, you'll probably need a way to identify or refer to the sublayers. There is no layer equivalent of `viewWithTag:`, so such identification and reference is entirely up to you; you'll probably have instance variables for this purpose (or keys: layers implement key–value coding in a special way, discussed at the end of this chapter).

**Mac OS X Programmer Alert**

On Mac OS X, layers have extensive layout support, including both "springs and struts" (*constraints*) and custom layout managers. But iOS lacks all of this.

# Drawing in a Layer

There are various ways to make a layer display something (apart from its `backgroundColor` and having a partnered view draw into it).

## Contents Image

A layer has a `contents` property. This is parallel to the `image` in a UIImageView (Chapter 15); indeed, it is expected to be a CGImageRef (or nil, signifying no contents). A CGImageRef is not an object type, but the `contents` property is typed as an `id`; in order to quiet the compiler, you'll have to typecast your CGImageRef to an `id` (or a `void*`) as you assign it, like this:

```
arrow.contents = (id)[im CGImage];
```

 Setting a layer's contents to a UIImage, rather than a CGImage, will fail silently — the contents don't appear, but there is no error either. This is absolutely maddening, and I wish I had a nickel for every time I've done it and then wasted hours figuring out why my layer isn't appearing.

## Contents on Demand

There are four methods that can be implemented to provide or draw a layer's contents on demand, similar to a UIView's drawRect:. A layer is very conservative about calling these methods (and you must not call any of them directly). If the layer's needsDisplay-OnBoundsChange property is NO (the default), then the only way to cause these methods to be called is by calling setNeedsDisplay (or setNeedsDisplayInRect:). Even this might not cause these methods to be called right away; if that's crucial, then you will also call displayIfNeeded. If the layer's needsDisplayOnBoundsChange property is YES, then these methods are also called when the layer's bounds change (rather like a UIView's UIView-ContentModeRedraw).

Here are the four methods; pick one (don't try to combine them, you'll just confuse things):

display *in a subclass*
> Your CALayer subclass can override display. There's no graphics context at this point, so display is pretty much limited to setting the contents.

drawInContext: *in a subclass*
> Your CALayer subclass can override drawInContext:. The parameter is a graphics context into which you can draw directly; the discussion of drawing from Chapter 15 thus pertains.

displayLayer: *or* drawLayer:inContext: *in the delegate*
> You can set the CALayer's delegate property, and implement displayLayer: or drawLayer:inContext:. They are parallel to display and drawInContext:, the former providing no graphics context so that it's fit mostly for setting the contents, and the latter providing a graphics context into which you can draw directly.

Remember, you must not set the delegate property of a view's underlying layer! This restriction is not as onerous as it seems; there's always an easy architectural way to draw into a layer by way of a delegate if that's what you want to do.

For example, in one of my apps there's an overlay view, sitting on top of everything else on the screen; the user is unaware of this, because the view is transparent and usually does no drawing, and the view ignores touches, which fall through to the visible views, as if the overlay were not there at all. But every once in a while I want the overlay view to display something (this is its purpose). I don't want the overhead of making an image, and my app has a main controller, which already knows what needs drawing,

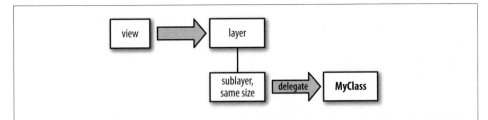

*Figure 16-3. A view and a layer delegate that draws into it*

so I want to draw using this controller as a layer delegate. But it can't be the delegate of the overlay view's underlying layer, so I give that layer a sublayer and make my controller that sublayer's delegate. Thus we have a view and its underlying layer that do nothing, except to serve as a host for this sublayer (Figure 16-3) — and there's nothing wrong with that.

If a layer redisplays itself (because you call `setNeedsDisplay`, or because the bounds are resized when `needsDisplayOnBoundsChange` is YES) and none of the `display` methods provides content (perhaps because you didn't override any of them), the layer's `contents` will now be nil. This can be confusing. The moral is: don't make a layer redisplay itself unless you mean it.

If a layer redisplays itself (because you call `setNeedsDisplay`, or because the bounds are resized when `needsDisplayOnBoundsChange` is YES) and if its `opaque` property is YES, its context has no alpha channel and will be drawn with a black background — and, if the layer's `opacity` is `1`, the layer's `backgroundColor` will be ignored. This feature is intended as a way of letting you gain some drawing efficiency in case you are supplying content that will occupy the entirety of the layer without transparency; you should not misuse it by claiming that the layer is opaque when it isn't.

 Setting a view's `backgroundColor` to an opaque color (alpha component of `1`) sets its layer's `opaque`, though not the view's `opaque`, to YES. This explains the behavior of `CGContextClearRect` described in Chapter 15.

## Contents Resizing and Positioning

Once a layer has contents — regardless of whether these contents came from an image (setting the `contents` property) or from direct drawing into its context (`drawIn-Context:`, `drawLayer:inContext:`) — various properties dictate how those contents should be drawn in relation to the layer's bounds. It is as if the cached contents are treated as an image, which can then be resized, repositioned, cropped, and so on. These properties are:

contentsGravity

This property is parallel to a UIView's contentMode property, and describes how the contents should be positioned or stretched in relation to the bounds. For example, kCAGravityCenter means the contents image is centered in the bounds without resizing; kCAGravityResize means the contents image is sized to fit the bounds, even if this means distorting its aspect; and so forth.

 For historical reasons, the terms "bottom" and "top" in the names of the contentsGravity settings have the opposite of their expected meanings.

contentsRect

A CGRect expressing the proportion of the contents image that is to be drawn. The default is (0,0,1,1), meaning the entire contents image. The specified part of the image is sized and positioned in relation to the bounds in accordance with the contentsGravity. Thus, for example, you can conveniently and efficiently move part of a larger image into view within a layer without redrawing or changing the contents.

You can also use the contentsRect to scale down the contents image, by specifying a contentsRect larger than the contents; but any pixels that touch the edge of the contentsRect will then be extended outwards to the edge of the layer (to prevent this, give the contents image a clear pixel border at its edges).

contentsCenter

A CGRect expressing the central region of nine rectangular regions of the contentsRect that are variously allowed to stretch if the contentsGravity calls for stretching. The central region (the actual value of the contentsCenter) stretches in both directions. Of the other eight regions (inferred from the value you provide), the four corner regions don't stretch, and the four side regions stretch in one direction. (UIView has a somewhat similar property, contentStretch, which I didn't discuss.)

*Figure 16-4. One way of resizing the compass arrow*

If you're drawing directly into the layer's context (e.g., with `drawLayer:inContext:`), and the `contentsRect` is the entire contents, then if the layer's contents are redrawn (because you call `setNeedsDisplay`, or because the bounds are resized when `needs-DisplayOnBoundsChange` is YES), the `contentsGravity` won't matter, because the context fills the layer. But if the layer's bounds are resized when `needsDisplayOnBoundsChange` is NO, then its cached contents from the last time you drew are treated as an image. By a judicious combination of settings, you can attain some fairly sophisticated automatic behavior, with no need to redraw the contents yourself. For example, Figure 16-4 shows the result of the following settings:

```
arrow.needsDisplayOnBoundsChange = NO;
arrow.contentsCenter = CGRectMake(0.0, 0.4, 1.0, 0.6);
arrow.contentsGravity = kCAGravityResizeAspect;
```

The arrow layer's bounds are then resized by adding 40 to both dimensions. Because `needsDisplayOnBoundsChange` is NO, the contents are not redrawn; instead, the cached contents are used. The `contentsGravity` setting tells us to resize proportionally; therefore, the arrow is both longer and wider than in Figure 16-1, but not in such a way as to distort its proportions. However, notice that although the triangular arrowhead is wider, it is not longer; the increase in length is due entirely to the stretching of the shaft. That's because the `contentsCenter` region is restricted to the shaft of the arrow.

If the contents are larger than the bounds of the layer, and if the `contentsGravity` and `contentsRect` do not resize the contents to fit the bounds, then by default the contents will be drawn larger than the layer; the layer does not automatically clip its contents to its bounds (just as it does not automatically clip its sublayers to its bounds). To get such clipping, for both contents and sublayers, set the layer's `masksToBounds` property to YES.

The value of the bounds origin does not affect where the contents are drawn.

## Layers that Draw Themselves

A few built-in CALayer subclasses provide some basic but extremely helpful self-drawing ability:

*CATextLayer*

A CATextLayer has a `string` property, which can be an NSString or NSAttributedString, along with other text formatting properties; it draws its `string`. The default text color, the `foregroundColor` property, is white, which is unlikely to be what you want. The text is different from the `contents` and is mutually exclusive with it: either the contents or the text will be drawn, but not both, so in general you should not give a CATextLayer any contents. In Figure 16-1, the cardinal point letters are CATextLayer instances.

The fact that a CATextLayer's `string` can be an NSAttributedString gives it a power that UILabel lacks, namely, to display text in multiple font, sizes, and styles. For example, using a CATextLayer, you could underline one word of the text; you can't do that with a UILabel. An example appears in Chapter 23 (because it requires use of Core Text).

*CAShapeLayer*

A CAShapeLayer has a `path` property, which is a CGPath. It fills or strokes this path, or both, depending on its `fillColor` and `strokeColor` values, and displays the result; the default is a `fillColor` of black and no `strokeColor`. A CAShapeLayer may also have `contents`; the shape is displayed on top of the contents, but there is no property permitting you to specify a compositing mode. In Figure 16-1, the background circle is a CAShapeLayer instance, stroked with gray and filled with a lighter, slightly transparent gray.

*CAGradientLayer*

A CAGradientLayer covers its background with a simple linear gradient; thus, it's an easy way to composite a gradient into your interface (and if you need something more elaborate you can always draw with Core Graphics instead). The gradient is defined much as in the Core Graphics gradient example in Chapter 15, an array of locations and an array of corresponding colors (except that these are NSArrays, of course, not C arrays), along with a start and end point. To clip the gradient, you can add a mask to the CAGradientLayer (masks are discussed later in this chapter). A CAGradientLayer's `contents` are not displayed.

The `colors` array requires CGColors, not UIColors. But a CGColorRef is not an object type, whereas NSArray expects objects, so to quiet the compiler you'll probably need to typecast at least the first item of the array (to `id` or `void*`).

Figure 16-5 shows our compass drawn with an extra CAGradientLayer behind it.

# Transforms

The way a layer is drawn on the screen can be modified though a transform. This is not surprising, because a view can have a transform (see Chapter 14), and a view is drawn on the screen by its layer. As with the bounds and other properties, a view and its

---

*Figure 16-5. A gradient drawn behind the compass*

underlying layer are tightly linked; when you change the transform of one, you are changing the transform of the other. But, as so often happens, the layer's transform is more powerful than the view's transform. Thus, you can use the transform of the underlying layer to accomplish things with a view that you can't accomplish with the view's transform alone.

In the simplest cases, when a transform is two-dimensional, you can use the `setAffine-Transform:` and `affineTransform` methods. The value is a CGAffineTransform, familiar from Chapter 14 and Chapter 15. The transform is applied around the `anchorPoint`. Thus, the `anchorPoint` has a second purpose that I didn't tell you about when discussing it earlier.

You now know everything you need to know in order to understand the code that generated Figure 16-5, so here is that code. Notice how the four cardinal point letters are drawn by a CATextLayer and placed using a transform. They are drawn at the same coordinates, but they have different rotation transforms. Moreover, even though the CATextLayers are small (just 40 by 30) and appear near the perimeter of the circle, they are anchored, and so their rotation is centered, at the center of the circle. In this code, `self` is the CompassLayer; it does no drawing of its own, but merely assembles and configures its sublayers. To generate the arrow, we make ourselves the arrow layer's delegate and call `setNeedsDisplay`; this causes `drawLayer:inContext:` to be called in CompassLayer (that code is just the same code we developed for drawing the arrow into a context in Chapter 15):

```
// the gradient
CAGradientLayer* g = [[CAGradientLayer alloc] init];
g.frame = self.bounds;
g.colors = [NSArray arrayWithObjects:
            (id)[[UIColor blackColor] CGColor],
            [[UIColor redColor] CGColor],
            nil];
g.locations = [NSArray arrayWithObjects:
              [NSNumber numberWithFloat: 0.0],
              [NSNumber numberWithFloat: 1.0],
              nil];
[self addSublayer:g];
[g release];

// the circle
CAShapeLayer* circle = [[CAShapeLayer alloc] init];
circle.lineWidth = 2.0;
```

```
circle.fillColor =
    [[UIColor colorWithRed:0.9 green:0.95 blue:0.93 alpha:0.9] CGColor];
circle.strokeColor = [[UIColor grayColor] CGColor];
CGMutablePathRef p = CGPathCreateMutable();
CGPathAddEllipseInRect(p, NULL, CGRectInset(self.bounds, 3, 3));
circle.path = p;
[self addSublayer:circle];
circle.bounds = self.bounds;
circle.position = CGPointMake(CGRectGetMidX(self.bounds),
                             CGRectGetMidY(self.bounds));

// the four cardinal points
NSArray* pts = [NSArray arrayWithObjects: @"N", @"E", @"S", @"W", nil];
for (int i = 0; i < 4; i++) {
    CATextLayer* t = [[CATextLayer alloc] init];
    t.string = [pts objectAtIndex: i];
    t.bounds = CGRectMake(0,0,40,30);
    t.position = CGPointMake(CGRectGetMidX(circle.bounds),
                             CGRectGetMidY(circle.bounds));
    CGFloat vert = (CGRectGetMidY(circle.bounds) - 5) / CGRectGetHeight(t.bounds);
    t.anchorPoint = CGPointMake(0.5, vert);
    t.alignmentMode = kCAAlignmentCenter;
    t.foregroundColor = [[UIColor blackColor] CGColor];
    [t setAffineTransform:CGAffineTransformMakeRotation(i*M_PI/2.0)];
    [circle addSublayer:t];
    [t release];
}

// the arrow
CALayer* arrow = [[CALayer alloc] init];
arrow.bounds = CGRectMake(0, 0, 40, 100);
arrow.position = CGPointMake(CGRectGetMidX(self.bounds),
                             CGRectGetMidY(self.bounds));
arrow.anchorPoint = CGPointMake(0.5, 0.8);
arrow.delegate = self;
[arrow setAffineTransform:CGAffineTransformMakeRotation(M_PI/5.0)];
[self addSublayer:arrow];
[arrow setNeedsDisplay];
[arrow release];

[circle release];
```

A full-fledged layer transform, the value of the **transform** property, takes place in three-dimensional space; its description includes a z-axis, perpendicular to both the x-axis and y-axis. (By default, the positive z-axis points out of the screen, toward the viewer's face.) Layers do not magically give you realistic three-dimensional rendering — for that you would use OpenGL, which is beyond the scope of this discussion. Layers are two-dimensional objects, and they are designed for speed and simplicity. Nevertheless, they do operate in three dimensions, quite sufficiently to give a cartoonish but effective sense of reality, especially when performing an animation. We've all seen the screen image flip like turning over a piece of paper to reveal what's on the back; that's a rotation in three dimensions.

A three-dimensional transform takes place around a three-dimensional extension of the anchorPoint, whose z-component is supplied by the anchorPointZ property. Thus, in the reduced default case where anchorPointZ is 0, the anchorPoint is sufficient, as we've already seen in using CGAffineTransform.

The transform itself is described mathematically by a struct called a CATransform3D. The *Core Animation Function Reference* lists the functions for working with these transforms. They are a lot like the CGAffineTransform functions, except they've got a third dimension. For example, here's the declaration of the function for making a 2D scale transform:

```
CGAffineTransform CGAffineTransformMakeScale (
    CGFloat sx,
    CGFloat sy
);
```

And here's the declaration of the function for making a 3D scale transform:

```
CATransform3D CATransform3DMakeScale (
    CGFloat sx,
    CGFloat sy,
    CGFloat sz
);
```

The rotation 3D transform is a little more complicated. In addition to the angle, you also have to supply three coordinates describing the vector around which the rotation takes place. Perhaps you've forgotten from your high-school math what a vector is, or perhaps trying to visualize three dimensions boggles your mind, so think of it this way.

Pretend for purposes of discussion that the anchor point is the origin, (0,0,0). Now imagine an arrow emanating from the anchor point; its other end, the pointy end, is described by the three coordinates you provide. Now imagine a plane that intersects the anchor point, perpendicular to the arrow. That is the plane in which the rotation will take place; positive angle is a clockwise rotation, as seen from the side of the plane with the arrow (Figure 16-6). In effect, the three points you supply describe, relative to the anchor point, where your eye would have to be to see this rotation as an old-fashioned two-dimensional rotation.

The three values you give specify a direction, not a point. Thus it makes no difference on what scale you give them: (1,1,1) means the same thing as (10,10,10). If the three values are (0,0,1), with all other things being equal, the case is collapsed to a simple CGAffineTransform, because the rotational plane is the screen. On the other hand, if the three values are (0,0,-1), it's a backward CGAffineTransform, so that a positive angle looks counterclockwise (because we are looking at the "back side" of the rotational plane).

A layer can itself be rotated in such a way that its "back" is showing. For example, the following rotation flips a layer around its y-axis:

```
someLayer.transform = CATransform3DMakeRotation(M_PI, 0, 1, 0);
```

*Figure 16-6. An anchor point plus a vector defines a rotation plane*

By default, the layer is considered double-sided, so when it is flipped to show its "back," what's drawn is an appropriately reversed version of the contents of the layer (along with its sublayers). But if the layer's `doubleSided` property is NO, then when it is flipped to show its "back," the layer disappears (along with its sublayers); its "back" is transparent and empty.

## Depth

There are two ways to place layers at different nominal depths with respect to their siblings. One is through the z-component of their `position`, which is the `zPosition` property. Thus the `zPosition`, too, has a second purpose that I didn't tell you about earlier. The other is to apply a transform that translates the layer's position in the z-direction. These two values (the z-component of a layer's position and the z-component of its translation transform) are related; in some sense, the `zPosition` is a shorthand for a translation transform in the z-direction. (If you provide both a `zPosition` and a z-direction translation, you can rapidly confuse yourself.)

In the real world, changing an object's `zPosition` would make it appear larger or smaller, as it is positioned closer or further away; but this is not the case in the world of layer drawing. There is no attempt to portray perspective; the layer planes are drawn at their actual size and flattened onto one another, with no illusion of distance. (This is called *orthographic projection*, and is the way blueprints are often drawn to display an object from one side.)

However, there's a widely used trick for introducing a quality of perspective into the way layers are drawn: make them sublayers of a layer whose `sublayerTransform` property maps all points onto a "distant" plane. (This is probably just about the only thing the `sublayerTransform` property is ever used for.) Combined with orthographic projection, the effect is to apply one-point perspective to the drawing, so that things do get perceptibly smaller in the negative z-direction.

For example, let's try applying a sort of "page-turn" rotation to our compass: we'll anchor it at its right side and then rotate it around the y-axis (for purposes of the example, all the other layers have been made sublayers of the gradient layer, g):

```
g.anchorPoint = CGPointMake(1,0.5);
g.position = CGPointMake(CGRectGetMaxX(self.bounds), CGRectGetMidY(self.bounds));
g.transform = CATransform3DMakeRotation(M_PI/4.0, 0, 1, 0);
```

*Figure 16-7. A disappointing page-turn rotation*

*Figure 16-8. A dramatic page-turn rotation*

The results are disappointing (Figure 16-7); the compass looks more squashed than rotated. Now, however, we'll apply the distance-mapping transform (recall that g is a sublayer of self):

```
g.anchorPoint = CGPointMake(1,0.5);
g.position = CGPointMake(CGRectGetMaxX(self.bounds), CGRectGetMidY(self.bounds));
g.transform = CATransform3DMakeRotation(M_PI/4.0, 0, 1, 0);
CATransform3D transform = CATransform3DIdentity;
transform.m34 = -1.0/1000.0;
self.sublayerTransform = transform;
```

The results (shown in Figure 16-8) are better, and you can experiment with values to replace 1000.0; for example, 500.0 gives an even more exaggerated effect. Also, the z-Position of g will now affect how large it is.

Another way to draw layers with depth is to use CATransformLayer. This CALayer subclass doesn't do any drawing of its own; it is intended solely as a host for other layers. It has the remarkable feature that you can apply a transform to it and it will maintain the depth relationships among its sublayers.

Figure 16-9 shows our page-turn rotation yet again, still with the sublayerTransform applied to self, but this time the only sublayer of self is a CATransformLayer. The CATransformLayer, to which the page-turn transform is applied, holds the gradient layer, the circle layer, and the arrow layer. Those three layers are at different depths (using different zPosition settings), and you can see that the circle layer floats in front of the gradient layer. (This is clear from its apparent offset, but I wish you could see this page-turn as an animation, which makes the circle jump right out from the gradient as the rotation proceeds.) I've also tried to emphasize the arrow's separation from the circle by adding a shadow.

*Figure 16-9. Page-turn rotation applied to a CATransformLayer*

Even more remarkable, note the little white peg sticking through the arrow and running into the circle. It is a CAShapeLayer, rotated to be perpendicular to the CATransform-Layer. Normally, it runs straight out of the circle toward the viewer, so it is seen end-on, and because a layer has no thickness, it is invisible. But as the CATransformLayer pivots forward in our page-turn rotation, the peg maintains its orientation relative to the circle, and comes into view.

There is, I think, a slight additional gain in realism if the same `sublayerTransform` is applied also to the CATransformLayer, but I have not done so here.

## Transforms and Key–Value Coding

Instead of using the CATransform3D and CGAffineTransform functions, you can take advantage of key–value coding to alter or access a particular component of a layer's transform. For example, instead of writing this:

```
g.transform = CATransform3DMakeRotation(M_PI/4.0, 0, 1, 0);
```

we could have written this:

```
[g setValue:[NSNumber numberWithFloat:M_PI/4.0] forKeyPath:@"transform.rotation.y"];
```

The second form may not seem to be any savings, especially as we have to wrap our CGFloat in an NSNumber (because the value in `setValue:forKeyPath:` must be an object). But the expression `@"transform.rotation.y"` brilliantly clarifies our intent. And of course there is always the possibility that we may take advantage of this feature to assemble a key path at runtime.

This notation is possible because both CALayer and CATransform3D are key–value coding compliant for a repertoire of keys and key paths. Don't get confused, though: these are not properties (though, where possible, they have the same names as properties). A CATransform3D doesn't have a `rotation` property; it doesn't have *any* properties, because it isn't even an object. You cannot say:

```
g.transform.rotation.y = //... No, sorry
```

The transform key paths you'll use most often are `rotation.x`, `rotation.y`, `rotation.z`, `rotation` (same as `rotation.z`), `scale.x`, `scale.y`, `scale.z`, `translation.x`, `translation.y`, `translation.z`, and `translation` (two-dimensional, a CGSize). The

Quartz Core framework also injects KVC compliance into CGPoint, CGSize, and CGRect, allowing you to use keys and key paths matching their struct component names. For a complete list of KVC compliant classes related to CALayer, along with the keys and key paths they implement, plus rules for how to wrap nonobject values as objects, see "Core Animation Extensions to Key-Value Coding" in the *Core Animation Programming Guide*.

## Shadows, Borders, and More

A CALayer has many additional properties that affect details of how it is drawn. Once again, all of these drawing details can, of course, be applied equally to a UIView; changing these properties of the UIView's underlying layer changes how the view is drawn. Thus, these are effectively view features as well.

A layer can have a shadow, defined by its shadowColor, shadowOpacity, shadowRadius, and shadowOffset properties. To make the layer draw a shadow, set the shadowOpacity to a nonzero value. The shadow is normally based on the shape of the layer's nontransparent region, but deriving this shape can be calculation-intensive (so much so that in early versions of iOS, layer shadows weren't implemented). You can vastly improve performance by defining the shape yourself and assigning this shape as a CGPath to the shadowPath property.

A layer can have a border (borderWidth, borderColor); the borderWidth is drawn inward from the bounds, potentially covering some of the content unless you compensate.

A layer can be bounded by a rounded rectangle, by giving it a cornerRadius greater than zero. If the layer has a backgroundColor, that background is clipped to the shape of the rounded rectangle. If the layer has a border, the border has rounded corners too.

Like a UIView, a CALayer has a master opacity property, and it has a hidden property that can be set to take it out of the visible interface without actually removing it from its superlayer.

Like a UIView, a CALayer can clip the drawing of its contents and sublayers to its bounds (masksToBounds, already mentioned earlier in this chapter); if the corners are rounded, the clipping is rounded to fit.

A CALayer can have a backgroundColor, as you already know.

A CALayer can have a mask. This is itself a layer, whose contents must be provided somehow. The transparency of the mask's contents in a particular spot becomes (all other things being equal) the transparency of the layer at that spot. For example, Figure 16-10 shows our arrow layer, with the gray circle layer behind it, and a mask applied to the arrow layer. The mask is silly, but it illustrates very well how masks work: it's an ellipse, with an opaque fill and a thick, semitransparent stroke. Here's the code that generates and applies the mask:

*Figure 16-10. A layer with a mask*

```
CAShapeLayer* mask = [[CAShapeLayer alloc] init];
mask.frame = arrow.bounds;
CGMutablePathRef p2 = CGPathCreateMutable();
CGPathAddEllipseInRect(p2, NULL, CGRectInset(mask.bounds, 10, 10));
mask.strokeColor = [[UIColor colorWithWhite:0.0 alpha:0.5] CGColor];
mask.lineWidth = 20;
mask.path = p2;
arrow.mask = mask;
CGPathRelease(p2); [mask release];
```

To position the mask, pretend it's a sublayer. The hues in the mask's colors are irrelevant; only transparency matters.

If a layer is complex (perhaps with shadow, sublayers, and so forth) and if this seems to be a performance drain (especially when scrolling or animating the layer), you may be able to gain some efficiency by "freezing" the entirety of the layer's drawing as a bitmap. In effect, you're drawing everything in the layer to a secondary cache and using the cache to draw to the screen. To do this, set the layer's `shouldRasterize` to YES and its `rasterizationScale` to some sensible value (probably `[UIScreen main-Screen].scale`). You can always turn rasterization off again by setting `should-Rasterize` to NO, so it's easy to rasterize just before some massive or sluggish rearrangement of the screen and then unrasterize afterward. (In addition, you can get some cool "out of focus" effects by setting the `rasterizationScale` to around `0.3`.)

# Layers and Key–Value Coding

Earlier, I showed that aspects of a layer's transform were accessible through key–value coding. This feature stems from the fact that CALayer is KVC compliant for the `@"transform"` key. The same is true of *all* of a layer's properties; they are all accessible through KVC by way of keys with the same name as the property. Thus, to apply the mask in the previous example, we could have said:

```
[arrow setValue: mask forKey: @"mask"];
```

But a layer goes further than this. You can treat a CALayer as a kind of NSDictionary, and get and set the value for *any* key. This is tremendously useful, because it means you can attach arbitrary information to an individual layer instance and retrieve it later. For example, earlier I mentioned that to apply manual layout to a layer's sublayers, you will need a way of identifying those sublayers. This feature could provide a way of doing that. It will also come in handy in connection with animation.

Also, CALayer has a `defaultValueForKey:` class method; to implement it, you'll need to subclass and override. In the case of keys whose value you want to provide a default for, return that value; otherwise, return the value that comes from calling `super`. Thus, even if a value for a particular key has never been explicitly provided, it can have a non-nil value.

The truth is that this feature, though delightful (and I often wish that all classes behaved like this), is not put there for your convenience and enjoyment. It's there to serve as the basis for animation, which is the subject of the next chapter.

# CHAPTER 17

# Animation

Animation is the visible change of an attribute over time. The changing attribute might be positional, but not necessarily. For example, a view's background color might change from red to green, not instantly, but perceptibly fading from one to the other. Or a view's opacity might change from opaque to transparent, not instantly, but perceptibly fading away.

Without help, most of us would find animation beyond our reach. There are just too many complications — complications of calculation, of timing, of screen refresh, of threading, and many more. Fortunately, help is provided. You don't perform an animation yourself; you describe it, you order it, and it is performed for you. You get *animation on demand*.

Asking for an animation can be as simple as setting a property value; under some circumstances, a single line of code will result in animation:

```
myLayer.backgroundColor = [[UIColor redColor] CGColor]; // animate change to red
```

And this is no coincidence. Apple wants to facilitate your use of animation. Animation is crucial to the character of the iOS interface. It isn't just cool and fun; it clarifies that something is changing or responding. For example, one of my first apps was based on a Mac OS X game in which the user clicks cards to select them. In the Mac OS X version, a card was highlighted to show it was selected, and the computer would beep to indicate a click on an ineligible card. On iOS, these indications were insufficient: the highlighting felt weak, and you can't use a sound warning in an environment where the user might have the volume turned off or be listening to music. So in the iOS version, animation is the indicator for card selection (a selected card waggles eagerly) and for tapping on an ineligible card (the whole interface shudders, as if to shrug off the tap).

 Recall from Chapter 16 that CALayer requires the Quartz Core framework; so do the other "CA" classes discussed here, such as CAAnimation.

# Drawing, Animation, and Threading

When you change a visible view property *without* animation, that change does *not* visibly take place there and then. Rather, the system records that this is a change you would like to make, and marks the view as needing to be redrawn. You can change many visible view properties, but these changes are all just accumulated for later. Later, when all your code has run to completion and the system has, as it were, a free moment, then it redraws all views that need redrawing, applying their new visible property features. I call this the *redraw moment*. (The documentation calls it "when the [current] thread's run-loop next iterates.")

You can see that this is true simply by changing some visible aspect of a view and changing it back again, in the same code: on the screen, nothing happens. For example, suppose a view's background color is green. Suppose your code changes it to red, and then later changes it back to green:

```
// view starts out green
view.backgroundColor = [UIColor redColor];
// ... time-consuming code goes here ...
view.backgroundColor = [UIColor greenColor];
// code ends, redraw moment arrives
```

The system accumulates all the desired changes until the redraw moment happens, and the redraw moment doesn't happen until after your code has finished, so when the redraw moment does happen, the last accumulated change in the view's color is to green — which is its color already. Thus, no matter how much time-consuming code lies between the change from green to red and the change from red to green, the user won't see any color change at all.

(That's why you don't order a view to be redrawn; rather, you tell it that it *needs* redrawing — setNeedsDisplay — at the next redraw moment. It's also why I used delayed performance in the contentMode example in Chapter 15: by calling performSelector: withObject:afterDelay:, I give the redraw moment a chance to happen, thus giving the view some content, *before* resizing the view. This use of delayed performance to let a redraw moment happen is quite common.)

Similarly, when you ask for an animation to be performed, the animation doesn't start happening on the screen until the next redraw moment. (You can force an animation to be performed immediately, but this is unusual.)

While the animation lasts, it is effectively in charge of the screen. Imagine that the animation is a kind of movie, a cartoon, interposed between the user and the "real" screen. When the animation is finished, this movie is removed, revealing the state of the "real" screen behind it. The user is unaware of this, because at the time that it starts, the movie's first frame looks just like the state of the "real" screen at that moment, and at the time that it ends, the movie's last frame looks just like the state of the "real" screen at *that* moment.

---

So, when you reposition a view from position 1 to position 2 with animation, you can envision a typical sequence of events like this:

1. The view is set to position 2, but there has been no redraw moment, so it is still portrayed at position 1.
2. The rest of your code runs to completion.
3. The redraw moment arrives. If there were no animation, the view would now be portrayed at position 2. But there *is* an animation, and it (the "animation movie") starts with the view portrayed at position 1, so that is still what the user sees.
4. The animation proceeds, portraying the view at intermediate positions between position 1 and position 2. The documentation describes the animation as now *in-flight*.
5. The animation ends, portraying the view ending up at position 2.
6. The "animation movie" is removed, revealing the view indeed at position 2.

Animation takes place on an independent thread. Multithreading is generally rather tricky and complicated, but the system makes it easy in this case. Nevertheless, you can't completely ignore the threaded nature of animation. Awareness of threading issues, and having a mental picture of how animation is performed, will help you to ask yourself the right questions and thus to avoid confusion and surprises. For example:

1. *The time when an animation starts is somewhat indefinite (because you don't know exactly when the next redraw moment will be). The time when an animation ends is also somewhat indefinite (because the animation happens on another thread, so your code cannot just wait for it to end). So what if your code needs to do something in response to an animation beginning or ending?*

    An animation can have a delegate; there is a delegate message that is sent when an animation starts, and another when it ends. Thus, you can arrange to receive an event at these crucial moments. On iOS 4 and later, you can also supply a block to be run after an animation ends.

2. *Since animation happens on its own thread, something might cause code of yours to start running while an animation is still in-flight. What happens if your code now changes a property that is currently being animated? What happens if your code asks for another animation?*

    If you change a property while it is being animated, it won't tie the system in knots, but the end result may look odd, if the value you set differs from the final value in the animation. If a property is being animated from value 1 to value 2 and meanwhile you set it to value 3, then the property may appear very suddenly to take on value 3 (because, in effect, the animation movie is removed, and its final frame shown doesn't agree with the state of things revealed behind it). If that isn't what you intend, don't do that; on the other hand, this can be a useful feature, as it provides a coherent way of effectively canceling an in-flight animation.

If you ask for an animation when an animation is already scheduled for the next redraw moment or already in-flight, there might be no problem; both animations can take place simultaneously. But that's impossible if both animations attempt to animate *the same property*. In that case, the first animation may be forced to end instantly; that is, the change it represents ceases to be animated and is portrayed as happening suddenly instead. This is typically not what's intended. But there are many alternative approaches. If you want to chain animations, you can wait until one animation ends (using the delegate message to learn when that is) before ordering the next one. Or you can create a single animation combining multiple changes; these changes needn't start at the same moment or be the same length. And a simple call (such as `setAnimationBeginsFromCurrentState:`) will "blend" the second animation with the first.

3. *While an animation is in-flight, if your code is not running, the interface is responsive to the user. What happens if the user tries to tap a view whose position is currently being animated?*

   The problem is a very real one: the view might not really be where it appears to be on the screen, so the user might try to tap it and miss, or might tap elsewhere and accidentally tap it (because that's where it really is). The usual way of coping is to turn off responsiveness in your app's interface.

   To prevent the interface as a whole from responding while an animation is in-flight, you can call the UIApplication instance method `beginIgnoringInteractionEvents` when the animation starts and call `endIgnoringInteractionEvents` when the animation is over (possibly using the delegate messages to learn when those things happen). If that's too broad, you can block responsiveness to touches at the level of individual views; for example, you can turn off a view's `userInteractionEnabled` until the animation is over. But all of this is up to you; the system has, generally speaking, no policy of automatically disabling touch responsiveness. (But there's an exception: on iOS 4, if you use block-based view animation, the system *does* turn off user interaction during the animation by default.)

4. *On a multitasking system such as iOS 4, the user can suspend my app without quitting it. What happens if an animation is in-flight at that moment?*

   If your app is suspended during animation, the animation is removed. This simply means that the "animation movie" is cancelled. Any animation, whether in-flight or scheduled, is simply a slowed-down visualization of a property change; that property is still changed, and indeed was probably changed before the animation even started. If your app is resumed, therefore, no animations will be running, and properties that were changed remain changed, and are shown as changed.

## Presentation Layer

There isn't really an "animation movie" in front of the screen — though the effect is much the same. In reality, it is not a layer that draws itself on the screen; it's a derived layer called the *presentation layer*. Thus, when you animate the change of a view's position or a layer's position from position 1 to position 2, its nominal position changes immediately; meanwhile, the presentation layer's position remains unchanged until the redraw moment, and then changes over time, and because that's what's actually drawn on the screen, that's what the user sees.

A layer's presentation layer can be accessed through its `presentationLayer` property (and the layer itself is the presentation layer's `modelLayer`). It is typed as an `id`, so in order to work with it as a layer, you will probably want to typecast it to a `CALayer*`. Accessing the `presentationLayer` is not a common thing to do, but it might come in handy if your code needs to learn the current state of an in-flight animation.

# UIImageView Animation

UIImageView provides a form of animation that is so simple and crude as to be scarcely deserving of the name. Nevertheless, sometimes this form of animation is all you need — a trivial solution to what might otherwise be a tricky problem. Supply the UIImageView with an array of UIImages, as the value of its `animationImages` or `highlightedAnimationImages` property; this causes the `image` or `highlightedImage` to be hidden. This array represents the "frames" of a simple cartoon; when you send the `startAnimating` message, the images are displayed in turn, at a frame rate determined by the `animationDuration` property, repeating as many times as specified by the `animationRepeatCount` property (the default is `0`, meaning to repeat forever, or until the `stopAnimating` message is received).

For example, suppose we want an image of Mars to appear out of nowhere and flash three times on the screen. This might seem to require some sort of NSTimer-based solution (see Chapter 11), but it's far simpler to use an animating UIImageView:

```
UIImage* mars = [UIImage imageNamed: @"mars.png"];
UIGraphicsBeginImageContext(mars.size);
UIImage* empty = UIGraphicsGetImageFromCurrentImageContext();
UIGraphicsEndImageContext();
NSArray* arr = [NSArray arrayWithObjects: mars, empty, mars, empty, mars, nil];
iv.animationImages = arr;
iv.animationDuration = 2;
iv.animationRepeatCount = 1;
[iv startAnimating];
```

You can combine UIImageView animation with other kinds of animation. For example, you could flash the image of Mars while at the same time sliding the UIImageView rightward, using view animation as described in the next section.

# View Animation

Animation is ultimately layer animation. However, for a limited range of attributes, you can animate a UIView directly: these are its `alpha`, `backgroundColor`, `bounds`, `center`, `frame`, and `transform`. You can also animate a UIView's change of contents. Despite the brevity of the list, UIView animation is an excellent way to become acquainted with animation and to experiment with the various parameters you can use to determine how an animation behaves; in many cases it will prove quite sufficient.

There are actually two ways to ask for UIView animation: the old way (before iOS 4.0, and still available), and the new way (iOS 4.0 and later only, because it uses Objective-C blocks; see Chapter 3). I'll describe the old way first.

## Animation Blocks

To animate a change to an animatable UIView property the old way, wrap the change in calls to the UIView class methods `beginAnimations:context:` and `commitAnimations`. Just to make life more confusing, the region between these calls is referred to as an *animation block*, even though it is *not* a block in the syntactical Objective-C sense.

So, animating a change to a view's background color could be as simple as this:

```
[UIView beginAnimations:nil context:NULL];
v.backgroundColor = [UIColor yellowColor];
[UIView commitAnimations];
```

Any animatable change made within an animation block will be animated, so we can animate a change both to the view's color and its position simultaneously:

```
[UIView beginAnimations:nil context:NULL];
v.backgroundColor = [UIColor yellowColor];
CGPoint p = v.center;
p.y -= 100;
v.center = p;
[UIView commitAnimations];
```

We can also animate changes to multiple views. For example, suppose we want to make one view dissolve into another. We start with the second view present in the view hierarchy, but with an `alpha` of 0, so that it is invisible. Then we animate the change of the first view's `alpha` to 0 and the second view's `alpha` to 1, simultaneously. This might be a way, for example, to make the text of a label or the title of a button appear to dissolve while changing.

The two parameters to `beginAnimations:context:` are an NSString and a pointer-to-void that are completely up to you; the idea is that an animation can have a delegate (so that you can be notified when the animation starts and ends), and you can supply values here that will be passed along in the delegate messages, helping you identify the animation and so forth.

---

## Modifying an Animation Block

An animation has various characteristics that you can modify, and an animation block provides a way to make such modifications: within the animation block, you call a UIView class method whose name begins with "setAnimation."

 Some of the "setAnimation" method calls are oddly picky as to whether they precede or follow the actual property value changes within the animation block. If a call seems to be having no effect, try moving it to the beginning or end of the animation block. I find that in general these calls work best if they *precede* the value changes.

Animation blocks can be nested. The result is a single animation, whose description is not complete until the outermost animation block is terminated with `commitAnimations`. Therefore, by using "setAnimation" method calls in the different nested animation blocks, you can give the parts of the animation different characteristics. Within each animation block, the animation for any property changes will have the default characteristics unless you change them.

 Nested animation blocks are different from successive top-level animation blocks; successive top-level animation blocks are different animations, which, as I mentioned earlier, can have undesirable effects, possibly causing the earlier animation to be cancelled abruptly.

Here are the "setAnimation" UIView class methods:

`setAnimationDuration:`
> Sets the "speed" of the animation, by dictating (in seconds) how long it takes to run from start to finish. Obviously, if two views are told to move different distances in the same time, the one that must move further must move faster.

`setAnimationRepeatAutoreverses:`
> If YES, the animation will run from start to finish (in the given duration time), and will then run from finish to start (also in the given duration time).

`setAnimationRepeatCount:`
> Sets how many times the animation should be repeated. Unless the animation also autoreverses, the animation will "jump" from its end to its start to begin the next repetition. The value is a float, so it is possible to end the repetition at some midpoint of the animation.

`setAnimationCurve:`
> Describes how the animation changes speed during its course. Your options are:
> - `UIViewAnimationCurveEaseInOut` (the default)
> - `UIViewAnimationCurveEaseIn`

- UIViewAnimationCurveEaseOut

- UIViewAnimationCurveLinear

The term "ease" means that there is a gradual acceleration or deceleration between the animation's central speed and the zero speed at its start or end.

setAnimationStartDate:, setAnimationDelay:

These are both ways postponing the start of the animation; in my experience, the former is broken, so you should use setAnimationDelay: exclusively.

setAnimationDelegate:

Arranges for your code to be notified as the animation starts or ends; the methods to be called on the delegate are specified as follows:

setAnimationWillStartSelector:

The "start" method must take two parameters; these are the values passed into beginAnimations:context:, namely an identifying NSString and a pointer-to-void. This method is not called unless something within the animation block triggers an actual animation.

setAnimationDidStopSelector:

The "stop" method must take three parameters: the second parameter is a BOOL wrapped as an NSNumber, indicating whether the animation completed successfully (and the other two are like the "start" method parameters). This method is called, with the second parameter representing YES, even if nothing within the animation block triggers any animations.

setAnimationsEnabled:

Set to NO to perform subsequent animatable property changes within the animation block without making them part of the animation.

setAnimationBeginsFromCurrentState:

If YES, and if this animation animates a property already being animated by an animation that is previously ordered or in-flight, then instead of canceling the previous animation (completing the requested change instantly), this animation will use the presentation layer to decide where to start, and will "blend" its animation with the previous animation if possible.

If an animation autoreverses, and if, when the animation ends, the view's actual property is still at the finish value, the view will appear to "jump" from start to finish as the "animation movie" is removed. So, for example, suppose we want a view to animate its position to the right and then back to its original position. This code causes the view to animate right, animate left, and then (unfortunately) jump right:

```
[UIView beginAnimations:nil context:NULL];
[UIView setAnimationRepeatAutoreverses:YES];
CGPoint p = v.center;
p.x += 100;
v.center = p;
[UIView commitAnimations];
```

How can we prevent this? We want the view to stay at the start value after the animation reverses and ends. If we try to eliminate the jump at the end by setting the view's position back to its starting point after the animation block, there is no animation at all (because when the redraw moment arrives, there is no property change):

```
[UIView beginAnimations:nil context:NULL];
[UIView setAnimationRepeatAutoreverses:YES];
CGPoint p = v.center;
p.x += 100;
v.center = p;
[UIView commitAnimations];
p = v.center;
p.x -= 100;
v.center = p;
```

The coherent solution is to use the "stop" delegate method to set the view's position back to its starting point when the animation ends:

```
- (void) someMethod {
    [UIView beginAnimations:nil context:NULL];
    [UIView setAnimationRepeatAutoreverses:YES];
    [UIView setAnimationDelegate:self];
    [UIView setAnimationDidStopSelector:@selector(stopped:fin:context:)];
    CGPoint p = v.center;
    p.x += 100;
    v.center = p;
    [UIView commitAnimations];
}

- (void) stopped:(NSString *)anim fin:(NSNumber*)fin context:(void *)context {
    CGPoint p = v.center;
    p.x -= 100;
    v.center = p;
}
```

In that example, we happened to know how the animation had changed the view's position, so we could hard-code the instructions for reversing the change. To be more general, we could take advantage of our ability to pass information into the animation block and retrieve this same information in the delegate method. Or, we could store the view's original position in its layer (recall that a CALayer is a dictionary-like container):

```
- (void) someMethod {
    [UIView beginAnimations:nil context:NULL];
    [UIView setAnimationRepeatAutoreverses:YES];
    [UIView setAnimationDelegate:self];
    [UIView setAnimationDidStopSelector:@selector(stopped:fin:context:)];
    CGPoint p = v.center;
    [v.layer setValue:[NSValue valueWithCGPoint:p] forKey:@"origCenter"];
    p.x += 100;
    v.center = p;
    [UIView commitAnimations];
}
```

```
- (void) stopped:(NSString *)anim fin:(NSNumber*)fin context:(void *)context {
    v.center = [[v.layer valueForKey:@"origCenter"] CGPointValue];
}
```

To illustrate `setAnimationBeginsFromCurrentState:`, consider the following:

```
[UIView beginAnimations:nil context:NULL];
[UIView setAnimationDuration:1];
CGPoint p = v.center;
p.x += 100;
v.center = p;
[UIView commitAnimations];

[UIView beginAnimations:nil context:NULL];
// uncomment the next line to fix the problem
//[UIView setAnimationBeginsFromCurrentState:YES];
[UIView setAnimationDuration:1];
CGPoint p2 = v.center;
p2.x = 0;
v.center = p2;
[UIView commitAnimations];
```

The result is that the view jumps 100 points rightward, and then animates leftward. That's because the second animation caused the first animation to be thrown away; the move 100 points rightward was performed instantly, instead of being animated. But if we uncomment the call to `setAnimationBeginsFromCurrentState:`, the result is that the view animates leftward from its current position, with no jump.

Even more interesting is what happens when we change x to y in the second animation. If we uncomment the call to `setAnimationBeginsFromCurrentState:`, both the x-component and the y-component of the view's position are animated together, as if we had ordered one animation instead of two.

## Transition Animations

A *transition* is a sort of animated redrawing of a view. The usual reason for a transition animation is that you are making some change in the view's appearance, and you want to emphasize this by animating the view. To order a transition animation using an animation block, call `setAnimationTransition:forView:cache:`.

- The first parameter describes how the animation should behave; your choices are:
  — `UIViewAnimationTransitionFlipFromLeft`
  — `UIViewAnimationTransitionFlipFromRight`
  — `UIViewAnimationTransitionCurlUp`
  — `UIViewAnimationTransitionCurlDown`
- The second parameter is the view.
- The third parameter is whether to cache the view's contents right now, effectively taking a "snapshot" of those contents at the moment and as they will be after the

---

contents change, and using these snapshots throughout the transition. The alternative is to redraw the contents repeatedly throughout the transition. You'll want to say YES wherever possible.

Here's a simple example that flips a UIImageView while changing its image. The result is that the UIImageView appears to flip over, like a piece of paper being rotated to show its reverse side — a piece of paper with Mars on its front and Saturn on its back:

```
[UIView beginAnimations:nil context:NULL];
[UIView setAnimationTransition:UIViewAnimationTransitionFlipFromLeft
                    forView:iv cache:YES];
// iv is a UIImageView whose image is Mars.png
iv.image = [UIImage imageNamed:@"Saturn.gif"];
[UIView commitAnimations];
```

The example is a little misleading, because the change in the image does not necessarily have to be inside the animation block. The animation described by setAnimation-Transition:... will be performed in any case. The change of image will be performed in any case as well. They will both happen at the redraw moment, so they are performed together. Thus, we could have written the same example this way:

```
iv.image = [UIImage imageNamed:@"Saturn.gif"];
[UIView beginAnimations:nil context:NULL];
[UIView setAnimationTransition:UIViewAnimationTransitionFlipFromLeft
                    forView:iv cache:YES];
[UIView commitAnimations];
```

Nevertheless, it is customary to order the changes in the view from inside the animation block, and I'll continue to do so in subsequent examples.

You can do the same sort of thing with any built-in view subclass. Here's a button that seems to be labeled "Start" on one side and "Stop" on the other:

```
[UIView beginAnimations:nil context:NULL];
// "b" is a UIButton; "stopped" is presumably a BOOL variable or ivar
[UIView setAnimationTransition:UIViewAnimationTransitionFlipFromLeft
                    forView:b cache:YES];
[b setTitle:(stopped ? @"Start" : @"Stop") forState:UIControlStateNormal];
[UIView commitAnimations];
```

To do the same thing with a custom UIView subclass that knows how to draw itself in its drawRect:, call setNeedsDisplay to cause a redraw. For example, imagine a UIView subclass with a reverse BOOL property, which draws an ellipse if reverse is YES and a square if reverse is NO. Then we can animate the square flipping over and becoming an ellipse (or *vice versa*):

```
v.reverse = !v.reverse;
[UIView beginAnimations:nil context:NULL];
[UIView setAnimationTransition:UIViewAnimationTransitionFlipFromLeft
                    forView:v cache:YES];
[v setNeedsDisplay];
[UIView commitAnimations];
```

Of course you can also animate a view while doing such things to it as removing or adding a subview.

## Block-Based View Animation

Starting in iOS 4.0, a UIView can be animated using a syntax involving Objective-C blocks. This is intended to replace the old animation block syntax described earlier (though it does not succeed completely). In the new syntax:

- The behavior to be animated is a block.
- The code to be run when the animation ends is also a block. Thus, there is no need for the two-part structure involving an animation block and a separate delegate method.
- Options describing the animation are part of the original animation method call, not separate calls as with an animation block.
- User touch interactions are disabled during the animation, by default. This is not the case with an animation block. The option `UIViewAnimationOptionAllowUser-Interaction` lets you reverse this setting.
- Transition animations have more options than with animation blocks.

The basis of the new syntax is the UIView class method `animateWithDuration:delay:options:animations:completion:`. There are also two reduced calls, the first letting you omit the `delay` and `options` parameters and the second letting you also omit the `completion` parameter. The parameters of the full form are:

duration
   The duration of the animation.

delay
   The delay before the animation starts. The default, in the reduced forms, is no delay.

options
   A bitmask stating additional options. The default, in the reduced forms, is `UIView-AnimationOptionCurveEaseInOut` (which is also the default animation curve for animation blocks). For an ordinary animation (not a transition), the chief options are:

   *Animation curve*
      Your choices are:

      - `UIViewAnimationOptionCurveEaseInOut`
      - `UIViewAnimationOptionCurveEaseIn`
      - `UIViewAnimationOptionCurveEaseOut`
      - `UIViewAnimationOptionCurveLinear`

*Repetition and autoreverse*

Your options are:

- `UIViewAnimationOptionRepeat`

- `UIViewAnimationOptionAutoreverse`

There is no way to specify a certain number of repetitions; you either repeat forever or not at all. This feels like an oversight.

`animations`

The block containing view property changes to be animated.

`completion`

The block to run when the animation ends. It takes one BOOL parameter indicating whether the animation ran to completion. (There is no way to specify a notification when the animation starts, but this should not be needed, as the animation code is itself a block.) It's fine for this block to order a further animation. This block is called, with a parameter indicating YES, even if nothing in the `animations` block triggers any animations.

Here's an example, recasting an earlier example to use Objective-C blocks instead of animation blocks. We move a view rightward and reverse it back into place. With animation blocks, we used a delegate so that we could set the view back to its original position, and we stored that position in the layer so as to be able to retrieve it in the delegate method. With blocks, however, the original position can live in a variable that remains in scope, so things are much simpler:

```
CGPoint p = v.center;
CGPoint pOrig = p;
p.x += 100;
void (^anim) (void) = ^{
    v.center = p;
};
void (^after) (BOOL) = ^(BOOL f) {
    v.center = pOrig;
};
NSUInteger opts = UIViewAnimationOptionAutoreverse;
[UIView animateWithDuration:1 delay:0 options:opts
                 animations:anim completion:after];
```

As you can see, I like to express the blocks as named variables; I think this increases readability.

In addition to the options I've already listed, there are some options saying what should happen if an animation is already ordered or in-flight.

`UIViewAnimationOptionBeginFromCurrentState`

Similar to `setAnimationBeginsFromCurrentState:`.

`UIViewAnimationOptionOverrideInheritedDuration`

Prevents inheriting duration from an already ordered or in-flight animation (the default is to inherit it).

```
UIViewAnimationOptionOverrideInheritedCurve
```
Prevents inheriting the animation curve from an already ordered or in-flight animation (the default is to inherit it).

Transitions are ordered using one of two methods. The one that's parallel to `set-AnimationTransition...`, described earlier in connection with animation blocks, is `transitionWithView:duration:options:animations:completion:`. The transition animation types are parallel as well, but they are expressed as part of the `options` bitmask:

- `UIViewAnimationOptionTransitionFlipFromLeft`
- `UIViewAnimationOptionTransitionFlipFromRight`
- `UIViewAnimationOptionTransitionCurlUp`
- `UIViewAnimationOptionTransitionCurlDown`

Here's a recasting, to use `transitionWithView...`, of the earlier example where we flip a rectangle into an ellipse by means of a custom UIView subclass whose `drawRect:` behavior depends on its `reverse` property:

```
v.reverse = !v.reverse;
void (^anim) (void) = ^{
    [v setNeedsDisplay];
};
NSUInteger opts = UIViewAnimationOptionTransitionFlipFromLeft;
[UIView transitionWithView:v duration:1 options:opts
                animations:anim completion:nil];
```

The second transition method is `transitionFromView:toView:duration:options:completion:`. It names two views; the first is replaced by the second, while their superview undergoes the transition animation. This has no parallel in the older animation block syntax. There are actually two possible configurations, depending on the options you provide:

*Remove one subview, add the other*

If `UIViewAnimationOptionShowHideTransitionViews` is *not* one of the options, then the second subview is not in the view hierarchy when we start; the first subview is removed from its superview and the second subview is added to that same superview.

*Hide one subview, show the other*

If `UIViewAnimationOptionShowHideTransitionViews` *is* one of the options, then both subviews are in the view hierarchy when we start; the `hidden` of the first is NO, the `hidden` of the second is YES, and these values are reversed.

So, for example, this code causes the superview of **v1** to rotate like a piece of paper being turned over, while at the same **v1** is removed from it and **v2** is added to it:

```
NSUInteger opts = UIViewAnimationOptionTransitionFlipFromLeft;
[UIView transitionFromView:v1 toView:v2 duration:1 options:opts completion:nil];
```

It's up to you to make sure beforehand that v2 has the desired position, so that it will appear in the right place in its superview.

# Implicit Layer Animation

If a layer is not a view's underlying layer, animating it can be as simple as setting a property. A change in what the documentation calls an *animatable property* is automatically interpreted as a request to animate that change. In other words, animation of layer property changes is the default! Multiple property changes are considered part of the same animation. This mechanism is called *implicit animation*.

 You cannot use implicit animation on the underlying layer of a UIView. You can animate a UIView's underlying layer directly, but you must use explicit animation (discussed in the upcoming section on Core Animation).

For example, in Chapter 16 we constructed a compass out of layers. The compass itself is a CompassView that does no drawing of its own; its underlying layer is a CompassLayer that also does no drawing, serving only as a superlayer for the layers that constitute the drawing. None of the layers that constitute the actual drawing is the underlying layer of a view, so a property change to any of them is animated automatically.

So, presume that we have a reference to the arrow layer, a property theArrow of the CompassLayer, and also a reference to the CompassView, a property compass of the app delegate, which is self. If we rotate the arrow by changing its transform property, that rotation is animated:

```
CompassLayer* c = (CompassLayer*)self.compass.layer;
// the next line is an implicit animation
c.theArrow.transform = CATransform3DRotate(c.theArrow.transform, M_PI/4.0, 0, 0, 1);
```

CALayer properties listed in the documentation as animatable in this way are anchorPoint and anchorPointZ, backgroundColor, borderColor, borderWidth, bounds, contents, contentsCenter, contentsRect, cornerRadius, doubleSided, hidden, masksToBounds, opacity, position and zPosition, rasterizationScale and shouldRasterize, shadowColor, shadowOffset, shadowOpacity, shadowRadius, and sublayerTransform and transform.

In addition, a CAShapeLayer's path, fillColor, strokeColor, lineWidth, lineDashPhase, and miterLimit are animatable; so are a CATextLayer's fontSize and foregroundColor.

Basically, a property is animatable because there's some sensible way to interpolate the intermediate values between one value and another. The nature of the animation attached to each property is therefore just what you would intuitively expect. When you change a layer's `hidden` property, it fades out of view (or into view). When you change a layer's `contents`, the old contents are dissolved into the new contents. And so forth.

## Animation Transactions

Implicit animation operates with respect to a *transaction* (a CATransaction), which groups animation requests into a single animation. Every animation request takes place in the context of a transaction. You can make this explicit by wrapping your animation requests in calls to the CATransaction class methods `begin` and `commit`; the result is a *transaction block*. But additionally there is already an *implicit transaction* surrounding all your code.

To modify the characteristics of an implicit animation, you modify its transaction. Typically, you'll use these class methods:

`setAnimationDuration:`
    The duration of the animation.

`setAnimationTimingFunction:`
    A CAMediaTimingFunction; timing functions are discussed in the next section.

`setCompletionBlock:`
    A block (only on iOS 4 and later, obviously) to be called when the animation ends. The block takes no parameters. The block is called even if no animation is triggered during this transaction.

By nesting transaction blocks, you can apply different animation characteristics to different elements of an animation. But you can also use transaction commands outside of any transaction block to modify the implicit transaction.

So, in our previous example, we could slow down the animation of the arrow like this:

```
CompassLayer* c = (CompassLayer*)self.compass.layer;
[CATransaction setAnimationDuration:0.8];
c.theArrow.transform = CATransform3DRotate(c.theArrow.transform, M_PI/4.0, 0, 0, 1);
```

Another useful feature of animation transactions is to turn implicit animation *off*. It's important to be able to do this, because implicit animation is the default, and can be unwanted (and a performance drag). To do so, call the CATransaction class method `setDisableActions:` with value YES. There are other ways to turn off implicit animation (discussed later in this chapter), but this is the simplest.

CATransaction implements KVC to allow you set and retrieve a value for an arbitrary key, similar to CALayer. An example appears later in this chapter.

A transaction block that orders an animation to a layer, if the block is not preceded by any changes to the layer, can cause animation to begin immediately when the CATransaction class method `commit` is called, without waiting for the redraw moment, while your code continues running. In my experience, this can cause confusion (for example, animation delegate messages cannot arrive, and the presentation layer can't be queried properly) and should be avoided.

## Media Timing Functions

The CATransaction class method `setAnimationTimingFunction:` takes as its parameter a media timing function (CAMediaTimingFunction). This class is the general expression of the animation curves we have already met (ease-in-out, ease-in, ease-out, and linear); in fact, you are most likely to use it with those very same predefined curves, by calling the CAMediaTimingFunction class method `functionWithName:` with one of these parameters:

- `kCAMediaTimingFunctionLinear`
- `kCAMediaTimingFunctionEaseIn`
- `kCAMediaTimingFunctionEaseOut`
- `kCAMediaTimingFunctionEaseInEaseOut`
- `kCAMediaTimingFunctionDefault`

In reality, a media timing function is a Bézier curve defined by two points. The curve graphs the fraction of the animation's time that has elapsed (the x-axis) against the fraction of the animation's change that has occurred (the y-axis); its endpoints are therefore at (0,0) and (1,1), because at the beginning of the animation there has been no elapsed time and no change, and at the end of the animation all the time has elapsed and all the change has occurred.

Because the curve's defining points are its endpoints, each needs only one Bézier control point to define the tangent to the curve. And because the curve's endpoints are known, defining the two control points is sufficient to describe the entire curve. And because a point is a pair of floating point values, a media timing function can be expressed as four floating-point values. That is, in fact, how it is expressed.

So, for example, the ease-in-out timing function is expressed as the four values 0.42, 0.0, 0.58, 1.0. That defines a Bézier curve with one endpoint at (0,0), whose control point is (0.42,0), and the other endpoint at (1,1), whose control point is (0.58,1) (Figure 17-1).

If you want to define your own media timing function, you can supply the coordinates of the two control points by calling `functionWithControlPoints::::` or `initWithControlPoints::::` (this is one of those rare cases of the parameters of an Objective-C method having no name; see Chapter 3). For example, here's a media timing function that starts out quite slowly and then whips quickly into place after about two-thirds of the time

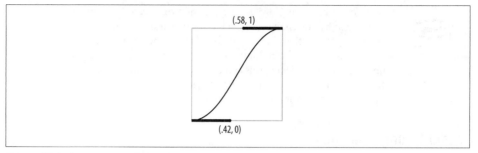

Figure 17-1. An ease-in-out Bézier curve

has elapsed. I call this the "clunk" timing function, and it looks great with the compass arrow:

```
CAMediaTimingFunction* clunk =
    [CAMediaTimingFunction functionWithControlPoints:.9 :.1 :.7 :.9];
[CATransaction setAnimationTimingFunction: clunk];
c.theArrow.transform = CATransform3DRotate(c.theArrow.transform, M_PI/4.0, 0, 0, 1);
```

 If you're going to define your own media timing function, it helps to design the curve in a standard drawing program first so that you can visualize how the placement of the control points shapes the curve.

# Core Animation

Core Animation is the fundamental underlying iOS animation technology. View animation and implicit layer animation are merely convenient façades for Core Animation. Core Animation is *explicit layer animation*, and revolves primarily around the CAAnimation class and its subclasses, which allow you to create far more elaborate specifications of an animation than anything we've encountered so far.

You may never program at the level of Core Animation, but you should read this section anyway, if only to learn how animation really works and to get a sense of the mighty powers you would acquire if you *did* elect to use Core Animation directly. In particular, Core Animation:

- Works even on a view's underlying layer. Thus, Core Animation is the *only* way to apply full-on layer property animation to a view.
- Provides fine control over the intermediate values and timing of an animation.
- Allows animations to be grouped into complex combinations.
- Adds transition animation effects that aren't available otherwise, such as new content "pushing" the previous content out of a layer.

# CABasicAnimation and Its Inheritance

The simplest way to animate a property with Core Animation is with a CABasicAnimation object. CABasicAnimation derives much of its power through its inheritance, so I'm going to describe that inheritance as well as CABasicAnimation itself. You will readily see that all the property animation features we have met so far are embodied in a CABasicAnimation instance.

*CAAnimation*

CAAnimation is an abstract class, meaning that you'll only ever use a subclass of it. Some of CAAnimation's powers come from its implementation of the CAMediaTiming protocol.

animation
A class method, a convenient way of creating an animation object.

delegate
The delegate messages are `animationDidStart:` and `animationDidStop:finished:`, which should sound familiar from the analogous UIView animation delegate messages. A CAAnimation instance *retains its delegate*; this is a very unusual thing and can cause trouble if you're not conscious of it. In iOS 4 and later, you can use the CATransaction class method `setCompletionBlock:` instead of a delegate message to run code after the animation ends.

duration, timingFunction
The length of the animation, and its timing function (a CAMediaTimingFunction). A duration of `0` (the default) means `.25` seconds unless overridden by the transaction.

autoreverses, repeatCount, repeatDuration, cumulative
The first two are familiar from UIView animation. The `repeatDuration` property is a different way to govern repetition, specifying how long the repetition should continue rather than how many repetitions should occur; don't specify both a `repeatCount` and a `repeatDuration`. If `cumulative` is YES, a repeating animation starts each repetition where the previous repetition ended (rather than jumping back to the start value).

beginTime
The delay before the animation starts. To delay an animation with respect to now, call `CACurrentMediaTime` and add the desired delay in seconds. The delay does not eat into the animation's duration.

timeOffset
A shift in the animation's overall timing; looked at another way, specifies the starting frame of the "animation movie," which is treated as a loop. For example, an animation with a duration of 8 and a time offset of 4 plays its second half followed by its first half.

*CAPropertyAnimation*

CAPropertyAnimation is a subclass of CAAnimation. It too is abstract, and adds the following:

keyPath

The all-important string specifying the CALayer key that is to be animated. Recall from Chapter 16 that CALayer properties are accessible through KVC keys; now we are using those keys! A CAPropertyAnimation convenience class method `animationWithKeyPath:` creates the instance and assigns it a `keyPath`.

additive

If YES, the values supplied by the animation are added to the current presentation-layer value.

valueFunction

Converts a simple scalar value that you supply into a transform.

*CABasicAnimation*

CABasicAnimation is a subclass (not abstract!) of CAPropertyAnimation. It adds the following:

fromValue, toValue

The starting and ending values for the animation. These values must be objects, so numbers and structs will have to be wrapped accordingly. If neither `from-Value` nor `toValue` is provided, the former and current values of the property are used. If just one of `fromValue` or `toValue` is provided, the other uses the current value of the property.

byValue

Expresses one of the endpoint values as a *difference* from the other rather than in absolute terms. So you would supply a `byValue` instead of a `fromValue` or instead of a `toValue`, and the actual `fromValue` or `toValue` would be calculated for you by subtraction or addition with respect to the other value. If you supply *only* a `byValue`, the `fromValue` is the property's current value.

## Using a CABasicAnimation

Having constructed and configured a CABasicAnimation, the way you order it to be performed is to *add it to a layer*. This is done with the CALayer instance method `add-Animation:forKey:`. (I'll discuss the purpose of the Key parameter later; it's fine to ignore it and use nil, as I do in the examples that follow.)

However, there's a slight twist. A CAAnimation is *merely* an animation; all it does is describe the hoops that the presentation layer is to jump through, the "animation movie" that is to be presented. It has no effect on the layer *itself*. Thus, if you naively create a CABasicAnimation and add it to a layer with `addAnimation:forKey:`, the animation happens and then the "animation movie" is whipped away to reveal the layer sitting there in exactly the same state as before. It is up to *you* to change the layer to match what the animation will ultimately portray.

This requirement may seem odd, but keep in mind that we are now in a much more fundamental, flexible world than the automatic, convenient worlds of view animation and implicit layer animation. Using explicit animation is more work, but you get more power. The converse, as we shall see, is that you *don't* have to change the layer if it *doesn't* change during the animation.

To assure good results, we'll start by taking a formulaic approach to the use of CABasicAnimation, like this:

1. Capture the start and end values for the layer property you're going to change, because you're likely to need these values in what follows.
2. Change the layer property to its end value, first calling `setDisableActions:` to prevent implicit animation.
3. Construct the explicit animation, using the start and end values you captured earlier, and with its `keyPath` corresponding to the layer property you just changed.
4. Add the explicit animation to the layer.

Here's how you'd use this approach to animate our compass arrow rotation:

```
CompassLayer* c = (CompassLayer*)self.compass.layer;
// capture the start and end values
CATransform3D startValue = c.theArrow.transform;
CATransform3D endValue = CATransform3DRotate(startValue, M_PI/4.0, 0, 0, 1);
// change the layer, without implicit animation
[CATransaction setDisableActions:YES];
c.theArrow.transform = endValue;
// construct the explicit animation
CABasicAnimation* anim = [CABasicAnimation animationWithKeyPath:@"transform"];
anim.duration = 0.8;
CAMediaTimingFunction* clunk =
    [CAMediaTimingFunction functionWithControlPoints:.9 :.1 :.7 :.9];
anim.timingFunction = clunk;
anim.fromValue = [NSValue valueWithCATransform3D:startValue];
anim.toValue = [NSValue valueWithCATransform3D:endValue];
// ask for the explicit animation
[c.theArrow addAnimation:anim forKey:nil];
```

Once you know the full form, you will find that in many cases it can be condensed. For example, when `fromValue` and `toValue` are not set, the former and current values of the property are used automatically. (This magic is possible because the presentation layer still has the former value of the property, while the layer itself has the new value.) Thus, in this case there was no need to set them, and so there was no need to capture the start and end values beforehand either. Here's the condensed version:

```
CompassLayer* c = (CompassLayer*)self.compass.layer;
[CATransaction setDisableActions:YES];
c.theArrow.transform = CATransform3DRotate(c.theArrow.transform, M_PI/4.0, 0, 0, 1);
CABasicAnimation* anim = [CABasicAnimation animationWithKeyPath:@"transform"];
```

```
anim.duration = 0.8;
CAMediaTimingFunction* clunk =
    [CAMediaTimingFunction functionWithControlPoints:.9 :.1 :.7 :.9];
anim.timingFunction = clunk;
[c.theArrow addAnimation:anim forKey:nil];
```

As I mentioned earlier, you will omit changing the layer if it doesn't change during the animation. For example, let's make the compass arrow appear to vibrate rapidly, without ultimately changing its current orientation. To do this, we'll waggle it back and forth, using a repeated animation, between slightly clockwise from its current position and slightly counterclockwise from its current position. The "animation movie" neither starts nor stops at the current position of the arrow, but for this animation it doesn't matter, because it all happens so quickly as to appear perfectly natural:

```
CompassLayer* c = (CompassLayer*)self.compass.layer;
// capture the start and end values
CATransform3D nowValue = c.theArrow.transform;
CATransform3D startValue = CATransform3DRotate(nowValue, M_PI/40.0, 0, 0, 1);
CATransform3D endValue = CATransform3DRotate(nowValue, -M_PI/40.0, 0, 0, 1);
// construct the explicit animation
CABasicAnimation* anim = [CABasicAnimation animationWithKeyPath:@"transform"];
anim.duration = 0.05;
anim.timingFunction =
    [CAMediaTimingFunction functionWithName:kCAMediaTimingFunctionLinear];
anim.repeatCount = 3;
anim.autoreverses = YES;
anim.fromValue = [NSValue valueWithCATransform3D:startValue];
anim.toValue = [NSValue valueWithCATransform3D:endValue];
// ask for the explicit animation
[c.theArrow addAnimation:anim forKey:nil];
```

That code, too, can be shortened considerably from its full form. We can eliminate the need to calculate the new rotation values based on the arrow's current transform by setting our animation's **additive** property to YES; this means that the animation's property values are added to the existing property value for us, so that they are relative, not absolute. For a transform, "added" means "matrix-multiplied," so we can describe the waggle without any dependence on the arrow's current rotation. Moreover, because our rotation is so simple (around a cardinal axis), we can take advantage of CAPropertyAnimation's **valueFunction**; the animation's property values can then be simple scalars (in this case, angles), because the **valueFunction** tells the animation to interpret these as rotations around the z-axis:

```
CompassLayer* c = (CompassLayer*)self.compass.layer;
CABasicAnimation* anim = [CABasicAnimation animationWithKeyPath:@"transform"];
anim.duration = 0.05;
anim.timingFunction =
    [CAMediaTimingFunction functionWithName:kCAMediaTimingFunctionLinear];
anim.repeatCount = 3;
anim.autoreverses = YES;
anim.additive = YES;
anim.valueFunction = [CAValueFunction functionWithName:kCAValueFunctionRotateZ];
anim.fromValue = [NSNumber numberWithFloat:M_PI/40];
```

```
anim.toValue = [NSNumber numberWithFloat:-M_PI/40];
[c.theArrow addAnimation:anim forKey:nil];
```

 Instead of using a `valueFunction`, we could have achieved the same effect
by setting the animation's key path to `@"transform.rotation.z"`. However, Apple advises against this, as it can result in mathematical trouble
when there is more than one rotation.

## Keyframe Animation

Keyframe animation (CAKeyframeAnimation) is an alternative to basic animation
(CABasicAnimation); they are both subclasses of CAPropertyAnimation and they are
used in identical ways. The difference is that a keyframe animation, in addition to
specifying a starting and ending value, also specifies multiple values through which the
animation should pass on the way, the stages (*frames*) of the animation. This can be as
simple as setting the animation's **values** property (an NSArray).

Here's a nicer version of our animation for waggling the compass arrow: the animation
includes both the start and end states, and the degree of waggle gets progressively
smaller:

```
CompassLayer* c = (CompassLayer*)self.compass.layer;
NSMutableArray* values = [NSMutableArray array];
[values addObject: [NSNumber numberWithFloat:0]];
int direction = 1;
for (int i = 20; i < 60; i += 5, direction *= -1) { // reverse direction each time
    [values addObject: [NSNumber numberWithFloat: direction*M_PI/(float)i]];
}
[values addObject: [NSNumber numberWithFloat:0]];
CAKeyframeAnimation* anim = [CAKeyframeAnimation animationWithKeyPath:@"transform"];
anim.values = values;
anim.additive = YES;
anim.valueFunction = [CAValueFunction functionWithName: kCAValueFunctionRotateZ];
[c.theArrow addAnimation:anim forKey:nil];
```

Here are some CAKeyframeAnimation properties:

values
    The array of values the animation is to adopt, including the starting and ending
    value.

timingFunctions
    An array of timing functions, one for each stage of the animation (so that this array
    will be one element shorter than the **values** array).

keyTimes
    An array of times to accompany the array of values, defining when each value
    should be reached. The times start at 0 and are expressed as increasing fractions of
    1, ending at 1.

calculationMode

Describes how the values are treated to create *all* the values through which the animation must pass.

- The default is kCAAnimationLinear, a simple straight-line interpolation from value to value.

- kCAAnimationCubic (on iOS 4 and later) constructs a single smooth curve passing through all the values (and additional advanced properties, tensionValues, continuityValues, and biasValues, allow you to refine the curve).

- kCAAnimationDiscrete means no interpolation: we jump directly to each value at the corresponding key time.

- kCAAnimationPaced and kCAAnimationCubicPaced means the timing functions and key times are ignored, and the velocity is made constant through the whole animation.

path

When you're animating a property whose values are pairs of floats (CGPoints), this is an alternative way of describing the values; instead of a values array, which must be interpolated to arrive at the intermediate values along the way, you supply the entire interpolation as a single CGPathRef. The points used to draw the path are the keyframe values, so you can still apply timing functions and key times. If you're animating a position, the rotationMode property lets you ask the animated object to rotate so as to remain perpendicular to the path. (I'll give an example later in this chapter.)

## Making a Property Animatable

So far, we've been animating built-in animatable properties. If you define your own property on a CALayer subclass, you can make that property animatable through a CAPropertyAnimation (a CABasicAnimation or a CAKeyframeAnimation). You do this by declaring the property @dynamic (so that Core Animation can create its accessors) and returning YES from the class method needsDisplayForKey:, where the key is the string name of the property.

For example, here's the code for a layer class MyLayer with an animatable thickness property:

```
// the interface section
@interface MyLayer : CALayer {
}
@property (nonatomic, assign) CGFloat thickness;
@end

// the implementation section
@implementation MyLayer
@dynamic thickness;

+ (BOOL) needsDisplayForKey:(NSString *)key {
```

```
        if ([key isEqualToString: @"thickness"])
            return YES;
        return [super needsDisplayForKey:key];
    }

    @end
```

Returning YES from `needsDisplayForKey:` causes this layer to be redisplayed repeatedly as the `thickness` property changes. So if we want to *see* the animation, this layer also needs to draw itself in some way that depends on the `thickness` property. Here, I'll use the layer's `drawInContext:` to make `thickness` the thickness of a rectangle:

```
- (void) drawInContext:(CGContextRef)ctx {
    CGRect r = CGRectInset(self.bounds, 20, 20);
    CGContextFillRect(ctx, r);
    CGContextSetLineWidth(ctx, self.thickness);
    CGContextStrokeRect(ctx, r);
}
```

Now we can animate the rectangle's thickness using explicit animation (`lay` is a My-Layer instance):

```
CABasicAnimation* ba = [CABasicAnimation animationWithKeyPath:@"thickness"];
ba.toValue = [NSNumber numberWithFloat: 10.0];
ba.autoreverses = YES;
[lay addAnimation:ba forKey:nil];
```

At every step of the animation, `drawLayer:inContext:` is called, and because the `thickness` value differs at each step, it is animated.

## Grouped Animations

A grouped animation (CAAnimationGroup) combines multiple animations into one, by means of its `animations` property (an NSArray of animations). By delaying and timing the various component animations, complex effects can be created.

A CAAnimationGroup is itself an animation; it is a CAAnimation subclass, so it has a `duration` and other animation features. Think of the CAAnimationGroup as the parent and its `animations` as listing its children. Then *the children inherit default values from their parent.* Thus, for example, if you don't set a child's duration explicitly, it will inherit the parent's duration. Also, make sure the parent's duration is sufficient to include all parts of the child animations that you want displayed.

For example, here's how we can combine the compass arrow rotation and the compass arrow waggle into a sequence. Very little change is required. We express the first animation in its full form, with explicit `fromValue` and `toValue`. We postpone the second animation using its `beginTime` property; notice that we express this in relative terms, as a number of seconds into the parent's duration, not with respect to `CACurrentMedia-Time`. Finally, we set the overall parent duration to the sum of the child durations, so that it can embrace both of them:

```
CompassLayer* c = (CompassLayer*)self.compass.layer;
// capture current value, set final value
CGFloat rot = M_PI/4.0;
[CATransaction setDisableActions:YES];
CGFloat current = [[c.theArrow valueForKeyPath:@"transform.rotation.z"] floatValue];
[c.theArrow setValue: [NSNumber numberWithFloat: current + rot]
        forKeyPath:@"transform.rotation.z"];
// first animation (rotate and clunk) ================
CABasicAnimation* anim1 = [CABasicAnimation animationWithKeyPath:@"transform"];
anim1.duration = 0.8;
CAMediaTimingFunction* clunk =
    [CAMediaTimingFunction functionWithControlPoints:.9 :.1 :.7 :.9];
anim1.timingFunction = clunk;
anim1.fromValue = [NSNumber numberWithFloat: current];
anim1.toValue = [NSNumber numberWithFloat: current + rot];
anim1.valueFunction = [CAValueFunction functionWithName:kCAValueFunctionRotateZ];
// second animation (waggle) ========================
NSMutableArray* values = [NSMutableArray array];
[values addObject: [NSNumber numberWithFloat:0]];
int direction = 1;
for (int i = 20; i < 60; i += 5, direction *= -1) { // reverse direction each time
    [values addObject: [NSNumber numberWithFloat: direction*M_PI/(float)i]];
}
[values addObject: [NSNumber numberWithFloat:0]];
CAKeyframeAnimation* anim2 =
    [CAKeyframeAnimation animationWithKeyPath:@"transform"];
anim2.values = values;
anim2.duration = 0.25;
anim2.beginTime = anim1.duration;
anim2.additive = YES;
anim2.valueFunction = [CAValueFunction functionWithName:kCAValueFunctionRotateZ];
// group =========================================
CAAnimationGroup* group = [CAAnimationGroup animation];
group.animations = [NSArray arrayWithObjects: anim1, anim2, nil];
group.duration = anim1.duration + anim2.duration;
[c.theArrow addAnimation:group forKey:nil];
```

In that example, I grouped two animations that animated the same property sequentially. Now let's go to the other extreme and group some animations that animate different properties simultaneously. I have a small view (about 56×38), located near the top right corner of the screen, whose layer contents are a picture of a sailboat facing to the left. I'll "sail" the boat in a curving path, both down the screen and left and right across the screen, like an extended letter "S" (Figure 17-2). Each time the boat comes to a vertex of the curve, changing direction across the screen, I'll turn the boat picture so that it faces the way it's about to move. At the same time, I'll constantly rock the boat, so that it always appears to be pitching a little on the waves.

Here's the first animation, the movement of the boat along its curving path. It illustrates the use of a CAKeyframeAnimation with a CGPath; the calculationMode of kCAAnimationPaced ensures an even speed over the whole path. We don't set an explicit duration because we want to adopt the duration of the group:

*Figure 17-2. A boat and the course she'll sail*

```
CGFloat h = 200;
CGFloat v = 75;
CGMutablePathRef path = CGPathCreateMutable();
int leftright = 1;
CGPoint next = self.view.layer.position;
CGPoint pos;
CGPathMoveToPoint(path, NULL, next.x, next.y);
for (int i = 0; i < 4; i++) {
    pos = next;
    leftright *= -1;
    next = CGPointMake(pos.x+h*leftright, pos.y+v);
    CGPathAddCurveToPoint(path, NULL, pos.x, pos.y+30, next.x, next.y-30,
                          next.x, next.y);
}
CAKeyframeAnimation* anim1 = [CAKeyframeAnimation animationWithKeyPath:@"position"];
anim1.path = path;
anim1.calculationMode = kCAAnimationPaced;
```

Here's the second animation, the reversal of the direction the boat is facing. This is simply a rotation around the y-axis. We make no attempt at visually animating this reversal, so we set the calculationMode to kCAAnimationDiscrete (the boat image reversal is a sudden change). There is one fewer value than the number of points in our first animation's path, and the first animation has an even speed, so the reversals take place at each curve apex with no further effort on our part. (If the pacing were more complicated, we could give both the first and the second animation identical keyTimes arrays, to coordinate them.) Once again, we don't set an explicit duration:

```
NSArray* revs = [NSArray arrayWithObjects:
                 [NSNumber numberWithFloat:0],
                 [NSNumber numberWithFloat:M_PI],
                 [NSNumber numberWithFloat:0],
                 [NSNumber numberWithFloat:M_PI],
                 nil];
CAKeyframeAnimation* anim2 =
    [CAKeyframeAnimation animationWithKeyPath:@"transform"];
anim2.values = revs;
anim2.valueFunction = [CAValueFunction functionWithName:kCAValueFunctionRotateY];
anim2.calculationMode = kCAAnimationDiscrete;
```

Here's the third animation, the rocking of the boat. It has a short duration, and repeats indefinitely (by giving its repeatCount an immense value):

```
NSArray* pitches = [NSArray arrayWithObjects:
                    [NSNumber numberWithFloat:0],
                    [NSNumber numberWithFloat:M_PI/60.0],
                    [NSNumber numberWithFloat:0],
                    [NSNumber numberWithFloat:-M_PI/60.0],
                    [NSNumber numberWithFloat:0],
                    nil];
CAKeyframeAnimation* anim3 =
    [CAKeyframeAnimation animationWithKeyPath:@"transform"];
anim3.values = pitches;
anim3.repeatCount = HUGE_VALF;
anim3.duration = 0.5;
anim3.additive = YES;
anim3.valueFunction = [CAValueFunction functionWithName:kCAValueFunctionRotateZ];
```

Finally, we combine the three animations, assigning the group an explicit duration that will be adopted by the first two animations. As we hand the animation over to the layer displaying the boat, we also change the layer's position to match the final position from the first animation, so that the boat won't jump back to its original position afterward:

```
CAAnimationGroup* group = [CAAnimationGroup animation];
group.animations = [NSArray arrayWithObjects: anim1, anim2, anim3, nil];
group.duration = 8;
[view.layer addAnimation:group forKey:nil];
[CATransaction setDisableActions:YES];
view.layer.position = next;
```

Here are some further CAAnimation properties (from the CAMediaTiming protocol) that come into play especially when animations are grouped:

speed
> The ratio between a child's timescale and the parent's timescale. For example, if a parent and child have the same duration, but the child's speed is 1.5, its animation runs one-and-a-half times as fast as the parent.

fillMode
> Suppose the child animation begins after the parent animation, or ends before the parent animation, or both. What should happen to the appearance of the property being animated, outside the child animation's boundaries? The answer depends on the child's fillMode:

> - kCAFillModeRemoved means the child animation is removed, revealing the layer property at its actual current value whenever the child is not running.

> - kCAFillModeForwards means the final presentation layer value of the child animation remains afterward.

> - kCAFillModeBackwards means the initial presentation layer value of the child animation appears right from the start.

> - kCAFillModeBoth combines the previous two.

CALayer adopts the CAMediaTiming protocol, in the sense that a layer can have a **speed**. This will affect any animation attached to it. A CALayer with a speed of 2 will play a 10-second animation in 5 seconds.

## Transitions

A layer transition is an animation involving two "copies" of a single layer, in which the second "copy" appears to replace the first. It is described by an instance of CATransition (a CAAnimation subclass), which has these chief properties describing the animation:

type
> Your choices are:
> - kCATransitionFade
> - kCATransitionMoveIn
> - kCATransitionPush
> - kCATransitionReveal

subtype
> If the type is not kCATransitionFade, your choices are:
> - kCATransitionFromRight
> - kCATransitionFromLeft
> - kCATransitionFromTop
> - kCATransitionFromBottom

 For historical reasons, the terms "bottom" and "top" in the names of the subtype settings have the opposite of their expected meanings.

To understand the nature of a transition animation, the best approach is to try one, without doing anything else. For example:

```
CATransition* t = [CATransition animation];
t.type = kCATransitionPush;
t.subtype = kCATransitionFromBottom;
[view.layer addAnimation: t forKey: nil];
```

It will help if the layer's frame is visible (give it a **borderWidth**, perhaps). What you'll see, then, is that the entire layer exits moving down from its original place, and another "copy" of the same layer enters moving down from above. In Figure 17-3, the green layer (the wider rectangle) is the superlayer of the red layer (the narrower rectangle, which appears twice). The red layer is normally centered in the green layer, but I've managed to freeze the red layer in the middle of a transition.

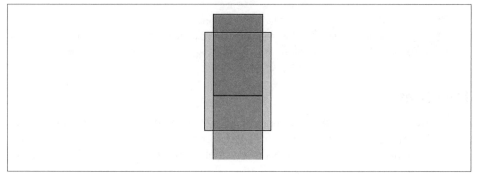

*Figure 17-3. A push transition*

You can use a layer's superlayer to help restrict the visible part of the layer's transition. If the superlayer's `masksToBounds` is NO, the user can see the entire transition; its movements will have the whole screen as their visible boundaries. But if the superlayer's `masksToBounds` is YES, then the visible part of the transition movement is restricted to the superlayer's bounds: it's as if you're seeing the movements through a window that is the superlayer. In Figure 17-3, for example, if the green layer's `masksToBounds` were YES, we wouldn't see any of the part of the transition animation outside its boundaries. A common device is to have the layer that is to be transitioned live inside a superlayer that is exactly the same size and whose `masksToBounds` is YES. This confines the visible transition to the bounds of the layer itself.

Our example appears silly, because there was no motivation for this animation; the two "copies" of the layer are identical. A typical motivation would be that you're changing the contents of a layer and you want to dramatize this. Here, we change the example so that an image of Saturn replaces an image of Mars by pushing it away from above (Figure 17-4). We get a slide effect, as if one layer were being replaced by another; but in fact there is just one layer that holds first one picture, then the other:

```
CATransition* t = [CATransition animation];
t.type = kCATransitionPush;
t.subtype = kCATransitionFromBottom;
[CATransaction setDisableActions:YES];
layer.contents = (id)[[UIImage imageNamed: @"Saturn.gif"] CGImage];
[layer addAnimation: t forKey: nil];
```

## The Animations List

The method that asks for an explicit animation to happen is CALayer's `addAnimation:forKey`. To understand how this method actually works (and what the "key" is), you need to know about a layer's *animations list*.

An animation is an object (a CAAnimation) that modifies how a layer is drawn. It does this merely by being attached to the layer; the layer's drawing mechanism does the rest. A layer maintains a list of animations that are currently in force. To add an animation

---

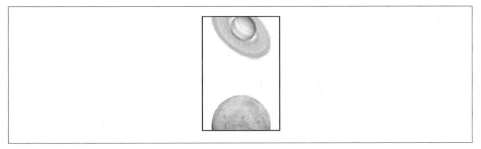

*Figure 17-4. Another push transition*

to this list, you call `addAnimation:forKey:`. When the time comes to draw itself, the layer looks through its animations list and draws itself in accordance with any animations it finds there. (The list of things the layer must do in order to draw itself is sometimes referred to by the documentation as the *render tree*.)

The animations list is maintained in a curious way. The list is not exactly a dictionary, but it behaves somewhat like a dictionary. An animation has a key — the second parameter to `addAnimation:forKey:`. If an animation with a certain key is added to the list, and an animation with that key is already in the list, the one that is already in the list is removed. Thus a rule is maintained that only one animation with a given key can be in the list at a time (the *exclusivity rule*). This explains why sometimes ordering an animation can cancel an animation already ordered or in-flight: the two animations had the same key, so the first one was removed. It is also possible to add an animation with no key (the key is nil); it is then not subject to the exclusivity rule (that is, there can be more than one animation in the list with no key). The order in which animations were added to the list is the order in which they are applied.

The `Key` parameter in `addAnimation:forKey:` is thus *not a property name*. It *could* be a property name, but it can be any arbitrary value. Its purpose is to enforce the exclusivity rule. It does *not* have any meaning with regard to what property a CAPropertyAnimation animates; that is the job of the animation's `keyPath`. This is a most unfortunate and confusing use of the term "key"; I wish they had called this `addAnimation:with-Identifier:` or something like that.

Actually, there *is* a relationship between the "key" in `addAnimation:forKey:` and a CAPropertyAnimation's `keyPath:` if a CAPropertyAnimation's `keyPath` is nil at the time that it is added to a layer with `addAnimation:forKey:`, *that keyPath is set to the call's Key parameter value.* Thus, you can misuse the Key parameter in `addAnimation:forKey:` as a way of specifying what `keyPath` an animation animates. (This fact is not documented, so far as I know, but it's easily verified experimentally, and it should remain reliably true, as implicit animation crucially depends on it.) I have seen many misleading examples that do so, apparently in the mistaken belief that the "key" in `addAnimation:forKey:` is the way you are *supposed* to specify what property to animate. *This is wrong.* Set the CAPropertyAnimation's `keyPath` explicitly (as do all my examples); that's what it's for.

You can use the exclusivity rule to your own advantage, to keep your code from stepping on its own feet. Some code of yours might add an animation to the list using a certain key; then later, some other code might come along and correct this, removing that animation and replacing it with another. By using the same key, the second code is easily able to override the first: "You may have been given some other animation with this key, but throw it away; play this one instead."

In some cases, the key you supply is ignored and a different key is substituted. In particular, the key with which a CATransition is added to the list is always `kCATransition` (which happens to be `@"transition"`); thus there can be only one transition animation in the list.

You can't access the entire animations list directly. You can access the key names of the animations in the list, with `animationKeys`; and you can obtain or remove an animation with a certain key, with `animationForKey:` and `removeAnimationForKey:`; but animations with a nil key are inaccessible. You can, however, remove all animations, including animations with a nil key, using `removeAllAnimations`.

On a multitasking system, when the app is suspended, `removeAllAnimations` is called on all layers for you.

You can think of an animation in a layer's animations list as being the "animation movie" I spoke of at the start of this chapter. As long as an animation is in the list, the movie is present, either waiting to be played or actually playing. An animation that has finished playing is, in general, pointless; the animation should now be removed from the list. Therefore, an animation has a `removedOnCompletion` property, which defaults to YES: when the "movie" is over, the animation removes itself from the list.

You can, if desired, set `removedOnCompletion` to NO. However, even the presence in the list of an animation that has already played might make no difference to the layer's appearance, because an animation's `fillMode` is `kCAFillModeRemoved`, which removes the animation from the layer's drawing when the movie is over. Thus, it can usually do no harm to leave an animation in the list after it has played, but it's not a great idea either, because this is just one more thing for the drawing system to worry about. Typically, you'll leave `removedOnCompletion` set at YES.

On the other hand, there are circumstances where it makes sense to set `removedOn-Completion` to NO and set the animation's `fillMode` to `kCAFillModeForwards` or `kCAFill-ModeBoth`. This causes the layer to keep the appearance of the last frame of the "animation movie" even after the animation is over. For instance, Apple's Metronome example does this for the animation that makes the arm of the metronome appear to rock from one side to the other. The reason is that *another* animation *with the same key* is about to come along and replace this one, and make the arm of the metronome appear to rock to the *other* side. In other words, as long as the metronome is ticking, animation of the arm is *all* the user sees; there is no need to reveal the arm's actual position.

This technique — setting an animation's `fillMode` to `kCAFillModeForwards` and its `removedOnCompletion` to NO — is sometimes treated by beginners as a way of keeping a property from apparently jumping back to its initial value when the animation ends. *This is incorrect.* The correct approach, as I have stated, is to change the property value to match the final frame of the animation. (Even in Apple's Metronome example, the *real* value of the arm's rotation is *also* changed, so that when all animations are removed, the position of the arm is correctly shown.)

# Actions

For the sake of completeness, I will now explain how implicit animation works — that is, how implicit animation is turned into explicit animation behind the scenes. The basis of implicit animation is the *action mechanism*.

## What an Action Is

An *action* is an object that adopts the CAAction protocol. This simply means that it implements `runActionForKey:object:arguments:`.

The action object could do *anything* in response to this message. The notion of an action is completely general. However, in real life, the only class that adopts the CAAction protocol is CAAnimation. So, an animation is a special case of an action, but in fact it is also the *only* case of an action.

What an animation does when it receives `runActionForKey:object:arguments:` is to assume that the second parameter, the `object`, is a layer, and to add itself to that layer's animations list. Thus, for an animation, receiving the `runActionForKey:object:arguments:` message is like being told: "Play yourself!"

You would never send `runActionForKey:object:arguments:` to an animation directly. Rather, this message is sent to an animation for you, as the basis of implicit animation.

## The Action Search

When you set a property of a layer and trigger an implicit animation, you are actually triggering the *action search*. This basically means that the layer searches for an *action object* to which it can send the `runActionForKey:object:arguments:` message; because that action object will be an animation, and because it will respond to this message by adding itself to the layer's animations list, this is the same as saying that the layer searches for an animation to play itself with respect to the layer. The procedure by which the layer searches for this animation is quite elaborate.

The search for an action object begins because you do something that causes the layer to be sent the `actionForKey:` message. Let us presume that what you do is to change the value of an animatable property. (Other things can cause the `actionForKey:` message to be sent, as I'll show later.) The action mechanism then treats the name of the property as a key, and the layer receives `actionForKey:` with that key — and the action search begins.

At each stage of the action search, the following rules are obeyed regarding what is returned from that stage of the search:

*An action object*
> If an action object (an animation) is produced, that is the end of the search. The action mechanism sends that animation the `runActionForKey:object:arguments:` message; the animation responds by adding itself to the layer's animations list.

*nil*
> If nil is produced, the search continues to the next stage.

`[NSNull null]`
> If `[NSNull null]` is produced, this means, "Do nothing and stop searching." The search comes to an end; there will be no implicit animation.

The action search proceeds as follows:

1. The layer might terminate the search before it even starts. For example, the layer will do this if it is the underlying layer of a view, or if a property is set to the same value it already has. In such a case, there should be no implicit animation, so the whole mechanism is nipped in the bud.

2. If the layer has a delegate that implements `actionForLayer:forKey:`, that message is sent to the delegate, with this layer as the layer and the property name as the key. If an animation or `[NSNull null]` is returned, the search ends.

3. The layer has a property called `actions`, which is a dictionary. If there is an entry in this dictionary with the given key, that value is used, and the search ends.

4. The layer has a property called `style` which is a dictionary. If there is an entry in this dictionary with the key `actions`, it is assumed to be a dictionary; if this `actions` dictionary has an entry with the given key, that value is used, and the search ends. Otherwise, if there is an entry in the `style` dictionary called `style`, the same search is performed within it, and so on recursively until either an `actions` entry with the given key is found (the search ends) or there are no more `style` entries (the search continues).

 If the `style` dictionary sounds profoundly weird, that's because it is profoundly weird. It is actually a special case of a larger, separate mechanism, which is also profoundly weird, having to do not with actions, but with a CALayer's implementation of KVC. When you call `valueForKey:` on a layer, if the key is undefined by the layer itself, the `style` dictionary is consulted. I have never written or seen code that uses this mechanism for anything, and I'll say no more about it.

5. The layer's class is sent `defaultActionForKey:`, with the property name as the key. If an animation or `[NSNull null]` is returned, the search ends.

6. If the search reaches this point, a default animation is supplied, as appropriate. For a property animation, this is a plain vanilla CABasicAnimation.

Both the delegate's `actionForLayer:forKey:` and the subclass's `defaultActionForKey:` are declared as returning an `id<CAAction>`. To return `[NSNull null]`, therefore, you'll need to typecast it to `id<CAAction>` to quiet the compiler; you're lying (NSNull does not adopt the CAAction protocol), but it doesn't matter.

## Hooking Into the Action Search

You can affect the action search at various stages to modify what happens when the search is triggered. For example, you could cause some stage of the search to produce an animation; that animation will then be used. Assuming that the search is triggered by setting an animatable layer property, you would then be affecting how implicit animation behaves.

You will probably want your animation to be fairly minimal. You may have no way of knowing the former and current values of the property that is being changed, so it would then be pointless (and very strange) to set a CABasicAnimation's `fromValue` or `toValue`. Moreover, although animation properties that you don't set can be set through CATransaction, in the usual manner for implicit property animation, animation properties that you *do* set can *not* be overridden through CATransaction. For example, if you set the animation's duration, a call to CATransaction's `setAnimationDuration:` class method cannot change it.

Let's say we want a certain layer's duration for an implicit `position` animation to be 5 seconds. We can achieve this with a minimally configured animation, like this:

```
CABasicAnimation* ba = [CABasicAnimation animation];
ba.duration = 5;
```

The idea now is to situate this animation, `ba`, where it will be produced by the action search when implicit animation is triggered on the `position` property of our layer. We could, for instance, put it into the layer's `actions` dictionary:

```
layer.actions = [NSDictionary dictionaryWithObject: ba forKey: @"position"];
```

The result is that when we set that layer's `position`, if an implicit animation results, its duration is 5 seconds, even if we try to change it through CATransaction:

```
[CATransaction setAnimationDuration:1];
layer.position = CGPointMake(100,200); // animation takes 5 seconds
```

Let's use that example to tease apart how the action mechanism makes implicit animation work:

1. You set the value of the layer's `position` property.
2. If your setting does not represent a change in the `position` value, or if this layer is a view's underlying layer, that's the end of the story; there is no implicit property animation.
3. Otherwise, the action search begins. There is no delegate in this case, so the search proceeds to the `actions` dictionary.
4. There is an entry under the key `@"position"` in the `actions` dictionary (because we put it there), and it is an animation. That animation is the action, and that is the end of the search.
5. The animation is sent `runActionForKey:object:arguments:`.
6. The animation responds by calling `[object addAnimation:self forKey: @"position"]`. The animation's `keyPath` was nil, *so this call also sets the keyPath to the same key!* Thus, there is now an animation in the layer's animations list that animates its `position`, because its `keyPath` is `@"position"`. Moreover, we didn't set the `fromValue` or `toValue`, so the property's previous and new values are used. The animation therefore shows the layer moving from its current position to `(100,200)`.

Using the layer's `actions` dictionary to set default animations is a somewhat inflexible way to hook into the action search, however. It's a good way to disable implicit animation for specific properties; just set the value for that key to `[NSNull null]`. But it has the disadvantage in general that you must write your animation beforehand.

By contrast, if you set the layer's delegate to a instance that responds to `actionForLayer: forKey:`, your code runs at the time the animation is needed, and you have access to the layer that is to be animated. So you can create the animation on the fly, possibly modifying it in response to current circumstances.

Recall also that CATransaction implements KVC to allow you to set and retrieve the value of arbitrary keys. We can take advantage of this fact to pass an additional message from the code that sets the property value, and triggers the action search, to the code that supplies the action. This works because they both take place within the same transaction.

In this example, we use the layer delegate to change the default `position` animation so that instead of being a straight line, the path has a slight waggle. To do this, the delegate constructs a keyframe animation. The animation depends on the old `position` value and the new `position` value; the delegate can get the former direct from the layer, but the latter must be handed to the delegate somehow. Here, a CATransaction key @"newP" is used to communicate this information. When we set the layer's `position`, we must remember to put its future value where the delegate can retrieve it, like this:

```
CGPoint newP = CGPointMake(200,300);
[CATransaction setValue: [NSValue valueWithCGPoint: newP] forKey: @"newP"];
layer.position = newP; // the delegate will waggle the layer into place
```

The delegate is called by the action search and constructs the animation:

```
- (id < CAAction >)actionForLayer:(CALayer *)lay forKey:(NSString *)key {
    if ([key isEqualToString: @"position"]) {
        CGPoint oldP = layer.position;
        CGPoint newP = [[CATransaction valueForKey: @"newP"] CGPointValue];
        CGFloat d = sqrt(pow(oldP.x - newP.x, 2) + pow(oldP.y - newP.y, 2));
        CGFloat r = d/3.0;
        CGFloat theta = atan2(newP.y - oldP.y, newP.x - oldP.x);
        CGFloat wag = 10*M_PI/180.0;
        CGPoint p1 = CGPointMake(oldP.x + r*cos(theta+wag),
                                 oldP.y + r*sin(theta+wag));
        CGPoint p2 = CGPointMake(oldP.x + r*2*cos(theta-wag),
                                 oldP.y + r*2*sin(theta-wag));
        CAKeyframeAnimation* anim = [CAKeyframeAnimation animation];
        anim.values = [NSArray arrayWithObjects:
                        [NSValue valueWithCGPoint:oldP],
                        [NSValue valueWithCGPoint:p1],
                        [NSValue valueWithCGPoint:p2],
                        [NSValue valueWithCGPoint:newP],
                        nil];
        anim.calculationMode = kCAAnimationCubic;
        return anim;
    }
    return nil;
}
```

Finally, for the sake of completeness, I'll demonstrate overriding `defaultActionFor-Key:`. This code would go into a CALayer subclass where setting its `contents` is to trigger a push transition from the left:

```
+ (id < CAAction >)defaultActionForKey:(NSString *)aKey {
    if ([aKey isEqualToString:@"contents"]) {
        CATransition* tr = [CATransition animation];
        tr.type = kCATransitionPush;
        tr.subtype = kCATransitionFromLeft;
        return tr;
    }
    return [super defaultActionForKey: aKey];
}
```

## Nonproperty Actions

Changing a property is not the only way to trigger a search for an action; an action search is also triggered when a layer is added to a superlayer (key kCAOnOrderIn) and when a layer's sublayers are changed by adding or removing a sublayer (key @"sublayers"). We can watch for these keys in the delegate and return an animation.

 Unfortunately, these triggers and their keys are incorrectly described in Apple's documentation, and there are additional triggers and keys that are not mentioned there.

In this example, when our layer is added to a superlayer, we make it "pop" into view by fading quickly in from an opacity of 0 and at the same time scaling its transform to make it momentarily appear a little larger:

```
- (id < CAAction >)actionForLayer:(CALayer *)lay forKey:(NSString *)key {
    if ([key isEqualToString:kCAOnOrderIn]) {
        CABasicAnimation* anim1 =
            [CABasicAnimation animationWithKeyPath:@"opacity"];
        anim1.fromValue = [NSNumber numberWithFloat: 0.0];
        anim1.toValue = [NSNumber numberWithFloat: lay.opacity];
        CABasicAnimation* anim2 =
            [CABasicAnimation animationWithKeyPath:@"transform"];
        anim2.toValue = [NSValue valueWithCATransform3D:
                        CATransform3DScale(lay.transform, 1.1, 1.1, 1.0)];
        anim2.autoreverses = YES;
        anim2.duration = 0.1;
        CAAnimationGroup* group = [CAAnimationGroup animation];
        group.animations = [NSArray arrayWithObjects: anim1, anim2, nil];
        group.duration = 0.2;
        return group;
    }
}
```

The documentation says that when a layer is removed from a superlayer, an action is sought under the key kCAOnOrderOut. This is true but useless, because by the time the action is sought, the layer has already been removed from the superlayer, so returning an animation has no visible effect. Similarly, an animation returned as an action when a layer's hidden is set to YES is never played. Apple has admitted that this is a bug. A possible workaround is to trigger the animation via the **opacity** property, perhaps in conjunction with a CATransaction key, and remove the layer afterward:

```
[CATransaction setCompletionBlock: ^{
    [layer removeFromSuperlayer];
}];
[CATransaction setValue:@"" forKey:@"byebye"];
layer.opacity = 0;
```

Now **actionForLayer:forKey:** can test for the incoming key @"opacity" and the CA-Transaction key @"byebye", and return the animation appropriate to removal from the superlayer.

# CHAPTER 18

# Touches

*[Winifred the Woebegone illustrates hit-testing:] Hey*
*nonny nonny, is it you? — Hey nonny nonny nonny no!*
*— Hey nonny nonny, is it you? — Hey nonny nonny*
*nonny no!*

—Marshall Barer, *Once Upon a Mattress*

A *touch* is an instance of the user putting a finger on the screen. The system and the hardware, working together, know *when* a finger contacts the screen and *where* it is. (Fingers are fat, but the system and the hardware cleverly reduce the finger's location to a single appropriate point.)

A UIView, by virtue of being a UIResponder, is the visible locus of touches. There are other UIResponder subclasses, but none of them is visible on the screen. What the user sees are views; what the user is touching are views. (The user may also see layers, but a layer is not a UIResponder and is not involved with touches. I'll talk later about how to make it seem as if the user can touch a layer.)

It would make sense, therefore, if every touch were reported directly to the view in which it occurred. However, what the system "sees" is not particular views but an app as a whole. So a touch is represented as an object (a UITouch instance) which is bundled up in an envelope (a UIEvent) which the system delivers to your app. It is then up to your app to deliver the envelope to an appropriate UIView. In the vast majority of cases, this will happen automatically the way you expect, and you will respond to a touch by way of the view in which the touch occurred.

In fact, usually you won't concern yourself with UIEvents and UITouches at all. Most built-in interface views deal with these low-level touch reports themselves, and notify your code at a higher level. When a UIButton emits an action message to report a control event such as Touch Up Inside (Chapter 11), it has already performed a reduction of a complex sequence of touches ("the user put a finger down inside me and then, possibly with some dragging hither and yon, raised it when it was still reasonably close to me"). A UITextField reports touches on the keyboard as changes in its own text. A UITable-

View reports that the user selected a cell. A UIScrollView, when dragged, reports that it scrolled; when pinched outward, it reports that it zoomed. Some interface views respond to touches internally without reporting to your code at all; for example, a UIWebView, when dragged, just scrolls.

Nevertheless, it is useful to know how to respond to touches directly, so that you can implement your own touchable views, and so that you understand what Cocoa's built-in views are actually doing. This chapter discusses touch detection and response by views (and other UIResponders) at their lowest level, along with a slightly higher-level mechanism, gesture recognizers, that categorizes touches into gesture types for you; then it deconstructs the touch-delivery architecture by which touches are reported to your views in the first place.

# Touch Events and Views

Imagine a screen that the user is not touching at all: the screen is "finger-free." Now the user touches the screen with one or more fingers. From that moment to the time the screen is once again finger-free, all touches and finger movements together constitute what Apple calls a single *multitouch sequence*.

The system reports to your app, during a given multitouch sequence, every change in finger configuration, so that your app can figure out what the user is doing. Every such report is a UIEvent. In fact, every report having to do with the same multitouch sequence is *the same UIEvent instance*, arriving repeatedly, each time there's a change in finger configuration.

Every UIEvent reporting a change in the user's finger configuration contains one or more UITouch objects. Each UITouch object corresponds to a single finger; conversely, every finger touching the screen is represented in the UIEvent by a UITouch object. Once a certain UITouch instance has been created to represent a finger that has touched the screen, *the same UITouch instance* is used to represent that finger throughout this multitouch sequence until the finger leaves the screen.

Now, it might sound as if the system has to bombard the app with huge numbers of reports constantly during a multitouch sequence. But that's not really true. The system needs to report only *changes* in the finger configuration. For a given UITouch object (representing, remember, a specific finger), only four things can happen. These are called *touch phases*, and are described by a UITouch instance's `phase` property:

UITouchPhaseBegan
> The finger touched the screen for the first time; this UITouch instance has just been created. This is always the first phase, and arrives only once.

UITouchPhaseMoved
> The finger moved upon the screen.

**UITouchPhaseStationary**

The finger remained on the screen without moving. Why is it necessary to report this? Well, remember, once a UITouch instance has been created, it must be present every time the UIEvent arrives. So if the UIEvent arrives because something *else* happened (e.g., a new finger touched the screen), we must report what *this* finger has been doing, even if it has been doing nothing.

**UITouchPhaseEnded**

The finger left the screen. Like **UITouchPhaseBegan**, this phase arrives only once. The UITouch instance will now be destroyed and will no longer appear in UIEvents for this multitouch sequence.

Those four phases are sufficient to describe everything that a finger can do. Actually, there is one more possible phase:

**UITouchPhaseCancelled**

The system has aborted this multitouch sequence because something interrupted it.

What might interrupt a multitouch sequence? There are many possibilities. Perhaps the user clicked the Home button or the screen lock button in the middle of the sequence. A local notification alert may have appeared (Chapter 26); on an actual iPhone, a call might have come in. (As we shall see, a gesture recognizer recognizing its gesture may also trigger touch cancellation.) The point is, if you're dealing with touches yourself, you cannot afford to ignore touch cancellation; they are your opportunity to get things into a coherent state when the sequence is interrupted.

When a UITouch first appears (**UITouchPhaseBegan**), your app works out which UIView it is associated with. (I'll give full details, later in this chapter, as to how it does that.) This view is then set as the touch's **view** property; from then on, this UITouch is *always* associated with this view. In other words, *a touch's view is that touch's view forever* (until that finger leaves the screen).

A UIEvent is distributed to all the views of all the UITouches it contains. (The same UIEvent containing the same UITouches can be sent to multiple views; these are programmatic objects, not real-world envelopes containing actual fingers.) Conversely, if a view is sent a UIEvent, it's because that UIEvent contains at least one UITouch whose **view** is this view.

If every UITouch in a UIEvent associated with a certain UIView has the phase **UITouchPhaseStationary**, that UIEvent is *not* sent to that UIView. There's no point, because as far as that view is concerned, nothing happened.

# Receiving Touches

A UIView, being a UIResponder, inherits four methods corresponding to the four UITouch phases that require UIEvent delivery. A UIEvent is delivered to a view by calling one or more of these four methods (the *touches... methods*):

touchesBegan:withEvent:
> A finger touched the screen, creating a UITouch.

touchesMoved:withEvent:
> A finger previously reported to this view with touchesBegan:withEvent: has moved.

touchesEnded:withEvent:
> A finger previously reported to this view with touchesBegan:withEvent: has left the screen.

touchesCancelled:withEvent:
> We are bailing out on a finger previously reported to this view with touchesBegan:withEvent:.

The parameters of these methods are:

*The relevant touches*
> These are the event's touches whose phase corresponds to the name of the method and (normally) whose view is this view. They arrive as an NSSet (Chapter 10). If you know for a fact that there is only one touch in the set, or that any touch in the set will do, you can retrieve it with anyObject (an NSSet doesn't implement lastObject because a set is unordered).

*The event*
> This is the UIEvent instance. It contains its touches as an NSSet, which you can retrieve with the allTouches message. This means *all* the event's touches, including but not necessarily limited to those in the first parameter; there might be touches in a different phase or intended for some other view. You can call touchesForView: or touchesForWindow: to ask for the set of touches associated with a particular view or window.

A UITouch has some useful methods and properties:

locationInView:, previousLocationInView:
> The current and previous location of this touch with respect to the coordinate system of a given view. The view you'll be interested in will often be self or self.superview; supply nil to get the location with respect to the window. The previous location will be of interest only if the phase is UITouchPhaseMoved.

timestamp
> When the touch last changed. A touch is timestamped when it is created (UITouchPhaseBegan) and each time it moves (UITouchPhaseMoved).

tapCount

> If two touches are in roughly the same place in quick succession, and the first one is brief, the second one may be characterized as a repeat of the first. They are different touch objects, but the second will be assigned a tapCount one larger than the previous one. The default is 1, so if (for example) a touch's tapCount is 3 then this is the third tap in quick succession in roughly the same spot.

view

> The view with which this touch is associated.

Here are some additional UIEvent properties:

type

> This will be UIEventTypeTouches. There are other event types, but you're not going to receive any of them this way.

timestamp

> When the event occurred.

So, when we say that a certain view *is receiving a touch*, that is a shorthand expression meaning that it is being sent a UIEvent containing this UITouch, over and over, by calling one of its touches... methods, corresponding to the phase this touch is in, from the time the touch is created until the time it is destroyed.

# Restricting Touches

Touch events can be turned off entirely at the application level with UIApplication's beginIgnoringInteractionEvents. It is quite common to do this during animations and other lengthy operations during which responding to a touch could cause undesirable results. This call should be balanced by endIgnoringInteractionEvents. Pairs can be nested, in which case interactivity won't be restored until the outermost endIgnoring-InteractionEvents has been reached.

A number of high-level UIView properties also restrict the delivery of touches to particular views:

userInteractionEnabled

> If set to NO, this view (along with its subviews) is excluded from receiving touches.

hidden

> If set to YES, this view (along with its subviews) is excluded from receiving touches.

opacity

> If set to 0.0 (or extremely close to it), this view (along with its subviews) is excluded from receiving touches.

**multipleTouchEnabled**

If set to NO, this view never receives more than one touch simultaneously; once it receives a touch, it doesn't receive any other touches until that first touch has ended.

**exclusiveTouch**

This is the only one of these properties that can't be set in the nib. An exclusive-Touch view receives a touch only if no other views in the same window have touches associated with them; once an exclusiveTouch view has received a touch, then while that touch exists no other view in the same window receives any touches.

 A UIWindow ignores multipleTouchEnabled; it always receives multiple touches. Moreover, a UIWindow's behavior with respect to exclusive-Touch is unreliable, presumably because it is not itself a view in the window.

# Interpreting Touches

To figure out what's going on as touches are received by a view, your code must essentially function as a kind of state machine. You'll receive various touches... method calls, and your response will partly depend upon what happened previously, so you'll have to record somehow, such as in instance variables, the information that you'll need in order to decide what to do when the next touches... method is called. Such an architecture can make writing and maintaining touch-analysis code quite tricky. Moreover, although you can distinguish a particular UITouch or UIEvent object over time by keeping a reference to it, you mustn't retain that reference; it doesn't belong to you.

Thanks to the existence, starting in iOS 3.2, of gesture recognizers (the subject of the next section), in most cases you won't have to interpret touches at all; you'll let a gesture recognizer do most of that work. Even so, it is beneficial to be conversant with the nature of touch interpretation; this will help you interact with a gesture recognizer, write your own gesture recognizer, or subclass an existing one. Furthermore, not every touch sequence can be codified through a gesture recognizer; sometimes, directly interpreting touches is the best approach. Therefore, even though you might not write the sort of code discussed in this section, you should read the section anyway.

To illustrate the business of interpreting touches, we'll start with a view that can be dragged with the user's finger. For simplicity, I'll assume that this view receives only a single touch at a time. (This assumption is easy to enforce by setting the view's multiple-TouchEnabled to NO, which is the default.)

The trick to making a view follow the user's finger is to realize that a view is positioned by its center, which is in superview coordinates, but the user's finger might not be at the center of the view. So at every stage of the drag we must use instance variables to record both the view's center (in superview coordinates) and the position of the user's finger (also in superview coordinates); then, however much the user's finger has moved, that's how much we must move the center. So we maintain two state variables, p and origC:

```
- (void) touchesBegan:(NSSet *)touches withEvent:(UIEvent *)event {
    self->p = [[touches anyObject] locationInView: self.superview];
    self->origC = self.center;
}

- (void) touchesMoved:(NSSet *)touches withEvent:(UIEvent *)event {
    CGPoint loc = [[touches anyObject] locationInView: self.superview];
    CGFloat deltaX = loc.x - self->p.x;
    CGFloat deltaY = loc.y - self->p.y;
    CGPoint c = self.center;
    c.x = self->origC.x + deltaX;
    c.y = self->origC.y + deltaY;
    self.center = c;
    self->p = [[touches anyObject] locationInView: self.superview];
    self->origC = self.center;
}
```

Next, let's add a restriction that the view can be dragged only vertically or horizontally. All we have to do is hold one coordinate steady; but which coordinate? Everything seems to depend on what the user does initially. So we'll do a one-time test the first time we receive touchesMoved:withEvent:. Now we're maintaining two *more* state variables, decided and horiz:

```
- (void) touchesBegan:(NSSet *)touches withEvent:(UIEvent *)event {
    self->p = [[touches anyObject] locationInView: self.superview];
    self->origC = self.center;
    self->decided = NO;
}

- (void) touchesMoved:(NSSet *)touches withEvent:(UIEvent *)event {
    if (!self->decided) {
        self->decided = YES;
        CGPoint then = [[touches anyObject] previousLocationInView: self];
        CGPoint now = [[touches anyObject] locationInView: self];
        CGFloat deltaX = fabs(then.x - now.x);
        CGFloat deltaY = fabs(then.y - now.y);
        self->horiz = (deltaX >= deltaY);
    }
    CGPoint loc = [[touches anyObject] locationInView: self.superview];
    CGFloat deltaX = loc.x - self->p.x;
    CGFloat deltaY = loc.y - self->p.y;
    CGPoint c = self.center;
    if (self->horiz)
        c.x = self->origC.x + deltaX;
    else
        c.y = self->origC.y + deltaY;
    self.center = c;
    self->p = [[touches anyObject] locationInView: self.superview];
    self->origC = self.center;
}
```

Finally, we'll make things a little more realistic by allowing the user to "fling" the view horizontally or vertically. This is a bit tricky because we must know how fast the user's finger was moving when it "let go" of the view. Speed is a function of change in position and change in time. We already know how to get the position; the time we can retrieve from the event's `timestamp`. It will suffice to use the last two position and timestamp pairs; that's a decent measure of the finger's final speed. But we do not know which two will be the last, so we must calculate the speed using *every* pair, as long as this touch exists.

So now we're recording two *more* state variables, `time` and `speed`. The speed we'll actually use is the last one recorded in `touchesMoved:withEvent:`. Then in `touchesEnded:withEvent:` we'll animate the continued movement. This isn't a classy physics simulation, but it feels natural enough, and anyhow, it's only an example:

```
- (void) touchesBegan:(NSSet *)touches withEvent:(UIEvent *)event {
    self->p = [[touches anyObject] locationInView: self.superview];
    self->origC = self.center;
    self->decided = NO;
    self->time = event.timestamp;
}

- (void) touchesMoved:(NSSet *)touches withEvent:(UIEvent *)event {
    if (!self->decided) {
        self->decided = YES;
        CGPoint then = [[touches anyObject] previousLocationInView: self];
        CGPoint now = [[touches anyObject] locationInView: self];
        CGFloat deltaX = fabs(then.x - now.x);
        CGFloat deltaY = fabs(then.y - now.y);
        self->horiz = (deltaX >= deltaY);
    }
    CGPoint loc = [[touches anyObject] locationInView: self.superview];
    CGFloat deltaX = loc.x - self->p.x;
    CGFloat deltaY = loc.y - self->p.y;
    CGPoint c = self.center;
    if (self->horiz)
        c.x = self->origC.x + deltaX;
    else
        c.y = self->origC.y + deltaY;
    self.center = c;
    //
    CGFloat elapsed = event.timestamp - self->time;
    loc = [[touches anyObject] locationInView: self.superview];
    deltaX = loc.x - self->p.x;
    deltaY = loc.y - self->p.y;
    CGFloat delta = self->horiz ? deltaX : deltaY;
    self->speed = delta/elapsed;
    //
    self->p = [[touches anyObject] locationInView: self.superview];
    self->origC = self.center;
    self->time = event.timestamp;
}

- (void) touchesEnded:(NSSet *)touches withEvent:(UIEvent *)event {
```

```
    CGFloat sp = self->speed;
    NSString* property = self->horiz ? @"position.x" : @"position.y";
    CGFloat start = self->horiz ? self.layer.position.x : self.layer.position.y;
    CGFloat dur = 0.1
    CGFloat end = start + sp * dur;
    CABasicAnimation* anim1 = [CABasicAnimation animationWithKeyPath: property];
    anim1.duration = dur;
    anim1.fromValue = [NSNumber numberWithFloat: start];
    anim1.toValue = [NSNumber numberWithFloat: end];
    anim1.timingFunction =
        [CAMediaTimingFunction functionWithName:kCAMediaTimingFunctionEaseOut];
    [CATransaction setDisableActions:YES];
    [self.layer setValue: [NSNumber numberWithFloat: end] forKeyPath: property];
    [self.layer addAnimation: anim1 forKey: nil];
}
```

That example shows how the interplay between the various touches... calls works, and how it requires that we maintain state between calls. But we have not been dealing, so far, with multiple simultaneous touches. So let's start over. Once again, we'll have a view that the user can drag freely around the screen. But this time, to reduce the number of state variables, instead of recording two values between calls, our center and the touch's position in the same coordinates, we'll record just one, the difference between them (expressed as a point, though in fact it is really an x-difference and a y-difference):

```
- (void) touchesBegan:(NSSet *)touches withEvent:(UIEvent *)event {
    // record delta between initial touch point and center, in a CGFloat ivar
    CGPoint initialTouch = [[touches anyObject] locationInView: self.superview];
    self->p = CGPointMake(initialTouch.x - self.center.x,
                          initialTouch.y - self.center.y);
}

- (void) touchesMoved:(NSSet *)touches withEvent:(UIEvent *)event {
    CGPoint where = [[touches anyObject] locationInView: self.superview];
    where.x -= self->p.x;
    where.y -= self->p.y;
    self.center = where;
}
```

Now imagine that our view's multipleTouchEnabled is YES. Then the user might start by dragging us with one finger, perhaps, but then put down a second finger, lift the initial finger, and continue dragging us with that second finger — whose delta from the center is different. So we're going to have to maintain the deltas, from the center, of *every* finger that touches down, so that no matter which finger is reported as moving, we have a delta for it.

So we need to maintain a dictionary in which we can look up each delta by way of the touch to which it belongs. But we cannot use a UITouch object as a key in an NSDictionary, because an NSDictionary copies its keys, and what we want is an identifier that matches the UITouch object itself. Apple's documentation suggests using a CFDictionary (the Core Foundation version of an NSDictionary), but here's another way:

from a UITouch object we'll derive a unique identifier, namely the string representing its location in memory, which we can obtain using `stringWithFormat:`.

So we'll start by putting a category on UITouch, to derive this unique identifier:

```
@interface UITouch (additions)
- (NSString*) uid;
@end

@implementation UITouch (additions)
- (NSString*) uid {
    return [NSString stringWithFormat: @"%p", self];
}
@end
```

Now we must maintain our dictionary throughout the period while we have touches, creating it on our first touch and destroying it when our last touch is gone:

```
- (void) touchesBegan:(NSSet *)touches withEvent:(UIEvent *)event {
    // create and retain dictionary if it doesn't exist
    if (!self->d)
        self->d = [[NSMutableDictionary alloc] init];
    // store delta for *every* new touch in dictionary
    for (UITouch* t in touches) {
        CGPoint initialTouch = [t locationInView: self.superview];
        CGPoint delta = CGPointMake(initialTouch.x - self.center.x,
                                    initialTouch.y - self.center.y);
        [d setObject: [NSValue valueWithCGPoint:delta] forKey:[t uid]];
    }
}

- (void) touchesMoved:(NSSet *)touches withEvent:(UIEvent *)event {
    // *any* touch that has moved will do to reposition ourselves
    UITouch* t = [touches anyObject];
    CGPoint where = [t locationInView: self.superview];
    CGPoint delta = [[self->d objectForKey: [t uid]] CGPointValue];
    where.x -= delta.x;
    where.y -= delta.y;
    self.center = where;
}

- (void) touchesEnded:(NSSet *)touches withEvent:(UIEvent *)event {
    // remove *every* touch that has ended from our dictionary
    for (UITouch* t in touches)
        [self->d removeObjectForKey:[t uid]];
    // if *all* touches are gone, release dictionary, nilify pointer
    if (![self->d count]) {
        [self->d release];
        self->d = nil;
    }
}

- (void) touchesCancelled:(NSSet *)touches withEvent:(UIEvent *)event {
    // bailing out: release dictionary, nilify pointer
    [self->d release];
```

```
    self->d = nil;
}
```

The result is structurally sound enough (that is, our dictionary is working perfectly), but the behavior of this interface is faulty; we are not taking care of every possibility coherently. When the view moves, if multiple fingers are down, they may have travelled different amounts, which will make our stored delta wrong for at least one of them. That's a bug. So we should recalculate our deltas every time `touchesMoved:with-Event:` is called.

Moreover, if the user puts down two fingers and moves one, the view moves. Whether this is right or wrong is up to us. Let's decide that it's wrong, and that the stationary finger should take precedence, holding the view in place. Here's a new version of `touchesMoved:withEvent::`

```
- (void) touchesMoved:(NSSet *)touches withEvent:(UIEvent *)event {
    BOOL move = YES;
    // if any touches are stationary, don't move
    for (UITouch* t in [event touchesForView:self])
        if (t.phase == UITouchPhaseStationary)
            move = NO;
    if (move) {
        // *any* touch that has moved will do to reposition ourselves
        UITouch* t = [touches anyObject];
        CGPoint where = [t locationInView: self.superview];
        CGPoint delta = [[self->d objectForKey: [t uid]] CGPointValue];
        where.x -= delta.x;
        where.y -= delta.y;
        self.center = where;
    }
    // recalculate deltas for all touches in dictionary
    for (UITouch* t in [event touchesForView:self]) {
        CGPoint tpos = [t locationInView: self.superview];
        CGPoint delta = CGPointMake(tpos.x - self.center.x,
                                    tpos.y - self.center.y);
        if ([d objectForKey:[t uid]])
            [d setObject: [NSValue valueWithCGPoint:delta] forKey:[t uid]];
    }
}
```

Another modification might be to choose more wisely which touch to follow if multiple touches move. Instead of selecting any old touch, we might decide to use the one that moves furthest. Still another improvement might be to "damp down" any movement smaller than 5 pixels from our previous position; this makes the view less sensitive to finger tremors, and, ironically, because there are fewer commands to change position, the view keeps up with a moving finger more successfully. Indeed, we could probably go on tweaking our code forever, making it more and more complicated. And yet our original desire ("be draggable") was so simple!

In the previous code, where we were maintaining a dictionary of touches associated with this view, it was easy to know when all our touches were gone: it was when the dictionary became empty. If you're not maintaining a dictionary, the technique (helpfully provided in Apple's documentation) is to compare the number of touches in the first parameter of `touchesEnded:withEvent:` with the number of touches for this view in the event itself:

```
if ([touches count] == [[event touchesForView:self] count])
```

If those numbers are equal, then all the touches associated with this view have reached `UITouchPhaseEnded` and henceforth this view has no touches.

# Gesture Recognizers

Writing and maintaining a state machine that interprets touches across a combination of three or four `touches...` methods is hard enough when a view confines itself to expecting only one kind of gesture, such as dragging. It becomes even more involved when a view wants to accept and respond differently to different kinds of gesture. This was a serious problem for developers up through version 3.1.3 of the system, and it was compounded by the fact that users were becoming accustomed to a vocabulary of basic gestures that every developer had to implement independently.

In iOS 3.2, Apple took a major step toward alleviating these difficulties by introducing gesture recognizers, which standardize common gestures and allow the code for different gestures to be separated and encapsulated into different objects.

## Distinguishing Gestures Manually

To see the value of gesture recognizers, it will help to try first to write code that differentiates gestures without them.

Imagine first a view that distinguishes between a finger tapping briefly and a finger remaining down for a longer time. We can't know how long a tap is until it's over, so one approach might be to wait until then before deciding:

```
- (void) touchesBegan:(NSSet *)touches withEvent:(UIEvent *)event {
    self->time = [[touches anyObject] timestamp];
}

- (void) touchesEnded:(NSSet *)touches withEvent:(UIEvent *)event {
    NSTimeInterval diff = event.timestamp - self->time;
    if (diff < 0.4)
        NSLog(@"short");
    else
        NSLog(@"long");
}
```

On the other hand, one might argue that if a tap hasn't ended after some set time (here, 0.4 seconds), we know that it is long, and so we could begin responding to it without waiting for it to end. The problem is that we don't automatically get an event after 0.4 seconds. So we'll create one, using delayed performance:

```
- (void) touchesBegan:(NSSet *)touches withEvent:(UIEvent *)event {
    self->time = [[touches anyObject] timestamp];
    [self performSelector:@selector(touchWasLong) withObject:nil afterDelay:0.4];
}

- (void) touchesEnded:(NSSet *)touches withEvent:(UIEvent *)event {
    NSTimeInterval diff = event.timestamp - self->time;
    if (diff < 0.4)
        NSLog(@"short");
}

- (void) touchWasLong {
    NSLog(@"long");
}
```

But there's a bug. If the tap is short, we report that it was short, but we *also* report that it was long. That's because the delayed call to `touchWasLong` arrives anyway. We could use some sort of boolean flag to tell us when to ignore that call, but there's a better way: NSObject has a class method that lets us cancel any pending delayed performance calls. So:

```
- (void) touchesBegan:(NSSet *)touches withEvent:(UIEvent *)event {
    self->time = [[touches anyObject] timestamp];
    [self performSelector:@selector(touchWasLong) withObject:nil afterDelay:0.4];
}

- (void) touchesEnded:(NSSet *)touches withEvent:(UIEvent *)event {
    NSTimeInterval diff = event.timestamp - self->time;
    if (diff < 0.4) {
        NSLog(@"short");
        [NSObject cancelPreviousPerformRequestsWithTarget:self
                                    selector:@selector(touchWasLong)
                                    object:nil];
    }
}

- (void) touchWasLong {
    NSLog(@"long");
}
```

Here's another use of the same technique. We'll distinguish between a single tap and a double tap. The UITouch `tapCount` property already makes this distinction, but that, by itself, is not enough to help us react differently to the two. What we must do, having received a tap whose `tapCount` is 1, is to delay responding to it long enough to give a second tap a chance to arrive. This is unfortunate, because it means that if the user intends a single tap, some time will elapse before anything happens in response to it; however, there's nothing we can easily do about that.

Distributing our various tasks correctly is a bit tricky. We *know* when we have a double tap as early as `touchesBegan:withEvent:`, so that's when we cancel our delayed response to a single tap, but we *respond* to the double tap in `touchesEnded:withEvent:`. We don't start our delayed response to a single tap until `touchesEnded:withEvent:`, because what matters is the time between the taps as a whole, not between the starts of the taps. This code is adapted from Apple's own example:

```
- (void) touchesBegan:(NSSet *)touches withEvent:(UIEvent *)event {
    int ct = [[touches anyObject] tapCount];
    if (ct == 2) {
        [NSObject cancelPreviousPerformRequestsWithTarget:self
                                      selector:@selector(singleTap)
                                        object:nil];
    }
}

- (void) touchesEnded:(NSSet *)touches withEvent:(UIEvent *)event {
    int ct = [[touches anyObject] tapCount];
    if (ct == 1)
        [self performSelector:@selector(singleTap) withObject:nil afterDelay:0.3];
    if (ct == 2)
        NSLog(@"double tap");
}

- (void) singleTap {
    NSLog(@"single tap");
}
```

Now let's consider combining our detection for a single or double tap with our earlier code for dragging a view horizontally or vertically. This is to be a view that can detect three kinds of gesture: a single tap, a double tap, and a drag. We must include the code all possibilities and make sure they don't interfere with each other. The result is a forced join between two sets of code, along with an additional pair of state variables to track the decision between the tap gestures on the one hand and the drag gesture on the other:

```
- (void) touchesBegan:(NSSet *)touches withEvent:(UIEvent *)event {
    // be undecided
    self->decidedTapOrDrag = NO;
    // prepare for a tap
    int ct = [[touches anyObject] tapCount];
    if (ct == 2) {
        [NSObject cancelPreviousPerformRequestsWithTarget:self
                                      selector:@selector(singleTap)
                                        object:nil];
        self->decidedTapOrDrag = YES;
        self->drag = NO;
        return;
    }
    // prepare for a drag
    self->p = [[touches anyObject] locationInView: self.superview];
    self->origC = self.center;
    self->decidedDirection = NO;
    self->time = event.timestamp;
}

- (void) touchesMoved:(NSSet *)touches withEvent:(UIEvent *)event {
    if (self->decidedTapOrDrag && !self->drag)
        return;
```

```
            self->decidedTapOrDrag = YES;
            self->drag = YES;
            if (!self->decidedDirection) {
                self->decidedDirection = YES;
                CGPoint then = [[touches anyObject] previousLocationInView: self];
                CGPoint now = [[touches anyObject] locationInView: self];
                CGFloat deltaX = fabs(then.x - now.x);
                CGFloat deltaY = fabs(then.y - now.y);
                self->horiz = (deltaX >= deltaY);
            }
            CGPoint loc = [[touches anyObject] locationInView: self.superview];
            CGFloat deltaX = loc.x - self->p.x;
            CGFloat deltaY = loc.y - self->p.y;
            CGPoint c = self.center;
            if (self->horiz)
                c.x = self->origC.x + deltaX;
            else
                c.y = self->origC.y + deltaY;
            self.center = c;
            //
            CGFloat elapsed = event.timestamp - self->time;
            loc = [[touches anyObject] locationInView: self.superview];
            deltaX = loc.x - self->p.x;
            deltaY = loc.y - self->p.y;
            CGFloat delta = self->horiz ? deltaX : deltaY;
            self->speed = delta/elapsed;
            //
            self->p = [[touches anyObject] locationInView: self.superview];
            self->origC = self.center;
            self->time = event.timestamp;
    }

    - (void) touchesEnded:(NSSet *)touches withEvent:(UIEvent *)event {
        if (!self->decidedTapOrDrag || !self->drag) {
            // end for a tap
            int ct = [[touches anyObject] tapCount];
            if (ct == 1)
                [self performSelector:@selector(singleTap) withObject:nil
                            afterDelay:0.3];
            if (ct == 2)
                NSLog(@"double tap");
            return;
        }
        // end for a drag
        CGFloat sp = self->speed;
        NSString* property = self->horiz ? @"position.x" : @"position.y";
        CGFloat start = self->horiz ? self.layer.position.x : self.layer.position.y;
        CGFloat dur = 0.1;
        CGFloat end = start + sp * dur;
        CABasicAnimation* anim1 = [CABasicAnimation animationWithKeyPath: property];
        anim1.duration = dur;
        anim1.fromValue = [NSNumber numberWithFloat: start];
        anim1.toValue = [NSNumber numberWithFloat: end];
        anim1.timingFunction =
            [CAMediaTimingFunction functionWithName:kCAMediaTimingFunctionEaseOut];
```

```
        [CATransaction setDisableActions:YES];
        [self.layer setValue: [NSNumber numberWithFloat: end] forKeyPath: property];
        [self.layer addAnimation: anim1 forKey: nil];
    }

    - (void) singleTap {
        NSLog(@"single tap");
    }
```

That code seems to work, but it's hard to say whether it covers all possibilities coherently; it's barely legible and the logic borders on the mysterious. This is the kind of situation for which gesture recognizers were devised.

## Gesture Recognizer Classes

A gesture recognizer (a subclass of UIGestureRecognizer) is an object attached to a UIView, which has for this purpose methods addGestureRecognizer: and removeGesture-Recognizer:, and a gestureRecognizers property. A UIGestureRecognizer implements the four touches... handlers, but it is not a responder (a UIResponder), so it does not participate in the responder chain.

If a new touch is going to be delivered to a view, it is also associated with and delivered to that view's gesture recognizers if it has any, and to that view's superview's gesture recognizers if it has any, and so on up the view hierarchy. Thus, the place of a gesture recognizer in the view hierarchy matters, even though it isn't part of the responder chain.

UITouch and UIEvent provide complementary ways of learning how touches and gesture recognizers are associated. UITouch's gestureRecognizers lists the gesture recognizers that are currently handling this touch. UIEvent's touchesForGesture-Recognizer: lists the touches that are currently being handled by a particular gesture recognizer.

Each gesture recognizer maintains its own state as touch events arrive, building up evidence as to what kind of gesture this is. When one of them decides that it has recognized its own type of gesture, it emits either a single message (to indicate, for example, that the user tapped this view) or a series of messages (to indicate, for example, that the user is dragging this view); the distinction here is between a *discrete* and a *continuous* gesture. What message a gesture recognizer emits, and to what object it sends it, is set through a target–action dispatch table attached to the gesture recognizer; a gesture recognizer is rather like a UIControl (Chapter 11) in this regard. (Indeed, one might say that a gesture recognizer simplifies the touch handling of *any* view to be like that of a control. The difference is that one control may report several different control events, whereas each gesture recognizer reports only one gesture type, with different gestures being reported by different gesture recognizers.)

This architecture implies that it is unnecessary to subclass UIView merely in order to implement touch analysis.

UIGestureRecognizer itself is abstract, providing methods and properties to its subclasses. Among these are:

`initWithTarget:action:`
> The designated initializer. Each message emitted by a UIGestureRecognizer is simply a matter of sending the action message to the target. Further target–action pairs may be added with `addTarget:action:`, and removed with `removeTarget:action:`.
>
> Two forms of selector are possible: either there is no parameter, or there is a single parameter which will be the gesture recognizer. Most commonly, you'll use the second form, so that the target can identify and query the gesture recognizer; moreover, using the second form also gives the target a reference to the view, because the gesture recognizer provides a reference to its view as the `view` property.

`locationOfTouch:inView:`
> The touch is specified by an index number. The `numberOfTouches` property provides a count of current touches; the touches themselves are inaccessible from outside the gesture recognizer.

`enabled`
> A convenient way to turn a gesture recognizer off without having to remove it from its view.

`state, view`
> I'll discuss state later on. The view is the view to which this gesture recognizer is attached.

Built-in UIGestureRecognizer subclasses are provided for six common gesture types: tap, pinch, pan (drag), swipe, rotate, and long press. These embody properties and methods likely to be needed for each type of gesture, either in order to configure the gesture recognizer beforehand or in order to query it as to the state of an ongoing gesture:

*UITapGestureRecognizer (discrete)*
> Configuration: `numberOfTapsRequired`, `numberOfTouchesRequired` ("touches" means simultaneous fingers).

*UIPinchGestureRecognizer (continuous)*
> State: `scale`, `velocity`.

*UIRotationGestureRecognizer (continuous)*
> State: `rotation`, `velocity`.

*UISwipeGestureRecognizer (discrete)*
> Configuration: `direction` (meaning permitted directions, a bitmask), `numberOfTouchesRequired`.

*UIPanGestureRecognizer (continuous)*
> Configuration: `minimumNumberOfTouches`, `maximumNumberOfTouches`.

State: `translationInView:`, `setTranslation:inView:`, and `velocityInView:`; the coordinate system of the specified view is used, so to follow a finger you'll use the superview of the view being dragged, just as we did in the examples earlier.

*UILongPressGestureRecognizer (continuous)*

Configuration: `numberOfTapsRequired`, `numberOfTouchesRequired`, `minimumPress-Duration`, `allowableMovement`. The `numberOfTapsRequired` is the count of taps *before* the tap that stays down; so it can be 0 (which is the default, not 1 as the documentation states). The `allowableMovement` setting lets you compensate for the fact that the user's finger is unlikely to remain steady during an extended press; thus we need to provide some limit before deciding that this gesture is, say, a drag, and not a long press after all. On the other hand, once the long press is recognized, the finger is permitted to drag.

UIGestureRecognizer also provides a `locationInView:` method. This is a single point, even if there are multiple touches. The subclasses implement this variously. For example, for UIPanGestureRecognizer, the location is where the touch is if there's a single touch, but it's a sort of midpoint ("centroid") if there are multiple touches.

We already know enough to implement, using a gesture recognizer, a view that responds to a single tap, or a view that responds to a double tap. We don't yet know quite enough to implement a view that lets itself be dragged around, or a view that can respond to more than one gesture; we'll come to that. Meanwhile, here's code that implements a view that responds to a single tap:

```
UITapGestureRecognizer* t = [[UITapGestureRecognizer alloc]
                            initWithTarget:self
                                  action:@selector(singleTap)];
[view addGestureRecognizer:t];
[t release];
// ...
- (void) singleTap {
    NSLog(@"single");
}
```

And here's code that implements a view that responds to a double tap:

```
UITapGestureRecognizer* t = [[UITapGestureRecognizer alloc]
                            initWithTarget:self
                                  action:@selector(doubleTap)];
t.numberOfTapsRequired = 2;
[view addGestureRecognizer:t];
[t release];
// ...
- (void) doubleTap {
    NSLog(@"double");
}
```

For a continuous gesture like dragging, we need to know both when the gesture is in progress and when the gesture ends. This brings us to the subject of a gesture recognizer's state.

A gesture recognizer implements a notion of *states* (the `state` property); it passes through these states in a definite progression. The gesture recognizer remains in the Possible state until it can make a decision one way or the other as to whether this is in fact the correct gesture. The documentation neatly lays out the possible progressions:

*Wrong gesture*
 Possible → Failed. No action message is sent.

*Discrete gesture (like a tap), recognized*
 Possible → Ended. One action message is sent, when the state changes to Ended.

*Continuous gesture (like a drag), recognized*
 Possible → Began → Changed (repeatedly) → Ended. Action messages are sent once for Began, as many times as necessary for Changed, and once for Ended.

*Continuous gesture, recognized but later cancelled*
 Possible → Began → Changed (repeatedly) → Cancelled. Action messages are sent once for Began, as many times as necessary for Changed, and once for Cancelled.

The actual phase names are `UIGestureRecognizerStatePossible` and so forth. The name `UIGestureRecognizerStateRecognized` is actually a synonym for the Ended state; I find this unnecessary and confusing and I'll ignore it in my discussion.

We now know enough to implement, using a gesture recognizer, a view that lets itself be dragged around in any direction by a single finger. Our maintenance of state is greatly simplified, because a UIPanGestureRecognizer maintains a delta (translation) for us. This delta, available using `translationInView:`, is reckoned from the touch's initial position. So we need to store our center only once:

```
UIPanGestureRecognizer* p = [[UIPanGestureRecognizer alloc]
                             initWithTarget:self
                                     action:@selector(dragging:)];
[view addGestureRecognizer:p];
[p release];
// ...
- (void) dragging: (UIPanGestureRecognizer*) p {
    UIView* v = p.view;
    if (p.state == UIGestureRecognizerStateBegan)
        self->origC = v.center;
    CGPoint delta = [p translationInView: v.superview];
    CGPoint c = self->origC;
    c.x += delta.x; c.y += delta.y;
    v.center = c;
}
```

Actually, it's possible to write that code without maintaining any state at all, because we are allowed to reset the UIPanGestureRecognizer's delta, using `setTranslation:inView:`. So:

```
- (void) dragging: (UIPanGestureRecognizer*) p {
    UIView* v = p.view;
    if (p.state == UIGestureRecognizerStateBegan ||
```

```
            p.state == UIGestureRecognizerStateChanged) {
        CGPoint delta = [p translationInView: v.superview];
        CGPoint c = v.center;
        c.x += delta.x; c.y += delta.y;
        v.center = c;
        [p setTranslation: CGPointZero inView: v.superview];
    }
}
```

A gesture recognizer also works, as I've already mentioned, if it is attached to the superview (or further up the hierarchy) of the view in which the user gestures. For example, if a tap gesture recognizer is attached to the window, the user can tap on any view within that window, and the tap will be recognized; the view's presence does not "block" the window from recognizing the gesture, even if it is a UIControl that responds autonomously to touches.

This behavior comes as a surprise to beginners, but it makes sense, because if it were not the case, certain gestures would be impossible. Imagine, for example, a pair of views on each of which the user can tap individually, but which the user can also touch simultaneously (one finger on each view) and rotate together around their mutual centroid. Neither view can detect the rotation *qua* rotation, because neither view receives both touches; only the superview can detect it, so the fact that the views themselves respond to touches must not prevent the superview's gesture recognizer from operating.

So, suppose your UIWindow has a UITapGestureRecognizer attached to it (perhaps because you want to be able to recognize taps on the window background), but there is also a UIButton in the window. How is the window to ignore a tap on the button? In this case it's easy, because a tap is a discrete gesture: the action handler just looks at the gesture's view and doesn't respond if that view isn't the window. And if the gesture recognizer attached to the window is some other gesture, then the problem never arises, because a tap on the button won't trigger its action handler in the first place. Nevertheless, the view hierarchy does complicate the use of gesture recognizers; fortunately, as I shall explain, gesture recognizers usually take care of these complications themselves, and when they don't, they provide ways for you to resolve them.

## Multiple Gesture Recognizers

The question naturally arises of what happens when multiple gesture recognizers are in play. This isn't a matter merely of multiple recognizers attached to a single view, because, as I have just said, if a view is touched, not only its own gesture recognizers but any gesture recognizers attached to views further up the view hierarchy are also in play, simultaneously. I like to think of a view as surrounded by a swarm of gesture recognizers: its own and those of its superview (and so on). In reality, it is a touch that has a swarm of gesture recognizers; that's why a UITouch has a gestureRecognizers property, in the plural.

In general, once a gesture recognizer succeeds in recognizing its gesture, any *other* gesture recognizers associated with its touches are *forced into the Failed state*, and whatever touches were associated with those gesture recognizers are no longer sent to them; in effect, the first gesture recognizer in a swarm that recognizes its gesture owns the gesture, and those touches, from then on.

In many cases, this behavior alone will correctly eliminate conflicts. For example, we can add *both* our UITapGestureRecognizer for a single tap *and* our UIPanGestureRecognizer to a view and everything will just work.

What happens if we also add the UITapGestureRecognizer for a double tap? Dragging works, and single tap works; double tap works too, but without preventing the single tap from working. So, on a double tap, both the single tap action handler and the double tap action handler are called.

If that isn't what we want, we don't have to use delayed performance, as we did earlier. Instead, we can create a *dependency* between one gesture recognizer and another, telling the first to suspend judgement until the second has decided whether this is its gesture, by sending the first the `requireGestureRecognizerToFail:` message. This message doesn't mean "force this recognizer to fail"; it means, "you can't succeed until this recognizer fails."

So our view is now configured as follows:

```
UITapGestureRecognizer* t2 = [[UITapGestureRecognizer alloc]
                              initWithTarget:self
                                     action:@selector(doubleTap)];
t2.numberOfTapsRequired = 2;
[view addGestureRecognizer:t2];

UITapGestureRecognizer* t1 = [[UITapGestureRecognizer alloc]
                              initWithTarget:self
                                     action:@selector(singleTap)];
[t1 requireGestureRecognizerToFail:t2];
[view addGestureRecognizer:t1];
[t1 release];
[t2 release];

UIPanGestureRecognizer* p = [[UIPanGestureRecognizer alloc]
                             initWithTarget:self
                                    action:@selector(dragging:)];
[view addGestureRecognizer:p];
[p release];
```

 Apple would prefer, if you're going to have a view respond both to single tap and double tap, that you *not* make the former wait upon the latter (because this delays your response after the user single taps). Rather, they would like you to arrange things so that it doesn't matter that you respond to a single tap that is the first tap of a double tap. This isn't always feasible, of course; Apple's own Safari is a clear counterexample.

## Subclassing Gesture Recognizers

To subclass a built-in gesture recognizer subclass, you must do the following things:

- At the start of the implementation file, import `<UIKit/UIGestureRecognizer-Subclass.h>`. This file contains a category on UIGestureRecognizer that allows you to set the gesture recognizer's state (which is otherwise read-only), along with declarations for the methods you may need to override.

- Override any `touches...` methods you need to (as if the gesture recognizer were a UIResponder); you will almost certainly call `super` so as to take advantage of the built-in behavior. In overriding a `touches...` method, you need to think like a gesture recognizer. As these methods are called, a gesture recognizer is setting its state; you must interact with that process.

To illustrate, we will subclass UIPanGestureRecognizer so as to implement a view that can be moved only horizontally or vertically. Our strategy will be to make *two* UIPan-GestureRecognizer subclasses — one that allows only horizontal movement, and another that allows only vertical movement. They will make their recognition decisions in a mutually exclusive manner, so we can attach an instance of each to our view. This separates the decision-making logic in a gorgeously encapsulated object-oriented manner — a far cry from the spaghetti code we wrote earlier to do this same task.

I will show only the code for the horizontal drag gesture recognizer, because the vertical recognizer is symmetrically identical. We maintain just one instance variable, which we will use once to determine whether the user's initial movement is horizontal. We override `touchesBegan:withEvent:` to set our instance variable with the first touch's location:

```
- (void) touchesBegan:(NSSet *)touches withEvent:(UIEvent *)event {
    self->origLoc = [[touches anyObject] locationInView:self.view.superview];
    [super touchesBegan: touches withEvent: event];
}
```

We then override `touchesMoved:withEvent:`; all the recognition logic is here. This method will be called for the first time with the state still at Possible. At that moment, we look to see if the user's movement is more horizontal than vertical. If it isn't, we set the state to Failed. But if it is, we just step back and let the superclass do its thing:

```
- (void) touchesMoved:(NSSet *)touches withEvent:(UIEvent *)event {
    if (self.state == UIGestureRecognizerStatePossible) {
        CGPoint loc = [[touches anyObject] locationInView:self.view.superview];
        CGFloat deltaX = fabs(loc.x - origLoc.x);
        CGFloat deltaY = fabs(loc.y - origLoc.y);
        if (deltaY >= deltaX)
            self.state = UIGestureRecognizerStateFailed;
    }
    [super touchesMoved: touches withEvent:event];
}
```

We now have a view that moves only if the user's initial gesture is horizontal. But that isn't the entirety of what we want; we want a view that, itself, moves horizontally only. To implement this, we'll simply lie to our client about where the user's finger is, by overriding `translationInView::`

```
- (CGPoint)translationInView:(UIView *)v {
    CGPoint proposedTranslation = [super translationInView:v];
    proposedTranslation.y = 0;
    return proposedTranslation;
}
```

That example was simple, because we subclassed a fully functional built-in UIGestureRecognizer subclass. If you were to write your own UIGestureRecognizer subclass entirely from scratch, there would be more work to do:

- You should definitely implement all four `touches...` handlers. Their job, at a minimum, is to advance the gesture recognizer through the canonical progression of its states. When the first touch arrives at a gesture recognizer, its state will be Possible; you never explicitly set the recognizer's state to Possible yourself. As soon as you know this can't be our gesture, you set the state to Failed (Apple says that a gesture recognizer should "fail early, fail often"). If the gesture gets past all the failure tests, you set the state instead either to Ended (for a discrete gesture) or to Began (for a continuous gesture); if Began, then you might set it to Changed, and ultimately you must set it to Ended. Action messages will be sent automatically at the appropriate moments.

- You should probably implement `reset`. This is called after you reach the end of the progression of states to notify you that the gesture recognizer's state is about to be set back to Possible; it is your chance to return your state machine to its starting configuration (resetting instance variables, for example).

Keep in mind that your gesture recognizer might stop receiving touches without notice. Just because it gets a `touchesBegan:withEvent:` call for a particular touch doesn't mean it will ever get `touchesEnded:withEvent:` for that touch. If your gesture recognizer fails to recognize its gesture, either because it declares failure or because it is still in the Possible state when another gesture recognizer recognizes, it won't get any more `touches...` calls for any of the touches that were being sent to it. This is why `reset` is so important; it's the one reliable signal that it's time to clean up and get ready to receive the beginning of another possible gesture.

## Gesture Recognizer Delegate

A gesture recognizer can have a delegate, which can perform two types of task:

*Block a gesture recognizer's operation*
> `gestureRecognizerShouldBegin:` is sent to the delegate before the gesture recognizer passes out of the Possible state; return NO to force the gesture recognizer to proceed to the Failed state.

gestureRecognizer:shouldReceiveTouch: is sent to the delegate before a touch is sent to the gesture recognizer's touchesBegan:... method; return NO to prevent that touch from ever being sent to the gesture recognizer.

*Mediate simultaneous gesture recognition*

When a gesture recognizer is about to declare that it recognizes its gesture, gesture-Recognizer:shouldRecognizeSimultaneouslyWithGestureRecognizer: is sent to the delegate of that gesture recognizer, if this declaration would force the failure of another gesture recognizer, and to the delegate of a gesture recognizer whose failure would be forced. Return YES to prevent that failure, thus allowing both gesture recognizers to operate simultaneously. For example, a view could respond to both a two-fingered pinch and a two-fingered pan, the one applying a scale transform, the other changing the view's center.

As an example, we will use delegate messages to combine a UILongPressGestureRecognizer and a UIPanGestureRecognizer, as follows: the user must perform a tap-and-a-half (tap and hold) to "get the view's attention," which we will indicate by a pulsing animation on the view; then (and only then) the user can drag the view.

As we create our gesture recognizers, we'll keep a reference to the UILongPressGestureRecognizer, and we'll make ourself the UIPanGestureRecognizer's delegate:

```
UIPanGestureRecognizer* p = [[UIPanGestureRecognizer alloc]
                                initWithTarget:self
                                    action:@selector(panning:)];
UILongPressGestureRecognizer* lp = [[UILongPressGestureRecognizer alloc]
                                initWithTarget:self
                                    action:@selector(longPress:)];
lp.numberOfTapsRequired = 1;
[view addGestureRecognizer:p];
[view addGestureRecognizer:lp];
self.longPresser = lp;
p.delegate = self;
[lp release]; [p release];
```

In keeping with encapsulation, the UILongPressGestureRecognizer's handler will take care of starting and stopping the animation, and the UIPanGestureRecognizer's handler will take care of the drag in the familiar manner:

```
- (void) longPress: (UILongPressGestureRecognizer*) lp {
    if (lp.state == UIGestureRecognizerStateBegan) {
        CABasicAnimation* anim =
            [CABasicAnimation animationWithKeyPath: @"transform"];
        anim.toValue =
            [NSValue valueWithCATransform3D:CATransform3DMakeScale(1.1, 1.1, 1)];
        anim.fromValue =
            [NSValue valueWithCATransform3D:CATransform3DIdentity];
        anim.repeatCount = HUGE_VALF;
        anim.autoreverses = YES;
        [lp.view.layer addAnimation:anim forKey:nil];
    }
    if (lp.state == UIGestureRecognizerStateEnded) {
```

```
            [lp.view.layer removeAllAnimations];
        }
    }

    - (void) panning: (UIPanGestureRecognizer*) p {
        UIView* v = p.view;
        if (p.state == UIGestureRecognizerStateBegan)
            self->origC = v.center;
        CGPoint delta = [p translationInView: v.superview];
        CGPoint c = self->origC;
        c.x += delta.x; c.y += delta.y;
        v.center = c;
    }
```

Now for the delegate methods. We are the UIPanGestureRecognizer's delegate. If the UIPanGestureRecognizer tries to declare success while the UILongPressGestureRecognizer's state is Failed or still at Possible, we prevent it. If the UILongPressGestureRecognizer succeeds, we permit the UIPanGestureRecognizer to operate as well:

```
    - (BOOL) gestureRecognizerShouldBegin: (UIGestureRecognizer*) g {
        if (self.longPresser.state == UIGestureRecognizerStatePossible ||
                self.longPresser.state == UIGestureRecognizerStateFailed)
            return NO;
        return YES;
    }

    - (BOOL)gestureRecognizer: (UIGestureRecognizer*) g1
        shouldRecognizeSimultaneouslyWithGestureRecognizer: (UIGestureRecognizer*) g2 {
        return YES;
    }
```

The result is that the view can be dragged only if it is pulsing, and if it *is* dragged, we are using a UIPanGestureRecognizer, with its convenient translationInView: method, to move the view, rather than the less able UILongPanGestureRecognizer (which permits movement of the touch, but has no translationInView: method). In effect, what we've done is to compensate, using delegate methods, for the fact that UIGestureRecognizer has no requireGestureRecognizerToSucceed: method.

If you are subclassing a gesture recognizer class, you can incorporate delegate-like behavior into the subclass. By overriding canPreventGestureRecognizer: and canBePreventedByGestureRecognizer:, you can mediate simultaneous gesture recognition at the class level. The built-in gesture recognizer subclasses already do this; for example, this is why a UITapGestureRecognizer whose numberOfTapsRequired is 1 does not, by recognizing its gesture, cause the failure of a UITapGestureRecognizer whose numberOfTapsRequired is 2.

You can also, in a gesture recognizer subclass, send ignoreTouch:forEvent: directly to a gesture recognizer (typically, to self). This has the same effect as the delegate method gestureRecognizer:shouldReceiveTouch: returning NO, blocking delivery of that touch to the gesture recognizer for as long as it exists. For example, if you're in the middle of an already recognized gesture and a new touch arrives, you might well elect to ignore it.

## Touch Delivery

Let's now return to the very beginning of the touch reporting process, when the system sends the app a UIEvent containing touches, and tease apart in full detail the entire procedure by which a touch is delivered to views and gesture recognizers.

When the user puts a finger to the screen and a touch event arrives at the app, the app follows a standard procedure for delivering touches:

1. The application calls the UIView instance method hitTest:withEvent: on the window, which returns the view (called, appropriately, the *hit-test view*) that will be associated with this touch. This method uses the UIView instance method point-Inside:withEvent: along with hitTest:withEvent: recursively down the view hierarchy to find the deepest view containing the touch's location and capable of receiving a touch.

2. Having determined the hit-test view of every touch in an event, the application calls its own sendEvent:, which in turn calls the window's sendEvent:. The window delivers the touches by calling the appropriate touches... method(s), as follows:

   a. As a touch first appears, it is delivered to the hit-test view's swarm of gesture recognizers. It is then also delivered to that view.

   b. The logic of withholding touches is implemented for views (but not for gesture recognizers). For example, additional touches won't be delivered to a view if that view currently has a touch and has multipleTouchEnabled set to NO (but they will be delivered to that view's swarm of gesture recognizers).

   c. If a gesture is recognized by a gesture recognizer, then for any touch associated with this gesture recognizer:

      i. touchesCancelled:forEvent: is sent to the touch's view, and the touch is no longer delivered to its view.

      ii. If that touch was associated with any other gesture recognizer, that gesture recognizer is forced to fail.

   d. If a gesture recognizer fails, either because it declares failure or because it is forced to fail, its touches are no longer delivered to it, but (except as already specified) they continue to be delivered to their view.

   e. If a touch would be delivered to a view, but that view does not respond to the appropriate touches... method, a responder further up the responder chain (Chapter 11) is sought that does respond to it, and the touch is delivered there.

The rest of this chapter elaborates on each stage of this standard procedure, nearly every bit of which can be customized to some extent.

# Hit-Testing

*Hit-testing* is the determination of what view the user touched. View hit-testing uses the UIView instance method `hitTest:withEvent:`, which returns either a view (the hit-test view) or nil. The idea is to find the frontmost view containing the touch point. This method uses an elegant recursive algorithm, as follows:

1. A view's `hitTest:withEvent:` first calls the same method on its own subviews, if it has any, because a subview is considered to be in front of its superview. The subviews are queried in reverse order, because that's front-to-back order (Chapter 14): thus, if two sibling views overlap, the one in front reports the hit first.

2. If, as a view hit-tests its subviews, any of those subviews responds by returning a view, it stops querying its subviews and immediately returns the view that was returned to it. Thus, the very first view to declare itself the hit-test view immediately percolates all the way to the top of call chain and *is* the hit-test view.

3. If, on the other hand, a view has no subviews, or if all of its subviews return nil (indicating that neither they nor their subviews was hit), then the view calls `pointInside:withEvent:` on itself. If this call reveals that the touch was inside this view, the view returns itself, declaring itself the hit-test view; otherwise it returns nil.

It is also up to `hitTest:withEvent:` to implement the logic of touch restrictions exclusive to a view. If a view's `userInteractionEnabled` is NO, or its **hidden** is YES, or its **opacity** is close to `0.0`, it returns nil without hit-testing any of its subviews and without calling `pointInside:withEvent:`. Thus these restrictions do not, of themselves, exclude a view from being hit-tested; on the contrary, they operate precisely by modifying a view's hit-test result.

However, hit-testing knows nothing about `multipleTouchEnabled` (because its behavior involves multiple touches) or `exclusiveTouch` (because its behavior involves multiple views). The logic of obedience to these properties is implemented at a later stage of the story.

You can use hit-testing yourself, and you can override `hitTest:withEvent:` to alter its results during touch delivery, thus customizing the touch delivery mechanism.

In calling `hitTest:withEvent:`, supply a point *in the coordinates of the view to which the message is sent*. The second parameter can be nil if you have no event.

For example, suppose we have a UIView with two UIImageView subviews. We want to detect a tap in either UIImageView, but we want to handle this at the level of the UIView. We can attach a UITapGestureRecognizer to the UIView, but how will we know which subview, if any, the tap was in?

Our first step must be to set `userInteractionEnabled` to YES for both UIImageViews. (This step is crucial; UIImageView is one of the few built-in view classes where this is NO by default, and a view whose `userInteractionEnabled` is NO won't be the result of a call to `hitTest:withEvent:`.) Now, when our gesture recognizer's action handler is called, the view can use hit-testing to determine where the tap was:

```
CGPoint p = [g locationOfTouch:0 inView:self]; // g is the gesture recognizer
UIView* v = [self hitTest:p withEvent:nil];
```

Hit-test munging can be used selectively as a way of turning user interaction on or off in an area of the interface. In this way, some unusual effects can be produced. Here are some examples:

- If a superview contains a UIButton but doesn't return that UIButton from `hitTest:withEvent:`, that button can't be tapped.

- You might override `hitTest:withEvent:` to return the result from `super` most of the time, but to return `self` under certain conditions, effectively making all subviews untouchable without making the superview itself untouchable (as setting its `userInteractionEnabled` to NO would do).

- A view whose `userInteractionEnabled` is NO can break the normal rules and return itself from hit-testing and can thus end up as the hit-test view.

No problem arises if a view has a transform, because `pointInside:withEvent:` takes the transform into account. That's why a rotated button continues to work correctly.

### Hit-testing for layers

There is also hit-testing for layers. It doesn't happen automatically, as part of `sendEvent:` or anything else; it's up to you. It's just a convenient way of finding out which layer would receive a touch at a point, if layers received touches. To hit-test layers, call `hitTest:` on a layer, with a point *in superlayer coordinates*.

Keep in mind, though, that layers do *not* receive touches. A touch is reported to a view, not a layer. A layer, except insofar as it is a view's underlying layer and gets touch reporting because of its view, is completely untouchable; from the point of view of touches and touch reporting, it's as if the layer weren't on the screen at all. No matter where a layer may appear to be, a touch falls right through the layer to whatever view is behind it.

In the case of the layer that is a view's underlying layer, you don't need hit-testing. It is the view's drawing; where it appears is where the view is. So a touch in that layer is equivalent to a touch in its view. Indeed, one might say that this is what views are actually for: to provide layers with touchability.

The only layers on which you'd need special hit-testing, then, would presumably be layers that are not themselves any view's underlying layer, because those are the only ones you don't find out about by normal view hit-testing. However, all layers, including a layer that is its view's underlying layer, are part of the layer hierarchy, and can participate in layer hit-testing. So the most comprehensive way to hit-test layers is to start with the topmost layer, the window's layer. In this example, we subclass UIWindow and override its `hitTest:withEvent:` so as to get layer hit-testing every time there is view hit-testing:

```
- (UIView*) hitTest:(CGPoint)point withEvent:(UIEvent *)event {
    CALayer* lay = [self.layer hitTest:point];
    // ... possibly do something with that information ...
    return [super hitTest:point withEvent:event];
}
```

Because this is the window, the view hit-test point works as the layer hit-test point; window bounds are screen bounds. But usually you'll have to convert to superlayer coordinates. In this example, we return to the CompassView developed in Chapter 16, in which all the parts of the compass are layers; we want to know whether the user tapped on the arrow layer. For simplicity, we've given the CompassView a UI-TapGestureRecognizer, and this is its action handler, in the CompassView itself. We convert to our superview's coordinates, because these are also our layer's superlayer coordinates:

```
// self is the CompassView
CGPoint p = [t locationOfTouch: 0 inView: self.superview];
CALayer* hit = [self.layer hitTest:p];
if (hit == ((CompassLayer*)self.layer).theArrow) // ...
```

Layer hit-testing knows nothing of the restrictions on touch delivery; it just reports on every sublayer, even those whose view has `userInteractionEnabled` set to NO.

 The documentation warns that `hitTest:` must not be called on a CA-TransformLayer.

Layer hit-testing works by calling `containsPoint:`. However, `containsPoint:` takes a point in the layer's coordinates, so to hand it a point that arrives through `hitTest:` you must first convert from superlayer coordinates:

```
BOOL hit = [lay containsPoint: [lay convertPoint:point fromLayer:lay.superlayer]];
```

### Hit-testing for drawings

The preceding example worked, but we might complain that it is reporting a hit on the arrow even if the hit misses the *drawing* of the arrow. That's true for view hit-testing as well. A hit is reported if we are within the view or layer as a whole; hit-testing knows nothing of drawing, transparent areas, and so forth.

If you know how the region is drawn and can reproduce the edge of that drawing as a CGPath, you can test whether a point is inside it with `CGPathContainsPoint`. So, for a layer, you could override `hitTest` along these lines:

```
- (CALayer*) hitTest:(CGPoint)p {
    CGPoint pt = [self convertPoint:p fromLayer:self.superlayer];
    CGMutablePathRef path = CGPathCreateMutable();
    // ... draw path here ...
```

```
        CALayer* result = CGPathContainsPoint(path, NULL, pt, true) ? self : nil;
        CGPathRelease(path);
        return result;
    }
```

Alternatively, it might be the case that if a pixel of the drawing is transparent, it's outside the drawn region. Unfortunately there's no way to ask a drawing (or a view, or a layer) for the color of a pixel; you have to make a bitmap and copy the drawing into it, and then ask the bitmap for the color of a pixel. If you can reproduce the content as an image, and all you care about is transparency, you can make a one-pixel alpha-only bitmap, draw the image in such a way that the pixel we want to test is the pixel drawn into the bitmap, and examine the transparency of the resulting pixel:

```
// assume im is a UIImage, point is the CGPoint to test
CGImageRef cgim = im.CGImage;
unsigned char pixel[1] = {0};
CGContextRef context = CGBitmapContextCreate(pixel,
                                             1, 1, 8, 1, NULL,
                                             kCGImageAlphaOnly);
CGContextDrawImage(context, CGRectMake(-point.x,
                                       -point.y,
                                       CGImageGetWidth(cgim),
                                       CGImageGetHeight(cgim)),
                   cgim);
CGContextRelease(context);
CGFloat alpha = pixel[0]/255.0;
BOOL transparent = alpha < 0.01;
```

However, there are can be complications; for example, there may not be a one-to-one relationship between the pixels of the underlying drawing and the points of the drawing as portrayed on the screen (because the drawing is stretched, for example). This can be a difficult problem to solve, and further discussion would take us too far afield.

### Hit-testing during animation

If the position of a view or layer is being animated and you want the user to be able to tap on it, you'll need to hit-test the presentation layer (see Chapter 17). In this simple example, we have a superview containing a subview. To allow the user to tap on the subview even when it is being animated, we interfere with hit-testing in the superview:

```
- (UIView*) hitTest:(CGPoint)point withEvent:(UIEvent *)event {
    // v is the animated subview
    CALayer* lay = [v.layer presentationLayer];
    CALayer* hitLayer = [lay hitTest: point];
    if (hitLayer == lay)
        return v;
    UIView* hitView = [super hitTest:point withEvent:event];
    if (hitView == v)
        return self;
    return hitView;
}
```

If the user taps outside the presentation layer, we cannot simply call super, because the user might tap at the spot to which the subview has in reality already moved (behind the "animation movie"), in which case super will report that it hit the subview. So if super does report this, we return self (assuming that we are what's behind the animated subview at its new location).

## Initial Touch Event Delivery

Once an event's touches have been hit-tested and their view has been set, the event is handed to the UIApplication instance by calling its sendEvent:, and the UIApplication in turn hands it to the relevant UIWindow by calling *its* sendEvent:. The UIWindow then performs the complicated logic of examining the hit-test view and its superviews and their gesture recognizers and deciding which of them should be sent a touches... message, and does so.

These are delicate and crucial maneuvers, and you wouldn't want to lame your application by interfering with them. Nevertheless, you can override sendEvent: in a subclass, and there are situations where you might wish to do so. This is just about the *only* case in which you might subclass UIApplication; if you do, remember to change the third argument in the call to UIApplicationMain in your *main.m* file to the string name of your UIApplication subclass so that your subclass is used to generate the app's singleton UIApplication instance. If you subclass UIWindow, remember to change the window's class in your *MainWindow.xib*, so that your subclass is used to generate the app's main window instance.

Now that gesture recognizers exist, it is unlikely that you will need to resort to such measures. A typical case, in the past, was that you needed to detect touches directed to an object of some built-in interface class in a way that subclassing it wouldn't permit. For example, you want to know when the user swipes a UIWebView; you're not allowed to subclass UIWebView, and in any case it eats the touch. The solution used to be to subclass UIWindow and override sendEvent:; you would then work out whether this was a swipe on the UIWebView and respond accordingly, or else call super. Now, however, you can just attach a UISwipeGestureRecognizer to the UIWebView.

## Gesture Recognizer and View

When a touch first appears and is delivered to a gesture recognizer, it is also delivered to its hit-test view, the same touches... method being called on both. This comes as a surprise to beginners, but it is the most reasonable approach, as it means that touch interpretation by a view isn't jettisoned just because gesture recognizers are in the picture. Later on in the multitouch sequence, if all the gesture recognizers in a view's swarm declare failure to recognize their gesture, that view's internal touch interpretation just proceeds as if gesture recognizers had never been invented.

However, if a gesture recognizer in a view's swarm recognizes its gesture, that view is sent `touchesCancelled:withEvent:` for any touches that went to that gesture recognizer and were hit-tested to that view, and subsequently the view no longer receives those touches.

This behavior can be changed by setting a gesture recognizer's `cancelsTouchesInView` property to NO. If this is the case for every gesture recognizer in a view's swarm, the view will receive touch events more or less as if no gesture recognizers were in the picture. Making this change, however, alters delivery logic rather drastically; it seems unlikely that you'd want to do that.

If a gesture recognizer happens to be ignoring a touch (because it was told to do so by `ignoreTouch:forEvent:`), then `touchesCancelled:withEvent:` *won't* be sent to the view for that touch when the gesture recognizer recognizes its gesture. Thus, a gesture recognizer's ignoring a touch is the same as simply letting it fall through to the view, as if the gesture recognizer weren't there.

Gesture recognizers can also *delay* the delivery of touches to a view, and by default they do. The UIGestureRecognizer property `delaysTouchesEnded` is YES by default, meaning that when a touch reaches `UITouchPhaseEnded` and the gesture recognizer's `touchesEnded:withEvent:` is called, if the gesture recognizer is still allowing touches to be delivered to the view because its state is still Possible, it doesn't deliver this touch until it has resolved the gesture. When it does, either it will recognize the gesture, in which case the view will have `touchesCancelled:withEvent:` called instead (as already explained), or it will declare failure and *now* the view will have `touchesEnded:withEvent:` called.

The reason for this behavior is most obvious with a gesture where multiple taps are required. The first tap ends, but this is insufficient for the gesture recognizer to declare success or failure, so it withholds that touch from the view. In this way, the gesture recognizer gets the proper priority. In particular, if there is a second tap, the gesture recognizer should succeed and send `touchesCancelled:withEvent:` to the view — but it can't do that if the view has already been sent `touchesEnded:withEvent:`.

It is also possible to delay the entire suite of `touches...` methods from being called on a view, by setting a gesture recognizer's `delaysTouchesBegan` property to YES. Again, this delay would be until the gesture recognizer can resolve the gesture: either it will recognize it, in which case the view will have `touchesCancelled:withEvent:` called, or it will declare failure, in which case the view will receive `touchesBegan:withEvent:` plus any further `touches...` calls that were withheld — except that it will receive *at most* one `touchesMoved:withEvent:` call, the last one, because if a lot of these were withheld, to queue them all up and send them all at once now would be simply insane.

It is unlikely that you'll change a gesture recognizer's `delaysTouchesBegan` property to YES, however. You might do so, for example, if you have an elaborate touch analysis within a view that simply cannot operate simultaneously with a gesture recognizer, but this is improbable, and the latency involved may look strange to your user.

---

When touches are delayed and then delivered, what's delivered is the original touch with the original event, which still have their original timestamps. Because of the delay, these timestamps may differ significantly from now. For this reason (and many others), Apple warns that touch analysis that is concerned with timing should always look at the timestamp, not the clock.

## Touch Exclusion Logic

It is up to the UIWindow's `sendEvent:` to implement the logic of `multipleTouchEnabled` and `exclusiveTouch`.

If a new touch is hit-tested to a view whose `multipleTouchEnabled` is NO and which already has an existing touch hit-tested to it, then `sendEvent:` never delivers the new touch to that view. However, that touch *is* delivered to the view's swarm of gesture recognizers.

Similarly, if there's an `exclusiveTouch` view in the window, then `sendEvent:` must decide whether a particular touch should be delivered, as already described. If a touch begins in an `exclusiveTouch` view at a time when another view in the window already has a touch, the touch is not delivered to the `exclusiveTouch` view, but it *is* delivered to that view's swarm of gesture recognizers. If a touch begins outside an `exclusiveTouch` view at a time when the `exclusiveTouch` view already has a touch, the touch is not delivered to its view, but it *is* delivered to its view's swarm of gesture recognizers.

The idea here is that gesture recognizers should ignore exclusivity, thus allowing for something like a pair of views on each of which the user can tap, but which the user can also touch simultaneously and rotate. However, this behavior is buggy; in some situations, if there is a touch already in the `exclusiveTouch` view, then a second touch in a different view is not delivered *at all*, not even to the gesture recognizer. Until this bug is fixed, I suggest that you not use `exclusiveTouch` when gesture recognizers are involved.

If you want to implement exclusivity between gestures, gesture recognizers themselves provide the means. For example, here's a delegate method that prevents a gesture recognizer from operating if its view's siblings' gesture recognizers have any touches:

```
- (BOOL)gestureRecognizerShouldBegin:(UIGestureRecognizer *)g {
    __block BOOL result = YES;
    [g.view.superview.subviews
    enumerateObjectsUsingBlock:^(id obj, NSUInteger idx, BOOL *stop) {
        [[obj gestureRecognizers]
        enumerateObjectsUsingBlock:^(id g2, NSUInteger idx, BOOL *stop) {
            if (([g2 numberOfTouches] > 0) && (g != g2))
                result = NO;
        }];
    }];
    return result;
}
```

# Recognition

When a gesture recognizer recognizes its gesture, everything changes. As we've already seen, the touches for this gesture recognizer are sent to their hit-test views as a `touches-Cancelled:forEvent:` message, and then no longer arrive at those views (unless the gesture recognizer's `cancelsTouchesInView` is NO). Moreover, all other gesture recognizers pending with regard to these touches are made to fail, and then are no longer sent the touches they were receiving either.

If the very same event would cause more than one gesture recognizer to recognize, there's an algorithm for picking the one that will succeed and make the others fail: a gesture recognizer lower down the view hierarchy (closer to the hit-test view) prevails over one higher up the hierarchy, and a gesture recognizer more recently added to its view prevails over one less recently added.

There are various means for modifying this "first past the post, winner takes all" behavior. One is by telling a gesture recognizer, in effect, that being first isn't good enough:

- `requireGestureRecognizerToFail:` institutes a dependency order, possibly causing the gesture recognizer to which it is sent to be put on hold when it tries to transition from the Possible state to the Began (continuous) or Ended (discrete) state; only if a certain other gesture recognizer fails is this one permitted to perform that transition. (So, "require to fail" means "*you* cannot succeed without this other's failure.")

  Apple says that in a dependency like this, the gesture recognizer that fails first is not sent `reset` (and won't receive any touches) until the second finishes its state sequence and is sent `reset`, so that they resume recognizing together.

- The delegate method `gestureRecognizerShouldBegin:`, by returning NO, turns success into failure; at the moment when the gesture recognizer is about to declare that it recognizes its gesture, the delegate is telling it to fail instead.

Another approach is to permit simultaneous recognition; a gesture recognizer succeeds, but some other gesture recognizer is *not* forced to fail. There are two ways to achieve this:

- A subclass can implement `canPreventGestureRecognizer:` or `canBePreventedBy-GestureRecognizer:` (or both). Here, "prevent" means "by succeeding, you force failure upon this other," and "be prevented" means "by succeeding, this other forces failure upon you."

  These two methods work together as follows. `canPreventGestureRecognizer:` is called first; if it returns NO, that's the end of the story for that gesture recognizer, and `canPreventGestureRecognizer:` is called on the other gesture recognizer. But if `canPreventGestureRecognizer:` returns YES when it is first called, the other gesture recognizer is sent `canBePreventedByGestureRecognizer:`. If it returns YES, that's the end of the story; if it returns NO, the process starts over the other way around, sending `canPreventGestureRecognizer:` to the second gesture recognizer, and so forth. In this way, conflicting answers are resolved without the device exploding: prevention is regarded as exceptional (even though it is in fact the norm) and will happen only if it is acquiesced to by everyone involved.

- The delegate method `gestureRecognizer:shouldRecognizeSimultaneouslyWith-GestureRecognizer:` can return YES to permit one gesture recognizer to succeed without forcing the other to fail.

## Touches and the Responder Chain

A UIView is a responder, and participates in the responder chain (Chapter 11). In particular, if a touch is to be delivered to a UIView (because, for example, it's the hit-test view) and that view doesn't implement the relevant `touches...` method, a walk up the responder chain is performed, looking for a responder that *does* implement it; if such a responder is found, the touch is delivered to that responder. Moreover, the default implementation of the `touches...` methods — the behavior that you get if you call `super` — is to perform the same walk up the responder chain, starting with the next responder in the chain.

The relationship between touch delivery and the responder chain can be useful, but you must be careful not to allow it to develop into an incoherency. For example, if `touchesBegan:withEvent:` is implemented in a superview but not in a subview, then a touch to the subview will result in the superview's `touchesBegan:withEvent:` being called, with the first parameter (the touches) containing a touch whose `view` is the subview. But most UIView implementations of the `touches...` methods rely upon the assumption that the first parameter consists of all and only touches whose `view` is `self`; built-in UIView subclasses certainly assume this.

Again, if `touchesBegan:withEvent:` is implemented in both a superview and a subview, and you call `super` in the subview's implementation, passing along the same arguments that came in, then the same touch delivered to the subview will trigger both the subview's `touchesBegan:withEvent:` and the superview's `touchesBegan:withEvent:` (and once again the first parameter to the superview's `touchesBegan:withEvent:` will contain a touch whose `view` is the subview).

The solution is to behave rationally, as follows:

- If all the responders in the affected part of the responder chain are instances of your own subclass of UIView itself or of your own subclass of UIViewController, you will generally want to follow the simplest possible rule: implement *all* the `touches...` events together in one class, so that touches arrive at an instance either because it was the hit-test view or because it is up the responder chain from the hit-test view, and do *not* call `super` in any of them. In this way, "the buck stops here" — the touch handling for this object or for objects below it in the responder chain is bottlenecked into one well-defined place.

- If you subclass a built-in UIView subclass and you override its touch handling, you don't have to override every single `touches...` event, but you *do* need to call `super` so that the built-in touch handling can occur.

- Don't allow touches to arrive from lower down the responder chain at an instance of a built-in UIView subclass that implements built-in touch handling, because such a class is completely unprepared for the first parameter of a `touches...` method containing a touch not intended for itself. Judicious use of `userInteraction-Enabled` or hit-test munging can be a big help here.

  I'm not saying, however, that you have to block all touches from percolating up the responder chain; it's normal for unhandled touches to arrive at the UIWindow or UIApplication, for example, because these classes do not (by default) do any touch handling — so those touches will remain unhandled and will percolate right off the end of the responder chain, which is perfectly fine.

- Never call a `touches...` method directly (except to call `super`).

 Apple's documentation has some discussion of a technique called *event forwarding* where you *do* call `touches...` methods directly. But you are far less likely to need this now that gesture recognizers exist, and it can be extremely tricky and even downright dangerous to implement, so I won't give an example here, and I suggest that you not use it.

# PART V

# Interface

The previous part of the book introduced views. This part of the book is about the particular kinds of view provided by the Cocoa framework — the built-in "widgets" with which you'll construct an app's interface. These are surprising few, but impressively powerful.

- Chapter 19 is about view controllers. View controllers are a brilliant mechanism for allowing an entire interface to be replaced by another; this ability is especially crucial on the iPhone's small screen. They are also the basis of an app's ability to compensate when the user rotates the device. In real life, every app you write will probably have its interface managed by view controllers.

- Chapter 20 is about scroll views, the iOS mechanism for letting the user scroll and zoom the interface.

- Chapter 21 explains table views, an extremely important and powerful type of scroll view that lets the user navigate through any amount of data.

- Chapter 22 is about two forms of interface unique to, and characteristic of, the iPad — popovers and split views.

- Chapter 23 describes several ways of presenting text in an app's interface — labels, text fields, text views, and text drawn manually with Core Text.

- Chapter 24 discusses web views. A web view is a easy-to-use interface widget backed by the power of a full-fledged web browser. It can also be used to present a PDF and various other forms of data.

- Chapter 25 describes all the remaining built-in iOS (UIKit) interface widgets.

- Chapter 26 is about the forms of modal dialog that can appear in front of an app's interface.

# View Controllers

An iOS app's interface is dynamic in a way that a Mac OS X application is not. In Mac OS X, an application's windows can be big, and there can be more than one of them, so there's room for lots of interface. With iOS, everything needs to fit on a single display, which in the case of the iPhone is almost forbiddingly tiny. The iOS solution to this is to replace interface with interface, as needed. Thus, entire screens of material need to come and go in a fashion that is not only agile but intuitive: the user must not be confused. Management of this task resides in a *view controller* (an instance of a UI-ViewController subclass).

You are extremely unlikely to write an iOS app that hasn't at least one view controller. They are, not to put too fine a point on it, indispensable. In this regard, the Empty Window example project that we've been using in earlier chapters to demonstrate individual views and controls is artificial and exceptional. Even if your app's interface as a whole is *never* replaced by some other interface, you are *still* likely to use a view controller, because a view controller also knows how to rotate the interface in response to the user rotating the device.

A view controller manages a single view (which can, of course, have subviews); its `view` property points to the view it manages. The view has no explicit pointer to the view controller that manages it, but a view controller is a UIResponder and is in the responder chain just above its view (Chapter 11), so it is the view's `nextResponder`.

The UIViewController class is designed to be subclassed. You might use a built-in subclass or you might subclass UIViewController directly, but you are fairly unlikely to use a plain vanilla UIViewController. Still, a UIViewController has some useful default behavior along with some properties that can be set from outside, so you *might* be able get away without subclassing. But you probably shouldn't. (I have written just one real-world app that uses a nonsubclassed UIViewController, and in retrospect I think even this was a poor decision.)

Here are some of the mighty powers you'll be taking advantage of with your UIView-Controller subclass:

*Figure 19-1. The TidBITS logo appears in the navigation bar automatically*

*Rotation*

    The user can rotate the device, and you might like the interface to rotate in response, to compensate. A window is effectively pinned to the physical display (window bounds are screen bounds and do not change), but a view can be given a transform so that its top moves to the current top of the display. A UIViewController responds to device rotation by applying this transform.

*Containment*

    To replace one interface with another, or to specify what interface to present, iOS uses an architecture of containment. Often, both the container and the contained are view controllers. Certain built-in UIViewController subclasses (in particular UITabBarController, UINavigationController, and UISplitViewController) have as their primary purpose the containment and management of other view controllers; moreover, any view controller can temporarily contain and manage another view controller modally, effectively replacing its own view by another. Other types of interface object may also involve a view controller to determine what view to present; for example, a popover's view, presented by a UIPopoverController, is managed through a view controller.

*Customizability*

    A view controller has properties and methods that are used to customize the interface and its behavior when its view is showing. For example, when a UINavigationController (a UIViewController subclass) substitutes another view controller's view into its interface, it looks for that view controller's `navigationItem.title-View` property — and puts it into the navigation bar at the top of the interface. (Thus, the TidBITS logo in Figure 19-1 appears in the navigation bar because it is a view controller's `navigationItem.titleView`.)

We may distinguish between two uses of a UIViewController:

*The root view controller*

    The view controller that manages the *root view* of the interface — the sole immediate subview of the window, which occupies the entire window. Just about any app you write will have a root view controller. The root view might have no other purpose than to contain the rest of the interface.

*Contained view controller*

A view controller that is contained and managed by another view controller, or by some other built-in type of object that requires a view controller.

Indeed, in iOS 4, as we shall see, the root view controller optionally *is* a contained view controller: the main window will contain and manage it through its `rootView-Controller` property. Thus both uses of a view controller become the same use: you use a view controller in places where a built-in class asks for it.

You should not use a view controller in any other way. It is not, for example, appropriate to use a view controller to manage a view that occupies only a part of the window, or is a subview of anything except the window as a whole, except as a side effect of the fact that this is a contained view controller. This, I take it, is what Apple's documentation means when it says:

> You should not use multiple custom view controllers to manage different portions of the same view hierarchy. Similarly, you should not use a single custom view controller object to manage multiple screens worth of content.... If you want to divide a view hierarchy into multiple subareas and manage each one separately, use generic controller objects (custom objects descending from NSObject) instead of view controller objects to manage each subarea.

# Creating a View Controller

I'll use the root view controller to illustrate the process of how a view controller comes into existence. You already know that your interface is displayed initially because the main nib is loaded and `makeKeyAndVisible` is called on the window. The window is now to have a root view, a single immediate subview occupying the window completely, and containing anything else that appears in the window; and this view is to be controlled by a view controller.

There are then four questions to be answered:

1. Where is this view controller to come from?
2. Where is its view to come from?
3. How will its view get into the window?
4. How will the view controller be memory-managed? That is, someone must retain the view controller so that it persists, in such a way that a reference to it can be obtained; how will this happen?

There is a range of possibilities from completely manual, using code, to completely automatic, using nibs:

- Both the view controller and its view may be created entirely in code, manually.

- Either the view controller or its view, or both, may be created in a nib. You can set this up in such a way that the loading of this nib is itself manual or automatic.

- You can start with an application template that does everything for you: both the view controller and the view are created in a nib, and the nib loading is automatic.

- If the view controller is created in a nib, its memory-management is likely to be automatic, and its view's insertion into the window can be made automatic as well.

Even though I'm going to be talking specifically about the root view controller, the discussion applies to any view controller. The possible answers to the first two questions (where the view controller comes from and where its view comes from) are effectively the same regardless of how the view controller is to be used. And in the case of a contained view controller, the other two questions answer themselves; both a contained view controller's memory management and the display of its view are taken care of by the very fact that it *is* a contained view controller.

## Manual View Controller, Manual View

We're going to create a view controller and its view in code as the application starts up. I actually use this approach quite a bit, and am fond of it because it is so clear and straightforward. Creating and populating a view in code can be verbose, but it gives me complete control, whereas loading a view from a nib always leaves me scratching my head a bit, wondering whether I checked all the right checkboxes and whether they will do the right thing.

We begin, therefore, with a project based on the Window-based Application template:

1. We need a UIViewController subclass, so choose File → New → New File; specify a Cocoa Touch UIViewController subclass. Click Next.

2. Make sure this is a UIViewController subclass. Uncheck both checkboxes. Click Next.

3. Name the file *RootViewController*, and save.

We now have a RootViewController class, and we proceed to edit its code.

A view controller is in charge of obtaining or creating its own view. If our view controller is to create its view manually, in code, we must override UIViewController's `load-View` method. Looking in *RootViewController.m*, we find that the UIViewController subclass template has provided a `loadView` method, commented out. So uncomment it and let's implement it. To convince ourselves that the example is working correctly, we'll give the view an identifiable color, and we'll put some interface inside that view, in this case a "Hello, World" label:

```
- (void) loadView {
    UIView* v = ❶
        [[UIView alloc] initWithFrame: [[UIScreen mainScreen] applicationFrame]];
    v.backgroundColor = [UIColor greenColor];
    UILabel* label = [[UILabel alloc] init];
```

```
    label.text = @"Hello, World!";
    [label sizeToFit];
    label.center = CGPointMake(CGRectGetMidX(v.bounds), CGRectGetMidY(v.bounds));
    label.autoresizingMask = ( ❷
                        UIViewAutoresizingFlexibleTopMargin |
                        UIViewAutoresizingFlexibleLeftMargin |
                        UIViewAutoresizingFlexibleBottomMargin |
                        UIViewAutoresizingFlexibleRightMargin
                        );
    [v addSubview:label];
    self.view = v; ❸
    [label release];
    [v release];
}
```

❶ The frame of v is set to a value that captures the notion of filling the screen: the applicationFrame is the entire visible area, excluding the status bar. If there is no status bar ("Status bar is initially hidden" is checked in *Info.plist*), we fill the entire visible screen. If there is a status bar but you want the view to underlap it, filling the screen behind it, which you might well want if the status bar is transparent ("Status bar style" in *Info.plist*), you would add this line:

```
    self.wantsFullScreenLayout = YES;
```

❷ We use autoresizing to obtain layout for our view's subviews — in this case, just one subview, the label. The view size may be adjusted for us depending on whether there is a status bar, and, even more important, if we respond to rotation of the device; we must be prepared for this. (I'll demonstrate rotation in a moment.) Of course you can use manual layout with layoutSubviews in a UIView subclass, but that isn't necessary for most interfaces.

❸ The most important line comes at the end: we set the value of self.view to the view which this view controller is to manage. This is why we are here. If you implement loadView, you *must* use it to set self.view. Notice also that we do *not* call super; the documentation strictly warns against this (I'll explain why in a moment).

Our view controller is ready for use; now we must arrange to use it. To do so, we turn to our app delegate class. It's a little frustrating having to set things up in two different places before our labors can bear any visible fruit, but such is life.

The first problem is our view controller's lifetime. The view controller must persist for as long as the view is needed. In this case, that's likely to be the lifetime of the app as a whole. The obvious solution to persistence is an instance variable and retain (Chapter 12). So in the app delegate class's header file, declare a property with a retain policy:

```
    @class RootViewController;
    // ...
    @property (nonatomic, retain) RootViewController* rvc;
```

In the app delegate class's implementation, import "RootViewController.h", synthesize rvc to get accessors for it, and don't forget to release rvc in dealloc.

Forgetting to implement persistence of a view controller through memory management is a common beginner error, and can be difficult to track down.

Our instance variable, with accessors and memory management, is ready; so now in the app delegate's `application:didFinishLaunchingWithOptions:` we can create the view controller:

```
RootViewController* theRVC = [[RootViewController alloc] init];
self.rvc = theRVC;
[theRVC release];
```

We must not only create the view controller; we must also put its view into the interface (this isn't going to happen magically all by itself):

```
[self.window addSubview:self.rvc.view];
// and now we can display our initial interface
[self.window makeKeyAndVisible];
```

Build and run the app. Sure enough, there's our telltale green background containing the words "Hello, world!" This proves that the view was created, but it doesn't really prove that the view controller is controlling the view. Is the view controller, in fact, doing anything? To demonstrate that it is, return to the view controller's code and implement rotation, by uncommenting and overriding `shouldAutorotateToInterface-Orientation:`, like this:

```
- (BOOL)shouldAutorotateToInterfaceOrientation:
        (UIInterfaceOrientation)interfaceOrientation {
    // Return YES for supported orientations
    return YES;
}
```

I'll talk more about rotation later, but this code means simply that we support any orientation of the device: if the user rotates the device, we want to rotate to compensate. So build and run the app, and in the Simulator, choose Hardware → Rotate Left repeatedly. Each time you do, the entire interface rotates to compensate, and the label (thanks to our autoresizing) remains centered. The view controller is working.

If your app is going to run only on iOS 4.0 or later, there's another way to slot the view controller into the app in such a way that you *don't* need to create an instance variable to retain it, and you *don't* need to add its view as a subview to the window. This way is to take advantage of the UIWindow `rootViewController` property. This property already exists, it already has a retain policy, and (most important) when you assign it a UIViewController instance, it automatically asks for that UIViewController's `view` and makes that the window's sole subview. So now our code in `application:didFinish-LaunchingWithOptions:` would look like this:

```
RootViewController* theRVC = [[RootViewController alloc] init];
self.window.rootViewController = theRVC;
[theRVC release];
[self.window makeKeyAndVisible];
```

This may not appear to be much of a savings, but remember, we can now delete the `rvc` property and all its related buttressing, and the resulting architecture is extremely sensible. The root view controller and its view "belong" to the same single object (the window); also, the root view controller is globally available through the window:

```
UIViewController* rvc =
    [[[UIApplication sharedApplication] keyWindow] rootViewController];
```

## Manual View Controller, Nib View

Designing and maintaining a complex interface in a nib might be more pleasant than creating it in code. We can fetch part or all of the view controller's view from a nib.

Let's start by supposing that you would create the view controller's view in code, as in the previous example, but that you would manually load a nib in order to populate that view with subviews. There is actually nothing new here. You have already seen how to create the view controller's view in code, and you already know how to load a nib to obtain a view instance. This is, indeed, almost exactly the example we developed in Chapter 7, where there's a secondary nib *MyNib.xib* containing a "Hello, World" label, and we load the nib, refer to the label through an instance variable that was set by an outlet when the nib loaded, and stuff the label into our interface. All we need is an owner for the nib; the most economical solution is obviously that this should be the view controller itself.

So I won't bother telling you how to create and configure *MyNib.xib*, or how to give RootViewController the necessary instance variable; all of that is effectively the same as in Chapter 7. I'll assume that RootViewController now has a property `theLabel` with an assign policy (we don't need to retain it, because we're going to insert it into another view immediately, and that view will retain it). Here's the code for the revised `loadView`:

```
UIView* v =
    [[UIView alloc] initWithFrame: [[UIScreen mainScreen] applicationFrame]];
v.backgroundColor = [UIColor greenColor];
[[NSBundle mainBundle] loadNibNamed:@"MyNib" owner:self options:nil];
```

```
    self.theLabel.center =
        CGPointMake(CGRectGetMidX(v.bounds), CGRectGetMidY(v.bounds));
    [v addSubview:self.theLabel];
    self.view = v;
    [v release];
```

If, on the other hand, we want to load the view controller's *entire* view from a nib, things change radically. When we instantiate the view controller, we won't initialize it with a mere init; instead, we'll call initWithNibName:bundle: (this is actually the designated initializer). This will cause the view controller to load the specified nib when we first ask for its view. We must *not* override loadView; the view property will be set from a view outlet in the nib. If we have further initializations to perform in code after the view property is set, we override viewDidLoad. (When the view is created in code using loadView, viewDidLoad is also called afterward, and can be used to perform additional initializations.)

 The truth is that loadView is *always* called when the view controller's view is mentioned and has not yet been set. If we override it, we supply and set the view. If we don't override it, the default implementation is to load the view controller's nib (setting view through an outlet). For this reason, if we do override loadView, we must *not* call super — that would cause us to get *both* behaviors.

In our example, then, comment out loadView in RootViewController and let's start over:

1. Create a nib from which RootViewController will get its view, specifying the View template. Let's call it *RV.xib* for the present (later we'll change the name, to demonstrate a shortcut).

2. Edit *RV.xib*. Change the File's Owner's class to RootViewController. This produces a view outlet; hook it up to the view.

3. Still in *RV.xib*, design the view; in this case, that would mean giving it a background color and putting a "Hello, World!" label into it, with appropriate autoresizing.

The code for the app delegate's application:didFinishLaunchingWithOptions: is just the same as before, except that now the view controller is created like this:

```
RootViewController* theRVC =
    [[RootViewController alloc] initWithNibName:@"RV" bundle:nil];
```

Build and run the app to prove to yourself that it works.

A moment ago, I mentioned a shortcut, and here it is: if the nib has the same name as the view controller's class, we can pass nil as the nib name (which means, in effect, we can return to using init to initialize the view controller). To put it conversely, the rule is that if the nib name passed to initWithNibName:bundle: is nil, a nib will be sought with the same name as the view controller's class. So, if you like, you could rename

*RV.xib* as *RootViewController.xib* and return to using `init` instead of `initWithNibName:` `bundle:`, and our app will keep on working just as before.

Taking advantage of this shortcut means that, because view controllers often have "Controller" in their name, we end up with nibs that *also* have "Controller" in their name, which is ridiculous: a nib is not a controller. But there's an additional aspect to the shortcut: the runtime, in looking for a view controller's corresponding nib, will in fact try stripping "Controller" off the end of the view controller class's name. (This feature is undocumented, but it works reliably and I can't believe it would ever be retracted.) Thus, we could name our nib *RootView.xib* instead of *RootViewController.xib*, and it would still work when we initialize our RootViewController instance using `init` instead of `initWithNibName:bundle:`.

When you create the files for a UIViewController subclass, the Xcode dialog has a checkbox (which we unchecked earlier) offering to create an eponymous *.xib* file at the same time ("With XIB for user interface"). If you accept that option, the nib is created with the as File's Owner's class set to the view controller's class and with its `view` outlet already hooked up to the view. This automatically created *.xib* file does *not* have "Controller" stripped off the end of its name; you can rename it manually later (I generally do) if the default name bothers you.

Not every built-in subclass of UIViewController obeys the convention that a nil nib name means a nib with the same name as the view controller's class. In particular, UITableViewController does not. I regard this as a bug; in any case, it has caught me by surprise several times (and can be difficult to track down, when the table view mysteriously fails to appear in the interface).

## Nib-Instantiated View Controller

A UIViewController, including a built-in subclass or your subclass, can be instantiated in a nib. The root view controller, in particular, will be a top-level nib object; in our app, this nib would be *MainWindow.xib*.

Let's begin by repeating the approach we used earlier: we gave our app delegate an `rvc` instance variable (with appropriate `@synthesize` and memory-management buttressing). If we wish to take this approach, the instance variable must now be set to a nib-instantiated object, which means we must use an outlet. So we write the app delegate's `rvc` property declaration in such a way that it *is* an outlet:

```
@property (nonatomic, retain) IBOutlet RootViewController* rvc;
```

Now, in *MainWindow.xib*, drag a UIViewController from the Object library into the dock, to make it a top-level object; then change its class to RootViewController and hook the app delegate nib object's `rvc` outlet to it.

The view controller is now being instantiated and assigned to an instance variable by the loading of the nib; we don't need to instantiate it explicitly in code. In the app delegate class's code, therefore, our opening dance for showing the interface is now down to just two lines of code:

```
[self.window addSubview:self.rvc.view];
[self.window makeKeyAndVisible];
```

What's more, if the app is to run on only iOS 4.0 or later, you'll recall, we can remove the app delegate's `rvc` property and all its buttressing once again, and reduce our opening dance to a single line of code:

```
[self.window makeKeyAndVisible];
```

To make that work, the outlet that needs to be hooked up to the UIViewController in the nib is not the app delegate's `rvc` outlet (which no longer exists) but the window's `rootViewController` outlet. When the nib loads and the window's `rootViewController` instance variable is set, the UIViewController's view will be made the window's subview automatically.

We come now to the question of how to specify a UIViewController's view when the UIViewController is instantiated in a nib. There are actually three different ways:

*By specifying another nib*

This is the most appropriate way to adapt our existing project, because our view is already off in another nib — *RV.xib*, or *RootViewController.xib* (or *Root-View.xib*) if you renamed it. If you *did* rename it, we are finished; our app now runs correctly. (Try it and see.) This is because, since the UIViewController has not been given a view in the same nib as itself, it is sent `initWithNibName:bundle:` as it is instantiated through the loading of the nib, and if you don't configure the UI-ViewController in the nib any further, the `NibName` parameter will be nil, and a nib with the same name as the UIViewController's class is sought.

If you need to specify the `NibName` parameter explicitly, select the UIViewController in the nib and specify the Nib Name in the Attributes inspector. This field is a combo box whose pop-up menu already knows the names of all your project's nib files, so just pick the right one.

Just a reminder: when you take this approach, the File's Owner's class in the second nib must be set correctly (so that the nib knows it's a UIViewController), and its `view` outlet must link to the view.

*Through the `view` outlet*

The UIViewController has a `view` outlet, so you can connect this to a view in the *same* nib. Thus, we could eliminate our use of a second nib. This is not a usual approach (because of its implications for memory management, which I'll explain later in this chapter), but it wouldn't be inappropriate if this view is to be always present in the interface as the window's sole subview. So we could in fact put the view right into the *MainWindow.xib* dock as a top-level object, and point the view controller's `view` outlet to it.

*By treating the UIViewController in the nib as a view container*

If you show a UIViewController nib object in the canvas, it acts as if it were a kind of view container. You can place (and design) the view here, rather than as a top-level object. This is in fact the preferred approach if you're going to put the view controller and its view in the same nib. There is no need to set the view controller's `view` outlet.

We are now in a position to examine and understand Xcode 4's View-based Application template. It takes the first of the three approaches I just listed ("By specifying another nib"). Make a project based on this template, study it, and see for yourself:

- The root view controller is instantiated in the main nib.
- The root view controller's view is loaded from a second nib; the name of this nib (which is the same as that of the view controller class), is specified explicitly in the root view controller's configuration in the main nib.
- The app delegate retains the root view controller instance through a `view-Controller` property with a retain policy, which is an outlet; thus the app delegate also gets a reference to the root view controller.
- The app delegate's `application:didFinishLaunchingWithOptions:` passes that view controller instance to the window's `rootViewController` property, so that the view controller's view will appear in the window:

```
self.window.rootViewController = self.viewController;
[self.window makeKeyAndVisible];
```

The root views for other Xcode 4 project templates generally work the same way.

Be very sure you understand how this project template works! You don't want to be dependent on the project templates, but you don't want to be afraid of them, either. You should be able to use and customize the View-based Application template quickly and easily; you should also be able to create your own project with a root view controller starting with the Window-based Application template, just as quickly and easily.

## No View

If you ask for a view controller's `view` and none of its ways of obtaining a view succeeds — `loadView` is not overridden, and we weren't given a nib name and no nib matches the name of the view controller's class, even with "Controller" stripped off — the view controller itself creates a plain vanilla UIView, sets its frame to the `applicationFrame`, and assigns it to its `view` property.

Thus, if you don't need the `view` to be a particular UIView subclass, you could simply permit this to happen, and perform any further configuration of the view in `viewDid-Load`. For example, here is our earlier `loadView` code, where we populate the view by loading its subviews from a nib; here, though, we've moved the code to `viewDidLoad`. We don't implement `loadView`, and there is no corresponding nib, so the `view` property

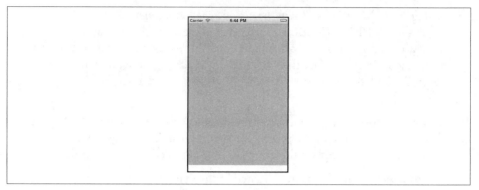

*Figure 19-2. An up-shifted root view*

has been automatically set and properly positioned, and all we need to do is configure it:

```
self.view.backgroundColor = [UIColor greenColor];
[[NSBundle mainBundle] loadNibNamed:@"MyNib" owner:self options:nil];
self.theLabel.center =
    CGPointMake(CGRectGetMidX(v.bounds), CGRectGetMidY(v.bounds));
[self.view addSubview:self.theLabel];
```

## Up-Shifted Root View

Sometimes, a view that is supposed to occupy the whole interface will appear shifted up, leaving a gap at the bottom — a gap that, not coincidentally, is the height of the status bar.

To see the problem, start with the View-based Application template. In the app delegate, delete this line:

```
self.window.rootViewController = self.viewController;
```

In its place, put this:

```
[self.window addSubview:self.viewController.view];
```

Now edit *MainWindow.xib*; select the top-level UIViewController object, and in the Attributes inspector, uncheck Resize View From XIB. Now build and run (Figure 19-2).

The problem is that in the nib from which it is loaded, the view that will act as root view has its origin at (0,0). That point, in window coordinates, is at the top of the window — at the top left of the status bar. So part of the view underlaps the status bar. At the same time, the view's height is shorter than the window — shorter by exactly the height of the status bar. Thus, a gap the size of the status bar appears at the bottom of the window.

If your app is to run only on iOS 4.0 or later, the solution is simple: don't place the root view into the window with **addSubview:**, but instead do it by assigning the view controller to the window's **rootViewController** property. This implicitly sets the view's frame to [[UIScreen mainScreen] applicationFrame] (exactly as we did manually in the first example in this chapter), thus positioning it correctly in relation to the status bar.

On a system before iOS 4.0, the window's rootViewController property doesn't exist, and you'll have to use a different solution. One approach, if the view is loaded from a nib with a UIViewController as its owner, and if the UIViewController is instantiated from a nib, is to check Resize View From XIB in the Attributes inspector. That is why, by default, that checkbox *is* checked. If that approach isn't applicable or doesn't work, you'll have to set the view's frame to applicationFrame yourself, in code. The usual place to do this is in the UIViewController's viewDidLoad.

# Rotation

A major part of a view controller's job is to know how to rotate the view. The user will experience this as rotation of the app itself: the top of the app shifts so that it is oriented against a different side of the device's display. There are two complementary uses for rotation:

*Compensatory rotation*
> The app rotates to compensate for the orientation of the device, so that the app appears right way up with respect to how the user is holding the device. The challenge of compensatory rotation stems, quite simply, from the fact that the screen is not square. This means that if the app rotates 90 degrees, the interface no longer fits the screen, and must be changed to compensate.

*Forced rotation*
> The app rotates when a particular view appears in the interface, or when the app launches, to indicate that the user needs to rotate the device in order to view the app the right way up. This is typically because the interface has been specifically designed, in the face of the fact that the screen is not square, to appear in one particular mode (portrait or landscape).

In the case of the iPhone, no law says that your app has to perform compensatory rotation. Most of my iPhone apps do not do so; indeed, I have no compunction about doing just the opposite, forcing the user to rotate the device differently depending on what view is being displayed. The iPhone is small and easily reoriented with a twist of the user's wrist, and it has a natural right way up, especially because it's a phone. (The iPod touch isn't a phone, but the same argument works by analogy.) On the other hand, Apple would like iPad apps to rotate to at least two opposed orientations (such as landscape with the button on the right and landscape with the button on the left), and preferably to all four possible orientations, so that the user isn't restricted in how the device is held and positioned.

It's fairly trivial to let your app rotate to two opposed orientations, because once the app is set up to work in one of them, it can work with no change in the other. But allowing an app to rotate between two orientations that are 90 degrees apart is trickier, because its dimensions must change — its height and width are swapped — and this may require a change of layout and might even call for more substantial alterations to the interface, such as removal or addition of part of the interface. A good example is the behavior of Apple's Mail app on the iPad: in landscape mode, the master pane and the detail pane appear side by side, but in portrait mode, the detail pane is removed and must be summoned as a popover using a button. (This style of master–detail interface management on the iPad is effectively built into the functionality of the UISplitViewController; see Chapter 22.)

The main thing your view controller must do in order to support rotation is to override `shouldAutorotateToInterfaceOrientation:`. The incoming parameter is the proposed orientation, and will be one of the following:

- `UIInterfaceOrientationPortrait`, with the home button at the bottom.
- `UIInterfaceOrientationPortraitUpsideDown`, with the home button at the top.
- `UIInterfaceOrientationLandscapeLeft`, with the home button at the left.
- `UIInterfaceOrientationLandscapeRight`, with the home button at the right.

You return YES for all permitted orientations and NO otherwise. (The default, if you don't override this method, is to return YES for `UIInterfaceOrientationPortrait` and NO otherwise; you *must* return YES for *some* orientation.)

These four interface orientations are matched by four device orientations with similar names (`UIDeviceOrientationPortrait` and so on), except that the two landscape orientations are reversed: `UIInterfaceOrientationLandscapeLeft` is the same as `UIDeviceOrientationLandscapeRight`, because if the user rotates the device 90 degrees left from an original portrait orientation, the interface must rotate 90 degrees right to compensate. The device actually has several more possible orientations, such as `UIDeviceOrientationFaceUp` (the device is lying on its back), but these will not, of themselves, trigger interface rotation.

In case your implementation of `shouldAutorotateToInterfaceOrientation:` wants to return YES to both of two opposed orientations, a pair of macros are provided: `UIInterfaceOrientationIsLandscape(io)` returns YES if `io` is either of the two landscape orientations, and `UIInterfaceOrientationIsPortrait(io)` returns YES if `io` is either of the two portrait orientations.

## Initial Orientation

Your app's initial orientation, as it is launched, is determined by the "Supported interface orientations" setting (`UISupportedInterfaceOrientations`) in the app's *Info.plist*. If there is only one orientation listed here, the app will launch into it. If there is more than one orientation listed, you are giving the system the option to launch the app into whichever of the supported orientations is closest to the way the device is

> # What Rotates?
>
> We say that your app rotates, and you'll think of it as rotating, but what really rotates is the status bar's position. When the device rotates, a `UIDeviceOrientationDidChange-Notification` is emitted by the UIDevice, and your app's root view controller is consulted with `shouldAutorotateToInterfaceOrientation:`; if the view controller returns YES for the proposed orientation, the UIApplication instance is sent the `setStatusBar-Orientation:animated:` message. In a 90-degree rotation, the window's subview then has its width and height dimensions swapped, and a transform is applied so that it appears "right way up." Moreover, this is all accompanied by animation, so it really looks to the user as if the app is rotating. But the window *itself* doesn't budge; it remains "pinned" to the screen (window bounds are screen bounds), it is taller than it is wide, and its top is at the top of the device (away from the home button). As for the view, its bounds are wider than tall in a landscape orientation, but its frame remains taller than wide (though you really shouldn't be referring to the view's frame in this situation, because it has a transform applied; see Chapter 14).

positioned at the time. In Xcode 4, you can specify this setting graphically by editing the target (in the Summary tab).

Alternatively, if the app supports only one possible initial orientation, you can use the older "Initial interface orientation" setting (`UIInterfaceOrientation`).

> The orientation(s) specified here must also be among the orientations to which the root view controller's `shouldAutorotateToInterface-Orientation:` will return YES.

As I've already mentioned, on the iPhone, it is common for an app to launch into just one orientation, as it is no trouble for the user to twist the device to view the app correctly, but on the iPad, Apple would like you to list at least two opposed orientations (both portrait orientations or both landscape orientations), and preferably all four.

An app whose initial orientation is portrait mode with the button at the bottom therefore has effectively no work to do, because this is the default orientation. An app with no "Supported interface orientations" or "Initial interface orientation" setting adopts "Portrait (bottom home button)" by default (`UIInterfaceOrientationPortrait`), and the default `shouldAutorotateToInterfaceOrientation:` behavior is to return YES to `UIInterfaceOrientationPortrait` and NO to anything else.

But an app whose initial orientation is landscape mode must be configured to rotate to this position even if it doesn't otherwise support rotation, and the initial setup of its interface can be tricky. Let's take the case of an iPhone app whose initial orientation is landscape, with the button on the right:

1. In *Info.plist*, set the "Supported interface orientations" or "Initial interface orientation" to "Landscape (right home button)."

2. In the root view controller's code, override `shouldAutorotateToInterfaceOrientation:` along these lines:

```
- (BOOL) shouldAutorotateToInterfaceOrientation:(UIInterfaceOrientation)io {
    return (io == UIDeviceOrientationLandscapeRight);
}
```

3. If the root view interface requires further configuration in code, give the interface a chance to establish itself and to rotate into position before doing that configuration.

It is the neglect of that third step that causes beginners the most trouble (especially because the documentation doesn't tell you about it). The problem is that when the root view is initially put into the window, its bounds are window bounds; only later, at the redraw moment (Chapter 14), does the view resize appropriately to the initial orientation you've requested. Thus, if you try to configure the interface too early (say, in the root view controller's `viewDidLoad`), the width and height values of the view's bounds will be reversed.

For example, let's say that we've taken the first two steps but we've neglected the third, and that our root view controller's `viewDidLoad` code looks like this:

```
- (void)viewDidLoad {
    [super viewDidLoad];
    UIView* square = [[UIView alloc] initWithFrame:CGRectMake(0,0,10,10)];
    square.backgroundColor = [UIColor blackColor];
    square.center = CGPointMake(CGRectGetMidX(self.view.bounds),5); // top center?
    [self.view addSubview:square];
    [square release];
}
```

The app launches into a rotated landscape orientation; the user must hold the device with the home button at the right to see it correctly. But where's the little black square? *Not* at the top center of the screen! The square appears at the top of the screen, but only about a third of the way across.

The trouble is that we said `CGRectGetMidX(self.view.bounds)` for the x-coordinate of the square's center *too soon*, at a time when the view's x-dimension (its width dimension) was still its shorter dimension. One solution is to use delayed performance, to give the redraw moment a chance to occur before we perform our final view configuration. Thus, we could write our code like this:

```
- (void)viewDidLoad {
    [super viewDidLoad];
    [self performSelector:@selector(finishViewDidLoad)
            withObject:nil afterDelay:0.0];
}

- (void) finishViewDidLoad {
    UIView* square = [[UIView alloc] initWithFrame:CGRectMake(0,0,10,10)];
```

```
        square.backgroundColor = [UIColor blackColor];
        square.center = CGPointMake(CGRectGetMidX(self.view.bounds),5);
        [self.view addSubview:square];
        [square release];
    }
```

The delayed performance (even with a delay of 0) postpones the calling of finishView-
DidLoad until after the next redraw moment, which includes the initial rotation of the
view. Now the x-dimension is the longer dimension and the black square appears at
the top center of the screen.

An alternative approach is to override didRotateFromInterfaceOrientation: and complete the configuration of your view there. This method is called at launch time after
the initial rotation has been performed, so the dimensions of the root view are correct.
It has been suggested to me that this approach is more correct than using delayed
performance in viewDidLoad, because it is more certain; didRotateFromInterface-
Orientation: tells us definitely that the rotation has taken place, whereas with delayed
performance in viewDidLoad, we're just making an assumption. So here's the same code
restructured to use didRotateFromInterfaceOrientation: (and not viewDidLoad). Observe that we take precautions to prevent the interface from being configured again in
case didRotateFromInterfaceOrientation: is called again later; this is a good use of a
static variable:

```
    - (void) finishInitializingView {
        // static BOOL flag
        static BOOL done = NO;
        if (done)
            return;
        done = YES;
        // the static BOOL flag makes sure the following is performed exactly once
        UIView* square = [[UIView alloc] initWithFrame:CGRectMake(0,0,10,10)];
        square.backgroundColor = [UIColor blackColor];
        square.center = CGPointMake(CGRectGetMidX(self.view.bounds),5);
        [self.view addSubview:square];
        [square release];
    }

    - (void)didRotateFromInterfaceOrientation:
            (UIInterfaceOrientation)fromInterfaceOrientation {
        [self finishInitializingView];
    }
```

Yet another alternative is to implement willAnimateRotationToInterfaceOrientation:
duration:. It has certain advantages over didRotateFromInterfaceOrientation: — it
arrives earlier in the rotation process, for example — while at the same time the interface
dimensions have already been swapped for the orientation to which we are rotating,
so you can safely perform initializations that depend on those dimensions.

When designing in the nib, if the interface is to appear in landscape mode, you can
design in landscape mode; select your window or root view, and choose Landscape in
the Orientation pop-up menu in the Simulated Metrics section of the Attributes in-

spector. However, this does not really rotate anything; you're merely swapping the view's height and width values. The nib knows nothing of orientations, and the view, if it is placed into the window automatically as the app launches, will still have a narrower x-dimension initially. In practice this should cause no difficulty; if the results at runtime are not what you expect, it may help to use autoresizing settings so that the bits of your interface settle into the correct position and dimensions.

## Rotation Events

In a 90-degree rotation, the width and height values of your root controller's view are swapped. This, as I've just said, should cause no difficulty if your app is merely launching into a landscape orientation, but if your app is to switch between portrait and landscape while running, the view's contents and subviews will surely need to compensate somehow. In simple cases, autoresizing settings may suffice. But in case you need to perform more elaborate adjustments, your root controller is sent willRotateToInterfaceOrientation:duration: before the bounds are changed, and willAnimateRotationToInterfaceOrientation:duration:, and later didRotateFromInterfaceOrientation:, after the bounds are changed. You can override these to make any desired adjustments. You can use the UIViewController property interfaceOrientation to learn the current orientation.

In this simple example, our app displays a black rectangle at the left side of the screen if the device is in landscape orientation, but not if the device is in portrait orientation. The view controller has an instance variable blackRect with a retain policy:

```
- (void) prepareInterface {
    if (!self.blackRect) {
        CGRect f = self.view.bounds;
        f.size.width = f.size.width/3.0;
        UIView* br = [[UIView alloc] initWithFrame:f];
        br.backgroundColor = [UIColor blackColor];
        self.blackRect = br;
        [br release];
    }
}

- (void) willRotateToInterfaceOrientation:(UIInterfaceOrientation)io
                                 duration:(NSTimeInterval)duration {
    if (UIInterfaceOrientationIsPortrait(io))
        [self.blackRect removeFromSuperview];
}

- (void) didRotateFromInterfaceOrientation:(UIInterfaceOrientation)io {
    [self prepareInterface];
    if (UIInterfaceOrientationIsLandscape(self.interfaceOrientation)
        && !self.blackRect.superview)
        [self.view addSubview:self.blackRect];
}
```

The example is marked by its defensive posture, quite typical of an event-driven architecture (Chapter 11) under which it is best to make as few assumptions as possible about what will really happen and in what order. The utility method `prepare-Interface` creates the black rectangle, but only if it hasn't been created already. The implementation of `didRotateFromInterfaceOrientation:` puts the black rectangle into the interface, but only if we have ended up in a landscape orientation, and only if it isn't in the interface already; after all, the user might rotate the device 180 degrees, from one landscape orientation to the other.

It is possible to divide your response to rotation into two stages by additionally implementing these methods:

* `willAnimateFirstHalfOfRotationToInterfaceOrientation:duration:`
* `didAnimateFirstHalfOfRotationToInterfaceOrientation:`
* `willAnimateSecondHalfOfRotationFromInterfaceOrientation:duration:`

This is not commonly needed and is mostly a holdover from iOS 2.0.

A complete alternative to all this rather daunting dynamism is to maintain two distinct static views, one for landscape orientation and one for portrait orientation, and to swap them as necessary. This approach, which can greatly reduce your code and your worry, requires use of a container view controller; I'll give an example in the next section.

# Modal Views

The simplest form of view controller containment is a *modal view*. Here, a view controller replaces its entire view with another view controller's view. This is done by sending the first view controller the `presentModalViewController:animated:` message, handing it the second view controller. The first view controller now contains the second. The second view controller becomes the first view controller's `modalView-Controller`; the first view controller is the second view controller's `parentView-Controller`. This state of affairs persists until `dismissModalViewControllerAnimated:` is called; it is implemented by the parent view controller (which knows which view controller to dismiss because that is its `modalViewController`), but may be sent to the modal view controller (whose default behavior is to pass the message on to its `parentView-Controller`).

The second view, the modal view, is often thought of as temporary or secondary, as somehow covering the parent view which is the real view; it's as if the second view were merely waiting to be dismissed, thus revealing the real view once again. This is indeed frequently the case, but this conception doesn't quite capture the power of modal views. In particular:

* A modal view might not be temporary or secondary; it might appear every bit as primary as the parent view, and it might never be dismissed.

*Figure 19-3. Two views that are equal partners*

- A modal view's controller can itself be of any degree of complexity. For example, it might be a UITabBarController with many tab bar items and contained view controllers.

- Any view controller can present a modal view — not just a root view controller. In particular, a modal view's controller can itself replace its own view with a modal view, thus creating a chain or stack of modal views.

Thus, although a modal view *can* be the equivalent of a modal dialog on Mac OS X (especially on the iPad), a view controller and its modal view controller can also be thought of as more like equal partners, and the modal view mechanism as a simple, direct, and extremely flexible form of view replacement.

So, for example, in Apple's own iPod app on the iPhone (the Music app on the iPod touch), the "sheet" that slides up to cover the More tab when you tap Edit has a modal, secondary quality: you're accomplishing a specific task (editing the contents of the tab bar), and you can't do anything else until you tap Done. But the two alternating views that appear when you view the currently playing song are more like equal partners (Figure 19-3); there's no sense that one is secondary to the other. Yet it's likely that the second is the modal view alternative of the first.

## Modal View Configuration

When a modal view is presented and dismissed, an animation can be performed, according to whether the last parameter of the corresponding method is YES. If it is, the style of animation is determined by the modal view controller's `modalTransitionStyle` property. (It is legal, but not common, for the `modalTransitionStyle` value to differ at the time of dismissal from its value at the time of presentation.) Your choices are:

**UIModalTransitionStyleCoverVertical** *(the default)*

The modal view slides up from the bottom to cover its parent on presentation and down to reveal its parent on dismissal. ("Bottom" is defined differently depending on the orientation of the device and the orientations the view controllers support.)

**UIModalTransitionStyleFlipHorizontal**

The view flips on the vertical axis as if the two views were the front and back of a piece of paper. (The "vertical axis" is the device's long axis, regardless of the app's orientation.)

**UIModalTransitionStyleCrossDissolve**

The views remain stationary, and one fades into the other.

**UIModalTransitionStylePartialCurl**

The first view curls up like a page in a notepad to expose most of the second view, but remains covering the top left region of the second view. Thus there must not be any important interface in that region, as the user will not be able to see or touch it. This option was introduced in iOS 3.2 and seems more appropriate on the iPad, though it is legal on the iPhone.

The `modalTransition` property is thus a property of view controllers in general, but is useful only if this view controller is presented modally. This is quite typical of the UIViewController architecture; the class is overloaded with properties that matter only in particular circumstances. (To give another example, a UIViewController's `navigationItem.titleView` property, mentioned earlier in this chapter, matters only if it is contained by a UINavigationController.)

In iOS 3.2, with the advent of the iPad, there was an expansion in the range of ways in which a modal view could be presented, in accordance with the iPad's larger screen and the existence of popovers. This was done through the introduction of the `modalPresentationStyle` property of the modal view controller. Your choices are:

**UIModalPresentationFullScreen**

The default. On the iPhone, although it is not illegal to set the `modalPresentationStyle` to another value, a modal view will always behave as if this were the setting. This is the only mode in which **UIModalTransitionStylePartialCurl** is legal.

**UIModalPresentationPageSheet**

In a portrait orientation, basically indistinguishable from fullscreen mode. But in a landscape orientation, the modal view has the width of the portrait-oriented screen, so the parent view remains partially visible behind the modal view. The parent view is dimmed and the user can't interact with it. Thus this mode is very like a modal dialog on Mac OS X.

**UIModalPresentationFormSheet**

Similar to **UIModalPresentationPageSheet**, but the modal view is smaller. As the name implies, this intended to allow the user to fill out a form (Apple describes this as "gathering structured information from the user").

`UIModalPresentationCurrentContext`

    The modal view has the same presentation mode as its parent. This is useful with popovers, for instance (see Chapter 22).

## Modal View Presentation

Although this fact appears to be nowhere explicitly stated in the documentation, `presentModalViewController:animated:` causes the view controller to which it is sent (the parent) to retain the modal view controller (the first parameter). Moreover, because the modal view controller is contained, management of its view in the interface is automatic. Therefore the usual procedure for showing a modal view is extremely simple:

1. Instantiate the modal view controller and initialize it, in code, leaving the modal view controller to acquire its view in one of the ways discussed earlier in this chapter.

2. Set the modal view controller's `modalTransitionStyle` (and, if appropriate, its `modalPresentationStyle`). This may be done now, by the code that just instantiated the modal view controller, or the modal view controller itself may do it as part of its override of `initWithNibName:bundle:`. This is also the time to hand the modal view controller any other data to which it may need a pointer.

3. Send `presentModalViewController:animated:` to the parent view controller. (Obviously, if this code is *in* the parent view controller, the receiver will be `self`.)

4. Release the modal view controller if required by memory management rules, as it is now being retained elsewhere.

This example code from the Xcode Utility Application template for new projects is quite typical. The Utility Application template implements what appears to be a view with a front and a back. To reach the back, the user taps the info button on the front; to return to the front, the user taps the Done button on the back. This is accomplished through two view controllers. The "front" is actually the first view controller's view, and the first view controller is the app's root view controller. When the user taps the info button, this is what happens (in the first view controller):

```
FlipsideViewController *controller =
    [[FlipsideViewController alloc] initWithNibName:@"FlipsideView" bundle:nil];
controller.delegate = self;
controller.modalTransitionStyle = UIModalTransitionStyleFlipHorizontal;
[self presentModalViewController:controller animated:YES];
[controller release];
```

The only unexpected line here is that the modal view controller has a delegate, which is set to `self`. The explanation has to do with the problem of dismissing the modal view. I'll discuss that problem now.

## Modal View Dismissal

The reason why dismissing the modal view is a problem is mainly that the user action that triggers the dismissal of the view will almost certainly be handled by the modal view controller, or some view controller that it contains, whereas it is the parent view controller that must be sent `dismissModalViewControllerAnimated:`, which will dismiss the view and release the modal view controller. It is therefore typically necessary to communicate somehow between the modal view controller and the parent view controller.

If the situation is extraordinarily simple, the modal view controller can just send itself `dismissModalViewControllerAnimated:`. This message will be automatically passed up the chain to the parent that is presenting the modal view controller.

However, for all kinds of reasons, the situation might not be so simple. The parent we need to contact might be at some distance up the chain of parents — there might be a cascade of modal views, or the view controller handling the user action might be contained by a navigation controller that is itself presented modally. Even more important, the parent might have additional work to do before the modal view is actually dismissed; for example, it might need to retrieve some data from the modal view controller.

In my own apps, I have used two sorts of solution to this problem:

*A notification*
> The parent, as it creates the modal view controller, registers for a notification that the modal view controller will emit. When it actually receives that notification, it unregisters for that notification, retrieves any needed data (possibly from the notification's `userInfo` dictionary), and dismisses the modal view. This solution has the advantage that it is easy to set up, but it has a certain slippery quality.

*Delegation*
> This is the Apple-recommended solution. The modal view controller is given a `delegate` property, and defines a protocol to which its delegate must adhere, consisting of a method that it will send to its delegate when it wants to be dismissed, possibly passing along any data as part of this method call. The parent adopts this protocol and sets itself as the modal view controller's delegate when it creates it. This is considerably more work to set up, but the path of communication is crystal clear.

Here's an example from one of my apps that uses a notification. I show here only the parent view controller's code, but it's obvious what's going on; the modal view controller, an IndexViewController, is to post a `@"goPic"` notification when it wants to be dismissed, attaching to it a `userInfo` dictionary with a `@"pic"` key whose value is a string telling us which picture to go to:

```
- (void) showIndex: (id) sender {
    [[NSNotificationCenter defaultCenter] addObserver:self
        selector:@selector(goPic:) name:@"goPic" object:nil];
```

```
    IndexViewController* ivc =
        [[IndexViewController alloc] initWithIndex: self.ix];
    [self presentModalViewController:ivc animated:YES];
    [ivc release];
}

- (void) goPic: (NSNotification*) n {
    NSString* pic = [[n userInfo] objectForKey: @"pic"];
    [[NSNotificationCenter defaultCenter] removeObserver:self
                                      name:@"goPic" object:nil];
    [self dismissModalViewControllerAnimated:NO];
    // ... do other stuff with pic here ...
}
```

You could argue, however, that this use of a notification was just lazy, and that I should have used delegation instead. I gave an example of the delegation solution, also from one of my apps, in Chapter 11. The ColorPickerController class's header file looks like this:

```
@protocol ColorPickerDelegate;
@interface ColorPickerController : UIViewController {
}
@property (nonatomic, assign) id <ColorPickerDelegate> delegate;
@end

@protocol ColorPickerDelegate
// color == nil on cancel
- (void) colorPicker:(ColorPickerController *)picker
    didSetColorNamed:(NSString *)theName
             toColor:(UIColor*)theColor;
@end
```

When the user taps the Done button, this ColorPickerController method is triggered:

```
- (void) dismissColorPicker: (id) sender { // user has tapped our Done button
    [self.delegate colorPicker:self
            didSetColorNamed:self.colorName
                     toColor:self.color];
}
```

An instance of a different view controller class, SettingsController, which adopts the ColorPickerDelegate protocol, creates the ColorPickerController instance and sets itself as its delegate:

```
ColorPickerController* cpc = [[ColorPickerController alloc]
                        initWithColorName:colorName andColor:c];
[cpc setDelegate: self];
// ...
```

SettingsController has promised to implement colorPicker:didSetColorNamed:to-Color:, and it does so:

```
- (void) colorPicker:(ColorPickerController *)picker
    didSetColorNamed:(NSString *)theName
             toColor:(UIColor*)theColor {
    // ... do stuff with theName and theColor here ...
```

```
    [self dismissModalViewControllerAnimated:YES];
}
```

What I have not shown you, in that example, is that the ColorPickerController is *not* the modal view controller. It is, rather, *contained* by the modal view controller, which is a UINavigationController and is set up and presented modally by the same code that creates the ColorPickerController. So, in this example, the parent is at a distance up the chain from the view controller that handles the user action that is to trigger dismissal, and there is data to be communicated to it; the use of the delegate architecture solves both problems.

Still, the delegate architecture isn't always appropriate or even possible. Perhaps there is a deep chain of modal views, and perhaps different user actions should cause dismissal at different levels up the chain; thus, the deepest view could not have a single delegate. Perhaps there is no point at which the parent who must perform the dismissal is ever in direct contact with the view controller that handles the user action; in the previous example, they were in contact because the one created the other, but that might not be the case. Then, I think, a notification is a perfectly reasonable solution.

## Modal Views and Rotation

No law requires that every part of your interface should appear in the same rotation. On the iPhone especially, where the user can easily rotate the device while working with an app, it is reasonable and common for one part of the interface to appear in portrait orientation and another part of the interface to appear in landscape orientation. One easy way to achieve this is to implement shouldAutorotateToInterface-Orientation: differently for a modal view controller.

For example, one of my iPhone apps is a flashcard app; the flashcards are viewed only in landscape orientation. But there is also an option to display a list (a UITableView) of all flashcards. This list is far better viewed in portrait orientation, so as to accommodate the greatest possible number of items on the screen at once; therefore, it is permitted to assume portrait orientation only. The user must rotate the device with the hand holding the iPhone, but this is not objectionable; in fact, it quickly becomes automatic and subconscious.

This is achieved by implementing shouldAutorotateToInterfaceOrientation: this way in one view controller:

```
// [view controller A]
- (BOOL) shouldAutorotateToInterfaceOrientation:(UIInterfaceOrientation)io {
    return (io == UIDeviceOrientationLandscapeRight);
}
```

Meanwhile, it is implemented this way in another view controller:

```
// [view controller B]
- (BOOL) shouldAutorotateToInterfaceOrientation:(UIInterfaceOrientation)io {
```

```
        return (io == UIDeviceOrientationPortrait);
    }
```

Then when view controller A's view appears, it will appear in landscape orientation.
View controller A, on demand, presents view controller B's view modally; when view
controller B's view appears, it will appear in portrait orientation.

In that example, we pay no attention to the orientation of the device; instead, we force
the user to rotate the device appropriately. But the same technique can be used conversely as a way of rotating the interface in response to rotation of the device. This can
be a way of performing a complex layout on rotation. Instead of rearranging the interface in response to the rotation of our view in a view controller by implementing did-
RotateFromInterfaceOrientation: ("Rotation Events" on page 452), we forbid the rotation of our view (in shouldAutorotateToInterfaceOrientation:), detect the rotation
of the *device* instead, and replace our view with a modal view suited to the new orientation.

In this example, I assume that the root view controller (where this code is) has its should-
AutorotateToInterfaceOrientation: set to return UIInterfaceOrientationIs-
Portrait(io), while the alternate LandscapeViewController is set to return UIInterface-
OrientationIsLandscape(io).

```
- (void)viewDidLoad {
    [super viewDidLoad];
    [[UIDevice currentDevice] beginGeneratingDeviceOrientationNotifications];
    [[NSNotificationCenter defaultCenter] addObserver:self
        selector:@selector(screenRotated:)
            name:UIDeviceOrientationDidChangeNotification
        object:nil];
}

- (void) screenRotated: (id) notif {
    NSUInteger rot = [[UIDevice currentDevice] orientation];
    if (UIDeviceOrientationIsLandscape(rot) && !self.modalViewController) {
        [[UIApplication sharedApplication]
            setStatusBarOrientation:rot animated:YES];
        LandscapeViewController *c =
            [[LandscapeViewController alloc]
                initWithNibName:@"LandscapeView" bundle:nil];
        c.modalTransitionStyle = UIModalTransitionStyleCrossDissolve;
        [self presentModalViewController:c animated:YES];
        [c release];
    } else if (UIDeviceOrientationIsPortrait(rot) && self.modalViewController) {
        [[UIApplication sharedApplication]
            setStatusBarOrientation:rot animated:YES];
        [self dismissModalViewControllerAnimated:YES];
    }
}
```

The judicious use of setStatusBarOrientation:animated: nets us the nice status bar
animation exactly on those occasions when the system does not hand it to us, so that

we get it no matter how the user rotates the device. The result is basically indistinguishable from "normal" interface rotation.

# Tab Bar Controllers

A *tab bar* (a UITabBar, see also Chapter 25) is a horizontal bar displaying items. Each item (a UITabBarItem) consists of an image and a name. At all times, exactly one of these items is selected. When the user taps an item, it becomes the selected item. If there are too many items to fit on the tab bar, the excess items are automatically subsumed into a final More item. When the user taps the More item, a modal list of the excess items appears, and the user can select one; the user can also be permitted to edit the tab bar, determining which items appear in the tab bar itself and which ones spill over into the More list. All of that functionality, if you want it, is more or less automatic.

A tab bar is an independent interface object, but it is most commonly used in conjunction with a view controller (UITabBarController, a subclass of UIViewController). The idea is that the tab bar items should correspond to views; when the user selects a tab bar item, the corresponding view appears. Thus a UITabBarController is an explicit way of letting the user switch between views, using a tab bar, which remains visible and can reveal (through highlighting) which view is currently showing.

A tab bar interface has the advantage that it makes the user's choices explicit. It has the disadvantage that some screen real estate is occupied by the tab bar, reducing the amount of space available for the views that it summons by about 60 pixels at the bottom, and the tab bar cannot readily be hidden. (Actually, you can hide the tab bar by setting its `visible` to YES, but Apple evidently does not condone this, and you would have to do some additional hacky stuff in order to make the view occupy the whole screen, so I'm not going to discuss this approach.) On the other hand, a tab bar controller can present a modal view that occupies the whole screen, or can itself be presented as a modal view controller, so parts of the interface can lack the tab bar if you want.

Obvious examples of a tab bar interface on the iPhone are Apple's own Clock app, which has four tab bar items, and Apple's iPod app (Music, on the iPod touch), which has four tab bar items plus a More item that reveals a list of six more.

When using a tab bar interface by way of a UITabBarController, you do *not* talk directly to the tab bar itself; you don't have to create it or configure it. You talk only to the UITabBarController, and it does the rest; when the UITabBarController's view is displayed, there's the tab bar along with the view of the selected item.

Apple also warns that you should not subclass UITabBarController. The only reason why you might be tempted to do so, indeed, is to implement rotation, so that a tab-based interface can appear in landscape mode. Resist that temptation. Instead, concentrate on the rotation of all the view controllers contained by the UITabBarController. If the device is rotated to a certain orientation, and all the contained view controllers

*Figure 19-4. A nice image makes an ugly tab bar item*

*Figure 19-5. A tab bar item based on a transparency mask*

permit rotation to that orientation, the tab bar interface itself will rotate; similarly, if all the contained view controllers agree in permitting rotation to a certain orientation, they can force the tab bar interface to assume that orientation.

## Tab Bar Item Images

A tab bar item is a UITabBarItem; this is a subclass of UIBarItem, an abstract class that provides some of its most important properties, such as `title`, `image`, and `enabled`. For each view you want contained and displayed by a tab bar controller, you're going to need a tab bar item, which will appear in the tab bar. This is likely to be the hardest part of getting started with a tab bar controller! Tab bar controllers are simple and easy to configure, but a tab bar item can be a pain to prepare. If you can borrow a tab bar item from the system, it's no work at all, but if you create your own, you're going to need an image with the following highly specific properties:

- The image should be a 30×30 PNG, though it can be larger, in which case it will be scaled down automatically as needed.
- The image should be a transparency mask. That is, it should consist of transparent pixels and opaque pixels (possibly including semiopaque pixels). Color is of no consequence and will be ignored; all that matters is the degree of transparency of each pixel. The system will color the image itself, adding a shine effect.

The problem is that a perfectly nice image, if used as is, often becomes a meaningless, ugly tab bar item (Figure 19-4).

The trouble with the image in Figure 19-4 is that it's just a solid block of opaque pixels, so its details, which are based on its colors, don't appear in the resulting tab bar item. One solution is to use an image editor to derive a transparency mask based on a gray-scale version of the original; this gives a much nicer result (Figure 19-5).

There are two ways to make a tab bar item:

*From an image that you supply*
> Initialize it using `initWithTitle:image:tag:`.

*By borrowing it from the system*
> Initialize it using `initWithTabBarSystemItem:tag:`. Consult the documentation for the list of available system items. The trouble with this approach is that you have to borrow the entire tab bar item, including its title, which is read-only (setting it is not an error, but it has no effect). The solution should be to form a temporary tab bar item and steal its image to form your actual tab bar item, but you can't do that. The inability to reuse system images easily is quite annoying.

## Configuring a Tab Bar Controller

A view controller (meaning any UIViewController) has a `tabBarItem` property, which is meaningful only if that view controller is contained by a tab bar controller. Set this property to an instance of UITabBarItem (obtained as described in the preceding section); alternatively, set the `tabBarItem.image` property to an appropriate image, and set the view controller's `title` property to the associated text. Do this for all the view controllers you want to be contained by the UITabBarController. Now package those view controllers into an array and set the UITabBarController's `viewControllers` property to that array. The result is that the tab bar items for those view controllers, as ordered in the array, appear in the tab bar.

You should also tell the UITabBarController which tab bar item should be initially selected. You can do this by reference to a contained view controller (by setting the `selectedViewController` property) or by index number (by setting the `selectedIndex` property). If you like, you can also set the UITabBarController's delegate; the delegate gets messages allowing it to prevent a given tab bar item from being selected, and notifying it when a tab bar item is selected and when the user is customizing the tab bar from the More item.

If the tab bar contains few enough items that it doesn't need a More item, there won't be one and the tab bar won't be user-customizable. If there *is* a More item, you can exclude some tab bar items from being customizable by setting the `customizableViewControllers` property to an array that lacks them; setting this property to nil means that the user can see the More list but can't rearrange the items at all. Setting the `viewControllers` property sets the `customizableViewControllers` property to the same value, so if you're going to set the `customizableViewControllers` property, do it *after* setting the `viewControllers` property. (If you do allow the user to rearrange items, you would presumably want to respond in the delegate to this rearrangement by saving the new arrangement in the NSUserDefaults and using it the next time the app runs.) The `moreNavigationController` property can be compared with the `selectedViewController` property to learn whether the user is currently viewing the More list; apart from this, the More interface is mostly out of your control, but I'll discuss some ways of customizing it in Chapter 25.

Here's a simple example excerpted from the app delegate's `applicationDidFinish-Launching:` of one of my apps, in which I construct a tab bar interface and display it:

```
self.tbc = [[[UITabBarController alloc] init] autorelease];
// create tabs
UIViewController* b = [[[GameBoardController alloc] init];
UINavigationController* n = // never mind what "s" is
    [[[UINavigationController alloc] initWithRootViewController:s];
// load up tab view with tabs
[tbc setViewControllers:[NSArray arrayWithObjects: b, n, nil] animated:NO];
[b release]; [n release];
// configure window and show it
[self.window addSubview: tbc.view];
[self.window makeKeyAndVisible];
```

You'll notice that I don't configure the contained view controllers' tab bar items. That's because those view controllers configure themselves. For example:

```
// [GameBoardController.m]

- (id) init {
    self = [super init];
    if (self) {
        // we will be embedded in a tab view, configure
        self.tabBarItem.image = [UIImage imageNamed:@"game.png"];
        self.title = @"Game";
    }
    return self;
}
```

You can also configure a UITabBarController in a nib. The nib editor is quite clever about this. The UITabBarController's contained view controllers can be set right in the nib. Moreover, each contained view controller contains a Tab Bar Item; you can select this and set its title and image right in the nib. The UITabBarController itself has a **delegate** outlet. Thus, it is possible to make a fully configured tab bar controller appear at the root of your interface with essentially no code at all. The Tab Bar Application template for new projects illustrates some of these features, but not all of them: the tab bar items have no images in the template, for example.

A view controller contained by a UITabBarController can access the UITabBarController as its `tabBarController` property. This works at any depth: that is, the view controller need not be *directly* contained by the UITabBarController. It might, for example, be contained by a UINavigationController that is itself contained by the UITabBarController. However, it doesn't work if the view controller is its parent's `modalViewController`.

# Navigation Controllers

A navigation controller (UINavigationController, a subclass of UIViewController) is the most elaborate and powerful of the built-in view controller classes. It is a brilliant solution to the problem of presenting multiple interfaces and options on the tiny iPhone screen. But you might use it also just because its basic interface is useful and familiar to users.

A navigation controller's interface has three parts:

*The central view*

A navigation controller is a container for other view controllers, and is responsible for displaying the view of one of these at all times. The "navigation" part has to do with how it decides which view controller's view to display. The navigation controller contains its view controllers in a stack. When a view controller is pushed onto the stack, it becomes the top view controller, and its view becomes the central view (with, by default, an animation from the right). When a view controller is popped from the stack, the view controller underneath it becomes the top view controller, and *its* view becomes the central view (with, by default, an animation from the left). This behavior is coordinated with the behavior of the navigation bar, as we shall now see.

*The navigation bar*

A navigation bar (a UINavigationBar) is a rectangular view displaying a left item, a center item, and a right item. It can be used independently, but it is most often used as part of a navigation controller interface, in which case it appears at the top (and can optionally be hidden). The center item is typically a title, giving the user a cue as to what the rest of the interface is about; a navigation bar might well be used solely in order to display this title. But it also has mighty powers connected with the notion of navigating.

A navigation bar implements an internal stack of navigation items (UINavigationItem). It starts out with one navigation item (the *root* or *bottom item*); you can then push another navigation item onto the stack, and from there you can either pop that navigation item to remove it from the stack or push yet *another* item onto the stack. At any moment, therefore, some navigation item is the *top item* on the stack, the most recently pushed item still present on the stack (the `topItem`). Furthermore, unless the top item is also the root item (because it is the only item in the stack), some navigation item is the *back item* (the `backItem`), the item that would be top item if we were now to pop the top item.

The state of the stack is reflected in the navigation bar's interface. In particular, the navigation bar's center comes automatically from the top item, and its left side comes from the back item. (See Chapter 25 for a complete description.) Thus, typically, the center tells the user what item is current, and the left side is a button telling the user what item we would return to if the user were to tap that button. Moreover, animations add a subliminal reinforcement to this notion of directionality. When a navigation item is pushed onto the stack, the navigation bar animates from the right; when items are popped from the stack, the navigation bar animates from the left. This gives the user a sense of position within a chain.

By itself, a navigation bar doesn't manipulate any part of the interface except itself. It is up to the navigation bar's delegate (adopting the UINavigationBarDelegate protocol) to listen for changes in the stack. In a navigation controller interface, the navigation controller *is* the navigation bar's delegate. It coordinates the ensemble: the navigation controller's stack is coordinated with the navigation bar's stack, and the animation of the central view is coordinated with the navigation bar's animation.

*The toolbar*

A toolbar (a UIToolbar) is a rectangular view displaying a row of items, any of which the user can tap. The tapped item highlights momentarily but is not selected; it represents the initiation of an action, not a state or a mode, and should be thought of as (and may in fact look like) a button. A UIToolbar can be used independently (and often is, typically appearing at the bottom on an iPhone but possibly at the top on an iPad), but it can also be part of a navigation controller interface, in which case it appears at the bottom (and can optionally be hidden — indeed, the toolbar itself should be thought of as optional in a navigation controller interface).

The great flexibility of a navigation controller lies in the following facts:

- A view controller is not pushed onto the stack until it is needed for display. Thus, you get to decide in real time what the "next" view should be. This makes a navigation controller perfect for a master–detail interface, in which the user sees a list of possibilities and taps one to navigate to the detailed view of that thing.

- The toolbar is optional, and both it and the navigation bar can be hidden. Moreover, both the navigation bar and the toolbar offer a choice of appearances. Thus, not all navigation interfaces look the same.

- The toolbar's contents and the navigation bar's contents respond automatically to the advent of a different view, and can also be changed in code.

- A navigation interface can be used in many ways: as the root view of your app, as a modal view, or as a view contained by a tab bar controller.

A familiar example of a navigation interface is Apple's Mail app (Figure 19-6), a master–detail interface with the navigation bar at the top (with a back button pointing to the list of mailboxes in the figure) and the toolbar displaying additional options and information at the bottom.

# Bar Button Items

All of the items in a UIToolbar, and the right and left items in a UINavigationBar, are instances of UIBarButtonItem (which, like UITabBarItem, is a subclass of UIBarItem). It is therefore essential to know how to obtain such an instance.

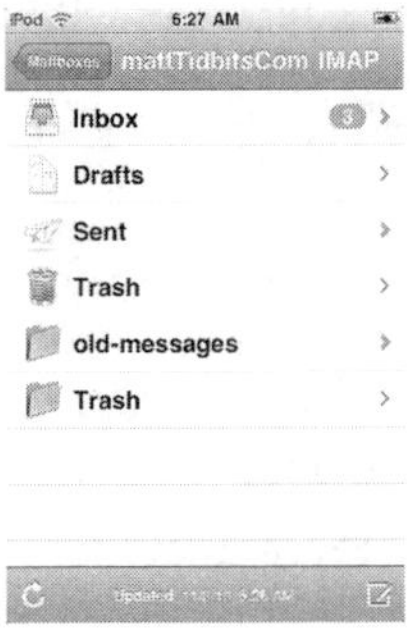

*Figure 19-6. A familiar navigation interface*

A UIBarButtonItem is not a UIButton! It has some button-like qualities, but it does not inherit from UIButton, from UIControl, or even from UIView. However, a UIBarButtonItem can be represented by a `custom-View` which *is* a UIView. Thus, it can be used to put any sort of view into a toolbar or navigation bar (and implementing any button behavior would then be the responsibility of that view).

A UIBarButtonItem inherits from UIBarItem a `title` property and an `image` property (and an `enabled` property). The `image` has the nature of a tab bar item image, as described earlier in this chapter: it needs to be a transparency mask. It should also be quite small (20×20 pixels is a good size); there isn't much height room, especially in a toolbar, especially if the bar button item has the bordered style. Typically, a UIBarButtonItem is assigned a `title` or an `image` but not both (though it is possible to assign both, in which case the title appears below the image).

To its inherited properties, a UIBarButtonItem adds `target` and `action` properties so that tapping it as a button can trigger a method elsewhere (Chapter 11). There is also a `style` property; the choices are:

`UIBarButtonItemStylePlain`
    The bare title or image (or both) is displayed.

`UIBarButtonItemStyleBordered`
    Looks like a button, with a round rectangular border around the image (or around the title if there is no image).

`UIBarButtonItemStyleDone`
    Bordered, and with a blue fill. As the name implies, this is suitable for a Done button in a modal or temporary view.

As with a UITabBarItem, the item can be created from your own title or image, in which case you must also supply a style, or the item can be borrowed from the system, in which case the style is built in. Alternatively, as I've already said, you can supply an entire UIView as the bar button item's `customView`, but in that case not only is there no style, but the UITabBarItem has no action and target; the UIView itself must somehow implement button behavior if that's what you want. For example, the `customView` might be a UISegmentedButton, but then it is the UISegmentedButton's target and action that give it button behavior.

Thus there are four initializers:

- `initWithTitle:style:target:action:`
- `initWithImage:style:target:action:`
- `initWithBarButtonSystemItem:target:action:`
- `initWithCustomView:`

The available system items for a UIBarButtonItem are not the same as for a UITabBar-Item. Check the documentation to see whether any of them meets your needs.

Bar button items in a toolbar are positioned automatically by the system. You can provide hints to help with this positioning. If you know that you'll be changing an item's title dynamically, you'll probably want the width to accommodate the longest possible title right from the start; to arrange that, set the `possibleTitles` to a set that includes the longest title. Alternatively, you can supply an absolute `width`. Also, you can incorporate spacer system items into the toolbar; these have no visible appearance, and cannot be tapped, but serve only to help distribute the other items. The `UIBarButton-SystemItemFlexibleSpace` system item is the one most frequently used; place these between the visible items to space the visible items equally across the width of the toolbar. There is also a `UIBarButtonSystemItemFixedSpace` whose `width` lets you insert a space of defined size.

## Configuring a Navigation Interface

Just as a navigation bar works through a stack of navigation items, a navigation controller works through a stack of view controllers. These are its contained view controllers, each of which embodies both a navigation item, for the navigation bar's stack, and a view, to be displayed in the center region whenever this view controller's navigation item is the navigation bar's top item. A contained view controller can also provide the toolbar items for the navigation controller's toolbar, if there is one; thus the toolbar items will change depending on what view is being displayed.

The navigation controller contains and retains its view controllers only at the time when they are actually on the stack; whether and how you maintain them the rest of the time is up to you, but the usual approach is to create each view controller on the fly as it is needed to push onto the stack, and to allow it to be released and forgotten when it is popped from the stack. The navigation controller is created with a *root view controller*, representing the initial view and the navigation bar's bottom item; this cannot be popped, but it can be replaced, as we shall see.

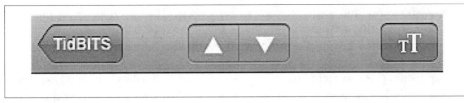

*Figure 19-7. A segmented control in the center of a navigation bar*

The most important part of configuring a navigation interface is thus configuring the contained view controllers. We already know how to give a view controller a view; the question now is how to configure a view controller so that it can supply a navigation item and toolbar items.

### View controller's navigation item

A view controller's navigation item is configured primarily through its `navigationItem` property. This property is a UINavigationItem; it is itself read-only, but its properties are not (see also Chapter 25):

`title` *or* `titleView`
> Determines what is to appear in the center of the navigation bar. The `title` is a string, and you will usually not set it; you'll set the view controller's `title` instead (and `navigationItem.title` will be set for you). The `titleView` can be any kind of UIView, and if set, it will be used instead of the `title`. However, you should always give a view controller a `title`, because it will be needed for the back button when a view controller is pushed onto the stack on top of this one.
>
> Figure 19-1 shows the TidBITS News master view, with the navigation bar displaying a `titleView` which is an image. In the TidBITS News detail view controller, the `titleView` is a segmented control providing a Previous and Next button, and the back button displays the master view controller's `title` (Figure 19-7).

`prompt`
> An optional string to appear centered above everything else in the navigation bar. The navigation bar's height will be increased to accommodate it.

`rightBarButtonItem`
> A UIBarButtonItem to appear at the right side of the navigation bar. This generally has nothing to do with navigation; rather, space being at a premium in an iPhone interface, it is a way of slotting a button into the interface. For example, in Apple's Mail app, the Edit button appears here in a message list, and a segmented control consisting of a Next and Previous button appears here when viewing a single message.

`backBarButtonItem`
> By default, when a view controller is pushed on top of this view controller, the pushed view controller's navigation bar will display at its left a button pointing to

the left, whose title is this view controller's `title`. The vast majority of the time, this default behavior is the behavior you'll want. However, you can customize that button's title by setting the `navigationItem.backBarButtonItem` of *this* view controller (the one that will provide the back item, not the one that will provide the top item). The best technique is to provide a new UIBarButtonItem whose target and action are nil (and whose style doesn't matter); the runtime will use this, when a view controller is pushed on top of this one, to form a working back button. So, for example:

```
UIBarButtonItem* b = [[UIBarButtonItem alloc]
    initWithTitle:@"Go Back" style:0 target:nil action:nil];
self.navigationItem.backBarButtonItem = b;
[b release];
```

`leftBarButtonItem`

A UIBarButtonItem to appear at the left side of the navigation bar. If present, it will be used *instead* of the normal back button, disabling the normal means of going back, so you typically will provide a value only for the root view, because no back button is needed when the root view is displayed.

The question arises of *where* in your code you should initially configure a view controller's navigation item. Apple warns (in the UIViewController class reference, under `navigationItem`) that configuring a view controller's navigation item in conjunction with the creation of its view is not a good idea, because the circumstances under which the view is needed are not identical to the circumstances under which the navigation item is needed. However, Apple's own examples appear to violate this warning; they often configure a view controller's navigation item in its `viewDidLoad` implementation (and their own templates invite the same thing). I take it, then, that this is a reasonable place to configure the navigation item, despite the warning. Places where I have configured the navigation item in my own apps include:

*The view controller's* `viewDidLoad` *(or* `loadView`*)*
This choice has never proved problematic, despite Apple's warning.

*The view controller's* `awakeFromNib`
Obviously, this choice is possible only in cases where the view controller instance comes from a nib.

*The view controller's designated initializer*
This is probably the best choice, if the view controller is to initialize its own navigation item.

*When creating the view controller in code*
If you're creating the view controller in code, it may make sense to configure it in the same code. It's really an architectural question: should the view controller configure itself, or be configured by whoever creates it?

The actual code for configuring a navigation item is extremely straightforward and easy. Here's an example, from one of my apps, of configuring the navigation item in awake-FromNib:

```
- (void) awakeFromNib {
    [super awakeFromNib];
    self.title = @"Albums";
    UIBarButtonItem* b = [[UIBarButtonItem alloc] initWithTitle:@"Now"
                              style:UIBarButtonItemStylePlain
                              target:self action:@selector(showNow)];
    self.navigationItem.rightBarButtonItem = b;
    [b release];
    // ...
}
```

Example 19-1 is an example of configuring the navigation item in viewDidLoad; it's the code that generates the navigation bar shown in Figure 19-1.

*Example 19-1. Configuring a view controller's navigation item*

```
- (void)viewDidLoad {
    [super viewDidLoad];
    // image to display in navigation bar
    UIImageView* imv = [[UIImageView alloc] initWithImage:
        [UIImage imageNamed:@"tb_iphone_banner.png"]];
    self.navigationItem.titleView = imv;
    [imv release];
    // reload button for navigation bar
    UIBarButtonItem* b = [[UIBarButtonItem alloc]
        initWithBarButtonSystemItem:UIBarButtonSystemItemRefresh
        target:self action:@selector(doRefresh:)];
    self.navigationItem.rightBarButtonItem = b;
    [b release];
}
```

A view controller's navigation item can have its properties set at any time while being displayed in the navigation bar. This, and not direct manipulation of the navigation bar, is the best way to change the navigation bar's contents dynamically. For example, in one of my apps, the visible right bar button should either be the system Play button, the system Pause button, or nothing, depending on whether music from the library is playing, paused, or stopped (Figure 19-8). So I have a timer that periodically checks the state of the music player:

```
int whichButton = -1;
if ([mp playbackState] == MPMusicPlaybackStatePlaying)
    whichButton = UIBarButtonSystemItemPause;
else if ([mp playbackState] == MPMusicPlaybackStatePaused)
    whichButton = UIBarButtonSystemItemPlay;
if (whichButton == -1)
    self.navigationItem.rightBarButtonItem = nil;
else {
    UIBarButtonItem* bb = [[UIBarButtonItem alloc]
        initWithBarButtonSystemItem:whichButton
                    target:self
```

*Figure 19-8. A highly dynamic navigation bar*

```
                    action:@selector(doPlayPause:)];
    self.navigationItem.rightBarButtonItem = bb;
    [bb release];
}
```

In that same app, and in the same navigation item, the `titleView` is a progress view (UIProgressView). I treat this like any other progress view, constantly updating it (setting its `progress` value) and even making it visible or invisible (setting its `hidden` value) without regard for the fact that it's being displayed in a navigation bar (Figure 19-8).

### View controller's toolbar items

Each view controller to be pushed onto the navigation controller's stack is responsible for supplying the items to appear in the navigation interface's toolbar, if there is one. This is done by setting the view controller's `toolbarItems` property to an array of UI-BarButtonItem instances. You can change the toolbar items even while the view controller's view and current `toolbarItems` are showing, optionally with animation, by sending `setToolbarItems:animated:` to the view controller.

A view controller also has the power to specify that the navigation interface's toolbar should be hidden whenever it (the view controller) is on the stack. To do so, set the view controller's `hidesBottomBarWhenPushed` to YES. The trick is that you must do this early enough, namely before the view loads. (The view controller's `viewDidLoad` is too late; its designated initializer is a good place.) The bottom bar remains hidden from the time this view controller is pushed to the time it is popped, even if other view controllers are pushed and popped on top of it in the meantime, so this is not a very flexible way to show and hide the toolbar. For more flexibility, implement a lifetime event handler (discussed later in this chapter) and call `setToolbarHidden:animated:`.

### Configuring the navigation view controller

As I've already mentioned, the most important thing you must do as you create a navigation view controller is supply the root view controller. To help with this, there's an initializer `initWithRootViewController:`. This pushes the supplied view controller onto the empty stack and retains it. The root view controller can never be popped, and will thus normally be released only if the navigation view controller itself goes out of existence; however, you can replace the entire stack with `setViewControllers:animated:` (see below), thus releasing and replacing the root view controller.

---

Subsequent view controllers are pushed onto the stack with the following UINavigationController method:

pushViewController:animated:

> Pushes the given view controller onto the stack (and retains it), thus displaying its view and so forth. The given view controller becomes the top view.

To pop a view controller, the most frequent approach is to do nothing. There will be a back button; the user will tap it, and the top view will be popped from the stack automatically. However, you can also pop view controllers from the stack in code, with these methods:

popViewControllerAnimated:

> Pops the top view controller, autoreleases it, and returns it in case you need it for something. The back view becomes the top view.

popToRootViewControllerAnimated:

> Pops all view controllers except the root view controller, which remains on the stack and becomes the top view. The popped view controllers are placed in an NSArray that is returned in case you need any of them for something.

popToViewController:animated:

> Pops all view controllers starting with the top of the stack until the given view controller comes to the top. The popped view controllers are placed in an NSArray that is returned in case you need any of them for something.

setViewControllers:animated:

> Releases all view controllers and replaces the entire stack with the given array of view controllers. Some or all of the view controllers in the array can be view controllers that were already on the stack; thus this is a good way to rearrange the stack or to insert a view controller inside the stack.

Those are all methods to be sent to the navigation controller, but in the natural course of things it will probably be one of the contained view controllers that wants to send one of them. Thus, a contained view controller needs a reference to the navigation view controller that contains it. That reference is its navigationController property.

The navigation view controller itself has a viewControllers property that gives access to the stack as an NSArray. Thus, the root item is the array's objectAtIndex:0; if this array's count is c, the back item is the array's objectAtIndex:c-2; and the top item is its lastObject, though you can also retrieve the top item with the topViewController property. There is also a visibleViewController property; this can differ from the topViewController because the topViewController might itself contain a view controller and display its view (as a modal view, for example).

The navigation bar can be hidden and shown with setNavigationBarHidden: animated:, and the toolbar can be hidden and shown with setToolbarHidden:

`animated:`. In addition, both the navigation bar and the toolbar can be customized through these properties of the UINavigationController:

`navigationBar.tintColor, toolbar.tintColor`
> A color. Strong colors will cause you to lose the bar's gradient appearance, but muted colors will permit it to appear. As far as I can tell, the alpha value of your chosen color is irrelevant.

`navigationBar.barStyle, toolbar.barStyle`
> Choices are `UIBarStyleDefault` and `UIBarStyleBlack`. Ignored if the `tintColor` is set; if it is, the style is `UIBarStyleDefault`.

`navigationBar.translucent, toolbar.translucent`
> If YES, causes the view to underlap the bar. The part of the view under the bar is visible, but only very faintly.

 The animations associated with the methods listed in this section are very helpful to the user, as giving a sense of what's happening and how various views relate to one another. But when you use one of these methods on a view that is not showing, be sure to request the option *without* animation, because in such a case the animation serves no purpose and can be a drag on performance.

In a nib, a navigation view controller has a top bar and a bottom bar (in the Attributes inspector), and you can configure how they look and whether they are initially visible. Thus, you can give it a navigation bar and a toolbar or tab bar. The root view controller can be specified. Moreover, the root view controller (or any view controller in a nib) has a Navigation Item where you can specify its title, its prompt, and the text of its back button. You can drag Bar Button Items into the navigation bar to set the left button and right button of the root view controller's Navigation Item. Moreover, the Navigation Item has outlets, one of which permits you to set its `titleView`. Plus, you can give the root view controller Bar Button Items that will appear in the toolbar. Thus the configuration of a navigation view controller, its root view controller, and any other view controllers that will be pushed onto its stack can be performed more or less completely in a nib.

## Navigation Interface Rotation

Apple warns that you should not subclass UINavigationController. The only reason why you might be tempted to do so, indeed, is to implement rotation, so that a navigation interface can appear in landscape mode. Resist that temptation. Instead, concentrate on the rotation of all the view controllers contained by the UINavigationController. I said all this earlier with regard to UITabBarController; but the rules for UINavigationController rotation are a bit more complicated, because a UINavigationController can't know what orientations a future view controller will permit — it only knows a view controller's permissible orientations when that view controller has been pushed onto the stack. So, the rules are as follows:

- Initially, the navigation interface adopts the orientation rule of its root view controller.
- When a view controller is pushed onto the stack, the navigation interface does not rotate, even if the new view controller does not permit the current orientation. However, if the device is *later* rotated to an orientation that the new view controller permits and that all other view controllers on the stack permit, the navigation interface will rotate to it.
- When a view controller is popped from the stack, if the back view controller (which is now the top view controller) permits the orientation that the navigation interface was in previously, the navigation interface stays in that orientation even if the device has been rotated. Otherwise, the navigation interface rotates to a permitted orientation.

Thus you can't use differing orientation rules for different contained view controllers in an attempt to get the navigation interface to rotate as a new view controller is pushed onto the stack. If you are in a navigation interface and you want to present a new view that absolutely must appear in a certain orientation, use a modal view. As we've already seen, when you show a view modally (using `presentModalViewController:`) and it can appear in only one orientation, the app rotates to that orientation.

But perhaps you're not satisfied with that solution; perhaps you want to give the user the illusion that we are still in the navigation interface. Then simply have the modal view be a navigation interface configured to look like the main navigation interface! Thus, when you present the modal view, and the app rotates to the permitted orientation of its contained view, there's an illusion that the navigation interface itself has rotated (though there will not be a rotation animation).

The only drawback is that the navigation interface in the modal view has no back button if we are looking at its root view. This breaks the illusion (and makes it hard for the user to dismiss the modal view). The solution is a trick: push the new view *twice* into the navigation interface before presenting it as a modal view. That way, what is showing in the navigation interface is the *second* view on the stack, so there is a back button. Then, in the navigation controller's delegate, catch the back button and dismiss the modal view when the user tries to return to the root level. So:

```
- (void) doButton: (id) sender {
    SecondViewController* sec = [[SecondViewController alloc] init];
    sec.title = self.title; // to give the correct back button title
    UINavigationController* nav =
        [[UINavigationController alloc] initWithRootViewController:sec];
    SecondViewController* sec2 = [[SecondViewController alloc] init];
    [nav pushViewController:sec2 animated:NO];
    [self presentModalViewController:nav animated:YES];
    nav.delegate = self; // so that we know when the user navigates back
    [sec release]; [sec2 release]; [nav release];
```

```
}

// and here's the delegate method
- (void)navigationController:(UINavigationController *)navigationController
      willShowViewController:(UIViewController *)viewController
                    animated:(BOOL)animated {
    if (viewController == [navigationController.viewControllers objectAtIndex:0])
        [self dismissModalViewControllerAnimated:YES];
}
```

# View Controller Lifetime Events

As views come and go, driven by view controllers and the actions of the user, events arrive that give you the opportunity to respond.

First, there are delegate messages:

*Tab bar controller*
> A tab bar controller can have a delegate (adopting the UITabBarControllerDelegate protocol) that receives messages when the selected view changes — you can even prevent the user from selecting a view — and when the user customizes the tab bar through the More item.

*Navigation controller*
> A navigation controller can have a delegate (adopting the UINavigationControllerDelegate protocol) that receives messages when a contained view controller's view appears, either because the view controller is pushed onto the stack or because the stack is popped so as to bring the view controller to the top.

In addition, a view controller receives four events that you can override in a subclass (the parameter tells you whether the change is being animated):

- `viewWillAppear:`
- `viewDidAppear:`
- `viewWillDisappear:`
- `viewDidDisappear:`

 If you override any of these methods, you must call super.

In these four view controller events, the notions "appear" and "disappear" mean exactly what you think they do. View controllers are all about views that can come and go — for example, because a modal view is shown, because a modal view is dismissed, because a tab bar controller is switched to a new view, or because a navigation controller's stack is pushed or popped. In each of these cases, some view is replaced on the screen by another view; the first one disappears and the second one appears. For every one of these transitions, you can get all four events.

My apps tend to make very heavy use of these four view controller events. In a world where views come and go, these events are the perfect moment to tweak the interface, to make sure that data is saved off, and so forth. For example, if a certain view in a navigation controller needs the toolbar, whereas other views do not, the simplest approach is to show and hide the toolbar as this view appears and disappears. Here are some of the many uses I make of these events:

- In a master–detail interface on the iPhone, the master view is the root view of a navigation controller and contains a table; when the user taps a row of the table, we push the corresponding detail view. I don't want the tapped row to be still selected when the user later returns to the master view, so I deselect it in the root view's `viewDidDisappear:`.

- In a master–detail interface on the iPhone (the same one, actually), the data displayed by the root view table might change while the user is working in a detail view. So I reload the root view table's data in its `viewWillAppear:`.

- A certain view that can appear in a navigation controller's stack contains a progress view that is constantly updated through a timer that checks on the state of the currently playing track of the music library. This timer needs to be in existence and running only when this view is actually visible to the user. So I create it in `viewWillAppear:` and destroy it in `viewDidDisappear:`.

- A certain view that can be shown by switching tab views must reflect the current state of certain user defaults. So I refresh the view's interface in its `viewWillAppear:`; thus, whenever it does appear, it is current.

- In a master–detail interface, the detail is a long scrollable text. Whenever the user returns to a previously read detail view, I want to scroll it to wherever it was previously scrolled to. So I save the scroll position for this detail view into the user defaults in its `viewWillDisappear:`.

 In the multitasking world of iOS 4, `viewWillDisappear:` and `viewDidDisappear:` are not called when the app is suspended. Some of your functionality performed in `viewWillDisappear:` and `viewDidDisappear:` may have to be duplicated in response to an application lifetime event (Chapter 11), such as `applicationDidEnterBackground:`, if you are to cover every case.

# View Controller Memory Management

Memory management works in a special way for view controllers. Memory is at a premium on a mobile device, and a view is memory-intensive (though a view controller itself will probably not be). A view controller can persist without its view being visible to the user — because a modal view is covering it, or because it is in a tab interface but is not the currently selected view, or because it is in a navigation interface but is not the top view of the stack. In such a situation, if memory is getting short, then even though the view controller itself persists, the runtime may nilify its view, thus releasing the view and its subviews. The view is effectively *unloaded*.

If a view controller's view is unloaded, then the next time that view is needed for display or mentioned in code, we'll go through the whole rigmarole of loading the view *again* — creating it in code if `loadView` is overridden, or loading the associated nib. And that's the whole point of the way a view controller's view is loaded lazily in the first place. Memory may become tight, but a view controller's view needn't occupy memory unless it is actually needed, to appear in the interface.

(This is why it's generally better not to have the view controller and its view in the same nib file. In that case, the view can't be unloaded, because there would be no way to load it again. So such a view can't participate in this aspect of iOS app memory management.)

This comes as a surprise to beginners (and not-so-beginners), who may feel that the possibility of the runtime coming along behind their backs and nilifying an existing view introduces a nasty element of indeterminacy into the app's behavior. However, look closely at your `loadView` and `viewDidLoad` overrides. If you've written them sensibly, doing within them only what needs to be done in connection with the view loading, and performing proper memory management, there shouldn't be any problem if these methods are called multiple times. For example, if `viewDidLoad` sets a certain property, what does it matter if it is called again later and sets the very same property to the very same value?

In general, view unloading shouldn't be a worry, provided you are obeying the dictates of model–view–controller (Chapter 13). The view controller is controller (hence the name). The view, on the other hand, should be just view; its temporary loss, and subsequent restoration, should not pose any special challenges to your code, because you aren't storing anything persistent in the view. The view must be configured, perhaps based on the model, when it comes into existence; as long as the view controller does this, the view should look and behave correctly no matter when and how often it may come into existence. Just don't write your code in such a way that you are *counting* on the view to come into existence just once or at a specific moment.

You will also get an event when the view is unloaded — `viewDidUnload`. You can override this method to learn that the view has been unloaded. If you do, do *not* nilify the view or refer to it in any way; it has already been unloaded, and you don't want to trigger its loading accidentally. The purpose of `viewDidUnload` is to allow you to release any interface objects that are associated with this view and that will be restored when the view loads again. Typically, if you are retaining such objects, it will be because you have a property whose setter has a retain policy, and you will simply nilify the property here.

The documentation on `viewDidUnload` does not say you have to call super. Some of Apple's examples do call super, but this is probably a (harmless) mistake.

For example, in the TidBITS News app, the root view controller's `navigationItem.title-View` is an image (Figure 19-1). If the view is being unloaded, there is no reason for this image to occupy any memory, so I release it in my `viewDidUnload` override. At the same time, I release the right bar button item (the Refresh button). Finally, I release the entire UITableView, which I've been keeping as a retained reference in the `tv` instance variable:

```
- (void)viewDidUnload {
    self.navigationItem.titleView = nil;
    self.navigationItem.rightBarButtonItem = nil;
    self.tv = nil;
}
```

How can I be so sanguine about disposing of these essential interface items, which must be present whenever the view is shown? It's because I know they'll be restored when the view is loaded once more. The `tv` property corresponds to an outlet in the view controller's nib; when we need the view again, the nib will load and the `tv` property will be set once again. The navigation item properties are set in `viewDidLoad` (Example 19-1).

In addition, you can override `didReceiveMemoryWarning`. If you do, you *must* call super, because the default implementation is to release the view and call `viewDid-Unload`, and you need that to happen. Apple's documentation suggests that you should divide your releases in low-memory situations into two categories: interface items, which are released by nilifying properties in `viewDidUnload`, and data (model) material that can easily be recreated on demand, which is released in `didReceiveMemory-Warning`. The reason is that `didReceiveMemoryWarning` will be always be called in low-memory situations, but the view will be released and `viewDidUnload` will be called only if the view is not showing.

If you're going to release data in `didReceiveMemoryWarning`, you must concern yourself with how you're going to get it back. You can't rely on `viewDidLoad` for this, because the data might be released without unloading the view, in which case `viewDidLoad` won't be called. The surest approach is to implement a getter that fetches the data if it is nil.

In this example, in `didReceiveMemoryWarning` we write `myBigData` out as a file to disk and release it from memory. At the same time, we override the synthesized accessors for `my-BigData` (using the technique shown in Example 12-5) so that if we try to get `myBig-Data` and it's nil, we then try to fetch it from disk and, if we succeed, we delete it from disk (to prevent stale data) and set `myBigData` before returning it. The result is that `my-BigData` is released when there's low memory, reducing our memory overhead until we actually *need* myBigData, at which time asking for its value (through the getter or property) restores it:

```
@synthesize myBigDataAlias=myBigData;

- (void) setMyBigData: (NSData*) data {
    self.myBigDataAlias = data;
}

- (NSData*) myBigData {
    NSFileManager* fm = [[NSFileManager alloc] init];
    NSString* f =
        [NSTemporaryDirectory() stringByAppendingPathComponent:@"myBigData"];
    BOOL fExists = [fm fileExistsAtPath:f];
    if (!self.myBigDataAlias) {
        if (fExists) {
            NSData* data = [NSData dataWithContentsOfFile:f];
            self.myBigDataAlias = data;
            NSError* err = nil;
            [fm removeItemAtPath:f error:&err];
            // error-checking omitted
        }
    }
    [fm release];
    return self.myBigDataAlias;
}

- (void)didReceiveMemoryWarning {
    [super didReceiveMemoryWarning];
    if (self->myBigData) {
        NSString* f =
            [NSTemporaryDirectory() stringByAppendingPathComponent:@"myBigData"];
        [myBigData writeToFile:f atomically:NO];
        self.myBigData = nil;
    }
}
```

Xcode gives you a way to test low-memory circumstances artificially. Run your app in the Simulator; in the Simulator, choose Hardware → Simulate Memory Warning. I don't believe this has any actual effect on memory, but a memory warning is sent to your app, so you can see the results of triggering your low-memory response code (did-ReceiveMemoryWarning and viewDidUnload, as well as the app delegate's applicationDid-ReceiveMemoryWarning:). Unfortunately there doesn't seem to be a parallel way of testing low-memory situations when running on a device.

# CHAPTER 20

# Scroll Views

A scroll view (UIScrollView) is a view whose contents are larger than its bounds. To reveal a desired area, the user can scroll the contents by dragging or flicking, or you can reposition the contents in code.

Think of the scroll view as consisting of *two* views:

*The scroll view itself*
> The scroll view itself acts like a window (a window in a house, not a UIWindow). The scroll view's bounds size is the size of that window.

*The content view*
> The content view is the scene viewed through the window (the scroll view). The content view is presumably larger than the scroll view, because otherwise there would be nothing to scroll. By sliding the content view, a desired portion of it can be positioned within the scroll view and thus made visible.

Although it is useful to *think* of the scroll view in this way, the truth is far simpler. The scroll view isn't really specially window-like; it's just a view (whose clipsToBounds is usually YES). And the content view isn't really a view; it's just a set of parameters for positioning the scroll view's subviews. When the scroll view scrolls, what's really changing is its bounds origin; the subviews are positioned with respect to the bounds origin, so they move with it. (See Chapter 14.)

However, a scroll view does bring to the table some nontrivial additional abilities:

- It knows how to shift its bounds origin in response to the user's gestures.
- It provides scroll indicators whose size and position give the user a clue as to the content view's size and position.
- It can optionally enforce paging, whereby the user can view only integral portions of the content.
- It can support zooming, so that the user can resize the apparent content by pinching.

# Creating a Scroll View

You do not literally provide a scroll view with a content view (because the content view isn't really a view). Rather, you tell the scroll view how large the content view is, by setting its contentSize, and you populate the scroll view with subviews whose visibility will be managed as if they constituted the content view. Evidently, you have two choices about how to provide these subviews: you can supply them directly in code, or you can design the scroll view in a nib.

Here's an example of the first approach. Let's start with the View-based Application template so that we have a root view controller. In the view controller's loadView I'll create the root view in code (ignoring the view controller nib supplied by the template); I'll create the scroll view and make it the root view, and populate it with 30 UILabels whose text contains a sequential number so that we can see where we are when we scroll:

```
UIScrollView* sv = [[UIScrollView alloc] initWithFrame:
                        [[UIScreen mainScreen] applicationFrame]];
self.view = sv;
CGFloat y = 10;
for (int i=0; i<30; i++) {
    UILabel* lab = [[UILabel alloc] init];
    lab.text = [NSString stringWithFormat:@"This is label %i", i+1];
    [lab sizeToFit];
    CGRect f = lab.frame;
    f.origin = CGPointMake(10,y);
    lab.frame = f;
    [sv addSubview:lab];
    y += lab.bounds.size.height + 10;
    [lab release];
}
CGSize sz = sv.bounds.size;
sz.height = y;
sv.contentSize = sz; // This is the crucial line
[sv release];
```

The crucial move, as the comment notes, is that we tell the scroll view how large its content view is to be. If we omit this step, the scroll view won't be scrollable; the window will appear to consist of a static column of labels.

There is no rule about the order in which you perform the two operations of setting the contentSize and populating the scroll view with subviews. In this example, we set the contentSize afterward because it is more convenient to track the heights of the subviews as we add them than to calculate their total height in advance. Similarly, you can alter a scroll view's contents (subviews) and contentSize dynamically as the app runs.

Any direct subviews of the scroll view may need to have their autoresizing set appropriately in case the scroll view is resized, as would happen, for instance, if our root view controller allowed autorotation. To see this, add these lines inside the for loop:

---

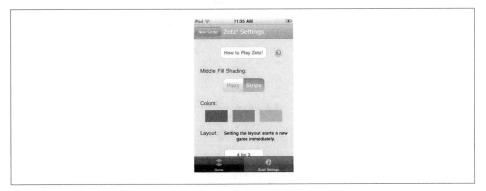

*Figure 20-1. The Zotz! settings view*

```
lab.backgroundColor = [UIColor redColor]; // make label bounds visible
lab.autoresizingMask = UIViewAutoresizingFlexibleWidth;
```

Now implement `shouldAutorotateToInterfaceOrientation:` to return YES for all orientations, run the app, and rotate the device (or the Simulator). The labels are wider in portrait orientation because the scroll view itself is wider. Note that this has nothing to do with the `contentSize`! The content view is not really a view, so resizing the `contentSize` has no effect on the size or position of the scroll view's subviews.

Populating a scroll view in code is a very common approach, especially because the contents of the scroll view are often not known until runtime. However, sometimes a scroll view is just a way of presenting a fixed view that's larger than the available space; in that case, it is simpler to design the whole scroll view in the nib. The nib editor makes this easy to do.

For example, in my Zotz! app, the view where the user specifies preference settings is in a navigation interface inside a tab bar interface, so there isn't enough vertical space for the various interface objects (Figure 20-1). The obvious solution is that the view should be a scroll view. To lay out this scroll view's subviews in code would be painful and unmaintainable; a nib-based solution is better.

A view in a nib can be a UIScrollView, and this can be any size; its subviews will be the scroll view's subviews when the app runs, which means, as we've already seen, that they will constitute the scroll view's content view. So you design the scroll view's contents in the nib exactly as you'd design the contents of any view (Figure 20-2). In this case, the scroll view itself is a view controller's view and will be automatically resized appropriately when it is placed into the interface.

The only problem is that the nib provides no way to set the scroll view's `contentSize`. Thus it is up to your code to set an appropriate `contentSize`, large enough to embrace all the scroll view's subviews. But how will your code know what size that is? In the Zotz! app, where the scroll view's content needs to scroll vertically, I solve this problem by means of an outlet to the bottommost subview in the nib. When the view loads, I

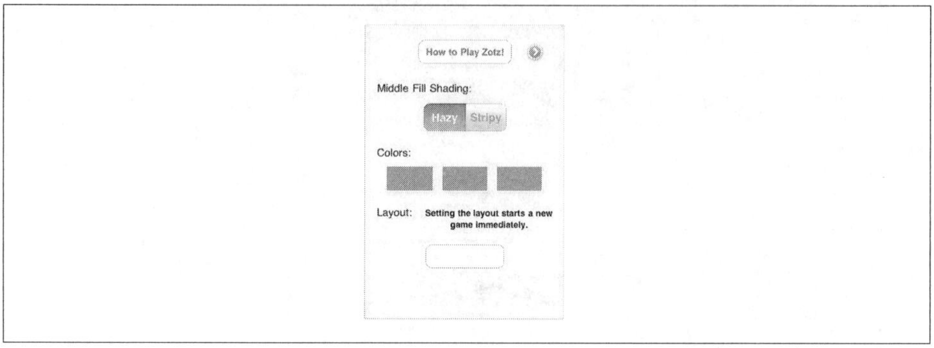

*Figure 20-2. The Zotz! settings view, designed in the nib*

use the view controller's `viewDidLoad` to learn the y-position of this subview; I allow
some additional space at the bottom and set the content view size:

```
UIScrollView* sc = (UIScrollView*)self.view;
float width = sc.bounds.width;
// use lowest subview, "layout", as reference for content height
float height = self.layout.frame.origin.y + self.layout.frame.size.height + 20.0;
sc.contentSize = CGSizeMake(width, height);
```

A more elegant approach, perhaps, would have been to put all those views into a single
container view that is itself inside the scroll view. The purpose of the container view is
to show the scroll view what its `contentSize` should be. We no longer need an outlet
because we know that the container view is the scroll view's first subview:

```
UIScrollView* sc = (UIScrollView*)self.view;
sc.contentSize = ((UIView*)[sc.subviews objectAtIndex:0]).bounds.size;
```

> Do not assume that the subviews you add to a UIScrollView are its only
> subviews! The scroll indicators managed by the scroll view, discussed
> in the next section, are also subviews (they are actually UIImageViews).

# Scrolling

For the most part, the purpose of a scroll view will be to let the user scroll. A number
of properties affect the user experience with regard to scrolling:

`scrollEnabled`
> If NO, the user can't scroll, but you can still scroll in code (as explained later in
> this section). You could put a UIScrollView to various creative purposes other than
> letting the user scroll; for example, scrolling in code to a different region of the
> content view might be a way of replacing one piece of interface by another.

`scrollsToTop`
> If YES (the default), and assuming scrolling is enabled, the user can tap on the
> status bar as a way of making the scroll view scroll its content view to the top.

**bounces**

If YES (the default), then when the user scrolls to a limit of the content, it is possible to scroll somewhat further (possibly revealing the scroll view's backgroundColor behind the content view, if a subview was covering it); the content then snaps back into place when the user releases it. Otherwise, the user experiences the limit as a sudden inability to scroll further in that direction.

**alwaysBounceVertical, alwaysBounceHorizontal**

If YES, and assuming that bounces is YES, then even if the contentSize in the given dimension isn't larger than the scroll view (so that no scrolling is actually possible in that dimension), the user can nevertheless scroll somewhat and the content then snaps back into place when the user releases it; otherwise, the user experiences a simple inability to scroll in that dimension.

**directionalLockEnabled**

If YES, and if scrolling is possible in both dimensions (even if only because the appropriate alwaysBounce... is YES), then the user, having begun to scroll in one dimension, can't scroll in the other dimension without ending the gesture and starting over. In other words, the user is constrained to scroll vertically or horizontally but not both at once.

**decelerationRate**

The rate at which scrolling is damped out, and the content comes to a stop, after a flick gesture. As convenient examples, standard constants UIScrollView-DecelerationRateNormal (0.998) and UIScrollViewDecelerationRateFast (0.99) are provided. Lower values mean faster damping; experimentation suggests that values lower than 0.5 are viable but barely distinguishable from one another.

**showsHorizontalScrollIndicator, showsVerticalScrollIndicator**

The scroll indicators are bars that appear only while the user is scrolling in a scrollable dimension (where the content view is larger than the scroll view), and serve to indicate both the size of the content view in that dimension relative to the scroll view and where the user is within it. The default is YES for both.

Because the user cannot see the scroll indicators except when actively scrolling, there is normally no indication that the view is scrollable. I regard this as somewhat unfortunate, because it makes the possibility of scrolling less discoverable; I'd prefer an option to make the scroll indicators constantly visible. Apple suggests that you call flashScrollIndicators when the scroll view appears, to make the scroll indicators visible momentarily.

**indicatorStyle**

The way the scroll indicators are drawn. Your choices are:

- UIScrollViewIndicatorStyleDefault (black with a white border)
- UIScrollViewIndicatorStyleBlack (black)
- UIScrollViewIndicatorStyleWhite (white)

contentInset

A UIEdgeInsets struct (four CGFloats in the order top, left, bottom, right) specifying margins around the content view. A typical use for this would be that your scroll view underlaps an interface element, such as a translucent status bar, navigation bar, or toolbar, and you want your content to be visible even when scrolled to its limit.

For example, suppose that our app with the 30 labels has its *Info.plist* configured with the "Status bar style" key set to "Transparent black style," and that our scroll view's view controller sets its wantsFullScreenLayout to YES. The scroll view now underlaps the status bar. This looks cool while scrolling, but at launch time, and if scrolled all the way to the top, the first label is partly covered by the status bar. We can fix this by supplying a contentInset whose top matches the height of the status bar. We may also have to scroll the content view into position at launch time in code so that it looks right:

```
CGFloat top = [[UIApplication sharedApplication] statusBarFrame].size.height;
sv.contentInset = UIEdgeInsetsMake(top,0,0,0);
[sv scrollRectToVisible:CGRectMake(0,0,1,1) animated:NO];
```

scrollIndicatorInsets

A UIEdgeInsets struct specifying a shift in the position of the scroll indicators. A typical use is to compensate for the contentInset. For example, returning to our scroll view that underlaps the translucent status bar, the content is no longer hidden under the status bar when scrolled to the top, but the top of the vertical scroll indicator is. We can fix this by setting the scrollIndicatorInsets to the same value as the contentInset.

 Here's a trick I've sometimes used: by setting a scrollIndicatorInsets component to a negative number and setting the scroll view's clipsToBounds to NO, you can make the scroll indicators appear *outside* the scroll view. But because you've turned off clipsToBounds, you might have to impose some opaque views on top of the interface to mask off the edges of the scroll view, so that its content isn't visible outside its bounds.

You can scroll in code even if the user can't scroll. The content view simply moves to the position you specify, with no bouncing and no exposure of the scroll indicators. You can specify the new position in two ways:

contentOffset

The point (CGPoint) of the content view that is located at the scroll view's top left. Of course the content view isn't really a view, but the numbers will work correctly if you pretend that it is. You can get this property to learn the current scroll position, and set it to change the current scroll position. There is an implication here that you could equally scroll by changing the scroll view's bounds origin; you are un-

*Figure 20-3. A scroll view coordinated with a page control*

likely to do that, but the truth is that the bounds origin and the `contentOffset` are effectively the same thing.

To set the `contentOffset` with animation, call `setContentOffset:animated:`. The animation does not cause the scroll indicators to appear; it just slides the content to the desired position.

`scrollRectToVisible:animated:`
> Adjusts the content view so that the specified CGRect of the view is within the scroll view's bounds. This is less precise than setting the `contentOffset`, because you're not saying exactly what the resulting scroll position will be, but sometimes guaranteeing the visibility of a certain portion of the content is exactly what you're after.

If you call a method to scroll with animation and you need to know when the animation ends, implement `scrollViewDidEndScrollingAnimation:` in the scroll view's delegate.

# Paging

If its `pagingEnabled` property is YES, the scroll view doesn't let the user scroll freely; instead, the content is considered to consist of sections the size of the scroll view's bounds, and the user can scroll only in such a way as to move to an adjacent section.

For instance, one of Apple's examples consists of a scroll view containing image views. Each image view is the size of the scroll view. This is an appropriate use of `paging-Enabled`: the user can scroll to see the entire next image or the entire previous image.

The scroll indicator, if it appears, gives the user a sense of how many "pages" constitute the view. Alternatively, you could use delegate messages to coordinate with a UIPage-Control (Chapter 25). Figure 20-3 shows my modification of Apple's Scrolling example, where I've added a UIPageControl below the paging scroll view. Here's the code that updates the page control (**pager**) when the user scrolls:

```
- (void)scrollViewDidEndDecelerating:(UIScrollView *)scrollView {
    CGFloat x = scrollView.contentOffset.x;
    CGFloat w = scrollView.bounds.size.width;
    self.pager.currentPage = x/w;
}
```

And here's the code that scrolls the scroll view (**sv**) when the user taps the page control:

```
- (void) userDidPage: (id) sender {
    NSInteger p = self.pager.currentPage;
    CGFloat w = self.sv.bounds.size.width;
    [self.sv setContentOffset:CGPointMake(p*w,0) animated:YES];
}
```

A useful trick is to have *no* scroll indicator and *no* page control, so that the user has *no* indication of how many "pages" there are, and then to supply pages dynamically as the user scrolls. The result is that the user gets a paging environment that just keeps going and going. In this way, you can display a huge number of pages without having to put them all into the scroll view at once.

That, in fact, is how my flashcard apps work. There are thousands of flashcards, and I want the user to be able to page by dragging or flicking from one flashcard to the next or previous flashcard, so a scroll view is the perfect interface. But it would be a terrible drain on resources to have a gigantic scroll view whose content consists of all the flashcards simultaneously. Instead, I have a scroll view whose content consists of just *three* flashcards: the one the user is looking at, plus the previous flashcard (to its left) and the next flashcard (to its right).

To see how this works, let's number the three flashcard positions: we'll say that the previous flashcard occupies Position 1, the current flashcard occupies Position 2, and the next flashcard occupies Position 3. Suppose that the user scrolls to bring the next flashcard into view from the right. The situation is then that Position 3 is showing; this is bad, because the user now can't scroll to the next flashcard; the scroll view is already scrolled to its rightmost limit. However, a delegate message informs me that the user has just scrolled, so I take this opportunity to fix the content behind the scenes: I shove the card from Position 3 into Position 2 and the card from Position 2 into Position 1, and move the content view to show Position 2 — the same card the user has just scrolled to. And I do it without any animation, so the user doesn't realize that anything has happened. Now Position 3 is vacant, and I draw the next flashcard into it — and because Position 3 isn't showing, the user doesn't see that either. Now the user can scroll either left or right, just as before.

This architecture is possible because the user can scroll only one page at a time. Thus, each time the user scrolls, we are guaranteed of a moment where we have time to adjust everything before the user scrolls again. (Consult Apple's PageControl example if you want to see a possible implementation.)

## Tiling

Suppose we have some finite but really big content we want to display in a scroll view, such as a very large image that the user can inspect, piecemeal, by scrolling. To hold the entire image in memory may be onerous or impossible, but on the other hand there's no need to do so; all we really need at any given moment is the part of the image the user is looking at right now.

Tiling is one solution to this kind of problem. Mentally, divide the content view into a matrix of rectangles (tiles); in reality, divide the huge image into corresponding rectangles. Then whenever the user scrolls, we look to see whether part of any empty tile has become visible, and if so, we supply its content. At the same time, we can release the content of all tiles that are completely offscreen. Thus, at any given moment, only the tiles that are showing have content. There some latency associated with this approach (the user scrolls, then any empty newly visible tiles are filled in), but we will have to live with that.

There is actually a built-in CALayer subclass for helping us implement tiling — CATiledLayer. Its `tileSize` property sets the dimensions of a tile. Its `drawLayer:inContext:` is called only when content for an empty tile is needed; calling `CGContextGetClipBoundingBox` on the context reveals the location of desired tile, and now we can supply that tile's content.

To illustrate, we'll use some tiles already created for us as part of Apple's own PhotoScroller example. In particular, I'll use the "Shed_1000" images. These all have names of the form *Shed_1000_x_y.png*, where *x* and *y* are integers corresponding to the picture's position within the matrix. The images are 256×256 pixels (except for the ones on the extreme right and bottom edges of the matrix, which are shorter in one dimension). So, starting with the View-based Application template, we'll make the root view controller's view a UIScrollView (in the nib), and initialize it in the root view controller's `viewDidLoad`. Our scroll view's sole subview will be an instance of a UIView subclass, TiledView, which exists purely to give our CATiledLayer a place to live:

```
- (void)viewDidLoad {
    [super viewDidLoad];
    CGRect f = CGRectMake(0,0,9*256,13*256);
    TiledView* content = [[TiledView alloc] initWithFrame:f];
    [(CATiledLayer*)content.layer setTileSize: CGSizeMake(256,256)];
    [self.view addSubview:content];
    [content release];
    [(UIScrollView*)self.view setContentSize: f.size];
}
```

Here's the code for TiledView. The CATiledLayer is our underlying layer; therefore we are its delegate, so if we implement `drawLayer:inContext:`, it will be called whenever a tile needs drawing. We fetch the corresponding image, flip it using the `flip` utility developed in Example 15-1, and draw it into place. As Apple's code points out, we must fetch images with `imageWithContentsOfFile:` so as to avoid the automatic caching behavior of `imageNamed:`, because we're doing all this exactly to avoid using any more memory than we have to:

```
+ (Class) layerClass {
    return [CATiledLayer class];
}

-(void)drawRect:(CGRect)r {
    // implemented, but empty; this is deliberate
}
```

```
- (void)drawLayer:(CALayer *)layer inContext:(CGContextRef)ctx {
    CGRect tile = CGContextGetClipBoundingBox(ctx);
    int x = tile.origin.x/256;
    int y = tile.origin.y/256;
    NSString *tileName = [NSString stringWithFormat:@"Shed_1000_%i_%i", x, y];
    NSString *path = [[NSBundle mainBundle] pathForResource:tileName ofType:@"png"];
    UIImage *image = [UIImage imageWithContentsOfFile:path];
    CGContextDrawImage(ctx, tile, flip([image CGImage]));
}
```

See Chapter 16 for the reason why we implement an empty `drawRect:` even though our drawing is actually done in `drawLayer:inContext:`.

There is no special call for invalidating an offscreen tile. You can call `setNeeds-Display` or `setNeedsDisplayInRect:` on the TiledView, but this doesn't erase offscreen tiles. You're just supposed to trust that the CATiledLayer will eventually clear offscreen tiles if needed to conserve memory.

There is a tiny bug in the foregoing code. It doesn't work correctly on the double-resolution Retina display; the tiles are drawn at half size. The simplest solution is probably to set the tile size with respect to the CATiledLayer's native scale:

```
CGFloat tsz = 256 * content.layer.contentsScale;
[(CATiledLayer*)content.layer setTileSize: CGSizeMake(tsz, tsz)];
```

On the other hand, a completely different solution would be to draw with UIKit instead of Core Graphics. In the example so far, our drawing into the graphics context in `draw-Layer:inContext:` has been done with Core Graphics, deliberately; Apple has a tech note (QA1637, "CATiledLayer and UIKit graphics") warning that a CATiledLayer introduces threading issues that make UIKit drawing methods dangerous. However, there is some evidence that this warning may be outdated; starting in iOS 4, accessing the current context and drawing to it with UIKit is said to be safe even in a background thread. If this is true, we don't need to worry about the difference between the single-resolution and double-resolution displays, and we don't have to flip the image. Once we have the image, we can draw it directly into the requested tile of the given context with UIKit:

```
UIGraphicsPushContext(ctx);
[image drawAtPoint:tile.origin];
UIGraphicsPopContext();
```

But we can go further. Because accessing the current context is said to be thread-safe in iOS 4, we can eliminate `drawLayer:inContext:` and move our code to `drawRect:`. There is no need to set the current graphics context, because it has already been set for us; there is no need to ask for the clip bounding box, because the incoming CGRect parameter *is* the clip bounding box; and there is no need to flip the image or compensate for the double-resolution screen, because we are drawing with UIImage, which takes care of those things for us:

```
-(void)drawRect:(CGRect)r {
    CGRect tile = r;
    int x = tile.origin.x/256;
    int y = tile.origin.y/256;
    NSString *tileName = [NSString stringWithFormat:@"Shed_1000_%i_%i", x, y];
    NSString *path = [[NSBundle mainBundle] pathForResource:tileName ofType:@"png"];
    UIImage *image = [UIImage imageWithContentsOfFile:path];
    [image drawAtPoint:tile.origin];
}
```

CATiledLayer has a class method `fadeDuration` that dictates the duration of the animation that fades a new tile into view. You can create a CATiledLayer subclass and override this method to return a value different from the default (`0.25`), but in general this is probably not worth doing, as the default value is a good one. Returning a smaller value won't make tiles appear faster; it just replaces the nice fade-in with an annoying flash.

# Zooming

In the simplest case, zooming is just a scaling transform that the scroll view applies to a subview. To implement zooming of a scroll view's contents, you set the scroll view's `minimumZoomScale` and `maximumZoomScale` so that at least one of them isn't `1` (the default); you also implement `viewForZoomingInScrollView:` in the scroll view's delegate to tell the scroll view which of its subviews is to be the scalable view. Typically, you'll want the scroll view's entire contents to be scalable, so you'll have one direct subview of the scroll view that acts as the scalable view, and anything else inside the scroll view will be a subview of the scalable view, so as to be scaled together with it.

To illustrate, let's return to the first example in this chapter, where we created a scroll view containing 30 labels. To make this scroll view zoomable, we'll need to modify the way we create it. As it stands, the scroll view's subviews are just the 30 labels; there is no single view that we would scale in order to scale all the labels together. So instead of making the 30 labels subviews of the scroll view, we'll make them subviews of a single scalable view and make the scalable view the subview of the scroll view:

```
UIScrollView* sv = [[UIScrollView alloc] initWithFrame:
                        [[UIScreen mainScreen] applicationFrame]];
self.view = sv;
UIView* v = [[UIView alloc] init]; // scalable view
CGFloat y = 10;
for (int i=0; i<30; i++) {
    UILabel* lab = [[UILabel alloc] init];
    lab.text = [NSString stringWithFormat:@"This is label %i", i+1];
    [lab sizeToFit];
    CGRect f = lab.frame;
    f.origin = CGPointMake(10,y);
    lab.frame = f;
    [v addSubview:lab]; // labels are subviews of scalable view
    y += lab.bounds.size.height + 10;
    [lab release];
```

```
}
CGSize sz = sv.bounds.size;
sz.height = y;
sv.contentSize = sz;
v.frame = CGRectMake(0,0,sz.width,sz.height);
[sv addSubview:v];
[v release];
[sv release];
```

So far, nothing has changed; the scroll view works just as before, but it isn't zoomable. To make it zoomable, replace the last two lines of the foregoing code with this:

```
v.tag = 999;
[v release];
sv.minimumZoomScale = 1.0;
sv.maximumZoomScale = 2.0;
sv.delegate = self;
[sv release];
```

We have assigned a tag to the view that is to be scaled, so we can find it later. We have set the scale limits for the scroll view. And we have made ourselves the scroll view's delegate. Now all we have to do is implement viewForZoomingInScrollView: and return the scalable view:

```
- (UIView *)viewForZoomingInScrollView:(UIScrollView *)scrollView {
    return [scrollView viewWithTag:999];
}
```

The scroll view now responds to pinch gestures by scaling appropriately. The user can actually scale considerably beyond the limits we set in both directions; when the gesture ends, the scale returns to the limit value. If we wish to confine scaling strictly to our defined limits, we can set the scroll view's bouncesZoom to NO; when the user reaches a limit, scaling will simply stop.

If the minimumZoomScale is less than 1, then when the scalable view becomes smaller than the scroll view, it is pinned to the scroll view's top left. If you don't like this, you can change it by subclassing UIScrollView and overriding layoutSubviews, or by implementing the scroll view delegate method scrollViewDidZoom:. Here's a simple example demonstrating one approach; it keeps the scalable view centered as it becomes smaller than the scroll view:

```
- (void) scrollViewDidZoom:(UIScrollView*)sv {
    CGFloat svw = sv.bounds.size.width;
    CGFloat svh = sv.bounds.size.height;
    UIView* v = [sv viewWithTag: 999]; // the scalable view
    CGFloat vw = v.frame.size.width;
    CGFloat vh = v.frame.size.height;
    CGPoint c = v.center;
    if (vw < svw)
        c.x = svw / 2.0;
    if (vh < svh)
        c.y = svh / 2.0;
    v.center = c;
}
```

## Zooming Programmatically

To zoom programmatically, you have two choices:

setZoomScale:animated:
> Zooms in terms of scale value. The contentOffset is automatically adjusted to keep the current center centered and the content view occupying the entire scroll view.

zoomToRect:animated:
> Zooms so that the given rectangle of the content view occupies as much as possible of the scroll view's bounds. The contentOffset is automatically adjusted to keep the content view occupying the entire scroll view.

For example, let's say we want to implement double-tapping as a zoom-and-center gesture. One implementation might be that double-tapping means both zoom in and zoom out: if we're zoomed in less than halfway, it means to zoom all the way in; otherwise it means to zoom all the way out. This is particularly easy thanks to gesture recognizers (Chapter 18). The gesture recognizer should ideally be attached to the scalable view. It reports its locationInView in view bounds coordinates, so the point we want to center on is precisely the point reported by the gesture recognizer, and all we have to do is provide an appropriately scaled rectangle centered at that point. Here's the action handler for a double-tap UITapGestureRecognizer:

```
- (void) tapped: (UIGestureRecognizer*) tap {
    UIScrollView* sv = (UIScrollView*)tap.view.superview;
    CGPoint loc = [tap locationInView: tap.view];
    CGFloat targetScale =
        (sv.zoomScale <= 1.5) ? sv.maximumZoomScale : sv.minimumZoomScale;
    CGRect f = sv.bounds;
    CGFloat w = f.size.width/targetScale;
    CGFloat h = f.size.height/targetScale;
    CGRect r = CGRectMake(loc.x - w/2.0, loc.y - h/2.0, w, h);
    [sv zoomToRect:r animated:YES];
}
```

## Zooming with Detail

By default, when a scroll view zooms, it merely applies a scale transform to the scaled view. The scaled view's drawing is cached beforehand into its layer, and the bits of the resulting bitmap are drawn larger. This means that a zoomed-in scroll view's content is fuzzy (pixellated).

> On a double-resolution device, this might not be such an issue. If the user is allowed to scroll only up to double scale, you can just draw at double scale right from the start; the results will look good at single scale, because the screen has double resolution, as well as at double scale, because that's the scale you drew at.

You might, on the other hand, like to redraw the content with improved resolution or increased detail after the scroll view is zoomed in. You can learn when a zoom has taken place, by implementing the delegate's scrollViewDidEndZooming:withView:atScale:. But unfortunately it is far from clear how you can redraw at this point. You cannot merely redraw the scaled view's content at higher resolution, because the scaled view is not at a higher resolution, nor has its size increased; it still at its original size and resolution, with a transform applied. What you'd like to do is draw into the view as if the view's size had *really* increased, and *without* a transform applied. However, the scroll view is using the scaled view's transform as an indication of zoomed state; if you remove the transform from the scaled view, the scroll view will reset its own zoomScale to 1. This means that if the minimumZoomScale is 1, the user will now be unable to zoom back out.

My approach, then, is as follows. After a zoom, we remove the scalable view entirely, to break the scroll view's special relationship with it, and replace it by a new view whose real size is the apparent (zoomed) size of the old view. The scroll view now thinks the zoomScale is 1, so we can no longer trust it; we must keep track of the scale ourselves, in an instance variable, which must be initialized (to 1.0, presumably) when the scroll view is created. At the same time, we adjust the minimumZoomScale and maximumZoomScale in conformity with our private notion of the scale, so we need to remember the nominal minimum and maximum zoom values (if these values don't change, we can use constants for this). I find that this technique looks best if there is a slight delay between the end of zooming and the redrawing of the content view, so I use delayed performance. In the following code, I assume that, as in earlier examples, our scaling view is identified by a tag value of 999:

```
- (void) sharpenToScale: (NSNumber*) sc {
    CGFloat scale = [sc floatValue];
    // remove old view
    UIScrollView* sv = (UIScrollView*)self.view;
    UIView* v = [sv viewWithTag:999];
    [v removeFromSuperview];
    // create new view appropriate to new absolute scale
    CGFloat newscale = scale * self->oldScale; // absolute scale at which to redraw
    self->oldScale = newscale;
    [self addNewScalableViewAtScale:newscale]; // workhorse utility
    sv.minimumZoomScale = MINZOOM / newscale;
    sv.maximumZoomScale = MAXZOOM / newscale;
}

- (void)scrollViewDidEndZooming:(UIScrollView *)scrollView
                       withView:(UIView *)view atScale:(float)scale {
    [self performSelector:@selector(sharpenToScale:)
               withObject:[NSNumber numberWithFloat:scale] afterDelay:0.1];
}
```

As the comment implies, the example posits a workhorse utility, addNewScalableViewAtScale:, which creates the view, tags it, sizes it, populates or draws it, puts it into the scroll view, and sets the scroll view's contentSize to match. This is exactly the same sort of thing we did in the first example in this section; the difference is that we must now be prepared to do it all at any given scale.

So, earlier, we populated our scalable view with 30 labels, arranged vertically, 10 pixels apart. How might we adapt this to constitute our implementation of addNewScalable-ViewAtScale:? Basically, we must multiply every hard-coded number, including implicitly hard-coded numbers such as the font size of the labels, by the scale. For clarity, I'll break the utility into two methods, one of which calls the other:

```
- (CGFloat) addLabelsToView: (UIView*) v scale: (CGFloat) scale {
    CGFloat y = 10*scale;
    for (int i=0; i<30; i++) {
        UILabel* lab = [[UILabel alloc] init];
        NSString* name = lab.font.fontName;
        CGFloat fsz = lab.font.pointSize;
        lab.text = [NSString stringWithFormat:@"This is label %i", i+1];
        [lab sizeToFit];
        CGFloat origHeight = lab.bounds.size.height;
        lab.font = [UIFont fontWithName:name size:fsz*scale];
        [lab sizeToFit];
        CGRect f = lab.frame;
        f.origin = CGPointMake(10*scale,y);
        lab.frame = f;
        [v addSubview:lab]; // labels are subviews of scalable view
        y += (origHeight + 10) * scale;
        [lab release];
    }
    return y;
}


- (void) addNewScalableViewAtScale: (CGFloat) scale {
    UIScrollView* sv = (UIScrollView*) self.view;
    UIView* v = [[UIView alloc] init]; // scalable view
    CGFloat y = [self addLabelsToView: v scale: scale];
    CGSize sz = sv.bounds.size;
    sz.width *= scale;
    sz.height = y;
    sv.contentSize = sz;
    v.frame = CGRectMake(0,0,sz.width,sz.height);
    [sv addSubview:v];
    v.tag = 999;
    [v release];
}
```

And of course when we originally create our scroll view we populate it by calling add-NewScalableViewAtScale: with an initial scale of 1:

```
- (void)loadView {
    UIScrollView* sv = [[UIScrollView alloc] initWithFrame:
                           [[UIScreen mainScreen] applicationFrame]];
    self.view = sv;
    [self addNewScalableViewAtScale: 1.0];
    sv.minimumZoomScale = MINZOOM;
    sv.maximumZoomScale = MAXZOOM;
    self->oldScale = 1.0;
```

```
        sv.delegate = self;
        [sv release];
}
```

The overall effect is remarkably good. The user zooms with a pinch gesture, and the labels are momentarily blurry, but then an instant later they sharpen. A even better effect can be achieved by using an animation as we replace one scalable view by another: put the second view into the scroll view with an `alpha` of 0, animate changing this `alpha` to 1 and the first view's `alpha` to 0, and now remove the first view. This is left as an exercise for the reader.

A completely different approach to achieving a detailed redraw after a zoom is to use a CATiledLayer. Earlier, we saw that a CATiledLayer will ask for tiles to be drawn only as needed. Additionally, it can be made to ask for tiles to be drawn when the layer is scaled to a new order of magnitude. This approach is extremely easy: your drawing routine is called and you simply draw, the graphics context itself having already been scaled appropriately.

Your drawing does *not* have to involve tiles. Of course it *can* involve tiles; for a large tiled image, you would be forearmed with multiple versions of the image broken into an identical quantity of tiles, each set having double the tile size of the previous set (as in Apple's PhotoScroller example). But you can also just draw directly (as shown in the "Basic Zooming Using the Pinch Gestures" chapter of Apple's *Scroll View Programming Guide for iOS*).

You have to set up two CATiledLayer properties:

levelsOfDetail

> The number of different resolutions at which you want to redraw, where each level has twice the resolution of the previous level. So, for example, with two levels of detail we can ask to redraw when zooming to double size (2x) and when zooming back to single size (1x).

levelsOfDetailBias

> The number of levels of detail that are *larger* than single size (1x). For example, if levelsOfDetail is 2, then if we want to redraw when zooming to 2x and when zooming back to 1x, the levelsOfDetailBias is 1, because one of those levels is larger than 1x; if we were to leave levelsOfDetailBias at 0 (the default), we would be saying we want to redraw when zooming to 0.5x and back to 1x — we have two levels of detail but neither is larger than 1x, so one must be smaller than 1x.

> So, just to hammer home the point, let's say we want to redraw at .5x, 1x, 2x, and 4x. That's four levels of detail, so levelsOfDetail is 4; and two of them are larger than 1x, so levelsOfDetailBias is 2.

The CATiledLayer will ask for a redraw at a higher resolution as soon as the view's size becomes larger than the previous resolution. In other words, if there are two levels of detail with a bias of 1, the layer will be redrawn at 2x as soon as it is zoomed even a little bit larger than 1x. This is an excellent approach, because although a level of detail would look blurry if scaled up, it looks pretty good scaled down.

To illustrate, I'll rewrite our example with the 30 labels to use plain Core Graphics text drawing instead. In the root view controller, we create our content view (a TiledView) and configure everything. The tiles have no purpose to us, so we may as well set the tile size to the bounds size:

```
- (void)viewDidLoad {
    [super viewDidLoad];
    CGRect f = CGRectMake(0,0,self.view.bounds.size.width,940);
    TiledView* content = [[TiledView alloc] initWithFrame:f];
    content.tag = 999;
    CATiledLayer* lay = (CATiledLayer*)content.layer;
    [lay setTileSize: f.size];
    lay.levelsOfDetail = 2;
    lay.levelsOfDetailBias = 1;
    [self.view addSubview:content];
    [content release];
    UIScrollView* sv = (UIScrollView*)self.view;
    [sv setContentSize: f.size];
    sv.minimumZoomScale = 1.0;
    sv.maximumZoomScale = 2.0;
    sv.delegate = self;
}

- (UIView *)viewForZoomingInScrollView:(UIScrollView *)scrollView {
    return [scrollView viewWithTag:999];
}
```

In the TiledView, we simply draw (with some appropriate futzing to deal with text flipping). We ignore the context's clip bounding box, and we care nothing about its scale; we just draw the same way no matter what, and the rest happens automatically:

```
+ (Class) layerClass {
    return [CATiledLayer class];
}

-(void)drawRect:(CGRect)r {
    // implemented, but empty; this is deliberate
}

- (void)drawLayer:(CALayer *)layer inContext:(CGContextRef)ctx {
    CGContextSetFillColorWithColor(ctx, [[UIColor whiteColor] CGColor]);
    CGContextFillRect(ctx, self.bounds);
    CGContextSetFillColorWithColor(ctx, [[UIColor blackColor] CGColor]);

    CGContextSaveGState(ctx);
    CGContextTranslateCTM(ctx, 0, self.bounds.size.height);
    CGContextScaleCTM(ctx, 1.0, -1.0);
    CGContextSelectFont(ctx, "Helvetica", 18, kCGEncodingMacRoman);

    // height consists of 31 spacers with 30 texts between them
    CGFloat viewh = self.bounds.size.height;
    CGFloat spacerh = 10;
```

```
    CGFloat texth = (viewh - (31*spacerh))/30.0;
    CGFloat y = spacerh;
    for (int i = 30; i > 0; i--) {
        NSString* s = [NSString stringWithFormat:@"This is label %i", i];
        const char* ss = [s UTF8String];
        CGContextShowTextAtPoint(ctx, 10, y, ss, strlen(ss));
        y += texth + spacerh;
    }
    CGContextRestoreGState(ctx);
}
```

That code jumps through a number of hoops in order to draw with Core Graphics only; in particular, we have to flip the context coordinate system to get our text to come out right side up, compensating by drawing our strings in reverse order. In iOS4 and later, those hoops aren't needed; drawing directly with UIKit and NSString is thread-safe. So we can eliminate the context flipping, draw the strings in their natural order, and move the code to drawRect: (and eliminate drawLayer:inContext:):

```
-(void)drawRect:(CGRect)r {
    [[UIColor whiteColor] set];
    UIRectFill(self.bounds);
    [[UIColor blackColor] set];
    UIFont* f = [UIFont fontWithName:@"Helvetica" size:18];
    // height consists of 31 spacers with 30 texts between them
    CGFloat viewh = self.bounds.size.height;
    CGFloat spacerh = 10;
    CGFloat texth = (viewh - (31*spacerh))/30.0;
    CGFloat y = spacerh;
    for (int i = 0; i < 30; i++) {
        NSString* s = [NSString stringWithFormat:@"This is label %i", i];
        [s drawAtPoint:CGPointMake(10,y) withFont:f];
        y += texth + spacerh;
    }
}
```

Our initial configuration of the CATiledLayer, in viewDidLoad, must be modified if we want things to work the same way on a double-resolution Retina display. First, the CATiledLayer starts life at the 2x level of detail, so instead of asking to be redrawn at 1x and 2x, as now, we must ask to be redrawn at 2x and 4x. We can do this by setting the levelsOfDetailBias to 2. Second, because we are at double resolution at the 2x level of detail, we must make our tiles *four* times bigger if a single tile is to be the size of the view initially. So we would add this to viewDidLoad:

```
if ([[UIScreen mainScreen] scale] > 1.0) {
    f.size.width *= 4;
    f.size.height *= 4;
    lay.tileSize = f.size;
    lay.levelsOfDetailBias = 2;
}
```

# Scroll View Delegate

The scroll view's delegate (adopting the UIScrollViewDelegate protocol) receives lots of messages that can help you track what the scroll view is up to:

`scrollViewDidScroll:`
> If you scroll in code without animation, you will receive this message *once*. If the user drags or flicks, or uses the scroll-to-top feature, or if you scroll in code with animation, you will receive this message *repeatedly* throughout the scroll, including during the time the scroll view is decelerating after the user's finger has lifted; there are other delegate messages that tell you, in those cases, when the scroll has really ended.

`scrollViewDidEndScrollingAnimation:`
> If you scroll in code with animation, you will receive this message when the animation ends.

`scrollViewWillBeginDragging:`, `scrollViewDidEndDragging:willDecelerate:`
> If the user scrolls by dragging or flicking, you will receive these messages at the start and end of the user's finger movement. If the user brings the scroll view to a stop before lifting the finger, `willDecelerate` is NO and the scroll is over. If the user lets go of the scroll view while the finger is moving, or if paging is turned on and the user has not paged perfectly already, `willDecelerate` is YES and we proceed to the delegate messages reporting deceleration.

`scrollViewWillBeginDecelerating:`, `scrollViewDidEndDecelerating:`
> Sent once each after `scrollViewDidEndDragging:willDecelerate:` arrives with a value of YES. When `scrollViewDidEndDecelerating:` arrives, the scroll is over.

`scrollViewShouldScrollToTop:`, `scrollViewDidScrollToTop:`
> You won't get either of these if `scrollsToTop` is NO, because the scroll-to-top feature is turned off in that case. The first lets you prevent the user from scrolling to the top on this occasion even if `scrollsToTop` is YES. The second tells you that the user has employed this feature and the scroll is over.

In addition, the scroll view has read-only properties reporting its state:

`tracking`
> The user has touched the scroll view, but the scroll view hasn't decided whether this is a scroll or some kind of tap.

`dragging`
> The user is dragging to scroll.

`decelerating`
> The user has scrolled and has lifted the finger, and the scroll is continuing.

So, if you wanted to do something after a scroll ends completely regardless of how the scroll was performed, you'd need to implement many delegate methods:

- `scrollViewDidEndDragging:willDecelerate:` in case the user drags and stops (`will-Decelerate` is NO).

- `scrollViewDidEndDecelerating:` in case the user drags and the scroll continues afterward.

- `scrollViewDidScrollToTop:` in case the user uses the scroll-to-top feature.

- `scrollViewDidEndScrollingAnimation:` in case you scroll in code with animation.

You don't need a delegate method to tell you when the scroll is over after you scroll in code without animation: it's over immediately, so if you have work to do after the scroll ends, you can do it in the next line of code.

There are also three delegate messages that report zooming:

`scrollViewWillBeginZooming:withView:`
> If the user zooms or you zoom in code, you will receive this message as the zoom begins.

`scrollViewDidZoom:`
> If you zoom in code, even with animation, you will receive this message *once* (and you might receive `scrollViewDidScroll:` as well). If the user zooms, you will receive this message *repeatedly* as the zoom proceeds. (You will probably also receive `scrollViewDidScroll:` repeatedly as the zoom proceeds.)

`scrollViewDidEndZooming:withView:atScale:`
> If the user zooms or you zoom in code, you will receive this message after the last `scrollViewDidZoom:`.

In addition, the scroll view has read-only properties reporting its state during a zoom:

`zooming`
> The scroll view is zooming. It is possible for **dragging** to be true at the same time.

`zoomBouncing`
> The scroll view is returning automatically from having been zoomed outside its minimum or maximum limit. As far as I can tell, you'll get only one `scrollViewDidZoom:` while the scroll view is in this state.

# Scroll View Touches

Improvements in the scroll view implementation have eliminated most of the worry once associated with scroll view touches. A scroll view will interpret a drag or a pinch as a command to scroll or zoom, and any other gesture will fall through to the subviews; thus buttons and similar interface objects inside a scroll view work just fine.

You can even put a scroll view inside a scroll view, and this can be quite a useful thing to do, in contexts where you might not think of it at first. A WWDC 2010 presentation uses as an example Apple's Photos app, where a single photo fills the screen: you can page-scroll from one photo to the next, and you can zoom the current photo with a pinch-out gesture. This, the presentation suggests, can be implemented with a scroll view inside a scroll view: the outer scroll view is for paging between images, and the inner scroll view contains the current image and is for zooming.

Gesture recognizers (Chapter 18) have also greatly simplified the task of adding custom gestures to a scroll view. For instance, some older code in Apple's documentation, showing how to implement a double-tap to zoom in and a two-finger tap to zoom out, uses old-fashioned touch handling, but this is no longer necessary. Simply attach to your scroll view's scalable subview any gesture recognizers for these sorts of gesture, and they will mediate automatically among the possibilities.

In the past, making something inside a scroll view draggable required setting the scroll view's `canCancelContentTouches` property to NO. (The reason for the name is that the scroll view, when it realizes that a gesture is a drag or pinch gesture, normally sends `touchesCancelled:forEvent:` to a subview tracking touches, so that the scroll view and not the subview will be affected.) However, unless you're implementing old-fashioned direct touch handling, you probably won't have to concern yourself with this. Regardless of how `canCancelContentTouches` is set, a draggable control, such as a UISlider, remains draggable inside a scroll view.

On the other hand, something like a UISlider might prove more quickly responsive if you set the scroll view's `delaysContentTouches` to NO. Without this, the user may have to hold a finger on the slider briefly before it becomes draggable. But even this will be a concern only if the scroll view is scrollable in the same dimension as the slider is oriented; a horizontal slider in a scroll view that can be scrolled only vertically is instantly draggable.

Here's an example of a draggable object inside a scroll view implemented through a gesture recognizer. Suppose we have an image of a map, larger than the screen, and we want the user to be able to scroll it in the normal way to see any part of the map, but we also want the user to be able to drag a flag into a new location on the map. We can arrange this, as we configure the scroll view in our `viewDidLoad`, with a UIPanGestureRecognizer using the `dragging:` action handler developed in Chapter 18:

```
- (void)viewDidLoad {
    [super viewDidLoad];
    UIScrollView* sv = (UIScrollView*)self.view;
    UIImageView* imv =
        [[UIImageView alloc] initWithImage: [UIImage imageNamed:@"map.jpg"]];
    [sv addSubview:imv];
    sv.contentSize = imv.bounds.size;
    UIImageView* flag =
        [[UIImageView alloc] initWithImage: [UIImage imageNamed:@"redflag.png"]];
    [sv addSubview: flag];
    UIPanGestureRecognizer* pan =
    [[UIPanGestureRecognizer alloc] initWithTarget:self
                                            action:@selector(dragging:)];
    [flag addGestureRecognizer:pan];
```

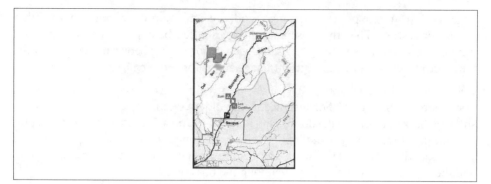

*Figure 20-4. A scrollable map with a draggable flag*

```
        flag.userInteractionEnabled = YES;
        [pan release]; [flag release]; [imv release];
}
```

The user can now drag the map or the flag (Figure 20-4). The state of the scroll view's `canCancelContentTouches` is irrelevant, because the flag view isn't tracking the touches manually.

An interesting addition to that example would be to implement autoscrolling, meaning that the scroll view scrolls itself when the user drags the flag close to its edge. This, too, is greatly simplified by gesture recognizers; in fact, we can add autoscrolling code directly to the **dragging:** action handler:

```
- (void) dragging: (UIPanGestureRecognizer*) p {
    // this part is identical to the code developed earlier
    UIView* v = p.view;
    if (p.state == UIGestureRecognizerStateBegan ||
            p.state == UIGestureRecognizerStateChanged) {
        CGPoint delta = [p translationInView: v.superview];
        CGPoint c = v.center;
        c.x += delta.x; c.y += delta.y;
        v.center = c;
        [p setTranslation: CGPointZero inView: v.superview];
    }
    // this is the addition to implement autoscrolling
    if (p.state == UIGestureRecognizerStateChanged) {
        CGPoint loc = [p locationInView:self.view.superview];
        CGRect f = self.view.frame;
        UIScrollView* sv = (UIScrollView*)self.view;
        CGPoint off = sv.contentOffset;
        CGSize sz = sv.contentSize;
        CGPoint c = v.center;
        // to the right
        if (loc.x > CGRectGetMaxX(f) - 30) {
            CGFloat margin = sz.width - CGRectGetMaxX(sv.bounds);
            if (margin > 6) {
                off.x += 5;
                sv.contentOffset = off;
                c.x += 5;
```

```
            v.center = c;
            [self performSelector:@selector(dragging:) withObject:p
                                                  afterDelay:0.2];
        }
    }
    // to the left
    if (loc.x < f.origin.x + 30) {
        CGFloat margin = off.x;
        if (margin > 6) {
            // ... omitted ...
        }
    }
    // to the bottom
    if (loc.y > CGRectGetMaxY(f) - 30) {
        CGFloat margin = sz.height - CGRectGetMaxY(sv.bounds);
        if (margin > 6) {
            // ... omitted ...
        }
    }
    // to the top
    if (loc.y < f.origin.y + 30) {
        CGFloat margin = off.y;
        if (margin > 6) {
            // ... omitted ...
        }
    }
    }
    }
}
```

The material marked as omitted in the second, third, and fourth cases is obviously parallel to the first case, and is left as an exercise for the reader.

# Scroll View Performance

At several points in earlier chapters I've mentioned performance problems and ways to increase drawing efficiency. Nowhere are you so likely to need these as in connection with a scroll view. As a scroll view scrolls, views must be drawn very rapidly as they appear on the screen. If the view-drawing system can't keep up with the speed of the scroll, the scrolling will visibly stutter.

Performance testing and optimization is a big subject, so I can't tell you exactly what to do if you encounter stuttering while scrolling. But certain general suggestions (mostly extracted from a really great presentation at the 2010 WWDC) should come in handy:

- Everything that can be opaque should be opaque: don't force the drawing system to composite transparency, and remember to tell it that an opaque view or layer *is* opaque by setting its opaque property to YES. (The Core Animation module of Instruments, available when testing on a device, has a Color Blended Layers option that will show you where transparency is being composited.) If you really must composite transparency, keep the size of the nonopaque regions to a minimum;

for example, if a large layer is transparent at its edges, break it into five layers — the large central layer, which is opaque, and the four edges, which are not.

 Apple's documentation also says that setting a view's `clearsContext-BeforeDrawing` to NO may make a difference. I can't confirm or deny this; it may be true, but I haven't encountered a case that positively proves it.

- Don't make the drawing system scale images for you; supply the images at the target size for the correct resolution. (Again, the Core Animation module of Instruments will help you spot incorrectly sized images with its Color Misaligned Images option.)

- If you're drawing shadows, don't make the drawing system calculate the shadow shape for a layer: supply a `shadowPath`, or use Core Graphics to create the shadow with a drawing. Similarly, avoid making the drawing system composite the shadow as a transparency against another layer; for example, if the background layer is white, your opaque drawing can itself include a shadow already drawn on a white background.

- In a pinch, you can just eliminate massive swatches of the rendering operation by setting a layer's `shouldRasterize` to YES. You could, for example, do this when scrolling starts and then set it back to NO when scrolling ends.

# CHAPTER 21

# Table Views

*I'm gonna ask you the three big questions. — Go ahead.*
*— Who made you? — You did. — Who owns the biggest*
*piece of you? — You do. — What would happen if I*
*dropped you? — I'd go right down the drain.*

—Dialogue by Garson Kanin and Ruth Gordon,
*Pat and Mike*

A table view (UITableView) is a scrolling interface (a vertically scrolling UIScrollView, Chapter 20) for presenting a single column of rectangular cells (UITableViewCell). It is a keystone of Apple's strategy for making the small iPhone screen useful and powerful, and has three main purposes:

*Presentation of information*
> The cells typically contain text, which can provide the user with helpful information. The cells are usually quite small, in order to maximize the number of them that appear on the screen at once, so this information is often condensed, truncated, or otherwise simplified.

*Selection*
> A cell can be selected by tapping. A table view can thus be used to provide the user with a column of choices. The user chooses by tapping a cell, and the app responds appropriately to that choice.

*Navigation*
> The appropriate response to the user's choosing a cell is often navigation to another portion of the interface. This might be done, for example, through a modal view or a navigation interface. An extremely common configuration is a master–detail interface, in which the master view is (or contains) a table view, often at the root of a navigation interface; the user taps a listing in the table to navigate to the details for that choice. This is one reason why truncation of information in a table view is acceptable: the detail view contains the full information.

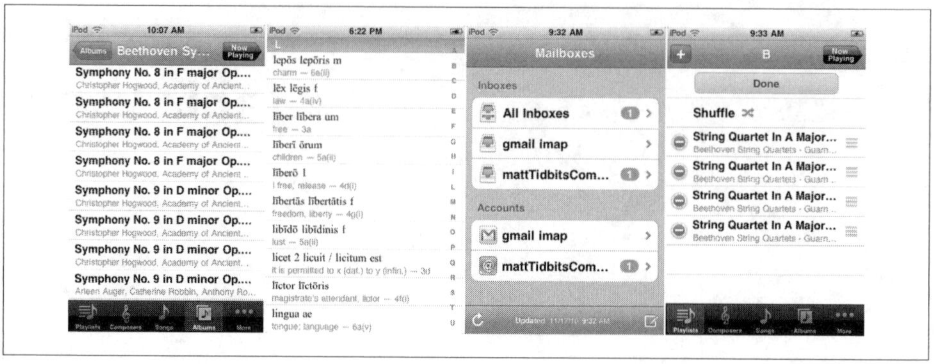

*Figure 21-1. Four table view variations*

In addition to its column of cells, a table view can be extended by a number of other features that make it even more useful and flexible:

- A table can start with a header view (at the top) and end with a footer view (at the bottom).

- The cells can be clumped into sections. Each section can have a header and footer, and these remain visible as long as the section itself occupies the screen, giving the user a clue as to where we are within the table. Moreover, a section index can be provided, in the form of a secondary column of abbreviated section titles, allowing the user to jump instantly to the start of a section.

- A table can have a "grouped" format. This is often used for presenting small numbers of related cells.

- Tables can be editable: the user can be permitted to insert, delete, and reorder cells.

Figure 21-1 illustrates four variations of the table view:

1. The iPod (Music) app lists song titles and artists for a given album in truncated form in a table view within a navigation interface which is itself within a tab bar interface; one table (the list of albums) leads to another (the list of songs within that album), which in turn allows the user to choose a song and play it.

2. An app of mine lists Latin words and their definitions in alphabetical order, divided into sections by first letter, with section headers and a section index.

3. The Mail app lists inboxes and accounts in a grouped format, clumped into sections with headers.

4. The iPod (Music) app allows a custom playlist to be edited, with interface for deleting and rearranging cells.

Table cells, too, can be extremely flexible. Some basic table cell formats are provided, such as a text label along with a small image view, but you are free to design your own table cell, as you would any other view. There are also some standard interface items

---

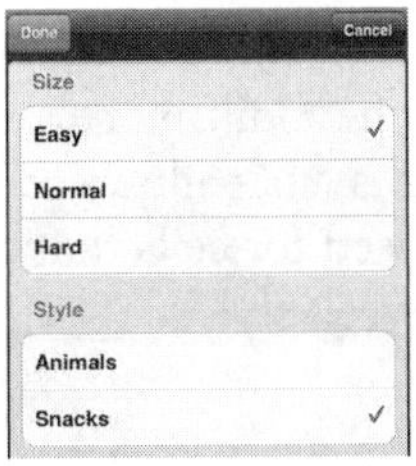

*Figure 21-2. A grouped table view as an interface for choosing options*

that are commonly used in a table cell, such as a checkmark to indicate selection or a right-pointing chevron to indicate that tapping the cell navigates to a detail view.

It would be difficult to overestimate the importance of table views. An iOS app without a table view somewhere in its interface would be a rare thing. I've written apps consisting almost entirely of table views. Indeed, it is not uncommon to use a table even in situations where there is nothing particularly table-like about the interface, simply because it is so convenient. For example, in one of my apps I want the user to be able to choose between three levels of difficulty, so I use a grouped table so small that it doesn't even scroll. This gives me a section header, three tappable cells, and a checkmark indicating the current choice (Figure 21-2).

## Table View Cells

Beginners may be surprised to learn that a table view's structure and contents are not configured in advance. Rather, you supply the table view with a data source and a delegate (which will often be the same object; see Chapter 11), and the table view turns to these in real time, as the app runs, whenever it needs a piece of information about its structure and contents. This architecture conserves resources; a long table might appear to consist of thousands of cells, but if only six cells are showing on the screen at any one time, the table actually needs to maintain only six cells.

This means that your code must be prepared, on demand, to supply the table with pieces of requested data. Of these, the most important is the table cell to be slotted into a given position. A position in the table is specified by means of an index path (NSIndexPath), a class used here to combine a section number with a row number, and is often referred to simply as a *row* of the table. Your data source object will be sent the message `tableView:cellForRowAtIndexPath:`, and must respond by returning the UITableViewCell to be displayed at that row of the table.

In this section, then, I'll discuss *what* you're going to be supplying — the table view cell. In the next section, I'll talk about *how* you supply it.

# Built-In Cell Styles

To create a cell using one of the built-in cell styles, call `initWithStyle:reuseIdentifier:`. The `reuseIdentifier` is what allows cells previously assigned to rows that are now longer showing to be reused for cells that are; it will usually be the same for all cells in a table. Your choices of cell style are:

`UITableViewCellStyleDefault`
>    The cell has a UILabel (its `textLabel`), with an optional UIImageView (its `imageView`) at the left. If there is no image, the label occupies the entire width of the cell.

`UITableViewCellStyleValue1`
>    The cell has two UILabels (its `textLabel` and its `detailTextLabel`), side by side, with an optional UIImageView (its `imageView`) at the left. The first label is left-aligned; the second label is right-aligned. If the first label's text is too long, the second label won't appear.

`UITableViewCellStyleValue2`
>    The cell has two UILabels (its `textLabel` and its `detailTextLabel`), side by side; the first label is small. No UIImageView will appear. The label sizes are fixed, and the text of either will be truncated if it's too long.

`UITableViewCellStyleSubtitle`
>    The cell has two UILabels (its `textLabel` and its `detailTextLabel`), one above the other, with an optional UIImageView (its `imageView`) at the left.

To experiment with the built-in cell styles, do this (even though we have not yet discussed *what* you're actually doing). Make a new project from the Navigation-based Application template. The resulting app has a UINavigationController with a UITableView as its root view, controlled by a UITableViewController (a UIViewController subclass, to be discussed later in this chapter). Now modify the RootViewController class (which comes with a lot of templated code), as follows:

```
// Customize the number of sections in the table view.
- (NSInteger)numberOfSectionsInTableView:(UITableView *)tableView {
    return 1; ❶
}

// Customize the number of rows in the table view.
- (NSInteger)tableView:(UITableView *)tableView
        numberOfRowsInSection:(NSInteger)section {
    return 10; ❷
}

// Customize the appearance of table view cells.
- (UITableViewCell *)tableView:(UITableView *)tableView
        cellForRowAtIndexPath:(NSIndexPath *)indexPath {
    static NSString *CellIdentifier = @"Cell";
    UITableViewCell *cell =
        [tableView dequeueReusableCellWithIdentifier:CellIdentifier];
    if (cell == nil) {
```

```
              cell = [[[UITableViewCell alloc]
                      initWithStyle:UITableViewCellStyleDefault ❸
                      reuseIdentifier:CellIdentifier] autorelease];
          }
          ❹
          return cell;
      }
```

The idea is to generate a single cell in a built-in cell style and to examine and experiment with its appearance by tweaking the code and running the app. The key parts of the code are:

❶ This code is unchanged from the template; our table will have one section.

❷ Our table will consist of ten rows. We're going to make our cell without regard to what row it is slotted into; so all ten rows will be identical. But having multiple rows will give us a sense of how our cell looks when placed next to other cells.

❸ This point in the code is where you specify the built-in table cell style you want to experiment with. Change `UITableViewCellStyleDefault` to a different style as desired.

❹ At this point in the code the cell is pointed to by a variable called `cell`, and you can modify its characteristics. For example:

```
cell.textLabel.text = @"Hello there";
cell.imageView.image = [UIImage imageNamed:@"pic.png"];
```

The flexibility of the built-in styles is based mostly on the flexibility of UILabels (see also Chapter 23). Not everything can be customized, because after you return the cell some further configuration takes place, which may override your settings. For example, the size and position of the cell's subviews are not up to you. (I'll explain how to get around that in the next section.) But you get a remarkable degree of freedom. Here are some of the UILabel properties you can try changing:

text
: The string shown in the label.

textColor, highlightedTextColor
: The color of the text. The `highlightedTextColor` applies when the cell is selected (tap on a cell to select it); if you don't set it, the label may choose its own variant of the `textColor` when the cell is highlighted.

textAlignment
: How the text is aligned; your choices are `UITextAlignmentLeft`, `UITextAlignment-Center`, and `UITextAlignmentRight`.

numberOfLines
: The maximum number of lines of text to appear in the label. Text that is long but permitted to wrap, or that contains explicit linefeed characters, can appear com-

pletely in the label if the label is tall enough and the number of permitted lines is sufficient. 0 means there's no maximum.

lineBreakMode

The wrapping rule for text that is too long for the label's width. The default is UILineBreakModeTailTruncation, which means that text wraps at word ends and then, if the last permitted line is still too long for the label, an ellipsis mark is its last visible character.

font

The label's font. You could reduce the font size as a way of fitting more text into the label. A font name includes its style, so you could change a bold font to nonbold, or *vice versa*. For example:

```
cell.textLabel.font = [UIFont fontWithName:@"Helvetica-Bold" size:12.0];
```

minimumFontSize, adjustsFontSizeToFitWidth

If the numberOfLines is 1, setting these will allow the font size to shrink automatically in an attempt to fit the entire text into the label's width.

shadowColor, shadowOffset

The text shadow. Adding a little shadow can increase clarity and emphasis for large text.

The image view's frame can't be changed, but you can inset its apparent size by supplying a smaller image and setting the image view's contentMode to UIViewContentMode-Center. It's probably a good idea in any case, for performance reasons, to supply images at their drawn size and resolution rather than making the drawing system scale them for you (see the last section of Chapter 20). For example:

```
UIImage* im = [UIImage imageNamed:@"pic.png"];
UIGraphicsBeginImageContextWithOptions(CGSizeMake(35,35), YES, 0.0);
[im drawInRect:CGRectMake(0,0,35,35)];
UIImage* im2 = UIGraphicsGetImageFromCurrentImageContext();
UIGraphicsEndImageContext();
cell.imageView.image = im2;
cell.imageView.contentMode = UIViewContentModeCenter;
```

The cell itself also has some properties you can play with:

accessoryType

A built-in type of accessory view, which appears at the cell's right end. For example:

```
cell.accessoryType = UITableViewCellAccessoryDisclosureIndicator;
```

accessoryView

Your own UIView, which appears at the cell's right end (overriding the accessory-Type). For example:

```
UIButton* b = [UIButton buttonWithType:UIButtonTypeRoundedRect];
[b setTitle:@"Tap Me" forState:UIControlStateNormal];
[b sizeToFit];
```

```
// ... also assign button a target and action ...
cell.accessoryView = b;
```

**indentationLevel, indentationWidth**
> These properties give the cell a left margin, useful for suggesting a hierarchy among cells. You can also set a cell's indentation level in real time, with respect to the table row into which it is slotted, by implementing the delegate's tableView:indentation-LevelForRowAtIndexPath: method.

**selectionStyle**
> How the background looks when the cell is selected. The default is a blue gradient (UITableViewCellSelectionStyleBlue), or you can choose UITableViewCell-SelectionStyleGray (gray gradient) or UITableViewCellSelectionStyleNone.

**backgroundColor, backgroundView, selectedBackgroundView**
> These can be tricky to apply, because tableView:cellForRowAtIndexPath: is too early to be effective. Instead, implement tableView:willDisplayCell:forRowAt-IndexPath:.

 What's the difference between cell configuration in tableView:cellFor-RowAtIndexPath: and in tableView:willDisplayCell:forRowAtIndex-Path:? The former is a required data source method and supplies the cell and provides its content. The latter is an optional delegate method and is intended to allow you to override the cell's general appearance, which the table view has already set in relation to the cell's state (such as selected or not selected).

Setting a backgroundColor alone is somewhat inflexible; it's a solid color, and it will be covered by the selection background if there is one (blue or gray). These limitations can be overcome by supplying a backgroundView; you might use a UIImageView along with a desired image, or supply some other view that knows how to draw itself. If a selectedBackgroundView is supplied, the selectionStyle will automatically be ignored, so that your view is shown instead. If the backgroundView or selectedBackgroundView has transparency, the backgroundColor will appear through it.

A problem is that a UILabel when combined with a cell background view may seem to punch a hole through the view to reveal the cell background color; an added complication is that the details vary for different versions of the system. The simplest and most universally reliable solution is to assign the UILabel a background color of UIClear-Color at the end of tableView:willDisplayCell:forRowAtIndexPath: — that is, *after* setting the cell's background view and background color.

Finally, there are a few properties of the table view itself worth playing with:

**rowHeight**
> The height of a cell. This is another way to deal with text that is too long; besides decreasing the font size, you can increase the cell size. You can change this value

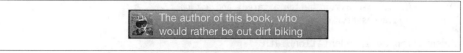

The author of this book, who
would rather be out dirt biking

*Figure 21-3. A cell with a custom gradient background*

in the nib file; the table view's row height appears in the Size inspector. The cell's subviews have their autoresizing set so as to compensate correctly. You can also set a cell's height in real time by implementing the delegate's `tableView:heightForRowAtIndexPath:` method; this can be used to make a table's cells different heights (more about that later in this chapter).

separatorColor, separatorStyle

The latter can be set in the nib (your choices, for a plain table, are UITableViewCell-SeparatorStyleNone and UITableViewCellSeparatorStyleSingleLine); oddly, the former can't. Another oddity is that the separator style names are associated with UITableViewCell even though the separator style itself is a UITableView property.

You can thus customize the built-in table cell styles quite heavily if you've a mind to. In this example of a `UITableViewCellStyleDefault` cell, I shrink the image and center it in the image view, supply a gray gradient as the cell's background, and put a round-rect border around the cell (Figure 21-3):

```
- (void)tableView:(UITableView *)tableView willDisplayCell:(UITableViewCell *)cell
                forRowAtIndexPath:(NSIndexPath *)indexPath {
    UIView* v = [[UIView alloc] initWithFrame:cell.frame];
    CAGradientLayer* lay = [CAGradientLayer layer];
    lay.colors = [NSArray arrayWithObjects:
        (id)[UIColor colorWithWhite:0.6 alpha:1].CGColor,
        [UIColor colorWithWhite:0.4 alpha:1].CGColor, nil];
    lay.frame = v.layer.bounds;
    [v.layer addSublayer:lay];
    lay.borderWidth = 1;
    lay.borderColor = [UIColor blackColor].CGColor;
    lay.cornerRadius = 5;
    cell.backgroundView = v;
    [v release];
    [cell.layer setValue:@"done" forKey:@"done"];
    cell.backgroundColor = [UIColor blackColor];
    cell.textLabel.backgroundColor = [UIColor clearColor];
}
```

## Custom Cells

The built-in cell styles give the beginner a leg up in getting started with table views, but there is nothing sacred about them, and sooner or later you'll probably want to go beyond them and put yourself in charge of how a table's cells look and what subviews they contain. There are three possible approaches:

- Supply a UITableViewCell subclass and override `layoutSubviews` to alter the frames of the built-in subviews.

- In `tableView:cellForRowAtIndexPath:`, add subviews to each cell's `contentView` as the cell is created. The `contentView` is the superview for the cell's subviews, exclusive of things like the `accessoryView`; so by confining yourself to the `contentView`, you allow the cell to continue working correctly. This approach can be combined with the previous approach, or you can just ignore the built-in subviews and use your own exclusively. As long as the built-in subviews for a particular built-in cell style are not referenced, they are never created or inserted into the cell.

- Design the cell in a nib, and load that nib in `tableView:cellForRowAtIndexPath:` each time a cell needs to be created.

I'll illustrate each approach.

### Overriding a cell's subview layout

You can't directly change the frame of a built-in cell style subview in `tableView:cellForRowAtIndexPath:` or `tableView:willDisplayCell:forRowAtIndexPath:`, because after your changes, `layoutSubviews` comes along and overrides them. The workaround is to override `layoutSubviews`. This is a straightforward solution if your main objection to a built-in style is the frame of a subview.

So, for example, let's modify a `UITableViewCellStyleDefault` cell so that the image is at the right end instead of the left end. We'll make a UITableViewCell subclass, MyCell; Xcode makes this easy by supplying UITableViewCell as one of the default classes in the "Subclass of" pop-up menu when you make a new Cocoa Touch Objective-C Class file. Here is MyCell's `layoutSubviews`:

```
- (void) layoutSubviews {
    [super layoutSubviews];
    CGRect cvb = self.contentView.bounds;
    CGRect imf = self.imageView.frame;
    imf.origin.x = cvb.size.width - imf.size.width;
    self.imageView.frame = imf;
    CGRect tf = self.textLabel.frame;
    tf.origin.x = 0;
    self.textLabel.frame = tf;
}
```

Now, in our table view's data source, we change the line where new cells are created, so as to generate an instance of MyCell:

```
cell = [[[MyCell alloc]
            initWithStyle:UITableViewCellStyleDefault
            reuseIdentifier:CellIdentifier] autorelease];
```

### Adding subviews in code

Let's rewrite the previous example so that we don't need our own UITableViewCell subclass. Instead of modifying the existing `imageView` and `textLabel`, we'll add to each

UITableView's content view a completely new UIImageView and UILabel, each of which can be assigned a frame that won't be changed by the runtime. Here are some things to keep in mind:

- The new views must be added when we instantiate a new cell, but not when we reuse a cell (because a reused cell already has them).
- We should assign the new views an appropriate `autoresizingMask`, because the cell's content view might be resized.
- Each new view should be assigned a tag so that it can be referred to elsewhere.
- We must never send `addSubview:` to the cell itself — only to its `contentView` (or some subview thereof).

Our implementation of `tableView:cellForRowAtIndexPath:` might look like this:

```
- (UITableViewCell *)tableView:(UITableView *)tableView
        cellForRowAtIndexPath:(NSIndexPath *)indexPath {
    static NSString *CellIdentifier = @"Cell";
    UITableViewCell *cell =
        [tableView dequeueReusableCellWithIdentifier:CellIdentifier];
    if (cell == nil) {
        cell = [[[UITableViewCell alloc]
                  initWithStyle:UITableViewCellStyleDefault
                  reuseIdentifier:CellIdentifier] autorelease];
        CGFloat side = cell.contentView.bounds.size.height;
        UIImageView* iv = [[UIImageView alloc] init];
        iv.frame =
            CGRectMake(cell.contentView.bounds.size.width - side, 0, side, side);
        iv.tag = 1;
        iv.autoresizingMask = UIViewAutoresizingFlexibleHeight |
                              UIViewAutoresizingFlexibleLeftMargin;
        [cell.contentView addSubview:iv];
        [iv release];
        UILabel* lab = [[UILabel alloc] init];
        lab.frame =
            CGRectMake(5, 0, cell.contentView.bounds.size.width - side - 10, side);
        lab.tag = 2;
        lab.autoresizingMask = UIViewAutoresizingFlexibleHeight |
                               UIViewAutoresizingFlexibleRightMargin;
        [cell.contentView addSubview:lab];
        [lab release];
    }
    UILabel* lab = (UILabel*)[cell viewWithTag: 2];
    // ... set up lab here ...
    UIImageView* iv = (UIImageView*)[cell viewWithTag: 1];
    // ... set up iv here ...
    return cell;
}
```

Using our own cell subviews instead of the built-in cell style subviews has some clear advantages; we no longer have to perform an elaborate dance to escape from the restrictions imposed by the runtime. We can set the frame of our subviews, and they stay where we put them. Similarly, making a UILabel's background transparent is trivial:

we can assign it `clearColor` right here in `tableView:cellForRowAtIndexPath:`, because, unlike the built-in `textLabel`, the runtime isn't going alter our setting afterward.

Still, the verbosity of this code is somewhat overwhelming. We can avoid this by designing the cell in a nib.

### Designing a cell in a nib

In designing a cell in a nib, we start by creating a nib file that will consist, in effect, solely of this one cell. In Xcode, we create a new User Interface file using the View template. Let's call it *MyCell.xib*. In the nib editor, delete the UIView from the dock and replace it with a Table View Cell from the Object library.

The cell's design window shows a standard-sized cell with the content view region clearly demarcated. Using the Attributes inspector, we can add a built-in accessory view, and the content view shrinks accordingly. Outlets for the `accessoryView` and `backgroundView` allow us to add these features without code. The cell is assumed to be a `UITableViewCellStyleDefault` type, and we can set features of its `textLabel` and `imageView` directly; however, let's ignore these and insert our own subviews instead. For purposes of discussion, let's just implement the same subviews we've already implemented in the preceding two examples: a UILabel on the left side of the cell, and a UIImageView on the right side.

Just as when we add subviews in code, we should set each subview's autoresizing behavior and give each subview a tag. The difference is that we now do both those tasks in the nib, not in code.

To configure the nib so that it can be loaded and the cell actually used, we must do the following:

1. In our code, decide on a class to function as the owner of the nib, and give it a UITableViewCell outlet so that when the nib loads, we will be able to access the cell through an instance variable. The obvious choice here is to use as this nib's owner the very same view controller we've been putting our code in all along. I'll call the outlet `tvc` (and don't forget to synthesize its accessors as well):

   ```
   @property (nonatomic, assign) IBOutlet UITableViewCell* tvc;
   ```

2. In the nib, set the File's Owner to the class to which we just gave the `tvc` outlet, and hook its `tvc` outlet to the cell. (Don't use its `view` outlet by mistake! We don't want to accidentally repoint this view controller's view to the cell.)

3. Assign to the cell in the nib, in the Attributes inspector, the same string Identifier that is used as a cell identifier in our code. We have not altered the template, so that value is `@"Cell"`, in accordance with this line of code:

   ```
   static NSString* CellIdentifier = @"Cell";
   ```

   I can't stress sufficiently the importance of getting this right. If the cell's Identifier in the nib doesn't match the identifier string in code, cells will not be reused properly in the construction of the table. Omitting this step or performing it incorrectly is a common beginner mistake.

We are now ready to modify our implementation of `tableView:cellForRowAtIndex-Path:`. Each time a new cell is needed, we load the nib with ourself as owner. This means that a new instance of the cell is assigned to the `tvc` instance variable (Chapter 7), so we use that as the `cell` for the rest of this method:

```
- (UITableViewCell *)tableView:(UITableView *)tableView
        cellForRowAtIndexPath:(NSIndexPath *)indexPath {
    static NSString *CellIdentifier = @"Cell";
    UITableViewCell *cell =
        [tableView dequeueReusableCellWithIdentifier:CellIdentifier];
    if (cell == nil) {
        [[NSBundle mainBundle] loadNibNamed:@"MyCell" owner:self options:nil];
        cell = self.tvc;
    }
    UILabel* lab = (UILabel*)[cell viewWithTag: 2];
    // ... set up lab here ...
    UIImageView* iv = (UIImageView*)[cell viewWithTag: 1];
    // ... set up iv here ...
    return cell;
}
```

This gives us all the advantages of customized cell contents without any verbosity; the cell is created in two easy lines of code, and we proceed to configure it. Moreover, our configuration code ("set up `lab` here") can perhaps be greatly reduced, because this subview can be configured in the nib. For example, as I was evolving this example from earlier examples, I had this configuration code:

```
lab.numberOfLines = 2;
lab.textAlignment = UITextAlignmentLeft;
lab.adjustsFontSizeToFitWidth = YES;
lab.lineBreakMode = UILineBreakModeClip;
lab.minimumFontSize = 0.1;
lab.textColor = [UIColor whiteColor];
lab.highlightedTextColor = [UIColor blackColor];
lab.font = [UIFont fontWithName:@"Helvetica-Bold" size:12.0];
lab.text = @"This is a test";
```

But all of that code can now be deleted! Those are all aspects of the UILabel that can be configured in the nib instead. For this and many other reasons, I am very much partial to the nib-loading approach to cell instantiation.

If you dislike the use of `viewWithTag:` as a way of referring to the cell's subviews, and would prefer to use properties, provide a UITableViewCell subclass and set up outlets there. Here are the steps for modifying the current example to use this technique:

1. Start with a UITableViewCell subclass. Let's call it MyCell. (If you still have the MyCell files from the earlier example, you can use them, but be sure to delete the `layoutSubviews` override.) Give the class two outlets, and be sure to synthesize the accessors for them:

```
@property (nonatomic, assign) IBOutlet UILabel* theLabel;
@property (nonatomic, assign) IBOutlet UIImageView* theImageView;
```

2. In the table cell nib, change the class of the table cell to MyCell, and link up the outlets from the cell to the respective subviews.

Now we can modify our implementation of `tableView:cellForRowAtIndexPath:` once again, making sure that the cell is typed as a MyCell and referring to its properties, like this:

```
- (UITableViewCell *)tableView:(UITableView *)tableView
        cellForRowAtIndexPath:(NSIndexPath *)indexPath {
    static NSString *CellIdentifier = @"Cell";
    UITableViewCell *cell =
        [tableView dequeueReusableCellWithIdentifier:CellIdentifier];
    if (cell == nil) {
        [[NSBundle mainBundle] loadNibNamed:@"MyCell" owner:self options:nil];
        cell = self.tvc;
    }
    MyCell* theCell = (MyCell*)cell; // cast as MyCell, use properties
    UILabel* lab = theCell.theLabel;
    // ... set up lab here ...
    UIImageView* iv = theCell.theImageView;
    // ... set up iv here ...
    return cell;
}
```

All my examples so far have used `loadNibNamed:`, but starting in iOS 4 you can use the UINib class. Instead of this line:

```
[[NSBundle mainBundle] loadNibNamed:@"MyCell" owner:self options:nil];
```

You'd say this:

```
UINib* theCellNib = [UINib nibWithNibName:@"MyCell" bundle:nil];
[theCellNib instantiateWithOwner:self options:nil];
```

This minor change of expression can mean a major performance boost, because the UINib class can cache a loaded nib the first time `nibWithNibName:bundle:` is called with a particular nib name; thus, subsequent repeated calls to `nibWithNibName:bundle:` with the same nib name may have no work to do, as the nib is already in memory.

# Table View Data

The structure and content of the actual data as portrayed in a table view comes from the data source, an object pointed to by the table view's `dataSource` property and adopting the UITableViewDataSource protocol. The data source is thus the heart and soul of the table. What surprises beginners is that the data source operates not by *setting* the table view's structure and content, but *on demand*. The data source, *qua* data source, consists of a set of methods that the table view will call when it needs information. This architecture has important consequences for how you write your code, which can be summarized by these simple guidelines:

*Be ready*

> Your data source cannot know *when* or *how often* any of these methods will be called, so it must be prepared to answer *any question at any time*.

*Be fast*

> The table view is asking for data in real time; the user is probably scrolling through the table *right now*. So you mustn't gum up the works; you must be ready to supply responses just as fast as you possibly can. (If you can't supply a piece of data fast enough, you may have to skip it, supply a placeholder, and insert the data into the table later. This, however, may involve you in threading issues that I don't want to get into here. I'll give an example in Chapter 37.)

*Be consistent*

> There are multiple data source methods, and you cannot know *which* one will be called at a given moment. So you must make sure your responses are mutually consistent at *any* moment. For example, a common beginner error is forgetting to take into account, in your data source methods, the possibility that the data might not be ready yet.

This may sound daunting, but you'll be fine as long as you maintain an unswerving adherence to the principles of model–view–controller (Chapter 13). How and when you accumulate the actual data, and how that data is structured, is a *model* concern. Acting as a data source is a *controller* concern. So you can acquire and arrange your data whenever and however you like, just so long as when the table view actually turns to you and asks what to do, you can lay your hands on the relevant data rapidly and consistently.

Another source of confusion for beginners is that methods are rather oddly distributed between the data source and the delegate, an object pointed to by the table view's `delegate` property and adopting the UITableViewDelegate protocol; in some cases, one may seem to be doing the job of the other. This is not usually a cause of any real difficulty, because the object serving as data source will probably also be the object serving as delegate. Nevertheless, it is rather inconvenient when you're consulting the documentation; you'll probably want to keep the data source and delegate documentation pages open simultaneously as you work.

## The Three Big Questions

Like Katherine Hepburn in *Pat and Mike*, the basis of your success as a data source is your ability, at any time, to answer the Three Big Questions. The questions the table view will ask you are a little different from the questions Mike asks Pat, but the principle is the same: know the answers, and be able to recite them at any moment. Here they are:

*How many sections does this table have?*

> The table will call `numberOfSectionsInTableView:`; respond with an integer. In theory you can omit this method, as the default response is 1, which is often correct.

However, I never omit it; for one thing, returning 0 is a good way to say that the table has no data, and will prevent the table view from asking any other questions.

*How many rows does this section have?*

The table will call `tableView:numberOfRowsInSection:`. The table supplies a section number — the first section is numbered 0 — and you respond with an integer. In a table with only one section, of course, there is probably no need to examine the incoming section number.

*What cell goes in this row of this section?*

The table will call `tableView:cellForRowAtIndexPath:`. The index path is expressed as an NSIndexPath; this is a sophisticated and powerful class, but you don't actually have to know anything about it, because UITableView provides a category on it that adds two read-only properties — `section` and `row`. Using these, you extract the requested section number and row number, and return a UITableView-Cell. The first row of a section is numbered 0.

The strategy for implementing `tableView:cellForRowAtIndexPath:` is a little complicated, because you will probably want to keep memory usage at a minimum by reusing table cells. The idea, as I've already mentioned, is that once a table cell is no longer visible on the screen, it can be slotted into a row that *is* visible — with its portrayed data appropriately changed, of course! — so that no more than the number of simultaneously visible cells need to exist at any given moment. Luckily, a table view is ready to implement this strategy for you, and the template shows you how to write `table-View:cellForRowAtIndexPath:` accordingly. Let's examine the template code more closely (Example 21-1).

*Example 21-1. The template code for the third big question*

```
// Customize the appearance of table view cells.
- (UITableViewCell *)tableView:(UITableView *)tableView
        cellForRowAtIndexPath:(NSIndexPath *)indexPath {
    static NSString *CellIdentifier = @"Cell"; ❶
    UITableViewCell *cell = ❷
        [tableView dequeueReusableCellWithIdentifier:CellIdentifier];
    if (cell == nil) {
        cell = [[[UITableViewCell alloc] ❸
                initWithStyle:UITableViewCellStyleDefault
                reuseIdentifier:CellIdentifier] autorelease];
      ❹
    }
    ❺
    return cell;
}
```

❶ The table view is ready to maintain a cache of reusable cells. In fact, it can maintain more than one such cache; this could be useful if your table view contains more than one type of cell (where the meaning of the concept "type of cell" is pretty much up to you). Therefore you must *name* each cache, by attaching a cell identifier string to any cell that can be reused. In most cases, there will be just one cache and therefore just one cell identifier string, and you will want every cell to be reusable, so you will attach that identifier string to every cell. In the template code, this string is maintained as a static NSString literal, ensuring that the memory for it will be set aside only once and maintained between calls to this method.

❷ To generate the cell being requested by the method call, you start by sending the table view `dequeueReusableCellWithIdentifier:`. This asks the table view to pull out of the named cache a currently unused cell, if there is one. There are two possibilities: either the table view will return a cell, in which case that's the cell you're going to be returning, or the table view will return nil (because there isn't an unused cell already in the cache), in which case you're going to have to create the cell yourself.

❸ If `dequeueReusableCellWithIdentifier:` returned nil, you create a new cell, initializing it with `initWithStyle:reuseIdentifier:`. The style is one of the built-in styles; we have already seen what this implies, and how you can configure a cell yourself regardless of its style. The reuse identifier is the cell identifier that makes this cell reusable. If you were to supply nil here, the cell would not be reusable. A cell created with `alloc` must be autoreleased, because you must balance the `alloc` with a `release` but you're also going to be returning this cell. Instead of the line of code shown in the template, you may want to instantiate the cell by loading a nib (I've already shown how to do that). A cell instantiated from a nib is already autoreleased, so no further memory management is required.

❹ If `dequeueReusableCellWithIdentifier:` returned nil, you have just instantiated a new cell; you may now want to perform any other tasks appropriate to the initial configuration of a new cell. For example, earlier we saw that you can add subviews to the cell's content view; you would need to do this only when the cell is first created, so this is the place for it.

❺ You now have a cell (here, called `cell`), from whatever source derived. No matter whether you just created it or you are reusing a previously used cell, you now configure the cell appropriately to the section and row into which this cell is now to be slotted. (This is something we did *not* do in any of our earlier examples; we were concentrating on cell configuration itself, so we configured the cell the same way regardless of its row.)

You do not know or care, when configuring the cell at the final stage, whether the cell is new or reused. Therefore, always configure *everything* about the cell that might need configuring. If you fail to do this, and if the cell is reused, you might be surprised when some aspect of the cell is left over from its previous use; on the other hand, if you fail to do this, and if the cell is new, you might be surprised when some aspect of the cell isn't configured at all.

For example, in one of my apps that lists article titles in a table, there is a little loudspeaker icon that should appear in the cell if there is a recording associated with this article. So I wrote this code:

```
    if (item.enclosures && [item.enclosures count])
        [cell viewWithTag: 5].hidden = NO;
```

This turned out to be a mistake, because when a cell was reused, it had a visible loud-speaker icon if, in a previous incarnation, it had *ever* had a visible loudspeaker icon. The solution was to rewrite the logic like this:

```
    [cell viewWithTag: 5].hidden = !(item.enclosures && [item.enclosures count]);
```

To illustrate the efficiency of the cell-caching architecture, I'll use the nib-instantiated cell left over from our earlier examples. We have a table of one section and 100 rows:

```
- (UITableViewCell *)tableView:(UITableView *)tableView
        cellForRowAtIndexPath:(NSIndexPath *)indexPath {
    static NSString *CellIdentifier = @"Cell";
    UITableViewCell *cell =
        [tableView dequeueReusableCellWithIdentifier:CellIdentifier];
    if (cell == nil) {
        [[NSBundle mainBundle] loadNibNamed:@"MyCell" owner:self options:nil];
        cell = self.tvc;
        NSLog(@"creating a new cell");
    }
    MyCell* theCell = (MyCell*)cell;
    UILabel* lab = theCell.theLabel;
    lab.text = [NSString stringWithFormat: @"This is row %i of section %i",
                indexPath.row, indexPath.section];
    return cell;
}
```

When we run this code and scroll through the table, every cell is numbered correctly, so there appear to be 100 cells. But the log messages show us that only 11 cells are actually created.

In real life, of course, you'd probably be setting `lab.text` by consulting a data store (the model) for the value appropriate to this row (or, if there is more than one section, this row of this section). A line from a typical real-life implementation of `tableView:cell-ForRowAtIndexPath:` consults an array (`titles`):

```
    cell.textLabel.text = [titles objectAtIndex: [indexPath row]];
```

## Table View Sections

The number of sections, as we've already seen, is determined by your reply to `number-OfSectionsInTableView:`. For each section, the table view will consult your data source and delegate to learn whether this section has a header or a footer, or both, or neither (the default). You can supply headers and footers in two ways:

*Header or footer string*
    You implement the data source method `tableView:titleForHeaderInSection:` or `tableView:titleForFooterInSection:` (or both). Return nil to indicate that the given section has no header (or footer). Return a string to use it as the section's

header (or footer). You cannot change the style of the label or of the header or footer as a whole.

*Header or footer view*

You implement the delegate method `tableView:viewForHeaderInSection:` or `table-View:viewForFooterInSection:` (or both). The corresponding data source method, if implemented, is ignored. The view you supply is used as the entire header or footer and is automatically resized to the table's width and the section header or footer height. If the view you supply has subviews, be sure to set proper autoresizing behavior so that they'll be positioned and sized appropriately when the view itself is resized.

Supplying a header or a footer as a string is simpler, but supplying it as a view is more powerful, because not only can you style a label, but you can also insert other kinds of interface (such as a button).

No matter which way you supply the header or footer, its height is determined as follows. The default height comes from the table itself, which has a `sectionHeaderHeight` property and a `sectionFooterHeight` property. But you can override this to supply header and footer heights on an individual basis by implementing the delegate method `tableView:heightForHeaderInSection:` or `tableView:heightForFooterInSection:`.

 Don't confuse the section headers and footers with the header and footer of the table as a whole. The latter are view properties of the table view itself and are set through its properties `tableHeaderView` and `tableFooterView`.

If the table view has the plain style, you can add an index down the right side of the table, which the user can tap to jump to the start of a section. This is very helpful for navigating long tables. To generate the index, implement the data source method `sectionIndexTitlesForTableView:`, returning an NSArray of string titles to appear as entries in the index. This works even if there are no section headers. You will want the index entries to be short — preferably just one character — because they will be partially obscuring the right edge of the table; the cell's content view will shrink to match, so you're sacrificing some cell width real estate. Unfortunately, there is no official way to modify the index's appearance (such as the color of its entries).

Normally, there will be a one-to-one correspondence between the index entries and the sections; when the user taps an index entry, the table jumps to the start of the corresponding section. However, under certain circumstances you may want to customize this correspondence. For example, suppose there are 40 sections, but there isn't room to display 40 index entries comfortably on the iPhone. The index will automatically curtail itself, omitting some index entries and inserting bullets to suggest this, but you might prefer to take charge of the situation by supplying a shorter index. In such a case,

implement the data source method `tableView:sectionForSectionIndexTitle:at-`
`Index:`, returning the index of the section to jump to for this section index. Both the section index title and its index are passed in, so you can use whichever is convenient.

Apple's documentation elaborates heavily on the details of implementing the model behind a table with an index and suggests that you rely on a class called UILocalize-dIndexedCollation. This class is effectively a way of generating an ordered list of letters of the alphabet, with methods for helping to sort an array of strings and separate it into sections. This might be useful if you need your app to be localized, because the notion of the alphabet and its order changes automatically depending on the user's preferred language. But this notion is also fixed; you can't readily use a UILocalizedIndexColla-tion to implement your own sort order. For example, UILocalizedIndexCollation was of no use to me in writing my Greek and Latin vocabulary apps, in which the Greek words must be sorted, sectioned, and indexed according to the Greek alphabet, and the Latin words use a reduced version of the English alphabet (no initial J, K, or V through Z).

I'll demonstrate a technique for implementing a sectioned indexed table by describing the approach I take in my Latin vocabulary app (this is the second app in Figure 21-1). Everything depends on preparing the data in advance, storing it in appropriate structures. The data, consisting of Latin words and their English definitions, start out in an array (`dataIn`) of dictionaries; in particular, each Latin word is stored in its NSDictionary under the key `@"latin"`. So we begin by sorting the array on that key's value:

```
// sort data alphabetically
NSSortDescriptor* sort =
    [[NSSortDescriptor alloc] initWithKey:@"latin" ascending:YES];
NSArray* data =
    [dataIn sortedArrayUsingDescriptors:[NSArray arrayWithObject: sort]];
[sort release];
```

We proceed now to make two arrays:

1. A list of section names, consisting of the unique capitalized first letters of the Latin words. The trick here is the word "unique"; as we cycle through the sorted Latin words, we add a letter to this list only if it isn't the same as the last letter we added.

2. An array of arrays of all words starting with each letter.

```
self.sectionNames = [NSMutableArray array];
self.sectionData = [NSMutableArray array];
NSString* previous = @"";
for (NSDictionary* aCard in data) {
    // get the first letter
    NSString* c = [[aCard valueForKey: @"latin"] substringToIndex:1];
    // only add a letter to sectionNames when it's a different letter
    if (![c isEqualToString: previous]) {
        previous = c;
        [sectionNames addObject: [c uppercaseString]];
        // and in that case, also add a new array to our array of arrays
```

```
        NSMutableArray* oneSection = [NSMutableArray array];
        [sectionData addObject: oneSection];
    }
    // in every case, add this dictionary to the last section array
    [[sectionData lastObject] addObject: aCard];
}
```

Now that we have our two arrays, the business of actually supplying the table view with data based on them is trivial:

```
- (NSInteger)tableView:(UITableView *)tableView
        numberOfRowsInSection:(NSInteger)section {
    return [[sectionData objectAtIndex: section] count];
}

- (NSString *)tableView:(UITableView *)tableView
        titleForHeaderInSection:(NSInteger)section {
    return [sectionNames objectAtIndex: section];
}

- (NSArray *)sectionIndexTitlesForTableView:(UITableView *)tableView {
    return sectionNames;
}

- (UITableViewCell *)tableView:(UITableView *)tableView
        cellForRowAtIndexPath:(NSIndexPath *)indexPath {
    // ... skipping the boilerplate ...
    NSDictionary* card =
        [[sectionData objectAtIndex: [indexPath section]]
                    objectAtIndex: [indexPath row]];
    cell.textLabel.text = [card valueForKey:@"latin"];
    // ...
    return cell;
}
```

## Refreshing Table View Data

The table view doesn't know when its underlying data changes; you have to tell it. You can do this using any of several methods:

reloadData

> Causes the table view to ask the data source the Three Big Questions all over again, including asking for index entries and section headers and footers. This is not necessarily inefficient; having worked out the layout of the table through the section header and footer heights and row heights, the table has to regenerate only those cells that are actually visible.

reloadRowsAtIndexPaths:withRowAnimation:

> Causes the table to ask the data source the Three Big Questions all over again, including section headers and footers (but not index entries). The table then regenerates the cells for any of the specified rows that are visible. The first parameter

is an array of index paths; to form an index path, use the NSIndexPath class method `indexPathForRow:inSection:`.

`reloadSections:withRowAnimation:`

Causes the table to ask the data source the Three Big Questions all over again, including section headers and footers (but not index entries). The table then regenerates any visible section header(s) and visible cells of the specified sections(s). The first parameter is an NSIndexSet (see Chapter 10).

The advantage of the second two methods isn't so much that they are significantly less expensive than a simple `reloadData` — they are not, really — but that they provide the option for animations that cue the user as to what's changing. The `withRow-Animation:` parameter is one of the following:

`UITableViewRowAnimationFade`

The old fades into the new.

`UITableViewRowAnimationRight`
`UITableViewRowAnimationLeft`
`UITableViewRowAnimationTop`
`UITableViewRowAnimationBottom`

The old slides out in the stated direction, and is replaced from the opposite direction.

`UITableViewRowAnimationNone`

No animation. This was not made available until iOS 3.0; previously, to refresh the table with no animation, it was necessary to call `reloadData` (which was no bad thing, as it involves only slightly more work on the part of the table).

`UITableViewRowAnimationMiddle`

Introduced in iOS 3.2. Hard to describe; it's a sort of venetian blind effect on each cell individually.

 According to Apple's documentation, the method `reloadSectionIndex-Titles` should cause the table to reload just the index entries, presumably by calling the data source's `sectionIndexTitlesForTableView:`. But my experience is that this method is broken and does nothing.

It is also possible to access and alter a table's individual cells directly. This can be a far more lightweight approach to refreshing the table. The `reload...` methods all require the table to calculate its entire layout, including the heights of all section headers and footers and cells, even if only one row's data needs refreshing. If the data for a row changes behind the scenes, and you don't need the built-in row animation, you might prefer to change the corresponding cell's contents directly. And there are other reasons why you might need direct access to the cells of a table.

It is important, however, to bear in mind that the cells are not the data (view is not model), and that if cells are reusable, which they usually will be, the table has cells only for the rows that are actually showing on the screen. So you can change only a cell that actually exists, and when you do, you should make sure that the model corresponds to it so that the row will be correct if its data is reloaded later.

Here are some UITableView methods that mediate between cells, rows, and visibility:

`visibleCells`
> An array of the cells actually showing within the table's bounds. The table may be maintaining additional cells (if, for example, it is not reusing cells), but there is no simple way to get a list of those.

`indexPathsForVisibleRows`
> An array of the rows actually showing within the table's bounds.

`cellForRowAtIndexPath:`
> Returns a UITableViewCell if the table is maintaining a cell for the given row (typically because this is a visible row); otherwise, returns nil.

`indexPathForCell:`
> Given a cell obtained from the table view, returns the row into which it is slotted.

## Variable Row Heights

Most tables have rows that are all the same height, as set by the table view's `rowHeight`. However, as I mentioned earlier, the delegate's `tableView:heightForRowAtIndexPath:` can be used to make different rows different heights. (You can see this in the TidBITS News app; look at Figure 19-1, where the first cell is one line of text shorter than the second cell.)

Here are some things to remember when implementing a table whose rows can have different heights:

*Avoid performance limits*
> Variable row heights work best if the table is short and simple. The table view must effectively lay out the entire table in order to load the data and in order at any moment to know the size and offset of the scrolling content view. With a long table, this can become too much information for the table to manipulate fast enough as the user scrolls.

*Lay out subviews correctly*
> As a cell is reused, its height may be changed, because the new row into which it is to be slotted is a different height from the old row. Similarly, if the cell comes from a nib, its height in the table view may be changed from its height in the nib. This will expose any weaknesses in your practice for laying out subviews. For example, a mistake in the `autoresizingMask` value of subviews can result in display

errors that would not have appeared if all the rows were the same height. You may have to resort to manual layout (implementing `layoutSubviews`).

## Plan ahead

You (the delegate) are going to be asked for all the heights of all the rows well before you (the data source) are called upon to provide the data for any individual rows. You will want to provide this information quickly and accurately. So you will have to plan how the data will appear in *every* row before actually causing the data to appear in *any* row.

For example, here's how I implemented the variable-height rows in the TidBITS News app. In order to determine the height of a cell, I need to know how much vertical space each of its labels should occupy. For example, the first label, the article headline, permits two lines of text (`numberOfLines`), but if the headline is short it might need only one. The cell, which is designed in a nib, is the correct width in that nib (320, the width of the iPhone display); hence the labels are at their final width from the outset, and only their height varies. So I supply a utility method, `labelHeightsForItem:`, that calls NSString's `sizeWithFont:constrainedToSize:lineBreakMode:` to calculate the heights of both labels given their text and font. My `tableView:heightForRowAtIndexPath:` implementation can then use those heights, along with some `#define`d spacer values, to work out the total height of the cell, while restricting it to the maximum height I'm willing to allow:

```
- (CGFloat)tableView:(UITableView *)tableView
        heightForRowAtIndexPath:(NSIndexPath *)indexPath {
    id item = [self.parsedData.items objectAtIndex: [indexPath row]];
    NSArray* arr = [self labelHeightsForItem: item]; // call our utility method
    // label heights are now in a two-element array of NSNumbers
    CGFloat proposedHeight =
        [[arr objectAtIndex:0] floatValue] + [[arr objectAtIndex:1] floatValue]
            + _topspace + _midspace + _bottomspace;
    CGFloat result =
        (proposedHeight >= tableView.rowHeight) ?
        tableView.rowHeight : proposedHeight;
    return result;
}
```

In `tableView:willDisplayCell:forRowAtIndexPath:`, I call my utility method `labelHeightsForItem:` *again*, using that information and the same `#define`d spacer values to set the frames of the two labels within the cell's content view:

```
- (void)tableView:(UITableView *)tableView willDisplayCell:(UITableViewCell *)cell
                            forRowAtIndexPath:(NSIndexPath *)indexPath {
    FPItem* item = [self.parsedData.items objectAtIndex: [indexPath row]];
    NSArray* arr = [self labelHeightsForItem: item];
    CGRect f1 = [cell viewWithTag: 1].frame;
    f1.size.height = [[arr objectAtIndex: 0] floatValue];
    f1.origin.y = _topspace;
    [cell viewWithTag: 1].frame = f1;
    // ... and similarly for the second label ...
}
```

# Table View Selection

A table view cell has a normal (deselected) state and a selected state, according to its `selected` property. It is possible to change a cell's `selected` property directly (possibly with animation, using `setSelected:animated:`), but you are more likely to manage selection through the table view. Indeed, one of the chief purposes of your table view is likely to be to let the user select a cell. This will be possible, provided you have not set the value of the table view's `allowsSelection` property to NO. The user taps a normal cell, and the cell switches to its selected state. As we've already seen, this will usually mean that the cell is redrawn with a blue (or gray) background.

Your code can also learn and manage the selection through these UITableView instance methods:

`indexPathForSelectedRow`
> Reports the currently selected row, or nil if there is no selection.

`selectRowAtIndexPath:animated:scrollPosition:`
> The animation involves fading in the selection, but the user may not see this unless the selected row is already visible. The last parameter dictates whether and how the table view should scroll to reveal the newly selected row:
>
> - `UITableViewScrollPositionTop`
> - `UITableViewScrollPositionMiddle`
> - `UITableViewScrollPositionBottom`
> - `UITableViewScrollPositionNone`
>
> For the first three, the table view scrolls (with animation, if the second parameter is YES) so that the selected row is at the specified position among the visible cells. For `UITableViewScrollPositionNone`, the table view does not scroll; if the selected row is not already visible, it does not become visible.

`deselectRowAtIndexPath:animated:`
> Deselects the given row (if it is selected); the optional animation involves fading out the selection. No automatic scrolling takes place. This method is rarely needed, though, because to deselect the currently selected row you can call `selectRowAtIndexPath:animated:scrollPosition:` with a nil index path.

When a table view changes a cell's `selected` state, it also changes its `highlighted` state. This causes the cell to propagate the highlighted state down through its subviews by setting each subview's `highlighted` property if it has one. This is why a UILabel's `highlightedTextColor` applies when the cell is selected. Similarly, a UIImageView (such as the cell's `imageView`) can have a `highlightedImage` that is shown when the cell is selected, and a UIControl (such as a UIButton) takes on its `highlighted` state when the cell is selected. You can set a cell's `highlighted` state directly, with the `highlighted` property or `setHighlighted:animated:`; but you are unlikely to do so, instead leaving the table view to manage selection and highlighting together.

If you set a cell's `selected` or `highlighted` property directly, you are acting behind the table view's back, as it were; it has no knowledge of what you're doing, so it won't track selection properly. This is another reason why it's better to let the user tap to select, or call the table view selection methods.

Response to user selection is through the table view's delegate. Despite their names, the "will" methods are actually "should" methods: return nil to prevent the selection (or deselection) from taking place. Return the index path handed in as parameter to permit the selection (or deselection), or a different index path to cause a different cell to be selected (or deselected):

- `tableView:willSelectRowAtIndexPath:`
- `tableView:didSelectRowAtIndexPath:`
- `tableView:willDeselectRowAtIndexPath:`
- `tableView:didDeselectRowAtIndexPath:`

When `tableView:willSelectRowAtIndexPath:` is called because the user taps a cell, it is followed by `tableView:willDeselectRowAtIndexPath:` for any already selected cells.

The default behavior is that the user can select only one cell at a time; if the user selects a cell while another cell is already selected, the previously selected cell is deselected. However, your implementation of these delegate methods can override this default behavior. If `tableView:willDeselectRowAtIndexPath:` returns nil at the appropriate moment, that cell will not be deselected when the user selects another cell. Similarly, the default behavior is that if the user taps an already selected cell, it remains selected; you can override this so that tapping a selected cell will deselect the cell instead. As an example, I'll override both behaviors; the user can now tap to select multiple rows and can tap a selected row to deselect it:

```
- (NSIndexPath*) tableView:(UITableView*)tv
        willSelectRowAtIndexPath:(NSIndexPath*)ip {
    if ([tv cellForRowAtIndexPath:ip].selected) {
        [tv deselectRowAtIndexPath:ip animated:NO];
        return nil;
    }
    return ip;
}

- (NSIndexPath*) tableView:(UITableView*)tv
        willDeselectRowAtIndexPath:(NSIndexPath*)ip {
    return nil;
}
```

Unfortunately, if you implement multiple row selection, the table view still reports only one selected row from `indexPathForSelectedRow`, so if you want to know what rows are selected, you'll have to keep track of the selection yourself.

One common response to user selection is navigation. A typical architecture is that of master and detail: the table view lists things the user can see in more detail, and a tap replaces the table view with the detailed view of the selected thing. Very often the table view will be in a navigation interface, and you will respond to user selection by creating the detail view and pushing it onto the navigation controller's stack.

For example, here's the code from my TidBITS News app that navigates from the list of articles to the actual article on which the user has tapped:

```
- (void)tableView:(UITableView *)tableView
        didSelectRowAtIndexPath:(NSIndexPath *)indexPath {
    id item = [self.parsedData.items objectAtIndex: [indexPath row]];
    UIViewController* svc = [[StoryViewController alloc] initWithItem: item];
    [self.navigationController pushViewController:svc animated:YES];
    [svc release];
}
```

Under some circumstances, you might use a modal view instead of a navigation interface; for example, the Latin vocabulary list in Figure 21-1 is in a modal view, and when the user taps a cell, the modal view is dismissed to reveal the details on the selected word.

So common, in fact, is the use of a table view as the basis for navigation, that there is a UIViewController subclass, UITableViewController, dedicated to the presentation of a table view. The built-in Navigation-based Application project template uses it: the UINavigationController's root view controller is a UITableViewController, so the navigation interface at launch time is completely occupied by a table view. It is important to stress, however, that you never really *need* to use a UITableViewController — it's just a convenience, and doesn't do anything that you couldn't do yourself by other means — and that if your table view does not constitute the *entire* view to be handled by a UIViewController, you *can't* use a UITableViewController.

 A UITableViewController does *not* obey the UIViewController rule about what happens if it is sent `initWithNibName:bundle:` with a nil nib name. It doesn't look for a nib with the same name as its own class; instead, it creates the table view from scratch.

If you do use a UITableViewController, this is what it gives you:

- UITableViewController's `initWithStyle:` creates the table view with a plain or grouped format.
- The view controller is automatically made the table view's delegate and data source, unless you specify otherwise.
- The table view is made the controller's `tableView`. It is also, of course, the controller's `view`, but the `tableView` property is typed as a UITableView, so you can send table view messages to it without typecasting.

- Whenever the table view appears, the selection is cleared automatically in `viewWill-Appear:` (unless you disable this by setting `clearsSelectionOnViewWillAppear` to NO), and the scroll indicators are flashed in `viewDidAppear:`.

If you disable UITableViewController's automatic deselection behavior, or if you're not using a UITableViewController, you can implement automatic deselection in some other way. I sometimes prefer to implement deselection in `viewDidAppear:`; the effect is that when the user returns to the table, the row is still selected, but instantly deselects itself:

```
- (void) viewDidAppear:(BOOL)animated {
    // deselect selected row
    [tableView selectRowAtIndexPath:nil animated:NO
        scrollPosition:UITableViewScrollPositionNone];
    [super viewDidAppear:animated];
}
```

By convention, if selecting a table cell causes navigation, the cell should be given an `accessoryType` of `UITableViewCellAccessoryDisclosureIndicator`. This is a plain gray right-pointing chevron at the right end of the cell. The chevron doesn't of itself respond to user interaction; it's just a visual cue that we'll "move to the right" if the user taps the cell.

An alternative `accessoryType` is `UITableViewCellAccessoryDetailDisclosureButton`. It is a button and does respond to user interaction through your implementation of the table view delegate's `tableView:accessoryButtonTappedForRowWithIndexPath:`. The button has a right-pointing chevron, so once again you'd be likely to respond by navigating; in this case, however, you would probably use the button *instead* of selection as a way of letting the user navigate. An appropriate interface would be that selecting the cell as a whole does one thing and tapping the disclosure button does something else (involving navigation to the right).

A completely different use of table cell selection is to implement a choice among cells, where a section of a table effectively functions as an iOS alternative to Mac OS X radio buttons. The table usually has the grouped format. An `accessoryType` of `UITableView-CellAccessoryCheckmark` is typically used to indicate the current choice. Implementing radio-button behavior is up to you.

For example, here's how Figure 21-2 is implemented. The table is created in the grouped style, in code, as part of the view controller's `loadView` implementation:

```
UITableView* tv = [[UITableView alloc] initWithFrame:CGRectMake(0,0,320,310)
                                        style:UITableViewStyleGrouped];
[v addSubview:tv];
tv.dataSource = self;
tv.delegate = self;
tv.scrollEnabled = NO;
self.tableView = tv;
[tv release];
```

As data source, we supply the structure and content of the table. The user defaults are storing the current choice in each of the two categories, so we use them to decide where the checkmarks go:

```
- (NSInteger)numberOfSectionsInTableView:(UITableView *)tableView {
    return 2;
}

- (NSString *)tableView:(UITableView *)tableView
        titleForHeaderInSection:(NSInteger)section {
    if (section == 0)
        return @"Size";
    return @"Style";
}

- (NSInteger)tableView:(UITableView *)tableView
        numberOfRowsInSection:(NSInteger)section {
    if (section == 0)
        return 3;
    return 2;
}

- (UITableViewCell *)tableView:(UITableView *)tv
        cellForRowAtIndexPath:(NSIndexPath *)indexPath {
    static NSString *CellIdentifier = @"Cell";
    UITableViewCell *cell = [tv dequeueReusableCellWithIdentifier:CellIdentifier];
    if (cell == nil) {
        cell = [[[UITableViewCell alloc]
                    initWithStyle:UITableViewCellStyleDefault
                    reuseIdentifier:CellIdentifier] autorelease];
    }
    NSUInteger section = [indexPath section];
    NSUInteger row = [indexPath row];
    NSUserDefaults* ud = [NSUserDefaults standardUserDefaults];
    if (section == 0) {
        if (row == 0) {
            cell.textLabel.text = @"Easy";
        } else if (row == 1) {
            cell.textLabel.text = @"Normal";
        } else if (row == 2) {
            cell.textLabel.text = @"Hard";
        }
    } else if (section == 1) {
        if (row == 0) {
            cell.textLabel.text = @"Animals";
        } else if (row == 1) {
            cell.textLabel.text = @"Snacks";
        }
    }
    cell.accessoryType = UITableViewCellAccessoryNone;
    if ([[ud valueForKey:@"Style"] isEqualToString:cell.textLabel.text] ||
            [[ud valueForKey:@"Size"] isEqualToString:cell.textLabel.text])
        cell.accessoryType = UITableViewCellAccessoryCheckmark;
    return cell;
}
```

As delegate, we are called when the user taps a cell. We simply store the user's selection into the user defaults and reload the table data. This deselects the current selection and reassigns the checkmark:

```
- (void)tableView:(UITableView *)tv
        didSelectRowAtIndexPath:(NSIndexPath *)indexPath {
    NSUserDefaults* ud = [NSUserDefaults standardUserDefaults];
    NSString* setting = [tv cellForRowAtIndexPath:indexPath].textLabel.text;
    [ud setValue:setting forKey:
        [self tableView:tv titleForHeaderInSection:indexPath.section]];
    [self.tableView reloadData];
}
```

# Table View Scrolling and Layout

A UITableView is a UIScrollView, so everything you already know about scroll views is applicable (Chapter 20). In addition, a table view supplies two convenience scrolling methods:

- `scrollToRowAtIndexPath:atScrollPosition:animated:`
- `scrollToNearestSelectedRowAtScrollPosition:animated:`

The `scrollPosition` parameter is as for `selectRowAtIndexPath:...`, discussed earlier in this chapter.

The following UITableView methods mediate between the table's bounds coordinates on the one hand and table structure on the other:

- `indexPathForRowAtPoint:`
- `indexPathsForRowsInRect:`
- `rectForSection:`
- `rectForRowAtIndexPath:`
- `rectForFooterInSection:`
- `rectForHeaderInSection:`

The table's header and footer are views, so their coordinates are given by their frames.

# Table View Searching

A table view is a common way to present the results of a search performed through a search field (a UISearchBar; see Chapter 25). This is such a standard interface, in fact, that a class is provided, UISearchDisplayController, to mediate between the search field where the user enters a search term and the table view listing the results of the search. The UISearchDisplayController needs the following things:

*A search bar*
> A UISearchBar in the interface. This will be the UISearchDisplayController's `searchBar`.

*A view controller*
> The controller managing the view in the interface over which the search results are to appear. This will be the UISearchDisplayController's `searchContents-Controller`. The UISearchDisplayController will harness this view controller's view and present its table of results modally on top of it.

*A table view*
> The table view in which the search results will be presented. This will be the UI-SearchDisplayController's `searchResultsTableView`. It can already exist, or the UI-SearchDisplayController will create it.

*A data source and delegate for the table view*
> The UISearchDisplayController's `searchResultsDataSource` and `searchResults-Delegate`. They will control the data and structure of the search results table. They are commonly the same object, as for any table view; moreover, they are commonly the view controller.

*A delegate*
> An optional object adopting the UISearchDisplayDelegate protocol. It will be notified of events relating to the display of results. It, too, is commonly the view controller.

Moreover, the UISearchBar itself can also have a delegate; plus, it is often the case that the thing being searched is itself a table view, so the search field is effectively filtering the contents of the table view. A single object may thus be playing all of the following roles:

- The searchable table view's view controller
- The searchable table view's data source
- The searchable table view's delegate
- The view controller for the view over which the search results will appear
- The search results table view's data source
- The search results table view's delegate
- The UISearchDisplayController's delegate
- The UISearchBar's delegate

To illustrate, we will implement a table view that is searchable through a UISearchBar and that displays the results of that search in a second table view managed by a UI-SearchDisplayController. The first question is how to make the search field appear along with the table view. Apple's own apps, such as the Contacts app, have popularized an interface in which the search field is the table view's header view. (Indeed, this is such a common arrangement that if you drag a UISearchBar onto a UITableView in a nib, the search field becomes the table's header view and a UISearchDisplayController is created for you automatically.) Another feature of Apple's standard interface is that the search field isn't initially showing. To implement this, we scroll to the first actual row of data when the table view appears.

We're going to start with a table managed by a UITableViewController. In this controller's `viewDidLoad`, we create the search bar and slot it in as the table's header view; we then load the data and scroll the header view out of sight. We also create the UISearchDisplayController and tie it to the search bar — and to ourselves as the UISearchDisplayController's controller, delegate, search table data source, and search table delegate, as well as making ourselves the UISearchBar delegate:

```
UISearchBar* b = [[UISearchBar alloc] init];
[b sizeToFit];
b.delegate = self;
[self.tableView setTableHeaderView:b];
[self.tableView reloadData];
[self.tableView
    scrollToRowAtIndexPath:[NSIndexPath indexPathForRow:0 inSection:0]
    atScrollPosition:UITableViewScrollPositionTop animated:NO];
UISearchDisplayController* c =
    [[UISearchDisplayController alloc] initWithSearchBar:b
                                    contentsController:self];
[b release];
self.sbc = c; // retain policy
c.delegate = self;
c.searchResultsDataSource = self;
c.searchResultsDelegate = self;
[c release];
```

When the user initially taps in the search field, the UISearchDisplayController automatically becomes "active": it grabs the search field and the view controller's view and constructs a new interface along with a nice animation. This indicates to the user that the search field is ready to receive input; when the user proceeds to enter characters into the search field, the UISearchDisplayController is ready to superimpose its own search results table view onto this interface. The UISearchBar has a Cancel button that the user can tap to dismiss (deactivate) the interface created by the UISearchDisplay-Controller.

Now, we are both the data source and delegate for the original table view and the data source and delegate for the search results table. This means that our search is already almost working, because the search results table will automatically have the same data and structure as the original table! Our only task is to modify our existing code to check whether the table view that's talking to us is the search results table view (this will be UISearchDisplayController's `searchResultsTableView`) and, if it is, to limit our returned data with respect to the search bar's text.

The strategy for doing this should be fairly obvious if we are maintaining our source data in a sensible model. Let's say, for the sake of simplicity, that our original table is displaying the names of the 50 United States, which it is getting from an array of strings called `states`:

```
- (NSInteger)numberOfSectionsInTableView:(UITableView *)tableView {
    return 1;
}

- (NSInteger)tableView:(UITableView *)tableView
        numberOfRowsInSection:(NSInteger)section {
    NSArray* model = self.states;
    return [model count];
}

// Customize the appearance of table view cells.
- (UITableViewCell *)tableView:(UITableView *)tableView
        cellForRowAtIndexPath:(NSIndexPath *)indexPath {
    static NSString *CellIdentifier = @"Cell";
    UITableViewCell *cell =
        [tableView dequeueReusableCellWithIdentifier:CellIdentifier];
    if (cell == nil) {
        cell = [[[UITableViewCell alloc]
                    initWithStyle:UITableViewCellStyleDefault
                    reuseIdentifier:CellIdentifier] autorelease];
    }
    NSArray* model = self.states;
    cell.textLabel.text = [model objectAtIndex: indexPath.row];
    return cell;
}
```

To make this work with a UISearchDisplayController, the only needed change is this: Each time we speak of the NSArray called `model`, we must decide whether it should be `self.states`, as now, or whether it should be a *different* array that is filtered with respect to the current search — let's call it `self.filteredStates`. There are two occurrences of this line:

```
NSArray* model = self.states;
```

They are now to be replaced by this:

```
NSArray* model =
    (tableView == sbc.searchResultsTableView) ? self.filteredStates : self.states;
```

The only remaining question is when and how this `filteredStates` array should be calculated. One approach is to ignore the user typing into the search field and calculate the filtered array only when the user taps the Search button in the keyboard. We are the UISearchBar delegate, so we can hear about the user tapping the Search button by implementing `searchBarSearchButtonClicked:`. We create the filtered array and reload the UISearchDisplayController's search results table view:

```
- (void)searchBarSearchButtonClicked:(UISearchBar *)searchBar {
    NSPredicate* p = [NSPredicate predicateWithBlock:
      ^BOOL(id obj, NSDictionary *d) {
        NSString* s = obj;
        return ([s rangeOfString:searchBar.text
            options:NSCaseInsensitiveSearch].location != NSNotFound);
```

```
    }];
    self.filteredStates = [states filteredArrayUsingPredicate:p];
    [self.sbc.searchResultsTableView reloadData];
}
```

This works fine. However, as soon as the user starts typing into the search field, the results table becomes empty, along with a background that reads "No Results" (a phrase that, unfortunately, cannot be removed or customized). This is because the results table reloads whenever the user changes the contents of the search field and is finding that it has no data (because `filteredStates` is nil).

One solution is to set the `filteredStates` array to the `states` array before the search begins. We can know when this will be through a UISearchDisplayController delegate method:

```
- (void)searchDisplayControllerWillBeginSearch:(UISearchDisplayController *)c {
    self.filteredStates = self.states;
}
```

Alternatively, we can generate a new set of search results every time the user types in the search field, thus effectively implementing a "live" search. This is perfectly reasonable for our extremely small data set of 50 states, though of course it mightn't work well if the data set were very large or if there were for some other reason a delay in filtering it (such as data needing to be fetched over the network). To implement live search, we turn our implementation of `searchBarSearchButtonClicked:` into an implementation of `searchBar:textDidChange:`. Everything else stays the same, except that now there is no need to reload the search results table's data, as by default the UI-SearchDisplayController will do that automatically:

```
- (void)searchBar:(UISearchBar *)searchBar textDidChange:(NSString *)searchText {
    NSPredicate* p = [NSPredicate predicateWithBlock:
    ^BOOL(id obj, NSDictionary *d) {
        NSString* s = obj;
        return ([s rangeOfString:searchText
            options:NSCaseInsensitiveSearch].location != NSNotFound);
    }];
    self.filteredStates = [states filteredArrayUsingPredicate:p];
}
```

A UISearchBar can also display scope buttons, letting the user alter the meaning of the search. If you add these, then of course you must take them into account when filtering the model data. For example, let's have two scope buttons, "Starts With" and "Contains":

```
UISearchBar* b = [[UISearchBar alloc] init];
[b sizeToFit];
b.scopeButtonTitles = [NSArray arrayWithObjects: @"Starts With", @"Contains", nil];
// ...
```

Our filtering routine must now take the state of the scope buttons into account. Moreover, the search results table view will reload when the user changes the scope, so if we're doing a live search, we must respond by filtering the data then as well. To prevent repetition, we'll abstract the filtering routine into a method of its own:

```
- (void) filterData {
    NSPredicate* p = [NSPredicate predicateWithBlock:
     ^BOOL(id obj, NSDictionary *d) {
         NSString* s = obj;
         NSStringCompareOptions options = NSCaseInsensitiveSearch;
         if (sbc.searchBar.selectedScopeButtonIndex == 0)
             options |= NSAnchoredSearch;
         return ([s rangeOfString:sbc.searchBar.text
             options:options].location != NSNotFound);
    }];
    self.filteredStates = [states filteredArrayUsingPredicate:p];
}

- (void)searchBar:(UISearchBar *)searchBar textDidChange:(NSString *)searchText {
    [self filterData];
}

- (void)searchBar:(UISearchBar *)searchBar
        selectedScopeButtonIndexDidChange:(NSInteger)selectedScope {
    [self filterData];
}
```

The UISearchBar has various properties through which it can be configured (see Chapter 25). Both the UISearchBar and UISearchDisplayController send their delegate numerous messages that you can take advantage of to customize behavior. A UISearchBar in a UIToolbar on the iPad can display its results in a popover (see Chapter 22).

In an indexed list — one with sections and an index running down the right side — a "magnifying glass" search symbol can be made to appear in the index by including UITableViewIndexSearch (usually as the first item) in the string array returned from sectionIndexTitlesForTableView:. For example, suppose that as in our earlier example, the section names are to be used as index entries and are in an array called sectionNames:

```
- (NSArray *)sectionIndexTitlesForTableView:(UITableView *)tableView {
    return [[NSArray arrayWithObject: UITableViewIndexSearch]
            arrayByAddingObjectsFromArray:sectionNames];
}
```

You'll also need to implement tableView:sectionForSectionIndexTitle:atIndex:, because now the correspondence between index entries and sections is off by one. If the user taps the magnifying glass in the index, you scroll to reveal the search field (and you'll also have to return a bogus section number, but there is no penalty for that):

```
- (NSInteger)tableView:(UITableView *)tableView
        sectionForSectionIndexTitle:(NSString *)title
                          atIndex:(NSInteger)index {
    if (index == 0)
        [tableView scrollRectToVisible:tableView.tableHeaderView.frame
                               animated:NO];
    return index-1;
}
```

# Table View Editing

A table view cell has a normal state and an editing state, according to its `editing` property. The editing state is typically indicated visually by one or more of the following:

*Editing controls*
> At least one editing control will usually appear, such as a minus button (for deletion) at the left side.

*Shrinkage*
> The content of the cell will usually shrink to allow room for an editing control. You can prevent a cell in a grouped-style table from shifting its left end rightward in editing mode by setting its `shouldIndentWhileEditing` to NO, or with the table delegate's `tableView:shouldIndentWhileEditingRowAtIndexPath:`.

*Changing accessory view*
> The cell's accessory view will change automatically in accordance with its `editingAccessoryType` or `editingAccessoryView`. If you assign neither, so that they are nil, the cell's accessory view will vanish when in editing mode.

As with selection, you can set a cell's `editing` property directly (or use `setEditing:animated:` to get animation), but you are more likely to let the table view manage editability. Table view editability is controlled through the table's `editing` property, usually by sending the table the `setEditing:animated:` message. The table is then responsible for putting its cells into edit mode.

 A cell in edit mode can also be selected by the user if the table view's `allowsSelectionDuringEditing` is YES. But this would be unusual.

Putting the table into edit mode is usually left up to the user. One typical device for allowing this is an Edit button. In a navigation interface, we could have our view controller supply the button as the navigation item's right button:

```
UIBarButtonItem* bbi =
    [[UIBarButtonItem alloc] initWithBarButtonSystemItem:UIBarButtonSystemItemEdit
                            target:self action:@selector(doEdit:)];
self.navigationItem.rightBarButtonItem = bbi;
[bbi release];
```

Our action handler will be responsible for putting the table into edit mode, so in its simplest form it might look like this:

```
- (void) doEdit: (id) sender {
    [self.tableView setEditing:YES animated:YES];
}
```

But that does not solve the problem of getting *out* of editing mode. The standard solution is to have the Edit button replace itself by a Done button:

```
- (void) doEdit: (id) sender {
    int which;
    if (![self.tableView isEditing]) {
        [self.tableView setEditing:YES animated:YES];
        which = UIBarButtonSystemItemDone;
    } else {
        [self.tableView setEditing:NO animated:YES];
        which = UIBarButtonSystemItemEdit;
    }
    UIBarButtonItem* bbi = [[UIBarButtonItem alloc]
        initWithBarButtonSystemItem:which target:self action:@selector(doEdit:)];
    self.navigationItem.rightBarButtonItem = bbi;
    [bbi release];
}
```

However, it turns out that all of this is completely unnecessary if we want standard behavior, as it is already implemented for us! A UIViewController supplies an `edit-ButtonItem` that calls the UIViewController's `setEditing:animated:` when tapped, tracks whether we're in edit mode with the UIViewController's `editing` property, and changes its own title accordingly. Moreover, a UITableViewController's implementation of `setEditing:animated:` is to call the same method on its table view. Thus, if we're using a UITableViewController, we get all of that behavior for free just by inserting the `editButtonItem` into our interface (and indeed, the line of code to do this may already be present in our project template, just waiting for us to uncomment it):

```
self.navigationItem.rightBarButtonItem = self.editButtonItem;
```

When the table view enters edit mode, it consults its data source and delegate about the editability of individual rows:

`tableView:canEditRowAtIndexPath:` *to the data source*
> The default is YES. The data source can return NO to prevent the given row from entering edit mode.

`tableView:editingStyleForRowAtIndexPath:` *to the delegate*
> Each standard editing style corresponds to a control that will appear in the cell. The choices are:

`UITableViewCellEditingStyleNone`
> No editing control appears.

`UITableViewCellEditingStyleDelete`
> The cell shows a minus button at its left end. The user can tap this to summon a Delete button, which the user can then tap to confirm the deletion. This is the default.

`UITableViewCellEditingStyleInsert`
> The cell shows a plus button at its left end.

If the user taps an insert button (the plus button) or a delete button (the Delete button that appears after the user taps the minus button), the data source is sent the `table-View:commitEditingStyle:forRowAtIndexPath:` message and is responsible for obeying it. In your response, you will probably want to alter the structure of the table, and UITableView methods for doing this are provided:

- `insertRowsAtIndexPaths:withRowAnimation:`
- `deleteRowsAtIndexPaths:withRowAnimation:`
- `insertSections:withRowAnimation:`
- `deleteSections:withRowAnimation:`

The row animations here are effectively the same ones discussed earlier in connection with refreshing table data; "left" for an insertion means to slide in from the left, and for a deletion it means to slide out to the left, and so on.

If you're issuing more than one of these commands, you can combine them by surrounding them with `beginUpdates` and `endUpdates`, forming an *updates block*. An updates block combines not just the animations but the requested changes themselves. This relieves you from having to worry about how a command is affected by earlier commands in the same updates block; indeed, order of commands within an updates block doesn't really matter. For example, if you delete row 1 of a certain section and then (in a separate command) delete row 2 of the same section, you delete two successive rows, just as you would expect; the notion "2" does not change its meaning because you deleted an earlier row first, because you *didn't* delete an earlier row first — the updates block combines the commands for you, interpreting both index paths with respect to the state of the table before any changes are made. Similarly, if you perform insertions and deletions together in one animation, the deletions are performed first, regardless of the order of your commands, and the insertion row and section numbers refer to the state of the table after the deletions.

An interesting trick is that an empty updates block lays out the table view, fetching the section header and footer titles or views, their heights, and the row heights, without reloading any cells. Apple takes advantage of this in the Table View Animations and Gestures example, in which a pinch gesture is used to change a table's row height in real time.

## Deleting Table Items

Deletion of table items is the default, so there's not much for us to do in order to implement it. If our view controller is a UITableViewController and we've displayed the Edit button as its navigation item's right button, everything happens automatically: the user taps the Edit button, the view controller's `setEditing:animated:` is called, the table view's `setEditing:animated:` is called, and the table cells all show the minus button at the left end. The user can then tap a minus button; a Delete button appears at the cell's right end. You can customize the Delete button's title with the table delegate method `tableView:titleForDeleteConfirmationButtonForRowAtIndexPath:`.

What is *not* automatic is the actual response to the Delete button. For that, we need to implement `tableView:commitEditingStyle:forRowAtIndexPath:`. Typically, you'll remove the corresponding entry from the underlying model data, and you'll call `deleteRowsAtIndexPaths:withRowAnimation:` or `deleteSections:withRowAnimation:` to update the appearance of the table. This is the tricky part; you have to do whatever makes sense for the way you're maintaining the model, and you must delete the row or section in such a way as to keep the table display coordinated with the model's structure. Otherwise, the app will crash (with an extremely helpful error message).

To illustrate, let's suppose that the underlying model is an array of arrays, maintained as `sectionNames` and `sectionData`, as in our earlier example. These arrays must now be mutable. Our approach will be in two stages:

1. Deal with the model data. We'll delete the requested row; if this empties the section array, we'll also delete that section array and the corresponding section name.

2. Deal with the table's appearance. If we deleted the section array, we'll call `deleteSections:withRowAnimation:`; otherwise, we'll call `deleteRowsAtIndexPaths:withRowAnimation:`:

```
- (void)tableView:(UITableView *)tableView
      commitEditingStyle:(UITableViewCellEditingStyle)editingStyle
                    forRowAtIndexPath:(NSIndexPath *)indexPath {
    [[self.sectionData objectAtIndex: indexPath.section]
        removeObjectAtIndex:indexPath.row];
    if ([[self.sectionData objectAtIndex: indexPath.section] count] == 0) {
        [self.sectionData removeObjectAtIndex: indexPath.section];
        [self.sectionNames removeObjectAtIndex: indexPath.section];
        [tableView deleteSections:[NSIndexSet indexSetWithIndex: indexPath.section]
                  withRowAnimation:UITableViewRowAnimationLeft];
    } else {
        [tableView deleteRowsAtIndexPaths:[NSArray arrayWithObject:indexPath]
                  withRowAnimation:UITableViewRowAnimationLeft];
    }
}
```

 If a section index appears in the table, and you delete a section, you're going to want to reload the section index. Ideally, you could call `reloadSectionIndexTitles`, but this method, as we've already seen, is broken; so you'll have to call `reloadData`. However, that call interferes with the deletion animation. A simple solution is to use delayed performance (a delay of about `0.4` seconds should suffice).

The user can also delete a row by swiping it to summon its Delete button *without* having explicitly entered edit mode; no other row is editable, and no other editing controls are shown. This feature is implemented "for free" by virtue of our having supplied an

---

*Figure 21-4. A simple phone directory app*

implementation of `tableView:commitEditingStyle:forRowAtIndexPath:`. If you're like me, your first response will be: "Thanks for the free functionality, Apple, and now how do I turn this off?" Because the Edit button is already using the UIViewController's `editing` property to track edit mode, we can take advantage of this and refuse to let any cells be edited unless the view controller *is* in edit mode:

```
- (UITableViewCellEditingStyle)tableView:(UITableView *)aTableView
        editingStyleForRowAtIndexPath:(NSIndexPath *)indexPath {
    return self.editing ?
        UITableViewCellEditingStyleDelete : UITableViewCellEditingStyleNone;
}
```

## Editable Content in Table Items

A table item might have content that the user can edit directly, such as a UITextField (Chapter 23). Because the user is working in the view, you need a way to reflect the user's changes into the model. This will probably involve putting yourself in contact with the interface objects where the user does the editing.

To illustrate, I'll implement a table cell with a text field that is editable when the cell is in editing mode. Imagine an app that maintains a list of names and phone numbers. A name and phone number are displayed as a grouped-style table, and they become editable when the user taps the Edit button (Figure 21-4).

A UITextField is editable if its `enabled` is YES. To tie this to the cell's `editing` state, it is probably simplest to implement a custom UITableViewCell class. I'll call it MyCell, and I'll design it in the nib, giving it a single UITextField that's pointed to through a property called `textField`. In the code for MyCell, we override `didTransitionTo-State:`, as follows:

```
- (void) didTransitionToState:(UITableViewCellStateMask)state {
    [super didTransitionToState:state];
    if (state == UITableViewCellStateEditingMask) {
        self.textField.enabled = YES;
    }
    if (state == UITableViewCellStateDefaultMask) {
        self.textField.enabled = NO;
    }
}
```

In the table's data source, we make ourselves the text field's delegate when we create and configure the cell. For example, here's the part where we configure a phone number cell; the model is an array called `numbers`:

```
- (UITableViewCell *)tableView:(UITableView *)tableView
        cellForRowAtIndexPath:(NSIndexPath *)indexPath {
    // ...
    MyCell* theCell = (MyCell*) cell;
    if (indexPath.section == 1) {
        theCell.textField.text = [self.numbers objectAtIndex: indexPath.row];
        theCell.textField.keyboardType = UIKeyboardTypeNumbersAndPunctuation;
        theCell.textField.delegate = self;
    }
    return cell;
}
```

We are the UITextField's delegate, so we are responsible for implementing the Return button in the keyboard to dismiss the keyboard:

```
- (BOOL)textFieldShouldReturn:(UITextField *)tf {
    [tf endEditing:YES];
    return YES;
}
```

Now comes the interesting part. When a text field stops editing, we can hear about it because we are its delegate, by implementing `textFieldDidEndEditing:`. We work out which cell it belongs to, and update the model accordingly:

```
- (void)textFieldDidEndEditing:(UITextField *)tf {
    // some cell's text field has finished editing; which cell?
    UIView* v = tf;
    do {
        v = v.superview;
    } while (![v isKindOfClass: [UITableViewCell class]]);
    MyCell* cell = (MyCell*)v;
    // update data model to match
    NSIndexPath* ip = [self.tableView indexPathForCell:cell];
    // ...
    if (ip.section == 1)
        [self.numbers replaceObjectAtIndex:ip.row withObject:cell.textField.text];
}
```

## Inserting Table Items

You are unlikely to attach a plus (insert) button to every row. In fact, a common interface is that when a table is edited, every row has a minus button except the last row, which has a plus button; this shows the user that a new row can be inserted at the end of the table.

Let's implement this for phone numbers in our name-and-phone-number app, allowing the user to give a person any quantity of phone numbers (Figure 21-5):

```
- (UITableViewCellEditingStyle)tableView:(UITableView *)tableView
        editingStyleForRowAtIndexPath:(NSIndexPath *)indexPath {
```

*Figure 21-5. Phone directory app in editing mode*

```
    if (indexPath.section == 1) {
        NSInteger ct =
            [self tableView:tableView numberOfRowsInSection:indexPath.section];
        if (ct-1 == indexPath.row)
            return UITableViewCellEditingStyleInsert;
        return UITableViewCellEditingStyleDelete;
    }
    return UITableViewCellEditingStyleNone;
}
```

The person's name has no editing control (a person must have exactly one name), so we prevent it from indenting in edit mode:

```
- (BOOL)tableView:(UITableView *)tableView
        shouldIndentWhileEditingRowAtIndexPath:(NSIndexPath *)indexPath {
    if (indexPath.section == 1)
        return YES;
    return NO;
}
```

When the user taps an editing control, we must respond. The model is a mutable array of strings, `numbers`. We already know what to do when the tapped control is a delete button; things are similar when it's an insert button, but we've a little more work to do. The new row will be empty, and it will be at the end of the table; so we append an empty string to the `numbers` model array, and then we insert a corresponding row at the end of the view. But now two successive rows have a plus button; the way to fix that is to reload the first of those rows. We also show the keyboard for the new, empty phone number, so that the user can start editing it immediately; we can't do that until the row animation from the insertion is over, so we use delayed performance (this use of delayed performance has a certain fragility, but no event tells us when the row animation ends, so we've no other choice). I find that the whole thing looks and works best if the row reloading is also part of the delayed performance:

```
- (void) tableView:(UITableView *)tableView
        commitEditingStyle:(UITableViewCellEditingStyle)editingStyle
        forRowAtIndexPath:(NSIndexPath *)indexPath {
    if (editingStyle == UITableViewCellEditingStyleInsert) {
        [self.numbers addObject: @""];
```

```
        NSInteger ct = [self.numbers count];
        [tableView insertRowsAtIndexPaths:
         [NSArray arrayWithObject: [NSIndexPath indexPathForRow: ct-1 inSection:1]]
                        withRowAnimation:UITableViewRowAnimationMiddle];
        [self performSelector:@selector(selectLast) withObject:nil afterDelay:0.4];
    }
    if (editingStyle == UITableViewCellEditingStyleDelete) {
        [self.numbers removeObjectAtIndex:indexPath.row];
        [tableView deleteRowsAtIndexPaths:[NSArray arrayWithObject: indexPath]
            withRowAnimation:UITableViewRowAnimationBottom];
    }
}

- (void) selectLast {
    NSInteger ct = [self.numbers count];
    [self.tableView reloadRowsAtIndexPaths: [NSArray arrayWithObject:
        [NSIndexPath indexPathForRow:ct-2 inSection:1]]
        withRowAnimation:UITableViewRowAnimationNone];
    UITableViewCell* cell = [self.tableView cellForRowAtIndexPath:
                                [NSIndexPath indexPathForRow:ct-1 inSection:1]];
    [(((MyCell*)cell).textField becomeFirstResponder];
}
```

## Rearranging Table Items

If the data source implements tableView:moveRowAtIndexPath:toIndexPath:, the table displays a reordering control at the right end of each row in editing mode, and the user can drag it to rearrange table items. The reordering control can be prevented for individual table items by implementing tableView:canMoveRowAtIndexPath:. The user is free to move rows that display a reordering control, but the delegate can limit where a row can be moved to by implementing tableView:targetIndexPathForMoveFromRowAtIndexPath:toProposedIndexPath:.

To illustrate, we'll add to our name-and-phone-number app the ability to rearrange phone numbers. There must be multiple phone numbers to rearrange:

```
- (BOOL)tableView:(UITableView *)tableView
      canMoveRowAtIndexPath:(NSIndexPath *)indexPath {
    if (indexPath.section == 1 && [self.numbers count] > 1)
        return YES;
    return NO;
}
```

In our example, a phone number must not be moved out of its section, so we implement the delegate method to prevent this. We also take this opportunity to dismiss the keyboard if it is showing.

```
- (NSIndexPath *)tableView:(UITableView *)tableView
      targetIndexPathForMoveFromRowAtIndexPath:(NSIndexPath *)sourceIndexPath
              toProposedIndexPath:(NSIndexPath *)proposedDestinationIndexPath {
    [tableView endEditing:YES];
    if (proposedDestinationIndexPath.section == 0)
        return [NSIndexPath indexPathForRow:0 inSection:1];
```

```
        return proposedDestinationIndexPath;
    }
```

After the user moves an item, `tableView:moveRowAtIndexPath:toIndexPath:` is called, and we trivially update the model to match. We also reload the table, to fix the editing controls:

```
- (void)tableView:(UITableView *)tableView
        moveRowAtIndexPath:(NSIndexPath *)fromIndexPath
             toIndexPath:(NSIndexPath *)toIndexPath {
    NSString* s = [self.numbers objectAtIndex: fromIndexPath.row];
    [s retain];
    [self.numbers removeObjectAtIndex: fromIndexPath.row];
    [self.numbers insertObject:s atIndex: toIndexPath.row];
    [s release];
    [tableView reloadData];
}
```

# CHAPTER 22

# Popovers and Split Views

Popovers and split views are forms of interface that exist only on the iPad.

A *popover* is like a secondary window or dialog: it presents a view layered on top of the main interface. It does not dim out the rest of the screen like a modal view (if its presentation mode is `UIModalPresentationPageSheet` or `UIModalPresentationFormSheet`; see Chapter 19). It can be effectively modal, preventing the user from working in the rest of the interface, or it can vanish if the user taps outside it; or you can allow the user to tap some or all of the interface outside it without dismissing the popover.

A *split view* is a combination of two views, the first of which is the width of an iPhone screen (when the iPhone is held in portrait orientation). When the iPad is in landscape orientation, the two views appear side by side; when the iPad is in portrait orientation, only the second view appears, with an option to summon the first view as a popover.

Popovers may be thought of as a sort of compromise between the iPhone interface and the iPad interface. For example, in my LinkSame app, both the settings view (which allows the user to configure and begin a new game) and the help view (which describes how to play the game) are popovers (Figure 22-1). On the iPhone, both these views would occupy the entire screen; for each, we'd need a way to navigate to it and to return to the main interface when the user is finished with it (both would probably be modal views). But with the larger iPad screen, that would make no sense; neither view is large enough, or important enough, to occupy the entire screen exclusively. As popovers, these views are shown as what they are: smaller, secondary views which the user summons temporarily and then dismisses.

The split view, too, eases the transition from iPhone to iPad. On the iPhone, you might have a master–detail architecture in a navigation interface, where the master is a table view (Chapter 21). On the iPad, the screen is large enough to accommodate the master and the detail simultaneously: there is no need to navigate from one to the other. The split view provides a straightforward way to present them simultaneously; it is no coincidence that its first view is sized to hold the master table that occupied the entire screen on the iPhone. Apple's own Mail app is a familiar example.

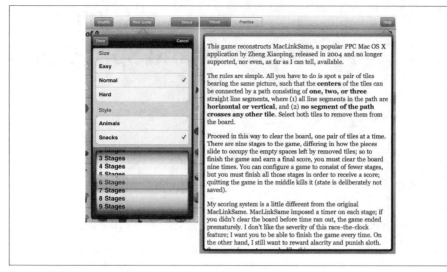

*Figure 22-1. Two popovers*

# Presenting a Popover

To present a popover, you'll need a UIPopoverController and a view controller. The UIPopoverController is not itself a view controller, because a popover doesn't occupy the whole interface; rather, it presents the secondary world in which the view controller's view *does* occupy the whole interface (rather as if someone were holding an iPhone in front of the iPad). The view controller is the UIPopoverController's `contentViewController`, which is set through its initializer, `initWithContentViewController:`. (You can also swap out a popover controller's view later while the popover is showing, substituting a different view controller with `setContentViewController:animated:`.)

For example, here's how the first popover in Figure 22-1 is initialized. I have a UIViewController subclass, NewGameController. NewGameController's view contains a table (Figure 21-2) and a UIPickerView (Chapter 11), and is itself the data source and delegate for both. I instantiate NewGameController and use this instance as the root view controller of a UINavigationController, giving its `navigationItem` a `leftBarButtonItem` (Done) and a `rightBarButtonItem` (Cancel). I don't really intend to do any navigation; I just want the two buttons, and this is an easy way of getting them. That UINavigationController then becomes a UIPopoverController's view controller:

```
NewGameController* dlg = [[NewGameController alloc] init];
UIBarButtonItem* b = [[UIBarButtonItem alloc]
    initWithBarButtonSystemItem: UIBarButtonSystemItemCancel
                     target: self
                     action: @selector(cancelNewGame:)];
dlg.navigationItem.rightBarButtonItem = b;
[b release];
b = [[UIBarButtonItem alloc]
    initWithBarButtonSystemItem: UIBarButtonSystemItemDone
```

```
                    target: self
                    action: @selector(saveNewGame:)];
    dlg.navigationItem.leftBarButtonItem = b;
    [b release];
    UINavigationController* nav =
        [[UINavigationController alloc] initWithRootViewController:dlg];
    [dlg release];
    UIPopoverController* pop =
        [[UIPopoverController alloc] initWithContentViewController:nav];
    [nav release];
```

The popover controller should also be told the size of the view it is to display, which will be the size of the popover. The default popover size is (320,1100); Apple would like you to stick to the default width of 320 (the width of an iPhone screen), but a maximum width of 600 is permitted, and the second popover in Figure 22-1 uses it. The popover's height might be shorter than requested if there isn't enough vertical space, so the view to be displayed needs to be prepared for the possibility that it might be resized.

You can provide the popover size in one of two ways:

*UIPopoverController's* popoverContentSize *property*
> This property can be set before the popover appears; it can also be changed while the popover is showing, with setPopoverContentSize:animated:.

*UIViewController's* contentSizeForViewInPopover *property*
> The UIViewController is the UIPopoverController's contentViewController (or is contained by that view controller, as in a tab bar interface or navigation interface). This approach often makes more sense, because a UIViewController will generally know its own view's ideal size. (contentSizeForViewInPopover is yet another of those UIViewController properties that is used only in one limited situation.)

In the case of the first popover in Figure 22-1, the NewGameController sets its own contentSizeForViewInPopover. It knows that its view will be used only in a popover, so its popover size is simply the size of its view:

```
    self.contentSizeForViewInPopover = self.view.bounds.size;
```

The popover itself, however, will need to be somewhat taller, because the NewGame-Controller is embedded in a UINavigationController, whose navigation bar occupies additional vertical space. Delightfully, the UINavigationController takes care of that automatically; its own contentSizeForViewInPopover adds the necessary height to that of its root view controller.

In case of a conflict, the rule seems to be that if the UIPopoverController and the UI-ViewController have different settings for their respective properties at the time the popover is presented, the UIPopoverController's setting wins. But if either property is changed while the popover is visible, the change is obeyed; specifically, my experiments suggest that if the UIViewController's contentSizeForViewInPopover is changed (not merely set to the value it already has), the UIPopoverController adopts that value as its `popoverContentSize` and the popover's size is adjusted accordingly.

If a popover's `contentViewController` is a UINavigationController, and a view controller is pushed onto or popped off of its stack, then if the current view controller's `contentSizeForViewInPopover` differs from that of the previously displayed view controller, my experiments suggest that the popover's *width* will change to match the new width, but the popover's *height* will change only if the new height is *taller*. This feels like a bug. A workaround is to implement the UINavigationController's delegate method `navigationController:didShowViewController:animated:`, so as to set the navigation controller's `contentSizeForViewInPopover` explicitly:

```
- (void)navigationController:(UINavigationController *)navigationController
        didShowViewController:(UIViewController *)viewController
                    animated:(BOOL)animated {
    navigationController.contentSizeForViewInPopover =
        viewController.contentSizeForViewInPopover;
}
```

The popover is made to appear on screen by sending the UIPopoverController one of the following messages:

- `presentPopoverFromRect:inView:permittedArrowDirections:animated:`
- `presentPopoverFromBarButtonItem:permittedArrowDirections:animated:`

The UIPopoverController's `popoverVisible` then becomes YES.

The popover has a sort of triangular bulge (called its *arrow*) on one edge, pointing to some region of the existing interface, from which the popover thus appears to emanate and to which it seems to be related. The difference between the two methods lies only in how this region is specified. With the first method, you can provide any CGRect with respect to any visible UIView's coordinate system; for example, to make the popover emanate from a UIButton, you would provide the UIButton's frame with respect to its superview (or the UIButton's bounds with respect to itself). But you can't do that with a UIBarButtonItem, because a UIBarButtonItem isn't a UIView and doesn't have a frame or bounds, so the second method is provided.

The permitted arrow directions restrict which sides of the popover the arrow can appear on. It's a bitmask, and your choices are:

- `UIPopoverArrowDirectionUp`
- `UIPopoverArrowDirectionDown`
- `UIPopoverArrowDirectionLeft`
- `UIPopoverArrowDirectionRight`
- `UIPopoverArrowDirectionAny`

Usually, you'd specify `UIPopoverArrowDirectionAny`, allowing the runtime to put the arrow on whatever side it feels is appropriate. (Even if you specify a particular direction, you have no precise control over a popover's location.)

The first popover in Figure 22-1 has a dark navigation bar even though no such thing was requested when the UINavigationController was created. This is because a popover whose content view controller is a navigation controller likes to take control of its navigation bar's `barStyle` and set it to a special undocumented style, evidently to make it harmonize with the popover's border. This is not easy to prevent and my advice is not to try.

# Managing a Popover

Unlike the controller of a modal view or of a view used in a tab bar interface or a navigation interface, a UIPopoverController instance is not automatically retained for you; you must retain it manually. You'll need a reference to any UIPopoverController that you present, because without such a reference you can't do two things you're likely to want to do afterward:

*Dismiss the popover*
> There are two ways in which a popover can be dismissed: the user can tap outside the popover, or you can explicitly dismiss the popover (as I do with the first popover in Figure 22-1 when the user taps the Done button or the Cancel button). In order to dismiss the popover explicitly, you send its UIPopoverController the `dismiss-PopoverAnimated:` message. But you can't do that unless you have a reference to that UIPopoverController.

*Release the popover*
> Because you created the UIPopoverController with `alloc`, you're eventually going to want to send it a `release` message. But you can't release a UIPopoverController while its popover is showing. Thus, you're going to want to release the UIPopoverController after its popover has been dismissed. But you can't do that unless you have a reference to that UIPopoverController.

Nor do the complications of popover management end there. In keeping with the transient nature of popovers, I like to dismiss the current popover programmatically when the application undergoes certain strong transitions, such as going into the background or being rotated. (See also Apple's technical note on what to do when the interface rotates while a popover is showing, QA1694, "Handling Popover Controllers During Orientation Changes.") You can listen for the former by registering for `UIApplication-DidEnterBackgroundNotification`, and for the latter by implementing `willRotateTo-InterfaceOrientation:duration:`. This policy is not merely aesthetic; some view controllers, especially certain built-in specialized view controllers, recover badly from such transitions when displayed in a popover. But dismissing a popover requires a reference to any UIPopoverController that's being presented.

The obvious solution is an instance variable in the same object that creates the UIPopoverController in the first place. The question then is how many such instance variables to use if the app is going to be displaying more than one popover. We could have one instance variable for *each* popover controller. On the other hand, a well-behaved app, in accordance with Apple's interface guidelines, is probably never going to display more than one popover simultaneously, so a *single* UIPopoverController instance variable (we might call it `currentPopover`) should suffice. This one instance variable could be handed a reference to the current popover controller each time we present a popover; using that reference, we would be able later to dismiss the current popover and release its controller.

## Dismissing a Popover

An important feature of a popover's configuration is whether and to what extent the user can operate outside it without automatically dismissing it. There are two aspects to this configuration:

*UIViewController's* `modalInPopover` *property*
> If this is YES for the popover controller's view controller (or for its current view's controller, as in a tab bar interface or navigation interface), the popover is absolutely modal; any tap outside it will be ignored — such a tap won't have any effect at all, not even to dismiss the popover. The default is NO.

*UIPopoverController's* `passThroughViews` *property*
> This matters only if `modalInPopover` is NO. It is an array of views in the interface behind the popover; the user can interact with these views, but a tap anywhere else outside the popover will dismiss it (with no effect on the thing tapped). If `passThroughViews` is nil, a tap *anywhere* outside the popover will dismiss it.

 Setting a UIPopoverController's `passThroughViews` might not have any effect unless the popover is already showing (the UIPopoverController has been sent `presentPopover...`).

A popover can present a modal view internally; specify a `modalPresentationStyle` of `UIModalPresentationCurrentContext` (and a transition style of `UIModalTransitionStyleCoverVertical`), because otherwise the modal view will be fullscreen by default. A modal view's `modalInPopover` is effectively YES; while it is showing, the user can't make anything happen by tapping outside the popover, so you need to provide a way of dismissing the modal view.

If `modalInPopover` is NO, you should pay attention to the `passThroughViews`, as the default behavior may be undesirable. For example, if a popover is summoned by the user tapping a UIBarButton item in a toolbar using `presentPopoverFromBarButtonItem:...`, the entire toolbar is a passthrough view; this means that the user can tap any button in the toolbar, *including the button that summoned the popover*. The user can thus by default summon the popover *again* while it is still showing, which is certainly not what you want. I like to set the `passThroughViews` to nil; at the very least, while the popover is showing, you should probably disable the UIBarButtonItem that summoned the popover.

We can thus now specify the two ways in which a popover can be dismissed:

- The popover controller's view controller's `modalInPopover` is NO, and the user taps outside the popover on a view not listed in the popover controller's `passThroughViews`. The UIPopoverController's delegate (adopting the UIPopoverControllerDelegate protocol) is sent `popoverControllerShouldDismissPopover:`; if it doesn't return NO (which might be because it doesn't implement this method), the popover is dismissed, and the delegate is sent `popoverControllerDidDismissPopover:`.

- The UIPopoverController is sent `dismissPopoverAnimated:` by your code. (The delegate methods are not sent in that case.) Typically this would be because you've included some interface item *inside* the popover that the user can tap to dismiss the popover (like the Done and Cancel buttons in the first popover in Figure 22-1).

Because a popover can be dismissed in two different ways, if you have a cleanup task to perform as the popover vanishes, you may have to see to it that this task is performed under two different circumstances.

To illustrate, I'll describe what happens when the first popover in Figure 22-1 is dismissed. Within this popover, the user is interacting with several settings in the user defaults. But if the user cancels, or if the user taps outside the popover (which I take to be equivalent to canceling), I want to revert those defaults to the way they were before the popover was summoned. So, as I initially present the popover, I preserve the relevant current user defaults as an ivar:

```
// save defaults so we can restore them later if user cancels
self.oldDefs = [[NSUserDefaults standardUserDefaults] dictionaryWithValuesForKeys:
                [NSArray arrayWithObjects:@"Style", @"Size", @"Stages", nil]];
```

Now, if the user taps Save, the user's settings within the popover have *already* been saved (in the user defaults), so I explicitly dismiss the popover and proceed to initiate the new game that the user has asked for. On the other hand, if the user taps Cancel, I must revert the user defaults as I dismiss the popover:

```
- (void) cancelNewGame: (id) sender { // cancel button in New Game popover
    [self.currentPopover dismissPopoverAnimated:YES];
    self.currentPopover = nil;
    [[NSUserDefaults standardUserDefaults]
        setValuesForKeysWithDictionary:self.oldDefs];
}
```

But I must also do the same thing if the user taps outside the popover. Therefore I implement the delegate method and revert the user defaults there as well:

```
- (void)popoverControllerDidDismissPopover:(UIPopoverController *)pc {
    [[NSUserDefaults standardUserDefaults]
        setValuesForKeysWithDictionary:self.oldDefs];
```

```
        self.currentPopover = nil;
    }
```

Notice also the use of the `currentPopover` instance variable that I talked about in the previous section. If the only way the popover could be dismissed was that the user tapped outside it, I wouldn't need this instance variable; the popover has already been dismissed, and the delegate method provides a reference to the popover controller, so I can send `release` to that reference to complete the popover controller's memory management. But the UIButtonItem action handler `cancelNewGame:` gives me no reference to the popover controller. Therefore, I have to store a reference to it myself, when I present the popover initially, both so that I can dismiss the popover and so that I can release the popover controller. Here, the `currentPopover` instance variable has a retain policy, and I released the UIPopoverController once after assigning it to the ivar initially, so nilifying the ivar now releases the UIPopoverController again and completes its memory management.

There is a problem with the foregoing implementation, however. My app, you may remember, has *another* popover (the second popover in Figure 22-1). This popover, too, can be dismissed by the user tapping outside it; in fact, that's the only way the user can dismiss it. This means that `popoverControllerDidDismissPopover:` will be called. But now we don't want to call `setValuesForKeysWithDictionary:`; it's the wrong popover, and we have no preserved defaults to revert. This means that I must test for *which* popover controller is being passed in as the parameter to `popoverControllerDid-DismissPopover:`. But how can I distinguish one popover controller from another? Luckily, my popover controllers have different types of view controller:

```
- (void)popoverControllerDidDismissPopover:(UIPopoverController *)pc {
    if ([pc.contentViewController isKindOfClass: [UINavigationController class]])
        [[NSUserDefaults standardUserDefaults]
            setValuesForKeysWithDictionary:self.oldDefs];
    self.popover = nil;
}
```

If this were not the case — for example, if I had two different popovers each of which had a UINavigationController as its view controller — I'd need some other way of distinguishing them. This is rather a knotty problem, and in the past I've resorted to various desperate measures to resolve it, such as writing a UIPopoverController subclass with a `name` property.

In my view, what all of this shows is that the framework's implementation of popover controllers is deeply flawed. You don't get sufficient help with getting a reference to a UIPopoverController from a view currently being displayed within it, with managing a popover controller's memory, or with distinguishing one popover controller from another. I've shown how you can work around these shortcomings, but in a better world such workarounds wouldn't be necessary. (For example, because only one popover is supposed to be showing at a time, the framework could just maintain a reference to its controller for you.)

# Automatic Popovers

In a few situations, the framework will automatically create and display a popover for you. I am not personally fond of this behavior; the advantages of the automatic behavior (such as the fact that you do not have to provide code to create the popover) are counterbalanced, in my view, by the disadvantages — in particular, you can't get access to the UIPopoverController, so the behavior and appearance of the popover is completely out of your hands.

One such situation is what happens when a search bar (a UISearchBar) tied to a search display controller (UISearchDisplayController) appears in a toolbar (UIToolbar) on the iPad. I'll illustrate by rewriting the search bar code from Chapter 21. In this example, there's a toolbar at the top of the screen, and in the nib editor we drag a search bar and search display controller (a single item in the Object library) into that toolbar. This single move puts a search bar in a bar button item into the toolbar and creates a search display controller at the nib's top level, and configures all connections automatically, as follows:

- The search bar's delegate is the File's Owner.
- The File's Owner's `searchDisplayController` is the search display controller. This is a UIViewController property that I didn't mention in Chapter 21, because its worth is not clear when a UISearchDisplayController is created and configured in code. When a UISearchDisplayController is instantiated from a nib, however, this property is an outlet that retains the search display controller, as well as providing access to it in code.
- The search display controller's search bar is the search bar.
- The search display controller's delegate, `searchContentsController`, `searchResults-DataSource`, and `searchResultsDelegate` is the File's Owner. Of these, only the latter two appear to be of importance in this example.

When our view controller loads its view, we also load the model (the list of states) into an NSArray property called `states`. We also have an NSArray property called `filtered-States`. Here is the example's complete code:

```
- (NSInteger)numberOfSectionsInTableView:(UITableView *)tableView {
    return 1;
}

- (NSInteger)tableView:(UITableView *)tableView
        numberOfRowsInSection:(NSInteger)section {
    return [self.filteredStates count];
}

- (UITableViewCell *)tableView:(UITableView *)tableView
        cellForRowAtIndexPath:(NSIndexPath *)indexPath {
    static NSString *CellIdentifier = @"Cell";
    UITableViewCell *cell =
        [tableView dequeueReusableCellWithIdentifier:CellIdentifier];
```

*Figure 22-2. An automatically created search results popover*

```
    if (cell == nil)
        cell = [[[UITableViewCell alloc] initWithStyle:UITableViewCellStyleDefault
                                    reuseIdentifier:CellIdentifier] autorelease];
    cell.textLabel.text = [self.filteredStates objectAtIndex: indexPath.row];
    return cell;
}

- (void) filterData {
    NSString* target = self.searchDisplayController.searchBar.text;
    NSPredicate* p = [NSPredicate predicateWithBlock:
     ^(id obj, NSDictionary *d) {
        NSString* s = obj;
        NSStringCompareOptions options = NSCaseInsensitiveSearch;
        BOOL b = [s rangeOfString:target options:options].location != NSNotFound;
        return b;
    }];
    self.filteredStates = [states filteredArrayUsingPredicate:p];
}

- (void)searchBar:(UISearchBar *)searchBar textDidChange:(NSString *)searchText {
    [self filterData];
}
```

That's all. There is no creation of a UITableView and no mention of a UIPopoverController. Nevertheless, when the user enters text in the search bar, a popover appears, containing a table of search results (Figure 22-2). However, as I mentioned before, you get no official access to this popover's controller; you can't change the Results title at the top, you can't set its passthrough views, and so on.

Another example of an automatic popover on the iPad is the alert sheet, discussed in Chapter 26.

# Split Views

A split view is implemented through a UISplitViewController (a UIViewController subclass) along with an array of two UIViewControllers whose views are to be displayed in the two regions of the split view. This array is the UISplitViewController's **view-Controllers** property; it can be configured in code or in a nib. A UIViewController contained in a UISplitViewController has a reference to the UISplitViewController through its `splitViewController` property.

There is very little work for you to do with regard to a split view. A split view controller has no further properties or methods beyond those inherited from UIViewController. You can hear about what the split view is doing through its delegate (adopting the UISplitViewControllerDelegate protocol):

`splitViewController:willHideViewController:withBarButtonItem:forPopover-Controller:`
> The split view is rotating to portrait orientation, so it's hiding the first view. The split view creates a UIBarButtonItem and hands it to you as the third parameter. Your mission, should you decide to accept it, is to put that UIBarButtonItem into the interface, typically in a toolbar at the top of the root view. Of course you are also free to configure the UIBarButtonItem's title and image as well.
>
> What you do with the other parameters is up to you, but none of them are needed; the split view has already set things up so that if you do put this UIBarButtonItem into the interface, then if the user taps it, a popover will be presented through the given popover controller (fourth parameter) containing the view of the given view controller (second parameter). It's common practice to keep a reference to the popover controller, in case you need it in order to dismiss the popover later (but don't set its delegate).

`splitViewController:popoverController:willPresentViewController:`
> The user has tapped the UIBarButtonItem you were handed in the first delegate method, and the popover is about to appear. You probably won't need to implement this method.

`splitViewController:willShowViewController:invalidatingBarButtonItem:`
> This is the opposite of the first delegate method: The split view is rotating to landscape orientation, so it's going to break the connection between the UIBarButtonItem and the popover controller and is going to put the first view back into the interface. You should remove the UIBarButtonItem from the interface (the split view will not do that for you).

As an app with a split view interface launches, the `willHide` delegate method is called; if the device is being held in landscape orientation, then if the split view is free to rotate, it immediately rotates to landscape orientation and the `willShow` delegate method is called.

The only even slightly tricky part of all this lies hidden in the words "put that UIBarButtonItem into the interface" and "remove the UIBarButtonItem from the interface." A toolbar (a UIToolbar) has no method for adding or removing a single bar button item; you have to set its entire array of items at once. So, for example, to put a UIBarButtonItem at the left end of a toolbar, you'll set the toolbar's `items` array to an array composed of the UIBarButtonItem and the items from the existing `items` array. You will probably set the toolbar's `items` array by calling `setItems:animated:` in order to get the animation. So:

```
NSArray* arr = [[NSArray arrayWithObject: barButtonItem]
                arrayByAddingObjectsFromArray:self.toolbar.items];
[self.toolbar setItems:arr animated:YES];
```

Removing a UIBarButtonItem from a toolbar is similar.

The Split View–based Application project template is an excellent starting place and demonstrates how little code is required to implement a working split view. The split view controller is configured in the main nib, so that the entire split view and its two subviews spring to life automatically as the app launches, when the split view controller is instantiated from the main nib and its view is embedded in the window. Its first view controller is a UINavigationController whose root view is a UITableViewController that creates its own table view. Its second view controller gets its view from a second nib; that view has a toolbar at the top.

Thus, what the user sees in landscape orientation is: on the left, a master view, which is a table view, with a navigation bar at the top; on the right, a detail view, with a toolbar at the top. The navigation bar in the first view and the toolbar in the second view are effectively indistinguishable — they both have the same default gray gradient color and the same default height — so they look like two pieces of the same interface item.

In portrait orientation, the master view vanishes. The detail view, with its toolbar, now occupies the entire screen. A UIBarButtonItem appears at the toolbar's left end; tapping it summons the master view in a popover.

To implement this, the following code is all that's needed:

- Both the master view and the detail view permit rotation, returning YES from `shouldAutorotateToInterfaceOrientation:`. Otherwise, the split view itself won't permit rotation.

- The controller of the detail view is the delegate of the split view controller (this is configured in the nib), which makes sense, because the detail view holds the toolbar where the UIBarButtonItem is to go. The detail view's controller implements the two delegate methods to add and remove the UIBarButtonItem in the toolbar.

If (as in the template example) the first view is controlled by a UINavigationController, then, as with a popover controller, the split view controller takes charge of the style of its navigation bar. Thus the navigation bar appears gray when the view is in the split view and dark when the view is in the popover. As I said with regard to popovers, this is difficult to prevent and it probably isn't worthwhile trying.

The Split View–based Application project template has a flaw: The toolbar is loaded from the nib. This means that if the second view controller's view is unloaded and loaded again (for example, because of a low-memory situation while a modal view is covering the screen), the toolbar is loaded from the nib *again* — and because the `will-Hide` delegate method is *not* called at this time, the UIBarButtonItem that accesses the popover won't appear. It isn't hard to come up with a workaround, but it's certainly surprising the first time it happens to you.

When you convert a target from iPhone-only to iPad (either as a separate target or as a universal app) as described in Chapter 9, and if your existing project has a root view controller, a new main nib is created using the Split View–based Application template. With, perhaps, some tweaking of this nib, your existing root view controller can become the controller for the first view of the split view, and thus the iPad version of your app can start life as a split view whose first view contains the entire interface and functionality of the iPhone version. Modifying the code and interface to make something appropriate appear in the split controller's second view is then up to you. In the iPhone version of the app, the master view probably navigated to the detail view by pushing the detail view onto the UINavigationController's stack, but in the iPad version, you don't want that — you want the detail version to appear in the split controller's second view. Also, you will very likely have to change the way the detail view gets a reference to the master view: in the iPhone version of the app, you probably assumed that the detail view could ask its own `navigationController` for its root view controller, but in the iPad version the detail view will have to talk to its `splitViewController` instead.

# CHAPTER 23

# Text

Text can be displayed in various ways:

*UILabel*
> Displays text, possibly consisting of multiple lines, in a single font and size, with color (and highlighted color), alignment, and wrapping and truncation. Discussed in this chapter.

*UITextField*
> Displays a single line of editable text, in a single font and size, with color and alignment; may have a border, may have a background image, and overlay views may appear at its right and left end. Discussed in this chapter; a UITextField is a UIControl subclass, so see also Chapter 25.

*UITextView*
> Displays scrollable text, possibly editable, in a single font and size, with color and alignment; can use data detectors to display tappable links. Discussed in this chapter.

*UIWebView*
> A scrollable view displaying rendered HTML. Because HTML can express text attribute spans, this is a good way to show text in multiple fonts, sizes, colors, alignments, and so on, and to include images and tappable links. Can also display various additional document types, such as PDF, RTF, and *.doc*. Discussed in the next chapter.

*Drawing*
> There are three main ways to draw strings directly:

> *Core Graphics*
>> Low-level methods for drawing text (not NSStrings). For drawing in general, see Chapter 15.

*NSString*

> At a high level, the UIStringDrawing category on NSString endows strings with the ability to draw themselves, along with metrics methods (the `sizeWith-Font...` methods) for learning the dimensions at which a given string will be drawn. NSString drawing methods are not complicated, and examples have already appeared in this book without special comment (for example, in Chapter 12 and Chapter 20).

*Core Text*

> The only way in iOS (added in iOS 3.2) to draw strings with multiple fonts and styles. Core Text also provides access to advanced font typographical features. Discussed in this chapter.

Starting in iOS 3.2, an app can include fonts within its bundle; these will be loaded at launch time if the app lists them in its *Info.plist* under the "Fonts provided by application" key (`UIAppFonts`). In this way, your app can use fonts not present by default on the device.

# UILabel

We met UILabel in Chapter 7 and have used it in examples throughout; we surveyed most of its properties in Chapter 21. You assign the label a `text`; you can also set its `font`, `textColor`, and `textAlignment`, and possibly a `shadowColor` and `shadowOffset`. The label's text can also have an alternate `highlightedTextColor`, which will be used when its `highlighted` property is YES (as happens when the label is in a selected cell of a table view).

If a UILabel consists of only one line of text (`numberOfLines` is 1, the default), then you can set `adjustsFontSizeToFitWidth` to YES and provide a `minimumFontSize` if you want the label to shrink the font size smaller than its `font` setting in an attempt to display as much of the `text` as possible. (How the text is repositioned when this happens is determined by the label's `baselineAdjustment` property.) A UILabel may alternatively consist of multiple lines of text (`numberOfLines` is greater than 1), but in that case `adjusts-FontSizeToFitWidth` is ignored; the font size set in `font` is used even if not all of the text will fit.

If `numberOfLines` is 1, any line breaks in the `text` are treated as spaces. Further line breaking (wrapping) and truncation behavior, which applies to both single-line and multiline labels, is determined by its `lineBreakMode`. You can get a feel for this behavior by experimenting in the nib. Your options are:

`UILineBreakModeWordWrap`
> All lines break at word-end. This is the default.

`UILineBreakModeClip`
> Multiple lines break at word-end. The last line can break in the middle of a word.

---

`UILineBreakModeCharacterWrap`
> All lines can break in the middle of a word.

`UILineBreakModeHeadTruncation`
`UILineBreakModeMiddleTruncation`
`UILineBreakModeTailTruncation`
> Multiple lines break at word-end. If the text is too long for the label, the last line displays an ellipsis at the start, middle, or end (respectively).

If `numberOfLines` is larger than the number of lines actually needed, the drawn text is vertically centered in the label. This may be undesirable; you might prefer to shrink (or grow) the label to fit its text (and then perhaps reposition the label). On the face of it, you can't use `sizeToFit` to do this, because the default UILabel response to `sizeToFit` is to make the label the right *width* to contain all its text on a *single* line. However, you can modify that response by overriding UILabel's `textRectForBounds:limitedToNumberOfLines:` in a subclass. Recall the example, in Chapter 21, of using NSString's `sizeWithFont:constrainedToSize:lineBreakMode:` to work out the actual height needed for a given text. Here, we create a UILabel subclass such that the label responds to `sizeToFit` by making itself the right *height* to contain all of its text on *multiple* lines, without changing its width:

```
- (CGRect)textRectForBounds:(CGRect)bounds
    limitedToNumberOfLines:(NSInteger)numberOfLines {
  CGSize sz = [self.text sizeWithFont:self.font
                  constrainedToSize:CGSizeMake(self.bounds.size.width, 10000)
                      lineBreakMode:self.lineBreakMode];
  return (CGRect){bounds.origin, sz};
}
```

In that example, 10,000 is just an arbitrarily big number, which we assume the label's real height would never reach. Of course, the lines of the label won't all be displayed unless its `numberOfLines` is also sufficiently large.

The other UILabel method that you can override in a subclass is `drawTextInRect:`. This is the equivalent of `drawRect:` — that is, it's your chance to modify the overall drawing of the label. An example appears in Chapter 10.

# UITextField

A text field has many of the same properties as a label, but a text field can't contain multiple lines. So it has a `text`, `font`, `textColor`, and `textAlignment`. It also has `adjustsFontSizeToFitWidth` and `minimumFontSize` properties, although these don't work exactly like a label; a text field won't allow its font size to shrink automatically as small as a label will. If the user enters text that is too long for the width of the field, the text moves (scrolls horizontally) to show the insertion point, but when the field is no longer being edited, text that is too long is displayed with an ellipsis at the end.

A text field also has a `placeholder` property, which is the text that appears faded within the text field when it has no text; the idea is that you can use this to suggest to the user what the text field is for. If its `clearsOnBeginEditing` property is YES, the text field automatically deletes its existing text when the user begins editing within it.

A text field's border drawing is determined by its `borderStyle` property. Your options are:

`UITextBorderStyleNone`
> No border.

`UITextBorderStyleLine`
> A plain rectangle.

`UITextBorderStyleBezel`
> A slightly bezeled rectangle: the top and left sides have a very slight, thin shadow.

`UITextBorderStyleRoundedRect`
> A rounded rectangle; the top and left sides have a stronger shadow, so that the text appears markedly recessed behind the border.

A text field can have a background color (because it is a UIView) or a background image (`background`), possibly along with a second image (`disabledBackground`) to be displayed when the text field's `enabled` property (inherited from UIControl) is NO. The user can't interact with a disabled text field, but without a `disabledBackground` image, the user may not have any visual clue to this fact.

The text background of a `UITextBorderStyleRoundedRect` text field is always white; its background image is ignored. But its background color is visible at its corners, outside the rounded border, and therefore, to look good, should match what's behind the text field or should be `clearColor`.

A text field may contain as many as two ancillary overlay views (such as a magnifying glass icon to suggest that the field initiates a search), its `leftView` and `rightView`, and a Clear button (a gray circle with a white "x"). The automatic visibility of each of these is determined by the `leftViewMode`, `rightViewMode`, and `clearViewMode`, respectively. The view mode values are:

`UITextFieldViewModeNever`
> The view never appears.

`UITextFieldViewModeWhileEditing`
> A Clear button appears if there is text in the field and the user is editing. A left or right view appears if there is *no* text in the field and the user is editing.

`UITextFieldViewModeUnlessEditing`
> A Clear button appears if there is text in the field and the user is not editing. A left or right view appears if the user is not editing, or if the user is editing but there is no text in the field.

UITextFieldViewModeAlways

A left or right view always appears; a Clear button appears if there is text in the field.

Depending on what sort of view you use, your `leftView` and `rightView` may have to be sized manually so as not to overwhelm the text view contents. A right view and a Clear button can conflict, trying to appear at the same time (for example, if they both have `UITextFieldViewModeAlways` and there is text in the field); in this case, the right view may cover the Clear button unless you reposition it. The positions and sizes of *any* of the components of the text field can be set in relation to the text field's bounds by overriding the appropriate method in a subclass:

- `clearButtonRectForBounds:`
- `leftViewRectForBounds:`
- `rightViewRectForBounds:`
- `borderRectForBounds:`
- `textRectForBounds:`
- `placeholderRectForBounds:`
- `editingRectForBounds:`

 These methods should all be called with a parameter that is the bounds of the text field, but some of them are called a second time with a 100×100 bounds. This feels like a bug.

You can also override the following:

`drawTextInRect:`
Called when the text has changed and the user is not editing or ends editing. You should either draw the text or call **super** to draw it; if you do neither, the text will become blank. Observe that you get no method to customize the drawing of the text while it is being edited.

`drawPlaceholderInRect:`
Called when the placeholder text is about to appear. You should either draw the placeholder text or call **super** to draw it; if you do neither, the placeholder will become blank.

Both these methods are called with a parameter whose size is the dimensions of the text field's text area, but whose origin is (0,0). In effect what you've got is a graphics context for just the text area; any drawing you do outside the given rectangle will be clipped.

## Editing and the Keyboard

Recall from Chapter 11 the UIResponder-related notion of the *first responder*. A text field's editing status, as well as the presence or absence of the onscreen simulated keyboard, is intimately tied to this notion:

- When a text field is first responder, it is being edited and the keyboard is present.
- When a text field is no longer first responder, it is no longer being edited, and if no other text field (or text view) becomes first responder, the keyboard is not present. If the keyboard is present because one text field is first responder, and another text field becomes first responder (for example, because the user taps in it), the keyboard is not dismissed and brought back; it just remains onscreen.

You can programmatically control a text field's editing status, as well as the presence or absence of the keyboard, by way of the text field's first responder status. To make the insertion point appear within a text field and to cause the keyboard to appear, you send `becomeFirstResponder` to that text field; to make a text field stop being edited and to cause the keyboard to disappear, you send `resignFirstResponder` to that text field. Actually, `resignFirstResponder` returns a BOOL, because a responder might return NO to indicate that for some reason it refuses to obey this command. Note also the UIView `endEditing:` method, which can be sent to the first responder or any superview to make (optionally, to force) the first responder to resign first responder status.

In a view presented modally in the `UIModalPresentationFormSheet` style on the iPad (Chapter 19), sending `resignFirstResponder` to the first responder does *not* make the keyboard disappear. Instead, the keyboard disappears when the modal view is dismissed (assuming that some text field in the parent view does not then become first responder). This is apparently because a form sheet is intended primarily for text input, so the keyboard is felt as accompanying the form as a whole, not individual text fields. Starting in iOS 4.3, you get more control over this behavior; your UIViewController subclass can override `disablesAutomaticKeyboardDismissal`.

 There is no simple way to learn what view is first responder! This is very odd, because a window surely knows what its first responder is — but it won't tell you. There's a method `isFirstResponder`, but you'd have to send it to every view in a window until you find the first responder. One workaround is to store a reference to the first responder yourself, typically in your implementation of the text field delegate's `textFieldDid-BeginEditing:`. *Do not name this reference* `firstResponder`! This name is apparently already in use by Cocoa, and a name collision can cause your app to misbehave.

What you're probably hoping is that a text field will just work with the keyboard: the user taps in the text field, the keyboard appears, the user enters text, the user dismisses the keyboard. Unfortunately, this is not quite the case. There are two main issues to be resolved before a text field becomes usable with the keyboard:

- The keyboard may cover the text field, or may cover some other part of the interface that you'd like the user to be able to see or tap in. (Some scrolling views, such as a table view, may try to help out here by scrolling automatically.)
- The key within the keyboard that should dismiss the keyboard (such as Return) does not automatically do so. (On the iPad this may not be a problem, as the keyboard typically contains a separate button that dismisses the keyboard.)

Let's start by talking about the problem of the keyboard covering the text field. There are four keyboard-related notifications for which you can register:

- `UIKeyboardWillShowNotification`
- `UIKeyboardDidShowNotification`
- `UIKeyboardWillHideNotification`
- `UIKeyboardDidHideNotification`

The `userInfo` dictionary contains information about the keyboard describing what it will do or has done, under these keys:

- `UIKeyboardFrameBeginUserInfoKey`
- `UIKeyboardFrameEndUserInfoKey`
- `UIKeyboardAnimationDurationUserInfoKey`
- `UIKeyboardAnimationCurveUserInfoKey`

Thus you can coordinate your actions with those of the keyboard. In particular, you can respond to the keyboard appearing by adjusting the interface so that the text field is visible.

One simple way to achieve this is to start with your interface embedded in a scroll view. The user need not be aware of the scroll view, and the scroll view need not be scrollable by the user; its purpose is then merely so that *you* can scroll the interface. (You might object that in that case the scroll view is unnecessary, because we can effectively scroll the interface by setting our containing view's bounds origin. This is true, but using a scroll view provides more flexibility, and in any case I'll need the scroll view as I develop the example.)

Let's assume, then, that the whole interface is in a scroll view. As our view controller's view loads, we configure the scroll view's content size, and register for two of the keyboard notifications:

```
- (void)viewDidLoad {
    [super viewDidLoad];
    CGSize sz = self.scrollView.bounds.size;
    sz.height *= 2;
    self.scrollView.contentSize = sz;
    self.scrollView.scrollEnabled = NO;
    [[NSNotificationCenter defaultCenter] addObserver:self
                            selector:@selector(keyboardShow:)
                                name:UIKeyboardWillShowNotification
```

```
                                                object:nil];
    [[NSNotificationCenter defaultCenter] addObserver:self
                                    selector:@selector(keyboardHide:)
                                        name:UIKeyboardWillHideNotification
                                      object:nil];
}
```

Fortunately, the text field delegate's `textFieldDidBeginEditing:` arrives before the `UIKeyboardWillShowNotification`; we can use the former to keep track of what view is first responder, and use the latter to adjust the interface. As the keyboard appears, we store the old content offset in an instance variable and scroll to keep the text field visible. Observe that the keyboard's frame comes to us in window coordinates, so it is necessary to convert it to our scroll view's coordinates in order to make sense of it:

```
- (void)textFieldDidBeginEditing:(UITextField *)tf {
    self.fr = tf; // keep track of first responder
}

- (void) keyboardShow: (NSNotification*) n {
    self->oldOffset = self.scrollView.contentOffset;
    NSDictionary* d = [n userInfo];
    CGRect r = [[d objectForKey:UIKeyboardFrameEndUserInfoKey] CGRectValue];
    r = [self.scrollView convertRect:r fromView:nil];
    CGRect f = self.fr.frame;
    CGFloat y =
        CGRectGetMaxY(f) + r.size.height - self.scrollView.bounds.size.height + 5;
    if (r.origin.y < CGRectGetMaxY(f))
        [self.scrollView setContentOffset:CGPointMake(0, y) animated:YES];
}
```

The heart of that code is, of course, the determination of the value y, the vertical value to which we're going to scroll the scroll view. I've elected to scroll just enough to keep the entire text field above the keyboard, with a space of five pixels between them. The decision involves both aesthetics and functionality; a completely different decision could be equally valid. For example, if my interface contains exactly three text fields, it might make sense to scroll in such a way as to make them all visible, so that the user can work in any of them without dismissing the keyboard.

We now come to the problem of dismissing the keyboard. One solution is to implement another text field delegate method, `textFieldShouldReturn:`. When the user taps the Return key in the keyboard, we hear about it through this method, and we tell the text field to resign its first responder status; this dismisses the keyboard as well, and we respond by scrolling back to our previous position:

```
- (BOOL)textFieldShouldReturn: (UITextField*) tf {
    [tf resignFirstResponder];
    return YES;
}

- (void) keyboardHide: (NSNotification*) n {
    [self.scrollView setContentOffset:self->oldOffset animated:YES];
}
```

Let's now extend the example to cover the situation where the interface is a scroll view that the user *can* normally scroll. In that case, we shouldn't change the scroll view's content size. Instead, we should change the behavior of the scroll view so that it operates coherently within the reduced space left by the keyboard. This is a job for content-Inset, whose purpose, you will recall (Chapter 20), is precisely to make it possible for the user to view all of the scroll view's content even though part of the scroll view is being covered by something.

So, in `viewDidLoad`, we still register for keyboard notifications, but we won't touch the scroll view. When the keyboard appears, we store not only the current content offset but the current content inset and scroll indicator inset as well; then we alter them:

```
- (void) keyboardShow: (NSNotification*) n {
    self->oldContentInset = self.scrollView.contentInset;
    self->oldIndicatorInset = self.scrollView.scrollIndicatorInsets;
    self->oldOffset = self.scrollView.contentOffset;
    NSDictionary* d = [n userInfo];
    CGRect r = [[d objectForKey:UIKeyboardFrameEndUserInfoKey] CGRectValue];
    r = [self.scrollView convertRect:r fromView:nil];
    CGRect f = self.fr.frame;
    CGFloat y =
        CGRectGetMaxY(f) + r.size.height - self.scrollView.bounds.size.height + 5;
    if (r.origin.y < CGRectGetMaxY(f))
        [self.scrollView setContentOffset:CGPointMake(0, y) animated:YES];
    UIEdgeInsets insets;
    insets = self.scrollView.contentInset;
    insets.bottom = r.size.height;
    self.scrollView.contentInset = insets;
    insets = self.scrollView.scrollIndicatorInsets;
    insets.bottom = r.size.height;
    self.scrollView.scrollIndicatorInsets = insets;
}
```

When the keyboard disappears, we restore not only the content offset but the insets as well. I find that, because of the animation, this works best if the insets are restored using delayed performance:

```
- (void) keyboardHide: (NSNotification*) n {
    [self.scrollView setContentOffset:self->oldOffset animated:YES];
    [self performSelector:@selector(restoreInsets) withObject:nil afterDelay:0.4];
}

- (void) restoreInsets {
    self.scrollView.scrollIndicatorInsets = self->oldIndicatorInset;
    self.scrollView.contentInset = self->oldContentInset;
}
```

This second approach works equally well even if the scroll view was not originally user-scrollable (because its content size is the same as its bounds size); the interface becomes user-scrollable only when the keyboard is present, allowing the user to see any part of it. A nice byproduct is that when the keyboard is present, the scroll view scrolls automatically if the user enters characters into a text field that has been scrolled out of sight or taps in a text field that's partially hidden.

## Configuring the Keyboard

A UITextField implements the UITextInputTraits protocol, which defines properties on the UITextField that you can set to determine how the keyboard will look and how typing in the text field will behave. (These properties can also be set in the nib.) For example, you can set the keyboardType to UIKeyboardTypePhonePad to make the keyboard for this text field consist of digits only. You can set the returnKeyType to determine the text of the Return key (if the keyboard is of a type that has one). You can turn off autocapitalization (autocapitalizationType) or autocorrection (autocorrectionType), make the Return key disable itself if the text field has no content (enablesReturnKey-Automatically), and make the text field a password field (secureTextEntry).

 The user's choices in the Settings app with regard to certain text input features, such as autocapitalization or autocorrection, take priority over your configuration of these same features for a particular text field.

In addition, you can attach an accessory view to the top of the keyboard by setting the text field's inputAccessoryView (see Apple's KeyboardAccessory example), and you can even supply your own keyboard by setting the text field's inputView.

The user can control the localization of the keyboard character set in the Settings app, either through a choice of the system's base language or by enabling additional "international keyboards." In the latter case, the user can switch among keyboard character sets while the keyboard is showing. But, as far as I can tell, your code can't make this choice, so you can't, for example, have a Russian-teaching app in which a certain text field automatically shows the Cyrillic keyboard. You can ask the user to switch keyboards manually, but if you really want a particular keyboard to appear regardless of the user's settings and behavior, you'll have to create it yourself and provide it as the inputView.

## Text Field Delegate and Control Event Messages

As editing begins and proceeds in a text field, a sequence of messages is sent to the text field's delegate (some of which are also available to other objects as notifications). Using these, you can customize the text field's behavior during editing:

textFieldShouldBeginEditing:
    Return NO to prevent the text field from becoming first responder.

textFieldDidBeginEditing: *(and* UITextFieldTextDidBeginEditingNotification*)*
    The text field has become first responder.

`textFieldShouldClear:`

Return NO to prevent the operation of the Clear button or of automatic clearing on entry (`clearsOnBeginEditing`).

`textFieldShouldReturn:`

The user has tapped the Return button in the keyboard. We have already seen that this can be used as way of dismissing the keyboard.

`textField:shouldChangeCharactersInRange:replacementString:`

Sent when the user changes the text in the field by typing or pasting, or by backspacing or cutting (in which case the replacement string's length will be 0). Return NO to prevent the proposed change. It is common practice to implement this delegate method as a way of learning that the text has been changed, even if you then always return YES. The `UITextFieldTextDidChangeNotification` corresponds loosely.

`textFieldShouldEndEditing:`

Return NO to prevent the text field from resigning first responder (even if you just sent `resignFirstResponder` to it). You might do this, for example, because the text is invalid or unacceptable in some way. The user will not know why the text field is refusing to end editing, so the usual thing is to put up an alert explaining the problem.

`textFieldDidEndEditing:` *(and* `UITextFieldTextDidEndEditingNotification`*)*

The text field has resigned first responder. See Chapter 21 for an example of using `textFieldDidEndEditing:` to fetch the text field's current text and store it in the model.

A text field is also a control. This means you can attach a target–action pair to any of the events that it reports in order to receive a message when that event occurs (see Chapter 11):

- The user can touch and drag, triggering Touch Down and the various Touch Drag events.
- If the user touches in such a way that the text field enters editing mode, Editing Did Begin and Touch Cancel are triggered; if the user causes the text field to enter editing mode in some other way (such as by tabbing into it), Editing Did Begin is triggered without any Touch events.
- As the user edits, Editing Changed is triggered. If the user taps while in editing mode, Touch Down (and possibly Touch Down Repeat) and Touch Cancel are triggered.
- Finally, when editing ends, Editing Did End is triggered; if the user stops editing by tapping Return in the keyboard, Did End on Exit is triggered first.

In general, you're more likely to treat a text field as a text field (through its delegate messages) than as a control (through its control events). However, the Did End on Exit event message has an interesting property: it provides an alternative way to dismiss the keyboard when the user taps a text field keyboard's Return button. If there is a Did End on Exit target–action pair for this text field, then if the text field's delegate does not return NO from `textFieldShouldReturn:`, the keyboard will be dismissed *automatically* when the user taps the Return key. (The action handler for Did End on Exit doesn't actually have to *do* anything.)

This suggests the following trick for getting automatic keyboard dismissal *with no code at all*. In the nib, edit the First Responder proxy object in the Attributes inspector, adding a new First Responder Action; let's call it `dummy:`. Now hook the Did End on Exit event of the text field to the `dummy:` action of the First Responder proxy object. That's it! Because the text field's Did End on Exit event now has a target–action pair, the text field automatically dismisses its keyboard when the user taps Return; because there is no penalty for not finding a handler for a message sent up the responder chain, the app doesn't crash even though there is no implementation of `dummy:` anywhere.

Of course, you can implement that trick in code instead:

```
[textField addTarget:nil action:@selector(dummy:)
    forControlEvents:UIControlEventEditingDidEndOnExit];
```

A disabled text field emits no delegate messages or control events.

## The Text Field Menu

When the user double-taps or long-presses in a text field, the menu appears. It contains menu items such as Select, Select All, Paste, Copy, Cut, and Replace; which menu items appear depends on the circumstances.

The menu can be customized, but you are unlikely to do this with respect to a text field, because you don't get any access to information about the text field's selection, making it difficult to decide intelligently what menu items should appear or what they should do when chosen. Thus, for the most part, it is best not to alter a text field's menu or to interfere with its behavior.

If you do want to alter the menu, the key facts you need to know are these:

- You can add menu items to the menu through the singleton global UIMenuController object. Its `menuItems` property is an array of *custom* menu items — that is, menu items that may appear *in addition* to those that the system puts there. A menu item is a UIMenuItem, which is simply a title (which appears in the menu) plus an action selector. The action will be called, nil-targeted, thus sending it up the responder chain, when the user taps the menu item (and, by default, the menu will be dismissed).

- The actions for the standard menu items are nil-targeted, so they percolate up the responder chain, and you can interfere with their behavior by implementing their actions. Their selectors are listed in the UIResponderStandardEditActions informal protocol (except for Replace, which is implemented through an undocumented selector `promptForReplace:`).

- You govern the presence or absence of *any* menu item by implementing the UIResponder method `canPerformAction:withSender:` in the responder chain.

As an example, we'll devise a text field in which the standard menu is completely replaced by our own menu, which contains a single menu item, Expand. I'm imagining here, for instance, a text field where the user can type a U.S. state two-letter abbreviation (such as "CA") and then summon the menu and tap Expand to get the state's full name (such as "California"). We'll implement this by means of a UITextField subclass.

At some point before the user can tap in an instance of our UITextField subclass, we modify the global menu; we could do this in the app delegate as the app starts up, for example:

```
UIMenuItem *mi = [[UIMenuItem alloc] initWithTitle:@"Expand"
                                        action:@selector(expand:)];
UIMenuController *mc = [UIMenuController sharedMenuController];
mc.menuItems = [NSArray arrayWithObject:mi];
[mi release];
```

In our UITextField subclass, we implement `canPerformAction:withSender:` to govern the contents of the menu. The placement of this implementation is crucial. By putting it here, we guarantee that this implementation will be called when an instance of this subclass is first responder, but at no other time. Therefore, every other text field (or any other object that displays a menu) will behave normally, displaying Cut or Select All or whatever's appropriate; only an instance of our subclass will have the special menu, displaying only Expand.

```
- (BOOL) canPerformAction:(SEL)action withSender: (id) sender {
    if (action == @selector(expand:))
        return ([self.text length] == 2); // could be more intelligent here
    return NO;
}
```

When the user chooses the Expand menu item, the `expand:` message is sent up the responder chain. We catch it in our UITextField subclass and obey it. Actually matching up abbreviations with state names is left as an exercise for the reader:

```
- (void) expand: (id) sender {
    NSString* s = self.text;
    // ... alter s here ...
    self.text = s;
}
```

By setting the `text` property at the end of the `expand:` method, we cause the selection handles to vanish if there are any.

To demonstrate interference with the standard menu items, we'll modify the example to allow the Copy menu item to appear if it wants to:

```
- (BOOL) canPerformAction:(SEL)action withSender:(id)sender {
    if (action == @selector(expand:))
        return ([self.text length] == 2);
    if (action == @selector(copy:))
        return [super canPerformAction:action withSender:sender];
    return NO;
}
```

Now we'll implement copy: and modify its behavior. First we call super to get standard copying behavior; then we modify what's now on the pasteboard:

```
- (void) copy: (id) sender {
    [super copy: sender];
    UIPasteboard* pb = [UIPasteboard generalPasteboard];
    NSString* s = pb.string;
    // ... alter s here ....
    pb.string = s;
}
```

# UITextView

A text view (UITextView) is sort of a scrollable, multiline version of a text field (UI-TextField, with which it should not be confused). It is a scroll view subclass (UIScroll-View, Chapter 20), and thus has (by default) no border; it is *not* a control. It has text, font, textColor, and textAlignment properties; it can be editable or not, according to its editable property. (You might use a scrollable noneditable text view instead of a UILabel, so as not to be limited to a fixed number of lines of text.) An editable text view governs its keyboard just as a text field does: when it is first responder, it is being edited and shows the keyboard, and it implements the UITextInput protocol and has input-View and inputAccessoryView properties. Its menu works the same way as a text field's.

One big difference, from the programmer's point of view, between a text view and a text field is that a text view gives you information about, and control of, its selection: it has a selectedRange property which you can get and set, and it adds a scrollRangeTo-Visible: method so that you can scroll in terms of a range of its text. The selected-Range is useful especially if the text view is first responder, because the selection is then meaningful and visible, but it does work (invisibly) even if the text view is not first responder. (You could take advantage of the selectedRange, for example, to customize a text view's menu with more intelligence than in our text field example in the previous section.)

A text view also has a dataDetectorTypes property that, if the text view is not editable, allows text of certain types (presumably located using NSDataDetector, an NSRegu-larExpression subclass) to be rendered as tappable links.

A text view's delegate messages (UITextViewDelegate protocol) and notifications are quite parallel to those of a text field. The big differences are:

- There's a `textViewDidChange:` delegate message (and an accompanying `UITextView-TextDidChangeNotification`), whereas a text field has its Editing Changed control event (and notification).

- There's a `textViewDidChangeSelection:` delegate message, whereas a text field is uninformative about the selection.

A text view's `contentSize` is maintained for you, automatically, as the text changes. You can track changes to the content size (in `textViewDidChange:`, for example), but you probably shouldn't try to change it. A common use of content size tracking is to implement a *self-sizing* text view, that is, a text view that adjusts its size automatically to embrace the amount of text it contains:

```
- (void) adjust {
    CGSize sz = self->tv.contentSize;
    CGRect f = self->tv.frame;
    f.size = sz;
    self->tv.frame = f;
}

- (void)textViewDidChange:(UITextView *)textView {
    [self adjust];
}
```

A self-sizing text view works best if the text view is not user-scrollable (`scrollEnabled` is NO). If it *is* user-scrollable, it might scroll itself as the user enters text, and you might then have to struggle to prevent it from doing so:

```
- (void)scrollViewDidScroll:(UIScrollView *)scrollView {
    scrollView.contentOffset = CGPointZero;
}
```

Dismissing the keyboard for a text view works differently than for a text field. Because a text view is multiline, the Return key is meaningful for character entry; you aren't likely to want to misuse it as a way of dismissing the keyboard, and you don't get a special delegate message for it. On the iPad, the virtual keyboard may contain a button that dismisses the keyboard. On the iPhone, the interface might well consist of a text view and the keyboard, so that instead of dismissing the keyboard, the user dismisses the entire interface; for example, in the Mail app on the iPhone, when the user is composing a message, the keyboard is present the whole time. On the other hand, in the Notes app, a note alternates between being read fullscreen and being edited with the keyboard present; in the latter case, a Done button is provided to dismiss the keyboard. If there's no good place to put a Done button in the interface, you could attach an accessory view to the keyboard itself.

The problem of having part of a text view be covered by the virtual keyboard can't be solved by meddling with its `contentInset`, because for some undocumented reason a text view doesn't accept changes to the `bottom` of its `contentInset` — the value is always reset to 32. The solution is therefore to shrink the text view itself.

In this example, we imagine a simple interface containing a single text view (**tv**) and no text fields; thus, if the keyboard shows, it must be because our text view is being edited. As our view controller loads its view, we register for keyboard notifications UIKeyboardWillShowNotification and UIKeyboardWillHideNotification as we did in our text field example. When the keyboard appears, we store the text view's frame and shrink the text view; when the keyboard hides, we restore the text view's frame:

```
- (void) keyboardShow: (NSNotification*) n {
    NSDictionary* d = [n userInfo];
    CGRect r = [[d objectForKey:UIKeyboardFrameEndUserInfoKey] CGRectValue];
    r = [self.view convertRect:r fromView:nil];
    CGRect f = self.tv.frame;
    self->oldFrame = f;
    f.size.height = self.view.frame.size.height - f.origin.y - r.size.height;
    self.tv.frame = f;
}

- (void) keyboardHide: (NSNotification*) n {
    self.tv.frame = self->oldFrame;
}
```

This approach works, but the scroll view's change of frame lacks animation to match that of the keyboard. We can easily fix that, because the notification's userInfo dictionary describes that animation in detail:

```
- (void) keyboardShow: (NSNotification*) n {
    NSDictionary* d = [n userInfo];
    CGRect r = [[d objectForKey:UIKeyboardFrameEndUserInfoKey] CGRectValue];
    NSNumber* curve = [d objectForKey:UIKeyboardAnimationCurveUserInfoKey];
    NSNumber* duration = [d objectForKey:UIKeyboardAnimationDurationUserInfoKey];
    r = [self.view convertRect:r fromView:nil];
    CGRect f = self.tv.frame;
    self->oldFrame = f;
    f.size.height = self.view.frame.size.height - f.origin.y - r.size.height;
    [UIView beginAnimations:nil context:NULL];
    [UIView setAnimationDuration:[duration floatValue]];
    [UIView setAnimationCurve:[curve intValue]];
    self.tv.frame = f;
    [UIView commitAnimations];
}

- (void) keyboardHide: (NSNotification*) n {
    NSDictionary* d = [n userInfo];
    NSNumber* curve = [d objectForKey:UIKeyboardAnimationCurveUserInfoKey];
    NSNumber* duration = [d objectForKey:UIKeyboardAnimationDurationUserInfoKey];
    [UIView beginAnimations:nil context:NULL];
    [UIView setAnimationDuration:[duration floatValue]];
    [UIView setAnimationCurve:[curve intValue]];
    self.tv.frame = self->oldFrame;
    [UIView commitAnimations];
}
```

Apple's own apps display some interesting uses of text views. How, for instance, is the Notes app interface actually achieved? Its key features are: the text appears to be on lined paper; the first line of the text has some space above it, where the date appears; and the text has a wide left margin.

The text is presumably a text view; it must have a background color of clearColor to allow the paper to show through. My guess is that the space at the start of the text is achieved with the text view's contentInset, whose top value, at least, is obeyed; the wide left margin, on the other hand, suggests that the left edge of the text view is inset from the left edge of the "paper." The paper itself might be an image view; by tracking the text view's contentSize (in textViewDidChange:, for example), the app can make sure that the paper image is always sufficiently tall, and by tracking the scroll position (in scrollViewDidScroll), the image view's transform can be adjusted to keep the lines of text coordinated with the lines of the paper:

```
- (void)scrollViewDidScroll:(UIScrollView *)scrollView {
    CGFloat yoff = scrollView.contentOffset.y + scrollView.contentInset.top;
    paperMiddle.transform = CGAffineTransformMakeTranslation(0,-yoff);
}
```

Another interesting interface is the Mail app's screen for composing a message. At the top are fields for addresses and subject; then comes the body of the message, which gets longer as the user types into it. The message body is evidently a text view, but it lacks scroll indicators and cannot itself be scrolled; what scrolls is the interface as a whole. So this must be a self-sizing text view; presumably the text view's contentSize is tracked, and both the text view's size and the enclosing scroll view are adjusted accordingly. (But the Mail app's screen for *replying* to a message uses styled text, so it is presumably drawn with Core Text, discussed in the next section.)

# Core Text

Core Text allows strings to be drawn with multiple fonts and styles. It is implemented by the Core Text framework; to utilize it, your app must link to *CoreText.framework*, and your code must import <CoreText/CoreText.h>. It uses C, not Objective-C, and it's rather verbose, but getting started with it is not difficult.

A typical simple Core Text drawing operation begins with an *attributed string*. This is an NSAttributedString (or CFAttributedString; they are toll-free bridged), which is a string accompanied by attributes (such as font, size, and style) applied over ranges. Each attribute is described as a name–value pair. The names of the attributes are listed in Apple's *Core Text String Attributes Reference*, along with their value types. The most commonly used attribute is probably kCTFontAttributeName, which determines the font and size of a stretch of text; its value is a CTFontRef, a Core Text type which is *not* bridged to UIFont. You'll typically supply attributes as a dictionary of name–value pairs.

For example, imagine that we have a UIView subclass called StyledText, which has a text property that is an attributed string. Its job will be to draw that attributed string into itself:

```
@interface StyledText : UIView {
}
@property (nonatomic, copy) NSAttributedString* text;
@end
```

Imagine further that an instance of StyledText appears in the interface and that we have a reference to it as an instance variable called **styler**. How, then, might we create an NSAttributedString and assign it to **styler.text**? Let's start with a mutable attributed string:

```
NSString* s = @"Yo ho ho and a bottle of rum!";
NSMutableAttributedString* mas =
    [[NSMutableAttributedString alloc] initWithString:s];
```

Now I'll apply some attributes. I'll cycle through the words of the string; to each word I'll apply a slightly larger size of the same font. My base font will be Baskerville 18. Note that the name supplied when creating a CTFont must be a PostScript name; a free app, Typefaces, is helpful for learning all the fonts on a device along with their PostScript names:

```
__block CGFloat f = 18.0;
CTFontRef basefont = CTFontCreateWithName(@"Baskerville", f, NULL);
[s enumerateSubstringsInRange:NSMakeRange(0, [s length])
                      options:NSStringEnumerationByWords
                   usingBlock:
 ^(NSString *substring, NSRange substringRange, NSRange encRange, BOOL *stop) {
     f += 3.5;
     CTFontRef font2 = CTFontCreateCopyWithAttributes(basefont, f, NULL, NULL);
     NSDictionary* d2 = [[NSDictionary alloc] initWithObjectsAndKeys:
         (id)font2, (NSString*)kCTFontAttributeName, nil];
     [mas addAttributes:d2 range:encRange];
     CFRelease(font2);
     [d2 release];
 }];
```

Finally, I'll make the last word bold. The easiest way to obtain the range of the last word is to cycle through the words backward and stop after the first one. Boldness is a font trait; we must obtain a bold variant of the original font. The font we started with, Baskerville, has such a variant, so this will work:

```
[s enumerateSubstringsInRange:NSMakeRange(0, [s length])
                      options: (NSStringEnumerationByWords |
                                NSStringEnumerationReverse)
                   usingBlock:
 ^(NSString *substring, NSRange substringRange, NSRange encRange, BOOL *stop) {
     CTFontRef font2 = CTFontCreateCopyWithSymbolicTraits (
         basefont, f, NULL, kCTFontBoldTrait, kCTFontBoldTrait);
     NSDictionary* d2 = [[NSDictionary alloc] initWithObjectsAndKeys:
         (id)font2, (NSString*)kCTFontAttributeName, nil];
     [mas addAttributes:d2 range:encRange];
     CFRelease(font2);
     *stop = YES; // do just once, last word
 }];
```

You're probably wondering why I seem to ask for the bold variant (kCTFontBoldTrait) twice. The first time (the fourth argument in the call to CTFontCreateCopyWithSymbolic- Traits) I'm providing a bitmask. The second time (the fifth argument) I'm providing a second bitmask that says which bits of the first bitmask are meaningful. For example, suppose I'm starting with a font that might or might not be italic, and I want to obtain its bold variant — meaning that if it *is* italic, I want a bold italic font. It isn't enough to supply a bitmask whose value is kCTFontBoldTrait, because this appears to switch boldness on and everything else off. Thus, the second bitmask says, "Only this one bit is important; leave all other attributes alone." By the same token, to get a nonbold variant of a font that might be bold, you'd supply 0 as the fourth argument and kCTFont-BoldTrait as the fifth argument.

Finally, I'll hand the attributed string over to our self-drawing interface object and complete our memory management:

```
self.styler.text = mas;
[self.styler setNeedsDisplay];
[mas release];
CFRelease(basefont);
```

We have now generated an NSAttributedString and handed it over to our StyledText. How will the StyledText draw itself? There are two main ways: a CATextLayer and direct drawing with Core Text itself.

Let's start by using a CATextLayer (Chapter 16). Because this UIView subclass will be instantiated from a nib, I'll give it a CATextLayer in awakeFromNib, retaining a reference to it as an instance variable, textLayer. I'll also implement layoutSublayersOfLayer: so that the CATextLayer always has the bounds of the view as a whole:

```
- (void) awakeFromNib {
    CATextLayer* lay = [[CATextLayer alloc] init];
    lay.frame = self.layer.bounds;
    [self.layer addSublayer:lay];
    self.textLayer = lay;
    [lay release];
}

- (void) layoutSublayersOfLayer:(CALayer *)layer {
    [[layer.sublayers objectAtIndex:0] setFrame:layer.bounds];
}
```

Our drawRect: implementation is now trivial; we simply set the CATextLayer's string property to our attributed string:

```
- (void)drawRect:(CGRect)rect {
    if (!self.text)
        return;
    self.textLayer.string = self.text;
```

Sure enough, our attributed string is drawn (Figure 23-1). I've given our UIView a background color to show how the CATextLayer positions the string by default.

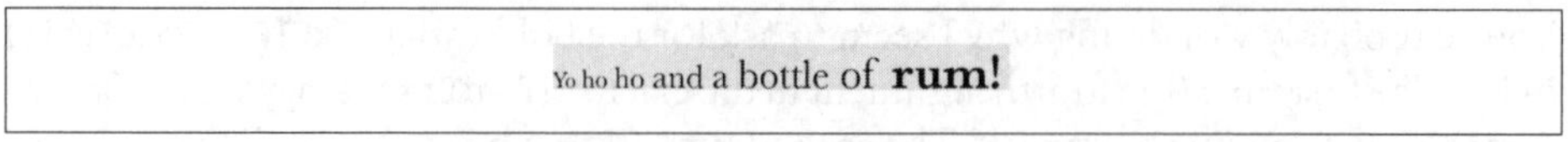

Figure 23-1. Text whose size increases word by word

Figure 23-2. The same text wrapped and centered

CATextLayer has some additional useful properties. If the width of the layer is insufficient to display the entire string, we can get truncation behavior with the `truncationMode` property. If the `wrapped` property is set to YES, the string will wrap. We can also set the alignment with the `alignmentMode` property (Figure 23-2).

The second way to display an attributed string is to draw it directly into a graphics context with Core Text. The text will be drawn upside-down unless we flip the graphics context's coordinate system. If the string is a single line we can draw it directly into a graphics context with a CTLineRef. Positioning the drawing is up to us; the following code results in a drawing that looks just like Figure 23-1:

```
- (void)drawRect:(CGRect)rect {
    if (!self.text)
        return;
    CGContextRef ctx = UIGraphicsGetCurrentContext();
    // flip context
    CGContextSaveGState(ctx);
    CGContextTranslateCTM(ctx, 0, self.bounds.size.height);
    CGContextScaleCTM(ctx, 1.0, -1.0);
    CTLineRef line =
        CTLineCreateWithAttributedString((CFAttributedStringRef)self.text);
    CGContextSetTextPosition(ctx, 1, 3);
    CTLineDraw(line, ctx);
    CFRelease(line);
    CGContextRestoreGState(ctx);
}
```

If we want our string to be drawn wrapped, we must use a CTFramesetter. The framesetter requires a frame into which to draw; this is expressed as a CGPath, but don't get all excited about the possibility of drawing wrapped into some interesting shape, such as an ellipse, because on iOS the path must describe a rectangle:

```
- (void)drawRect:(CGRect)rect {
    if (!self.text)
        return;
    CGContextRef ctx = UIGraphicsGetCurrentContext();
    // flip context
    CGContextSaveGState(ctx);
```

```
        CGContextTranslateCTM(ctx, 0, self.bounds.size.height);
        CGContextScaleCTM(ctx, 1.0, -1.0);
        CTFramesetterRef fs =
            CTFramesetterCreateWithAttributedString((CFAttributedStringRef)self.text);
        CGMutablePathRef path = CGPathCreateMutable();
        CGPathAddRect(path, NULL, rect);
        // range (0,0) means "the whole string"
        CTFrameRef f = CTFramesetterCreateFrame(fs, CFRangeMake(0, 0), path, NULL);
        CTFrameDraw(f, ctx);
        CGPathRelease(path);
        CFRelease(f);
        CFRelease(fs);
        CGContextRestoreGState(ctx);
    }
```

With a CTFramesetter, drawing behaviors such as alignment and truncation can be expressed as part of the original attributed string by applying a CTParagraphStyle. Paragraph styles can also include first-line indent, tab stops, line height, spacing, and more. In this example, we return to the code where we configured our mutable attributed string (mas) and add center alignment (which results in a drawing that looks like Figure 23-2):

```
    CTTextAlignment centerValue = kCTCenterTextAlignment;
    CTParagraphStyleSetting center =
        {kCTParagraphStyleSpecifierAlignment, sizeof(centerValue), &centerValue};
    CTParagraphStyleSetting pss[1] = {center};
    CTParagraphStyleRef ps = CTParagraphStyleCreate(pss, 1);
    [mas addAttribute:(NSString*)kCTParagraphStyleAttributeName
                value:(id)ps
                range:NSMakeRange(0, [s length])];
    CFRelease(ps);
```

Core Text can also access font typographical features that can't be accessed in any other way, such as the ability of Didot and Hoefler Text (present by default on the iPad) to render themselves in small caps. As an example, we'll draw the names of the 50 U.S. states in small caps, centered, in two columns (Figure 23-3).

As we create the NSAttributedString, we use a convenience function, CTFontDescriptor-CreateCopyWithFeature, to access Didot's small caps variant. I had to log the result of CTFontCopyFeatures to learn the "magic numbers" for this variant of this font (there is also old documentation of font features at *http://developer.apple.com/fonts/registry*):

```
    NSString* path = [[NSBundle mainBundle] pathForResource:@"states" ofType:@"txt"];
    NSString* s = [NSString stringWithContentsOfFile:path];
    CTFontRef font = CTFontCreateWithName(@"Didot", 18, NULL);
    CTFontDescriptorRef fontdesc1 = CTFontCopyFontDescriptor(font);
    CTFontDescriptorRef fontdesc2 =
    CTFontDescriptorCreateCopyWithFeature(fontdesc1,
                                (CFNumberRef)[NSNumber numberWithInt:3],
                                (CFNumberRef)[NSNumber numberWithInt:3]);
    CTFontRef basefont = CTFontCreateWithFontDescriptor(fontdesc2, 0, NULL);
    NSDictionary* d = [[NSDictionary alloc] initWithObjectsAndKeys:(id)basefont,
                                (NSString*)kCTFontAttributeName, nil];
    NSMutableAttributedString* mas =
```

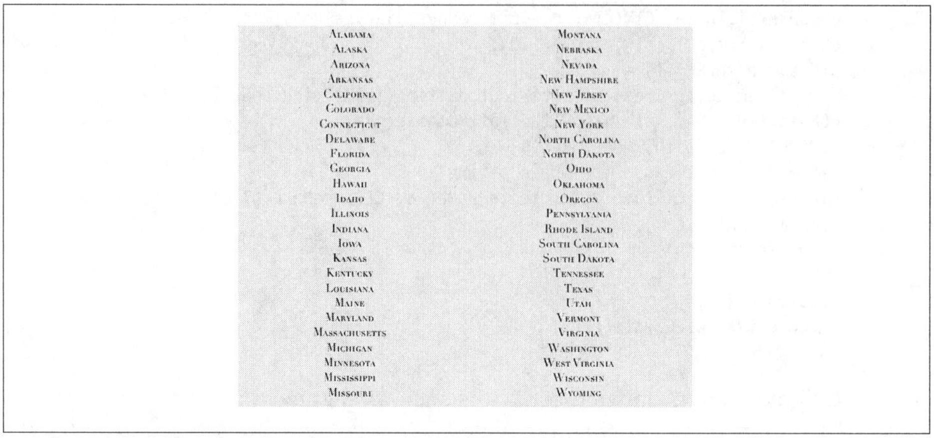

*Figure 23-3. Two-column text in small caps*

```
    [[NSMutableAttributedString alloc] initWithString:s attributes:d];
[d release];
// ...
```

Giving the attributed string a centered text alignment and assigning it to our StyledText object's text is as before, so I've omitted it here.

The two-column arrangement is achieved by drawing into two frames. In our draw-Rect code, we draw the entire text into the first frame and then use CTFrameGetVisible-StringRange to learn how much of the text actually fits into it; this tells us where in the attributed string to start drawing into the second frame:

```
CGRect r1 = rect;
r1.size.width /= 2.0; // column 1
CGRect r2 = r1;
r2.origin.x += r2.size.width; // column 2
CTFramesetterRef fs =
    CTFramesetterCreateWithAttributedString((CFAttributedStringRef)self.text);
// draw column 1
CGMutablePathRef path = CGPathCreateMutable();
CGPathAddRect(path, NULL, r1);
CTFrameRef f = CTFramesetterCreateFrame(fs, CFRangeMake(0, 0), path, NULL);
CTFrameDraw(f, ctx);
CGPathRelease(path);
CFRange drawnRange = CTFrameGetVisibleStringRange(f);
CFRelease(f);
// draw column 2
path = CGPathCreateMutable();
CGPathAddRect(path, NULL, r2);
f = CTFramesetterCreateFrame(fs,
    CFRangeMake(drawnRange.location + drawnRange.length, 0), path, NULL);
CTFrameDraw(f, ctx);
CGPathRelease(path);
CFRelease(f);
CFRelease(fs);
```

*Figure 23-4. The user has tapped on California*

A frame is itself composed of CTLines describing how each line of text was laid out. To demonstrate, let's turn our two-column list of states into an interactive interface: when the user taps the name of a state, we'll fetch that name, and we'll briefly draw a rectangle around the name to provide feedback (Figure 23-4).

We have two NSMutableArray properties, `theLines` and `theBounds`. We initialize them to empty arrays at the start of our `drawRect:`, and each time we call `CTFrameDraw` we also call a utility method:

```
[self appendLinesAndBoundsOfFrame:f context:ctx];
```

In `appendLinesAndBoundsOfFrame:context:` we save the CTLines of the frame into the-Lines; we also calculate the drawn bounds of each line and save it into theBounds:

```
- (void) appendLinesAndBoundsOfFrame:(CTFrameRef)f context:(CGContextRef)ctx{
    CGAffineTransform t1 =
        CGAffineTransformMakeTranslation(0, self.bounds.size.height);
    CGAffineTransform t2 = CGAffineTransformMakeScale(1, -1);
    CGAffineTransform t = CGAffineTransformConcat(t2, t1);
    CGPathRef p = CTFrameGetPath(f);
    CGRect r = CGPathGetBoundingBox(p); // this is the frame bounds
    NSArray* lines = (NSArray*)CTFrameGetLines(f);
    [self.theLines addObjectsFromArray:lines];
    CGPoint origins[[lines count]];
    CTFrameGetLineOrigins(f, CFRangeMake(0,0), origins);
    for (int i = 0; i < [lines count]; i++) {
        CTLineRef aLine = (CTLineRef)[lines objectAtIndex:i];
        CGRect b = CTLineGetImageBounds((CTLineRef)aLine, ctx);
        // the line origin plus the image bounds size is the bounds we want
        CGRect b2 = { origins[i], b.size };
        // but it is expressed in terms of the frame, so we must compensate
        b2.origin.x += r.origin.x;
        b2.origin.y += r.origin.y;
        // we must also compensate for the flippedness of the graphics context
        b2 = CGRectApplyAffineTransform(b2, t);
        [self.theBounds addObject: [NSValue valueWithCGRect:b2]];
    }
}
```

We have attached a UITapGestureRecognizer to our view; when the user taps, we cycle through the saved bounds to see if any of them contains the tap point. If it does, we fetch the name of the state, and we draw a rectangle around it:

```
- (void) tapped: (UITapGestureRecognizer*) tap {
    CGPoint loc = [tap locationInView:self];
    for (int i = 0; i < [self.theBounds count]; i++) {
        CGRect rect = [[self.theBounds objectAtIndex: i] CGRectValue];
        if (CGRectContainsPoint(rect, loc)) {
```

```
// draw rectangle for feedback
CALayer* lay = [CALayer layer];
lay.frame = CGRectInset(rect, -5, -5);
lay.borderWidth = 2;
[self.layer addSublayer: lay];
[lay performSelector:@selector(removeFromSuperlayer)
        withObject:nil afterDelay:0.3];
// fetch the drawn string tapped on
CTLineRef theLine = (CTLineRef)[self.theLines objectAtIndex:i];
CFRange range = CTLineGetStringRange(theLine);
CFStringRef s = CFStringCreateWithSubstring(
                NULL, (CFStringRef)[self.text string], range);
// ... do something with string here ...
CFRelease(s);
break;
        }
    }
}
```

If we needed to, we could even learn what character the user tapped by going down to the level of glyph runs (CTRun) and glyphs (CTGlyph). We have barely scratched the surface of what Core Text can do. Read Apple's *Core Text Programming Guide* for further information.

# CHAPTER 24

# Web Views

A web view (UIWebView) is a versatile renderer of text in various formats, including:

- HTML
- PDF
- RTF, including *.rtfd* (which must be supplied in a zipped format, *.rtfd.zip*)
- Microsoft Word (*.doc*), Excel (*.xls*), and PowerPoint (*.ppt*)
- Pages, Numbers, and Keynote; before iWork 2009, these must be zipped (e.g. *.key.zip*), but starting with iWork 2009 they must *not* be zipped.

In addition to displaying rendered text, a web view is, by default, a web browser. This means that if the user taps, within the web view, on a link that leads to content that the web view can render, the web view by default will automatically fetch that content (possibly over the Internet) and display it. Indeed, a web view is, in effect, a front end for WebKit, the same rendering engine used by Mobile Safari (and, for that matter, by Safari on Mac OS X). A web view can display non-HTML file formats such as PDF, RTF, and so on, precisely because WebKit can display them.

As the user taps links and displays web pages, the web view keeps back-and-forward lists, just like a web browser. Two properties, `canGoBack` and `canGoForward`, and two methods, `goBack` and `goForward`, let you interact with this list. Your interface could thus contain Back and Forward buttons, like a miniature web browser.

UIWebView is not intended for subclassing. A web view is scrollable, but UIWebView is *not* a UIScrollView subclass. A web view is zoomable if its `scalesToFit` property is YES; in that case, it initially scales its content to fit, and the user can zoom the content (this includes use of the gesture, familiar from Mobile Safari, whereby double-tapping part of a web page zooms to that region of the page). Like a text view, its `dataDetectorTypes` property lets you set certain types of data to be automatically converted to clickable links. An obvious difference from a text view is that the target of a web page link is, as I mentioned a moment ago, displayed by default right there in the web view, rather than switching to Mobile Safari.

It is possible to design an entire app that is effectively nothing but a UIWebView —
especially if you have control of the server with which the user is interacting. Indeed,
before the advent of iOS, an iPhone app *was* a web application. There are still iPhone
apps that work this way, but such an approach to app design is outside the scope of
this book. (See Apple's *Mobile Safari Web Application Tutorial* if you're curious.)

A web view's most important task is to render HTML content; like any browser, a web
view understands HTML, CSS, and JavaScript. In order to construct content for a web
view, *you* must know HTML, CSS, and JavaScript. Discussion of those languages is
beyond the scope of this book; each would require a book (at least) of its own.

# Loading Content

To load a web view with content initially, you're going to need one of three things:

*An HTML string*
Construct an NSString consisting of valid HTML and call `loadHTMLString:base-URL:`.

*Data and a MIME type*
Obtain an NSData object and call `loadData:MIMEType:textEncodingName:base-URL:`. Obviously, this requires that you know the appropriate MIME type, and that
you obtain the content as NSData (or convert it to NSData).

*An NSURLRequest*
Construct an NSURLRequest and call `loadRequest:`. An NSURLRequest might
involve a file URL referring to a file on disk (within your app's bundle, for instance);
the web view will deduce the file's type from its extension. But it might also involve
the URL of a resource to be fetched across the Internet, in which case you can
configure various additional aspects of the request (for example, you can form a
POST request). This is the only form of loading that works with `goBack` (because
in the other two forms, there is no URL to return to).

There is often more than one way to load a given piece of content. For instance, one of
Apple's own examples suggests that you display a PDF file in your app's bundle by
loading it as data, along these lines:

```
NSString *thePath = [[NSBundle mainBundle] pathForResource:@"MyPDF" ofType:@"pdf"];
NSData *pdfData = [NSData dataWithContentsOfFile:thePath];
[self.wv loadData:pdfData MIMEType:@"application/pdf"
                  textEncodingName:@"utf-8" baseURL:nil];
```

But the same thing can be done with a file URL and `loadRequest:`, like this:

```
NSURL* url = [[NSBundle mainBundle] URLForResource:@"MyPDF" withExtension:@"pdf"];
NSURLRequest* req = [[NSURLRequest alloc] initWithURL:url];
[self.wv loadRequest:req];
[req release];
```

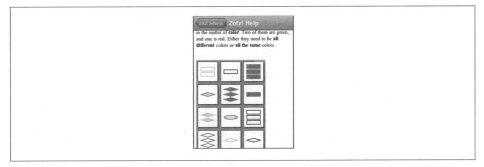

*Figure 24-1. A Help screen that's a web view*

Similarly, in one of my apps, where the Help screen is a web view (Figure 24-1), the content is an HTML file along with some referenced image files, and I load it like this:

```
NSString* path = [[NSBundle mainBundle] pathForResource:@"help" ofType:@"html"];
NSURL* url = [NSURL fileURLWithPath:path];
NSError* err = nil;
NSString* s = [NSString stringWithContentsOfURL:url
                                       encoding:NSUTF8StringEncoding error:&err];
// error-checking omitted
[view loadHTMLString:s baseURL:url];
```

At the time I wrote that code, the NSBundle method URLForResource:withExtension: didn't yet exist (it was introduced in iOS 4.0, and I needed this code to run on iOS 3.2 as well), so I had to form a pathname reference to the file and convert it to a URL. Observe that I need both the string contents of the HTML file and the URL reference to the same file, the latter to act as a base URL so that the relative references to the images will work properly. In this instance, I could have used loadRequest: and the file URL:

```
NSString* path = [[NSBundle mainBundle] pathForResource:@"help" ofType:@"html"];
NSURL* url = [NSURL fileURLWithPath:path];
NSURLRequest* req = [[NSURLRequest alloc] initWithURL:url];
[view loadRequest: req];
[req release];
```

You can use loadHTMLString:baseURL: to form your own web view content dynamically. For example, in the TidBITS News app, the content of an article is displayed in a web view that is loaded using loadHTMLString:baseURL:. The body of the article comes from an RSS feed, but it is wrapped in programmatically supplied material. For example, in Figure 24-2, the title of the article and the fact that it is a link, the right-aligned author byline and publication date, and the Listen button, along with the overall formatting of the text (including the font size), are imposed as the web view appears.

There are many possible strategies for doing this. In the case of the TidBITS News app, I start with a template loaded from disk:

```
<!DOCTYPE HTML PUBLIC "-//W3C//DTD HTML 4.01 Transitional//EN"
"http://www.w3.org/TR/html4/loose.dtd">
<!-- this is an NSString format, so percent-escapes are used -->
```

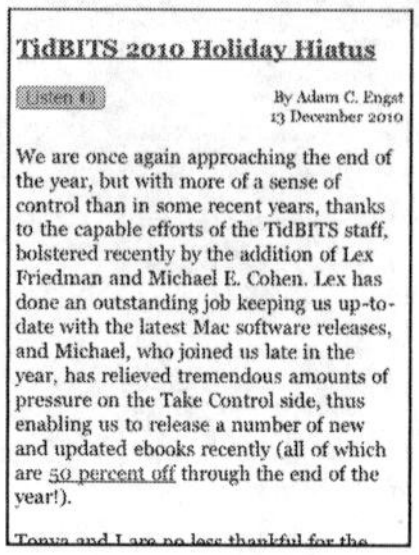

*Figure 24-2. A web view with dynamically formed content*

```html
<html>
<head>
  <meta http-equiv="content-type" content="text/html; charset=utf-8">
  <meta name="viewport" content="initial-scale=1.0" />
  <!-- scale images down to fit -->
    <style type="text/css">
      p.inflow_image {
        text-align:center;
      }
      img {
        width:100%%;
        max-width:%ipx;
        height:auto
      }
    </style>
    <!-- preload alt image -->
    <script type="text/javascript" language="javascript">
     (new Image()).src='tb_iphone_listen_pressed_02.png';
    </script>
  <title>no title</title>
</head>
<body style="font-size:%ipx; font-family:Georgia; margin:1px %ipx">
  <!-- title, which is a link to original article at our site -->
  <div style="margin-top: 0px; margin-bottom: 15px">
    <h3><a href="%@">%@</a></h3>
  </div>
  <!-- playbutton or nothing; author and date -->
  <div style="width:100%%">
    <span style="float:left; display:block; vertical-align:middle">%@</span>
    <span style="float:right; margin-bottom: 15px; display:block;
    text-align:right; font-size:80%%;">
      By %@<br>%@
    </span>
  </div>
  <!-- body, from feed -->
  <div style="clear:both; margin:30px 0px;">
    %@
  </div>
</body>
</html>
```

As you can see, the template defines the structure of a valid HTML document — the opening and closing tags, the head area (including some CSS styling and a little Java-Script), and a body consisting of divs laying out the parts of the page. The template is designed to be used as the format string in a stringWithFormat: method call; hence the various format specifiers scattered throughout it (and literal percent signs are escaped by doubling them). When the web view is to be loaded, the template is read from disk and handed over to stringWithFormat:, with every format specifier matched by an argument:

```
NSError* err = nil;
NSString* template =
    [NSString stringWithContentsOfFile:
        [[NSBundle mainBundle] pathForResource:@"htmltemplate" ofType:@"txt"]
                        encoding: NSUTF8StringEncoding error:&err];
// error-checking omitted
NSString* s = [NSString stringWithFormat: template,
                maxImageWidth,
                [fontsize intValue],
                margin,
                anitem.guid,
                anitem.title,
                (canPlay ? playbutton : @""),
                [anitem authorOfItem],
                date,
                anitem.content
                ];
```

Some of these arguments (such as anitem.title, date, anitem.content) slot values more or less directly from the app's model into the web view. Others are derived from the current circumstances. For example, maxImageWidth and margin have been set depending on whether the app is running on the iPhone or on the iPad; fontsize comes from the user defaults, because the user is allowed to determine how large the text should be. The result is an HTML string ready for loadHTMLString:baseURL:.

Web view content is loaded *asynchronously* (gradually, in a thread of its own), and it might not be loaded at all (because the user might not be connected to the Internet, the server might not respond properly, and so on). This isn't likely to matter if you're loading a resource directly from disk, where loading is quick and nothing is going to go wrong; even then, rendering the content can take time, and even a resource loaded from disk, or content formed directly as an HTML string, might itself refer to material out on the Internet that takes time to fetch.

Your app's interface is not blocked or frozen while the content is loading. On the contrary, it remains accessible and operative; that's what "asynchronous" means. The web view, in fetching a web page and its linked components, is doing something quite complex, involving both threading and network interaction, but it shields you from this complexity. Your own interaction with the web view stays on the main thread and is straightforward. You ask the web view to load some content, and then you just sit back and let it worry about the details.

Indeed, there's very little you *can* do once you've asked a web view to load content. Your main concerns will probably be to know when loading really starts, when it has finished, and whether it succeeded. To help you with this, a UIWebView's delegate (adopting the UIWebViewDelegate protocol) gets three messages:

- `webViewDidStartLoad:`
- `webViewDidFinishLoad:`
- `webView:didFailLoadWithError:`

In this example from the TidBITS News app, I mask the delay while the content loads by displaying an activity indicator (a UIActivityIndicatorView, referred to by a property, `activity`) at the center of the web view:

```
- (void)webViewDidStartLoad:(UIWebView *)wv {
    self.activity.center =
      CGPointMake(CGRectGetMidX(wv.bounds), CGRectGetMidY(wv.bounds));
    [self.activity startAnimating];
}

- (void)webViewDidFinishLoad:(UIWebView *)wv {
    [self.activity stopAnimating];
}

- (void)webView:(UIWebView *)wv didFailLoadWithError:(NSError *)error {
    [self.activity stopAnimating];
}
```

Before designing the HTML to be displayed in a web view, you might want to read up on the brand of HTML native to the mobile WebKit engine. Of course a web view *can* display any valid HTML you throw at it, but the mobile WebKit has certain limitations. For example, mobile WebKit notoriously doesn't use plug-ins, such as Flash; it doesn't implement scrollable frames within framesets; and it imposes limits on the size of resources (such as images) that it can display. On the plus side, it has many special abilities and specifications that you'll want to take advantage of.

A good place to start is Apple's *Safari Web Content Guide* (*http://developer.apple.com/library/safari/documentation/AppleApplications/Reference/SafariWebContent*). It contains links to all the other relevant documentation, such as the *Safari CSS Visual Effects Guide* (*http://developer.apple.com/library/safari/documentation/InternetWeb/Conceptual/SafariVisualEffectsProgGuide*), which describes some things you can do with WebKit's implementation of CSS3 (like animations), and the *Safari HTML5 Audio and Video Guide* (*http://developer.apple.com/library/safari/documentation/AudioVideo/Conceptual/Using_HTML5_Audio_Video*), which describes WebKit's audio and video player support.

If nothing else, you'll definitely want to be aware of one important aspect of web page content — the *viewport*. You'll notice that the TidBITS News HTML string in the previous section contains this line:

```
<meta name="viewport" content="initial-scale=1.0" />
```

Without that line, the HTML string is laid out incorrectly when it is rendered. This is noticeable especially with the iPad version of TidBITS News, where the web view can be rotated when the device is rotated, causing its width to change: in one orientation or the other, the text will be too wide for the web view, and the user has to scroll horizontally in order to read it all. The *Safari Web Content Guide* explains why: if no viewport is specified, the viewport can change when the app rotates. Setting the `initial-scale` causes the viewport size to adopt correct values in both orientations.

A web view's `loading` property tells you whether it is in the process of loading a request. If, at the time a web view is to be destroyed, its `loading` is YES, it is up to you to cancel the request by sending it the `stopLoading` message first; actually, it does no harm to send the web view `stopLoading` in any case. In addition, UIWebView is one of those weird classes I warned you about (Chapter 12) whose memory management behavior is odd: Apple's documentation warns that if you assign a UIWebView a delegate, you must nilify its `delegate` property before releasing the web view. Thus, in a controller class that retains a web view, I do an extra little dance in `dealloc`:

```
[wv stopLoading];
wv.delegate = nil;
[wv release];
```

# Communicating with a Web View

Having loaded a web view with content, you don't so much configure or command the web view as communicate with it. There are two modes of communication with a web view and its content:

*Load requests*
> When a web view is asked to load content, in particular because the user has tapped a link within it, its delegate is sent the message `webView:shouldStartLoadWith-Request:navigationType:`. This is your opportunity to interfere with the web view's loading behavior. You are handed an NSURLRequest, whose `URL` property you can analyze (very easily, because it's an NSURL). And you are handed a constant describing the type of navigation involved, whose value will be one of the following:

- `UIWebViewNavigationTypeLinkClicked`
- `UIWebViewNavigationTypeFormSubmitted`
- `UIWebViewNavigationTypeBackForward`
- `UIWebViewNavigationTypeReload`
- `UIWebViewNavigationTypeFormResubmitted`
- `UIWebViewNavigationTypeOther` (includes loading the web view with content initially)

*JavaScript execution*

You can speak JavaScript to a web view's content by sending it the `stringBy-EvaluatingJavaScriptFromString:` message. Thus you can enquire as to the nature and details of that content, and you can alter the content dynamically.

The TidBITS News app uses `webView:shouldStartLoadWithRequest:navigationType:` to distinguish between the user tapping an ordinary link and tapping the Listen button (shown in Figure 24-2). The `onclick` script for the `<a>` tag surrounding the Listen button image executes this JavaScript code:

```
document.location='play:me'
```

This causes the web view to attempt to load an NSURLRequest whose URL is `play:me`, which is totally bogus; it's merely an internal signal to ourselves. We intercept the attempt to load this request, examine the NSURLRequest, observe that its URL has a `scheme` called `@"play"`, and prevent the loading from taking place; instead, we head back to the Internet to start playing the online podcast recording associated with this article. Any other load request caused by tapping a link is also prevented and redirected instead to Mobile Safari, because we don't want our web view used as an all-purpose browser. But we do let our web view load a request in the general case, because otherwise it wouldn't even respond to our attempt to load it with HTML content in the first place:

```
- (BOOL)webView:(UIWebView *)webView shouldStartLoadWithRequest:(NSURLRequest *)r
                          navigationType:(UIWebViewNavigationType)nt {
    if ([r.URL.scheme isEqualToString: @"play"]) {
        [self doPlay:nil];
        return NO;
    }
    if (nt == UIWebViewNavigationTypeLinkClicked) {
        [[UIApplication sharedApplication] openURL:r.URL];
        return NO;
    }
    return YES;
}
```

The TidBITS News app uses JavaScript in several ways; I'll describe one. If the user reads an article, then leaves that screen to examine the list of articles (or terminates the app), but then returns to the same article, we'd like to display the article vertically scrolled to the same position where it was before. At first glance one might have the impression that this is impossible, because a web view is not a UIScrollView, so we can't learn or control its scroll position. But this impression is wrong; it ignores the fact that a web view is a browser. We can learn the scroll position of its content using JavaScript (`wv` here is the web view):

```
NSString* scrolly = [wv stringByEvaluatingJavaScriptFromString: @"scrollY"];
```

Later, we can restore the scroll position by using the converse:

```
[wv stringByEvaluatingJavaScriptFromString:
    [NSString stringWithFormat: @"window.scrollTo(0, %@);", scrolly]];
```

JavaScript and the document object model (*DOM*) are quite powerful. Here's some additional documentation you may find helpful:

- WebKit DOM Programming Topics (*http://developer.apple.com/library/safari/ #documentation/AppleApplications/Conceptual/SafariJSProgTopics/WebKitJava Script.html*)
- WebKit DOM Reference (*http://developer.apple.com/library/safari/#documenta tion/AppleApplications/Reference/WebKitDOMRef*)
- Safari DOM Additions Reference (*http://developer.apple.com/library/safari/#docu mentation/AppleApplications/Reference/SafariJSRef*).

# CHAPTER 25

# Controls and Other Views

This chapter discusses all UIView subclasses provided by UIKit that haven't been discussed already (except for the two modal dialog classes, which are described in the next chapter). It's remarkable how few of them there are; UIKit exhibits a noteworthy economy of means in this regard.

Additional UIView subclasses are provided by other frameworks. For example, the Map Kit framework provides the MKMapView (Chapter 34). Also, additional UIViewController subclasses are provided by other frameworks as a way of creating interface. For example, the MessageUI framework provides MFMailComposeViewController, which acts as a contained view controller to give your app interface for letting the user compose and send a mail message (Chapter 33). There will be lots of examples in Part VI.

## UIActivityIndicatorView

An activity indicator (UIActivityIndicatorView) appears as the spokes of a small wheel. You set the spokes spinning with startAnimating, giving the user a sense that some time-consuming process is taking place. You stop the spinning with stopAnimating. If the activity indicator's hidesWhenStopped is YES (the default), it is visible only when spinning.

An activity indicator comes in a style, its activityIndicatorViewStyle; if the indicator is created in code, you'll set its style with initWithActivityIndicatorStyle:. Your choices are:

- UIActivityIndicatorViewStyleWhiteLarge
- UIActivityIndicatorViewStyleWhite
- UIActivityIndicatorViewStyleGray

An activity indicator has a standard size, which depends on its style. You can change its size in code, though an enlarged activity indicator may look rather fuzzy.

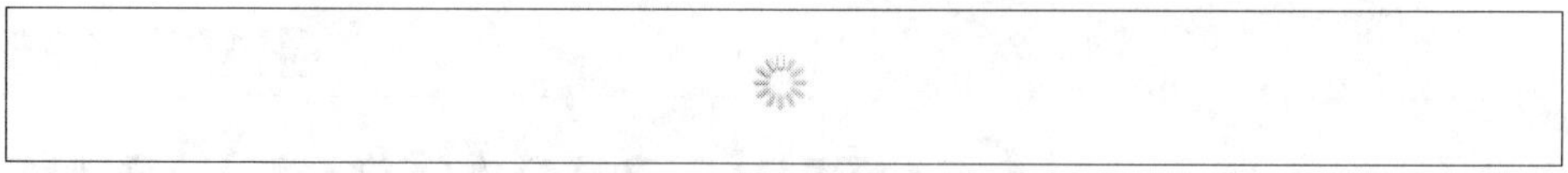

*Figure 25-1. A large white activity indicator*

Here's some code from a UITableViewCell subclass in one of my apps. In this app, it takes some time, after the user taps a cell to select it, for me to construct the next view and navigate to it, so to cover the delay, I show a spinning activity indicator in the center of a cell while it's selected:

```
- (void)setSelected:(BOOL)selected animated:(BOOL)animated {
    if (selected) {
        UIActivityIndicatorView* v =
            [[UIActivityIndicatorView alloc]
                initWithActivityIndicatorStyle:UIActivityIndicatorViewStyleWhiteLarge];
        v.center =
            CGPointMake(self.bounds.size.width/2.0, self.bounds.size.height/2.0);
        v.tag = 1001;
        [self.contentView addSubview:v];
        [v startAnimating];
        [v release];
    } else {
        [[self.contentView viewWithTag:1001] removeFromSuperview];
        // no harm if nonexistent
    }
    [super setSelected:selected animated:animated];
}
```

If the activity involves the network, you might want to set UIApplication's `network-ActivityIndicatorVisible` to YES. This displays a small spinning activity indicator in the status bar. The indicator is not reflecting actual network activity — if it's visible, it's spinning — so be sure to set it back to NO when the activity is over.

An activity indicator is simple and standard, but you can't change the way it's drawn. If you want your own custom activity indicator, though, it's easy to make one. One obvious way is to use a UIImageView with a sequence of custom images forming an animation (`animationImages`), as described in Chapter 17.

# UIProgressView

A progress view (UIProgressView) is a "thermometer," graphically displaying a percentage. It is often used to represent a time-consuming process during which the percentage of completion is known (if the percentage of completion is unknown, you're more likely to use an activity indicator), but it might also be used to represent a fairly static percentage. For example, in one of my apps, I use a progress view to show the current position within the song being played by the built-in music player; in another app, which is a card game, I use a progress view in reverse, as it were, to show how many cards are left in the deck.

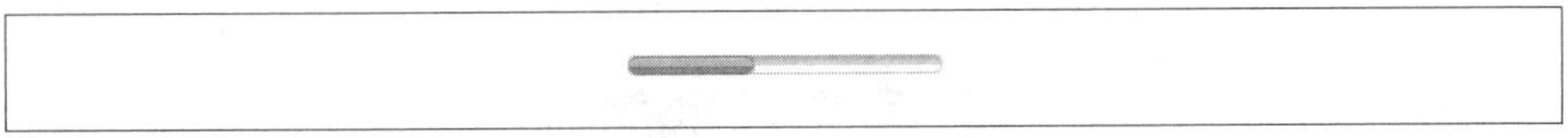

*Figure 25-2. A progress view*

A progress view comes in a style, its `progressViewStyle`; if the progress view is created in code, you'll set its style with `initWithProgressViewStyle:`. Your choices are:

- `UIProgressViewStyleDefault`
- `UIProgressViewStyleBar`

The latter is intended for use in a UIBarButtonItem, as the title view of a navigation item, and so on.

The height (the narrow dimension) of a progress view is generally not up to you; it's determined by the progress view's style. Changing a progress view's height has no visible effect on how the thermometer is drawn and is not a good idea.

The fullness of the thermometer is the progress view's `progress` property. This is a value between 0 and 1, inclusive; obviously, you'll need to do some elementary arithmetic in order to convert from the actual value you're reflecting to a value within that range. For example, to reflect the number of cards remaining in a deck of 52 cards:

```
prog.progress = [[deck cards] count] / 52.0;
```

A progress view is simple and standard, but you can't change the way it's drawn. If you want your own custom progress view, it's easy to make one; all you need is a custom UIView subclass that draws something similar to a thermometer. Figure 25-3 shows a simple custom thermometer view; it has a `value` property, and you set this to something between 0 and 1 and then call `setNeedsDisplay` to get the view to redraw itself. Here's its `drawRect:` code:

```
- (void)drawRect:(CGRect)rect {
    CGContextRef c = UIGraphicsGetCurrentContext();
    [[UIColor whiteColor] set];
    CGFloat ins = 2.0;
    CGRect r = CGRectInset(self.bounds, ins, ins);
    CGFloat radius = r.size.height / 2.0;
    CGMutablePathRef path = CGPathCreateMutable();
    CGPathMoveToPoint(path, NULL, CGRectGetMaxX(r) - radius, ins);
    CGPathAddArc(path, NULL,
        radius+ins, radius+ins, radius, -M_PI/2.0, M_PI/2.0, true);
    CGPathAddArc(path, NULL,
        CGRectGetMaxX(r) - radius, radius+ins, radius, M_PI/2.0, -M_PI/2.0, true);
    CGPathCloseSubpath(path);
    CGContextAddPath(c, path);
    CGContextSetLineWidth(c, 2);
    CGContextStrokePath(c);
    CGContextAddPath(c, path);
    CGContextClip(c);
    CGContextFillRect(c, CGRectMake(
        r.origin.x, r.origin.y, r.size.width * self.value, r.size.height));
}
```

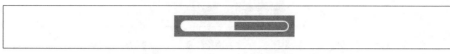

*Figure 25-3. A custom progress view*

# UIPickerView

A UIPickerView displays selectable choices using a rotating drum metaphor. It has a standard legal range of possible heights, which is undocumented and must be discovered by trial and error (attempting to set the height outside this range will fail with a warning in the console); its width is largely up to you. Each drum, or column, is called a *component*.

Your code configures the UIPickerView's content through its data source (UIPickerViewDataSource) and delegate (UIPickerViewDelegate), which are usually the same object (see also Chapter 11). Your data source and delegate must answer questions similar to those posed by a UITableView (Chapter 21):

`numberOfComponentsInPickerView:` *(data source)*
> How many components (drums) does this picker view have?

`pickerView:numberOfRowsInComponent:` *(data source)*
> How many rows does this component have? The first component is numbered 0.

`pickerView:titleForRow:forComponent:`
`pickerView:viewForRow:forComponent:reusingView:` *(delegate)*
> What should this row of this component display? The first row is numbered 0. You can supply either a simple title string or an entire view such as a UILabel, giving you more control over formatting, but you must supply every row of every component the same way, because if `viewForRow` is implemented, `titleForRow` isn't called. The `reusingView` parameter, if not nil, is a view that you supplied for a row now no longer visible, giving you a chance to reuse it, much as cells are reused in a table view.

Here's the code for a UIPickerView (Figure 25-4) that displays the names of the 50 U.S. states, obtained from a text file. We implement `pickerView:viewForRow:forComponent:reusingView:` just because it's the more interesting case; as our views, we supply UILabel instances. The state names, drawn from an NSArray property `states`, are drawn centered because the labels are themselves centered within the picker view:

```
- (NSInteger)numberOfComponentsInPickerView:(UIPickerView *)pickerView {
    return 1;
}

- (NSInteger)pickerView:(UIPickerView *)pickerView
        numberOfRowsInComponent:(NSInteger)component {
    return 50;
```

*Figure 25-4. A picker view*

```
    }

- (UIView *)pickerView:(UIPickerView *)pickerView viewForRow:(NSInteger)row
        forComponent:(NSInteger)component reusingView:(UIView *)view {
    UILabel* lab;
    if (view)
        lab = (UILabel*)view;
    else
        lab = [[[UILabel alloc] init] autorelease];
    lab.text = [self.states objectAtIndex:row];
    lab.backgroundColor = [UIColor clearColor];
    [lab sizeToFit];
    return lab;
}
```

The delegate may further configure the UIPickerView's physical appearance by means of these methods:

- `pickerView:rowHeightForComponent:`
- `pickerView:widthForComponent:`

The delegate may implement `pickerView:didSelectRow:inComponent:` to be notified each time the user spins a drum to a new position. You can also query the picker view directly by sending it `selectedRowInComponent:`.

You can set the value to which any drum is turned using `selectRow:inComponent:animated:`. Other handy picker view methods allow you to request that the data be reloaded, and there are properties and methods to query the picker view's contents (though of course they do not relieve you of responsibility for knowing the data model from which the picker view's contents are supplied):

- `reloadComponent:`
- `reloadAllComponents`
- `numberOfComponents`
- `numberOfRowsInComponent:`
- `viewForRow:forComponent:`

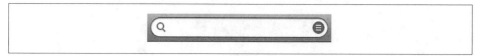

*Figure 25-5. A search bar with a search results button*

By implementing `pickerView:didSelectRow:inComponent:` and using `reloadComponent:` you can make a picker view where the values displayed by one drum depend dynamically on what is selected in another. For example, one can imagine expanding our U.S. states example to include a second drum listing major cities in each state; when the user switches to a different state in the first drum, a different set of major cities appears in the second drum.

# UISearchBar

A search bar (UISearchBar) is essentially a variety of text field, though it is not in fact a UITextField subclass. It is displayed as a rounded rectangle containing a magnifying glass icon, where the user can enter text (Figure 25-5). It does not, of itself, do any searching or display the results of a search; a common interface involves displaying the results of a search as a table, and a controller class, UISearchDisplayController, makes this easy to do (see Chapter 21).

A search bar's current text is its `text` property. It can have a `placeholder`, which appears when there is no text. A `prompt` can be displayed above the search bar to explain its purpose. Delegate methods (UISearchBarDelegate) notify you of editing events:

- `searchBarShouldBeginEditing:`
- `searchBarTextDidBeginEditing:`
- `searchBar:textDidChange:`
- `searchBar:shouldChangeTextInRange:replacementText:`
- `searchBarShouldEndEditing:`
- `searchBarTextDidEndEditing:`

A search bar has a `barStyle`, for which your choices are the same as for a toolbar or navigation bar: either `UIBarStyleDefault` or `UIBarStyleBlack`, and if the latter, either `translucent` or not. Alternatively, the search bar may have a `tintColor`; as with a toolbar, if this is set, the `barStyle` is ignored. (See Chapter 19 and later in this chapter.) Because of this, a search bar looks good at the top of the screen, where a navigation bar or toolbar might go; in effect, it is drawn as if it *were* a navigation bar or toolbar.

A search bar displays an internal Cancel button automatically (an "x" in a circle) if there is text in the search bar. Internally, at its right end, a search bar may display a search results button (`showsSearchResultsButton`), which may be selected or not (`search-ResultsButtonSelected`), or a bookmark button (`showsBookmarkButton`). These buttons cover the internal Cancel button, but they vanish if text is entered in the search bar.

There is also an option to display a Cancel button externally (`showsCancelButton`). Delegate methods notify you when the buttons are tapped:

- `searchBarResultsListButtonClicked:`
- `searchBarBookmarkButtonClicked:`
- `searchBarCancelButtonClicked:`

The best way to get a sense of how these properties affect the look of a search bar is to experiment with them in the nib editor.

A search bar may also display scope buttons (see the example in Chapter 21). These are intended to let the user alter the meaning of the search; precisely how you use them is up to you. To make the scope buttons appear, use the `showsScopeBar` property; the button titles are the `scopeButtonTitles` property, and the currently selected scope button is the `selectedScopeButtonIndex` property. The delegate is notified when the user taps a different scope button:

- `searchBar:selectedScopeButtonIndexDidChange:`

The problem of allowing the keyboard to appear without hiding the search bar is exactly as for a text field (Chapter 23). Text input properties of the search bar configure its keyboard and typing behavior like a text field as well: `keyboardType`, `autocapitalizationType`, and `autocorrectionType`. When the user taps the Search key in the keyboard, the delegate is notified, and it is then up to you to dismiss the keyboard (`resignFirstResponder`) and perform the search:

- `searchBarSearchButtonClicked:`

A common interface on the iPad is to embed a search bar as a bar button item's view in a toolbar at the top of the screen. This approach has its pitfalls; for example, there is no room for a prompt, and scope buttons or an external Cancel button may not appear either. One rather slimy workaround is to layer the search bar over the toolbar rather than having it genuinely live in the toolbar. Another is to have the search bar itself occupy the position of the toolbar at the top of the screen. On the other hand, a search bar in a toolbar that is managed by a UISearchDisplayController will automatically display search results in a popover, which can be a considerable savings of time and effort (though, as usual, the popover controller is unfortunately out of your hands); see Chapter 22 for an example. An interesting thing about that example, which I didn't mention at the time, is that the search bar contains a results list button that summons the popover when tapped, and in that case the popover's bar contains a Clear button that empties the search bar and dismisses the popover; that behavior is apparently entirely automatic and due to the search display controller.

# UIControl

UIControl is a subclass of UIView whose chief purpose is to be the superclass of several further built-in classes representing views with which the user can interact (controls), endowing them with common behavior.

The most important thing that controls have in common is that they automatically track and analyze touch events (Chapter 18) and report them to the programmer as significant control events by way of action messages. Each control implements some subset of the possible control events (see Chapter 11 for a list of which control events are implemented by which controls); for each control event that you want to hear about automatically, you attach to the control one or more target–action pairs. You can do this in the nib (Chapter 7) or in code (Chapter 11).

For any given control, each control event and its target–action pairs form a dispatch table. The following methods permit you to manipulate and query the dispatch table:

- `addTarget:action:forControlEvents:`
- `removeTarget:action:forControlEvents:`
- `actionsForTarget:forControlEvent:`
- `allTargets`
- `allControlEvents` (a bitmask of control events to which a target–action pair is attached)

An action selector may adopt any of three signatures (see Chapter 11). Disappointingly, none of these signatures provide a way to learn what control event triggered the current action selector call! Thus, for example, to distinguish a Touch Up Inside event from a Touch Up Outside event, you must dispatch them to two different action handlers; if you dispatch them to the same action handler, your code cannot discern which event occurred.

When a control wants to send an action message reporting control event, it calls its own `sendAction:to:forEvent:` method. This in turn calls the shared application instance's `sendAction:to:from:forEvent:`, which actually calls the specified method of the specified target. In theory, you could call or override either of these methods, but it is extremely unlikely that you would do so.

To force a control to report a particular control event message, call its `sendActionsForControlEvents:` method (which is never called automatically by the framework). For example, suppose you tell a UISwitch programmatically to change its setting from Off to On. This doesn't cause the switch to report a control event, as it would if the user had slid the switch from off to on; if you wanted it to do so, you could use `sendActionsForControlEvents:`, like this:

```
[switch setOn: YES animated: YES];
[switch sendActionsForControlEvents:UIControlEventValueChanged];
```

*Figure 25-6. A switch*

You might also use `sendActionsForControlEvents:` in a subclass to customize the circumstances under which a control reports control events.

A control has `enabled`, `selected`, and `highlighted` properties. A control that is not enabled does not respond to user interaction; whether the control also portrays itself differently, to cue the user to this fact, depends upon the control. For example, a disabled UISwitch is faded. But a round rect text field, unless you explicitly configure it to display a different background image when disabled (Chapter 23), gives the user no cue that it is disabled. The visual nature of control selection and highlighting, too, depends on the control. Neither highlighting nor selection make any difference to the appearance of a UISwitch, but a highlighted UIButton usually looks quite different from a nonhighlighted UIButton.

A control has `contentHorizontalAlignment` and `contentVerticalAlignment` properties. Again, these matter only if the control has content that can be aligned. You are most likely to use these properties in connection with a UIButton to position its title and internal image.

A text field (UITextField) is a control; see Chapter 23. The remaining controls are covered here, and then I'll give a simple example of writing your own custom control.

## UISwitch

A UISwitch portrays a BOOL value: it looks like a sliding electrical switch whose positions are labeled ON and OFF, and its on property is either YES or NO. The user can slide or tap to toggle the switch's position. When the user changes the switch's position, the switch reports a Value Changed control event. To change the on property's value with accompanying animation, call `setOn:animated:`.

A switch has only one size and color scheme. Any attempt to set its size will be ignored. (Experimentation suggests that the standard size is 97×27.) You can't customize the ON and OFF labels; the only solution is to roll your own switch-like interface widget (several third-party implementations are available).

> Don't name a UISwitch instance variable or property `switch`, as this is a reserved word in C.

## UIPageControl

A UIPageControl is a row of dots; each dot is called a *page*, because it is intended to be used in conjunction with some other interface that portrays something analogous to pages, such as a UIScrollView with its `pagingEnabled` set to YES. Coordinating the page control with this other interface is up to you. (See Chapter 20 for an example and Figure 20-3 for an illustration.) The number of dots is the page control's `numberOf-Pages`. The current page, its `currentPage`, is portrayed as a solid dot; the others are slightly transparent. The user can tap to one side or the other of the current page's dot to increment or decrement the current page; the page control then reports a Value Changed control event.

You can make the page control wider than the dots to increase the target region on which the user can tap. You can make the page control taller as well, but only the horizontal component of a tap is taken into account, so this would probably be pointless as well as confusing to the user. To learn the minimum size required for a given number of pages, use `sizeForNumberOfPages:`.

If a page control's `hidesForSinglePage` is YES, the page control becomes invisible when its `numberOfPages` changes to 1.

If a page control's `defersCurrentPageDisplay` is YES, then when the user taps to increment or decrement the page control's value, the display of the current page is not changed. A Value Changed control event is reported, but it is up to your code to handle this action and call `updateCurrentPageDisplay`. A case in point might be if the user's changing the current page starts an animation, but you don't want the current page dot to change until the animation ends.

## UIDatePicker

A UIDatePicker looks like a UIPickerView (discussed earlier in this chapter), but it is *not* a UIPickerView subclass (it *uses* a UIPickerView to draw itself, but it provides no official access to that picker view). Its purpose is to express the notion of a date and time, taking care of the calendrical and numerical complexities so that you don't have to. When the user changes its setting, the date picker reports a Value Changed control event.

A UIDatePicker has one of four modes (`datePickerMode`), determining how it is drawn:

UIDatePickerModeTime
> The date picker displays a time; for example, it has an hour component and a minutes component.

UIDatePickerModeDate
> The date picker displays a date; for example, it has a month component, a day component, and a year component.

UIDatePickerModeDateAndTime
> The date picker displays a date and time; for example, it has a component showing day of the week, month, and day, plus an hour component and a minutes component.

`UIDatePickerModeCountDownTimer`

   The date picker displays a number of hours and minutes; for example, it has an hours component and a minutes component.

Exactly what components a date picker displays, and what values they contain, depends upon the locale. For example, a U.S. time displays an hour (numbered 1 through 12), minutes, and AM or PM, but a British time displays an hour (numbered 1 through 24) and minutes. A date picker has `locale`, `calendar`, and `timeZone` properties, respectively an NSLocale, NSCalendar, and NSTimeZone. These are nil by default, meaning that the date picker responds to the user's system-level settings. For example, if your app contains a date picker displaying a time, and the user changes the region format from United States to United Kingdom, the date picker's display will change immediately, eliminating the AM/PM component and changing the hour numbers to run from 1 to 24.

According to Apple's documentation, you should also be able to set a date picker's `locale` and `calendar` programmatically, but in fact changing the `locale` may have no useful effect (it does seem to change the language if the mode is `UIDatePickerModeDate-AndTime`, but not the number and values of the components), and it is hard to see the use of this property. Setting a date picker's `timeZone` does work, however; for example, if you live in California and you set a date picker's `timeZone` to GMT, the displayed time is shifted forward by 8 hours, so that 11 AM is displayed as 7 PM (if it is winter).

   Don't change the `timeZone` of a `UIDatePickerModeCountDownTimer` date picker, or the displayed value will be shifted and you will confuse the heck out of yourself and your users.

The minutes component, if there is one, defaults to showing every minute, but you can change this with the `minuteInterval` property. The maximum value is 30, in which case the minutes component values are 0 and 30.

The maximum and minimum values enabled in the date picker are determined by its `maximumDate` and `minimumDate` properties. Values outside this range may appear disabled. There isn't really any limit on the range that a date picker can display, because the "drums" representing its components are not physical, and values are added dynamically as the user spins them. In this example, we set the initial minimum and maximum dates of a date picker (`dp`) to the beginning and end of 1954. We also set the actual `date`, because otherwise the date picker will appear initially set to now, which will be disabled because it isn't within the minimum–maximum range:

```
NSDateComponents* dc = [[NSDateComponents alloc] init];
[dc setYear:1954];
[dc setMonth:1];
[dc setDay:1];
NSCalendar* c = [[NSCalendar alloc] initWithCalendarIdentifier:NSGregorianCalendar];
NSDate* d = [c dateFromComponents:dc];
dp.minimumDate = d;
```

```
dp.date = d;
[dc setYear:1955];
d = [c dateFromComponents:dc];
dp.maximumDate = d;
[c release]; [dc release];
```

 Don't set the maximumDate and minimumDate properties values for a UIDate-
PickerModeCountDownTimer date picker, or you might cause a crash with
an out-of-range exception.

The date represented by a date picker (unless its mode is UIDatePickerModeCountDown-
Timer) is its date property, an NSDate. The default date is now, at the time the date
picker is instantiated. For a UIDatePickerModeDate date picker, the time by default is 12
AM (midnight), local time; for a UIDatePickerModeTime date picker, the date by default
is today. The internal value is reckoned in the local time zone, so it may be different
from the displayed value, if you have changed the date picker's timeZone.

The value represented by a UIDatePickerModeCountDownTimer date picker is its countDown-
Duration. The date picker does not actually do any counting down; changing its count-
DownDuration at appropriate intervals, if desired, is up to you, though you are more
likely to use some other interface to display the countdown, especially because the date
picker doesn't display seconds. The Timer tab of Apple's Clock app shows a typical
interface; the user configures the date picker to set the countDownDuration initially, but
once the counting starts, the date picker is hidden and a label displays the remaining
time. The countDownDuration is an NSTimeInterval, which is a double representing a
number of seconds; dividing by 60 to convert to minutes, and again to convert to hours,
is up to you — or you could use the built-in calendrical classes:

```
NSTimeInterval t = [datePicker countDownDuration];
NSDate* d = [NSDate dateWithTimeIntervalSinceReferenceDate:t];
NSCalendar* c = [[NSCalendar alloc] initWithCalendarIdentifier:NSGregorianCalendar];
[c setTimeZone: [NSTimeZone timeZoneForSecondsFromGMT:0]]; // normalize
NSUInteger units = NSHourCalendarUnit | NSMinuteCalendarUnit;
NSDateComponents* dc = [c components:units fromDate:d];
[c release];
NSLog(@"%i hr, %i min", [dc hour], [dc minute]);
```

Similarly, to convert between an NSDate and a string, you'll need an NSDateFormatter
(see Chapter 10, and Apple's *Date and Time Programming Guide*):

```
NSDate* d = [datePicker date];
NSDateFormatter* df = [[NSDateFormatter alloc] init];
[df setTimeStyle:kCFDateFormatterFullStyle];
[df setDateStyle:kCFDateFormatterFullStyle];
NSLog(@"%@", [df stringFromDate:d]);
// "Wednesday, August 10, 2011 3:16:25 AM Pacific Daylight Time"
[df release];
```

# UISlider

A slider (UISlider) is an expression of a continuously settable value (its `value`) between some minimum and maximum (its `minimumValue` and `maximumValue`; they are 0 and 1 by default). It is portrayed as an object, the *thumb*, positioned along a *track*. As the user changes the thumb's position, the slider reports a Value Changed control event; it may do this continuously as the user presses and drags the thumb (if the slider's `continuous` is YES, the default) or only when the user releases the thumb (if its `continuous` is NO). While the user is pressing on the thumb, the slider is in the `highlighted` state. To change the slider's value with animation, call `setValue:animated:`.

A commonly expressed desire is to modify a slider's behavior so that, for example, if the user taps on its track, the slider moves to the spot where the user tapped. Unfortunately, a slider does not, of itself, respond to taps on its track; such a tap doesn't even cause it to report a Touch Up Inside. However, with a gesture recognizer, most things are possible; here's the action handler for a UITapGestureRecognizer attached to a UISlider:

```
- (void) tapped: (UITapGestureRecognizer*) g {
    UISlider* s = (UISlider*)g.view;
    if (s.highlighted)
        return; // tap on thumb, let slider deal with it
    CGPoint pt = [g locationInView: s];
    CGFloat percentage = pt.x / s.bounds.size.width;
    CGFloat delta = percentage * (s.maximumValue - s.minimumValue);
    CGFloat value = s.minimumValue + delta;
    [s setValue:value animated:YES];
}
```

A slider's appearance is extremely customizable: you can provide your own thumb and your own track, along with images to appear at each end of the track, and you can override in a subclass the methods that position these.

The images at the ends of the track are the slider's `minimumValueImage` and `maximumValue-Image`, and they are nil by default. If you set them to actual images (which can also be done in the nib), the slider will attempt to position them within its own bounds, shrinking the drawing of the track to compensate. The slider does not clip its subviews by default, so the images can extend outside the slider's bounds.

For example, suppose the slider's dimensions are 250×23 (the standard height), and suppose the images are 30×30. Then the minimum image is drawn with its origin at (0,-4) — its left edge matches the slider's left edge, and its top is raised so that the center of its height matches the center of the slider's height — and the maximum image is drawn with its origin at (220, -4). But the track is drawn with a width of only 164 pixels, instead of the normal 246; that is, instead of being nearly the full width of the slider, the track is contracted to allow room for the images. (This, by the way, wrecks the behavior of the `tapped:` handler in the previous example, which relies on the actual bounds of the slider, not the apparent width and position of the track. Fixing the example is left as an exercise for the reader.)

*Figure 25-7. Repositioning a slider's images and track*

You can change these dimensions by overriding `minimumValueImageRectForBounds:`, `maximumValueImageRectForBounds:`, and `trackRectForBounds:` in a subclass. The bounds passed in are the slider's bounds. In this example, we expand the track width to the full width of the slider, and draw the images outside the slider's bounds (Figure 25-7; I've given the slider a gray background color so you can see how the track and images are related to its bounds):

```
- (CGRect)maximumValueImageRectForBounds:(CGRect)bounds {
    CGRect result = [super maximumValueImageRectForBounds:bounds];
    result = CGRectOffset(result, 31, 0);
    return result;
}

- (CGRect)minimumValueImageRectForBounds:(CGRect)bounds {
    CGRect result = [super minimumValueImageRectForBounds:bounds];
    result = CGRectOffset(result, -31, 0);
    return result;
}

- (CGRect)trackRectForBounds:(CGRect)bounds {
    CGRect result = [super trackRectForBounds:bounds];
    result.origin.x = 0;
    result.size.width = bounds.size.width;
    return result;
}
```

The thumb is also an image, and you set it with `setThumbImage:forState:`. There are two chiefly relevant states, `UIControlStateNormal` (not highlighted) and `UIControlState-Highlighted`, so if you supply images for both, the thumb will change automatically while the user is dragging it. If you supply just one image, for normal state only, the thumb image *won't* change while the user is dragging it. You can position the image by overriding `thumbRectForBounds:trackRect:value:` in a subclass. By default, the image will be centered in the track at the point represented by the slider's current value. In this example, the image is repositioned upward slightly (Figure 25-8):

```
- (CGRect)thumbRectForBounds:(CGRect)bounds
                  trackRect:(CGRect)rect value:(float)value {
    CGRect result = [super thumbRectForBounds:bounds trackRect:rect value:value];
    result = CGRectOffset(result, 0, -7);
    return result;
}
```

Enlarging a slider's thumb can mislead the user as to the area on which it can be tapped to drag it. The slider is the thumb's superview, after all, so if the slider's height is still only 23 pixels, only the part of the thumb that intersects that 23-pixel height will be draggable. The user may try to drag the part of the thumb that is drawn outside the

*Figure 25-8. Replacing a slider's thumb*

*Figure 25-9. Replacing a slider's track*

slider's bounds, and will fail (and be confused). The solution is to increase the slider's height; you can't do this in the nib editor, but you can do it in code.

The track is two images, one appearing to the left of the thumb, the other to its right. They are set with `setMinimumTrackImage:forState:` and `setMaximumTrackImage:for-State:`. If you supply images both for normal state and for highlighted state, the images will change while the user is dragging the thumb.

The trick to these images is that they must be *horizontally stretchable*. It looks like the user is dragging the thumb along a single static track, but that's a clever illusion. In reality, there are two images; as the user drags the thumb, one image grows horizontally and the other shrinks horizontally. The part of each image that grows and shrinks is a column one pixel wide somewhere in the middle of the image; that single column is replicated to form the middle section of the stretched image. Thus, the image you provide consists of a left end cap, a one-pixel middle section to be replicated, and a right end cap. For the left track image, the right end cap will be partially or entirely hidden under the thumb; for the right track image, the left end cap will be partially or entirely hidden under the thumb.

To create an image that behaves in this way, you derive it from an existing image with `stretchableImageWithLeftCapWidth:topCapHeight:`. You don't need the image to be vertically stretchable, so the top cap height doesn't matter; only the left cap width matters. You might think that not enough information is being supplied, but remember, we know the width of the stretchable region in the middle: it is 1 pixel wide. Therefore, defining the left cap width defines the right cap width: it is the rest of the image's width minus that 1 pixel. Figure 25-9 shows a track derived from a single 15×15 image of a circular object (a coin):

```
UIImage* coin = [UIImage imageNamed: @"coin.png"];
UIImage* coinEnd = [coin stretchableImageWithLeftCapWidth:7 topCapHeight:0];
[slider setMinimumTrackImage:coinEnd forState:UIControlStateNormal];
[slider setMaximumTrackImage:coinEnd forState:UIControlStateNormal];
```

*Figure 25-10. A segmented control*

# UISegmentedControl

A segmented control (UISegmentedControl) is a row of tappable segments; a segment is rather like a button. This provides a way for the user to choose among several related options. By default (`momentary` is NO), the most recently tapped segment remains selected; alternatively (`momentary` is YES), the tapped segment is shown as selected momentarily, but then no segment selection is displayed, though internally the tapped segment remains the selected segment. The selected segment can be retrieved with the `selectedSegmentIndex` property; it can also be set with the `selectedSegmentIndex` property, and remains visibly selected (even for a `momentary` segmented control). A `selectedSegmentIndex` value of `UISegmentedControlNoSegment` (`-1`) means no segment is selected. When the user taps a segment that is not already visibly selected, the segmented control reports a Value Changed event.

 Setting the `selectedSegmentIndex` in code, in such a way as to change its value, also reports a Value Changed event. This feels like a bug, because it is abnormal; usually, changing a control in code doesn't cause any control events to be triggered. Setting a UIDatePicker's `date` doesn't trigger a Value Changed event. Setting a UIPageControl's `currentPage` doesn't trigger a Value Changed event. Setting a UISlider's `value` doesn't trigger a Value Changed event. Setting a UISwitch's `on` doesn't trigger a Value Changed event. Similarly, setting a UITextField's `text` doesn't trigger an Editing Changed event.

A segment can be separately enabled or disabled with `setEnabled:forSegmentAtIndex:`, and its enabled state can be retrieved with `isEnabledForSegmentAtIndex:`. (The checkbox that does this in the nib editor used to be broken, but in Xcode 4 it appears to be working correctly.) A disabled segment is drawn faded, and the user can't tap it, but it can still be selected in code.

A segment has either a title or an image; when one is set, the other becomes nil. The methods for setting and fetching the title and image for existing segments are:

- `setTitle:forSegmentAtIndex:`
- `setImage:forSegmentAtIndex:`
- `titleForSegmentAtIndex:`
- `imageForSegmentAtIndex:`

After changing an existing segment's title or image, you might want to call `sizeToFit` to resize the segments automatically.

You will also want to set the title or image when creating the segment. You can do this in code if you're creating the segmented control from scratch, with `initWithItems:`, which takes an array each item of which is either a string or an image.

Methods for managing segments dynamically are:

- `insertSegmentWithTitle:atIndex:animated:`
- `insertSegmentWithImage:atIndex:animated:`
- `removeSegmentAtIndex:animated:`
- `removeAllSegments`

The number of segments can be retrieved with the read-only `numberOfSegments` property.

A segmented control comes in a choice of styles (its `segmentedControlStyle`):

UISegmentedControlStylePlain
> Large default height (44 pixels) and large titles. Deselected segments are gray; the selected segment is blue and has a depressed look.

UISegmentedControlStyleBordered
> Just like `UISegmentedControlStylePlain`, but a dark border emphasizes the segmented control's outline.

UISegmentedControlStyleBar
> Small default height (30 pixels) and small titles. All segments are blue, but you can change this by setting the `tintColor`; the selected segment is slightly darker.

UISegmentedControlStyleBezeled *(introduced in iOS 4.0)*
> Large default height (40 pixels) and small titles. Similar to `UISegmentedControlStyleBar`. All segments are blue, but you can change this by setting the `tintColor`; the selected segment is brighter.

A segmented control's height is standard in accordance with its style. You can change a segmented control's height in code, but of course if you later call `sizeToFit`, it will resume its standard height.

A segment's width is adjusted automatically when you create it or call `sizeToFit`, or you can set it manually with `setWidth:forSegmentAtIndex:` (and retrieve it with `widthForSegmentAtIndex:`). You can also change the position of the content (title or image) within a segment. (In my testing before Xcode 4, doing this in the nib was broken.) To set this position in code, call `setContentOffset:forSegmentAtIndex:` (and retrieve it with `contentOffsetForSegmentAtIndex:`), where the offset is expressed as a CGSize describing how much to move the content from its default centered position.

## UIButton

A button (UIButton) is a fundamental tappable control; its appearance is extremely flexible. It is endowed at creation with a type. The code creation method is a class method, `buttonWithType:`. The types are:

UIButtonTypeCustom

> Could be completely invisible, if the `backgroundColor` is `clearColor` and there's no title or other content. If a `backgroundColor` is supplied, a thin, subtle rectangular border is also present; you can add more of a border, of course, by modifying the button's `layer`. Alternatively, as we shall see, you can provide a background image, thus making the button appear to be any shape you like (though naturally this does not affect its tappable region).

UIButtonTypeDetailDisclosure
UIButtonTypeContactAdd
UIButtonTypeInfoLight
UIButtonTypeInfoDark

> Basically, these are all `UIButtonTypeCustom` buttons whose image is set automatically to standard button images: a right-pointing chevron, a plus sign, a light letter "i," and a dark letter "i," respectively.

UIButtonTypeRoundedRect

> A rounded rectangle with a white background and an antialiased gray border. However, supplying a rectangular opaque background image results in a rectangle similar to a `UIButtonTypeCustom` button. (A rounded rect button is actually an instance of a UIButton subclass, UIRoundedRectButton, but you're probably not supposed to know that.)

A button has a title, a title color, a title shadow color, an image, and a background image. The background image, if any, is stretched to fit the button's bounds. The image, on the other hand, if is smaller than the button, is not resized, and is thus shown internally within the button. The button can have both a title and an image, if the image is small enough; in that case, the image is shown to the left of the title by default.

These five features (title, title color, title shadow color, image, and background image) can all be made to vary depending on the button's current state: `UIControlState-Highlighted`, `UIControlStateSelected`, `UIControlStateDisabled`, and `UIControlState-Normal` (that is, none of the preceding). A state change, whether automatic (the button is highlighted while the user is tapping it) or programmatically imposed, will thus in and of itself alter a button's appearance. To make this possible, the methods for setting these button features all involve specifying a corresponding state (or multiple states, using a bitmask):

- `setTitle:forState:`
- `setTitleColor:forState:` (by default, the title color is white when the button is highlighted)

---

- `setTitleShadowColor:forState:`
- `setImage:forState:`
- `setBackgroundImage:forState:`

Similarly, when getting these button features, you must either use a method to specify a single state you're interested in or use a property to ask about the feature as currently displayed:

- `titleForState:`
- `titleColorForState:`
- `titleShadowColorForState:`
- `imageForState:`
- `backgroundImageForState:`
- `currentTitle`
- `currentTitleColor`
- `currentTitleShadowColor`
- `currentImage`
- `currentBackgroundImage`

If you don't specify a feature for a particular state, or if the button adopts more than one state at once, an internal heuristic is used to determine what to display. I can't describe all possible combinations, but here are some general observations:

- If you specify a feature for a particular state (highlighted, selected, or disabled), and the button is in only that state, that feature will be used.
- If you *don't* specify a feature for a particular state (highlighted, selected, or disabled), and the button is in only that state, the normal version of that feature will be used as fallback. (That's why many examples earlier in this book have assigned a title for `UIControlStateNormal` only; this is sufficient to give the button a title in every state.)
- Combinations of states often cause the button to fall back on the feature for normal state. For example, if a button is both highlighted and selected, the button will display its normal title, even if it has a highlighted title, a selected title, or both.

In addition, a UIButton has some properties determining how it draws itself in various states, which can save you the trouble of specifying different images for different states:

`showsTouchWhenHighlighted`
> If YES, then the button projects a circular white glow when highlighted. If the button has an internal image, the glow is centered behind it (Figure 25-11); thus, this feature is suitable particularly if the button image is small and circular; for example, it's the default behavior for a `UIButtonTypeInfoLight` or `UIButtonTypeInfo-`

*Figure 25-11. A button with highlighted glow*

Dark button. (If the button has no internal image, the glow is centered at the button's center.) The glow is drawn on top of the background image or color, if any.

adjustsImageWhenHighlighted

If YES (the default), then if there is no separate highlighted image (and if shows-TouchWhenHighlighted is NO), the normal image is darkened when the button is highlighted. This applies equally to the internal image and the background image.

adjustsImageWhenDisabled

If YES (the default), then if there is no separate disabled image, the normal image is lightened (faded) when the button is disabled. This applies equally to the internal image and the background image.

The title is a UILabel (Chapter 23), and the label features of the title can be accessed through the button's titleLabel. Thus, for example, you can set the title's font, lineBreakMode, and shadowOffset. If the shadowOffset is not (0,0), then the title has a shadow, and the title shadow color feature comes into play; the button's reversesTitleShadowWhenHighlighted property also applies: if YES, the shadowOffset values are replaced with their additive inverses when the button is highlighted.

An easy way to make a button's title consist of multiple lines is to set the button's titleLabel.lineBreakMode to UILineBreakModeWordWrap and put manual line breaks into the button's title: @"This is a line\nand this is a line". (To insert a line break in the nib editor, type Option-Return.)

The internal image is drawn by a UIImageView (Chapter 15) whose features can be accessed through the button's imageView. Thus, for example, you can change the internal image's alpha to make it more transparent.

The internal position of the image and title as a whole are governed by the button's contentVerticalAlignment and contentHorizontalAlignment (recall that these properties are inherited from UIControl). You can also tweak the position of the image and title, together or separately, by setting the button's contentEdgeInsets, titleEdgeInsets, or imageEdgeInsets. Increasing an inset component increases that margin; thus, for example, a positive top component makes the distance between that object and the top of the button larger than normal (where "normal" is where the object would be according to the alignment settings). The titleEdgeInsets or imageEdgeInsets values are added to the overall contentEdgeInsets values. So, for example, if you really wanted to, you could make the internal image appear to the right of the title by decreasing the left titleEdgeInsets and increasing the left imageEdgeInsets.

Four methods also provide access to the button's positioning of its elements:

*Figure 25-12. A button with a stretched background image*

- `titleRectForContentRect:`
- `imageRectForContentRect:`
- `contentRectForBounds:`
- `backgroundRectForBounds:`

These methods are called whenever the button is redrawn, including every time it changes state. The content rect is the area in which the title and image are placed. By default, `contentRectForBounds:` and `backgroundRectForBounds:` yield the same result.

You can override these methods in a subclass to change the way the button's elements are positioned. In this example, we shrink the button slightly when highlighted as a way of providing feedback:

```
- (CGRect)backgroundRectForBounds:(CGRect)bounds {
    CGRect result = [super backgroundRectForBounds:bounds];
    if (self.highlighted)
        result = CGRectInset(result, 3, 3);
    return result;
}
```

A button's background image is stretched if the image is smaller, in both dimensions, than the button's `backgroundRectForBounds:`. You can take advantage of this stretching, for example, to construct a rounded rectangle background for the button. To do so, use `stretchableImageWithLeftCapWidth:topCapHeight:`, as we did with a UISlider's track images earlier in this chapter, but this time, both the left and top cap values will matter. In this example (Figure 25-12), both the internal image and the background image are generated from the same image (which is in fact the same image used to generate the track in Figure 25-9):

```
UIImage* im = [UIImage imageNamed: @"coin.png"];
CGSize sz = [im size];
UIImage* im2 = [im stretchableImageWithLeftCapWidth:sz.width/2.0
                             topCapHeight:sz.height/2.0];
[button setBackgroundImage: im2 forState: UIControlStateNormal];
button.backgroundColor = [UIColor clearColor];
```

# Custom Controls

The UIControl class implements several touch-tracking methods that you might override in order to customize a built-in UIControl type or to create your own UIControl subclass, along with properties that tell you whether touch tracking is going on:

- `beginTrackingWithTouch:withEvent:`

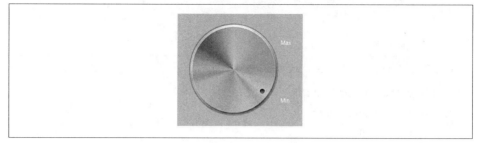

*Figure 25-13. A custom control*

- `continueTrackingWithTouch:withEvent:`
- `endTrackingWithTouch:withEvent:`
- `cancelTrackingWithEvent:`
- `tracking` (property)
- `touchInside` (property)

With the advent of gesture recognizers (Chapter 18), such direct involvement with touch tracking is probably less needed than it used to be, especially if your purpose is to modify the behavior of a built-in UIControl subclass. So, to illustrate their use, I'll give a simple example of creating a custom control. The main reason for doing this (rather than using, say, a UIView and gesture recognizers) would probably be to obtain the convenience of control events. Also, the touch-tracking methods, though of course nowhere near as high-level as gesture recognizers, are at least a level up from the UIResponder methods `touchesBegan:withEvent:` and so forth (Chapter 18): they track a single touch, and both `beginTracking...` and `continueTracking...` return a BOOL, giving you a chance to stop tracking the current touch.

We'll build a simplified knob control (Figure 25-13). The control starts life at its minimum position, with an internal angle value of 0; it can be rotated clockwise with a single finger as far as its maximum position, with an internal angle value of 5 (radians). To keep things simple, the words "Min" and "Max" appearing in the interface are actually labels; the control just draws the knob, and to rotate it we'll simply apply a rotation transform.

Our control is a UIControl subclass, MyKnob. It has a CGFloat property `angle`, and a CGFloat instance variable `initialAngle` that we'll use internally during rotation. Because a UIControl is a UIView, it can draw itself, which it does with a UIImage included in our app bundle:

```
- (void) drawRect:(CGRect)rect {
    UIImage* knob = [UIImage imageNamed:@"knob.png"];
    [knob drawInRect:rect];
}
```

We'll need a utility function for transforming a touch's Cartesian coordinates into polar coordinates, giving us the angle to be applied as a rotation to the view:

```
static CGFloat pToA (UITouch* touch, UIView* self) {
    CGPoint loc = [touch locationInView: self];
    CGPoint c = CGPointMake(CGRectGetMidX(self.bounds),
                            CGRectGetMidY(self.bounds));
    return atan2(loc.y - c.y, loc.x - c.x);
}
```

Now we're ready to override the tracking methods. `beginTrackingWithTouch:with-Event:` simply notes down the angle of the initial touch location. `continueTrackingWith-Touch:withEvent:` uses the difference between the current touch location's angle and the initial touch location's angle to apply a transform to the view, and updates the `angle` property. `endTrackingWithTouch:withEvent:` triggers the Value Changed control event. So our first draft looks like this:

```
- (BOOL) beginTrackingWithTouch:(UITouch *)touch withEvent:(UIEvent *)event {
    self->initialAngle = pToA(touch, self);
    return YES;
}

- (BOOL) continueTrackingWithTouch:(UITouch *)touch withEvent:(UIEvent *)event {
    CGFloat ang = pToA(touch, self);
    ang -= self->initialAngle;
    CGFloat absoluteAngle = self->angle + ang;
    self.transform = CGAffineTransformRotate(self.transform, ang);
    self->angle = absoluteAngle;
    return YES;
}

- (void) endTrackingWithTouch:(UITouch *)touch withEvent:(UIEvent *)event {
    [self sendActionsForControlEvents:UIControlEventValueChanged];
}
```

This works: we can put a MyKnob into the interface and hook up its Value Changed control event (this can be done in the nib editor), and sure enough, when we run the app, we can rotate the knob and, when our finger lifts from the knob, the Value Changed action handler is called. However, `continueTrackingWithTouch:withEvent:` needs modification.

First, we need to peg the minimum and maximum rotation at 0 and 5, respectively. For simplicity, we'll just stop tracking, by returning NO, if the rotation goes below 0 or above 5, fixing the angle at the exceeded limit. However, because we're no longer tracking, `endTracking...` will never be called, so we also need to trigger the Value Changed control event. (Doubtless you can come up with a more sophisticated way of pegging the knob at its minimum and maximum, but remember, this is only a simple example.) Second, it might be nice to give the programmer the option to have the Value Changed control event reported continuously as `continueTracking...` is called repeatedly. So we'll add a `continuous` BOOL property and obey it.

Here, then, is our revised `continueTracking...` implementation:

```
- (BOOL) continueTrackingWithTouch:(UITouch *)touch withEvent:(UIEvent *)event {
    CGFloat ang = pToA(touch, self);
```

```
    ang -= self->initialAngle;
    CGFloat absoluteAngle = self->angle + ang;
    if (absoluteAngle < 0) {
        self.transform = CGAffineTransformIdentity;
        self->angle = 0;
        [self sendActionsForControlEvents:UIControlEventValueChanged];
        return NO;
    }
    if (absoluteAngle > 5) {
        self.transform = CGAffineTransformMakeRotation(5);
        self->angle = 5;
        [self sendActionsForControlEvents:UIControlEventValueChanged];
        return NO;
    }
    self.transform = CGAffineTransformRotate(self.transform, ang);
    self->angle = absoluteAngle;
    if (self->continuous)
        [self sendActionsForControlEvents:UIControlEventValueChanged];
    return YES;
}
```

Finally, we'll probably want to be able to set the angle programmatically as a way of rotating the knob:

```
- (void) setAngle: (CGFloat) ang {
    if (ang < 0)
        ang = 0;
    if (ang > 5)
        ang = 5;
    self.transform = CGAffineTransformMakeRotation(ang);
    self->angle = ang;
}
```

This is more work than using a gesture recognizer (which is left as an exercise for the reader), but not much, and it gives a sense of what's involved in creating a custom control.

# Bars

As you saw in Chapter 19, the three bar types — UINavigationBar, UIToolbar, and UITabBar — are often used in in conjunction with a dedicated view controller. A UI-NavigationBar can be used with a UINavigationController (in which case it always appears at the top of the view). A UIToolbar can be used with a UINavigationController (in which case it always appears at the bottom of the view). A UITabBar can be used with a UITabBarController (in which case it always appears at the bottom of the view).

You can also use these bar types independently. In the case of UINavigationBar and UITabBar, it isn't particularly likely that you would do this. The purpose of a UINavigationBar is usually to let the user navigate between views, and to populate a UINavigationBar, you need a UINavigationItem; it's very convenient to let this be the navigationItem of a UIViewController and let a UINavigationController take care of the relationship between the two, including the physical display of the UIViewController's view. Similarly, a UITabBar is a way of letting the user choose between multiple items; those items often correspond to entire views, in which case the overall management is best left to a UITabBarController. Also, these are standard interface items, and you don't want to use them in a nonstandard way that might confuse the user. Even so, you might encounter a situation in which a full-fledged UIViewController is overkill or somehow doesn't work properly, and you might then solve the problem by using a UINavigationBar or UITabBar independently.

An independent UIToolbar is a more frequent interface element, especially on the iPad, where it frequently appears as a top bar, adopting a role analogous to a menu bar on Mac OS X. This is such a common interface that certain special automatic behaviors are associated with it; for example, as we've seen, a UISearchBar in a UIToolbar and managed by a UISearchDisplayController will automatically display its search results table in a popover, which is different from what happens if the UISearchBar is *not* in a UIToolbar.

Another thing to keep in mind is that there is nothing sacred about any of these bar types; you might be happier devising your own bar-like interface. A UIToolbar, for example, could easily be replaced by a rectangular view containing buttons. (In all probability, that's what appears at the bottom of a note in the iPhone Notes app.)

For the sake of completeness, this section summarizes the facts about the three bar types. (Please supply your own "Goldilocks and the three bars" joke here.)

## UINavigationBar

A UINavigationBar is populated by UINavigationItems. The UINavigationBar maintains a stack; UINavigationItems are pushed onto and popped off of this stack. Whatever UINavigationItem is currently topmost in the stack (the UINavigationBar's `topItem`), in combination with the UINavigationItem just beneath it in the stack (the UINavigationBar's `backItem`), determines what appears in the navigation bar:

- The `title` (string) or `titleView` (UIView) of the `topItem` appears in the center of the navigation bar.
- The `prompt` (string) of the `topItem` appears at the top of the navigation bar.
- The `rightBarButtonItem` and `leftBarButtonItem` appear at the right and left ends of the navigation bar. These are UIBarButtonItems. A UIBarButtonItem can be a system button, a titled button, an image button, or a container for a UIView. A UIBarButtonItem is not itself a UIView, however. See "Bar Button Items" on page 466 for details about UIBarButtonItems.
- The `backBarButtonItem` *of the* `backItem` appears at the left end of the navigation bar. It typically points to the left, and is automatically configured so that, when tapped, the `topItem` is popped off the stack. If the `backItem` has *no* `backBarButtonItem`, then there is *still* a back button at the left end of the navigation bar, taking its title from

the `title` of the `backItem`. However, if the `topItem` has a `leftBarButtonItem`, or if the `topItem` has its `hidesBackButton` set to YES, the back button is suppressed.

Changes to the navigation bar's buttons can be animated by sending its `topItem` any of these messages:

- `setRightBarButtonItem:animated:`
- `setLeftBarButtonItem:animated:`
- `setHidesBackButton:animated:`

UINavigationItems are pushed and popped with `pushNavigationItem:animated:` and `popNavigationItemAnimated:`, or you can set all items on the stack at once with `setItems:animated:` or by directly setting the `items`.

A UINavigationBar can be styled using its `barStyle`, `translucent`, and `tintColor` properties. See "Configuring the navigation view controller" on page 472 for details.

When you use a UINavigationBar implicitly as part of a UINavigationController interface, the controller is the navigation bar's delegate. If you were to use a UINavigationBar on its own, you might want to supply your own delegate. The delegate methods are:

- `navigationBar:shouldPushItem:`
- `navigationBar:didPushItem:`
- `navigationBar:shouldPopItem:`
- `navigationBar:didPopItem:`

This simple (and silly) example of a stand-alone UINavigationBar (Figure 25-14) implements the legendary baseball combination trio of Tinker to Evers to Chance (see the relevant Wikipedia article if you don't know about them):

```
- (void)viewDidLoad {
    [super viewDidLoad];
    UINavigationItem* ni = [[UINavigationItem alloc] initWithTitle:@"Tinker"];
    UIBarButtonItem* b = [[UIBarButtonItem alloc] initWithTitle:@"Evers"
        style:UIBarButtonItemStyleBordered
        target:self action:@selector(pushNext:)];
    ni.rightBarButtonItem = b;
    [b release];
    nav.items = [NSArray arrayWithObject: ni]; // nav is the UINavigationBar
    [ni release];
}

- (void) pushNext: (id) sender {
    UIBarButtonItem* oldb = sender;
    NSString* s = oldb.title;
    UINavigationItem* ni = [[UINavigationItem alloc] initWithTitle:s];
    if ([s isEqualToString: @"Evers"]) {
        UIBarButtonItem* b = [[UIBarButtonItem alloc] initWithTitle:@"Chance"
            style:UIBarButtonItemStyleBordered
            target:self action:@selector(pushNext:)];
```

*Figure 25-14. A navigation bar*

```
        ni.rightBarButtonItem = b;
        [b release];
    }
    [nav pushNavigationItem:ni animated:YES];
    [ni release];
}
```

# UIToolbar

A UIToolbar displays a row of UIBarButtonItems, which are its `items`. The items are displayed from left to right in the order in which they appear in the `items` array. You can use the system bar button items `UIBarButtonSystemItemFlexibleSpace` and `UIBar-ButtonSystemItemFixedSpace`, along with the UIBarButtonItem `width` property, to position the items within the toolbar. See the previous section and Chapter 19 for more about UIBarButtonItems.

A UIToolbar can be styled, like a UINavigationBar.

# UITabBar

A UITabBar displays UITabBarItems (its `items`), each consisting of an image and a name, and maintains a current selection among those items (its `selectedItem`, which is a UITabBarItem, not an index number). To hear about a change of selection, implement `tabBar:didSelectItem:` in the delegate (UITabBarDelegate). To change the items in an animated fashion, call `setItems:animated:`. See "Tab Bar Item Images" on page 462 on how to create a UITabBarItem and on the peculiar requirements of its image.

The user can be permitted to customize the contents of the tab bar. To implement this, provide interface that calls `beginCustomizingItems:`, passing an array of UITabBarItems that may or may not appear in the tab bar. (To prevent the user from removing an item from the tab bar, include it in the tab bar's `items` and *don't* include it in the argument passed to `beginCustomizingItems:`.) A modal view with a Done button appears, behind the tab bar but in front of everything else, displaying the customizable items. The user can then drag an item into the tab bar, replacing an item that's already there. To hear about the customizing modal view appearing and disappearing, implement delegate methods:

- `tabBar:willBeginCustomizingItems:`
- `tabBar:didBeginCustomizingItems:`
- `tabBar:willEndCustomizingItems:changed:`

- `tabBar:didEndCustomizingItems:changed:`

A UITabBar on its own does not provide any automatic customization access; it's up to you. In this (silly) example, we populate a UITabBar with four system tab bar items and a More item; we also populate an instance variable array with those same four system tab bar items, plus four more. When the user taps the More item, we show the customization interface with all eight tab bar items:

```
- (void)viewDidLoad {
    [super viewDidLoad];
    NSMutableArray* arr = [NSMutableArray array];
    for (int ix = 1; ix < 8; ix++) {
        UITabBarItem* tbi =
            [[UITabBarItem alloc] initWithTabBarSystemItem:ix tag:ix];
        [arr addObject: tbi];
        [tbi release];
    }
    self.items = arr; // copy policy
    [arr removeAllObjects];
    [arr addObjectsFromArray: [self.items subarrayWithRange:NSMakeRange(0,4)]];
    UITabBarItem* tbi = [[UITabBarItem alloc] initWithTabBarSystemItem:0 tag:0];
    [arr addObject: tbi]; // More button
    tb.items = arr; // tb is the UITabBar
    [tbi release];
}

- (void)tabBar:(UITabBar *)tabBar didSelectItem:(UITabBarItem *)item {
    NSLog(@"did select item with tag %i", item.tag);
    if (item.tag == 0) {
        // More button
        tabBar.selectedItem = nil;
        [tabBar beginCustomizingItems:self.items];
    }
}
```

When used in conjunction with a UITabBarController, the customization interface is provided automatically, in an elaborate way. If there are a lot of items, a More item is automatically present, and can be used to access the remaining items in a table view. Here, the user can select any of the excess items, navigating to the corresponding view. Or, the user can switch to the customization interface by tapping the Edit button. See the iPhone iPod/Music app for a familiar example. Figure 25-15 shows an example generated automatically, with no code; the tab bar is created and configured completely in the nib.

The way this works is that the automatically provided More item corresponds to a UINavigationController with a root view controller (UIViewController) whose `view` is a UITableView. Thus, it is this UITableView that appears in a navigation interface when the user taps the More button. When the user selects an item in the table, the corresponding UIViewController is pushed onto the UINavigationController's stack.

You can access this UINavigationController: it is the UITabBarController's `moreNavigationController`. Through it, you can access the root view controller: it is the first

*Figure 25-15. Automatically generated More list*

item in the UINavigationController's `viewControllers` array. And through that, you can access the table view: it is the root view controller's `view`. This means you can customize what appears when the user taps the More button. For example, let's make the navigation bar black, and let's remove the word More from its title:

```
UINavigationController* more = self.tabBarController.moreNavigationController;
UIViewController* list = [more.viewControllers objectAtIndex:0];
list.title = @"";
UIBarButtonItem* b = [[UIBarButtonItem alloc] init];
b.title = @"Back";
list.navigationItem.backBarButtonItem = b; // so user can navigate back
[b release];
more.navigationBar.barStyle = UIBarStyleBlack;
```

We can go even further by supplementing the table view's data source with a data source of our own, thus proceeding to customize the table itself. This is tricky because we have no internal access to the actual data source, and we mustn't accidentally disable it from populating the table. Still, it can be done. I'll start by replacing the table view's data source with an instance of my own MyDataSource, storing a reference to the original data source object in an instance variable of MyDataSource:

```
UITableView* tv = (UITableView*)list.view;
MyDataSource* mds = [[MyDataSource alloc] init];
self.myDataSource = mds; // retain policy
[mds release];
```

```
    self.myDataSource.originalDataSource = tv.dataSource;
    tv.dataSource = self.myDataSource;
```

Next, I'll use Objective-C's automatic message forwarding mechanism (see the *Objective-C Runtime Programming Guide*) so that MyDataSource acts as a front end for originalDataSource. MyDataSource will magically appear to respond to any message that originalDataSource responds to, and any message that arrives that MyDataSource can't handle will be magically forwarded to originalDataSource. This way, the insertion of the MyDataSource instance as data source doesn't break whatever the original data source does:

```
    - (BOOL)respondsToSelector:(SEL)aSelector {
        if ([super respondsToSelector:aSelector])
            return YES;
        else if ([self.originalDataSource respondsToSelector:aSelector])
            return YES;
        return NO;
    }

    - (NSMethodSignature*)methodSignatureForSelector:(SEL)selector {
        NSMethodSignature* signature = [super methodSignatureForSelector:selector];
        if (!signature)
            signature = [self.originalDataSource methodSignatureForSelector:selector];
        return signature;
    }

    - (void)forwardInvocation:(NSInvocation *)anInvocation {
        if ([self.originalDataSource respondsToSelector: [anInvocation selector]])
            [anInvocation invokeWithTarget:self.originalDataSource];
        else
            [super forwardInvocation:anInvocation];
    }
```

Starting in iOS 4 there is a much simpler way to do the above:

```
    - (id)forwardingTargetForSelector:(SEL)aSelector {
        if ([self.originalDataSource respondsToSelector: aSelector])
            return self.originalDataSource;
        return [super forwardingTargetForSelector:aSelector];
    }
```

(If you know your app will run only under iOS 4 or later, you can implement forwardingTargetForSelector: alone and not bother with respondsToSelector:, methodSignatureForSelector:, and forwardInvocation:; if your app will also run under iOS 3, it does no harm to implement all four methods, as the first will be called in preference to the others on iOS 4 and will be ignored on iOS 3.)

Finally, we'll implement the two Big Questions required by the UITableViewDataSource protocol, to quiet the compiler. In both cases, we first pass the message along to originalDataSource (somewhat analogous to calling super); then we add our own customizations as desired. Here, I'll remove each cell's disclosure indicator and change its text font. The outcome is shown in Figure 25-16:

*Figure 25-16. Customized More list*

```
- (NSInteger)tableView:(UITableView *)tv numberOfRowsInSection:(NSInteger)sec {
    // this is just to quiet the compiler
    return [self.originalDataSource tableView:tv numberOfRowsInSection:sec];
}

- (UITableViewCell *)tableView:(UITableView *)tv
        cellForRowAtIndexPath:(NSIndexPath *)ip {
    UITableViewCell* cell =
        [self.originalDataSource tableView:tv cellForRowAtIndexPath:ip];
    cell.accessoryType = UITableViewCellAccessoryNone;
    cell.textLabel.font = [UIFont systemFontOfSize:14];
    return cell;
}
```

# CHAPTER 26

# Modal Dialogs

A modal dialog demands attention; while it is present, the user can do nothing other than dismiss the dialog. You might need to put up a simple modal dialog in order to give the user some information or to ask the user how to proceed. Two UIView subclasses are provided that construct and present rudimentary modal dialogs:

*UIAlertView*

> A UIAlertView pops up unexpectedly with an elaborate animation and may be thought of as an attention-getting interruption. An alert is displayed in the center of the screen; it contains a title, a message, and an indefinite number of additional buttons, one of which may be the cancel button, meaning that it does nothing but dismiss the alert. The cancel button appears last, slightly separated from the other buttons. Often there is *only* a cancel button, the primary purpose of the alert being to show the user the message ("You won the game"); the additional buttons may be used to give the user a choice of how to proceed ("You won the game; would you like to play another?" "Yes," "No," "Replay").

*UIActionSheet*

> A UIActionSheet may be considered the iOS equivalent of a Mac OS X menu. An action sheet is displayed arising from the interface: on the iPhone, it slides up from the bottom of the screen; on the iPad, it is typically shown in a popover. It consists of an indefinite number of buttons (there can be a title, optionally, but there usually isn't); one may be the cancel button, which appears last (though on the iPad, for a popover, this may not be needed), and one may be a "destructive" button, which appears first in red, emphasizing the severity of that option. Where a UIAlertView is an interruption, a UIActionSheet is a logical branching of what the user is already doing: it typically divides a single piece of interface into multiple possible courses of action. For example, in Mobile Safari a single "More" button summons an action sheet that lets the user add the current page as a bookmark, add it to the home screen, mail a link to it, or print it (or cancel and so do nothing).

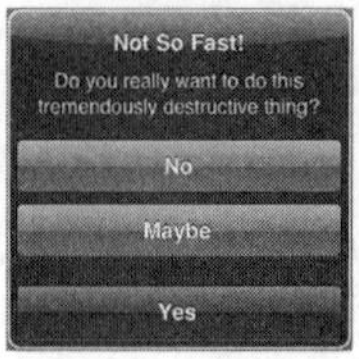

*Figure 26-1. An alert view (UIAlertView)*

# Alert View

The basic method for constructing an alert view (UIAlertView) is `initWithTitle:` `message:delegate:cancelButtonTitle:otherButtonTitles:`. The method for making a constructed alert view appear onscreen is `show`. Here's an example (Figure 26-1):

```
UIAlertView* alert = [[UIAlertView alloc] initWithTitle:@"Not So Fast!"
    message:@"Do you really want to do this tremendously destructive thing?"
    delegate:self cancelButtonTitle:@"Yes" otherButtonTitles:@"No", @"Maybe", nil];
[alert show];
[alert release];
```

The `otherButtonTitles` parameter is of indefinite length, so it must either be nil or must consist of a nil-terminated list of strings. The cancel button needn't involve canceling anything; it is drawn darker than the other buttons and comes last in a column of buttons, as you can see from Figure 26-1, but if there were three `otherButtonTitles` and a nil `cancelButtonTitle`, the alert dialog would look exactly the same.

The alert dialog is modal, but the code that presents it is not: after the alert is shown, your code continues to run. Thus, in the example, the UIAlertView instance is released immediately after the alert is shown, while it is still showing. (This is not a problem, because once the alert is shown, the framework retains it.)

The alert is automatically dismissed as soon as the user taps any button. If an alert consists of a single button (the cancel button), you might show it and forget about it, secure in the knowledge that the user must dismiss it sooner or later and that nothing can happen until then. But if you want to respond at the time the user dismisses the alert, or if there are several buttons and you want to know which one the user tapped to dismiss the alert, you'll need to implement at least one of these delegate methods (UIAlertViewDelegate):

- `alertView:clickedButtonAtIndex:`
- `alertView:willDismissWithButtonIndex:`
- `alertView:didDismissWithButtonIndex:`

The cancel button index is usually 0, with the remaining button indexes increasing in the order in which they were defined. If you're in any doubt, or if you need the button title for any other reason, you can call `buttonTitleAtIndex:`. Properties allow you to work out the correspondence between indexes and buttons without making any assumptions:

- `cancelButtonIndex` (-1 if none)
- `firstOtherButtonIndex` (-1 if none)
- `numberOfButtons` (including the cancel button)

You can also dismiss an alert view programmatically, with `dismissWithClickedButton-Index:animated:`. When an alert view is dismissed programmatically, the delegate method `alertView:clickedButtonAtIndex:` is *not* called, because no button was actually clicked by the user. But the button index you specify is still passed along to the two `dismiss` delegate methods. The button index you specify doesn't need to correspond to any existing button; thus, you could use it as a way of telling your delegate method that your code, and not the user, dismissed the alert.

Two additional delegate methods notify you when the alert is initially shown:

- `willPresentAlertView:`
- `didPresentAlertView:`

One further delegate method notifies you if the alert is dismissed by the system:

- `alertViewCancel:`

Before iOS 4.0, this could happen because the user quit the app with the alert showing; the system dismissed the alert, and your code had a chance to respond before actually terminating. But iOS 4.0 introduced multitasking; if the user clicks the Home button, your app is backgrounded without the system dismissing the alert, and `alertView-Cancel:` may be a dead letter. It would thus be up to your code, as the app is backgrounded, whether to leave the alert there or to dismiss the alert and perhaps take some default action.

# Action Sheet

The basic method for constructing an action sheet (UIActionSheet) is `initWithTitle:delegate:cancelButtonTitle:destructiveButtonTitle:otherButtonTitles:`. There are various methods for summoning the actual sheet, depending on what part of the interface you want the sheet to arise from. The following are appropriate on the iPhone, where the sheet typically rises from the bottom of the screen:

`showInView:`
> On the iPhone, far and away the most commonly used method. You will usually specify the root view controller's view. Don't specify a view whose view controller is contained by a view controller that hides the bottom of the interface, such as a tab bar controller or a navigation controller with a toolbar; if you do, some of the buttons may not function. (On recent iOS versions, you get a helpful warning in

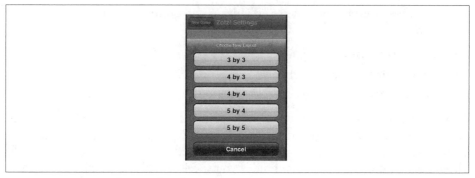

Figure 26-2. An action sheet on the iPhone

Figure 26-3. An action sheet presented as a popover

the console if you make this mistake: "Presenting action sheet clipped by its superview.") Instead, specify the tab bar controller's view itself, or the navigation controller's view itself, or use one of the other methods. For example, in my Zotz app, which has a tab bar interface, the settings view controller summons an action sheet like this (Figure 26-2):

```
[sheet showInView: self.tabBarController.view];
```

showFromTabBar:, showFromToolbar:
   On the iPhone, these cause the sheet to rise from the bottom of the screen, just like showInView:, because the tab bar or toolbar is at the bottom of the screen; however, they avoid the problem with showInView: described earlier.

On the iPad, you are more likely to use one of the following methods, added in iOS 3.2. These methods resemble the methods for presenting a popover (Chapter 22), and they do in fact present the action sheet as a popover, with its arrow pointing to the specified part of the interface (Figure 26-3):

• showFromRect:inView:animated:

• showFromBarButtonItem:animated:

(On the iPhone, those methods should be avoided; they don't cause an error, and they do work — the sheet still ends up at the bottom at the screen — but they can do messy things to the interface.)

*Figure 26-4. An action sheet presented inside a popover*

On the iPad, there is usually no point including a cancel button title: if the alert sheet is shown as a popover, no cancel button will appear. This is because the popover is configured to be dismissed when the user taps outside it, which is the same as canceling it.

However, it is also possible on the iPad to show an alert sheet *inside an existing popover*. In this scenario, we are already presenting the popover, and then we summon an action sheet within the popover's view. In that case, the action sheet behaves as if the popover were an iPhone: you summon it with `showInView:`, it slides up from the bottom of the popover, and the cancel button appears (Figure 26-4). Moreover, the action sheet is then modal: the user can't dismiss the popover, or do anything else, without dismissing the action sheet first.

An action sheet also has a style, its `actionSheetStyle`:

- `UIActionSheetStyleAutomatic`
- `UIActionSheetStyleDefault`
- `UIActionSheetStyleBlackTranslucent`
- `UIActionSheetStyleBlackOpaque`

These values are closely related to the possible styles (`barStyle`) of a UIToolbar. However, an action sheet's style depends also on the mode of presentation; experimentation suggests, for example, that setting the `actionSheetStyle` of an action sheet that appears as a popover may make no perceptible difference, and that an action sheet that is shown from a tab bar will always be black opaque.

In other respects an action sheet is managed in a manner completely parallel to an alert view. When one of its buttons is tapped, the sheet is dismissed automatically, but you'll probably want to implement a delegate method (UIActionSheetDelegate) in order to learn which button it was:

- `actionSheet:clickedButtonAtIndex:`
- `actionSheet:willDismissWithButtonIndex:`
- `actionSheet:didDismissWithButtonIndex:`

If the action sheet is shown as a popover on the iPad, and if the popover is dismissed by the user tapping outside it, the button index is -1.

To respond appropriately to the delegate methods without making assumptions about how the indexes correspond to the buttons, you can use the `buttonTitleAtIndex:` method, and these properties:

- `cancelButtonIndex`
- `destructiveButtonIndex`
- `firstOtherButtonIndex`
- `numberOfButtons`

You can dismiss an action sheet programmatically with `dismissWithClickedButton-Index:animated:`, in which case `actionSheet:clickedButtonAtIndex:` is not called, but the two `dismiss` delegate methods are. Two additional delegate methods notify you when the sheet is initially shown:

- `willPresentActionSheet:`
- `didPresentActionSheet:`

A further delegate method, `actionSheetCancel:`, notifies you if the sheet is dismissed by the system, though in iOS 4.0 or later this is unlikely to happen; if your app is backgrounded with an action sheet showing, it's up to you to decide how to proceed.

Here's the code that presents the action sheet shown in Figure 26-2, along with the code that responds to its dismissal:

```
- (void) chooseLayout: (id) sender {
    UIActionSheet* sheet =
        [[UIActionSheet alloc] initWithTitle:@"Choose New Layout" delegate:self
        cancelButtonTitle:(NSString *)@"Cancel" destructiveButtonTitle:nil
        otherButtonTitles:@"3 by 3", @"4 by 3", @"4 by 4", @"5 by 4", @"5 by 5",
        nil];
    [sheet showInView: self.tabBarController.view];
    [sheet release];
}

- (void)actionSheet:(UIActionSheet *)as clickedButtonAtIndex:(NSInteger)ix {
    if (ix == as.cancelButtonIndex)
        return;
    NSString* s = [as buttonTitleAtIndex:ix];
    // ...
}
```

On the iPad, if an action sheet is shown as a popover from a bar button item in a toolbar, the toolbar becomes a passthrough view for the popover. This behavior is troublesome, for the same reasons I gave in Chapter 22: the user can now tap another bar button item without causing the action sheet's popover to be dismissed (and possibly even summoning another popover — perhaps even another instance of the same action sheet — simultaneously). Preventing this sort of conflict is entirely up to your code. You can't

*Figure 26-5. A modal view functioning as a modal dialog*

solve the problem by adjusting the popover controller's `passthroughViews`, because you can't get access to the popover controller! This situation seems like a massive bug. The best solution seems to be to implement the delegate methods to toggle user interaction in the toolbar:

```
- (IBAction)doButton:(id)sender {
    UIActionSheet* act = [[UIActionSheet alloc]
        initWithTitle:nil delegate:self cancelButtonTitle:nil
        destructiveButtonTitle:nil otherButtonTitles:@"Hey", @"Ho", nil];
    [act showFromBarButtonItem:sender animated:YES];
}

- (void)didPresentActionSheet:(UIActionSheet *)actionSheet {
    [self.toolbar setUserInteractionEnabled:NO];
}

- (void)actionSheet:(UIActionSheet *)actionSheet
        didDismissWithButtonIndex:(NSInteger)buttonIndex {
    [self.toolbar setUserInteractionEnabled:YES];
}
```

# Dialog Alternatives

Alert views and actions sheets are limited, inflexible, and inappropriate to any but the simplest cases. In more complex situations, it really isn't that much work to implement an alternative.

 One occasionally sees a misuse of the built-in dialogs to include additional interface. For example, a UIActionSheet is a UIView, so in theory you can add a subview to it. I cannot recommend such behavior; it clearly isn't intended, and there's no need for it. If what you need isn't what a built-in dialog normally does, don't use a built-in dialog.

On the iPhone, the main alternative is to navigate to a new screenful of interface. This might be by way of a navigation interface, or using a modal view. For example, in the Zotz app, in the Settings view, when the user taps a color, I summon a modal view, using a UIViewController subclass of my own, ColorPickerController (Figure 26-5).

On Mac OS X, the color picker in Figure 26-5 might be presented as a secondary window acting as a dialog. On the small iPhone screen, where there are no secondary windows, the modal view *is* the equivalent of a dialog. Indeed, one might argue that the action sheet shown in Figure 26-2 is not a very appropriate use of an action sheet, that it's too intrusive and has too many buttons. It might have been better if I'd designed my own modal view; I probably picked an action sheet because it required just a few lines of code — basically, I was being lazy.

On the iPad, a popover is virtually a secondary window, and can be truly modal. An action sheet is usually presented as a popover, but it's limited, and you don't get access to the popover controller; in many cases, you'll probably be better off designing your own view to be presented in a popover. The popovers in Figure 22-1, for example, are effectively modal dialogs. A popover can internally present a secondary modal view or even an action sheet, as we've already seen. Also on the iPad, a modal view can be presented using the `UIModalPresentationFormSheet` presentation style, which is effectively a dialog window smaller than the screen.

# Local Notifications

A *local notification* is an alert to the user that can appear even if your app is not running. In its most commonly used manifestation, it appears as a dialog on top of whatever the user is doing at that moment, which is why it is treated in this chapter. (If a local notification from some other app were to appear while *your* app is frontmost, your app would become inactive; see Chapter 11 and the `applicationWillResignActive:` app delegate message.) Local notifications were introduced in iOS 4.

 This use of the term *notification* has nothing to do with NSNotification (Chapter 11). The ambiguity is unfortunate.

Your app does not present a local notification alert: indeed, your app *can't* present a local notification alert, because if your app's local notification alert appears, your app *ex hypothesi* isn't frontmost. Rather, your app hands a local notification to the system along with instructions about when the local notification should *fire*. When the specified time arrives, if your app isn't frontmost, the system presents the alert on your behalf.

The alert can optionally contain an action button. (If the alert appears when the device is locked, this will appear as a slider.) If user taps this, your app will be brought to the front, launching it if it isn't already suspended in the background.

To create a local notification, you configure a UILocalNotification object and hand it to the system with UIApplication's `scheduleLocalNotification:`. The UILocalNotifi-

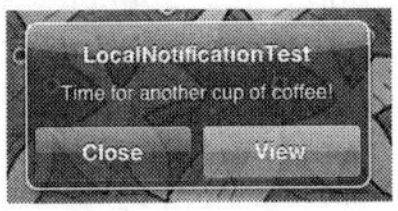

*Figure 26-6. An alert posted by the system when a local notification fires*

cation object has properties describing how the dialog should look and behave and when you want it to appear:

`alertBody, alertAction`
> The message displayed in the alert, and the text of the action button (if any). If you don't set `alertAction` and you do not set `hasAction` to NO, there will still be an action button, whose text will be "View." (The alert's title will be your app's name, and you can't change this.)

`soundName`
> The name of a sound file at the top level of your app bundle, to be played when the alert appears. This should be an uncompressed sound (AIFF or WAV). Alternatively, you can specify the default sound, `UILocalNotificationDefaultSound-Name`. If you don't set this property, there won't be a sound.

`userInfo`
> An optional NSDictionary whose contents are up to you. As you would expect, this is so that your app can identify the local notification object when it fires.

`fireDate, timeZone`
> When you want the local notification to fire. The `fireDate` is an NSDate (see Chapter 10 and Chapter 25 for examples of date manipulation). If you don't include a `timeZone`, the date is measured against universal time; if you *do* include a `timeZone`, the date is measured against the user's local time zone, even if that time zone changes (because the user travels, for instance).

`repeatInterval, repeatCalendar`
> If set, the local notification will recur.

As I've already mentioned, you hand a configured local notification to the system with UIApplication's `scheduleLocalNotification:`. Additional UIApplication methods let you manipulate the list of local notifications you've already scheduled. You can cancel one or all scheduled local notifications (`cancelLocalNotification:`, `cancelAllLocal-Notifications:`); starting in iOS 4.2, you can also manipulate the list directly by setting UIApplication's `scheduledLocalNotifications`, an NSArray property (previously, this property was read-only).

Figure 26-6 shows an alert generated by the firing of a local notification. Here's a simple example of creating and scheduling the local notification that resulted in that alert:

```
UILocalNotification* ln = [[UILocalNotification alloc] init];
ln.alertBody = @"Time for another cup of coffee!";
ln.fireDate = [NSDate dateWithTimeIntervalSinceNow:15];
```

```
ln.soundName = UILocalNotificationDefaultSoundName;
[[UIApplication sharedApplication] scheduleLocalNotification:ln];
[ln release];
```

Now let's talk about what happens when one of your scheduled local notifications fires. There are three possibilities, depending on the state of your app at that moment:

*Your app is suspended in the background*
> The alert appears (and the sound plays). If the user taps the action button, your app is brought to the front. Your app delegate will receive `application:didReceiveLocalNotification:`, where the second parameter is the UILocalNotification, and your application's `applicationState` will be `UIApplicationStateInactive`.

*Your app is frontmost*
> There will be no alert (and no sound). Your app delegate will receive `application:didReceiveLocalNotification:`, where the second parameter is the UILocalNotification, and your application's `applicationState` will be `UIApplicationStateActive`. The idea is that if your app wants to let the user know that something special is happening, that's your app's business and it can do it in its own way.

*Your app isn't running*
> The alert appears (and the sound plays). If the user taps the action button, your app is launched. Your app delegate will *not* receive `application:didReceiveLocalNotification:`. Instead, it will receive `application:didFinishLaunchingWithOptions:` with an NSDictionary parameter that includes the `UIApplicationLaunchOptionsLocalNotificationKey`, whose value is the UILocalNotification.

Thus, you should implement `application:didReceiveLocalNotification:` to check the UIApplication's `applicationState`, and you should implement `application:didFinishLaunchingWithOptions:` to check its second parameter to see whether we are launching in response to a local notification. In this way, you will be able to distinguish the three different possibilities, and you can respond appropriately.

In the first and third cases (your app is suspended in the background, or your app isn't running), you may want to show the user some interface appropriate to the local notification's situation. For example, you might want to push a particular view controller onto your navigation interface or show a particular view controller modally. However, when your app is launched from scratch, the first thing the user sees is its launch image (Chapter 9), and when your app is activated from a suspended state, the first thing the user sees is a screenshot image of your app, taken by the system when your app was suspended — and there may be a mismatch between these images and the interface that you're about to show the user in this special situation. The user will thus see an odd flash as the image is removed to reveal your app's actual interface. To prevent this flash, you can include in the original UILocalNotification an `alertLaunchImage` to be presented instead of these images. The idea is that this `alertLaunchImage` should be a better match for the interface the user will actually see.

There is actually a fourth possibility for when a local notification fires. Under some special circumstances (addressed, for example, in Chapter 27 and Chapter 35), your app might be running, *not* suspended, in the background. In this case, the situation is similar to what happens when your app *is* suspended: the alert does appear, and the user can summon your app to the front if `hasAction` is YES. Your running-in-the-background app can even schedule an alert to appear immediately with the convenience method `presentLocalNotificationNow:`.

# PART VI

# Some Frameworks

In addition to the basic UIKit and Foundation frameworks, which supply the fundamental interface and utility classes for all apps, Cocoa supplies numerous optional frameworks that you can use if your app has special needs. This part of the book introduces some of these frameworks and their related topics. At the same time, it necessarily exercises some restraint. To explore *all* of the additional iOS frameworks in *full* depth would more than double the size of this book! So this part of the book fully explains the basics, but then stops and leaves you to go further on your own if you need to; it teaches you what you need to know to get started, and it trains you to understand and explore these and related frameworks independently if your app requires a further level of depth and detail.

- Chapter 27 introduces the various iOS means for playing sound files, including audio sessions and playing sounds in the background.
- Chapter 28 describes some basic ways of playing video (movies), along with an introduction to the powerful new AV Foundation framework.
- Chapter 29 is about how an app can access the user's music library.
- Chapter 30 is about how an app can access the user's photo library, along with the ability to take photos and capture movies.
- Chapter 31 discusses how an app can access the user's address book.
- Chapter 32 talks about how an app can access the user's calendar data.
- Chapter 33 describes how an app can allow the user to compose and send email and SMS messages.
- Chapter 34 explains how an app can display a Google map, along with custom annotations and overlays.
- Chapter 35 is about how an app can learn where the device is located, how it is moving, and how it is oriented.

# CHAPTER 27

# Audio

iOS provides various means and technologies for allowing your app to produce sound (and even to input it). The topic is a large one, so this chapter can only introduce it. You'll want to read Apple's *Multimedia Programming Guide* and *Core Audio Overview*.

 None of the classes discussed in this chapter provide any user interface within your application for allowing the user to stop and start playback of sound (though you can create your own interface and use it with them). However, a web view (Chapter 24) supports the HTML 5 `<audio>` tag; this can be a simple, lightweight way to play audio and to allow the user to control playback. Or treat the sound as a movie and use the MPMoviePlayerController class discussed in Chapter 28; this can also be a good way to play a sound file located remotely over the Internet.

## System Sounds

The simplest form of sound is *system sound*, which is the iOS equivalent of the basic computer "beep." This is implemented through System Sound Services; you'll need to import `<AudioToolbox/AudioToolbox.h>` and link to *AudioToolbox.framework*. You'll be calling one of two C functions, which behave very similarly to one another:

`AudioServicesPlayAlertSound`
Plays a sound and, on an iPhone, may also vibrate the device, depending on the user's settings. On the original iPod touch, plays only a built-in alert sound.

`AudioServicesPlaySystemSound`
Plays a short sound of your choice. On an iPhone, there won't be an accompanying vibration, but you can specifically elect to have this "sound" *be* a device vibration.

The sound needs to be an uncompressed AIFF or WAV file (or an Apple CAF file wrapping one of these). To hand the sound to these functions, you'll need a System-

SoundID, which you obtain by calling `AudioServicesCreateSystemSoundID` with a CFURLRef (or NSURL) that points to a sound file. In this example, the sound file is in our app bundle:

```
NSURL* sndurl = [[NSBundle mainBundle] URLForResource:@"test" withExtension:@"aif"];
SystemSoundID snd;
AudioServicesCreateSystemSoundID ((CFURLRef)sndurl, &snd);
AudioServicesPlaySystemSound(snd);
```

However, there's a problem with that code: we have failed to exercise proper memory management. We need to call `AudioServicesDisposeSystemSoundID` to release our SystemSoundID. But when shall we do this? `AudioServicesPlaySystemSound` executes asynchronously. So the solution can't be to call `AudioServicesDisposeSystemSoundID` in the next line of the same snippet, because this would release our sound just as it is about to start playing, resulting in silence. A solution that works is to implement a sound completion handler, a function that is called when the sound has finished playing. So, our sound-playing snippet now looks like this:

```
NSURL* sndurl = [[NSBundle mainBundle] URLForResource:@"test" withExtension:@"aif"];
SystemSoundID snd;
AudioServicesCreateSystemSoundID((CFURLRef)sndurl, &snd);
AudioServicesAddSystemSoundCompletion(snd, NULL, NULL, &SoundFinished, NULL);
AudioServicesPlaySystemSound(snd);
```

And here is our sound completion handler, the `SoundFinished` function referred to in the previous snippet:

```
void SoundFinished (SystemSoundID snd, void* context) {
    AudioServicesRemoveSystemSoundCompletion(snd);
    AudioServicesDisposeSystemSoundID(snd);
}
```

Note that because we are about to release the sound, we first release the sound completion handler information applied to it. The last argument passed to `AudioServices-AddSystemSoundCompletion` is a pointer-to-void that comes back as the second parameter of our sound completion handler function; you can use this parameter in any way you like, such as to help identify the sound.

# Audio Session

If your app is going to use a more sophisticated way of producing sound, such as an audio player (discussed in the next section), it must specify a *policy* regarding that sound. This policy will answer such questions as: Should sound stop when the screen is locked? Should sound interrupt existing sound (being played, for example, by the iPod/Music app) or should it be layered on top of it?

Your policy is declared in an *audio session*, which is a singleton AVAudioSession instance created automatically as your app launches. You can configure this AVAudioSession instance once at launch time (or, at any rate, before producing any sound), or you can change its configuration dynamically while your app runs. You can talk to the

AVAudioSession instance in Objective-C (see the AVAudioSession class reference) or in C (see the Audio Session Services reference), or both.

To use the Objective-C API, you'll need to link to *AVFoundation.framework* and import `<AVFoundation/AVFoundation.h>`. You'll refer to your app's AVAudioSession by way of the class method `sharedInstance`.

To use the C API, you'll need to link to *AudioToolbox.framework* and import `<AudioToolbox/AudioToolbox.h>`. The `AudioSession...` functions don't require a reference to an audio session. You must explicitly initialize your audio session with `AudioSessionInitialize` before talking to it with the C API, unless you have already talked to it with the Objective-C API.

The basic policies for audio playback are:

*Ambient*
> Your app's audio plays even while iPod music or other background audio is playing, and is silenced by the Silent switch and screen locking.

*Solo Ambient*
> Your app stops iPod music or other background audio from playing, and is silenced by the Silent switch and screen locking (the default).

*Playback*
> Your app stops iPod music or other background audio from playing, and is not silenced by the Silent switch or screen locking.

In addition, you can modify these policies, using the `AudioSessionSetProperty` function of the C API. For example:

- You can override the Playback policy so as to allow iPod music or other background audio to play (`kAudioSessionProperty_OverrideCategoryMixWithOthers`).

- You can override a policy that allows iPod music or other background audio to play, so as to *duck* (diminish the volume of) that background audio (`kAudioSessionProperty_OtherMixableAudioShouldDuck`). Ducking does *not* depend automatically on whether your app is actively producing any sound; rather, it starts as soon as you turn this override on and remains in place until your audio session is deactivated.

Your audio session policy is not in effect unless your audio session is also *active*. By default, it isn't. Thus, asserting your audio session policy is done by a combination of configuring the audio session and activating the audio session. This is a little tricky because of multitasking on iOS 4. Your audio session can be deactivated automatically if your app is no longer active. So if you want your policy to be obeyed under all circumstances, you must explicitly activate your audio session each time your app becomes active. (See Chapter 11 for how an app resigns and resumes active status.)

For example, an audio session configured with a Playback policy that is activated as the app launches, in the app delegate's `applicationDidFinishLaunching:`, will silence background audio at launch time, but if the user then switches away to the iPod/Music app and starts playing some music, and then switches back to your app, the iPod music won't be silenced, even though it is now in the background, because your audio session has been deactivated. You might try to work around this by activating your audio session in the app delegate's `applicationWillEnterForeground:` as well. But then the user might double-click the Home button while your app is frontmost, and use the app switcher playback controls (Figure 27-1) to start playing iPod music; when the user leaves the app switcher interface, that iPod music continues to play, even though it is now in the background. To prevent *that*, you must activate your audio session in the app delegate's `applicationDidBecomeActive:`. It turns out that *only* `applicationDidBecomeActive:` is called in all three situations, so that is the place to activate your audio session so as to keep it active when running under iOS 4.

Here are the main methods you'll need:

`setCategory:error:`
> How you configure your audio session policy. You can do the same thing with the C API and `AudioSessionSetProperty`.

`setActive:error:`
> How you bring your audio session policy into force. You'll need to call this any time your audio session has been deactivated. At a minimum, calling it in `applicationDidBecomeActive:` keeps your audio session policy in force in the multitasking world of iOS 4.
>
> If you deactivate your audio session using `setActive:withFlags:error:`, passing a flag of `AVAudioSessionSetActiveFlags_NotifyOthersOnDeactivation`, you tell the system to allow any audio suspended by the activation of your audio session to resume. Thus you can activate and deactivate a Playback-policy audio session as your app runs as a way of pausing and resuming background audio (if the app providing the background audio responds correctly to this flag). I'll give an example later in this chapter.
>
> You can do the same thing with the C API and `AudioSessionSetActive` or `AudioSessionSetActiveWithFlags`.

Here's an example from an app where we want background sound such as iPod/Music songs to continue playing while our app runs. We configure our audio session to use the Ambient policy in `applicationDidFinishLaunching:`, as follows:

```
[[AVAudioSession sharedInstance] setCategory:
    AVAudioSessionCategoryAmbient error: NULL];
```

Or, using the C API:

```
AudioSessionInitialize (NULL, NULL, NULL, NULL);
UInt32 ambi = kAudioSessionCategory_AmbientSound;
AudioSessionSetProperty(kAudioSessionProperty_AudioCategory, sizeof(ambi), &ambi);
```

We activate our audio session every time our app becomes active, no matter how, in `applicationDidBecomeActive:`, like this:

```
[[AVAudioSession sharedInstance] setActive: YES error: NULL];
```

Or, using the C API:

```
AudioSessionSetActive(true);
```

That's all it takes to set and enforce your app's overall audio session policy. Now let's make the example more interesting by introducing ducking. Just before we're about to play a sound, we duck any external sound:

```
UInt32 duck = 1;
AudioSessionSetProperty(kAudioSessionProperty_OtherMixableAudioShouldDuck,
                        sizeof(duck), &duck);
```

When we finish playing a sound, we turn off ducking. This is the tricky part. Not only must we remove the ducking property from our audio session policy, but we must also deactivate our audio session to make the change take effect immediately and bring the external sound back to its original level; there is then no harm in reactivating our audio session:

```
UInt32 duck = 0;
AudioSessionSetProperty(kAudioSessionProperty_OtherMixableAudioShouldDuck,
                        sizeof(duck), &duck);
AudioSessionSetActive(false);
AudioSessionSetActive(true);
```

Your audio session can be *interrupted*. This could mean that some other app deactivates it: for example, on an iPhone a phone call can arrive. In the multitasking world of iOS 4, it could mean that another app asserts its audio session over yours, or simply that your app is no longer in the foreground. If you initially set your audio session's category using Objective-C and AVAudioSession, you can handle interruptions in the AVAudioSession's delegate. If you use the C API and `AudioSessionInitialize`, you can set up an interruption handler there (for example code, see the "Audio Session Cookbook" section of Apple's *Audio Session Programming Guide*).

Handling an interruption can be as simple as reactivating your audio session when the interruption ends. So, in `applicationDidFinishLaunching:`, when we set our audio session's category, we can also set ourselves as its delegate, and implement the delegate method `endInterruption`:

```
- (void)endInterruption {
    AudioSessionSetActive(true);
}
```

Even this may not be necessary; if you use an audio player (AVAudioPlayer, discussed in the next section), it provides its own delegate methods for notifying you of interruptions and activates your audio session for you when an interruption ends.

In the multitasking world of iOS 4, when your app switches to the background, your audio session is interrupted (unless your app plays audio in the background, as discussed later in this chapter). But because your app is now suspended in the background, you won't find out about this until the user brings your app back to the front. At that point, you'll get your audio session's `beginInterruption` and `endInterruption` delegate messages, plus your app delegate's `applicationDidBecomeActive:`. In general this shouldn't cause any difficulty, but it's something to be aware of: make sure your implementations of these methods don't step on one another in some undesirable way.

You should look over the documentation for both the Objective-C API and the C API. The C API is more powerful. With the C API, as we've already seen, you can implement ducking, and, for example, you can arrange to be notified when a property of your audio session changes, you can learn whether background audio is playing, and you can track and manipulate how audio is routed. Read Apple's *Audio Session Programming Guide* for a full overview of how you can use your app's audio session.

# Audio Player

An *audio player* is an instance of the AVAudioPlayer class. This is the easiest way to play sounds with any degree of sophistication. A wide range of sound types is acceptable, including MP3, AAC, and ALAC, as well as AIFF and WAV. You can set a sound's volume and stereo pan features, loop a sound, synchronize the playing of multiple sounds simultaneously, and set playback to begin somewhere in the middle of a sound.

An audio player should always be used in conjunction with an audio session; see the previous section.

 Not every device type can play a compressed sound format in every degree of compression, and the limits can be difficult or impossible to learn except by experimentation. I encountered this issue when an app of mine worked correctly on an iPod touch 32GB but failed to play its sounds on an iPod touch 8GB (even though the latter was newer). Even more frustrating, the files played just fine in the iPod/Music app on *both* devices. The problem appears to be that the compression bit rate of my sound files was too low for AVAudioPlayer on the 8GB device, but not on the 32GB device. But there is no documentation of any such limit.

An audio player can possess and play only one sound, but you can have multiple audio players playing simultaneously. Devising a strategy for instantiating, retaining, and releasing your audio players is up to you. An audio player is initialized with its sound, using a local file URL or NSData. To play the sound, first tell the audio player to `prepareToPlay`, causing it to load buffers and initialize hardware; then tell it to `play`. The audio player's delegate is notified when the sound finishes playing. Other useful methods include `pause` and `stop`; the chief difference between them is that `pause` doesn't release the buffers and hardware set up by `prepareToPlay`, but `stop` does (so you'd want to call `prepareToPlay` again before resuming play).

For example, one of my apps uses a class called Player, which implements a `play:` method expecting a string path to a sound file in the app bundle. This method creates a new audio player, stores it as an instance variable, and tells it to play the sound file; it also sets itself up as that audio player's delegate, and emits a notification when the sound finishes playing. In this way, by maintaining a single Player instance, I can play different sounds in succession:

```
- (void) play: (NSString*) path {
    NSURL *fileURL = [[NSURL alloc] initFileURLWithPath: path];
    NSError* err = nil;
    AVAudioPlayer *newPlayer =
        [[AVAudioPlayer alloc] initWithContentsOfURL: fileURL error: &err];
    // error-checking omitted
    [fileURL release];
    self.player = newPlayer; // retain policy
    [newPlayer release];
    [self.player prepareToPlay];
    [self.player setDelegate: self];
    [self.player play];
}

- (void)audioPlayerDidFinishPlaying:(AVAudioPlayer *)player // delegate method
                    successfully:(BOOL)flag {
    [[NSNotificationCenter defaultCenter]
        postNotificationName:@"soundFinished" object:nil];
}
```

Here are some useful audio player properties:

`pan, volume`
> Stereo positioning and loudness, respectively.

`numberOfLoops`
> How many times the sound should repeat after it finishes playing; thus, 0 (the default) means it doesn't repeat. A negative value causes the sound to repeat indefinitely (until told to `stop`).

`duration`
> The length of the sound.

`currentTime`
> The playhead position within the sound.

Starting in iOS 4.0, the `playAtTime:` method allows playing to be scheduled to start at a certain time. The time should be described in terms of the audio player's `deviceCurrentTime` property.

As I mentioned in the previous section, an audio player handles sound interruptions automatically. In particular, your audio session is reactivated for you when the interruption ends. You can implement the delegate methods `audioPlayerBeginInterruption:` and `audioPlayerEndInterruption:` (or, in iOS 4, `audioPlayerEndInterruption:withFlags:`) to add functionality; for example, you might respond by

*Figure 27-1. The software remote controls in the iOS 4 app switcher*

*Figure 27-2. The software remote controls on the locked screen*

updating your interface, or you might want to resume play when the interruption ends (by calling `play`). What you do will depends on what makes sense for your particular application. An example appears later in this chapter.

# Remote Control of Your Sound

Various sorts of signal constitute *remote control*. There is hardware remote control; the user might be using earbuds with buttons, for example. There is also software remote control; for example, in iOS 4, the playback controls that you see when you double-click the Home button to view the fast app switcher and then swipe to the right (Figure 27-1) are a form of software remote control. Similarly, the buttons that appear if you double-click the Home button when the screen is locked and sound is playing are a form of software remote control (Figure 27-2).

Your app can arrange to be targeted by *remote control events* reporting that the user has tapped a remote control. This is particularly appropriate in an app that plays sound. Your sound-playing app can respond to the remote play/pause button, for example, by playing or pausing its sound.

Remote control events are a form of UIEvent, and they are sent initially to the first responder. (See Chapter 11 and Chapter 18 on UIResponders and the responder chain.) To arrange to be a recipient of remote control events:

- Your app must contain a UIResponder in its responder chain that returns YES from `canBecomeFirstResponder`, and that responder must actually be first responder.

- Some UIResponder in the responder chain, at or above the first responder, must implement `remoteControlReceivedWithEvent:`.

- Your app must call the UIApplication instance method `beginReceivingRemote-ControlEvents`.

- Your app must emit some sound. The rule is that whatever running app capable of receiving remote control events last produced sound is the target of remote events. The user can tell what app this is because the icon at the right of Figure 27-1 is the icon of that app. The remote control event target app defaults to the iPod/Music app if no other app takes precedence by this rule.

A typical place to put all of this is in your view controller, which is, after all, a UIResponder:

```
- (BOOL)canBecomeFirstResponder {
    return YES;
}

- (void) viewDidAppear:(BOOL)animated {
    [super viewDidAppear: animated];
    [self becomeFirstResponder];
    [[UIApplication sharedApplication] beginReceivingRemoteControlEvents];
}

- (void)remoteControlReceivedWithEvent:(UIEvent *)event {
    // ...
}
```

That's just a sketch, but it does work: when this app is running, the user can employ remote controls, such as the buttons in Figure 27-1 or a physical button on earbuds, to cause remoteControlReceivedWithEvent: to be called.

The question then is how to implement remoteControlReceivedWithEvent:. Your implementation will examine the subtype of the incoming UIEvent in order to decide what to do. There are many possible subtype values, listed under UISubtype in the UIEvent class documentation; they have names like UIEventSubtypeRemoteControlPlay. A minimal implementation will respond to UIEventSubtypeRemoteControlTogglePlayPause. Here's an example in an app where sound is produced by an AVAudioPlayer:

```
- (void)remoteControlReceivedWithEvent:(UIEvent *)event {
    UIEventSubtype rc = event.subtype;
    if (rc == UIEventSubtypeRemoteControlTogglePlayPause) {
        if ([player isPlaying])
            [player pause];
        else
            [player play];
    }
}
```

# Playing Sound in the Background

In the multitasking world of iOS 4, when the user switches away from your app to another app, by default, your audio session is interrupted and your app is suspended. But if the business of your app is to play sound, you might like your app to continue playing sound in the background. In earlier sections of this chapter, I've spoken about how your app, in the foreground, relates its sound production to background sound such as the iPod/Music app. Now we're talking about how your app can *be* that background sound, possibly playing sound while some other app is in the foreground.

To play sound in the background, your app must do two things:

- In your *Info.plist*, you must include the "Required background modes" key (UIBackgroundModes) with a value that includes "App plays audio" (audio).
- Your audio session's policy must be Playback (and must be active, of course).

That's actually all it takes! If those two things are true, then if your app is producing sound, that sound will go right on playing when the user clicks the Home button and dismisses your application or switches to another app.

An extremely cool feature of playing sound in the background is that remote control events continue to work. Even if your app was not actively playing at the time it was put into the background, if it is the remote control target, then if the user causes a remote control event to be sent, your app will be woken up in the background in order to receive it and can begin playing sound. However, the rules for interruptions still apply; another app can interrupt your app's audio session while your app is in the background, and if that app receives remote control events, then your app is no longer the remote control target.

If your app is the remote control target in the background, then another app can interrupt your app's audio, play some audio of its own, and then deactivate its own audio session with the flag telling your app to resume playing. I'll give a minimal example of how this works with an AVAudioPlayer.

Let's call the two apps BackgroundPlayer and Interrupter. Suppose Interrupter has an audio session policy of Ambient. This means that when it comes to the front, background audio doesn't stop. But now Interrupter wants to play a sound of its own, temporarily stopping background audio. To pause the background audio, it sets its own audio session to Playback:

```
[[AVAudioSession sharedInstance]
    setCategory:AVAudioSessionCategoryPlayback error:NULL];
[[AVAudioSession sharedInstance] setActive:YES error:NULL];
[player setDelegate: self];
[player prepareToPlay];
[player play];
```

When Interrupter's sound finishes playing, the AVAudioPlayer's delegate is notified. In response, Interrupter deactivates its audio session with the flag; then it's fine for it to switch its audio session policy back to Ambient and activate it once again:

```
[[AVAudioSession sharedInstance] setActive:NO
    withFlags:AVAudioSessionSetActiveFlags_NotifyOthersOnDeactivation error:NULL];
[[AVAudioSession sharedInstance]
    setCategory:AVAudioSessionCategoryAmbient error:NULL];
[[AVAudioSession sharedInstance] setActive:YES error:NULL];
```

So much for Interrupter. Now let's turn to BackgroundPlayer. Remember, it is configured to play in the background and to receive remote control events. When Interrupter changes its own policy to Playback, BackgroundPlayer is interrupted. When Interrupter deactivates its audio session, BackgroundPlayer's AVAudioPlayer delegate is notified that the interruption has ended. It tests for the resume flag and, if it is set, starts playing again:

```
- (void)audioPlayerEndInterruption:(AVAudioPlayer *)p withFlags:(NSUInteger)flags {
    if (flags & AVAudioSessionInterruptionFlags_ShouldResume) {
        [p prepareToPlay];
        [p play];
    }
}
```

 In Chapter 11, I said that your app delegate will probably never receive the `applicationWillTerminate:` message, because by the time the app terminates, it will already have been suspended and incapable of receiving any events. However, an app that is playing sound in the background is *not* suspended, even though it is in the background. If it is terminated while playing sound in the background, it will receive `applicationDidEnterBackground:`, even though it has *already* received this previously when it was moved into the background, and then it *will* receive `applicationWillTerminate:`.

# Further Topics in Sound

iOS is a powerful milieu for production and processing of sound; its sound-related technologies are extensive. Here are some further topics, beyond the scope of this book:

*Recording sound*
> To record sound simply, use AVAudioRecorder. Your audio session policy will need to adopt a Record policy before recording begins.

*Audio queues*
> Audio queues implement sound playing and recording through a C API with more granularity than the Objective-C AVAudioPlayer and AVAudioRecorder (though it is still regarded as a high-level API), giving you access to the buffers used to move chunks of sound data between stored sound data and sound hardware.

*Extended Audio File Services*
> A C API for reading and writing sound files in chunks. It is useful in connection with technologies such as audio queues.

*Audio Converter Services*
> A C API for converting sound files between formats.

*Streaming audio*

Audio streamed in real time over the network, such as an Internet radio station, can be played with Audio File Stream Services, in connection with audio queues.

*OpenAL*

An advanced technology for playing sound with fine control over its stereo stage and directionality.

*Audio units*

Plug-ins that filter and modify the nature and quality of a sound as it passes through them. See the *Audio Unit Hosting Guide for iOS*.

*CoreMIDI*

The CoreMIDI framework was introduced into iOS in version 4.2. It allows interaction with MIDI devices (but not, unfortunately, direct internal playback of MIDI files).

See also Chapter 29 on accessing sound files in the user's music library.

# CHAPTER 28

# Video

Basic video playback is performed in a view owned by a MPMoviePlayerController. You'll need to link to *MediaPlayer.framework* and import `<MediaPlayer/MediaPlayer.h>`. There are two relevant classes supplied by the Media Player framework:

*MPMoviePlayerController*
> Vends and controls a view that plays a movie.

> The behavior of this class has changed very greatly since it was introduced in iOS 2.0. It is difficult to use it compatibly with multiple system versions. In this chapter, I describe only its current behavior (in iOS 4.2 or later), with no attempt to discuss earlier differences or to advise you on backward compatibility.

*MPMoviePlayerViewController*
> Owns an MPMoviePlayerController, and presents its view as a fullscreen view. Introduced in iOS 3.2.

A simple interface for trimming video (UIVideoEditorController) is also supplied. Starting in iOS 4, sophisticated video editing can be performed through AV Foundation, which this book does not discuss in depth.

A mobile device does not have unlimited power for decoding and presenting video in real time. A video that plays on your computer might not play at all on an iOS device. See the "Media Layer" chapter of Apple's *iOS Technology Overview* for a list of specifications and limits within which video is eligible for playing.

A web view (Chapter 24) supports the HTML 5 `<video>` tag. This can be a simple lightweight way to present video and to allow the user to control playback. Starting in iOS 4.3, both web view video and MPMoviePlayerController support AirPlay (streaming from the device to an Apple TV), but I have not tested this.

# MPMoviePlayerController

An MPMoviePlayerController vends and controls a view, its view property, and a movie described by a URL, its contentURL, which it will present in that view. You are responsible for instantiating and retaining the MPMoviePlayerController, and for placing its view into your interface. No law says you *have* to put the MPMoviePlayerController's view into your interface, but if you don't, the user won't be able to see the movie or the controls that accompany it by default. The view is a real view; you can set its frame, its autoresizingMask, and so forth, and you can give it subviews.

The movie URL can be a local file URL, so that the player can show, for example, a movie stored as a file in the app's bundle, or obtained from the Camera Roll / Saved Photos group in the user's photo library (see Chapter 30); or it can be a resource (possibly streamed) to be fetched over the Internet, in which case the MPMoviePlayerController initiates the download as soon as the MPMoviePlayerController has the contentURL.

Things happen slowly with a movie. Even when a movie is a local file, a certain amount of it has to load before the MPMoviePlayer actually has the movie and its specifications and can start playing it. In the case of a remote resource, this will take even longer. If shouldAutoplay is YES, play will begin as soon as it *is* possible.

By default, an MPMoviePlayerController's shouldAutoplay is YES. This means that the movie will start loading and playing as soon as the MPMoviePlayerController has a contentURL — which, if you create it using initWithContentURL:, will be the moment it comes into existence. This will happen even if you don't put the MPMoviePlayerController's view into your interface. If the movie has sound, the user will then hear it without being able to see it, which could be confusing. To prevent this, put the view into your interface, or set shouldAutoplay to NO (or both).

A movie file can be in a standard movie format, such as *.mov* or *.mp4*, but it can also be a sound file. An MPMoviePlayerController is thus an easy way to play a sound file, including a sound file obtained in real time over the Internet, along with standard controls for pausing the sound and moving the playhead.

In this example, we create an MPMoviePlayerController, give it a reference to a movie from our app bundle, retain it through a property, and put its view into our interface:

```
NSURL* m = [[NSBundle mainBundle] URLForResource:@"Movie" withExtension:@"m4v"];
MPMoviePlayerController* mp = [[MPMoviePlayerController alloc] initWithContentURL:m];
self.mpc = mp; // retain policy
[mp release];
self.mpc.shouldAutoplay = NO;
self.mpc.view.frame = CGRectMake(10, 10, 300, 230);
[self.view addSubview:self.mpc.view];
```

*Figure 28-1. A movie player with controls*

*Figure 28-2. A movie player without controls*

*Figure 28-3. A movie player in fullscreen mode, with controls*

The controls (`controlStyle` is `MPMovieControlStyleEmbedded`) include a play/pause button, a slider for changing the current frame of the movie, and a fullscreen button; there may also be an AirPlay route button, if an appropriate device is found on the network (Figure 28-1).

The user can tap the view to show or hide the controls at the bottom; the controls may also disappear automatically after play begins (Figure 28-2).

If the user taps the fullscreen button (or pinches outwards) to enter fullscreen mode, the controls (`controlStyle` is `MPMovieControlStyleFullscreen`) at the top include a Done button, a slider, and an increased fullscreen button, and a second set of controls appears at the bottom with a play/pause button and rewind and fast-forward buttons, plus possibly a volume slider and an AirPlay route button. The user can tap to dismiss or summon the controls, can double-tap to toggle increased fullscreen mode, and can tap Done to stop play and leave fullscreen mode (Figure 28-3).

You can also set the style of the controls (`controlStyle`) manually, though this would be an odd thing to do, because each style of control goes with a display mode (fullscreen

*Figure 28-4. A movie player when the movie is a sound file*

*Figure 28-5. A fullscreen movie player when the movie is a sound file*

or otherwise); you are most likely to use this feature to make it impossible for the user to summon the controls at all (`MPMovieControlStyleNone`).

If the movie is actually a sound file, the controls are drawn differently: there is a start/ pause button, a slider, and possibly an AirPlay route button, and that's all (Figure 28-4).

The movie is scaled to fill the size of the view in accordance with the MPMoviePlayer-Controller `scalingMode`; the default is `MPMovieScalingModeAspectFit`, which scales to fit, keeping the correct aspect ratio, and fills the unfilled dimension with the color of the MPMoviePlayerController's `backgroundView`.

You might like to learn the actual size and aspect ratio of the movie, perhaps so as to eliminate the excess unfilled dimension. You can get the MPMoviePlayerController's `naturalSize`, but, as I mentioned earlier, it takes time after the content URL is set for this to be determined. I'll show an example in a moment.

The fullscreen rendering can be rotated if the view in which the movie player subview is embedded can be rotated (because it is, or is in, a view controlled by a view controller that permits this). You can programmatically toggle between fullscreen and not, with `setFullscreen:animated:`. It is possible to toggle the view for a sound file into fullscreen mode programmatically even though it lacks a fullscreen control that the user can tap (Figure 28-5).

The movie can be made to repeat automatically (`repeatMode`) when it reaches its end. You can get the movie's `duration`. You can change its `initialPlaybackTime` and `end-PlaybackTime` (effectively trimming the start and end off the movie). Further programmatic control over the actual playing of the movie is obtained through the MPMedia-Playback protocol, which MPMoviePlayerController adopts. This gives you the expected `play`, `pause`, and `stop` methods, as well as commands for seeking quickly forward and backward, and you can get and set the `currentPlaybackTime` to position the playhead. Note the `prepareToPlay` method; it's often a good idea to send this to the MPMo-

viePlayerController just after changing its content URL. You can also set the current-
PlaybackRate, making the movie play slower or faster than normal, and even backward
(though in my experience backward play doesn't always work very well).

An MPMoviePlayerController doesn't have a delegate. Instead, to learn of events as
they happen, you must register for notifications. These notifications are how you know
when, after assigning a content URL, it is safe for you to query properties of the movie
such its naturalSize and duration. In this example, I'll use a notification to embed the
movie view into the interface, at the correct aspect ratio, as soon as the naturalSize is
known:

```
- (void) setUpMPC {
    NSURL* m = [[NSBundle mainBundle] URLForResource:@"Movie" withExtension:@"m4v"];
    // ... the rest as before; do NOT add to view yet
    // [self.view addSubview:self.mpc.view];
    [[NSNotificationCenter defaultCenter] addObserver:self
        selector:@selector(finishSetup:)
        name:MPMovieNaturalSizeAvailableNotification
        object:self.mpc];
}

- (void) finishSetup: (id) n {
    CGRect f = self.mpc.view.bounds;
    f.size = self.mpc.naturalSize;
    // make width 300, keep ratio
    CGFloat ratio = 300/f.size.width;
    f.size.width *= ratio;
    f.size.height *= ratio;
    self.mpc.view.bounds = f;
    [self.view addSubview:self.mpc.view];
}
```

Additional notifications tell such things as when fullscreen mode is entered and exited,
and when the movie finishes playing. One of the most important notifications is MPMovie-
PlayerPlaybackStateDidChangeNotification; to learn the actual playback state, query
the MPMoviePlayerController's playbackState, which will be one of these:

- MPMoviePlaybackStateStopped
- MPMoviePlaybackStatePlaying
- MPMoviePlaybackStatePaused
- MPMoviePlaybackStateInterrupted
- MPMoviePlaybackStateSeekingForward
- MPMoviePlaybackStateSeekingBackward

If the content comes from the Internet, there is of course many a slip possible. Things
take time; the Internet might slow down, or go away completely; the resource to be
fetched might not exist. You'll want to register for notifications that tell you when things
happen, and especially when things go wrong.

In this example, we've registered for the `MPMoviePlayerPlaybackDidFinish-Notification`. There are two ways to detect an error by looking in the notification's `userInfo` dictionary: we can examine its key called `MPMoviePlayerPlaybackDidFinish-ReasonUserInfoKey`, which will be `MPMovieFinishReasonPlaybackError`; or, we can look to see if it has a key called `@"error"`, which will be an NSError:

```
- (void) didFinish: (NSNotification*) n {
    // first way
    NSNumber* num =
        [[n userInfo] objectForKey:MPMoviePlayerPlaybackDidFinishReasonUserInfoKey];
    int reason = [num intValue];
    if (reason == MPMovieFinishReasonPlaybackError)
        NSLog(@"there was an error of some sort!");
    // second way
    NSError* err = [[n userInfo] objectForKey: @"error"];
    if (err)
        NSLog(@"%@", [err localizedDescription]);
}
```

However, the `MPMoviePlayerPlaybackDidFinishNotification` will not be sent if the movie starts downloading and playing, but the download is then cut off. To detect this, we register for `MPMoviePlayerLoadStateDidChangeNotification` and check for whether the MPMoviePlayerController's `loadState` (a bitmask) has the `MPMovieLoadState-Stalled` bit set. If so, we're in trouble, but play will not automatically stop; the MPMoviePlayerController will keep trying to obtain data. If we want to prevent that, we have to stop it manually:

```
- (void) loadStateChanged: (id) n {
    int ls = self.mpc.loadState;
    if (ls & MPMovieLoadStateStalled) {
        [self.mpc stop];
        NSLog(@"The download seems to have stalled out.");
    }
}
```

 Only one MPMoviePlayerController can display a movie in your interface. To avoid confusion about why one of your MPMoviePlayerControllers is not playing its movie successfully, restrict your interface so that it contains only one MPMoviePlayerController in the first place.

# MPMoviePlayerViewController

An MPMoviePlayerViewController is, as its name implies, a view controller (a UI-ViewController subclass). It manages an MPMoviePlayerController (`moviePlayer`) and automatically provides a fullscreen presentation of the MPMoviePlayerController's view. Thus, an MPMoviePlayerViewController has some strong advantages of simplicity. You don't have to put the MPMoviePlayerController's view into your interface, and you don't have to worry about the user toggling between fullscreen and non-fullscreen modes. The view is either present, occupying the entire screen, or it isn't.

You can use an MPMoviePlayerViewController wherever you would use a UIView-Controller, pushing it onto a navigation stack, for example, or making it part of a tab bar interface, or presenting it as a modal view. Here's a simple example:

```
NSURL* m = [[NSBundle mainBundle] URLForResource:@"Movie" withExtension:@"m4v"];
MPMoviePlayerViewController* mpvc =
    [[MPMoviePlayerViewController alloc] initWithContentURL: m];
[self presentModalViewController:mpvc animated:YES];
[mpvc release];
```

An alternative method for presenting the view modally is `presentMoviePlayerView-ControllerAnimated:`. It uses a style of animation otherwise unavailable, in which the current view slides out to reveal the movie view.

If the MPMoviePlayerViewController's view is presented modally, it is dismissed automatically when the user taps the Done button. If you use the MPMoviePlayerView-Controller in some other way, the Done button stops play but that's all. You can detect the tapping of the Done button by registering for the `MPMoviePlayerPlaybackDidFinish-Notification`.

MPMoviePlayerViewController overrides `shouldAutorotateToInterfaceOrientation:` to return YES for the primary portrait orientation and both landscape orientations. This means the view is rotatable without your having to subclass MPMoviePlayerViewController and override `shouldAutorotateToInterfaceOrientation:` yourself.

 When an MPMoviePlayerViewController's view is showing, it becomes a recipient of remote control events (see Chapter 27). This feature is convenient, but if it's not what you want, it is not easily overcome; there is no property for turning it off. The best way to avoid it is to use an MPMoviePlayerController instead.

That's all there is to an MPMoviePlayerViewController; the rest of your interaction with it is through its MPMoviePlayerController (`moviePlayer`), including the latter's notifications.

# UIVideoEditorController

UIVideoEditorController is a view controller that presents an interface for trimming video. Its view and internal behavior are outside your control. You are expected to present the view controller's view, probably modally (or, on the iPad, in a popover, though in fact I haven't been able to get this view controller to work properly on the iPad no matter how I present it), and respond by way of its delegate.

Before summoning a UIVideoEditorController, be sure to call its class method `canEdit-VideoAtPath:`. Not every video format is editable, and not every device supports video editing. If this call returns NO, you can't use an instance of this class. (This call can take some noticeable time to return.) You must also set the UIVideoEditorController instance's `delegate` and `videoPath` before presenting it modally:

```
NSString* path = [[NSBundle mainBundle] pathForResource:@"movie" ofType:@"mov"];
BOOL can = [UIVideoEditorController canEditVideoAtPath:path];
if (!can) {
    NSLog(@"can't edit this video");
    return;
}
UIVideoEditorController* vc = [[UIVideoEditorController alloc] init];
vc.delegate = self;
vc.videoPath = path;
[self presentModalViewController:vc animated:YES];
[vc release];
```

The view's interface contains Cancel and Save buttons, a trimming box displaying thumbnails from the movie, a Play/Pause button, and the movie itself. The user slides the ends of the trimming box to set the beginning and end of the saved movie. The Cancel and Save buttons do *not* dismiss the modal view; you must do that in your implementation of the delegate methods. There are three of them, and you should implement all three and dismiss the modal view in all of them:

- `videoEditorController:didSaveEditedVideoToPath:`
- `videoEditorControllerDidCancel:`
- `videoEditorController:didFailWithError:`

It's important to implement the `didFail...` method, because things can go wrong even at this stage.

By the time `videoEditorController:didSaveEditedVideoToPath:` is called, the video has already been saved to a file in your app's temporary directory (the same directory returned from a call to `NSTemporaryDirectory`). Doing something useful with the saved file is up to you; if you merely leave it in the temporary directory, you can't rely on it to persist. In this example, I copy the edited movie into the user's Camera Roll photo album (called Saved Photos if the device has no camera):

```
- (void) videoEditorController: (UIVideoEditorController*) editor
        didSaveEditedVideoToPath: (NSString*) editedVideoPath {
    if (UIVideoAtPathIsCompatibleWithSavedPhotosAlbum(editedVideoPath))
        UISaveVideoAtPathToSavedPhotosAlbum(editedVideoPath, nil, nil, NULL);
    else
        NSLog(@"need to think of something else to do with it");
    [self dismissModalViewControllerAnimated:YES];
}
```

# Further Topics in Video

A large suite of AV Foundation classes was introduced in iOS 4 that provide detailed access to media components, analogous to QuickTime on Mac OS X. To access these, you'll need to link to *AVFoundation.framework* (and probably *CoreMedia.framework* as well), and import `<AVFoundation/AVFoundation.h>`. For a list of classes, see the *AV Foundation Framework Reference*.

The AV Foundation class that performs actual playing of media is AVPlayer. An AVPlayer has an AVPlayerItem; this is its media. An AVPlayerItem comprises tracks (AVPlayerItemTrack), which can be individually enabled or disabled. It gets these from its underlying AVAsset; this is the basic media unit, as it were, providing you with access to tracks and metadata.

Starting in iOS 4.1, an AVPlayer can be an AVQueuePlayer, a subclass that allows multiple AVPlayerItems to be loaded up and then played in sequence. AVQueuePlayer also has an `advanceToNextItem` method, and its list of items can be changed dynamically, so you could use it to give the user access to a set of "chapters."

To display an AVPlayer's movie, you need an AVPlayerLayer (a CALayer subclass). You are unlikely to take this approach unless you need either the extended powers of AV Foundation or the sequential playing power of AVQueuePlayer or the flexibility of working directly with a layer and Core Animation. The AVPlayerLayer doesn't even come with controls for playing a movie and visualizing its progress; you have to create these yourself. Nevertheless, simply displaying a movie in this way is quite easy:

```
NSURL* m = [[NSBundle mainBundle] URLForResource:@"movie" withExtension:@"mov"];
AVPlayer* p = [AVPlayer playerWithURL:m];
self.player = p; // might need a reference later
AVPlayerLayer* lay = [AVPlayerLayer playerLayerWithPlayer:p];
lay.frame = CGRectMake(10,10,300,200);
[self.view.layer addSublayer:lay];
```

To let the user choose to play the movie, we might provide a Play button. In this example, the button toggles the playing status of the movie by changing its rate:

```
- (IBAction) doButton: (id) sender {
    CGFloat rate = self.player.rate;
    if (rate < 0.01)
        self.player.rate = 1;
    else
        self.player.rate = 0;
}
```

Another intriguing feature of an AVPlayer is that you can coordinate animation in your interface (Chapter 17) with the playing of the movie. In other words, you attach an animation to a layer in more or less the usual way, but the animation takes place in movie playback time: if the movie is stopped, the animation is stopped, and if the movie is run at double rate, the animation runs at double rate. This is done by embedding the layer to be animated in an AVSynchronizedLayer, which is coupled with an AVPlayerItem.

To demonstrate, I'll extend the previous example; after we insert our AVPlayerLayer into the interface, we also create and insert an AVSynchronizedLayer:

```
// create synch layer, put it in the interface
AVSynchronizedLayer* syncLayer =
```

*Figure 28-6. The black square's position is synchronized to the movie*

```
[AVSynchronizedLayer synchronizedLayerWithPlayerItem:item];
syncLayer.frame = CGRectMake(10,220,300,10);
syncLayer.backgroundColor = [[UIColor whiteColor] CGColor];
[self.view.layer addSublayer:syncLayer];
// give synch layer a sublayer
CALayer* subLayer = [CALayer layer];
subLayer.backgroundColor = [[UIColor blackColor] CGColor];
subLayer.frame = CGRectMake(0,0,10,10);
[syncLayer addSublayer:subLayer];
// animate the sublayer
CABasicAnimation* anim = [CABasicAnimation animationWithKeyPath:@"position"];
anim.fromValue = [NSValue valueWithCGPoint: subLayer.position];
anim.toValue = [NSValue valueWithCGPoint: CGPointMake(295,5)];
anim.removedOnCompletion = NO;
anim.beginTime = AVCoreAnimationBeginTimeAtZero; // important trick
anim.duration = CMTimeGetSeconds(item.asset.duration);
[subLayer addAnimation:anim forKey:nil];
```

The result is shown in Figure 28-6. The white rectangle is the AVSynchronizedLayer, tied to our movie. The little black square inside it is its sublayer; if we animate the black square, that animation will be synchronized to the movie. We do animate the black square, changing its position from the left end of the white rectangle to the right end, starting at the beginning of the movie and with the same duration as the movie, but although we attach this animation to the black square layer in the usual way, the black square *doesn't move* until we tap the button to call `doButton:` and start the movie playing. Moreover, if we tap the button again to pause the movie, the black square stops. The black square is thus *automatically* representing the current play position within the movie!

Despite the simplicity of those examples, writing real-life AV Foundation code usually presents certain sophisticated challenges. For instance, as we've already seen, it takes time for media values to become available. Even with MPMoviePlayerController we couldn't fetch a movie's `naturalSize` immediately; we had to wait for an `MPMovieNatural-SizeAvailableNotification`. This is even more true with AV Foundation, where you use Objective-C blocks to call back into your code when values are ready or tasks are finished; moreover, such blocks may run on a background thread. AV Foundation also prefers key–value observing (Chapter 13) rather than notifications for letting you track value changes in your media (such as the progress of a movie as it plays).

The mighty powers with which AV Foundation endows you are beyond the scope of this book. Here's a quick survey to whet your appetite. With AV Foundation, you can:

- Construct your own media asset (AVComposition, an AVAsset subclass). For example, you might combine part of the sound from one asset and part of the video from another into a single movie.
- Apply audio volume changes, and video opacity and transform changes, to the playback of individual tracks.
- Extract single images ("thumbnails") from a movie (AVAssetImageGenerator).
- Export a movie in a different format (AVAssetExportSession).
- Capture audio, video, and stills, on a device that supports it (such as an iPhone, or another device connected to external hardware), including capturing video frames as still images (see Technical Q&A QA1702).

It should be evident from even so brief a summary that you could use AV Foundation to write a movie editor or a sound mixer. To learn more, you'll want to read the *AV Foundation Programming Guide*.

# CHAPTER 29

# Music Library

An iOS device, in addition to running apps, can also be used for the same purpose as the original iPod — to hold and play music and podcasts. These items, usually moved onto the device by way of iTunes on a computer, constitute the device's *music library*; the user can play them with the iPod app (which is called the Music app on some devices). Since version 3, iOS has provided the programmer with access to the device's music library; this access has improved over time, and some aspects are as new as iOS 4.2. You can:

- Explore the music library
- Play an item from the music library
- Learn and control what the iPod/Music app's music player is doing
- Present a standard interface for allowing the user to select a music library item

These abilities are provided by the Media Player framework. You'll need to link to *MediaPlayer.framework* and import `<MediaPlayer/MediaPlayer.h>`.

## Exploring the Music Library

Everything in the music library, as seen by your code, is an MPMediaEntity. This is an abstract class that endows its subclasses with the ability to describe themselves through key–value pairs called *properties*. (This use of the word "properties" has nothing to do with Objective-C properties, explained in Chapter 12; these properties are more like entries in an NSDictionary, except that the keys are not objects.) The repertoire of properties depends on the sort of entity you're looking at; many of them will be intuitively familiar from your use of iTunes. For example, a media item has a title, an album title, a track number, an artist, a composer, and so on; a playlist has a title, a flag indicating whether it is a "smart" playlist, and so on. The property keys have names like `MPMediaItemPropertyTitle`.

To fetch a property's value, call `valueForProperty:` with its key. Starting in iOS 4, you can fetch multiple properties with `enumerateValuesForProperties:usingBlock:`.

An individual item in the music library is an MPMediaItem, an MPMediaEntity sub-class. It has a type, according to the value of its `MPMediaItemPropertyMediaType` property: it might be music, a podcast, or an audiobook. Different types of item have slightly different properties; for example, a podcast has a podcast title (in addition to its normal title). An item's artwork image is an instance of the MPMediaItemArtwork class, from which you can get the image itself scaled to a specified size.

A playlist is an MPMediaPlaylist. As you would expect, it has `items` and a `count` of those items. It inherits those properties from its superclass, MPMediaItemCollection, which is the other MPMediaEntity subclass. I'll talk more about MPMediaItemCollection in a moment.

Obtaining actual information from the music library requires a *query*, an MPMedia-Query. First, you *form* the query. There are two main ways to do this:

*With a convenience constructor*
> MPMediaQuery provides several class methods that form a query ready to ask the music library for all of its songs, or all of its podcasts, and so on. Here's the complete list:
>
> * songsQuery
> * podcastsQuery
> * audiobooksQuery
> * playlistsQuery
> * albumsQuery
> * artistsQuery
> * composersQuery
> * genresQuery
> * compilationsQuery

*With filter predicates*
> You can attach to the query one or more MPMediaPropertyPredicate instances, forming a set (NSSet) of predicates. These predicates filter the music library according to criteria you specify; to be included in the result, a media item must successfully pass through all the filters (in other words, the predicates are combined using logical-and). A predicate is a simple comparison. It has two, or possibly three, aspects:
>
> *A property*
> > The key to the property you want to compare against. Not every property can be used in a filter predicate; the documentation makes the distinction clear (and starting in iOS 4.2, so does an MPMediaEntity class method, `canFilter-ByProperty:`).

*A value*
> The value that the specified property must have in order to pass through the filter.

*A comparison type (optional)*
> In order to pass through the filter, a media item's property value can either *match* the value you provide (`MPMediaPredicateComparisonEqualTo`, the default) or *contain* the value you provide (`MPMediaPredicateComparisonContains`).

These two ways of forming a query are actually the same; a convenience constructor is just a quick way of supplying a query already endowed with a filter predicate.

A query also *groups* its results, according to its `groupingType`. Your choices are:

* `MPMediaGroupingTitle`
* `MPMediaGroupingAlbum`
* `MPMediaGroupingArtist`
* `MPMediaGroupingAlbumArtist`
* `MPMediaGroupingComposer`
* `MPMediaGroupingGenre`
* `MPMediaGroupingPlaylist`
* `MPMediaGroupingPodcastTitle`

The query convenience constructors all supply a `groupingType` in addition to a filter predicate. Indeed, the grouping is often the salient aspect of the query. For example, an `albumsQuery` is in fact a `songsQuery` with the added feature that its results are grouped by album.

The groups resulting from a query are *collections*; that is, each is an MPMediaItem-Collection. This class, you will recall, is the superclass of MPMediaPlaylist, and is an MPMediaEntity subclass. So, a collection has properties; it also has items and a count. It also has a `representativeItem` property, which gives you just one item from the collection. The reason you need this is that properties of a collection are often embodied in its items rather than in the collection itself. For example, an album has no title; rather, its items have album titles that are all the same. So to learn the title of an album, you ask for the album title of a representative item.

After you form the query, you *perform* the query. You do this simply by asking for the query's results. You can ask either for its `collections` (if you care about the groups returned from the query) or for its `items`. Here, I'll discover the titles of all the albums:

```
MPMediaQuery* query = [MPMediaQuery albumsQuery];
NSArray* result = [query collections];
// prove we've performed the query, by logging the album titles
for (MPMediaItemCollection* album in result)
    NSLog(@"%@", [[album representativeItem]
              valueForProperty:MPMediaItemPropertyAlbumTitle]);
```

```
/*
Output starts like this on my device:
Bach Instrumental
Bach Keyboard
Bach Masses, Oratorios, Passions
Bach, CPE, Misc
Bach, CPE, Trio Sonatas
Beethoven Canons
Beethoven Choral / Vocal
...
*/
```

Now let's make our query more elaborate; we'll get the titles of all the albums whose name contains "Bach". Observe that what we really do is to ask for all songs whose album title contains "Bach", grouped by album:

```
MPMediaQuery* query = [MPMediaQuery albumsQuery];
MPMediaPropertyPredicate* hasBach =
    [MPMediaPropertyPredicate predicateWithValue:@"Bach"
    forProperty:MPMediaItemPropertyAlbumTitle
    comparisonType:MPMediaPredicateComparisonContains];
[query addFilterPredicate:hasBach];
NSArray* result = [query collections];
for (MPMediaItemCollection* album in result)
    NSLog(@"%@", [[album representativeItem]
                    valueForProperty:MPMediaItemPropertyAlbumTitle]);
/*
Complete output on my device:
Bach Instrumental
Bach Keyboard
Bach Masses, Oratorios, Passions
Bach, CPE, Misc
Bach, CPE, Trio Sonatas
*/
```

Because the results of that query are actually songs (MPMediaItems), we can immediately access any song in any of those albums. Let's modify our output from that query to print the titles of all the songs in the first album returned, which happens to be the Bach Instrumental album. We don't have to change our query, so I'll start at the point where we perform it:

```
// ... same as before ...
NSArray* result = [query collections];
MPMediaItemCollection* album = [result objectAtIndex: 0];
for (MPMediaItem* song in album.items)
    NSLog(@"%@", [song valueForProperty:MPMediaItemPropertyTitle]);
/*
Output starts like this:
Lute Suite In G Minor BWV 995 1. Prélude
Lute Suite In G Minor BWV 995 2. Allemande
Lute Suite In G Minor BWV 995 3. Courante
Lute Suite In G Minor BWV 995 4. Sarabande
...
*/
```

One of the properties of an MPMediaEntity is its *persistent ID* (`MPMediaItemProperty-PersistentID` and `MPMediaPlaylistPropertyPersistentID`). This is important, as it uniquely identifies this song or playlist. No other means of identification is guaranteed unique; two songs or two playlists can have the same title, for example. Using the persistent ID, you can retrieve again at a later time the same song or playlist you retrieved earlier, even across launches of your app. Starting in iOS 4.2, the repertoire of available persistent IDs is extended to entities in general (`MPMediaEntityProperty-PersistentID`), album, artist, composer, and more.

While you are maintaining the results of a search, the contents of the music library may themselves change. For example, the user might connect the device to a computer and add or delete music with iTunes. This can put your results out of date. For this reason, the library's own modified state is available through the MPMediaLibrary class. Call the class method `defaultMediaLibrary` to get the actual library instance; now you can ask it for its `lastModifiedDate`. You can also register to receive a notification, `MPMediaLibraryDidChangeNotification`, when the music library is modified; this notification is not emitted unless you first send the library `beginGeneratingLibraryChangeNotifications`. You should eventually balance this with `endGeneratingLibraryChangeNotifications`.

# The Music Player

The Media Player framework class for playing an MPMediaItem is MPMusicPlayerController. It comes in two flavors, depending on which class method you use to get an instance:

`applicationMusicPlayer`
> Plays an MPMediaItem from the music library within your application. The song being played by the `applicationMusicPlayer` can be different from the iPod/Music app's current song. This player stops when your app is not in the foreground.

`iPodMusicPlayer`
> The global music player — the very same player used by the iPod/Music app. This might already be playing an item, or be paused with a current item, at any time while your app runs; you can learn what item this is, and play music with this player. It continues playing independently of the state of your app. The user can at any time completely change what this player is doing.

 An `applicationMusicPlayer` is not really inside your app. It is actually the global music player behaving differently. It has its own audio session; if you activate an audio session with a Solo Ambient or Playback policy (Chapter 27), the player will stop. You cannot play its audio when your app is in the background. You cannot make it the target of remote control events. If these limitations prove troublesome, use the `iPodMusicPlayer` (or AVPlayer, as discussed later in this chapter).

A music player doesn't merely play an item; it plays from a *queue* of items. This behavior is familiar from iTunes and the iPod/Music app, though you might not have considered it explicitly. For example, in iTunes, when you switch to a playlist and double-click the first song to start playing, when iTunes comes to the end of that song, it proceeds to the next song in the playlist. So at that moment, the totality of songs in the playlist is its queue. The music player behaves the same way; when it reaches the end of a song, it proceeds to the next song in its queue.

Your methods for controlling playback also reflect this queue-based orientation. In addition to the expected `play`, `pause`, and `stop` commands, there's a `skipToNextItem` and `skipToPreviousItem` command. Anyone who has ever used iTunes or the iPod/Music app (or, for that matter, an old-fashioned iPod) will have an intuitive grasp of this and everything else a music player does. For example, you can also set a music player's `repeatMode` and `shuffleMode`, just as in iTunes and so forth.

You provide a music player with its queue in one of two ways:

*With a query*
> You hand the music player an MPMediaQuery. The query's `items` are the items of the queue.

*With a collection*
> You hand the music player an MPMediaItemCollection. This might be obtained from a query you performed, but you can also assemble your own collection of MPMediaItems in any way you like, putting them into an array and calling `collectionWithItems:` or `initWithItems:`.

In this example, we collect all songs in the library shorter than 30 seconds into a queue and set the queue playing in random order using the application-internal music player:

```
MPMediaQuery* query = [MPMediaQuery songsQuery];
NSMutableArray* marr = [NSMutableArray array];
MPMediaItemCollection* queue = nil;
for (MPMediaItem* song in query.items) {
    CGFloat dur =
        [[song valueForProperty:MPMediaItemPropertyPlaybackDuration] floatValue];
    if (dur < 30)
        [marr addObject: song];
}
if ([marr count] == 0)
    NSLog(@"No songs that short!");
else
    queue = [MPMediaItemCollection collectionWithItems:marr];
if (queue) {
    MPMusicPlayerController* player =
        [MPMusicPlayerController applicationMusicPlayer];
    [player setQueueWithItemCollection:queue];
    player.shuffleMode = MPMusicShuffleModeSongs;
    [player play];
}
```

If a music player is currently playing, setting its queue will stop it; restarting play appropriately is up to your code, if desired. Unfortunately, you can't query a music player as to its queue. You can keep your own copy of the array constituting the queue when you set the queue, but the user can completely change the queue of an iPodMusic-Player, so if control over the queue is important to you, you'll have to use the applicationMusicPlayer.

A music player has a playbackState that you can query to learn what it's doing (whether it is playing, paused, stopped, or seeking). It also emits notifications so you can hear about changes in its state:

- MPMusicPlayerControllerPlaybackStateDidChangeNotification
- MPMusicPlayerControllerNowPlayingItemDidChangeNotification
- MPMusicPlayerControllerVolumeDidChangeNotification

These notifications are not emitted, however, until you tell the music player to begin-GeneratingPlaybackNotifications. This is an instance method, so you can arrange to receive notifications from just one particular music player if you like. If you do receive notifications from both, you can distinguish them by examining the NSNotification's object and comparing it to each player. You should eventually balance this call with endGeneratingPlaybackNotifications.

To illustrate, I'll extend the previous example to set a UILabel in our interface every time a different song starts playing. Before we set the player playing, we insert these lines to generate the notifications:

```
[player beginGeneratingPlaybackNotifications];
[[NSNotificationCenter defaultCenter] addObserver:self
    selector:@selector(changed:)
    name:MPMusicPlayerControllerNowPlayingItemDidChangeNotification
    object:nil];
```

And here's how we respond to those notifications:

```
- (void) changed: (NSNotification*) n {
    MPMusicPlayerController* player =
        [MPMusicPlayerController applicationMusicPlayer];
    if ([n object] == player) { // just playing safe
        NSString* title =
            [player.nowPlayingItem valueForProperty:MPMediaItemPropertyTitle];
        [self->label setText: title];
    }
}
```

There's no periodic notification as a song plays and the current playhead position advances. To get this information, you'll have to resort to polling. This is not objectionable as long as your polling interval is reasonably sparse; your display may occasionally fall a little behind reality, but this won't usually matter. For example, in one of my apps I use a UIProgressView (p) to show the current percentage of the current song played by the global player. There's no notification, so I use an NSTimer and poll the state of the player every 2 seconds. (I described this architecture in Chapter 11, and showed some of the code triggered by the firing of this timer in Chapter 19; Figure 19-8 is a screenshot containing this UIProgressView.) If we are playing or paused in a song, I show the proportion played; otherwise, I hide the UIProgressView entirely:

```
MPMusicPlayerController* mp = [MPMusicPlayerController iPodMusicPlayer];
if ([mp playbackState] == MPMusicPlaybackStatePlaying ||
        [mp playbackState] == MPMusicPlaybackStatePaused) {
    p.hidden = NO;
    MPMediaItem* item = mp.nowPlayingItem;
    NSTimeInterval current = mp.currentPlaybackTime;
    NSTimeInterval total =
        [[item valueForProperty:MPMediaItemPropertyPlaybackDuration] doubleValue];
    p.progress = current / total;
} else {
    p.hidden = YES;
}
```

An MPMusicPlayerController has no user interface; if you want your app to provide the user with controls for playing and stopping a song, you'll have to provide those controls yourself. The iPodMusicPlayer has its own natural interface already, of course — namely, the iPod/Music app and the remote playback controls (Figure 27-1). The Media Player framework does offer a slider for setting the system output volume, along with an AirPlay route button if appropriate; this is an MPVolumeView.

MPMusicPlayerController is convenient and simple, but it's also simple-minded. As we've seen, its audio session isn't your audio session; the music player doesn't really belong to you. Starting in iOS 4.0, an MPMediaItem has an MPMediaItemPropertyAsset-URL key, whose value is a URL suitable for forming an AVAsset. Thus, another way to play an MPMediaItem is through AV Foundation (Chapter 28). This approach gives you independence from the iPod/Music player; it puts playback of the song into your app's audio session and allows you to control it in response to remote control events and to play it while your app is in the background. (Of course, you can do a lot more with AV Foundation than merely to *play* a song from the music library. For example, you could incorporate a song, or part of a song, as the sound track to a movie.) In this simple example, we start with an array of MPMediaItems and initiate play of those items in an AVQueuePlayer:

```
NSArray* arr = // array of MPMediaItem;
NSMutableArray* assets = [NSMutableArray array];
for (MPMediaItem* item in arr) {
    AVPlayerItem* pi = [[AVPlayerItem alloc] initWithURL:
        [item valueForProperty:MPMediaItemPropertyAssetURL]];
    [assets addObject:pi];
    [pi release];
}
self.qp = [AVQueuePlayer queuePlayerWithItems:assets];
[self.qp play];
```

# The Music Picker

The music picker (MPMediaPickerController) is a view controller (UIViewController) whose view is an self-contained navigation interface in which the user can select a media item. This interface looks very much like the iPod/Music app. You have no access to the actual view; you are expected to present the view controller modally (or, on the iPad, in a popover).

You can limit the type of media items displayed by creating the controller using `init-WithMediaTypes:`. You can make a prompt appear at the top of the navigation bar (`prompt`). And you can govern whether the user can choose multiple media items or just one, with the `allowsPickingMultipleItems` property. That's all there is to it.

While the view is showing, you learn what the user is doing through two delegate methods (MPMediaPickerController):

- `mediaPicker:didPickMediaItems:`
- `mediaPickerDidCancel:`

How you use these depends on the value of the controller's `allowsPickingMultiple-Items`:

*The controller's `allowsPickingMultipleItems` is NO (the default)*
> Every time the user taps a media item, your `mediaPicker:didPickMediaItems:` is called, handing you an MPMediaItemCollection consisting of all items the user has tapped so far (including the same item multiple times if the user taps the same item more than once). When the user taps Cancel, your `mediaPickerDidCancel:` is called.

*The controller's `allowsPickingMultipleItems` is YES*
> The interface has Plus buttons at the right end of every media item, similar to the iPod/Music app interface for creating a playlist. When the user taps Done, `media-Picker:didPickMediaItems:` is called, handing you an MPMediaItemCollection consisting of all items for which the user has tapped the Plus button (including the same item multiple times if the user taps the same item's Plus button more than once). Your `mediaPickerDidCancel:` is *never* called.

The view is *not* automatically dismissed; it is up to you to dismiss the modal view controller. The standard behavior, in order to manage the interface sensibly, would be for you to dismiss the modal view controller as soon as you get either delegate message.

In this example, we put up the music picker, allowing the user to choose one media item; we then play that media item with the application's music player:

```
- (void) presentPicker {
    MPMediaPickerController* picker = [[MPMediaPickerController alloc] init];
    picker.delegate = self;
    [self presentModalViewController:picker animated:YES];
    [picker release];
}
```

```
- (void) mediaPicker: (MPMediaPickerController*) mediaPicker
        didPickMediaItems: (MPMediaItemCollection*) mediaItemCollection {
    MPMusicPlayerController* player =
        [MPMusicPlayerController applicationMusicPlayer];
    [player setQueueWithItemCollection:mediaItemCollection];
    [player play];
    [self dismissModalViewControllerAnimated:YES];
}

- (void) mediaPickerDidCancel: (MPMediaPickerController*) mediaPicker {
    [self dismissModalViewControllerAnimated:YES];
}
```

On the iPad, the music picker should be presented in a popover. (You can present the music picker modally on the iPad, but my experience is that it then doesn't work correctly. I regard as a bug the fact that you can present it modally at all; if that isn't going to work, it would be better if the framework threw an exception.) On the iPad, the popover has no Cancel button, but this is no trouble because the user can tap outside the popover to dismiss it.

Example 29-1 rewrites the preceding code so that on the iPhone it presents the picker modally but on the iPad it presents the picker in a popover. The presentPicker method is now a button's control event action, so that we can point the popover's arrow to the button. How we summon the picker depends on the device (we use UI_USER_INTERFACE_IDIOM to distinguish the two cases); if it's an iPad, we create a popover and set an instance variable to retain it (as discussed in Chapter 22). How we dismiss the picker depends on how it is being presented.

*Example 29-1. Presenting a view controller modally or in a popover*

```
- (void) presentPicker: (id) sender {
    MPMediaPickerController* picker =
        [[[MPMediaPickerController alloc] init] autorelease];
    picker.delegate = self;
    if (UI_USER_INTERFACE_IDIOM() == UIUserInterfaceIdiomPhone)
        [self presentModalViewController:picker animated:YES];
    else {
        UIPopoverController* pop =
            [[UIPopoverController alloc] initWithContentViewController:picker];
        self.currentPop = pop;
        [pop presentPopoverFromRect:[sender bounds] inView:sender
            permittedArrowDirections:UIPopoverArrowDirectionAny animated:YES];
        [pop release];
    }
}

- (void) dismissPicker: (MPMediaPickerController*) mediaPicker {
    if (self.currentPop && self.currentPop.popoverVisible) {
        [self.currentPop dismissPopoverAnimated:YES];
    } else {
        [self dismissModalViewControllerAnimated:YES];
    }
}
```

```
- (void)mediaPicker: (MPMediaPickerController *)mediaPicker
        didPickMediaItems:(MPMediaItemCollection *)mediaItemCollection {
    MPMusicPlayerController* player = [MPMusicPlayerController applicationMusicPlayer];
    [player setQueueWithItemCollection:mediaItemCollection];
    [player play];
    [self dismissPicker: mediaPicker];
}

- (void)mediaPickerDidCancel:(MPMediaPickerController *)mediaPicker {
    [self dismissPicker: mediaPicker];
}
```

MPMediaPickerController is a good example of a view controller that behaves badly in a popover if the app is suspended to the background and then comes back to the foreground with the popover still visible (see my warning about this in Chapter 22).

# CHAPTER 30

# Photo Library

The still photos and movies accessed by the user through the Photos app constitute the *photo library*. Your app can provide an interface for exploring this library through the UIImagePickerController class. The same class can also be used to take photos and videos on devices with the necessary hardware.

Also, starting in iOS 4, the Assets Library framework lets you access the photo library and its contents programmatically.

You can write files into the Camera Roll / Saved Photos album. The ability to save an image file into the Camera Roll / Saved Photos album, by calling UIImageWriteToSaved-PhotosAlbum, has existed since the early days of iOS 2.0. Some kinds of video file can also be saved into the Camera Roll / Saved Photos album; in an example in Chapter 28, I checked whether this was true of a certain video file by calling UIVideoAtPath-IsCompatibleWithSavedPhotosAlbum, and saved the file by calling UISaveVideoAtPathTo-SavedPhotosAlbum, functions that have existed since iOS 3.1. The Assets Library framework adds further options.

To use constants such as kUTTypeImage, referred to in this chapter, your app must link to *MobileCoreServices.framework* and import <MobileCoreServices/MobileCore-Services.h>.

## UIImagePickerController

UIImagePickerController is a view controller (UINavigationController) whose view provides a navigation interface, similar to the Photos app, in which the user can choose an item from the photo library. Alternatively, it can provide an interface for taking a video or still photo if the necessary hardware is present. You will typically present the view controller modally (or, on the iPad, in a popover; for code that does both, see Example 29-1).

## Choosing from the Photo Library

To let the user choose an item from the photo library, instantiate UIImagePickerController and assign its **sourceType** one of these values:

- UIImagePickerControllerSourceTypeSavedPhotosAlbum
- UIImagePickerControllerSourceTypePhotoLibrary

You should call the class method **isSourceTypeAvailable:** beforehand; if it doesn't return YES, don't present the controller with that source type.

You'll probably want to specify an array of **mediaTypes** you're interested in. This array will usually contain kUTTypeImage, kUTTypeMovie, or both; or you can specify all available types by calling the class method **availableMediaTypesForSourceType:**.

After doing all of that, and having supplied a delegate, present the view controller:

```
UIImagePickerControllerSourceType type =
    UIImagePickerControllerSourceTypePhotoLibrary;
BOOL ok = [UIImagePickerController isSourceTypeAvailable:type];
if (!ok) {
    NSLog(@"alas");
    return;
}
UIImagePickerController* picker = [[UIImagePickerController alloc] init];
picker.sourceType = type;
picker.mediaTypes =
    [UIImagePickerController availableMediaTypesForSourceType:type];
picker.delegate = self;
[self presentModalViewController:picker animated:YES];
[picker release];
```

The delegate (UIImagePickerControllerDelegate) will receive one of these messages:

- imagePickerController:didFinishPickingMediaWithInfo:
- imagePickerControllerDidCancel:

If a delegate method is not implemented, the view controller is dismissed automatically, but rather than relying on this, you should implement both delegate methods and dismiss the view controller yourself in both. The **didFinish...** method is handed a dictionary of information about the chosen item. The keys in this dictionary depend on the media type.

*An image*
    The keys are:

    UIImagePickerControllerMediaType
        A UTI; probably @"public.image", which is the same as kUTTypeImage.

    UIImagePickerControllerOriginalImage
        A UIImage.

---

UIImagePickerControllerReferenceURL

> An ALAsset URL (discussed later in this chapter).

*A movie*

The keys are:

UIImagePickerControllerMediaType

> A UTI; probably @"public.movie", which is the same as kUTTypeMovie.

UIImagePickerControllerMediaURL

> A file URL to a copy of the movie saved into a temporary directory. This would be suitable, for example, to display the movie with an MPMoviePlayerController (Chapter 28).

UIImagePickerControllerReferenceURL

> An ALAsset URL (discussed later in this chapter).

Optionally, you can set the view controller's allowsEditing to YES. In the case of an image, the interface then allows the user to scale the image up and to move it so as to be cropped by a preset square; the dictionary will include two additional keys:

UIImagePickerControllerCropRect

> An NSValue wrapping a CGRect.

UIImagePickerControllerEditedImage

> A UIImage.

In the case of a movie, the user can trim the movie just as with a UIVideoEditorController (Chapter 28). The dictionary keys are the same as before, but the file URL points to the trimmed copy in the temporary directory.

> Because of restrictions on how many movies can play at once, if you use a UIImagePickerController in a popover on the iPad to let the user choose a movie and you then want to play that movie in an MPMoviePlayerController, you must destroy the UIImagePickerController first. To do so, release the UIPopoverController that presented the UIImagePickerController (probably by nilifying the instance variable that's retaining it).

## Using the Camera

To prompt the user to take a photo or video, instantiate UIImagePickerController and set its source type to UIImagePickerControllerSourceTypeCamera. Be sure to check isSourceTypeAvailable: beforehand; it will be NO if the user's device has no camera or the camera is unavailable. If it is YES, call availableMediaTypesForSourceType: to learn whether the user can take a still photo (kUTTypeImage), a video (kUTTypeMovie), or both. The result will guide your mediaTypes setting. Set a delegate, and present the view controller modally.

Starting in iOS 3.1 (when video recording was introduced), you can also specify the `videoQuality` and `videoMaximumDuration`.

Starting in iOS 4.0, additional properties and class methods allow you to determine the camera capabilities:

`isCameraDeviceAvailable:`
Checks to see whether the front or rear camera is available, using one of these parameters:

- `UIImagePickerControllerCameraDeviceFront`
- `UIImagePickerControllerCameraDeviceRear`

`cameraDevice`
Lets you learn and set which camera is being used.

`availableCaptureModesForCameraDevice:`
Checks whether the given camera can capture still images, video, or both. You specify the front or rear camera; returns an NSArray of NSNumbers, from which you can extract the integer value. Possible modes are:

- `UIImagePickerControllerCameraCaptureModePhoto`
- `UIImagePickerControllerCameraCaptureModeVideo`

`cameraCaptureMode`
Lets you learn and set the capture mode (still or video).

`isFlashAvailableForCameraDevice:`
Checks whether flash is available.

`cameraFlashMode`
Lets you learn and set the flash mode (or, for a movie, toggles the "video torch"). Your choices are:

- `UIImagePickerControllerCameraFlashModeOff`
- `UIImagePickerControllerCameraFlashModeAuto`
- `UIImagePickerControllerCameraFlashModeOn`

When the view controller appears, the user will see the interface for taking a picture, familiar from the Camera app, possibly including flash button, camera selection button, and digital zoom (if the hardware supports these), still/video switch (if your `media-Types` setting allows both), and Cancel and Shutter buttons.

Alternatively, you can hide the standard controls by setting `showsCameraControls` to NO, replacing them with your own overlay view, which you supply as the value of the `cameraOverlayView`. In this case, you're probably going to want a button in your overlay view to make the camera to take a picture! You can do that through these methods:

- `takePicture`
- `startVideoCapture`

- `stopVideoCapture`

You can supply a `cameraOverlayView` even if you don't set `showsCameraControls` to NO, but you'll need to work out a sensible frame if you don't want your view to obscure existing controls.

You can also zoom or otherwise transform the preview image by setting the `cameraView-Transform` property. This can be tricky, not least because the default transform is not the identity transform, and also because different versions of iOS apply your transform differently; in iOS 4 and later, it is applied from the center, but before that it is applied from the top.

If you set `showsCameraControls` to NO, you may notice a blank area the size of the toolbar at the bottom of the screen. You can set the `cameraViewTransform` property so that this area is filled in, but knowing just what values to use can be tricky. Experimentation suggests that in iOS 4 this might be a good approach:

```
CGAffineTransform translate = CGAffineTransformMakeTranslation(0.0, 27.0);
CGAffineTransform scale = CGAffineTransformMakeScale(1.125, 1.125);
picker.cameraViewTransform = CGAffineTransformConcat(translate, scale);
```

I'm not very happy with that code, as it relies so heavily on "magic numbers," but at least it provides a starting point.

Allowing the user to edit the captured image or movie, and handling the outcome with the delegate messages, is just as described in the previous section. In this example, having presented the interface for the user to take a still photo, we stick the resulting photo into a UIImageView in our interface:

```
- (void)imagePickerController:(UIImagePickerController *)picker
      didFinishPickingMediaWithInfo:(NSDictionary *)info {
   UIImage* im = [info objectForKey:UIImagePickerControllerOriginalImage];
   [self->iv setImage:im];
   [self dismissModalViewControllerAnimated:YES];
}
```

There won't be any `UIImagePickerControllerReferenceURL` key in the dictionary delivered to the delegate because the image isn't in the photo library. Also, starting in iOS 4.1, a still image might report a `UIImagePickerControllerMediaMetadata` key containing the metadata for the photo.

 Setting camera-related properties such as `cameraViewTransform` when there is no camera or when the UIImagePickerController is not set to camera mode can crash your app.

Instead of using UIImagePickerController, you can control the camera and capture images using the AV Foundation framework; see the "Media Capture" chapter of the *AV Foundation Programming Guide*.

*Figure 30-1. The user might see this*

# The Assets Library Framework

The Assets Library framework, introduced in iOS 4, does for the photo library roughly what the Media Player framework does for the music library (Chapter 29), letting your code explore the library's contents. You'll need to link to *AssetsLibrary.framework* and import `<AssetsLibrary/AssetsLibrary.h>`. One obvious use of the Assets Library framework might be to implement your own interface for letting the user choose an image in a way that transcends the limitations of UIImagePickerController.

> You might not be able to explore the photo library in this way; instead, you might get a "Global denied access" error, because the user must explicitly grant permission to access the library. If the user has never done that, the interface for giving such permission (Figure 30-1) requires that Location Services be turned on. So if the user has never given permission and Location Services is off, or if Location Services is on and the user refuses permission, you are blocked; your code must always be prepared for this possibility. (In my tests, even when I tapped OK in the Figure 30-1 interface, my code seemed to halt; I didn't get an error notification, but my code didn't access the photo library either. Things worked fine the *next* time my code ran. This feels like a bug.)

A photo or video in the photo library is an ALAsset. Like a media entity (Chapter 29), an ALAsset can describe itself through key–value pairs called *properties*. (This use of the word "properties" has nothing to do with Objective-C properties, as explained in Chapter 12.) For example, it can report its type (photo or video), its creation date, its orientation if it is a photo whose metadata reports this, and its duration if it is a video. You fetch a property value with `valueForProperty:`. The properties have names like `ALAssetPropertyType`.

A complicating factor in the case of photos is that a photo can provide multiple *representations* (roughly, image file formats). A given photo ALAsset lists these representations as one its properties, `ALAssetPropertyRepresentations`, an array of strings giving the UTIs identifying the file format; a typical UTI might be `@"public.jpeg"`. A representation is an ALAssetRepresentation. You can get a photo's `defaultRepresentation`, or ask for a particular representation by submitting a file format's UTI to `representationForUTI:`.

Once you have an ALAssetRepresentation, you can interrogate it to get the actual image, either as raw data or as a CGImage (see Chapter 15). The simplest way is to ask for its `fullResolutionImage`; you may then want to derive a UIImage from this using `imageWithCGImage:scale:orientation:`. The original scale and orientation of the image are available as the ALAssetRepresentation's `scale` and `orientation`. An ALAssetRepresentation also has a `url`, which is important, because it's the unique identifier for the ALAsset (similar to the persistent ID of a song in the music library).

The photo library itself is an ALAssetsLibrary instance. It is divided into groups, which have types. For example, the user might have multiple albums; each of these is a group of type `ALAssetsGroupAlbum`. To fetch assets from the library, you either fetch one specific asset by providing its URL, or you enumerate its groups of a certain type. If you take the second approach, you are handed each group as an ALAssetsGroup; you can then enumerate the group's assets. Before doing so, you may optionally filter the group using a simple ALAssetsFilter; this limits any subsequent enumeration to photos only, videos only, or both. An ALAssetsGroup also has properties, such as a name, which you can fetch with `valueForProperty:`.

The Assets Library framework uses Objective-C blocks for fetching and enumerating assets and groups. These blocks behave rather oddly: at the end of the enumeration, they are called one extra time with a nil first parameter. Thus, you must code your block defensively to avoid treating the first parameter as real on that final call.

We now know enough for an example! I'll fetch the first photo from the album named "mattBestVertical" in my photo library and stick it into a UIImageView in the interface. For readability, I've set up the blocks in my code separately as variables *before* they are used, so it will help to read backward: we enumerate (at the end of the code) using the `getGroups` block (previously defined), which itself enumerates using the `getPix` block (defined before that). Here we go:

```
// what I'll do with the assets from the group
ALAssetsGroupEnumerationResultsBlock getPix =
^ (ALAsset *result, NSUInteger index, BOOL *stop) {
    if (!result)
        return;
    ALAssetRepresentation* rep = [result defaultRepresentation];
    CGImageRef im = [rep fullResolutionImage];
    UIImage* im2 = [UIImage imageWithCGImage:im];
    [self->iv setImage:im2]; // put image into our UIImageView
    *stop = YES; // got first image, all done
};
// what I'll do with the groups from the library
ALAssetsLibraryGroupsEnumerationResultsBlock getGroups =
^ (ALAssetsGroup *group, BOOL *stop) {
    if (!group)
        return;
    NSString* title = [group valueForProperty: ALAssetsGroupPropertyName];
    if ([title isEqualToString: @"mattBestVertical"]) {
        [group enumerateAssetsUsingBlock:getPix];
        *stop = YES; // got target group, all done
```

```
            }
    };
    // might not be able to access library at all
    ALAssetsLibraryAccessFailureBlock oops = ^ (NSError *error) {
        NSLog(@"oops! %@", [error localizedDescription]);
        // e.g. "Global denied access"
    };
    // and here we go with the actual enumeration!
    ALAssetsLibrary* library = [[ALAssetsLibrary alloc] init];
    [library enumerateGroupsWithTypes: ALAssetsGroupAlbum
                            usingBlock: getGroups
                           failureBlock: oops];
    [library release];
```

As I mentioned at the start of this chapter, writing an image file into the Camera Roll / Saved Photos album has been supported since iOS 2.0, with the ability to write a movie file added in iOS 3.1. In iOS 4.0 and iOS 4.1, these functionalities were extended through the ALAssetsLibrary class, which offers these five methods:

`writeImageToSavedPhotosAlbum:orientation:completionBlock:`
Takes a CGImageRef and orientation.

`writeImageToSavedPhotosAlbum:metadata:completionBlock:`
Takes a CGImageRef and optional metadata dictionary (such as might arrive through the `UIImagePickerControllerMediaMetadata` key when the user takes a picture using UIImagePickerController).

`writeImageDataToSavedPhotosAlbum:metadata:completionBlock:`
Takes raw image data (NSData) and optional metadata.

`videoAtPathIsCompatibleWithSavedPhotosAlbum:`
Takes a file path string. Returns a boolean.

`writeVideoAtPathToSavedPhotosAlbum:completionBlock:`
Takes a file path string.

Saving takes time, so a completion block allows you to be notified when it's over. The completion block supplies two parameters: an NSURL and an NSError. If the first parameter is not nil, the write succeeded, and this is the URL of the resulting ALAsset. If the first parameter *is* nil, the write failed, and the second parameter describes the error.

# CHAPTER 31

# Address Book

The user's address book, which the user sees through the Contacts app, is effectively a database that can be accessed directly through a C API provided by the Address Book framework. You'll link to *AddressBook.framework* and import `<AddressBook/Address-Book.h>`.

A user interface for interacting with the address book is also provided, through Objective-C classes, by the Address Book UI framework. You'll link to *AddressBookUI.framework* and import `<AddressBookUI/AddressBookUI.h>`.

## Address Book Database

The address book is an ABAddressBookRef obtained by calling `ABAddressBookCreate`. This method's name contains "Create," so you must `CFRelease` the ABAddressBookRef when you're finished with it. The address book's data starts out exactly the same as the user's Contacts data. If you make any changes to the data, they are not written through to the user's real address book until you call `ABAddressBookSave`.

The primary constituent record of the address book database is the ABPerson. You'll typically extract persons from the address book by using these functions:

- `ABAddressBookGetPersonCount`
- `ABAddressBookGetPersonWithRecordID`
- `ABAddressBookCopyPeopleWithName`
- `ABAddressBookCopyArrayOfAllPeople`

The result of the latter two is a CFArrayRef. Their names contain "Copy," so you must `CFRelease` the array when you're finished with it. (I'm going to stop reminding you about memory management from here on.)

An ABPerson doesn't formally exist as a type; it is actually an ABRecord (ABRecordRef), and by virtue of this has an ID, a type, and properties with values. To fetch the value of a property, you'll call `ABRecordCopyValue`, supplying a property ID to specify the property that interests you. ABPerson properties, as you might expect, include things like first name, last name, and email.

Working with a property value is a little tricky because the way you treat it depends on what type of value it is. (You can find this out dynamically by calling `ABPersonGetType-OfProperty`, but usually you'll know in advance.) Some values are simple, but some are not. For example, a last name is a string, which is straightforward. But a person can have more than one email, so an email value is a "multistring." To work with it, you'll treat it as an ABMultiValue (ABMultiValueRef). This is like an array of values in which each item has, in addition to a value, a label and an identifier. The label categorizes (for example, a Home email as opposed to a Work email) but is not a unique specifier (because a person might have, say, two or more Work emails); the identifier is the unique specifier.

A person's address is even more involved because not only is it an ABMultiValue (a person can have more than one address), but also a particular address is itself a dictionary (a CFDictionary). Each dictionary may have a key for street, city, state, country, and so on.

There is a lot more than this to parsing address book information, but this is enough to get you started and to illustrate by an example. I'll fetch my own record out of the address book database on my device and detect that I've got two email addresses:

```
ABAddressBookRef adbk = ABAddressBookCreate();
ABRecordRef moi = NULL;
CFArrayRef matts = ABAddressBookCopyPeopleWithName(adbk, @"Matt");
// might be multiple matts, but let's find the one with last name Neuburg
for (CFIndex ix = 0; ix < CFArrayGetCount(matts); ix++) {
    ABRecordRef matt = CFArrayGetValueAtIndex(matts, ix);
    CFStringRef last = ABRecordCopyValue(matt, kABPersonLastNameProperty);
    if (last && CFStringCompare(last, (CFStringRef)@"Neuburg", 0) == 0)
        moi = matt;
    if (last)
        CFRelease(last);
}
if (NULL == moi) {
    NSLog(@"Couldn't find myself");
    CFRelease(matts);
    CFRelease(adbk);
    return;
}
// parse my emails
ABMultiValueRef emails = ABRecordCopyValue(moi, kABPersonEmailProperty);
for (CFIndex ix = 0; ix < ABMultiValueGetCount(emails); ix++) {
    CFStringRef label = ABMultiValueCopyLabelAtIndex(emails, ix);
    CFStringRef value = ABMultiValueCopyValueAtIndex(emails, ix);
    NSLog(@"I have a %@ address: %@", (NSString*)label, (NSString*)value);
    CFRelease(label);
    CFRelease(value);
}
CFRelease(emails);
CFRelease(matts);
```

*Figure 31-1. A contact created programmatically*

## Library Access Inconsistencies

You need special permission even to *look* in the photo library with the Assets Library framework (Chapter 30), and you can't modify the music library (Chapter 29), but you can freely read the user's address book, altering a person's details, adding new people, and even possibly deleting every record in the database, without the user's knowledge or permission. Don't ask me to justify that inconsistency; it makes no sense to me. Indeed, as Apple's documentation points out, your code has *more* power over the address book database than the user does, because you can manipulate groups of persons (ABGroup, not discussed here), but the user can't; the user acquires groups only by syncing with a Mac with groups in its Address Book.

```
CFRelease(adbk);
/*
output:
I have a _$!<Home>!$_ address: matt@tidbits.com
I have a _$!<Work>!$_ address: mattworking@tidbits.com
*/
```

You can also modify an existing record, add a new record (`ABAddressBookAddRecord`), and delete a record (`ABAddressBookRemoveRecord`). In this example, I'll create a person, add him to the database, and save the database:

```
ABAddressBookRef adbk = ABAddressBookCreate();
ABRecordRef snidely = ABPersonCreate();
ABRecordSetValue(snidely, kABPersonFirstNameProperty, @"Snidely", NULL);
ABRecordSetValue(snidely, kABPersonLastNameProperty, @"Whiplash", NULL);
ABMutableMultiValueRef addr = ABMultiValueCreateMutable(kABStringPropertyType);
ABMultiValueAddValueAndLabel(addr, @"snidely@villains.com", kABHomeLabel, NULL);
ABRecordSetValue(snidely, kABPersonEmailProperty, addr, NULL);
ABAddressBookAddRecord(adbk, snidely, NULL);
ABAddressBookSave(adbk, NULL);
CFRelease(addr);
CFRelease(snidely);
CFRelease(adbk);
```

Sure enough, if we then check the state of the database through the Contacts app, the new person exists (Figure 31-1).

# Address Book Interface

The Address Book UI framework puts a user interface in front of common tasks involving the address book database and its manipulation by means of the functions and data types discussed in the preceding section. This is a great help, because designing your own interface to do the same thing would be tedious and involved, especially given properties with multiple values and the added complexity of addresses. The framework provides four UIViewController subclasses:

`ABPeoplePickerNavigationController`
> Presents a navigation interface, effectively the same as the Contacts app but without an Edit button: it lists the people in the database and allows the user to pick one and view the details.

`ABPersonViewController`
`ABNewPersonViewController`
`ABUnknownPersonViewController`
> Presents an interface showing, respectively:

- The properties of a specific person, possibly editable
- The editable properties of a new person
- A proposed person with a partial set of noneditable properties

## ABPeoplePickerNavigationController

An ABPeoplePickerNavigationController is a UINavigationController. Presenting it can be as simple as instantiating it, assigning it a delegate, and showing it modally. (On the iPad, you'll probably use a popover; presenting the controller modally does work, but a popover looks better. For code that does both, see Example 29-1.) The user can survey groups and the names of all contacts in each:

```
ABPeoplePickerNavigationController* picker =
    [[ABPeoplePickerNavigationController alloc] init];
picker.peoplePickerDelegate = self; // note: not merely "delegate"
[self presentModalViewController:picker animated:YES];
[picker release];
```

You should certainly provide a delegate, because without it the modal view will never be dismissed. This delegate is *not* the controller's `delegate` property! It is the controller's `peoplePickerDelegate` property. You should implement all three delegate methods:

`peoplePickerNavigationController:shouldContinueAfterSelectingPerson:`
> The user has tapped a person in the contacts list, provided to you as an ABRecordRef. You have two options:

- Return NO. The user has chosen a person and that's all you wanted done. The selected person remains selected unless the user chooses another person. You are likely to dismiss the picker at this point.

- Return YES (and don't dismiss the picker). The view will navigate to a view of the person's properties. You can limit the set of properties the user will see at this point by setting the ABPeoplePickerNavigationController's `displayed-Items`. This is an array of NSNumbers wrapping the property identifiers such as `kABPersonEmailProperty`.

`peoplePickerNavigationController:shouldContinueAfterSelectingPerson:property:`
`identifier:`

The user is viewing a person's properties and has tapped a property. Note that you are not handed the value of this property! You can fetch that yourself if desired, because you have the person and the property; plus, if the property has multiple values, you are handed an identifier so you can pick the correct one out of the array of values by calling `ABMultiValueGetIndexForIdentifier` and fetching the value at that index. You have two options:

- Return NO. The view is now still sitting there, displaying the person's properties. You are likely to dismiss the picker at this point.

- Return YES. This means that if the property is one that can be displayed in some other app, we will switch to that app. For example, if the user taps an address, it will be displayed in the Maps app; if the user taps an email, we will switch to the Mail app and compose a message addressed to that email.

`peoplePickerNavigationControllerDidCancel:`

The user has cancelled; you should dismiss the picker.

In this example, we want the user to pick an email. We have limited the display of properties to emails only:

```
picker.displayedProperties =
    [NSArray arrayWithObject: [NSNumber numberWithInt: kABPersonEmailProperty]];
```

We return YES from the first delegate method. The second delegate method fetches the value of the tapped email and dismisses the picker:

```
- (BOOL)peoplePickerNavigationController:
        (ABPeoplePickerNavigationController *)peoplePicker
        shouldContinueAfterSelectingPerson:(ABRecordRef)person
        property:(ABPropertyID)property
        identifier:(ABMultiValueIdentifier)identifier {
    ABMultiValueRef emails = ABRecordCopyValue(person, property);
    CFIndex ix = ABMultiValueGetIndexForIdentifier(emails, identifier);
    CFStringRef email = ABMultiValueCopyValueAtIndex(emails, ix);
    NSLog(@"%@", email); // do something with the email here
    CFRelease(email);
    CFRelease(emails);
    [self dismissModalViewControllerAnimated:YES];
    return NO;
}
```

# ABPersonViewController

An ABPersonViewController is a UIViewController. To use it, instantiate it, set its `displayedPerson` and `personViewDelegate` (*not* `delegate`), and push it onto an existing navigation controller's stack. The user's only way out of the resulting interface will be through the Back button. You can limit the properties to be displayed, as with ABPeoplePickerNavigationController, by setting the `displayedProperties`. You can highlight a property with `setHighlightedItemForProperty:withIdentifier:`.

The delegate is notified when the user taps a property, similar to ABPeoplePickerNavigationController's second delegate method illustrated in the code just above. As with ABPeoplePickerNavigationController's delegate, return YES to allow some other app, such as Maps or Mail, to open the tapped value; return NO to prevent this.

If ABPersonViewController's `allowsEditing` is YES, the right bar button is an Edit button. If the user taps this, the interface is transformed into the same sort of editing interface as ABNewPersonViewController. The user can tap Done or Cancel; if Done, the edits are automatically saved into the database. Either way, the user returns to the original display of the person's properties.

On the iPad, the same interface works, or alternatively you can use a popover. In that case you'll probably make the ABPersonViewController the root view of a UINavigationController created on the fly, especially if you intend to set `allowsEditing` to YES, since without the navigation interface the Edit button won't appear. No Back button is present or needed, because the user can dismiss the popover by tapping outside it.

# ABNewPersonViewController

An ABNewPersonController is a UIViewController. To use it, instantiate it, set its `newPersonViewDelegate` (*not* `delegate`), instantiate a UINavigationController with the ABNewPersonController as its root view, and show the navigation controller modally:

```
ABNewPersonViewController* npvc = [[ABNewPersonViewController alloc] init];
npvc.newPersonViewDelegate = self;
UINavigationController* nc =
    [[UINavigationController alloc] initWithRootViewController:npvc];
[self presentModalViewController:nc animated:YES];
[nc release];
[npvc release];
```

The interface allows the user to fill in all properties of a new contact. You cannot limit the properties displayed. You can provide properties with default values by creating a fresh ABRecordRef representing an ABPerson with `ABPersonCreate`, giving it any property values you like, and assigning it to the `displayedPerson` property.

The delegate has one method, `newPersonViewController:didCompleteWithNewPerson:`, which is responsible for dismissing the modal view. If the new person is NULL, the user tapped Cancel. Otherwise, the user tapped Done; the new person is an ABRecordRef and has already been saved into the database.

But what if you don't want the new person saved into the database? What if you were presenting this interface merely because it's such a convenient way of letting the user fill in the property values of an ABPerson? Then simply remove the newly created person from the database, like this:

```
- (void)newPersonViewController:(ABNewPersonViewController*)newPersonViewController
        didCompleteWithNewPerson:(ABRecordRef)person {
    if (NULL != person) {
        ABAddressBookRef adbk = ABAddressBookCreate();
        ABAddressBookRemoveRecord(adbk, person, NULL);
        ABAddressBookSave(adbk, NULL);
        CFStringRef name = ABRecordCopyCompositeName(person);
        NSLog(@"I have a person named %@", name); // do something with new person
        CFRelease(name);
        CFRelease(adbk);
    }
    [self dismissModalViewControllerAnimated:YES];
}
```

The modal display works on the iPad as well. Alternatively, you can display the UINavigationController in a popover; the resulting popover is effectively modal, so it will be dismissed only through your implementation of newPersonViewController:didCompleteWithNewPerson:.

## ABUnknownPersonViewController

An ABUnknownPersonViewController is a UIViewController. It presents, as it were, a proposed partial person. You can set the first and last name displayed as the controller's alternateName property and text below this as the controller's message property. You'll add other property values just as for an ABNewPersonViewController, namely, by creating a fresh ABRecordRef representing an ABPerson with ABPersonCreate, giving it some property values, and assigning it to the displayedPerson property.

To use ABUnknownPersonViewController, instantiate it, set the properties listed in the foregoing paragraph, set its unknownPersonViewDelegate (*not* delegate), and push it onto the stack of an existing navigation controller. The user's only way out of the resulting interface will be through the Back button.

On the iPad, make the ABUnknownPersonViewController the root view of a UINavigationController and present the navigation controller as a popover. No Back button is present or needed, because the user can dismiss the popover by tapping outside it.

What the user can do here depends on two other properties:

allowsAddingToAddressBook
   If Yes, a Create New Contact button and an Add to Existing Contact button appear:

   • If the user taps Create New Contact, the editing interface appears (as in ABNewPersonViewController and an editable ABPersonViewController). It is filled in with the property values of the `displayedPerson`. If the user taps Done, the person is saved into the database.

- If the user taps Add to Existing Contact, a list of all contacts appears (as in the first screen of ABPersonViewController). The user can Cancel or tap a person. If the user taps a person, the properties from the `displayedPerson` are merged into that person's record.

`allowsActions`

If YES, a Share Contact button appears. The user can tap this to edit and send a mail message containing a *.vcf* file embodying this contact.

The delegate has two methods, the first of which is required:

`unknownPersonViewController:didResolveToPerson:`

Called if `allowsAddingToAddressBook` is YES and the user finishes working in a modal editing view. The modal editing view has already been dismissed and the user has either cancelled (the second parameter is NULL) or has tapped Done (the second parameter is the ABPerson already saved into the database).

`unknownPersonViewController:shouldPerformDefaultActionForPerson:property:`
`identifier:`

Return NO, as with ABPeoplePickerNavigationController, to prevent a tap on a property value from navigating to another app.

# CHAPTER 32

# Calendar

The user's calendar information, which the user sees through the Calendar app, is effectively a database. Starting in iOS 4.0, this database can be accessed directly through the Event Kit framework. You'll link to *EventKit.framework* and import `<EventKit/EventKit.h>`.

A user interface for interacting with the calendar is also provided, by the Event Kit UI framework. This interface basically replicates part of the Calendar app. You'll link to *EventKitUI.framework* and import `<EventKitUI/EventKitUI.h>`.

## Calendar Database

The calendar database is accessed as an instance of the EKEventStore class. Starting with this instance, you can obtain two kinds of object:

*A calendar*
> A calendar is a collection of events, usually categorized for some purpose, such as Work or Home. It is an instance of EKCalendar. You can fetch all calendars with the `calendars` property, or the default calendar with the `defaultCalendarForNewEvents` property. Calendars have various types (`type`), reflecting the nature of their origin: a calendar can be created and maintained by the user locally (`EKCalendarTypeLocal`), but it might also live remotely on the network (`EKCalendarTypeCalDAV`, `EKCalendarTypeExchange`), possibly being updated by subscription (`EKCalendarTypeSubscription`); the Birthday calendar (`EKCalendarTypeBirthday`) is generated automatically from information in the address book. You can't create a calendar.

*An event*
> An event is a memorandum describing when something happens. It is an instance of EKEvent. An event is associated with a calendar, its `calendar`, and you must specify a calendar when creating an event. However, not every calendar permits modification or creation of events; if in doubt, check the calendar's `allowsContentModifications` property. Given a calendar, you can't fetch any events; rather, you

fetch an event from the database as a whole. You do this either by unique identifier or by a date range.

I'll give an example of fetching events from the calendar database in a moment, but first let's focus on events. An event is an instance of EKEvent, and is where all the real action is. You fetch events out of the calendar database; you can modify an existing event, or make a new one; you can save an event into the calendar database with `save-Event:span:error:`, and delete it from the database with `removeEvent:span:error:`. (You never save the database itself.)

If you've ever used the Calendar app, or iCal on the Mac, you have a sense for how an EKEvent can be configured. It has a `title` and optional `notes`. It is associated with a `calendar`, as I've already said. Most important, it has a `startDate` and an `endDate`; these are NSDates and involve both date and time. If the event's `allDay` property is YES, the time aspect of its dates is ignored; the event is associated with a day or a stretch of days as a whole. If the event's `allDay` property is NO, the time aspect of its dates matters; a typical event will then usually be bounded by two times on the same day.

An event can be a recurring event, repeating at intervals according to some rule. That rule is the event's `recurrenceRule`, and is an EKRecurrenceRule. A simple EKRecurrenceRule is described by three properties:

*Frequency*
> By day, by week, by month, or by year.

*Interval*
> Fine-tunes the notion "by" in the frequency. A value of 1 means "every." A value of 2 means "every other." And so on.

*End*
> Optional, because the event might recur forever. It is an EKRecurrenceEnd instance, describing the limit of the event's recurrence either as an end date or as a maximum number of occurrences.

The options for describing a more complex EKRecurrenceRule are best summarized by its initializer:

```
- (id)initRecurrenceWithFrequency:(EKRecurrenceFrequency)type
                         interval:(NSInteger)interval
                  daysOfTheWeek:(NSArray *)days
                 daysOfTheMonth:(NSArray *)monthDays
                monthsOfTheYear:(NSArray *)months
                 weeksOfTheYear:(NSArray *)weeksOfTheYear
                  daysOfTheYear:(NSArray *)daysOfTheYear
                   setPositions:(NSArray *)setPositions
                           end:(EKRecurrenceEnd *)end
```

The meanings of all these parameters are mostly obvious from their names. The arrays are mostly of NSNumber, except for `daysOfTheWeek`, which is an array of EKRecurrenceDayOfWeek, a class that allows specification of a week number as well as a day number so that you can say things like "the fourth Thursday of the month." The set-Positions parameter is an array of numbers filtering the occurrences defined by the rest of the specification against the interval; however, it doesn't seem to be always obeyed correctly. You can use any valid combination of parameters; the penalty for an invalid combination that can't be resolved is a return value of nil.

Unfortunately, an EKRecurrenceRule has rather severe limitations. In theory, it is intended to reflect the RRULE event component in the iCalendar standard specification (original published as RFC 2445 and recently superseded by RFC 5545, *http://data tracker.ietf.org/doc/rfc5545*). According to the standard, you should be allowed to specify both month and day in a yearly recurring event. The standard even gives an explicit example:

```
RRULE:FREQ=YEARLY;INTERVAL=2;BYMONTH=1;BYDAY=SU
```

This is means "every Sunday in January, every other year." But the documentation for EKRecurrenceRule says that daysOfTheMonth is valid only if the frequency is EKRecurrenceFrequencyMonthly, so you can't use EKRecurrenceRule to form this rule.

For example, let's consider how to express a single recurring event that marks when I have to pay my quarterly estimated taxes. The deadlines are the 15th of January, April, June, and September. This is not a regular interval (it isn't every three months). The solution would seem to be to describe this as an annual recurring event, listing the relevant months explicitly as the monthsOfTheYear parameter, and putting the 15th of the month as the daysOfTheMonth parameter, like this:

```
EKRecurrenceRule* recur =
[[EKRecurrenceRule alloc]
initRecurrenceWithFrequency:EKRecurrenceFrequencyYearly
interval:1
daysOfTheWeek:nil
daysOfTheMonth:[NSArray arrayWithObject:[NSNumber numberWithInt:15]]
monthsOfTheYear:[NSArray arrayWithObjects:
                [NSNumber numberWithInt: 1],
                [NSNumber numberWithInt: 4],
                [NSNumber numberWithInt: 6],
                [NSNumber numberWithInt: 9],
                nil]
weeksOfTheYear:nil
daysOfTheYear:nil
setPositions: nil
end:nil];
```

However, if we inspect the resulting recurrence rule, the daysOfTheMonth component has been thrown away, presumably because, as I just said, daysOfTheMonth is valid only if the frequency is EKRecurrenceFrequencyMonthly:

```
NSLog(@"event %@", recur); // RRULE FREQ=YEARLY;INTERVAL=1;BYMONTH=1,4,6,9
```

So EKRecurrenceRule falls short of the standard. Nevertheless, it turns out that in this case, by also assigning the event itself a start and end date of the 15th of the month, we can obtain the desired event. I'll create the event and save it into the calendar database:

```
EKRecurrenceRule* recur =
 [[EKRecurrenceRule alloc]
 initRecurrenceWithFrequency:EKRecurrenceFrequencyYearly
 interval:1
 daysOfTheWeek:nil
 daysOfTheMonth:nil
 monthsOfTheYear:[NSArray arrayWithObjects:
                    [NSNumber numberWithInt: 1],
                    [NSNumber numberWithInt: 4],
                    [NSNumber numberWithInt: 6],
                    [NSNumber numberWithInt: 9],
                    nil]
 weeksOfTheYear:nil
 daysOfTheYear:nil
 setPositions: nil
 end:nil];
EKEventStore* database = [[EKEventStore alloc] init];
EKEvent* taxes = [EKEvent eventWithEventStore:database];
taxes.title = @"Estimated tax payment due";
taxes.recurrenceRule = recur;
NSCalendar* greg =
    [[NSCalendar alloc] initWithCalendarIdentifier:NSGregorianCalendar];
NSDateComponents* comp = [[NSDateComponents alloc] init];
[comp setYear:2011];
[comp setMonth:4];
[comp setDay:15];
NSDate* date = [greg dateFromComponents:comp];
taxes.calendar = [database defaultCalendarForNewEvents];
taxes.startDate = date;
taxes.endDate = date;
taxes.allDay = YES;
NSError* err = nil;
BOOL ok = [database saveEvent:taxes span: EKSpanFutureEvents error:&err];
if (ok)
    NSLog(@"ok!");
else
    NSLog(@"error: %@", [err localizedDescription]);
[database release];
[greg release];
[comp release];
[recur release];
```

In that code, the event we save into the database is a recurring event. When we save or delete a recurring event, we must specify its span. This is either EKSpanThisEvent or EKSpanFutureEvents, and corresponds exactly to the two buttons the user sees in the Calendar interface when saving or deleting a recurring event (Figure 32-1, and there is a similar choice on the Mac in iCal). The buttons and the span types reflect their meaning exactly: either the change affects this event alone, or this event plus all *future* (not past) recurrences. This choice determines not only how this and future recurrences of the event are affected now, but also how they relate to one another from now on.

*Figure 32-1. The user specifies a span*

An EKEvent can have alarms. An alarm is an EKAlarm and can be set to fire either at an absolute date or at a relative offset from the event time. On an iOS device, an alarm fires through a local notification (Chapter 26).

An EKEvent can also be used to embody a meeting, with **attendees** (EKParticipant) and an **organizer**, but that is not a feature of an event that you can set.

Now let's return to the database as a whole. Once you've instantiated EKEventStore, you should maintain that instance for as long as your app will need access to the calendar database. This is partly because opening access to the database is somewhat expensive and time-consuming, and partly because an EKEvent belongs only to a single instance of EKEventStore.

An event in the database can be retrieved across instantiations of EKEventStore by its unique identifier (**eventIdentifier**), by calling **eventWithIdentifier:**; however, even this unique identifier might not survive changes in a calendar between launches of your app.

You can also extract events from the database by matching a predicate (NSPredicate). To form this predicate, you specify a start and end date and call the EKEventStore method **predicateForEventsWithStartDate:endDate:calendars:**. Because the date range is the only way to fetch events, any further filtering of events is up to you. In this example, I'll gather all events with "insurance" in their title; because I have to specify a date range, I ask for events occurring over the next year:

```
EKEventStore* database = [[EKEventStore alloc] init];
NSDate* d1 = [NSDate date];
NSDate* d2 = [NSDate dateWithTimeInterval:60*60*24*365 sinceDate:d1];
NSPredicate* pred =
    [database predicateForEventsWithStartDate:d1 endDate:d2
                                    calendars:database.calendars];
NSMutableArray* marr = [NSMutableArray array];
[database enumerateEventsMatchingPredicate:pred usingBlock:
 ^(EKEvent *event, BOOL *stop) {
    NSRange r = [event.title rangeOfString:@"insurance"
                                   options:NSCaseInsensitiveSearch];
    if (r.location != NSNotFound)
        [marr addObject: event];
}];
```

After that, `marr` contains three events, because I pay my motorcycle insurance annually and my car insurance biannually. Those events are in no particular order; a convenience method on EKEvent, `compareStartDateWithEvent:`, is suitable as a sort selector:

```
[marr sortUsingSelector:@selector(compareStartDateWithEvent:)];
```

When you extract events from the database, event recurrences are treated as separate events. Thus, for example, although we created the tax payment event as a single recurring event, we might retrieve as many as four EKEvent instances of it over the next year. These EKEvents will have different start and end dates but the same `event-Identifier`. When you fetch an event by calling `eventWithIdentifier:` you get the *earliest* event with that identifier. This makes sense, because if you're going to make a change affecting this and future recurrences of the event, you need the option to start with the earliest possible recurrence (so that "future" means "all").

The calendar database is an odd sort of database, because calendars can be maintained in so many ways and places. A calendar can change while your app is running (the user might sync, for example), which can put your information out of date. You can register for a single EKEventStore notification, `EKEventStoreChangedNotification`; if you receive it, you should assume that any calendar-related instances you're holding are invalid. If you are in the middle of editing an event, you can reload its properties by calling `refresh`, but in general the database, and all events and calendars you're working with, need to be fetched all over again.

# Calendar Interface

The graphical interface consists of two views for letting the user work with an event:

*EKEventViewController*
    Shows the description of a single event, possibly editable.

*EKEventEditViewController*
    Allows the user to create or edit an event.

EKEventViewController simply shows the little rounded rectangle containing the event's title, date, and time, familiar from the Calendar app, possibly with additional rounded rectangles describing alarms and notes. The user can't tap these to do anything. To use EKEventViewController, instantiate it, give it an event, and push it onto the stack of an existing UINavigationController. The user's only way out will be the Back button. So, for example:

```
EKEventViewController* evc = [[EKEventViewController alloc] init];
evc.event = [marr objectAtIndex:0];
evc.allowsEditing = NO;
[self.navigationController pushViewController:evc animated:YES];
[evc release];
```

The documentation says that `allowsEditing` is NO by default, but in my testing the default was YES; perhaps you'd best play safe and set it regardless. If it is YES, an Edit button appears as the right bar button item in the navigation bar, and by tapping this, the user can edit the various aspects of an event in the same navigation interface that should be familiar from the Calendar app, including the large red Delete button at the bottom. If the user ultimately deletes the event or edits it and taps Done, the change is saved into the database.

Starting in iOS 4.2, you can assign the EKEventViewController a delegate in order to hear about what the user did. The delegate method `eventViewController:didComplete-WithAction:` is called only if the user deletes an event or accepts an invitation.

On the iPad, you use the EKEventViewController as the root view of a navigation controller created on the fly and use the navigation controller as a popover's view controller. By default, the EKEventViewController's `modalInPopover` is YES and a Done button appears as the right bar button; the delegate method `eventViewController:didComplete-WithAction:` is called if the user taps the Done button, and you'll need to dismiss the popover there. However, if `allowsEditing` is YES, you must set `modalInPopover` to NO, so to replace the Done button with the Edit button. Here's code that works both on the iPhone and on the iPad:

```
EKEventViewController* evc = [[EKEventViewController alloc] init];
evc.delegate = self;
evc.event = // ... whatever ...;
evc.allowsEditing = NO;
// on iPhone, push onto existing navigation interface
if (UI_USER_INTERFACE_IDIOM() == UIUserInterfaceIdiomPhone)
    [self.navigationController pushViewController:evc animated:YES];
// on iPad, create navigation interface in popover
else {
    UINavigationController* nc =
        [[UINavigationController alloc] initWithRootViewController:evc];
    evc.modalInPopover = NO;
    UIPopoverController* pop =
        [[UIPopoverController alloc] initWithContentViewController:nc];
    self.currentPop = pop;
    [pop presentPopoverFromRect:[sender bounds] inView:sender
        permittedArrowDirections:UIPopoverArrowDirectionAny animated:YES];
    [nc release];
    [pop release];
}
[evc release];
```

EKEventEditViewController (a UINavigationController) presents the interface for editing an event. To use it, set its `eventStore` and `editViewDelegate` (*not* delegate), and optionally its `event`, and present it modally (or, on the iPad, in a popover). The event can be nil for a completely empty new event; it can be an event you've just created (and possibly partially configured) and not stored in the database, or it can be an existing event from the database.

The delegate method `eventEditViewControllerDefaultCalendarForNewEvents:` may be implemented to specify what calendar a completely new event should be assigned. If you're partially constructing a new event, you can assign it a calendar then, and of course an event from the database already has a calendar.

You must implement the delegate method eventEditViewController:didCompleteWith-Action: so that you can dismiss the modal view. Possible actions are that the user cancelled, saved the edited event, or deleted an already existing event from the database.

On the iPad, the modal view works, or you can present the EKEventEditViewController as a popover. By default, its modalInPopover is YES, which means you'll use eventEdit-ViewController:didCompleteWithAction: to dismiss the popover.

Both view controllers automatically listen for changes in the database and, if needed, will automatically call refresh on the event being edited, updating their display to match. If the event was in the database and has been deleted while the user is viewing it, the delegate will get the same notification as if the user had deleted it.

# CHAPTER 33

# Mail

Your app can present interface allowing the user to edit and send a mail message (and, starting in iOS 4, an SMS message). Two view controller classes are provided by the Message UI framework; your app will link to *MessageUI.framework* and import `<MessageUI/MessageUI.h>`. The classes are:

*MFMailComposeViewController*
    Allows composition and sending of a mail message.

*MFMessageComposeViewController*
    Allows composition and sending of an SMS message.

## Mail Message

The MFMailComposeViewController class, a UINavigationController, allows the user to edit a mail message. The user can attempt to send the message there and then or can cancel but save a draft, or can cancel completely. Before using this class to present a view, call `canSendMail`; if the result is NO, go no further. A negative result means that the device is not configured for sending mail. A positive result does not mean that the device is connected to the network and can send mail right now, only that sending mail is generally possible with this device.

To use MFMailComposeViewController, instantiate it, provide a `mailCompose-Delegate` (*not* `delegate`), and configure the message to any desired extent. The user can alter your preset configurations. Configuration methods are:

- `setSubject:`
- `setToRecipients:`
- `setCcRecipients:`
- `setBccRecipients:`
- `setMessageBody:isHTML:`
- `addAttachmentData:mimeType:fileName:`

The delegate method `mailComposeController:didFinishWithResult:error:` is called with the user's final action, which might be any of these:

- `MFMailComposeResultCancelled`
- `MFMailComposeResultSaved`
- `MFMailComposeResultSent`
- `MFMailComposeResultFailed`

Typically, you'll present the MFMailComposeViewController modally. Dismissing the modal view is up to you, in the delegate method. You don't *have* to present it modally, but it's a sensible interface and works well even on the iPad (use `UIModalPresentation-FormSheet` if a full-screen presentation feels too overwhelming).

## SMS Message

The MFMessageComposeViewController class, a UINavigationController, is even simpler. Instantiate the class, give it a `messageComposeDelegate`, configure it as desired, and present it modally. Configuration is through the `recipients` and `body` properties.

The delegate method `messageComposeViewController:didFinishWithResult:` is called with the same possible results as for a mail message. Dismissing the modal view is up to you, in the delegate method.

# CHAPTER 34

# Maps

Your app can imitate the Maps app, communicating with Google Maps to present a map interface and placing annotations and overlays on the map. UIView subclasses for displaying the map, along with the programming API, are provided by the Map Kit framework. You'll link to *MapKit.framework* and import `<MapKit/MapKit.h>`. You might also need the Core Location framework to express locations by latitude and longitude; you'll link to *CoreLocation.framework* and import `<CoreLocation/Core-Location.h>`.

## Presenting a Map

A map is presented through a UIView subclass, an MKMapView. The map is potentially a map of the entire world; the map view is usually configured to display a particular area. An MKMapView instance can be created in code or through the nib editor. A map has a `type`, which is one of the following:

- `MKMapTypeStandard`
- `MKMapTypeSatellite`
- `MKMapTypeHybrid`

The area displayed on the map is its `region`, an MKCoordinateRegion. This is a struct comprising a location (a CLLocationCoordinate2D), describing the latitude and longitude of the point at the center of the region, along with a span (an MKCoordinate-Span), describing the quantity of latitude and longitude embraced by the region. Convenience functions help you construct an MKCoordinateRegion.

In this example, I'll initialize the display of an MKMapView to show a place where I like to go dirt biking. The MKMapView is placed into the interface through the nib editor and is initially hidden so that the user doesn't see the default map of the world. I provide the region by setting the map view's `region` property, and show the view (Figure 34-1):

*Figure 34-1. A map view showing a happy place*

```
CLLocationCoordinate2D loc = CLLocationCoordinate2DMake(34.923964,-120.219558);
MKCoordinateRegion reg = MKCoordinateRegionMakeWithDistance(loc, 1000, 1000);
self->map.region = reg;
self->map.hidden = NO;
```

By default, the user can zoom and scroll the map with the usual gestures; you can turn this off by setting the map view's `zoomEnabled` and `scrollEnabled` to NO. Usually you will set them both to YES or both to NO. For example, if your aim is to prevent the user from changing the center coordinate, setting `scrollEnabled` to NO is insufficient, because the user can still zoom, and zooming includes double-tapping, which can change the center coordinate. (Workarounds to allow the user to zoom while keeping the center coordinate fixed, perhaps by implementing the delegate method `mapView:regionDidChangeAnimated:`, can quickly become ugly and difficult to maintain, involving raising and lowering of boolean flags and so forth.)

You can change the region displayed, optionally with animation, by calling these methods:

* `setRegion:animated:`
* `setCenterCoordinate:animated:`
* `setVisibleMapRect:animated:`
* `setVisibleMapRect:edgePadding:animated:`

MKMapRect (used in `setVisibleMapRect:animated:`) was introduced in iOS 4. Along with MKMapPoint and MKMapSize, it can simplify calculations by projecting the world's surface onto a flat rectangle. I'll give an example later in this chapter.

## Annotations

An *annotation* is a marker associated with a location on a map. To make an annotation appear on a map, two objects are needed:

*The object attached to the MKMapView*
> The annotation itself is attached to the MKMapView. It consists of any instance whose class adopts the MKAnnotation protocol, which specifies a coordinate, a title, and a subtitle for the annotation. You might have reason to define your own

class to handle this task, or you can use the simple built-in MKPointAnnotation class. The annotation's `coordinate` is its most important property; this says where on earth the annotation should be drawn. The title and subtitle are optional, to be displayed in a callout.

*The object that draws the annotation*

An annotation is drawn by an MKAnnotationView, a UIView subclass. This can be extremely simple. In fact, even a nil MKAnnotationView might be perfectly satisfactory: it draws a red pin. If red is not your favorite color, a built-in MKAnnotationView subclass, MKPinAnnotationView, displays a pin in red, green, or purple; by convention you are supposed to use these colors for different purposes (destination points, starting points, and user-specified points, respectively). For more flexibility, you can provide your own UIImage as the MKAnnotationView's `image` property. And for even *more* flexibility, you can take over the drawing of an MKAnnotationView by overriding `drawRect:` in a subclass.

Not only does an annotation require two separate objects, but in fact those objects do not initially exist together. An annotation object has no pointer to the annotation view object that will draw it. Rather, it is up to you to supply the annotation view object in real time, on demand, in the MKMapView's delegate. This architecture may sound confusing, but in fact it's a very clever way of reducing the amount of resources needed at any given moment. Think of it this way: an annotation itself is merely a lightweight object that a map can always possess; the corresponding annotation view is a heavyweight object that is needed only so long as that annotation's coordinates are within the visible portion of the map.

To illustrate the simplest possible case, let's return to the code where we initially configured our map. Here's the same code again, but this time I'll add an annotation:

```
CLLocationCoordinate2D loc = CLLocationCoordinate2DMake(34.923964,-120.219558);
MKCoordinateRegion reg = MKCoordinateRegionMakeWithDistance(loc, 1000, 1000);
self->map.region = reg;
MKPointAnnotation* ann = [[MKPointAnnotation alloc] init];
ann.coordinate = loc;
ann.title = @"Park here";
ann.subtitle = @"Fun awaits down the road!";
[self->map addAnnotation:ann];
[ann release];
self->map.hidden = NO;
```

That code is sufficient to produce Figure 34-2. I didn't implement any MKMapView delegate methods, so the MKAnnotationView is nil. But a nil MKAnnotationView, as I've already said, produces a red pin. I've also tapped the annotation, to display its callout, containing the annotation's title and subtitle.

This location, however, is a starting point, so by convention the pin should be green. We can create such a pin using MKPinAnnotationView, which has a `pinColor` property. We supply the annotation view in the map view's delegate (MKMapViewDelegate), by implementing `mapView:viewForAnnotation:`.

*Figure 34-2. A simple annotation*

The structure of `mapView:viewForAnnotation:` is rather similar to the structure of `tableView:cellForRowAtIndexPath:` (Chapter 21), because they both do the same sort of thing. Recall that the goal of `tableView:cellForRowAtIndexPath:` is to allow the table view to reuse cells, so that at any given moment only as many cells are needed as are *visible* in the table view, regardless of how many rows the table as a whole may consist of. The same thing holds for a map and its annotation views. The map may have a huge number of annotations, but it needs to display annotation views for only those annotations that are within its current `region`. Any extra annotation views that have been scrolled out of view can thus be reused and are held for us by the map view in a cache for exactly this purpose.

So, in `mapView:viewForAnnotation:`, we start by calling `dequeueReusableAnnotationView-WithIdentifier:` to see whether there's an already existing annotation view that's not currently being displayed and that we might be able to reuse. If there isn't, we create one, attaching to it an appropriate reuse identifier.

Here's our implementation of `mapView:viewForAnnotation:`. We examine the incoming annotation to see whether the annotation view that draws it might be of a type susceptible to reuse. How we categorize views for reuse is up to us. In this case, let's say that one category is our stock of green pins. We look to see whether this annotation is one that takes a green pin; in this case, I use the annotation's title to determine this. If so, we either create a green pin or reuse one from the map view's cache. Observe that in creating our green pin, we must explicitly set its `canShowCallout` to YES, as this is not the default:

```
- (MKAnnotationView *)mapView:(MKMapView *)mapView
        viewForAnnotation:(id <MKAnnotation>)annotation {
    MKAnnotationView* v = nil;
    if ([annotation.title isEqualToString:@"Park here"]) { ❶
        static NSString* ident = @"greenPin"; ❷
        v = [mapView dequeueReusableAnnotationViewWithIdentifier:ident];
        if (v == nil) {
            v = [[[MKPinAnnotationView alloc] initWithAnnotation:annotation
                                                reuseIdentifier:ident]
                    autorelease];
            ((MKPinAnnotationView*)v).pinColor = MKPinAnnotationColorGreen;
            v.canShowCallout = YES;
        } else {
```

```
                v.annotation = annotation; ❸
            }
        }
        return v;
    }
```

The structure of this implementation of `mapView:viewForAnnotation:` is typical (even though much of it seems pointlessly elaborate when we have only one annotation in our map):

❶ We might have more than one reusable type of annotation view. (A view can perhaps be reconfigured and thus reused, but cannot be magically converted into a view of a different type.) Here, some of our annotations might be marked with green pins, and other annotations might be marked by a different sort of annotation view altogether. So we must first somehow distinguish these cases, based on something about the incoming annotation.

❷ After that, for each reusable type, we proceed much as with table view cells. We have an identifier that categorizes this sort of reusable view. We try to dequeue an unused annotation view of the appropriate type, and if we can't, we create one and configure it.

❸ Even if we *can* dequeue an unused annotation view, and even if we have no other configuration to perform, we must associate the annotation view with the incoming annotation by assigning the annotation to this view's `annotation` property.

Now let's go further. Instead of a green pin, let's substitute our own artwork. Here, instead of creating an MKPinAnnotationView, I create an MKAnnotationView and give it a custom image. The image is too large, so I shrink the view's bounds before returning it; I also move the view up a bit, so that the bottom of the image is at the coordinates on the map (Figure 34-3):

```
v = [[[MKAnnotationView alloc] initWithAnnotation:annotation
                          reuseIdentifier:ident] autorelease];
v.image = [UIImage imageNamed:@"clipartdirtbike.gif"];
CGRect f = v.bounds;
f.size.height /= 3.0;
f.size.width /= 3.0;
v.bounds = f;
v.centerOffset = CGPointMake(0,-20);
v.canShowCallout = YES;
```

For more flexibility, we can create our own MKAnnotationView subclass and endow it with the ability to draw itself. At a minimum, such a subclass should override the initializer and assign itself a frame, and should implement `drawRect:`. Here's the implementation for a class MyAnnotationView that draws a dirt bike:

```
- (id)initWithAnnotation:(id <MKAnnotation>)annotation
        reuseIdentifier:(NSString *)reuseIdentifier {
    self = [super initWithAnnotation:annotation reuseIdentifier:reuseIdentifier];
    if (self) {
        UIImage* im = [UIImage imageNamed:@"clipartdirtbike.gif"];
```

*Figure 34-3. A custom annotation image*

```
        self.frame =
            CGRectMake(0, 0, im.size.width / 3.0 + 5, im.size.height / 3.0 + 5);
        self.centerOffset = CGPointMake(0,-20);
        self.opaque = NO;
    }
    return self;
}

- (void) drawRect: (CGRect) rect {
    UIImage* im = [UIImage imageNamed:@"clipartdirtbike.gif"];
    [im drawInRect:CGRectInset(self.bounds, 5, 5)];
}
```

The corresponding implementation of `mapView:viewForAnnotation:` now has much less work to do:

```
- (MKAnnotationView *)mapView:(MKMapView *)mapView
        viewForAnnotation:(id <MKAnnotation>)annotation {
    MKAnnotationView* v = nil;
    if ([annotation.title isEqualToString:@"Park here"]) {
        static NSString* ident = @"bike";
        v = [mapView dequeueReusableAnnotationViewWithIdentifier:ident];
        if (v == nil) {
            v = [[[MyAnnotationView alloc] initWithAnnotation:annotation
                                            reuseIdentifier:ident]
                    autorelease];
            v.canShowCallout = YES;
        } else {
            v.annotation = annotation;
        }
    }
    return v;
}
```

For ultimate flexibility, we should provide our own annotation class as well. A minimal annotation class will look like this:

```
@interface MyAnnotation : NSObject <MKAnnotation> {
}
@property (nonatomic, readonly) CLLocationCoordinate2D coordinate;
@property (nonatomic, copy) NSString *title, *subtitle;
- (id)initWithLocation:(CLLocationCoordinate2D)coord;
@end
```

```
@implementation MyAnnotation
@synthesize coordinate, title, subtitle;
- (id)initWithLocation: (CLLocationCoordinate2D) coord {
    self = [super init];
    if (self) {
        self->coordinate = coord;
    }
    return self;
}
@end
```

Now when we create our annotation and add it to our map, our code looks like this:

```
MyAnnotation* ann = [[MyAnnotation alloc] initWithLocation:loc];
ann.title = @"Park here";
ann.subtitle = @"Fun awaits down the road!";
[self->map addAnnotation:ann];
[ann release];
```

A major advantage of this change appears in our implementation of `mapView:viewForAnnotation:`, where we test for the annotation type. Formerly, it wasn't easy to distinguish those annotations that needed to be drawn as a dirt bike; we were rather artificially examining the title:

```
if ([annotation.title isEqualToString:@"Park here"]) {
```

Now, however, we can just look at the class:

```
if ([annotation isKindOfClass:[MyAnnotation class]]) {
```

A further advantage of supplying our own annotation class is that gives our implementation room to grow. For example, at the moment, every MyAnnotation is drawn as a bike, but we could now add another property to MyAnnotation that tells us what drawing to use. We could also give MyAnnotation further properties saying such things as which way the bike should face, what angle it should be drawn at, and so on. Our implementation of `mapView:viewForAnnotation:` would read these properties and pass them on to MyAnnotationView, which would then draw itself appropriately.

The callout is visible in Figure 34-2 and Figure 34-3 because before taking the screenshot I tapped on the annotation, thus *selecting* it. MKMapView has methods allowing annotations to be selected or deselected programmatically, thus causing their callouts to appear or disappear; the delegate has methods notifying you when the user selects or deselects an annotation.

A callout can contain left and right accessory views; these are the MKAnnotationView's `leftCalloutAccessoryView` and `rightCalloutAccessoryView`. These are UIViews, and should be small (less than 32 pixels in height). You can respond to taps on these views as you would any view or control.

MKMapView has extensive support for adding and removing annotations. Annotation views don't change size as the map is zoomed in and out, so if there are several annotations and they are brought close together by the user zooming out, the display can become crowded. The only way to prevent this is to respond to zooming by removing and adding annotations dynamically.

# Overlays

An overlay differs from an annotation in being drawn *entirely* with respect to points on the surface of the earth. Thus, although an annotation's size is always the same, an overlay's size is tied to the zoom of the map view. (Overlays were introduced in iOS 4.)

Overlays are implemented much like annotations. You provide an object that adopts the MKOverlay protocol (which itself conforms to the MKAnnotation protocol) and add it to the map view. When the map view delegate method `mapView:viewFor-Overlay:` is called, you provide an MKOverlayView that actually draws the overlay. As with annotations, this architecture means that the overlay itself is a lightweight object, and the overlay view is needed only if the part of the earth that the overlay covers is actually being displayed in the map view.

Some built-in MKShape subclasses adopt the MKOverlay protocol: MKCircle, MKPolygon, and MKPolyline. MKOverlayView has subclasses MKCircleView, MKPolygonView, and MKPolylineView, ready to draw the corresponding shapes. Thus, as with annotations, you can base your overlay entirely on the power of existing classes.

In this example, I'll use MKPolygonView to draw an overlay triangle pointing up the road from the parking place annotated in our earlier examples (Figure 34-4). We add the MKPolygon as an overlay to our map view, and derive the MKPolygonView from it in our implementation of `mapView:viewForOverlay:`. First, the MKPolygon overlay:

```
CLLocationCoordinate2D loc = self->map.region.center;
CGFloat lat = loc.latitude;
CLLocationDistance metersPerPoint = MKMetersPerMapPointAtLatitude(lat);
MKMapPoint c = MKMapPointForCoordinate(loc);
c.x += 150/metersPerPoint;
c.y -= 50/metersPerPoint;
MKMapPoint p1 = MKMapPointMake(c.x, c.y);
p1.y -= 100/metersPerPoint;
MKMapPoint p2 = MKMapPointMake(c.x, c.y);
p2.x += 100/metersPerPoint;
MKMapPoint p3 = MKMapPointMake(c.x, c.y);
p3.x += 300/metersPerPoint;
p3.y -= 400/metersPerPoint;
MKMapPoint pts[3] = {
    p1, p2, p3
};
MKPolygon* tri = [MKPolygon polygonWithPoints:pts count:3];
[self->map addOverlay:tri];
```

Second, the delegate method, where we provide the MKPolygonView:

```
- (MKOverlayView *)mapView:(MKMapView *)mapView
        viewForOverlay:(id <MKOverlay>)overlay {
    MKPolygonView* v = nil;
```

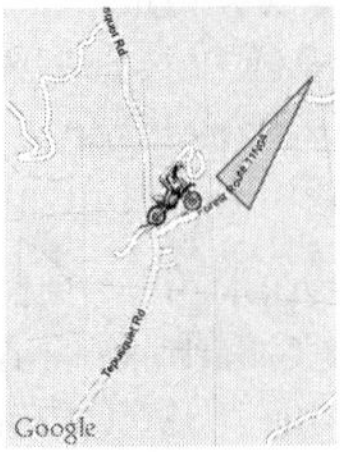

Figure 34-4. An overlay view

```
    if ([overlay isKindOfClass:[MKPolygon class]]) {
        v = [[[MKPolygonView alloc] initWithPolygon:(MKPolygon*)overlay]
                autorelease];
        v.fillColor = [[UIColor redColor] colorWithAlphaComponent:0.1];
        v.strokeColor = [[UIColor redColor] colorWithAlphaComponent:0.8];
        v.lineWidth = 2;
    }
    return v;
}
```

Now let's go further. The triangle in Figure 34-4 is rather crude; I could draw a better arrow shape using a CGPath (Chapter 15). The built-in MKOverlayView subclass that lets me do that is MKOverlayPathView. To structure my use of MKOverlayView similarly to the preceding example, I'll supply the CGPath when I add the overlay instance to the map view. No built-in class lets me do that, so I'll use a custom class that implements the MKOverlay protocol.

A minimal overlay class looks like this:

```
@interface MyOverlay : NSObject <MKOverlay> {
}
@property (nonatomic, readonly) MKMapRect boundingMapRect;
- (id) initWithRect: (MKMapRect) rect;
@end

@implementation MyOverlay
@synthesize boundingMapRect, coordinate;
- (id) initWithRect: (MKMapRect) rect {
    self = [super init];
    if (self) {
        self->boundingMapRect = rect;
    }
    return self;
}
@end
```

Our actual MyOverlay class will also have a `path` property, a UIBezierPath, that holds our CGPath and supplies it to the MKOverlayView.

Just as the `coordinate` property of an annotation tells the map view where on earth the annotation is to be drawn, the `boundingMapRect` property of an overlay tells the map view where on earth the overlay is to be drawn. Whenever any part of the `boundingMap-`

Rect is displayed within the map view's bounds, the map view will have to concern itself with drawing the overlay. With MKPolygon, we supplied the points of the polygon in earth coordinates and the boundingMapRect was calculated for us. With our custom overlay class, we must supply or calculate it ourselves.

At first it may appear that there is a typological impedance mismatch: the boundingMap-Rect is an MKMapRect, whereas a CGPath is defined by CGPoints. However, it turns out that these units are interchangeable: the CGPoints of our CGPath will be translated for us directly into MKMapPoints on the same scale — that is, the *distance* between any two CGPoints will be the distance between the two corresponding MKMapPoints. However, the *origins* are different: the CGPath must be described relative to the top left corner of the boundingMapRect — that is, the boundingMapRect is described in earth coordinates, but its top left corner is (0,0) as far as the CGPath is concerned. (You might think of this difference as analogous to the difference between a UIView's frame and its bounds.)

To make life simple, I'll think in meters; actually, I'll think in chunks of 75 meters, because this turned out to be a good unit for positioning and laying out the arrow. In other words, a line one unit long would in fact be 75 meters long if I were to arrive at this actual spot on the earth and discover the overlay literally drawn on the ground. Having derived this chunk (unit), I use it to lay out the boundingMapRect, four units on a side and positioned slightly east and north of the annotation point (because that's where the road is). Then I simply construct the arrow shape within the 4×4-unit square, rotating it so that it points in roughly the same direction as the road:

```
// start with our position and derive a nice unit for drawing
CLLocationCoordinate2D loc = self->map.region.center;
CGFloat lat = loc.latitude;
CLLocationDistance metersPerPoint = MKMetersPerMapPointAtLatitude(lat);
MKMapPoint c = MKMapPointForCoordinate(loc);
CGFloat unit = 75.0/metersPerPoint;
// size and position the overlay bounds on the earth
CGSize sz = CGSizeMake(4*unit, 4*unit);
MKMapRect mr = MKMapRectMake(c.x + 2*unit, c.y - 4.5*unit, sz.width, sz.height);
// describe the arrow as a CGPath
CGMutablePathRef p = CGPathCreateMutable();
CGPoint start = CGPointMake(0, unit*1.5);
CGPoint p1 = CGPointMake(start.x+2*unit, start.y);
CGPoint p2 = CGPointMake(p1.x, p1.y-unit);
CGPoint p3 = CGPointMake(p2.x+unit*2, p2.y+unit*1.5);
CGPoint p4 = CGPointMake(p2.x, p2.y+unit*3);
CGPoint p5 = CGPointMake(p4.x, p4.y-unit);
CGPoint p6 = CGPointMake(p5.x-2*unit, p5.y);
CGPoint points[] = {
    start, p1, p2, p3, p4, p5, p6
};
// rotate the arrow around its center
CGAffineTransform t1 = CGAffineTransformMakeTranslation(unit*2, unit*2);
CGAffineTransform t2 = CGAffineTransformRotate(t1, -M_PI/3.5);
CGAffineTransform t3 = CGAffineTransformTranslate(t2, -unit*2, -unit*2);
CGPathAddLines(p, &t3, points, 7);
```

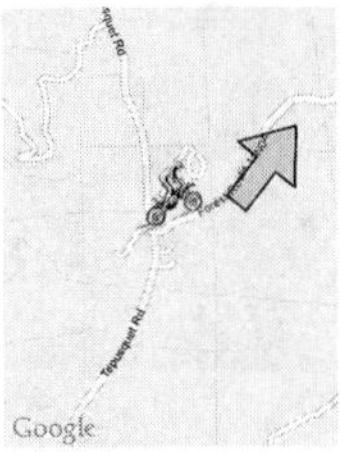

*Figure 34-5. A nicer overlay view*

```
CGPathCloseSubpath(p);
// create the overlay and give it the path
MyOverlay* over = [[[MyOverlay alloc] initWithRect:mr] autorelease];
over.path = [UIBezierPath bezierPathWithCGPath:p];
CGPathRelease(p);
// add the overlay to the map
[self->map addOverlay:over];
```

The delegate method, where we provide the MKOverlayPathView, is simple. We pull the CGPath out of the MyOverlay instance and hand it to the MKOverlayPathView, also telling the MKOverlayPathView how to stroke and fill that path:

```
- (MKOverlayView*)mapView:(MKMapView*)mapView
        viewForOverlay:(id <MKOverlay>)overlay {
    MKOverlayView* v = nil;
    if ([overlay isKindOfClass: [MyOverlay class]]) {
        v = [[[MKOverlayPathView alloc] initWithOverlay:overlay] autorelease];
        MKOverlayPathView* vv = (MKOverlayPathView*)v; // typecast for simplicity
        vv.path = ((MyOverlay*)overlay).path.CGPath;
        vv.strokeColor = [UIColor blackColor];
        vv.fillColor = [[UIColor redColor] colorWithAlphaComponent:0.2];
        vv.lineWidth = 2;
    }
    return v;
}
```

The result is a much nicer arrow (Figure 34-5), and of course this technique can be generalized to draw an overlay from any CGPath we like.

For full generality, you could define your own MKOverlayView subclass; your subclass must override and implement **drawMapRect:zoomScale:inContext:**. An example appears in the "Annotating Maps" chapter of Apple's *Location Awareness Programming Guide*.

Overlays are maintained by the map view as an array and are drawn from back to front starting at the beginning of the array. MKMapView has extensive support for adding and removing overlays, and for managing their layering order.

# CHAPTER 35

# Sensors

A device may contain hardware for sensing the world around itself — where it is located, how it is oriented, how it is moving.

Information about the device's current location, orientation, and motion using its Wi-Fi and cellular networking, GPS, and magnetometer is provided through the Core Location framework. You'll link to *CoreLocation.framework* and import `<CoreLocation/CoreLocation.h>`.

Information about the device's change in speed and orientation using its accelerometer is provided through the UIEvent and UIAccelerometer classes. In iOS 4, this information is supplemented by the device's gyroscope and is accessed through the Core Motion framework; you'll link to *CoreMotion.framework* and import `<CoreMotion/CoreMotion.h>`.

Not all devices have all of this hardware. As of this writing, only an an iPad2, an iPhone 4, or a fourth-generation iPod touch has a gyroscope. An iPod touch has no magnetometer. A device with only Wi-Fi (no cellular networking) cannot detect cell towers and also lacks a built-in GPS. And so forth.

## Location

Core Location provides facilities for the device to determine and report its location (*location services*). Even a device without GPS or cellular capabilities might be able to do this, by scanning for nearby Wi-Fi devices and comparing these against an online database. Core Location will automatically use whatever facilities the device does have; all you have to do is ask for the device's location.

Asking a map view (MKMapView, Chapter 34) to display the device's location can be as simple as setting its `showsUserLocation` property to YES. The map automatically puts an annotation at that location, but displaying the appropriate region of the map is up to you. You can use the map delegate's `mapView:didUpdateUserLocation:` to detect when it's time to do this:

```
- (void)mapView:(MKMapView *)mapView
        didUpdateUserLocation:(MKUserLocation *)userLocation {
    CLLocationCoordinate2D coordinate = userLocation.location.coordinate;
    MKCoordinateRegion reg =
        MKCoordinateRegionMakeWithDistance(coordinate, 600, 600);
    mapView.region = reg;
}
```

This approach, however, is extremely coarse-grained. By setting showsUserLocation to YES, you are turning on location services and leaving them on, which can represent a significant power drain. You can turn location services off by setting showsUser-Location to NO, but then the annotation vanishes.

Instead, let's turn on location services ourselves, just long enough to see if we can determine our position. If we can, we'll turn location services back off, and display the location in our map with an annotation manually. We begin by ascertaining that location services are in fact available. If they are, we instantiate CLLocationManager, set ourselves as the delegate, and call startUpdatingLocation to turn on location services:

```
BOOL ok = [CLLocationManager locationServicesEnabled];
if (!ok) {
    NSLog(@"oh well");
    return;
}
CLLocationManager* lm = [[CLLocationManager alloc] init];
self.locman = lm;
[lm release];
self.locman.delegate = self;
[self.locman startUpdatingLocation];
```

(If we were going to track our location continually, we would also set the CLLocation-Manager's desiredAccuracy and distanceFilter, but because we just want a single hit, we are skipping that step.) The delegate will eventually receive one of two messages. Something might go wrong (including that the user might refuse permission, as in Figure 30-1), in which case we'll just turn location services back off:

```
- (void)locationManager:(CLLocationManager *)manager
        didFailWithError:(NSError *)error {
    NSLog(@"error: %@", [error localizedDescription]);
    [manager stopUpdatingLocation];
}
```

If things *don't* go wrong, we'll be handed our location as soon as it is determined. We'll turn off location services and display our location on the map, along with a simple annotation:

```
- (void)locationManager:(CLLocationManager *)manager
        didUpdateToLocation:(CLLocation *)newLocation
        fromLocation:(CLLocation *)oldLocation {
    [manager stopUpdatingLocation];
    CLLocationCoordinate2D coordinate = newLocation.coordinate;
    MKCoordinateRegion reg =
        MKCoordinateRegionMakeWithDistance(coordinate, 600, 600);
    self->map.region = reg;
```

```
        MKPointAnnotation* ann = [[MKPointAnnotation alloc] init];
        ann.coordinate = coordinate;
        ann.title = @"You are here";
        [self->map addAnnotation:ann];
        [ann release];
}
```

Your app can track the device's location even when the app is not frontmost. As with sound (Chapter 27), you can set the UIBackgroundModes key of your app's *Info.plist*, giving it a value of location. This tells the system that if you have turned on location services and the user clicks the Home button, your app should not be suspended, the use of location services should still continue, and your app should still be notified if an event arrives. Background use of location services can cause a power drain, but if you want your app to function as a positional data logger, for instance, it may be the only way; you can also help conserve power by making judicious choices, such as setting a coarse distanceFilter value and not asking for high accuracy.

Starting in iOS 4.0, on a device with cellular capabilities, you can call startMonitoring-SignificantLocationChanges instead of startUpdatingLocation. This technology (*significant location monitoring*) uses cell tower positioning and thus requires much less power than leaving the GPS turned on continuously.

Also starting in iOS 4.0, you can supply a circular CLRegion and turn on region monitoring (startMonitoringForRegion:desiredAccuracy:). When the device enters or exits the specified region, you get a notification. This technology (*region monitoring*) also uses cell tower positioning, and thus requires little power.

Both significant location monitoring and region monitoring automatically notify your app even if it is not frontmost; you do *not* have to set the UIBackgroundModes key. Precisely what happens depends on the state of your app when an event arrives:

*Your app is suspended in the background*
  Your app is woken up long enough to receive the notification and do something with it.

*Your app is not running at all*
  Your app is relaunched (remaining in the background), and your app delegate will be sent application:didFinishLaunchingWithOptions: with an NSDictionary containing UIApplicationLaunchOptionsLocationKey, thus allowing it to discern the special nature of the situation.

# Heading and Course

For appropriately equipped devices, Core Location also supports use of the magnetometer to determine which way the device is facing (its *heading*) and the GPS to determine which way it is moving (its *course*).

In this example, I'll take advantage of the magnetometer and use the device as a compass. The headingFilter setting is to prevent us from being bombarded constantly with readings. For best results, the device should be held level (like a tabletop, or a compass); I have not changed the headingOrientation property, so the reported heading will then be the direction that the top of the device (the end away from the Home button) is pointing:

```
CLLocationManager* lm = [[CLLocationManager alloc] init];
self.locman = lm;
[lm release];
self.locman.delegate = self;
self.locman.headingFilter = 3;
[self.locman startUpdatingHeading];
```

Readings arrive as messages to the delegate. I'll simply log our magnetic heading along with a rough corresponding cardinal direction. I choose to use the magnetic heading (magneticHeading) rather than the true heading (trueHeading) because, as the documentation explains, the latter can be calculated correctly only if we are getting location updates as well as heading updates:

```
- (void) locationManager:(CLLocationManager *)manager
        didUpdateHeading:(CLHeading *)newHeading {
    CGFloat h = newHeading.magneticHeading;
    NSString* dir = @"N";
    NSArray* cards = [NSArray arrayWithObjects: @"N", @"NE", @"E", @"SE",
                                                @"S", @"SW", @"W", @"NW", nil];
    for (int i = 0; i < 8; i++)
        if (h < 45.0/2.0 + 45*i) {
            dir = [cards objectAtIndex: i];
            break;
        }
    NSLog(@"%f %@", h, dir);
}
```

(Combining the magnetometer with the compass interface we developed in Chapter 16 and Chapter 17, so as to simulate a physical compass, is left as an exercise for the reader.)

GPS-based course information, if available, is returned automatically as part of a CLLocation object in locationManager:didUpdateToLocation:fromLocation:, through its speed and course properties.

# Acceleration

Acceleration information can arrive in three ways:

*As a prepackaged UIEvent*
You can receive a UIEvent notifying you of a predefined gesture performed by accelerating the device. At present, the only such gesture is the user shaking the device.

*From the shared UIAccelerometer*

You can set yourself as the shared UIAccelerometer's delegate to receive acceleration notifications in `accelerometer:didAccelerate:`.

*With the Core Motion framework*

You instantiate CMMotionManager and then obtain information of a desired type. You can ask for accelerometer information, gyroscope information, or device motion information; device motion is a combination of accelerometer and gyroscope information that accurately describes the device's orientation in space, and is what you're most likely to want.

## Shake Events

A shake event is a UIEvent (Chapter 18). Receiving shake events is rather like receiving remote events (Chapter 27), involving the notion of the first responder. To receive shake events, your app must contain a UIResponder which:

- Returns YES from `canBecomeFirstResponder`
- Is in fact first responder

This responder, or a UIResponder further up the responder chain, should implement some or all of these methods:

`motionBegan:withEvent:`
Something has started to happen that might or might not turn out to be a shake.

`motionEnded:withEvent:`
The motion reported in `motionBegan:withEvent:` is over and has turned out to be a shake.

`motionCancelled:withEvent:`
The motion reported in `motionBegan:withEvent:` wasn't a shake after all.

Thus, it might be sufficient to implement `motionEnded:withEvent:`, because this arrives if and only if the user performs a shake gesture. The first parameter will be the event subtype, but at present this is guaranteed to be `UIEventSubtypeMotionShake`, so testing it is pointless.

The view controller in charge of the current view is a good candidate to receive shake events. Thus, a minimal implementation might look like this:

```
- (BOOL) canBecomeFirstResponder {
    return YES;
}

- (void) viewDidAppear: (BOOL) animated {
    [super viewDidAppear: animated];
    [self becomeFirstResponder];
}
```

```
- (void)motionEnded:(UIEventSubtype)motion withEvent:(UIEvent *)event {
    NSLog(@"hey, you shook me!");
}
```

However, if the first responder is of a type that supports undo (such as an NSTextField), and if `motionBegan:withEvent:` arrives at the end of the responder chain, and if you have not set the shared UIApplication's `applicationSupportsShakeToEdit` property to NO, a shake will be handled through an Undo or Redo alert. Your view controller might not want to rob any responders in its view of this capability. A simple way to prevent this is to test whether the view controller is, in fact, first responder; if it isn't, we call `super` to pass the event on up the responder chain:

```
- (void)motionEnded:(UIEventSubtype)motion withEvent:(UIEvent *)event {
    if ([self isFirstResponder])
        NSLog(@"hey, you shook me!");
    else
        [super motionEnded:motion withEvent:event];
}
```

## UIAccelerometer

To use the shared UIAccelerometer, call the class method `sharedAccelerometer` to get the global shared instance, set its `updateInterval` to prevent being swamped by notifications, and set its `delegate`. The delegate will immediately start receiving `accelerometer:didAccelerate:` calls; to turn these off, set the shared accelerometer's delegate to nil.

The second parameter of `accelerometer:didAccelerate:` is a UIAcceleration, a simple class — nothing more than a struct, really — consisting of a timestamp and three acceleration values (UIAccelerationValue, equivalent to a double), one for each axis of the device. The positive x-axis points to the right of the device. The positive y-axis points toward the top of the device, away from the Home button. The positive z-axis points out of the screen toward the user. Acceleration values are measured in Gs. These values are only approximate — in fact, they are noisy and possibly quantized — so you have to allow room for this.

Even if the device is completely motionless, its acceleration values will constitute a vector of approximately 1 pointing toward the center of the earth, popularly known as *gravity*. The accelerometer is thus constantly reporting a combination of gravity and user-induced acceleration. This is good and bad. It's good because it means you can use the accelerometer to detect the device's orientation in space. It's bad because gravity values and user-induced acceleration values are mixed together.

You can attempt to separate these values, at the expense of some latency, with a low-pass filter to detect gravity only, or with a high-pass filter to eliminate the effect of gravity and detect user acceleration only, reporting a motionless device as having zero acceleration; often you'll do both (and a common technique is to run the output of the high-pass filter through an additional low-pass filter to reduce noise and small twitches). Apple provides some very nice sample code for implementing a low-pass or a high-pass filter (see especially the AccelerometerGraph example, which is also very helpful for learning how the accelerometer behaves); it's pointless to try to improve on this, so I won't bother to reproduce or discuss it.

In this example, I will simply report whether the device is lying flat on its back. To start with, I won't bother to use a filter. The two axes orthogonal to gravity, which in this position are the x and y axes, are much more accurate and sensitive to small variation than the axis pointing toward or away from gravity. So our approach is to ask first whether the x and y values are close to zero; only then do we use the z value to learn whether the device is on its back or on its face. To keep from updating our interface constantly, we implement a crude state machine; the state (an instance variable) starts out at -1, and then switches between 0 (device on its back) and 1 (device not on its back), and we update the interface only when there is a state change:

```
- (void)accelerometer:(UIAccelerometer *)accelerometer
        didAccelerate:(UIAcceleration *)acceleration {
    CGFloat x = acceleration.x;
    CGFloat y = acceleration.y;
    CGFloat z = acceleration.z;
    CGFloat accu = 0.08;
    if (fabs(x) < accu && fabs(y) < accu && z < -0.5) {
        if (state == -1 || state == 1) {
            state = 0;
            self->label.text = @"I'm lying on my back... ahhh...";
        }
    } else {
        if (state == -1 || state == 0) {
            state = 1;
            self->label.text = @"Hey, put me back down on the table!";
        }
    }
}
```

This works, but it's sensitive to small motions of the device on the table. To damp this sensitivity, we can run our input through a low-pass filter. The low-pass filter code comes straight from Apple's own examples, and involves maintaining the previously filtered reading as a set of instance variables:

```
-(void)addAcceleration:(UIAcceleration*)accel {
    double alpha = 0.1;
    self->oldX = accel.x * alpha + self->oldX * (1.0 - alpha);
    self->oldY = accel.y * alpha + self->oldY * (1.0 - alpha);
    self->oldZ = accel.z * alpha + self->oldZ * (1.0 - alpha);
}

- (void)accelerometer:(UIAccelerometer *)accelerometer
        didAccelerate:(UIAcceleration *)acceleration {
    [self addAcceleration: acceleration];
    CGFloat x = self->oldX;
    CGFloat y = self->oldY;
    CGFloat z = self->oldZ;
```

```
    CGFloat accu = 0.08;
    if (fabs(x) < accu && fabs(y) < accu && z < -0.5) {
        // ... and the rest is as before ...
    }
}
```

In this next example, the user is allowed to slap the side of the device against an open hand as a way of telling it to go the next or previous image or whatever it is we're displaying. We pass the acceleration input through a high-pass filter to eliminate gravity (again, the filter code comes straight from Apple's examples). What we're looking for is a high positive or negative x value. A single slap is likely to consist of several consecutive readings above our threshold, but we want to report each slap only once, so we maintain the timestamp of our previous high reading as an instance variable and ignore readings that are too close to one another in time:

```
-(void)addAcceleration:(UIAcceleration*)accel {
    double alpha = 0.1;
    self->oldX = accel.x - ((accel.x * alpha) + (self->oldX * (1.0 - alpha)));
    self->oldY = accel.y - ((accel.y * alpha) + (self->oldY * (1.0 - alpha)));
    self->oldZ = accel.z - ((accel.z * alpha) + (self->oldZ * (1.0 - alpha)));
}

- (void)accelerometer:(UIAccelerometer *)accelerometer
        didAccelerate:(UIAcceleration *)acceleration {
    [self addAcceleration: acceleration];
    CGFloat x = self->oldX;
    // CGFloat y = self->oldY;
    // CGFloat z = self->oldZ;
    CGFloat thresh = 1.0;
    if (acceleration.timestamp - self->oldTime < 0.5)
        return;
    if (x < -thresh) {
        NSLog(@"left");
        self->oldTime = acceleration.timestamp;
    }
    if (x > thresh) {
        NSLog(@"right");
        self->oldTime = acceleration.timestamp;
    }
}
```

This works, but there's a problem. A sudden jerk involves both an acceleration (as the user starts the device moving) and a deceleration (as the device stops moving). Thus a left slap might be preceded by a high value in the opposite direction, which we will interpret wrongly as a right slap. We can compensate crudely, at the expense of some latency, with delayed performance:

```
CGFloat thresh = 1.0;
if (x < -thresh) {
    if (acceleration.timestamp - self->oldTime > 0.5 || self->lastSlap == 1) {
        self->oldTime = acceleration.timestamp;
        self->lastSlap = -1;
        [NSObject cancelPreviousPerformRequestsWithTarget:self];
```

```
        [self performSelector:@selector(report:) withObject:@"left" afterDelay:0.5];
    }
}
if (x > thresh) {
    if (acceleration.timestamp - self->oldTime > 0.5 || self->lastSlap == -1) {
        self->oldTime = acceleration.timestamp;
        self->lastSlap = 1;
        [NSObject cancelPreviousPerformRequestsWithTarget:self];
        [self performSelector:@selector(report:) withObject:@"right" afterDelay:0.5];
    }
}
```

A more sophisticated analysis might involve storing a stream of all the most recent UIAcceleration objects and studying the entire stream to work out the overall trend.

## Core Motion

Core Motion, introduced in iOS 4.0, takes advantage of the device's gyroscope if there is one. This means that instead of using the accelerometer alone and suffering the disadvantages and inaccuracies of filtering, you can have the device do the math, interpreting the accelerometer and gyroscope together for you and distinguishing gravity from user acceleration with negligible latency. To do so, you'll elect to receive CMDeviceMotion instances, consisting of the following properties:

gravity
> A vector with value 1 pointing to the center of the earth.

userAcceleration
> A vector describing user-induced acceleration, with no gravity component.

rotationRate
> A vector describing how the device is rotating around its center. This sort of motion was often difficult or impossible to detect before the addition of the gyroscope.

attitude
> A description of the device's instantaneous orientation in space. It is described with respect to an initial frame of reference in which the negative z-axis points at the center of the earth, but the x-axis and y-axis, though orthogonal to the other axes, could be pointing anywhere. Thus, it is of interest primarily as a change relative to an earlier attitude. To convert the current attitude to a description of this change, you store an earlier attitude, and then send the multiplyByInverseOfAttitude: message to the current attitude, passing the stored attitude as the argument.

Further detail about Core Motion is beyond the scope of this book. The important thing to understand is that the presence of the gyroscope, combined with the CMDeviceMotion class, compensates for a number of shortcomings of reading the accelerometer alone. (The device may use the gyroscope in other ways as well; for example, if you ask Core Location for updates with a desiredAccuracy of kCLLocationAccuracy-

`BestForNavigation`, it uses the gyroscope to supplement the calculation of location changes.)

# PART VII

# Final Topics

This part of the book is a miscellany of topics that didn't fit easily into any of the preceding chapters.

- Chapter 36 is about files. It explains how your app can store data on disk to be retrieved the next time the app runs (including both standalone files and user defaults). It also discusses sharing files with the user through iTunes and with other apps and concludes with a survey of how iOS can work with some common file formats (XML, SQLite, and image files).

- Chapter 37 introduces networking, with an emphasis on HTTP downloading of data, and giving a nod to other aspects of networks (such as Bonjour and push notifications) that you can explore independently if your app requires them.

- Chapter 38 is about threads. Making your app multithreaded (beyond the automatic threading support provided by the built-in interface widgets and their supporting frameworks) can introduce great complexity and is not a beginner topic, but you still might need to understand the basic concepts of multithreading, either in order to prevent a lengthy task from blocking user interaction with your app, or because some framework explicitly relies on it. Special attention is paid to the advantages of NSOperation and (especially) Grand Central Dispatch.

- Chapter 39 describes how iOS supports Undo in your app.

- You are now a proud graduate of this book's school of iOS programming fundamentals. You are fully prepared to proceed independently. Chapter 40 lists additional frameworks and facilities that were found to be beyond the scope of this book. Your mission, should you decide to accept it, is to explore these if and when you need them. iOS is huge; you'll never stop learning and experimenting. Good hunting!

# CHAPTER 36

# Persistent Storage

The device on which your app runs contains flash memory that functions as the equivalent of a hard disk, holding files that survive the device's being powered down (*persistent storage*). Apps can store files to, and retrieve them from, this virtual hard disk. Apps can also define document types in which they specialize and can hand such documents to one another.

## The Sandbox

The hard disk as a whole is not open to your app's view. A limited portion of the hard disk is dedicated to your app alone: this is your app's *sandbox*. The idea is that every app, seeing only its own sandbox, is hindered from spying or impinging on the files belonging to other apps. Your app can also see some higher-level directories owned by the system as a whole, but cannot write to them.

You can create directories (folders) within the sandbox. In addition, the sandbox contains some standard directories. For example, suppose you want a reference to the Documents directory. Here's how to access it:

```
NSString* docs = [NSSearchPathForDirectoriesInDomains(
    NSDocumentDirectory, NSUserDomainMask, YES) lastObject];
```

That code returns a path string for the Documents directory. Starting in iOS 4, the preferred way to refer to a file or directory is with a URL. You obtain this from an NSFileManager instance:

```
NSFileManager* fm = [[NSFileManager alloc] init];
// ...
NSError* err = nil;
NSURL* docsurl = [fm URLForDirectory:NSDocumentDirectory
    inDomain:NSUserDomainMask appropriateForURL:nil create:YES error:&err];
// error-checking omitted
// ...
[fm release];
```

A question that will immediately occur to you is: where should I put secondary files and folders that I want to save now and read later? Once upon a time, the Documents directory would have been a good place. But in iOS 3.2, file sharing was introduced, meaning that your app can be configured so that the user can see and modify your app's Documents directory through iTunes. So you might not want to put things there that the user isn't supposed to see and change.

Settling upon an alternative location for your app's files is up to you. Personally, I favor the Application Support directory. On a Mac, this directory is shared by multiple applications, but on iOS each app has its own private Application Support directory in its own sandbox, so you can safely put files directly into it. This directory may not exist initially, so you can obtain it and create it at the same time:

```
NSURL* suppurl = [fm URLForDirectory:NSApplicationSupportDirectory
    inDomain:NSUserDomainMask appropriateForURL:nil create:YES error:&err];
```

After that, if you need a file path reference (an NSString), just ask for [`suppurl path`].

# Basic File Operations

Let's say we intend to create folder *MyFolder* inside the Documents directory. Starting with the path string docs pointing at the Documents directory (as obtained in the previous section), we can generate a reference to *MyFolder*, using one of the many NSString methods specifically aimed at manipulating path strings. (There is no way to create a folder specified by a URL.) We can then use an NSFileManager instance (fm) to learn whether our target folder exists, and to create it if it doesn't:

```
NSString* myfolder = [docs stringByAppendingPathComponent:@"MyFolder"];
BOOL exists = [fm fileExistsAtPath:myfolder];
if (!exists) {
    NSError* err = nil;
    [fm createDirectoryAtPath:myfolder withIntermediateDirectories:NO
                  attributes:nil error:&err];
    // error-checking omitted
}
```

To learn what files and folders exist within a directory, you can ask for an array of the directory's contents:

```
NSError* err = nil;
NSArray* arr = [fm contentsOfDirectoryAtPath:docs error:&err];
// error-checking omitted
/*
MyFolder
*/
```

That array is shallow, showing only the directory's immediate contents. For a deep array, ask for the directory's subpaths:

```
NSError* err = nil;
NSArray* arr = [fm subpathsOfDirectoryAtPath:docs error:&err];
// error-checking omitted
```

```
/*
MyFolder
MyFolder/moi.txt
*/
```

A deep array might be very big. If you're looking for something in particular, you might prefer to enumerate the directory, so that you are handed only one file reference at a time:

```
NSDirectoryEnumerator* dir = [fm enumeratorAtPath:docs];
for (NSString* file in dir) {
    // do something with each string
}
```

A directory enumerator also permits you to decline to dive into a particular subdirectory, so you can make your traversal even more efficient.

Note that in all those cases you are handed a relative pathname. To make it usable as an actual file reference, you can either append it to the original directory pathname or make the original directory the current directory:

```
NSDirectoryEnumerator* dir = [fm enumeratorAtPath:docs];
[fm changeCurrentDirectoryPath: docs];
for (NSString* f in dir)
    if ([[f pathExtension] isEqualToString: @"txt"])
        // f is valid for referring to this file
```

In that example, f is a valid pathname even though it's a relative (partial) pathname, because its containing folder is the current directory. Similarly, if you convert f to a URL (using `fileURLWithPath:`), the resulting NSURL object has an appropriate `baseURL` and so is a valid reference.

Consult the NSFileManager class documentation for more about what you can do with files, and see also Apple's *Low-Level File Management Programming Topics*.

# Saving and Reading Files

To save or read a file, you are most likely to use one of the convenience methods for the class appropriate to the file's contents. NSString, NSData, NSArray, and NSDictionary provide `writeToFile...` and `initWithContentsOfFile...` methods (as well as `writeToURL...` and `initWithContentsOfURL...`). Recall that NSArray and NSDictionary files are actually property lists (Chapter 10) and work only if all the contents of the array or dictionary are property list types (NSString, NSData, NSDate, NSNumber, NSArray, and NSDictionary).

If an object's class adopts the NSCoding protocol, you can convert it to an NSData and back again using NSKeyedArchiver and NSKeyedUnarchiver. An NSData can be saved as a file or in a property list. Thus, NSCoding provides a way to save an object to disk. An example of doing this with a UIColor object appears in Chapter 10.

You can make your own class adopt the NSCoding protocol. This can become somewhat complicated because an object can refer (through an instance variable) to another object, which may also adopt the NSCoding protocol, and thus you can end up saving an entire *graph* of interconnected objects if you wish. However, I'll confine myself to illustrating a simple case (and you can read the *Archives and Serializations Programming Guide* for more information).

Let's say, then, that we have a simple Person class with a `firstName` property and a `lastName` property. We'll declare that it adopts the NSCoding protocol:

```
@interface Person : NSObject <NSCoding> {
```

To make this class actually conform to NSCoding, we must implement `encodeWithCoder:` (to archive the object) and `initWithCoder:` (to unarchive the object). In `encodeWithCoder:`, we must first call `super` if the superclass adopts NSCoding, and then call the appropriate `encode...` method for each instance variable we want preserved:

```
- (void)encodeWithCoder:(NSCoder *)encoder {
    //[super encodeWithCoder: encoder]; // not in this case
    [encoder encodeObject:self->lastName forKey:@"last"];
    [encoder encodeObject:self->firstName forKey:@"first"];
}
```

In `initWithCoder`, we must call `super`, using either `initWithCoder:` if the superclass adopts the NSCoding protocol or the designated initializer if not, and then call the appropriate `decode...` method for each instance variable stored earlier, finally returning `self`; memory management is up to us:

```
- (id) initWithCoder:(NSCoder *)decoder {
    //self = [super initWithCoder: decoder]; // not in this case
    self = [super init];
    self->lastName = [decoder decodeObjectForKey:@"last"];
    [self->lastName retain];
    self->firstName = [decoder decodeObjectForKey:@"first"];
    [self->firstName retain];
    return self;
}
```

Now we'll test this by creating, configuring, and saving a Person instance as a file:

```
Person* moi = [[Person alloc] init];
moi.firstName = @"Matt";
moi.lastName = @"Neuburg";
NSData* moidata = [NSKeyedArchiver archivedDataWithRootObject:moi];
NSString* moifile = [myfolder stringByAppendingPathComponent:@"moi.txt"];
[moidata writeToFile:moifile atomically:NO];
[moi release];
```

Now we should be able to retrieve the saved Person at a later time:

```
NSData* persondata = [[NSData alloc] initWithContentsOfFile:moifile];
Person* person = [NSKeyedUnarchiver unarchiveObjectWithData:persondata];
[persondata release];
NSLog(@"%@ %@", person.firstName, person.lastName); // Matt Neuburg
```

If the NSData object is itself the entire content of the file, as here, then instead of using `archivedDataWithRootObject:` and `unarchiveObjectWithData:`, you can skip the intermediate NSData object altogether and use `archiveRootObject:toFile:` and `unarchiveObjectWithFile:`.

Saving a single Person as an archive may seem like overkill; why didn't we just make a text file consisting of the first and last names? But imagine that a Person has a lot more properties, or that we have an array of hundreds of Persons, or an array of hundreds of dictionaries where one value in each dictionary is a Person; now all of a sudden the power of an archivable Person becomes clear. Even though Person now adopts the NSCoding protocol, an NSArray containing a Person object still cannot be written to disk using NSArray's `writeToFile...` or `writeToURL...`, because Person is still not a property list type. But the array can be archived and written to disk with NSKeyedArchiver.

# User Defaults

User defaults, which have been referred to often already in this book (see especially Chapter 10 and Chapter 13), are intended as the persistent storage of the user's preferences, as well as for maintaining state when your app quits so that you can restore the situation the next time the app launches. They are little more, really, than a special case of an NSDictionary property list file. You talk to the NSUserDefaults `standardUserDefaults` object much as if it were a dictionary; it has keys and values. And the only legal values are property list values (see the preceding section). Thus, to store a Person in user defaults, you'd have to archive it first to an NSData object. Unlike NSDictionary, NSUserDefaults provides convenience methods for converting between a simple data type such as a float or a BOOL and the object that is stored in the defaults (`setFloat:forKey:`, `floatForKey:`, and so forth). But the defaults themselves are still a dictionary.

Meanwhile, somewhere on disk, this dictionary is being saved for you automatically as a property list file — though you don't concern yourself with that. You simply set or retrieve values from the dictionary by way of their keys, secure in the knowledge that the file is being read into memory or written to disk as needed. Your chief concern is to make sure that you've written everything needful into user defaults before your app terminates; as we saw in Chapter 11, in a multitasking world this will usually mean when the app delegate receives `applicationDidEnterBackground:` at the latest. If you're worried that your app might crash, you can tell the `standardUserDefaults` object to `synchronize`, but this is rarely necessary.

To provide the value for a key before the user has had a chance to do so — the default default, as it were — use `registerDefaults:`. What you're supplying here is a dictionary whose key–value pairs will each be written into the defaults, but only if there is no such key already. Recall this example from Chapter 10:

```
[[NSUserDefaults standardUserDefaults] registerDefaults:
    [NSDictionary dictionaryWithObjectsAndKeys:
```

```
[NSNumber numberWithInt: 4],
@"cardMatrixRows",
[NSNumber numberWithInt: 3],
@"cardMatrixColumns",
nil]];
```

The idea is that we call `registerDefaults:` extremely early as the app launches. Either the app has run at some time previously and the user has set these preferences, in which case this call has no effect and does no harm, or not, in which case we now have initial values for these preferences with which to get started. So, in the game app from which that code comes, we start out with a 4×3 game layout, but the user can change this at any time.

This leaves only the question of how the user is to interact with the defaults. One way is that your app provides some kind of interface. For example, the game app from which the previous code comes has a tabbed interface; the second tab is where the user sets preferences (Figure 20-1). In the TidBITS News app, there's a single button for setting the size of text, and that's the only preference with which the user ever interacts directly.

(Both apps also store state information in the user defaults, but without the user's knowledge or direct participation, and not with keys that the user has any way of accessing. For example, the game app records the state of the game board and the card deck into user defaults every time these change, so that if the app is terminated we can restore the game, the next time the app is launched, as it was when the user left off.)

Alternatively, you can provide a *settings bundle*, consisting mostly of one or more property list files describing an interface and the corresponding user default keys and their initial values; the Settings app is then responsible for translating your instructions into an actual interface, and for presenting it to the user.

Using a settings bundle has some obvious disadvantages: the user may not think to look in the Settings app, for example; the user has to leave your app to access preferences; and you don't get the kind of control over the interface that you have within your own app. Also, in a multitasking world, this means that the user can set preferences while your app is backgrounded; you'll need to register for `NSUserDefaultsDidChange-Notification` in order to hear about this.

In some situations, though, a settings bundle has some clear advantages. Keeping the preferences interface out of your app can make your app's own interface cleaner and simpler. You don't have to write any of the "glue" code that coordinates the preferences interface with the user default values. And it can be nice for the user to be able to set preferences for your app even when your app isn't running.

Writing a settings bundle is described in the "Implementing Application Preferences" chapter of Apple's *iOS Application Programming Guide*, along with the *Settings Application Schema Reference*.

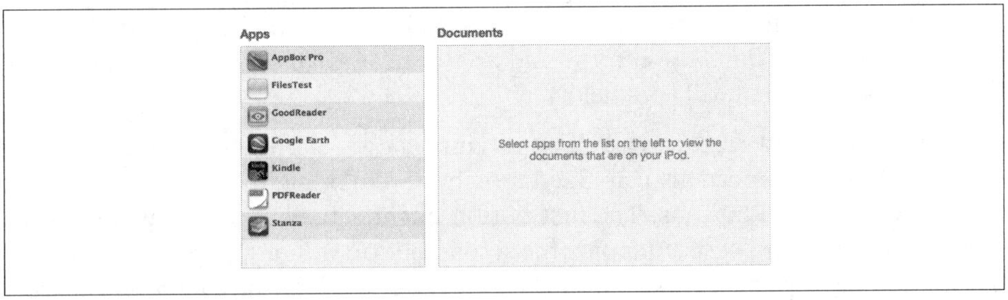

*Figure 36-1. The iTunes file sharing interface*

# File Sharing

If your app supports file sharing, its Documents directory becomes available to the user through iTunes (Figure 36-1). The user can add files to your app's Documents directory, and can save files and folders from your app's Documents directory to the computer, as well as renaming and deleting files and folders. This could be appropriate, for example, if the purpose of your app is to display some common file type that the user might obtain elsewhere, such as PDFs or JPEGs.

To support file sharing, set the *Info.plist* key "Application supports iTunes file sharing" (`UIFileSharingEnabled`).

Once your entire Documents directory is exposed to the user this way, you are suddenly not so likely to use the Documents directory to store private files. As I mentioned earlier, I like to use the Application Support directory instead.

# Document Types

Your app can declare itself willing to open documents of a certain type. In this way, if another app obtains a document of this type, it can propose to hand the document off to your app. For example, the user might download the document with Mobile Safari, or receive it in a mail message with the Mail app; now we need a way to get it from Safari or Mail to you.

To let the system know that your app is a candidate for opening a certain kind of document, you will configure the `CFBundleDocumentTypes` key in your *Info.plist*. This is an array, where each entry will be a dictionary specifying a document type by using keys such as `LSItemContentTypes`, `CFBundleTypeName`, `CFBundleTypeIconFiles`, and `LSHandlerRank`.

For example, suppose I want to declare that my app opens PDFs. My *Info.plist* could contain this simple entry (as seen in the standard editor):

```
Document types                        (1 item)
    Item 0                            (1 item)
        Document Content Type UTIs    (1 item)
            Item 0                    com.adobe.pdf
```

In Xcode 4, you can also specify document types by editing the target; switch to the Info tab. This same *Info.plist* entry would appear here as an untitled document type with `com.adobe.pdf` in the Types field.

Now suppose the user receives a PDF in an email message. The Mail app can display this PDF, but the user can also tap the Action button to bring up an action sheet containing two Open In buttons. The first button might actually specify my app as the default, but even if it doesn't, tapping the second button will bring up a second action sheet where my app appears as a button. (The interface will look like Figure 36-2, except that my app will be listed as one of the buttons.)

But now suppose the user actually *taps* the button that hands the PDF off to my app. For this to work, my app delegate must implement `application:handleOpenURL:`. At this point, my app has been brought to the front, either by launching it from scratch or by reviving it from background suspension; its job is now to handle the opening of the document whose URL has arrived as the second parameter. To prevent me from peeking into another app's sandbox, the system has already copied the document into my sandbox, into the Inbox directory, which is created for exactly this purpose.

 Unfortunately, the Inbox directory is currently created in your Documents folder. Thus, if your app implements file sharing, the user can see the Inbox folder; you may wish to delete the Inbox folder, therefore, as soon as you're done retrieving files from it.

In this simple example, my app has just one view controller, which has an outlet to a UIWebView where we will display any PDFs that arrive in this fashion. So my app delegate contains this code:

```
- (BOOL)application:(UIApplication *)application handleOpenURL:(NSURL *)url {
    [viewController displayPDF:url];
    return YES;
}
```

And my view controller contains this code:

```
- (void) displayPDF: (NSURL*) url {
    NSURLRequest* req = [NSURLRequest requestWithURL:url];
    [self->wv loadRequest:req];
}
```

In real life, things might be more complicated. Our implementation of `application:handleOpenURL:` might check to see whether this really *is* a PDF, and return NO if it isn't. Also, our app might be in the middle of something else, possibly displaying a completely different view controller's view; because `application:handleOpenURL:` can arrive at any time, we may have to be prepared to drop whatever we were doing and showing previously and display the incoming document instead.

If our app is launched from scratch by the arrival of this URL, `application:didFinish-LaunchingWithOptions:` will be sent to our app delegate as usual. The options dictionary

*Figure 36-2. The document Options action sheet and Open In action sheet*

(the second parameter) will contain the `UIApplicationLaunchOptionsURLKey`, and we can take into account, if we like, the fact that we are being launched specifically to open a document. The usual thing, however, is to ignore this key and launch in the normal way; `application:handleOpenURL:` will then arrive in good order after our interface has been set up, and we can handle it just as we would if we had already been running.

Starting in iOS 4.2, your app delegate can implement `application:openURL:source-Application:annotation:` in order to receive more information about the incoming URL. If implemented, this will be called in preference to `application:handleOpen-URL:`, and it won't be called at all on a device running an earlier system, so there is no penalty for implementing both methods.

# Handing Off a Document

The converse of the situation discussed in the previous section is this: your app has somehow acquired a document that it wants to hand off to whatever app can deal with it. This is done through the UIDocumentInteractionController class. This class operates asynchronously, so retaining an instance of it is up to you; typically, you'll store it in an instance variable with a retain setter policy.

For example, let's say our app has a PDF sitting in its Documents directory. Assuming we have an NSURL pointing to this document, presenting the interface for handing the document off to some other application (Figure 36-2) could be as simple as this (`sender` is a button that the user has just tapped):

```
self.dic = [UIDocumentInteractionController interactionControllerWithURL:url];
BOOL y =
    [dic presentOptionsMenuFromRect:[sender bounds] inView:sender animated:YES];
```

There are actually two action sheets available. The first action sheet in Figure 36-2, the Options action sheet, is summoned by `presentOptionsMenu...`; the second action sheet in Figure 36-2, the Open In action sheet, is summoned by `presentOpenInMenu...`, but it can also be summoned by one of the buttons in the first action sheet. These methods are cleverly designed to work on both iPhone and iPad interfaces; on the iPad, the buttons appear in a popover.

Your app can't learn *which* other applications are capable of accepting the document! Indeed, it can't even learn in advance whether *any* other applications are capable of accepting the document; your only clue is that the returned BOOL value afterward will be NO if UIDocumentInteractionController couldn't present the interface you requested.

UIDocumentInteractionController can, however, be interrogated for *some* information about the document type. In this example, we place a button into our interface whose image is the icon of the document type (the idea, perhaps, is that the user would then tap this button to do something with the document):

```
self.dic = [UIDocumentInteractionController interactionControllerWithURL:url];
UIImage* icon = [[self.dic icons] lastObject];
UIButton* b = [UIButton buttonWithType:UIButtonTypeRoundedRect];
[b setImage:icon forState:UIControlStateNormal];
[b sizeToFit]; // ... and probably also set frame origin here ...
[self.view addSubview: b];
```

A UIDocumentInteractionController can also present a preview of the document, if the document is of a type for which preview is enabled. You must give the UIDocumentInteractionController a delegate, and the delegate must implement `document-InteractionControllerViewControllerForPreview:`, returning an existing view controller that will contain the preview's view controller. So, here we ask for the preview:

```
self.dic = [UIDocumentInteractionController interactionControllerWithURL:url];
self.dic.delegate = self;
[self.dic presentPreviewAnimated:YES];
```

Here we supply the view controller:

```
- (UIViewController *) documentInteractionControllerViewControllerForPreview:
        (UIDocumentInteractionController *) controller {
    return self;
}
```

If the view controller returned were a UINavigationController, the preview's view controller would be pushed onto it. In this case it isn't, so the preview's view controller is presented modally. The preview interface also contains an Action button that lets the user summon the Options action sheet. In fact, this preview interface is exactly the same interface already familiar from the Mail app.

Delegate methods allow you to track what's happening in the interface presented by the UIDocumentInteractionController. Probably the most important of these are the ones that inform you that key stages of the interaction are ending:

- documentInteractionControllerDidDismissOptionsMenu:
- documentInteractionControllerDidDismissOpenInMenu:
- documentInteractionControllerDidEndPreview:
- documentInteractionController:didEndSendingToApplication:

Previews are actually provided through the Quick Look framework, and you can skip the UIDocumentInteractionController altogether and present the preview yourself through a QLPreviewController (link to *QuickLook.framework* and import <Quick-Look/QuickLook.h>). It's a view controller, so to display the preview you show it modally or push it onto a navigation controller's stack (just as UIDocumentInteractionController would have done). A nice feature of QLPreviewController is that you can give it more than one document to preview; the user can move between these, within the preview, using arrow buttons that appear at the bottom of the interface. Plus, if a document can be opened in another app, the interface includes the action button that summons UIDocumentInteractionController's Options or Open In action sheet.

In this example, I have in my Documents directory several PDF documents. I acquire a list of their URLs and present a modal preview for them:

```
// obtain URLs of PDFs as an array
NSString* docsdir = [NSSearchPathForDirectoriesInDomains(
    NSDocumentDirectory, NSUserDomainMask, YES) lastObject];
NSFileManager* fm = [[NSFileManager alloc] init];
NSDirectoryEnumerator* direnum = [fm enumeratorAtPath:docsdir];
[fm changeCurrentDirectoryPath: docsdir];
NSMutableArray* marr = [NSMutableArray array];
for (NSString* file in direnum) {
    [direnum skipDescendants];
    if ([[file pathExtension] isEqualToString: @"pdf"]) {
        NSURL* url = [NSURL fileURLWithPathComponents:
            [NSArray arrayWithObjects: docsdir, file, nil]];
        [marr addObject: url];
    }
}
self.pdfs = marr; // retain policy
[fm release];
// show preview interface
QLPreviewController* preview = [[QLPreviewController alloc] init];
preview.dataSource = self;
[self presentModalViewController:preview animated:YES];
[preview release];
```

You'll notice that I haven't told the QLPreviewController what documents to preview. That is the job of QLPreviewController's data source. I am the data source! I simply fetch the requested information from the list of URLs:

```
- (NSInteger) numberOfPreviewItemsInPreviewController:
        (QLPreviewController *) controller {
    return [self.pdfs count];
}

- (id <QLPreviewItem>) previewController: (QLPreviewController *) controller
                    previewItemAtIndex: (NSInteger) index {
    return [self.pdfs objectAtIndex:index];
}
```

The second data source method requires me to return an object that adopts the QLPreviewItem protocol. By a wildly improbable coincidence, NSURL *does* adopt this protocol, so the example works.

# XML

XML is a highly flexible and widely used general-purpose text file format for storage and retrieval of structured data. You might use it yourself to store data that you'll need to retrieve later, or you could encounter it when obtaining information from elsewhere, such as the Internet.

Mac OS X Cocoa provides a set of classes (NSXMLDocument and so forth) for reading, parsing, maintaining, searching, and modifying XML data in a completely general way, but iOS does *not* include these. I think the reason must be that their tree-based approach is too memory-intensive. Instead, iOS provides NSXMLParser, a much simpler class that walks through an XML document, sending delegate messages as it encounters elements. With this, you can parse an XML document once, but what you do with the pieces as they arrive is up to you. The general assumption here is that you know in advance the structure of the particular XML data you intend to read and that you have provided classes for storage of the same data in object form and for transforming the XML pieces into that storage.

To illustrate, let's return to our earlier example of a Person class with a `firstName` and a `lastName` property. Imagine that as our app starts up, we would like to populate it with Person objects, and that we've stored the data describing these objects as an XML file in our app bundle, like this:

```
<?xml version="1.0" encoding="utf-8"?>
<people>
    <person>
        <firstName>Matt</firstName>
        <lastName>Neuburg</lastName>
    </person>
    <person>
        <firstName>Snidely</firstName>
        <lastName>Whiplash</lastName>
    </person>
    <person>
        <firstName>Dudley</firstName>
        <lastName>Doright</lastName>
    </person>
</people>
```

This data could be mapped to an array of Person objects, each with its `firstName` and `lastName` properties appropriately set. (This is a deliberately easy example, of course; not all XML is so easily or obviously expressed as objects.) Let's consider how we might do that.

Using NSXMLParser is not difficult in theory. You create the NSXMLParser, handing it the URL of a local XML file (or an NSData, perhaps downloaded from the Internet), set its delegate, and tell it to `parse`. The delegate starts receiving delegate messages. For simple XML like ours, there are only three delegate messages of interest:

`parser:didStartElement:namespaceURI:qualifiedName:attributes:`
The parser has encountered an opening element tag. In our document, this would be `<people>`, `<person>`, `<firstName>`, or `<lastName>`.

`parser:didEndElement:namespaceURI:qualifiedName:`
The parser has encountered the corresponding closing element tag. In our document this would be `</people>`, `</person>`, `</firstName>`, or `</lastName>`.

`parser:foundCharacters:`
The parser has encountered some text between the starting and closing tags for the current element. In our document this would be, for example, `"Matt"` or `"Neuburg"` and so on.

In practice, responding to these delegate messages poses challenges of maintaining state. If there is just one delegate, it will have to bear in mind at every moment what element it is currently encountering; this could make for a lot of instance variables and a lot of if-statements in the implementation of the delegate methods. To aggravate the issue, `parser:foundCharacters:` can arrive multiple times for a single stretch of text; that is, the text may arrive in pieces, so we have to accumulate it into an instance variable, which is yet another case of maintaining state.

An elegant way to meet these challenges is by resetting the NSXMLParser's delegate to different objects at different stages of the parsing process. We make each delegate responsible for parsing one element; when a child of that element is encountered, we make a new object and make *it* the delegate. The child element delegate is then responsible for making us, the parent, the delegate once again when it finishes parsing its own element. This is slightly counterintuitive because it means `parser:didStartElement...` and `parser:didEndElement...` for the same element are arriving at two different objects. Imagine, for example, what the job of our `<people>` parser will be:

- When `parser:didStartElement...` arrives, the `<people>` parser looks to see if this is a `<person>`. If so, it creates an object that knows how to deal with a `<person>`, handing that object a reference to itself (the `<people>` parser), and makes it the delegate.

- Delegate messages now arrive at this newly created `<person>` parser. If any text is encountered, `parser:foundCharacters:` will be called, and the text must be accumulated into an instance variable.

- Eventually, `parser:didEndElement...` arrives. The `<person>` parser now uses its reference to make the `<people>` parser the delegate once again. Thus, the `<people>` parser is in charge once again, ready if another `<person>` element is encountered (and the old `<person>` parser might now go quietly out of existence).

With this in mind, we can design a simple all-purpose base class for parsing an element (simple especially because we are taking no account of namespaces, attributes, and other complications):

```
@interface MyXMLParserDelegate : NSObject <NSXMLParserDelegate> {
}
@property (nonatomic, copy) NSString* name;
@property (nonatomic, retain) NSMutableString* text;
@property (nonatomic, assign) MyXMLParserDelegate* parent;
@property (nonatomic, retain) MyXMLParserDelegate* child;
- (void) start: (NSString*) elementName parent: (id) parent;
- (void) makeChild: (Class) class
        elementName: (NSString*) elementName
            parser: (NSXMLParser*) parser;
- (void) finishedChild: (NSString*) s;

@end
```

Here's how these properties and methods are intended to work:

name

   The name of the element we are parsing now.

text

   A place for any characters to accumulate as we parse our element.

parent

   The MyXMLParserDelegate who created us and whose child we are.

child

   If we encounter a child element, we'll create a MyXMLParserDelegate and retain it here, making it the delegate.

start:parent:

   When we create a child parser, we'll call this method on the child so that it knows who its parent is. The first parameter is the name of the element the child will be parsing; we know this because we, not the child, received `parser:didStart-Element...`. (In a fuller implementation, this method would be more elaborate and we'd hand the child *all* the information we got with `parser:didStartElement...`.)

makeChild:elementName:parser:

   If we encounter a child element, there's a standard dance to do: instantiate some subclass of MyXMLParserDelegate, make it our `child`, make it the parser's delegate, and send it `start:parent:`. This is a utility method that embodies that dance.

finishedChild:

   When a child receives `parser:didEndElement...`, it sends this message to its parent before making its parent the delegate. The parameter is the `text`, but the parent can use this signal to obtain any information it expects from the child before the child goes out of existence.

Now we can sketch in the default implementation for MyXMLParserDelegate:

```
- (void) start: (NSString*) el parent: (id) p {
    self.name = el;
    self.parent = p;
    self.text = [NSMutableString string];
}

- (void) makeChild: (Class) class
        elementName: (NSString*) elementName
             parser: (NSXMLParser*) parser {
    MyXMLParserDelegate* del = [[class alloc] init];
    self.child = del;
    parser.delegate = del;
    [del start: elementName parent: self];
    [del release];
}

- (void) finishedChild: (NSString*) s { // subclass implements as desired
}

- (void)parser:(NSXMLParser *)parser foundCharacters:(NSString *)string {
    [self.text appendString:string];
}

- (void)parser:(NSXMLParser *)parser didEndElement:(NSString *)elementName
        namespaceURI:(NSString *)namespaceURI qualifiedName:(NSString *)qName {
    if (parent) {
        [parent finishedChild: [[self.text copy] autorelease]];
        parser.delegate = self.parent;
    }
}

- (void) dealloc {
    [text release];
    [child release];
    [name release];
    [super dealloc];
}
```

We can now create subclasses of MyXMLParserDelegate: one for each kind of element we expect to parse. The chief responsibility of such a subclass, if it encounters a child element in parser:didStartElement..., is to create an instance of the appropriate MyXMLParserDelegate subclass, send it start:parent:, and make it the delegate; we have already embodied this in the utility method makeChild:elementName:parser:. The reverse process is already built into the default implementation of parser:didEndElement...: we call the parent's finishedChild: and make the parent the delegate.

We can now parse our sample XML into an array of Person objects very easily. We start by obtaining the URL of the XML file, handing it to an NSXMLParser, creating our first delegate parser and making it the delegate, and telling the NSXMLParser to start:

```
NSURL* url = [[NSBundle mainBundle] URLForResource:@"folks" withExtension:@"xml"];
NSXMLParser* parser = [[NSXMLParser alloc] initWithContentsOfURL:url];
MyPeopleParser* people = [[MyPeopleParser alloc] init];
[parser setDelegate: people];
```

```
[parser parse];
// ... do something with people.people ...
[people release];
[parser release];
```

Here is MyPeopleParser. It is the top-level parser so it has some extra work to do: when it encounters the `<people>` element, which is the first thing that should happen, it creates the `people` array that will hold the Person objects; this array will be the final result of the entire parsing operation. If it encounters a `<person>` element, it does the standard dance I described earlier, creating a `<person>` parser (MyPersonParser) as its child and making it the delegate; when the `<person>` parser calls back to tell us it's finished, My-PeopleParser expects the `<person>` parser to supply a Person through its `person` property:

```
- (void)parser:(NSXMLParser *)parser didStartElement:(NSString *)elementName
        namespaceURI:(NSString *)namespaceURI
        qualifiedName:(NSString *)qualifiedName
        attributes:(NSDictionary *)attributeDict
{
    if ([elementName isEqualToString: @"people"])
        self.people = [NSMutableArray array];
    if ([elementName isEqualToString: @"person"])
        [self makeChild:[MyPersonParser class] elementName:elementName
                    parser:parser];
}

- (void) finishedChild: (NSString*) s {
    [people addObject: [self.child person]];
}
```

MyPersonParser does the same child-making dance when it encounters a `<firstName>` or a `<lastName>` element; it uses a plain vanilla MyXMLParserDelegate to parse these children, because the built-in ability to accumulate text and hand it back is all that's needed. In `finishedChild:`, it makes sure it has a Person object ready to hand back to its parent through its `person` property; key–value coding is elegantly used to match the name of the element with the name of the Person property to be set:

```
- (void)parser:(NSXMLParser *)parser didStartElement:(NSString *)elementName
        namespaceURI:(NSString *)namespaceURI
        qualifiedName:(NSString *)qualifiedName
        attributes:(NSDictionary *)attributeDict {
    [self makeChild:[MyXMLParserDelegate class] elementName:elementName
            parser:parser];
}

- (void) finishedChild:(NSString *)s {
    if (!self.person) {
        Person* p = [[Person alloc] init];
        self.person = p; // retain policy
        [p release];
    }
    [self.person setValue: s forKey: self.child.name];
}
```

```
- (void) dealloc {
    [person release];
    [super dealloc];
}
```

This may seem like a lot of work to parse such a simple bit of XML, but it is neatly object-oriented and requires very little new code once we've established the MyXML-ParserDelegate superclass, which is of course reusable in many other situations.

On the other hand, if you really want tree-based XML parsing along with XPath and so forth, you can have it, because the `libxml2` library is present in the SDK (and on the device). This is a C *dylib* (short for "dynamic library," extension *.dylib*), and Xcode doesn't automatically know during the build process where to find its headers (even though it's part of the SDK), so the instructions for accessing it in your project are a tiny bit more involved than linking to an Objective-C framework:

1. In Xcode, add *libxml2.dylib* to the Link Binary With Libraries build phase for your target, just as you would do with a framework.

2. Now comes the extra step that differs from using a framework; it is needed because, although the Xcode build process automatically looks inside *iphoneos/usr/include/* for headers, it doesn't automatically recurse down into folders, so it won't look inside the *libxml2* folder unless you tell it to. Edit the target's build settings and set the Header Search Paths build setting to `$SDKROOT/usr/include/libxml2`. When you close the dialog for adding a search path, this will transform itself into *iphoneos/usr/include/libxml2*.

3. In your code, import `<libxml/tree.h>`.

You now have to talk to `libxml2` using C. This is no trivial task. Here's an example proving we can do it; we read our XML file, parse it into a tree, and traverse all its elements:

```
NSURL* url = [[NSBundle mainBundle] URLForResource:@"folks" withExtension:@"xml"];
NSString* path = [url absoluteString];
const char* filename = [path UTF8String];
xmlDocPtr doc = NULL;
xmlNode *root_element = NULL;
doc = xmlReadFile(filename, NULL, 0);
root_element = xmlDocGetRootElement(doc);
traverse_elements(root_element); // must be previously defined
xmlFreeDoc(doc);
xmlCleanupParser();
```

Here's our definition for `traverse_elements`; it logs each person and the person's first and last name, just to prove we are traversing successfully:

```
void traverse_elements(xmlNode * a_node) {
    xmlNode *cur_node = NULL;
    for (cur_node = a_node; cur_node; cur_node = cur_node->next) {
        if (cur_node->type == XML_ELEMENT_NODE) {
            if (strcmp(cur_node->name, "person") == 0)
```

```
              NSLog(@"found a person");
          if (strcmp(cur_node->name, "firstName") == 0)
              NSLog(@"First name: %s", cur_node->children->content);
          if (strcmp(cur_node->name, "lastName") == 0)
              NSLog(@"Last name: %s", cur_node->children->content);
      }
      traverse_elements(cur_node->children);
    }
}
```

If talking C to `libxml2` is too daunting, you can interpose an Objective-C front end by taking advantage of a third-party library. See, for example, *https://github.com/Touch Code/TouchXML*.

Keep in mind, however, that you're really not supposed to do what I just did. Even if you use `libxml2`, you're supposed to use stream-based parsing, not tree-based parsing. See Apple's XMLPerformance example code.

# SQLite

SQLite (*http://www.sqlite.org/docs.html*) is a lightweight, full-featured relational database that you can talk to using SQL, the universal language of databases. This can be an appropriate storage format when your data comes in rows and columns (records and fields) and needs to be rapidly searchable.

In the same way as you can link to `libxml2.dylib`, you can link to `libsqlite3.dylib` (and import `<sqlite3.h>`) to access the power of SQLite. As with `libxml2`, talking C to `sqlite3` may prove annoying. There are a number of lightweight Objective-C front ends. In this example, I use `fmdb` (*https://github.com/ccgus/fmdb*) to read the names of people out of a previously created database:

```
NSString* docsdir = [NSSearchPathForDirectoriesInDomains(
    NSDocumentDirectory, NSUserDomainMask, YES) lastObject];
NSString* dbpath = [docsdir stringByAppendingPathComponent:@"people.db"];
FMDatabase* db = [FMDatabase databaseWithPath:dbpath];
if (![db open]) {
    NSLog(@"Ooops");
    return;
}
FMResultSet *rs = [db executeQuery:@"select * from people"];
while ([rs next]) {
    NSLog(@"%@ %@",
        [rs stringForColumn:@"firstname"],
        [rs stringForColumn:@"lastname"]);
}
[db close];
/* output:
Matt Neuburg
Snidely Whiplash
Dudley Doright
*/
```

You can include a previously constructed SQLite file in your app bundle, but you can't write to it there; the solution is to copy it from your app bundle into another location, such as the Documents directory, before you start working with it.

The Core Data framework also uses SQLite as a storage format (or, alternatively, it can use XML). Core Data is a generalized way of dealing with objects and properties; it is appropriate particularly when these form a complex relational graph. For example, a person might have not only multiple addresses but also multiple friends who are also persons; expressing persons and addresses as explicit object types, working out how to link them and how to translate between objects in memory and data in storage, and tracking the effects of changes, such as when a person is deleted from the data, can be tedious. Core Data can help, but it is *not* a beginner-level technology, nor should it be seen as a substitute for a true relational database. Core Data is beyond the scope of this book; entire books can be written about Core Data alone (and have been). See the *Core Data Programming Guide* and the other resources referred to there.

# Image File Formats

Starting in iOS 4, the Image I/O framework provides a simple, unified way to open image files (from disk or downloaded from the network, as described in Chapter 37), to save image files, to convert between image file formats, and to read metadata from standard image file formats, including EXIF and GPS information from a digital camera. You'll need to link to *ImageIO.framework* and import <ImageIO/ImageIO.h>.

Obviously, such features were not entirely missing before iOS 4. UIImage can read the data from most standard image formats, and you can convert formats with functions such as `UIImageJPEGRepresentation` and `UIImagePNGRepresentation`. But you could not, for example, save an image as TIFF without the Image I/O framework.

The Image I/O framework introduces the notion of an *image source* (CGImageSourceRef). This can be created from the URL of a file on disk or from NSData (actually CFDataRef, to which NSData is toll-free bridged) obtained or generated in some way. You can use this to obtain a CGImage of the source's image (or, if the source format contains multiple images, a particular image). But you can also obtain metadata from the source *without* transforming the source into a CGImage, thus conserving memory. For example:

```
NSURL* url = [[NSBundle mainBundle] URLForResource:@"colson" withExtension:@"jpg"];
CGImageSourceRef src = CGImageSourceCreateWithURL((CFURLRef)url, NULL);
NSDictionary* result = (id)CGImageSourceCopyPropertiesAtIndex(src, 0, NULL);
```

Without having opened the image file as an image, we now have a dictionary full of information about it, including its pixel dimensions (`kCGImagePropertyPixelWidth`, `kCGImagePropertyPixelHeight`), its resolution, its color model, its color depth, and its orientation — plus, because this picture originally comes from a digital camera, the

EXIF data such as the aperture and exposure at which it was taken, plus the make and model of the camera.

We can obtain the image as a CGImage, with `CGImageSourceCreateImageAtIndex`. Alternatively, we can request a thumbnail version of the image. I'm afraid that Apple's documentation fails to impress sufficiently on the reader the value of the thumbnail. If your purpose in opening this image is to display it in your interface, you don't care about the original image data; a thumbnail is precisely what you want, especially because you can specify any size for this "thumbnail" all the way up to the original size of the image! This is tremendously convenient, because to assign a small UIImageView a large image wastes all the memory reflected by the size difference.

To generate a thumbnail at a given size, you start with a dictionary specifying the size along with other instructions, and pass that, together with the image source, to `CGImageSourceCreateThumbnailAtIndex`. The only pitfall is that, because we are working with a CGImage and specifying actual pixels, we must remember to take account of the scale of our device's screen. So, for example, let's say we want to scale our image so that its largest dimension is no more than 100 points:

```
NSURL* url = [[NSBundle mainBundle] URLForResource:@"colson" withExtension:@"jpg"];
CGImageSourceRef src = CGImageSourceCreateWithURL((CFURLRef)url, NULL);
CGFloat scale = [UIScreen mainScreen].scale;
NSDictionary* d =
    [NSDictionary dictionaryWithObjectsAndKeys:
        (id)kCFBooleanTrue, kCGImageSourceShouldAllowFloat,
        (id)kCFBooleanTrue, kCGImageSourceCreateThumbnailWithTransform,
        (id)kCFBooleanTrue, kCGImageSourceCreateThumbnailFromImageAlways,
        [NSNumber numberWithInt:100*scale], kCGImageSourceThumbnailMaxPixelSize,
        nil];
CGImageRef imref = CGImageSourceCreateThumbnailAtIndex(src, 0, (CFDictionaryRef)d);
UIImage* im =
    [UIImage imageWithCGImage:imref scale:scale orientation:UIImageOrientationUp];
self->iv.image = im; // assign image to UIImageView
CFRelease(imref); CFRelease(src);
```

The Image I/O framework also introduces the notion of an *image destination*, used for saving an image into a specified file format. As a final example, I'll show how to save our image as a TIFF, which, as I mentioned before, was impossible previously. Notice that in this case we never even need to open the image as an image: we save directly from the image source to the image destination:

```
NSURL* url = [[NSBundle mainBundle] URLForResource:@"colson" withExtension:@"jpg"];
CGImageSourceRef src = CGImageSourceCreateWithURL((CFURLRef)url, NULL);
NSFileManager* fm = [[NSFileManager alloc] init];
NSURL* suppurl = [fm URLForDirectory:NSApplicationSupportDirectory
                            inDomain:NSUserDomainMask
                   appropriateForURL:nil
                              create:YES error:NULL];
NSURL* tiff = [suppurl URLByAppendingPathComponent:@"mytiff.tiff"];
CGImageDestinationRef dest =
    CGImageDestinationCreateWithURL((CFURLRef)tiff,
    (CFStringRef)@"public.tiff", 1, NULL);
```

```
CGImageDestinationAddImageFromSource(dest, src, 0, NULL);
bool ok = CGImageDestinationFinalize(dest);
// error-checking omitted
[fm release]; CFRelease(src); CFRelease(dest);
```

# CHAPTER 37

# Basic Networking

Networking is difficult and complicated, chiefly because it's ultimately out of your control. My favorite phrase with regard to the network is, "There's many a slip 'twixt the cup and the lip." You can ask for a resource from across the network, but at that point anything can happen: the resource might not be found (the server is down, perhaps), it might take a while to arrive, it might never arrive, the network itself might vanish after the resource has partially arrived. iOS, however, makes at least the *basics* of networking very easy, so that's all that this chapter will deal with.

Many earlier chapters have dealt with interface and frameworks that network for you automatically. Put a UIWebView in your interface (Chapter 24) and poof, you're networking; the UIWebView does all the grunt work, and it does it a lot better than you'd be likely to do it from scratch. The same is true of MPMovieViewController (Chapter 28), MFMailComposeViewController (Chapter 33), and MKMapView (Chapter 37).

## HTTP Requests

A simple HTTP request is made through an NSURLConnection object. You hand it an NSURLRequest describing what you'd like to do, along with a delegate; the download begins automatically (unless you specify otherwise). Then you stand back and let delegate messages arrive. The actual network operations happen asynchronously (unless you specifically demand that they happen synchronously, which you'd never do); the NSURLConnection object does all its work in the background and sends you delegate messages when something occurs that you need to know about.

Data received from the network in response to your request will arrive as an NSData object. It will arrive piecemeal, so you have to maintain state; in particular, you'll have an NSMutableData object to which you'll keep appending each new bit of NSData until you're told that the entire data has arrived — or that the request has failed. (The whole process is somewhat reminiscent of what we did with an NSXMLParser in Chapter 36.)

All the real work happens in four delegate methods:

`connection:didReceiveResponse:`

The server is responding. We can now hope that our data will start to arrive, so get ready. If you like, you can interrogate the NSURLResponse object that is handed to you, to learn things from the response headers such as the data's expected size and MIME type.

`connection:didReceiveData:`

Some data has arrived. Append it to the NSMutableData object.

`connectiondidFinishLoading:`

All of the data has arrived; the NSMutableData object presumably contains it. Clean up as needed.

`connection:didFailWithError:`

Something went wrong. Clean up as needed.

Here's an example of initiating a download of a JPEG image file:

```
self.receivedData = [NSMutableData data];
NSString* s = @"http://www.someserver.com/somefolder/someimage.jpg";
NSURL* url = [NSURL URLWithString:s];
NSURLRequest* req = [NSURLRequest requestWithURL:url];
NSURLConnection* conn = [NSURLConnection connectionWithRequest:req delegate:self];
[conn retain];
```

Here are the corresponding delegate method implementations:

```
- (void) connection:(NSURLConnection *)connection
        didReceiveResponse:(NSURLResponse *)response {
    // connection is starting, clear buffer
    [receivedData setLength:0];
}

- (void) connection:(NSURLConnection *)connection didReceiveData:(NSData *)data {
    // data is arriving, add it to the buffer
    [receivedData appendData:data];
}

- (void)connection:(NSURLConnection*)connection didFailWithError:(NSError *)error {
    // something went wrong, release connection
    [connection release];
    // clean up interface as needed
}

- (void)connectionDidFinishLoading:(NSURLConnection *)connection {
    // all done, release connection, we are ready to rock and roll
    [connection release];
    // do something with receivedData
}
```

You may have noticed that, in creating the NSURLConnection initially, we retain it without releasing it. The release takes place in our delegate methods. This style of memory management is copied from the "Using NSURLConnection" chapter of Apple's *URL Loading System Programming Guide*. The NSURLConnection instance is allowed to float in space, as it were, retained (so that it won't vanish in a puff of smoke) but with no reference to it, until the final delegate method is called.

An alternative approach would be to keep the NSURLConnection in an instance variable and balance the retain and release normally. In that case we would probably wrap the entire connection process in a dedicated object to hold this instance variable, because otherwise keeping track of multiple simultaneous NSURLConnections would be a nightmare. Here's the complete implementation for such a wrapper object, MyDownloader:

```objc
- (id) initWithRequest: (NSURLRequest*) req {
    self = [super init];
    if (self) {
        self->request = [req copy];
        self->connection = [[NSURLConnection alloc]
            initWithRequest:req delegate:self startImmediately:NO];
        self->receivedData = [[NSMutableData alloc] init];
    }
    return self;
}

- (void) dealloc {
    [request release];
    [connection release];
    [receivedData release];
    [super dealloc];
}

- (void) connection:(NSURLConnection *)connection
        didReceiveResponse:(NSURLResponse *)response {
    [receivedData setLength:0];
}

- (void) connection:(NSURLConnection *)connection didReceiveData:(NSData *)data {
    [receivedData appendData:data];
}

- (void)connection:(NSURLConnection *)connection didFailWithError:(NSError *)err {
    [[NSNotificationCenter defaultCenter]
        postNotificationName:@"connectionFinished" object:self
        userInfo:[NSDictionary dictionaryWithObject:err forKey:@"error"]];
}

- (void)connectionDidFinishLoading:(NSURLConnection *)connection {
    [[NSNotificationCenter defaultCenter]
        postNotificationName:@"connectionFinished" object:self];
}
```

In the line that creates the NSURLConnection, we have added the `startImmediately:` parameter, with a value of NO. Thus, a MyDownloader object can exist before doing any actual downloading. To set the download into motion, we tell MyDownloader's `connection` to `start`. (Sending `start` to an NSURLConnection that is already downloading has no effect.) In the past, there have been complaints that sending `start` to an

NSURLConnection that does not start immediately can cause a crash. I have not seen this myself, so perhaps it has been fixed in more recent iOS versions, but the solution is to schedule the connection on a run loop explicitly just before starting it:

```
[connection scheduleInRunLoop:[NSRunLoop currentRunLoop]
                      forMode:NSDefaultRunLoopMode];
[connection start];
```

How would we use MyDownloader if we have several objects to download? We might, for example, keep a mutable array of MyDownloader objects. To initiate a download, we create a MyDownloader object, register for its @"connectionFinished" notification, stuff it into the array, and set its connection going:

```
if (!self.connections)
    self.connections = [NSMutableArray array];
NSString* s = @"http://www.someserver.com/somefolder/someimage.jpg";
NSURL* url = [NSURL URLWithString:s];
NSURLRequest* req = [NSURLRequest requestWithURL:url];
MyDownloader* d = [[MyDownloader alloc] initWithRequest:req];
[self.connections addObject:d];
[[NSNotificationCenter defaultCenter] addObserver:self
    selector:@selector(finished:) name:@"connectionFinished" object:d];
[d.connection start];
[d release];
```

When the notification arrives, either we've failed with an error or we've finished in good order. In the latter case, we grab the received data and retain it; either way, we remove the MyDownloader from the array, thus releasing it, its connection, and its data:

```
- (void) finished: (NSNotification*) n {
    MyDownloader* d = [n object];
    NSData* data = nil;
    if ([n userInfo]) {
        // ... error of some kind! ...
    } else {
        data = [d receivedData];
        [data retain]; // about to go out of existence otherwise
        // ... and do something with the data right now ...
    }
    [self.connections removeObject:d];
}
```

In real life, you might also query the MyDownloader's request, or perhaps some other instance variable in a MyDownloader subclass, to identify what material this data represents. Also, you're not so likely to use a temporary array of downloaders; rather, you'll incorporate downloaders directly into your application's model, letting them fetch the data on demand.

Suppose, for example, you need to download images to serve as thumbnails in the cells of a UITableView. Let's consider how these images can be supplied lazily on demand. The model, as we saw in Chapter 21, might be an array of dictionaries. In this case, the dictionary might contain some text and a downloader whose job is to supply the image. So what I'm proposing is a model like this:

```
array
    dictionary
        text: @"Manny"
        pic: Downloader whose job is to supply an image of Manny
    dictionary
        text: @"Moe"
        pic: Downloader whose job is to supply an image of Moe
    dictionary
        text: @"Jack"
        pic: Downloader whose job is to supply an image of Jack
    ....
```

When the table turns to the data source for data, the data source will turn to the dictionary for the requested row and ask the downloader for its image. At that point, either the downloader has an image, in which case it supplies it, or it hasn't, in which case it returns nil (or some placeholder) and begins the download.

Here's the key point. When a downloader succeeds in downloading its image, it notifies the data source. If the corresponding row is visible, the data source immediately tells the table to reload the corresponding row; the table asks the data source for the data, the data source turns to the dictionary for the requested row, and this time it obtains the image! Moreover, once an image is downloaded, the downloader continues to hold on to it and to supply it on request, so as the user scrolls, previously downloaded images just appear as part of the table.

The downloader we're imagining here is a MyDownloader subclass, MyImageDownloader, with an image property so that the data source can request the image. MyImageDownloader's implementation is straightforward:

```
- (UIImage*) image {
    if (image)
        return image;
    [self.connection start];
    return nil; // or a placeholder
}

- (void)connectionDidFinishLoading:(NSURLConnection *)connection {
    UIImage* im = [UIImage imageWithData:self->receivedData];
    if (im) {
        self.image = im;
        [[NSNotificationCenter defaultCenter]
            postNotificationName:@"imageDownloaded" object:self];
    }
}
```

The data source looks perfectly normal:

```
- (UITableViewCell *)tableView:(UITableView *)tableView
        cellForRowAtIndexPath:(NSIndexPath *)indexPath {
    static NSString *CellIdentifier = @"Cell";
    UITableViewCell *cell =
        [tableView dequeueReusableCellWithIdentifier:CellIdentifier];
    if (cell == nil) {
        cell = [[[UITableViewCell alloc] initWithStyle:UITableViewCellStyleDefault
```

```
                               reuseIdentifier:CellIdentifier] autorelease];
    NSDictionary* d = [self.model objectAtIndex: indexPath.row];
    cell.textLabel.text = [d objectForKey:@"text"];
    MyImageDownloader* imd = [d objectForKey:@"pic"];
    cell.imageView.image = imd.image;
    return cell;
}
```

Now for the key point. The data source is also registered for an @"imageDownloaded" notification. When such a notification arrives, it works out the table row corresponding to the MyImageDownloader that posted the notification and reloads that row:

```
- (void) imageDownloaded: (NSNotification*) n {
    MyImageDownloader* d = [n object];
    NSUInteger row = [self.model indexOfObjectPassingTest:
      ^BOOL(id obj, NSUInteger idx, BOOL *stop) {
        return ([(NSDictionary*)obj objectForKey:@"pic"] == d);
    }];
    if (row == NSNotFound) return; // shouldn't happen
    NSIndexPath* ip = [NSIndexPath indexPathForRow:row inSection:0];
    NSArray* ips = [self.tableView indexPathsForVisibleRows];
    if ([ips indexOfObject:ip] != NSNotFound) {
        [self.tableView reloadRowsAtIndexPaths:[NSArray arrayWithObject: ip]
                           withRowAnimation:UITableViewRowAnimationFade];
    }
}
```

This works, and demonstrates the basic technique for doing one of the most-desired network-related operations, namely obtaining lazily, on demand, from the network, a piece of data and updating the interface accordingly. What's missing from the example is robustness with regard to failure. The trouble is that once an NSURLConnection has failed, it's dead; you can't use the same NSURLConnection to try again later. We can rectify that in MyImageDownloader by replacing the NSURLConnection on failure:

```
- (void)connection:(NSURLConnection *)connection didFailWithError:(NSError *)err {
    self.connection = [[[NSURLConnection alloc] initWithRequest:self.request
        delegate:self startImmediately:NO] autorelease];
}
```

This partially solves the problem: when the user scrolls a failed cell out of view and later scrolls it back into view, the table will ask the data source for its data and the MyImageDownloader will try again to download its image. But that won't happen for a failed cell that's never scrolled out of view. How you deal with this is up to you; it's a matter of providing the best user experience without having an undue impact upon performance, battery, and so forth. In this instance, because these images are fairly unimportant, I might arrange that when an NSTimer with a fairly large interval fires (every 60 seconds, say), we reload the visible rows; this will cause any failed MyImageDownloader whose corresponding row is visible to try again.

In planning your interface, it is useful to draw a distinction as to whether the user will experience a certain bit of networking explicitly or implicitly. This changes nothing about *how* you network; it's a matter of presentation. The earlier example of downloading images to be slotted into the cells of an existing table view would be implicit networking: it happens regardless of whether the user wants it, and it doesn't seriously affect overall functionality, even if some or all of the images fail to arrive. In the TidBITS News app, on the other hand, everything displayed comes from a downloaded RSS feed: no feed, no data. The app saves the previously downloaded feed (in user defaults, see Chapter 36), so the user has something to read even in the absence of the network, but the feed is explicitly refreshed at launch or if the user taps a button (along with the spinning network activity indicator, Chapter 25), and if the download fails, we put up an alert.

# Bonjour

Bonjour is the ingenious technology, originated at Apple and now becoming a universal standard, for allowing network devices to advertise services they provide and to discover dynamically other devices offering such services. Once an appropriate service is detected, a client device can resolve it to get a network address and can then begin communicating with the server device. Actually communicating is outside the scope of this book, but device discovery via Bonjour is easy.

In this example, we'll look to see whether any device, such as a Mac, is running iTunes with library sharing turned on. We can search for domains or for a particular service; here, we'll pass the empty string as the domain to signify "any domain," and concentrate on the service, which is @"_daap._tcp". We maintain two instance variables, the NSNetServiceBrowser that will look for devices, and a mutable array in which to store any services it discovers:

```
self.services = [NSMutableArray array];
NSNetServiceBrowser* browser = [[NSNetServiceBrowser alloc] init];
self.nsb = browser;
[browser release];
self.nsb.delegate = self;
[self.nsb searchForServicesOfType:@"_daap._tcp" inDomain:@""];
```

The NSNetServiceBrowser is now searching for devices advertising iTunes sharing and will keep doing so until we destroy it or tell it to stop. It is common to leave the service browser running, because devices can come and go very readily. As they do, the service browser's delegate will be informed. For purposes of this example, I'll simply maintain a list of services, and update the app's interface when the situation changes:

```
- (void)netServiceBrowser:(NSNetServiceBrowser *)netServiceBrowser
          didFindService:(NSNetService *)netService
              moreComing:(BOOL)moreServicesComing {
    [self.services addObject:netService];
    if (!moreServicesComing)
        [self updateInterface];
}
```

```
- (void)netServiceBrowser:(NSNetServiceBrowser *)netServiceBrowser
        didRemoveService:(NSNetService *)netService
              moreComing:(BOOL)moreServicesComing {
    [self.services removeObject:netService];
    if (!moreServicesComing)
        [self updateInterface];
}
```

The delegate messages very kindly tell me when they have completed the task of in-forming me of a series of changes, so I can wait to update the interface until after a full batch of changes has ended. In this example, I don't really have any interface to update; I'll just log the list of services, each of which is an NSNetService instance:

```
- (void) updateInterface {
    for (NSNetService* service in self.services) {
        if (service.port == -1) {
            NSLog(@"service %@ of type %@, not yet resolved",
                service.name, service.type);
        }
    }
}
```

To connect to a service, we would first need to *resolve* it, thus obtaining an address and other useful information. An unresolved service has port -1, as shown in the previous code. To resolve a service, you tell it to resolve; you will probably also set a delegate on the service, so as to be notified when the resolution succeeds (or fails). Here, I'll have the delegate call my updateInterface method again if a resolution succeeds, and I'll extend updateInterface to show the port number for any resolved services:

```
- (void) updateInterface {
    for (NSNetService* service in self.services) {
        if (service.port == -1) {
            NSLog(@"service %@ of type %@, not yet resolved",
                service.name, service.type);
            [service setDelegate:self];
            [service resolveWithTimeout:10];
        } else {
            NSLog(@"service %@ of type %@, port %i, addresses %@",
                service.name, service.type, service.port, service.addresses);
        }
    }
}

- (void)netServiceDidResolveAddress:(NSNetService *)sender {
    [self updateInterface];
}
```

The addresses of a resolved service constitute an array of NSData. Logging an address like this is largely pointless, as it is not human-readable, but it's useful for handing to a CFSocket. In general you'll call the service's getInputStream:outputStream: to start talking over the connection; that's outside the scope of this discussion. See Apple's WiTap example for more.

# Push Notifications

If your app uses a server on the network that's under your control, you can arrange for the user to be notified when a significant event takes place on the server. This is called a *push notification* (or *remote notification*). The user interface for a push notification is the same as for a local notification (Chapter 26): the user is shown an alert in front of whatever is happening at that moment and can use this alert to launch your app.

For example, the TidBITS News app is about news stories on the TidBITS website. The app's data comes from an RSS feed, which is refreshed on the server side whenever something changes on the site, such as a new news story being posted. It might be appropriate (and cool) if we were to add push notifications to the server code that refreshes the RSS feed, so that users could be alerted to the fact that they might like to launch TidBITS News and read a newly posted story.

Implementing push notifications is not trivial, and requires cooperation across the network between your app and your server, and between your server and Apple's push notification server. I've never actually tried this, so I'm just describing what the architecture is like; for details, read Apple's *Local and Push Notification Programming Guide*.

When developing your app, you obtain from the iOS Provisioning Portal (Chapter 9) credentials identifying your app, and allowing communication between your server and Apple's push notification server, and between Apple's push notification server and your app running on the user's device. When your app launches, it calls the UIApplication method `registerForRemoteNotificationTypes:`, which communicates asynchronously with Apple's push notification server to obtain a token identifying this instance of your app. If successful, the token comes back in the app delegate method `application:did-RegisterForRemoteNotificationsWithDeviceToken:`. At that point, your app must communicate with your server to provide it with this token.

The server is now maintaining two pieces of information: its credentials and a list of tokens effectively representing users. When an event occurs at your server for which the server wishes to push a notification out to users, the server uses its credentials to connect with Apple's push notification server and — for *every individual user* whom the server wishes to notify — streams a message to Apple's push notification server, providing the user token plus a "payload" that describes the notification, much as a UILocalNotification does (Chapter 26). The payload is written in JSON, which is a lightweight dictionary-like structure.

Meanwhile, the user's device, if it is still on, is (with luck) connected to the network in a low-power mode that allows it to hear from Apple's push notification server. The push notification server sends the message to the user's device, where the system treats it much like a local notification: if your app isn't frontmost, the user sees an alert, and if the user taps the action button in the alert, your app is brought to the front (launching if necessary). Either way, your app can then learn what has happened through either the app delegate message `application:didReceiveRemoteNotification:` or (if the app had to be launched from scratch) through `application:didFinishLaunchingWith-Options:`, whose dictionary will contain `UIApplicationLaunchOptionsRemote-NotificationKey`. The notification itself, instead of being a UILocalNotification object, is an NSDictionary corresponding to the original JSON payload.

## Beyond Basic Networking

An NSURLRequest has a cache policy, which you can set to determine whether the request might be satisfied without freshly downloading previously downloaded data. An NSURLRequest to be handed to an NSURLConnection can specify the FTP, HTTP, or HTTPS scheme, including POST requests. An NSURLConnection can handle redirects and authentication. See the *URL Loading System Programming Guide*. You can also get as deep into the details of networking as you like; see in particular the *CFNetwork Programming Guide*.

Apple provides a generous amount of sample code. See in particular SimpleURLConnections, AdvancedURLConnections, SimpleNetworkStreams, SimpleFTPSample, and MVCNetworking.

# CHAPTER 38

# Threads

A *thread* is, simply put, a subprocess of your app that can execute even while other such subprocesses are also executing. Such simultaneous execution is called *concurrency*. The iOS frameworks use threads all the time; if they didn't, your app would be less responsive to the user — perhaps even completely unresponsive. The genius of the frameworks, though, is that they use threads precisely so that you don't have to.

For example, suppose your app is downloading something from the network (Chapter 37). This download doesn't happen all by itself; somewhere, someone is running code that interacts with the network and obtains data. Yet a long download doesn't prevent *your* code from running, nor does it prevent the user from tapping and swiping things in your interface. That's concurrency in action.

It is a testament to the ingenuity of the iOS frameworks that this book has proceeded so far with no explicit discussion of threads. Indeed, it would have been nice to avoid the topic altogether. Threads are difficult and dangerous, and if at all possible you should avoid them. But sometimes that *isn't* possible. So this chapter introduces threads, along with a warning: here be dragons. There is much more to threading, and especially to making your threaded code safe, than this chapter can possibly touch on. For detailed information about the topics introduced in this chapter, read Apple's *Concurrency Programming Guide* and *Threading Programming Guide*.

## The Main Thread

You are always using *some* thread. All your code must run somewhere; "somewhere" means a thread. When code calls a method, that method normally runs on the same thread as the code that called it. Your code is called through events (Chapter 11); those events normally call your code on the *main thread*. The main thread has certain special properties:

*The main thread automatically has a run loop*
> A *run loop* is a recipient of events. It is how your code is notified that something is happening; without a run loop, a thread can't receive events. Cocoa events nor-

mally arrive on the main thread's run loop; that's why your code, called by those events, executes on the main thread.

*The main thread is the interface thread*

When the user interacts with the interface, those interactions are reported on the main thread. When your code interacts with the interface, it must do so on the main thread. Of course that will normally happen automatically, because your code normally runs on the main thread.

The main thread thus has a very great deal of work to do. Here's how life goes in your app:

1. An event arrives on the main thread; the user has tapped a button, for example, and now its control action handler is being called.

2. The event calls your code on the main thread. Your code now runs on the main thread. While this happens, nothing else can happen on the main thread. Your code might command some changes in the interface; this is safe, because your code is running on the main thread.

3. Your code finishes. The main thread's run loop is now free to report more events, and the user is free to interact with the interface once again.

The bottleneck here is obviously step 2, the running of your code. Your code runs on the main thread. That means the main thread can't do anything else while your code is running. No events can arrive while your code is running. The user can't interact with the interface while your code is running. But this is usually no problem, because:

- Your code executes really fast. It's true that the user can't interact with the interface while your code runs, but this is such a tiny interval of time that the user will probably never even notice.

- Your code, as it runs, blocks the user from interacting with the interface. But that's not bad: it's good! Your code, in response to what the user does, might update the interface; it would be insane if the user could do something else in the interface while you're in the middle of updating it.

On the other hand, as I've already mentioned, the frameworks operate in secondary threads all the time. The reason this doesn't affect you is that they talk to *your* code on the *main* thread. You have seen many examples of this in the preceding chapters. For example:

- You saw in Chapter 17 that during an animation, the interface remains responsive to the user, and it is possible for your code to run. The Core Animation framework is running the animation and updating the presentation layer on a background thread. But any delegate methods or completion blocks are called on the main thread.

- You saw in Chapter 24 that a UIWebView's fetching and loading of its content is asynchronous; that means the work is done in a background thread. But delegate methods are called on the main thread. The same is true of downloading a resource from the network with NSURLConnection (Chapter 37).

- You saw in Chapter 27 that sounds are played asynchronously. But delegate methods are called on the main thread. Obviously, the same is true of music players (Chapter 29). Similarly, you saw in Chapter 28 that movie loading, preparation, and playing happens asynchronously. But delegate methods are called on the main thread.

- You saw in Chapter 28 and Chapter 30 that saving a movie file takes time. So the saving takes place on a background thread. But delegate methods or completion blocks are called on the main thread.

Thus, you can (and should) usually ignore threads and just keep plugging away on the main thread. However, there are two kinds of situation in which your code will need to be explicitly aware of threading issues:

*Your code is not called back on the main thread.*

Some frameworks explicitly inform you that callbacks are not guaranteed to take place on the main thread. For example, CATiledLayer (Chapter 20) warns that `drawLayer:inContext:` is called in a background thread. As I explained, this means that in iOS 3.x and earlier, you can't draw here using UIKit, because UIKit classes are generally not thread-safe. In iOS 4, not only are the UIKit drawing-related classes thread-safe, but so is accessing the current context, so you can draw with `drawRect:` instead. Nevertheless, even in iOS 4 you need to be aware of the fact that `drawRect:`, when triggered by a CATiledLayer, might be running in a background thread.

Similarly, AV Foundation (Chapter 28) warns that its blocks and notifications can arrive on a background thread. So if you intend to update the user interface, or use a value that might also be used by your main-thread code, you'll need to be thread-conscious.

*Your code takes significant time.*
> If your code takes a long time to run and if running it on the main thread would prevent user interaction, you'll need to run that code on a background thread instead. This isn't just a matter of aesthetics; the system will actually kill your app if it discovers that its main thread is blocked for too long.

# Why Threading Is Hard

The one certain thing about computer code is that it just clunks along the path of execution, one statement at a time. Lines of code, in effect, are performed in the order in which they appear. With threading, that certainty goes right out the window. If you have code that can be performed on a background thread, then you don't know when it will be performed in relation to your main-thread code. Any line of your background-thread code could be interleaved between any two lines of your main-thread code.

You also might not know *how many times* a piece of your background-thread code might be running simultaneously. Unless you take steps to prevent it, the same code could be spawned off as a thread even while it's already running in a thread. So any line of your background-thread code could be interleaved between any two lines of *itself.*

This situation is particularly threatening with regard to *shared data*. Suppose two threads were to get hold of the same object and change it. Who knows what horrors might result? Objects in general have state, adding up to the state of your app as a whole. If multiple threads are permitted to access your objects, they and your entire app can be put into an indeterminate or nonsensical state.

This problem cannot be solved by simple logic. For example, suppose you try to make data access safe with a condition, as in this pseudo-code:

```
if (no other thread is touching this data)
    do something to the data...
```

Such logic cannot succeed. Suppose the condition succeeds; no other thread is touching this data. But between the time when that condition is executed and the time when the next line executes and you start to do something to the data, another thread can come along and start touching the data!

It is possible to request assistance at a deeper level to ensure that a section of code is not run by two threads simultaneously. For example, you can implement a *lock* around a section of code. But locks generate an entirely new level of potential pitfalls. In general, a lock is an invitation to forget to use the lock, or to forget to remove the lock after you've set it. And threads can end up contending for a lock in a way that permits neither thread to proceed.

Another problem is that the lifetime of a thread is independent of the lifetimes of other objects in your app. When an object is about to go out of existence and its `dealloc` is called, you are guaranteed that after `dealloc` calls `super`, none of your code in that object will ever run again. But a thread might still be running, and might try to talk to your object, even after your object has gone out of existence. You cannot solve this problem by having the thread retain your object, because then there is the danger that the thread might be the *last* code retaining your object, so that when the thread releases your object, its `dealloc` is called on that thread rather than the main thread, which could be a disaster.

Not only is threaded code hard to get right; it's also hard to test and hard to debug. It introduces indeterminacy, so you can easily make a mistake that never appears in your testing, but that does appear for some user. The real danger is that the user's experience will consist only of distant consequences of your mistake, long after the point where you made it, making the real cause of the problem extraordinarily difficult to track down.

All of this is meant to scare you away from using threads if you can possibly avoid it. For an excellent (and suitably frightening) account of some of the dangers and considerations that threading involves, see Apple's tech note TN2109. If terms like *race condition* and *deadlock* don't strike fear into your veins, look them up on Wikipedia.

# Three Ways of Threading

Without pretending to completeness or even safety, this section will illustrate three approaches to threading. To give the examples a common base, we envision an app that draws the Mandelbrot set. (The actual code, not all of which is shown here, is adapted from a small open source project I downloaded from the Internet.) All it does is draw the basic Mandelbrot set in black and white, but that's enough number-crunching to introduce a significant delay. The idea is then to see how we can get that delay off the main thread.

The app contains a UIView subclass, MyMandelbrotView, which has one instance variable:

```
@interface MyMandelbrotView : UIView {
    CGContextRef bitmapContext;
}
// ...
@end
```

Here's the structure of its implementation:

```
// jumping-off point: draw the Mandelbrot set
- (void) drawThatPuppy {
    [self makeBitmapContext: self.bounds.size];
    CGPoint center =
        CGPointMake(CGRectGetMidX(self.bounds), CGRectGetMidY(self.bounds));
    [self drawAtCenter: center zoom: 1];
    [self setNeedsDisplay];
}
```

```
    // create (and memory manage) instance variable
    - (void) makeBitmapContext:(CGSize)size {
        if (self->bitmapContext)
            CGContextRelease(self->bitmapContext);
        // ... configure arguments ...
        CGContextRef context = CGBitmapContextCreate(NULL, /* ... */);
        self->bitmapContext = context;
    }

    // draw pixels of self->bitmapContext
    - (void) drawAtCenter:(CGPoint)center zoom:(CGFloat)zoom {
        // .... do stuff to self->bitmapContext
    }

    // turn pixels of self->bitmapContext into CGImage, draw into ourselves
    - (void) drawRect:(CGRect)rect {
        CGContextRef context = UIGraphicsGetCurrentContext();
        CGImageRef im = CGBitmapContextCreateImage(self->bitmapContext);
        CGContextDrawImage(context, self.bounds, im);
        CGImageRelease(im);
    }

    // final memory managment
    - (void) dealloc {
        if (self->bitmapContext)
            CGContextRelease(bitmapContext);
        [super dealloc];
    }
```

(I haven't discussed creating a bitmap context from scratch; see "Graphics Contexts" in the *Quartz 2D Programming Guide* for example code. In this case, we take advantage of an iOS 4 feature that lets us pass NULL as the first argument to `CGBitmapContext-Create`, which relieves us of the responsibility for creating and memory-managing a data buffer associated with the graphics context.)

The `drawAtCenter:zoom:` method, which calculates the pixels of the instance variable `bitmapContext`, is time-consuming. We will consider three ways of moving this work off onto a background thread: with an old-fashioned manual thread, with NSOperation, and with Grand Central Dispatch.

## Manual Threads

The simple way to make a thread manually is to send `performSelectorInBackground:withObject:` to some object containing a method to be performed on a background thread. Even with this simple approach, there is additional work to do:

*Pack the arguments.*
    The method designated by the first argument to `performSelectorInBackground:withObject:` can take only one parameter, which you supply as the second argument to `performSelectorInBackground:withObject:`. So, if you want to pass more

than one piece of information into the thread, or if the information you want to pass isn't an object, you'll need to pack it into a single object. Typically, this will be an NSDictionary. You should create this dictionary with init... and release it after passing it, because passing an autoreleased argument is unreliable.

*Set up an autorelease pool.*

Secondary threads don't participate in the global autorelease pool. So the first thing you must do in your threaded code is to create an NSAutoreleasePool, and the last thing you must do in your threaded code is to release it. Otherwise, you'll probably leak memory as autoreleased objects are created behind the scenes and are never released.

We'll rewrite MyMandelbrotView to use manual threading. Our drawAtCenter:zoom: method takes two parameters (and neither is an object), so we'll have to pack the argument that we pass into the thread, as a dictionary. Once inside the thread, we'll set up our autorelease pool and unpack the dictionary. This will all be made much easier if we interpose a trampoline method between drawThatPuppy and drawAtCenter:zoom:. So our implementation now looks like this (ignoring the parts that haven't changed):

```
- (void) drawThatPuppy {
    [self makeBitmapContext: self.bounds.size];
    CGPoint center =
        CGPointMake(CGRectGetMidX(self.bounds), CGRectGetMidY(self.bounds));
    NSDictionary* d = [[NSDictionary alloc] initWithObjectsAndKeys:
        [NSValue valueWithCGPoint:center], @"center",
        [NSNumber numberWithInt: 1], @"zoom",
        nil];
    [self performSelectorInBackground:@selector(reallyDraw:) withObject:d];
    [d release];
    // [self setNeedsDisplay];
}

// trampoline, background thread entry point
- (void) reallyDraw: (NSDictionary*) d {
    NSAutoreleasePool* pool = [[NSAutoreleasePool alloc] init];
    [self drawAtCenter: [[d objectForKey:@"center"] CGPointValue]
                  zoom: [[d objectForKey:@"zoom"] intValue]];
    [pool release];
}
```

So far so good, but we haven't yet figured out how to draw our view. We have commented out the call to setNeedsDisplay in drawThatPuppy, because it's too soon; the call to performSelectorInBackground:withObject: launches the thread and returns immediately, so our bitmapContext instance variable isn't ready yet. Clearly, we need to call setNeedsDisplay *after* drawAtCenter:zoom: finishes generating the pixels of the graphics context. We can do this at the end of our trampoline method reallyDraw:, but we must remember that we're now in a background thread. Because setNeedsDisplay is a form of communication with the interface, we should call it on the main thread. We can do that with easily with performSelectorOnMainThread:withObject:waitUntilDone:. For maximum flexibility, it will probably be best to implement a second trampoline method:

```
// trampoline, background thread entry point
- (void) reallyDraw: (NSDictionary*) d {
    NSAutoreleasePool* pool = [[NSAutoreleasePool alloc] init];
    [self drawAtCenter: [[d objectForKey:@"center"] CGPointValue]
                  zoom: [[d objectForKey:@"zoom"] intValue]];
    [self performSelectorOnMainThread:@selector(allDone)
                           withObject:nil waitUntilDone:NO];
    [pool release];
}

// called on main thread! background thread exit point
- (void) allDone {
    [self setNeedsDisplay];
}
```

This code is specious; the seeds of nightmare are already sown. We now have a single object, MyMandelbrotView, some of whose methods are to be called on the main thread and some on a background thread; this invites us to become confused at some later time. Even worse, the main thread and the background thread are constantly sharing a piece of data, the instance variable `bitmapContext`; what's to stop some other code from coming along and triggering `drawRect:` while `drawAtCenter:zoom:` is in the middle of filling `bitmapContext`?

To solve these problems, we might need to use locks, and we would probably have to manage the thread more explicitly. For instance, we might use the NSThread class, which lets us retain our thread as an instance and query it from outside (with `isExecuting` and similar). For example code, see Apple's Metronome example, in *MetronomeView.m*. You'll observe immediately that the Metronome thread-handling code is quite elaborate and difficult to understand, yet it is an extremely basic implementation. In any case, it will be easier at this point to use NSOperation, the subject of the next threading approach.

## NSOperation

The essence of NSOperation is that it encapsulates a task, not a thread. The operation described by an NSOperation object may be performed on a background thread, but you don't have to concern yourself with that directly. You describe the operation and add the NSOperation to an NSOperationQueue to set it going. When the operation finishes, you are notified, typically by the NSOperation posting a notification. You can query both the queue and its operations from outside with regard to their state.

We'll rewrite MyMandelbrotView to use NSOperation. We need a new instance variable, an NSOperationQueue; we'll call it `queue`. And we have a new class, MyMandelbrotOperation, an NSOperation subclass. It is possible to take advantage of a built-in NSOperation subclass such as NSInvocationOperation or (in iOS 4) NSBlockOperation, but I'm deliberately illustrating the more general case by subclassing NSOperation itself.

Our implementation of **drawThatPuppy** makes sure that the queue exists; it then creates an instance of MyMandelbrotOperation, configures it, registers for its notification, and adds it to the queue:

```
- (void) drawThatPuppy {
    CGPoint center =
        CGPointMake(CGRectGetMidX(self.bounds), CGRectGetMidY(self.bounds));
    if (!self.queue) {
        NSOperationQueue* q = [[NSOperationQueue alloc] init];
        self.queue = q; // retain policy
        [q release];
    }
    NSOperation* op =
        [[MyMandelbrotOperation alloc] initWithSize:self.bounds.size
                                         center:center zoom:1];
    [[NSNotificationCenter defaultCenter] addObserver:self
        selector:@selector(operationFinished:)
        name:@"MyMandelbrotOperationFinished"
        object:op];
    [self.queue addOperation:op];
    [op release];
}
```

Our time-consuming calculations are performed by MyMandelbrotOperation. An NSOperation subclass, such as MyMandelbrotOperation, will typically have at least two methods:

*A designated initializer*
> The NSOperation may need some configuration data. Once the NSOperation is added to a queue, it's too late to talk to it, so you'll usually hand it this configuration data as you create it, in its designated initializer.

*A main method*
> This method will be called (with no parameters) automatically by the NSOperationQueue when it's time for the NSOperation to start.

Here's the interface for MyMandelbrotOperation:

```
@interface MyMandelbrotOperation : NSOperation {
    CGSize size;
    CGPoint center;
    CGFloat zoom;
    CGContextRef bitmapContext;
}
- (id) initWithSize: (CGSize) sz center: (CGPoint) c zoom: (CGFloat) z;
- (CGContextRef) bitmapContext;
@end
```

We have provided three instance variables for configuration, to be set in the initializer. Because MyMandelbrotOperation is completely separate from MyMandelbrotView, it must be told MyMandelbrotView's size explicitly in the initializer. MyMandelbrotOperation also has its own CGContextRef instance variable, `bitmapContext`, along with an accessor so MyMandelbrotView can retrieve a reference to this graphics context when the operation has finished. Note that this is different from MyMandelbrotView's `bitmap-Context`; one of the benefits of using NSOperation is that we are no longer sharing data so promiscuously between threads.

Here's the implementation for MyMandelbrotOperation. All the calculation work has been transferred from MyMandelbrotView to MyMandelbrotOperation without change; the only difference is that `bitmapContext` now means MyMandelbrotOperation's instance variable:

```
- (id) initWithSize: (CGSize) sz center: (CGPoint) c zoom: (CGFloat) z {
    self = [super init];
    if (self) {
        self->size = sz;
        self->center = c;
        self->zoom = z;
    }
    return self;
}

- (void) dealloc {
    if (self->bitmapContext)
        CGContextRelease(self->bitmapContext);
    [super dealloc];
}

- (CGContextRef) bitmapContext {
    return self->bitmapContext;
}

- (void)makeBitmapContext:(CGSize)size {
    // ... same as before ...
}

- (void)drawAtCenter:(CGPoint)center zoom:(CGFloat)zoom {
    // ... same as before ...
}

- (void) main {
    if ([self isCancelled])
        return;
    [self makeBitmapContext: self->size];
    [self drawAtCenter: self->center zoom: self->zoom];
    if (![self isCancelled])
        [[NSNotificationCenter defaultCenter]
            postNotificationName:@"MyMandelbrotOperationFinished" object:self];
}
```

The only method of interest is `main`. First, we test through the NSOperation method `isCancelled` to make sure we haven't been cancelled while sitting in the queue; this is good practice. Then, we do exactly what `drawThatPuppy` used to do, initializing our graphics context and drawing into its pixels.

When the operation is over, we need to notify MyMandelbrotView to come and fetch our data. There are two ways to do this; either `main` can post a notification through the NSNotificationCenter, or MyMandelbrotView can use key–value observing (Chapter 13) to be notified when our `isFinished` key path changes. We've chosen the former approach; observe that we check one more time to make sure we haven't been cancelled.

Now we are back in MyMandelbrotView, hearing that MyMandelbrotOperation has finished. We must immediately pick up any required data, because the NSOperation-Queue is about to release this NSOperation. However, we must be careful; the notification may have been posted on a background thread, in which case our method for responding to it will also be called on a background thread. We are about to set our own graphics context and tell ourselves to redraw; those are things we want to do on the main thread. So we immediately step out to the main thread:

```
// warning! called on background thread
- (void) operationFinished: (NSNotification*) n {
    [self performSelectorOnMainThread:@selector(redrawWithOperation:)
                          withObject:[n object] waitUntilDone:NO];
}
```

As we set MyMandelbrotView's `bitmapContext` by reading MyMandelbrotOperation's `bitmapContext`, we must concern ourselves with the memory management of a CGContext obtained from an object that may be about to release that context:

```
// now we're back on the main thread
- (void) redrawWithOperation: (MyMandelbrotOperation*) op {
    [[NSNotificationCenter defaultCenter]
        removeObserver:self
        name:@"MyMandelbrotOperationFinished"
        object:op];
    CGContextRef context = [op bitmapContext];
    if (self->bitmapContext)
        CGContextRelease(self->bitmapContext);
    self->bitmapContext = (CGContextRef) context;
    CGContextRetain(self->bitmapContext);
    [self setNeedsDisplay];
}
```

Using NSOperation instead of manual threading may not seem like any reduction in work, but it is a tremendous reduction in headaches:

*The operation is encapsulated.*

Because MyMandelbrotOperation is an object, we've been able to move all the code having to do with drawing the pixels of the Mandelbrot set into it. No longer does MyMandelbrotView contain some code to be called on the main thread and some code to be called on a background thread. The *only* MyMandelbrotView method that can be called in the background is `operationFinished:`, and that's a method we'd never call explicitly ourselves, so we won't misuse it accidentally.

*The data sharing is rationalized.*
Because MyMandelbrotOperation is an object, it has its own `bitmapContext`. The only moment of data sharing comes in `redrawWithOperation:`, when we must set MyMandelbrotView's `bitmapContext` to MyMandelbrotOperation's `bitmap-Context`. Even if multiple MyMandelbrotOperation objects are added to queue, the moments when we set MyMandelbrotView's `bitmapContext` all occur on the main thread, so they cannot conflict with one another.

The coherence of MyMandelbrotView's `bitmapContext` does depend upon our obedience to an implicit contract not to set it or write into it anywhere except a few specific moments in MyMandelbrotView's code. But this is always a problem with data sharing in a multithreaded world, and we have done all we can to simplify the situation.

If we are concerned with the possibility that more than one instance of MyMandelbrotOperation might be added to the queue and executed concurrently, we have a further defense — we can set the NSOperationQueue's maximum concurrency level to 1:

```
NSOperationQueue* q = [[NSOperationQueue alloc] init];
[q setMaxConcurrentOperationCount:1];
self.queue = q;
[q release];
```

This turns the NSOperationQueue into a true serial queue; every operation on the queue must be completely executed before the next can begin. This might cause an operation added to the queue to take longer to execute, if it must wait for another operation to finish before it can even get started; however, this delay might not be important. What *is* important is that by executing the operations on this queue completely separately, we guarantee that only one operation at a time can do any data sharing. A serial queue is thus a form of data locking.

Because MyMandelbrotView can be destroyed (if, for example, its view controller is destroyed), there is still a risk that it will create an operation that will outlive it and will try to access it after it has been destroyed. We can reduce that risk by canceling all operations in our queue before releasing it:

```
- (void)dealloc {
    // release the bitmap context
    if (self->bitmapContext)
        CGContextRelease(bitmapContext);
    [self->queue cancelAllOperations];
    [self->queue release];
    [super dealloc];
}
```

# Grand Central Dispatch

Grand Central Dispatch, or *GCD*, introduced in iOS 4, is a sort of low-level analogue to NSOperation and NSOperationQueue. When I say low-level, I'm not kidding; GCD is baked into the operating system kernel. Thus it can be used by any code whatsoever and is tremendously efficient.

Using GCD is like a mixture of the manual threading approach with the NSOperationQueue approach. It's like the manual threading approach because code to be executed on one thread appears together with code to be executed on another; however, you have a better chance of keeping the threads and data management straight, because GCD uses Objective-C blocks. It's like the NSOperationQueue approach because it uses queues; you express a task and add it to a queue, and the task is executed on a thread as needed. Moreover, by default these queues are serial queues, with each task on a queue finishing before the next is started, which, as we've already seen, is a form of data locking.

We'll rewrite MyMandelbrotView to use GCD. The structure of its interface is very slightly changed from the original, nonthreaded version. We have a new instance variable to hold our GCD queue; makeBitmapContext: now returns a graphics context rather than setting an instance variable directly; and drawAtCenter:zoom: now takes an additional parameter, the graphics context to draw into:

```
@interface MyMandelbrotView : UIView {
    CGContextRef bitmapContext;
    dispatch_queue_t draw_queue;
}
- (void)drawAtCenter:(CGPoint)center zoom:(CGFloat)zoom context:(CGContextRef)c;
- (CGContextRef)makeBitmapContext:(CGSize)size;
- (void) drawThatPuppy;
@end
```

In MyMandelbrotView's implementation, we add management to create our GCD queue as the view is created and to tear it down as the view is destroyed:

```
- (id)initWithCoder:(NSCoder *)aDecoder {
    self = [super initWithCoder: aDecoder];
    if (self) {
        self->draw_queue = dispatch_queue_create("com.neuburg.mandeldraw", NULL);
    }
    return self;
}

- (void) dealloc {
    if (bitmapContext)
        CGContextRelease(bitmapContext);
    dispatch_release(draw_queue);
    [super dealloc];
}
```

Now for the implementation of drawThatPuppy. Here it is:

```
- (void) drawThatPuppy {
    CGPoint center = ❶
        CGPointMake(CGRectGetMidX(self.bounds), CGRectGetMidY(self.bounds));
    dispatch_async(draw_queue, ^{ ❷
        CGContextRef bitmap = [self makeBitmapContext: self.bounds.size];
```

```
            [self drawAtCenter: center zoom: 1 context:bitmap];
        dispatch_async(dispatch_get_main_queue(), ^{ ❸
            if (self->bitmapContext)
                CGContextRelease(self->bitmapContext);
            self->bitmapContext = bitmap;
            [self setNeedsDisplay];
        });
    });
}
```

That's all there is to it. No trampoline methods. No `performSelector....` No packing arguments into a dictionary. No autorelease pools. No instance variables. And effectively no sharing of data across threads. That's the beauty of blocks.

❶ We begin by calculating our `center`, as before. This value will be visible within the blocks, because blocks can see their surrounding context.

❷ Now comes our task to be performed in a background thread on our queue, `draw_queue`. We specify this task with the `dispatch_async` function. GCD has a lot of functions, but this is the one you'll use 99 percent of the time; it's the most important thing you need to know about GCD. We specify a queue and we provide a block saying what we'd like to do. Thanks to the block, we don't need any trampoline methods. In the block, we begin by declaring `bitmap` as a variable *local to the block*. We then call `makeBitmapContext:` to create the graphics context `bitmap`, and `drawAtCenter:zoom:context:` to set its pixels; we make these calls *directly*, just as we would do if we weren't threading in the first place.

❸ Now we need to get back onto the main thread. How do we do that? With `dispatch_async` again! We specify the main queue (which is effectively the main thread) with a function provided for this purpose and describe what we want to do in *another* block. This second block is nested inside the first, so it isn't performed until the preceding commands in the first block have finished; moreover, because the first block is part of its surrounding context, the second block can see our block-local `bitmap` variable! We set our `bitmapContext` instance variable (with no need for further memory management, because `makeBitmapContext` has returned a retained graphics context), and call `setNeedsDisplay`.

The benefits and elegance of GCD are stunning. The `bitmap` variable is not shared; it is local to each specific call to `drawThatPuppy`. The nested blocks are executed in succession, so any instance of `bitmap` must be completely filled with pixels before being used to set the `bitmapContext` instance variable. Moreover, `bitmapContext` is set on the main thread, plus the *entire* operation is performed on a serial queue; thus data sharing is reduced to a minimum, with no possibility of conflict. Our code is also highly maintainable, because the entire task on all threads is expressed within the single `drawThatPuppy` method, thanks to the use of blocks; indeed, the code is only very slightly modified from the original, nonthreaded version.

# Threads and App Backgrounding

When your app is backgrounded and suspended (Chapter 11), a problem arises if your code is running. The system doesn't want to kill your code while it's executing; on the other hand, some other app may need to be given the bulk of the device's resources now. So as your app goes into the background, the system waits a short time for your app to finish doing whatever it may be doing, but it then suspends your app and stops it by force.

This shouldn't be a problem from your main thread's point of view, because your app shouldn't have any time-consuming code on the main thread in the first place; you now know that you can avoid this by using a background thread. On the other hand, it could be a problem for lengthy background operations, including asynchronous tasks performed by the frameworks. You can request time to complete a lengthy task (or at least abort it yourself, coherently) in case your app is backgrounded, by wrapping it in calls to UIApplication's `beginBackgroundTaskWithExpirationHandler:` and `endBackgroundTask:`.

You call `beginBackgroundTaskWithExpirationHandler:` to announce that a lengthy task is beginning; it returns an identification number. At the end of your lengthy task, you call `endBackgroundTask:`, passing in that same identification number. This tells the application that your lengthy task is over and that, if your app has been backgrounded while the task was in progress, it is now okay to suspend you.

The argument to `beginBackgroundTaskWithExpirationHandler:` is a block, but this block does *not* express the lengthy task. It expresses what you will do *if your extra time expires* before you finish your lengthy task. At the very least, your expiration handler must call `endBackgroundTask:`, just as your lengthy task would have done; otherwise, your app won't just be suspended — it will be killed.

 If your expiration handler block *is* called, you should make no assumptions about what thread it is running on.

Let's use MyMandelbrotView, from the preceding section, as an example. Let's say that if `drawThatPuppy` is started, we'd like it to be allowed to finish, even if the app is suspended in the middle of it, so that our `bitmapContext` instance variable is updated as requested. To try to ensure this, we call `beginBackgroundTaskWithExpirationHandler:` beforehand and call `endBackgroundTask:` at the end of the innermost block:

```
- (void) drawThatPuppy {
    CGPoint center =
        CGPointMake(CGRectGetMidX(self.bounds), CGRectGetMidY(self.bounds));
    UIBackgroundTaskIdentifier bti = [[UIApplication sharedApplication]
                            beginBackgroundTaskWithExpirationHandler: ^{
        [[UIApplication sharedApplication] endBackgroundTask:bti];
```

```
    }];
    dispatch_async(draw_queue, ^{
        CGContextRef bitmap = [self makeBitmapContext: self.bounds.size];
        [self drawAtCenter: center zoom: 1 context:bitmap];
        dispatch_async(dispatch_get_main_queue(), ^{
            if (self->bitmapContext)
                CGContextRelease(self->bitmapContext);
            self->bitmapContext = bitmap;
            [self setNeedsDisplay];
            [[UIApplication sharedApplication] endBackgroundTask:bti];
        });
    });
}
```

If our app is backgrounded while drawThatPuppy is in progress, it will (we hope) be given enough time to live that it can run all the way to the end. Thus, the instance variable bitmapContext will be updated, and setNeedsDisplay will be called, before we are actually suspended. Our drawRect: will not be called until our app is brought back to the front, but there's nothing wrong with that.

It's actually pretty good policy to use a similar technique when you're notified that your app is being backgrounded. It's common practice to respond to the app delegate message applicationDidEnterBackground: (or the corresponding UIApplicationDidEnter-BackgroundNotification) by saving state and reducing memory usage, but this can take time, whereas what you'd like to do is return from applicationDidEnterBackground: as quickly as possible. A reasonable solution is to implement applicationDidEnter-Background: very much like drawThatPuppy earlier: call beginBackgroundTaskWith-ExpirationHandler: and then call dispatch_async to get off the main thread, and do your state-saving and so forth in its block. In this case, there's no point creating your own queue, because you don't care about serial order; you can use dispatch_get_global_queue(0), the default-priority global background queue.

What about lengthy asynchronous operations such as networking (Chapter 37)? As far as I can tell, it might not strictly be necessary to use beginBackgroundTaskWithExpiration-Handler: in connection with NSURLConnection; it appears that NSURLConnection has the ability to resume automatically after an interruption when your app is suspended. Still, it might be better not to rely on that behavior (or on an assumption that, just because the network is present now, it will be present when the app awakes from suspension), so you might like to integrate beginBackgroundTaskWithExpirationHandler: into your use of NSURLConnection.

Such integration can be just a little tricky, because beginBackgroundTaskWithExpiration-Handler: and endBackgroundTask: rely on a shared piece of information, the UIBackgroundTaskIdentifier — but the downloading operation begins in one place (when the NSURLConnection is created, or when it is told to start) and ends in one of two other places (the NSURLConnection's delegate is informed that the download has failed or succeeded), so information is not so easily shared. However, with something like our MyDownloader class, an entire single downloading operation is encapsulated, and we can give the class a UIBackgroundTaskIdentifier instance variable. So, we would set this instance variable with a call to `beginBackgroundTaskWithExpirationHandler:` just before telling the connection to `start`, and then both `connection:didFailWithError:` and `connectionDidFinishLoading:` would use the value stored in that instance variable to call `endBackgroundTask:` as their last action.

# CHAPTER 39

# Undo

The ability to undo the most recent action is familiar from Mac OS X. Typically, a Mac application will maintain an internal stack of undoable actions; choosing Edit → Undo or pressing Command-Z will reverse the action at the top of the stack, and will also make that action available for Redo so that the user can undo the most recent Undo. The idea is that, provided the user realizes soon enough that a mistake has been made, that mistake can be reversed.

A pervasive, extensive implementation of Undo makes sense on Mac OS X, especially when real-life objects are involved. For example, a window may represent an actual document, a file on disk; it would be terrible if every word typed or pasted or cut represented a permanent, irreversible change to that document. Given the transient, visual nature of the iOS interface, however, and the sorts of thing for which iOS apps are typically intended, users do not generally expect Undo at all.

Nevertheless, some iOS apps may benefit from at least a limited version of this facility. Not every action needs to be undoable, and the ability to undo needn't persist for very long. And limited Undo is not difficult to implement. Some built-in views — in particular, those that involve text entry, UITextField and UITextView (Chapter 23) — implement Undo already. And you can add it in other areas of your app.

## The Undo Manager

Undo is provided through an instance of NSUndoManager, which basically just maintains a stack of undoable actions, along with a secondary stack of redoable actions. The goal in general is to work with the NSUndoManager so as to take care of handling both Undo and Redo in the standard manner: When the user chooses to undo the most recent action, the action at the top of the Undo stack is popped off and reversed and is pushed onto the top of the Redo stack.

To illustrate, I'll use an artificially simple app in which the user can drag a small square around the screen. We'll start with an instance of a UIView subclass, MyView, to which has been attached a UIPanGestureRecognizer to make it draggable, as described in Chapter 18. The gesture recognizer's action target is the MyView instance itself:

```
- (void) dragging: (UIPanGestureRecognizer*) p {
    if (p.state == UIGestureRecognizerStateBegan ||
            p.state == UIGestureRecognizerStateChanged) {
        CGPoint delta = [p translationInView: self.superview];
        CGPoint c = self.center;
        c.x += delta.x; c.y += delta.y;
        self.center = c;
        [p setTranslation: CGPointZero inView: self.superview];
    }
}
```

To make dragging of this view undoable, we need an NSUndoManager instance. Let's store this in an instance variable of MyView itself, accessible through a property, undoer.

There are two ways to register an action as undoable. One involves the NSUndoManager method `registerUndoWithTarget:selector:object:`. This method uses a target–action architecture: you provide a target, a selector for a method that takes one parameter, and the object value to be passed as argument when the method is called. Then, later, if the NSUndoManager is sent the undo message, it simply sends that action with that argument to that target. What we want to undo here is the setting of our center property. This can't expressed directly using a target–action architecture: we can call `setCenter:`, but its parameter needs to be a CGPoint, which isn't an object. This means we're going to have to provide a secondary method that *does* take an object parameter. This is neither bad nor unusual; it is quite common for actions to have a special representation just for the purpose of making them undoable.

So, in our `dragging:` method, instead of setting `self.center` to c directly, we now call a secondary method (let's call it `setCenterUndoably:`):

```
[self setCenterUndoably: [NSValue valueWithCGPoint:c]];
```

At a minimum, `setCenterUndoably:` should do the job that setting `self.center` used to do:

```
- (void) setCenterUndoably: (NSValue*) newCenter {
    self.center = [newCenter CGPointValue];
}
```

This works in the sense that the view is draggable exactly as before, but we have not yet made this action undoable. To do so, we must ask ourselves what message the NSUndoManager would need to send in order to undo the action we are about to perform. We would want the NSUndoManager to set `self.center` back to the value it has *now*, before we change it as we are about to do. And what method would NSUndoManager call in order to do that? It would call `setCenterUndoably:`, the very method we are implementing; that's *why* we are implementing it. So:

```
- (void) setCenterUndoably: (NSValue*) newCenter {
    [self.undoer registerUndoWithTarget:self
                    selector:@selector(setCenterUndoably:)
```

```
                        object:[NSValue valueWithCGPoint:self.center]]];
        self.center = [newCenter CGPointValue];
    }
```

This not only makes our action undoable, it also makes it redoable. Why? Because when we send undo to the NSUndoManager, it calls setCenterUndoably: and is immediately sent registerUndo... — and there's a rule that, if the NSUndoManager is sent this message *while it is undoing*, it puts the target–action information on the Redo stack instead of the Undo stack (because Redo *is* the Undo of an Undo, if you see what I mean). That's one of the chief tricks to working with an NSUndoManager: it will respond differently to registerUndo... depending on its state.

So far, so good. But our implementation of undoing is very annoying, because we are adding a single object to the Undo stack every time dragging: is called — and it is called many times during the course of a single drag. Thus, undoing merely undoes the tiny increment corresponding to one particular dragging: call. What we'd like, surely, is for undoing to undo an *entire* dragging gesture. We can implement this through *undo grouping*. As the gesture begins, we start a group; when the gesture ends, we end the group:

```
    - (void) dragging: (UIPanGestureRecognizer*) p {
        if (p.state == UIGestureRecognizerStateBegan)
            [self.undoer beginUndoGrouping];
        if (p.state == UIGestureRecognizerStateBegan ||
                p.state == UIGestureRecognizerStateChanged) {
            CGPoint delta = [p translationInView: self.superview];
            CGPoint c = self.center;
            c.x += delta.x; c.y += delta.y;
            [self setCenterUndoably: [NSValue valueWithCGPoint:c]];
            [p setTranslation: CGPointZero inView: self.superview];
        }
        if (p.state == UIGestureRecognizerStateEnded ||
                p.state == UIGestureRecognizerStateCancelled)
            [self.undoer endUndoGrouping];
    }
```

This works: each complete gesture of dragging MyView, from the time the user's finger contacts the view to the time it leaves, is now undoable (and then redoable) as a single unit.

Earlier I said that registerUndo... was one of two ways to register an action as undoable. The other is to use prepareWithInvocationTarget:. You provide the target and, *in the same line of code*, send to the object returned from this call the message and arguments you want sent when the NSUndoManager is sent undo (or, if we are undoing now, redo). So, in our example, instead of this line:

```
    [self.undoer registerUndoWithTarget:self
                        selector:@selector(setCenterUndoably:)
                        object:[NSValue valueWithCGPoint:self.center]];
```

You'd say this:

```
[[self.undoer prepareWithInvocationTarget:self]
   setCenterUndoably: [NSValue valueWithCGPoint:self.center]];
```

This code seems impossible: how can we send setCenterUndoably: without *calling* set-CenterUndoably:? Either we are sending it to self, in which case it should actually be called at this moment, or we are sending it to some other object that doesn't implement setCenterUndoably:, in which case our app should crash. However, under the hood, the NSUndoManager is cleverly using Objective-C's dynamism (similarly to the message-forwarding example at the end of Chapter 25) to capture this call as an NSInvocation object, which it can use later to send the same message with the same arguments to the specified target.

In our example, prepareWithInvocationTarget: provides no particular advantage over registerUndo.... In general, the advantage of prepareWithInvocationTarget: is that it lets you specify a method with any number of parameters, and those parameters needn't be objects.

# The Undo Interface

We must now decide how to let the user request Undo and Redo. In testing the code from the preceding section, I used two buttons, an Undo button that sent undo to the NSUndoManager and a Redo button that sent redo to the NSUndoManager. This can be a perfectly reasonable interface, but let's talk about some others.

By default, your application supports *shake-to-edit*. This means the user can shake the device to bring up an undo/redo interface. We discussed this briefly in Chapter 35. If you don't turn off this feature by setting the shared UIApplication's application-SupportsShakeToEdit property to NO, then when the user shakes the device, the framework walks up the responder chain, starting with the first responder, looking for a responder whose undoManager property returns an actual NSUndoManager instance. If it finds one, it puts up the undo/redo interface and communicates appropriately with that NSUndoManager, depending on the user's choice in that interface.

You will recall what it takes for a UIResponder to be first responder in this sense: it must return YES from canBecomeFirstResponder, and it must actually be made first responder through a call to becomeFirstResponder. Let's suppose that MyView satisfies these requirements (for example, we might call becomeFirstResponder at the start of dragging:). Then, to make shake-to-edit work, we must also set its undoManager property instead of its undoer property as we are now doing. However, the inherited undo-Manager property is read-only, so in order to set it, we must override its property declaration, which we can do through a class extension. For example:

```
@interface MyView ()
@property (nonatomic, retain) NSUndoManager *undoManager;
@end

@implementation MyView
@synthesize undoManager;
```

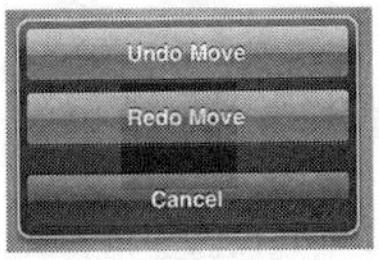

Figure 39-1. The shake-to-edit undo/redo interface

```
- (id)initWithCoder:(NSCoder *)aDecoder {
    self = [super initWithCoder:aDecoder];
    NSUndoManager* u = [[NSUndoManager alloc] init];
    self.undoManager = u; // retain policy
    [u release];
    return self;
}

- (BOOL) canBecomeFirstResponder {
    return YES;
}

- (void) dragging: (UIPanGestureRecognizer*) p {
    [self becomeFirstResponder];
    // ... the rest as before ...
}
//...
@end
```

This works: shaking the device now brings up the undo/redo interface, and its buttons work correctly. However, I don't like the way the buttons are labeled; they just say Undo and Redo. To make them more expressive, we should provide a string describing each undoable action by calling setActionName:. We can appropriately and conveniently do this in setCenterUndoably:, as follows:

```
- (void) setCenterUndoably: (NSValue*) newCenter {
    [self.undoer registerUndoWithTarget:self
                               selector:@selector(setCenterUndoably:)
                                 object:[NSValue valueWithCGPoint:self.center]];
    [self.undoManager setActionName: @"Move"];
    self.center = [newCenter CGPointValue];
}
```

Now the buttons say Undo Move and Redo Move, which is a nice touch (Figure 39-1).

Another possible interface is through a menu (Figure 39-2). Personally, I prefer this approach, as I am not fond of shake-to-edit (it seems both violent and unreliable). This is the same menu used by a UITextField or UITextView for displaying the Copy and Paste menu items (Chapter 23). The requirements for summoning this menu are effectively the same as those for shake-to-edit: we need a responder chain with a first responder at the bottom of it. So the code we've just supplied for making MyView first responder remains applicable.

*Figure 39-2. The shared menu as an undo/redo interface*

We can make a menu appear, for example, in response to a long press on our MyView instance. So let's suppose we've attached another gesture recognizer to MyView. This will be a UILongPressGestureRecognizer, whose action handler is called `longPress:`. Recall from Chapter 23 how to implement the menu: we get the singleton global UIMenuController object and specify an array of custom UIMenuItems as its `menuItems` property. But a *particular* menu item will appear only if we return YES from `canPerformAction:withSender:` for that menu item's action:

```
- (void) longPress: (id) g {
    UIMenuController *m = [UIMenuController sharedMenuController];
    [m setTargetRect:self.bounds inView:self];
    UIMenuItem *mi1 =
        [[UIMenuItem alloc] initWithTitle:[self.undoManager undoMenuItemTitle]
                                   action:@selector(undo:)];
    UIMenuItem *mi2 =
        [[UIMenuItem alloc] initWithTitle:[self.undoManager redoMenuItemTitle]
                                   action:@selector(redo:)];
    [m setMenuItems:[NSArray arrayWithObjects: mi1, mi2, nil]];
    [mi1 release]; [mi2 release];
    [m setMenuVisible:YES animated:YES];
}

- (BOOL)canPerformAction:(SEL)action withSender:(id)sender {
    if (action == @selector(undo:))
        return [self.undoManager canUndo];
    if (action == @selector(redo:))
        return [self.undoManager canRedo];
    return [super canPerformAction:action withSender:sender];
}

- (void) undo: (id) dummy {
    [self.undoManager undo];
}

- (void) redo: (id) dummy {
    [self.undoManager redo];
}
```

Observe how we consult our NSUndoManager throughout. We get the titles for our custom menu items from the NSUndoManager (there might, after all, be more than one undoable kind of action, and therefore more than one title), and we know whether to display the Undo menu item or the Redo menu item by calling our NSUndoManager's `canUndo` and `canRedo`, which essentially asks whether there's anything on the respective stack.

# The Undo Architecture

Implementing basic Undo is not particularly difficult. But maintaining an appropriate Undo stack at the right point (or points) in your responder hierarchy, so that the right thing happens at every moment, can require some work and some thought. Many questions can arise, and there are no simple answers.

In general, your chief concern will be maintaining a consistent state in your app and in the Undo and Redo stacks of any NSUndoManager instances. You don't want an Undo stack to contain a method call that, if actually sent, would be impossible to obey, or, if obeyed, would make nonsense of your app's state, because of things that have happened in the meantime. In order to prevent this, you have to make sure you are not implementing Undo only partially. Suppose, for example, your app presents a To-Do list in which the user can add items, edit items, and so forth. And suppose you implemented Undo and Redo for inserting an item but not for editing an item. Then if the user inserted an item and then edited it, and then did an Undo of an item insertion followed by a Redo of that item insertion, this would fail to restore the state of the app, because the editing has been omitted from the Redo.

This is why you typically want each undoable action to pass consistently through a bottleneck method that will register this action with the NSUndoManager. And you will usually want this bottleneck method to be the same method that is registered with the NSUndoManager, so that the Undo and Redo stacks are kept synchronized properly. The sole exception involves independent constructive and destructive actions, such as insertion into a list and deletion from that list; in that case, the Undo method for insertion will be the deletion method, and the Undo method for deletion will be the insertion method. You can customize the arrangement of bottlenecks further and in more complex ways, but it's easy to become confused, so you probably won't want to.

Not all aspects of communication with an NSUndoManager need to be performed in the same place, however. We already saw this in the examples earlier in this chapter: `setCenterUndoably:`, the bottleneck method, knows what method to register with the NSUndoManager, but `dragging:` knows what a complete gesture is and therefore knows where to place the boundaries of a group. Similarly, it happens that our bottleneck method is the one that called `setActionName:`, but in real life it will often be some other method that knows best what name should be attached to a particular action. You will thus end up with a single NSUndoManager being bombarded with messages from various places in your code. Indeed, NSUndoManager accomodates exactly this sort of design; for example, it emits many notifications for which you can register, to help tie together operations that are performed at disparate locations in your code.

Then there are the larger architectural questions of how many NSUndoManager objects your app needs and how long each one needs to live. There's typically nothing wrong with an iOS app having occasional short-lived, short-depth Undo stacks and no Undo the rest of the time. Apple's SimpleUndo example constructs an app with an Edit interface, where the user makes changes and then taps either Cancel or Save, returning to the main interface. Here, the user can shake to undo what happened during that edit session. And that's all that's undoable within this app. If the user taps Edit again, one imagines that it would make sense to clear the existing Undo stack; there's no point in letting the user return to an earlier Edit session's state. If the user switches away to a different view controller altogether, one imagines that it would make sense to release the NSUndoManager completely and start with a clean slate when we come back; if the user had any intention of undoing, the time to do so was before abandoning this part of the interface.

Your architectural decisions will often be closely tied to the actual functionality and nature of your app. For example, consider again the MyView instance that the user can move, and whose movements the user can undo. Suppose our app has *two* MyView instances in the same window. In our earlier examples, we've implemented Undo at the level of the individual MyView instance. Is this right when there are multiple MyView instances, or should we move the implementation to a higher point in the responder chain that effectively contains them both — for example, to the view controller of whose view they are subviews? The answer is that there's no right answer. It depends on what makes sense for what our app actually does. If these are fairly independent objects, in terms of the app's functionality and the mental world it creates, then it might make sense to be able to undo a move of either view, independently of the other. But if these are, say, two playing cards in a deck, then obviously it isn't up to an individual card whether it can be put back into the place it was before; the only undoable card is the most recently moved of *all* cards.

For more about the NSUndoManager class and how to use it, read Apple's *Undo Architecture* as well as the documentation for the class itself.

# CHAPTER 40

# Epilogue

*You may go, for you're at liberty.*

—W. S. Gilbert, *The Pirates of Penzance*

This book must come to an end, but your exploration of iOS will go on and on. There's much more to know and to explore. A single book that described completely, or even introduced, every aspect of iOS programming would be immense — many times the size of this one. Inevitably, severe limits have had to be set. Having read this book, you are now in a position to investigate many further areas of iOS that this book hasn't explored in any depth. Some of these areas have been mentioned in individual chapters; here are a few others:

*OpenGL*
> An open source C library for drawing, including 3D drawing, that takes full advantage of graphics hardware. This is often the most efficient way to draw, especially when animation is involved. iOS incorporates a simplified version of OpenGL called OpenGL ES. See the *OpenGL Programming Guide for iOS*. Also, some forms of animated display (chiefly, but not exclusively, those using OpenGL) will benefit from CADisplayLink, a timer object that calls a method repeatedly based on the refresh rate of the screen's physical display.

*Accelerate framework*
> Certain computation-intensive processes will benefit from the vector-based Accelerate framework, added in iOS 4. See the *vDSP Programming Guide*.

*Game Kit*
> The Game Kit framework covers three areas that can enhance your user's game experience: Wireless or Bluetooth communication directly between devices (peer-to-peer); voice communication across an existing network connection; and Game Center, a networking facility introduced in iOS 4.1 that facilitates these and many other aspects of interplayer communication, such as posting and viewing high scores and setting up combinations of players who wish to compete. See the *Game Kit Programming Guide*.

*Advertising*

The iAD framework, added in iOS 4, lets your free app attempt to make money by displaying advertisements provided by Apple. See the *iAD Programming Guide*.

*Purchases*

Your app can allow the user to buy something, using Apple's App Store to process payments. See the *In App Purchase Programming Guide*.

*Printing*

Printing was added to iOS in version 4.2. See the "Printing" chapter of the *Drawing and Printing Guide for iOS*.

*Security*

This book has not discussed security topics such as keychains, certificates, and encryption. See the *Security Overview* and the Security framework.

*Accessibility*

VoiceOver assists visually impaired users by describing the interface aloud. To participate, views must be configured to describe themselves usefully. Built-in views already do this to a large extent, and you can add to this functionality. See the *Accessibility Programming Guide for iOS*.

*Telephone*

The Core Telephony framework, introduced in iOS 4, lets your app get information about a particular cellular carrier and call.

*External accessories*

The user can attach an external accessory to the device, either directly via USB or wirelessly via Bluetooth. Your app can communicate with such an accessory. See *External Accessory Programming Topics*.

# Index

## A

ABNewPersonController, 692
ABPeoplePickerNavigationController, 690
ABPerson, 687
ABPersonViewController, 692
ABRecordRef, 688
ABUnknownPersonViewController, 693
accelerometer, 722
accessors, 84, 249
accessors and memory management, 260
accessors, synthesized, 272
accessory views, 510, 531
action connections, 143
action mechanism, 389
action message, 143, 604
action message of a gesture recognizer, 412
action search, 390
action selector signatures, 235, 604
action sheet, 631
action target of a control, 234
action target of a gesture recognizer, 412
actions (animation), 389
actions (control), 142, 233, 604
actions, nil-targeted, 238
activity indicator, 597
   network activity in status bar, 598
ad hoc distribution, 186
address book, 687
Address Book framework, 687
Address Book UI framework, 687
address operator, 22, 60
adopting a protocol, 203
ALAsset, 684
alert view, 630, 636

Alfke, Jens, 170
alloc, 74
analyze, 176
angle brackets in import directive, 26
animating a layer, 371, 374
animating a view, 362
animation, 357–395
   action mechanism, 389
   action search, 390
   block-based view animation, 368
   delegate of an animation, 364, 375
   grouped animations, 381
   hit-testing during animation, 426
   keyframe animation, 379
   layer animation, explicit, 374
   layer animation, implicit, 371
   layer, adding an animation to, 386
   properties, animatable, 371
   properties, custom animatable, 380
   redrawing with animation, 366, 370, 385
   subviews, animating, 370, 394
   transactions, 372
   transitions, 366, 370, 385
   UIImageView animation, 361
   view animation, 362
animation blocks, 362
animation synchronized with video, 663
animation triggered immediately, 373
animation "movie", 358
animations list, 386
annotation (on map), 706
API, 1
API of a class, 36
app bundle, getting a resource inside, 312
app delegate, 133, 230

We'd like to hear your suggestions for improving our indexes. Send email to *index@oreilly.com*.

---

keyboard, language of, 572
keyboard, scrolling in response to, 569
keyframe animation, 379
key–value coding, 86, 251–254
key–value coding and layers, 354
key–value coding and transforms, 352
key–value coding compliant, 252
key–value coding method names hard to
    discover, 254
key–value coding retains instance variables,
    263
key–value coding violates privacy, 251
key–value observing, 284
KVC, 86
    (see also key–value coding)
KVO, 284

# L

label punches hole in cell, 511
labels, 564–565
labels in built-in cell styles, 509
labels in nib editor, 128
landscape orientation at startup, 449
later feature used on earlier system, 160
launch images, 189
layer animation, explicit, 374
layer animation, implicit, 371
layer contents, setting to a UIImage, 342
layer coordinates, 339
layer delegate, changing, 337, 342
layer hierarchy, 337
layer size, forgetting to set, 340
layer, adding an animation to, 386
layering order of views, 296
layers, 335–395
    animating a layer, 371, 374
    animations list, 386
    contents of a layer, 341
    depth of layers, 339, 350
    drawing a layer, 341
    gradients, 346
    hit-testing layers, 424
    key–value coding and layers, 354
    layout of sublayers, 341
    mask, 353
    opaque, 343
    position of a sublayer, 339
    shape layers, 346
    text layers, 346, 581

    transparent background, 343
    layout of sublayers, 341
    layout of subviews, 302
    layout of table view cells, 513
leaks, memory, 254
library, music, 667
library, photo, 679
library, standard C, 27
libsqlite3, 746
libxml2, 745
LIFO, 39
Link Binary With Libraries build phase, 109
linking to a framework, 122
listing a folder's contents, 730
literal NSString, 7
LLDB, 175
LLVM, 6
loading a nib file, 132, 135
loading a view controller's view, 441
loadView, 438, 442
local notifications, 636
localization, 162
location services, 717
locks, 764
Log navigator, 102
logging, 169
logical operators, 18
Love, Tom, 43
lowercase variable names, 6
lproj folders, 163

# M

macros, 28
magic numbers, 27
magnetometer, 719
mail, 703
main function, 25, 121
main nib file, 133
main thread, 761
main window, 133, 293, 294
main window coordinates, 300
main window, background color of, 295
main window, overlapped by status bar, 299
maintenance of state, 39
manual threading, 766
Map Kit framework, 705
maps, 705
Maps app, 705
mask, 353

object-based programming, 31
object-oriented programming, 82
Objective-C, 3, 43–91, 200–208
Objective-C 2.0, 86, 87
Objective-C is C, forgetting, 3
Objective-C, history of, 43
opaque, 309, 319, 343
operators
    address operator, 22, 60
    arithmetic operators, 13
    arrow operator, 85
    bitwise operators, 14
    decrement operator, 14
    equality operator, 18
    increment operator, 14
    logical operators, 18
    relational operators, 18
    sizeof operator, 24
    structure pointer operator, 85
    ternary operator, 15
optimizing, 184
optional methods, 206
orientation of device, 722
orientation of interface at startup, 449
outlet broken by misused accessor name, 250
outlet collections, 142
outlet connections, 135
outlet, forgetting to connect, 139
outlets, 135
overlapping views, 295
overlay (on map), 712
overloading, 53
overriding, 66, 82
overriding a synthesized accessor, 275
owner of nib file, 132

# P

page control, 606
paging, 487
parameter, 20, 50
parameter lists, 53
parentheses around condition, forgetting, 16
password field, 572
pasteboard, 576
paths
    compound paths, 323
    drawing a path, 321
patterns, 328
PDF, 587

phases of a touch, 398
photo library, 679
photo, taking, 681
Photos app, 679
picker view, 600
pixels vs. points, 332
pixels, transparent, 426
Plato, 34
plus sign (class method), 36, 51
pointer to class name, 43
pointer to function, 60
pointer to pointer to NSError, 23, 46
pointer-to-struct (see struct pointers)
pointer-to-void, 11
pointer-to-void, memory management of, 269
pointers, 10
    assignment to a pointer, 11, 47
    creating a pointer, 22
    dangling pointers, 255
    declaring a pointer, 10
    garbage pointer, 45
    generic pointer, 11
    memory management, 48
    nilifying, 257
points vs. pixels, 332
polar coordinates, 618
polymorphism, 78–82
pool, autorelease, 264, 767
popovers, 549–558, 631–635
popovers, automatic, 557
popovers, dismissing, 553, 554
popovers, presenting, 550
popovers, size of, 551
Portal, iOS Provisioning, 178
position of a sublayer, 339
position of a subview, 298
posting a notification, 226
pragma directive, 28, 167
precompiled header, 121
preprocessing, 5
    define directive, 27
    import directive, 26
    include directive, 24
    pragma directive, 28
presentation layer, 361, 427
presenting action sheet clipped by its
        superview, 632
previewing a document, 738
private methods, 202

# Y

# Z

## About the Author

**Matt Neuburg** has a PhD in Classics and has taught at many universities and colleges. He has been programming computers since 1968. He has written applications for Mac OS X and iOS, is a former editor of *MacTech Magazine*, and is a long-standing contributing editor for TidBITS. His previous O'Reilly books are *Frontier: The Definitive Guide*, *REALbasic: The Definitive Guide*, and *AppleScript: The Definitive Guide*. He makes a living writing books, articles, and software documentation, as well as by programming, consulting, and training.

## Colophon

The animal on the cover of *Programming iOS 4* is a kingbird, one of the 13 species of North American songbirds making up the genus *Tyrannus*. A group of kingbirds is called a "coronation," a "court," or a "tyranny."

Kingbirds eat insects, which they often catch in flight, swooping from a perch to grab the insect midair. They may also supplement their diets with berries and fruits. They have long, pointed wings, and males perform elaborate aerial courtship displays.

Both the genus name (meaning "tyrant" or "despot") and the common name ("kingbird") refer to these birds' aggressive defense of their territories, breeding areas, and mates. They have been documented attacking red-tailed hawks (which are more than twenty times their size), knocking bluejays out of trees, and driving away crows and ravens. (For its habit of standing up to much larger birds, the gray kingbird has been adopted as a Puerto Rican nationalist symbol.)

"Kingbird" most often refers to the Eastern kingbird (*T. tyrannus*), an average-size kingbird (7.5–9 inches long, wingspan 13–15 inches) found all across North America. This common and widespread bird has a dark head and back, with a white throat, chest, and belly. Its red crown patch is rarely seen. Its high-pitched, buzzing, stuttering sounds have been described as resembling "sparks jumping between wires" or an electric fence.

The cover image is from *Cassell's Natural History*. The cover font is Adobe ITC Garamond. The text font is Linotype Birka; the heading font is Adobe Myriad Condensed; and the code font is LucasFont's TheSansMonoCondensed.

# Related Titles from O'Reilly

## Macintosh

AppleScript: The Definitive Guide, *2nd Edition*

AppleScript: The Missing Manual

Appleworks 6: The Missing Manual

The Best of the Joy of Tech

FileMaker Pro 8: The Missing Manual

FileMaker Pro 9: The Missing Manual

GarageBand 2: The Missing Manual

iBook Fan Book

iMovie 6 & iDVD: The Missing Manual

iPhone Forensics

iPhone Hacks

iPhone: The Missing Manual, *3rd Edition*

iPhoto '08: The Missing Manual

iPod: The Missing Manual, *8th Edition*

iWork '09: The Missing Manual

Mac Annoyances

Mac OS X Tiger Pocket Guide

Mac OS X Leopard Pocket Guide

Mac OS X Snow Leopard Pocket Guide

Mac OS X: The Missing Manual, *Tiger Edition*

Mac OS X Leopard: The Missing Manual

Mac OS X Power Hound, *2nd Edition*

Mac OS X Snow Leopard: The Missing Manual

Mac OS X Unwired

Modding Mac OS X

Office 2008 for the Macintosh: The Missing Manual

Revolution in The Valley

Switching to the Mac: The Missing Manual, *Snow Leopard Edition*

## Mac Developers

Building Cocoa Applications: A Step-By-Step Guide

Cocoa in a Nutshell

Essential Mac OS X Panther Server Administration

Learning Carbon

Learning Cocoa with Objective-C, *2nd Edition*

Learning Unix for Mac OS X Tiger

Mac OS X for Java Geeks

Mac OS X for Unix Geeks, *4th Edition*

Mac OS X Panther Hacks

Mac OS X Tiger in a Nutshell

Objective-C Pocket Reference

Running Mac OS X Tiger

# Get even more for your money.

**Join the O'Reilly Community, and register the O'Reilly books you own. It's free, and you'll get:**

- $4.99 ebook upgrade offer
- 40% upgrade offer on O'Reilly print books
- Membership discounts on books and events
- Free lifetime updates to ebooks and videos
- Multiple ebook formats, DRM FREE
- Participation in the O'Reilly community
- Newsletters
- Account management
- 100% Satisfaction Guarantee

**Signing up is easy:**

1. **Go to: oreilly.com/go/register**
2. **Create an O'Reilly login.**
3. **Provide your address.**
4. **Register your books.**

Note: English-language books only

**To order books online:**
oreilly.com/store

**For questions about products or an order:**
orders@oreilly.com

**To sign up to get topic-specific email announcements and/or news about upcoming books, conferences, special offers, and new technologies:**
elists@oreilly.com

**For technical questions about book content:**
booktech@oreilly.com

**To submit new book proposals to our editors:**
proposals@oreilly.com

**O'Reilly books are available in multiple DRM-free ebook formats. For more information:**
oreilly.com/ebooks

**O'REILLY**®

Spreading the knowledge of innovators          oreilly.com

# Buy this book and get access to the online edition for 45 days—for free!

*Fundamentals of iPhone, iPad, and iPod touch Development*

*Programming*

## iOS 4

O'REILLY®   *Matt Neuburg*

***Programming iOS 4***

By Matt Neuburg
May 2011, $49.99
ISBN 9781449388430

## With Safari Books Online, you can:

**Access the contents of thousands of technology and business books**

- Quickly search over 7000 books and certification guides
- Download whole books or chapters in PDF format, at no extra cost, to print or read on the go
- Copy and paste code
- Save up to 35% on O'Reilly print books
- **New!** Access mobile-friendly books directly from cell phones and mobile devices

**Stay up-to-date on emerging topics before the books are published**

- Get on-demand access to evolving manuscripts.
- Interact directly with authors of upcoming books

**Explore thousands of hours of video on technology and design topics**

- Learn from expert video tutorials
- Watch and replay recorded conference sessions

To try out Safari and the online edition of this book FREE for 45 days,
go to ***www.oreilly.com/go/safarienabled*** and enter the coupon code DKYCKFH.
To see the complete Safari Library, visit safari.oreilly.com.

Spreading the knowledge of innovators                    safari.oreilly.com